D1569725

Breaking White Supremacy

BOOKS BY GARY DORRIEN

Logic and Consciousness

The Democratic Socialist Vision

Reconstructing the Common Good

The Neoconservative Mind: Politics, Culture, and the War of Ideology

Soul in Society: The Making and Renewal of Social Christianity

The Word as True Myth: Interpreting Modern Theology

The Remaking of Evangelical Theology

The Barthian Revolt in Modern Theology

*The Making of American Liberal Theology:
Imagining Progressive Religion, 1805–1900*

*The Making of American Liberal Theology:
Idealism, Realism, and Modernity, 1900–1950*

Imperial Designs: Neoconservatism and the New Pax Americana

*The Making of American Liberal Theology:
Crisis, Irony, and Postmodernity, 1950–2005*

Social Ethics in the Making: Interpreting an American Tradition

Economy, Difference, Empire: Social Ethics for Social Justice

The Obama Question: A Progressive Perspective

Kantian Reason and Hegelian Spirit: The Idealistic Logic of Modern Theology

The New Abolition: W. E. B. Du Bois and the Black Social Gospel

BREAKING
WHITE
SUPREMACY

Martin Luther King Jr. and the Black Social Gospel

Gary Dorrien

Yale
UNIVERSITY
PRESS
New Haven & London

Published with assistance from the Louis Stern Memorial Fund.

Yale University Press books may be purchased in quantity for educational, business, or promotional use. For information, please e-mail sales.press@yale.edu (U.S. office) or sales@yaleup.co.uk (U.K. office).

Set in PostScript Electra type by IDS Infotech, Ltd.
Printed in the United States of America.

Library of Congress Control Number: 2016963360
ISBN 978-0-300-20561-9 (hardcover : alk. paper)

A catalogue record for this book is available from the British Library.

This paper meets the requirements of ANSI/NISO Z39.48–1992 (Permanence of Paper).

10 9 8 7 6 5 4 3 2 1

For Sara and Will,
With joy and thanksgiving

CONTENTS

PREFACE

This book stands on its own, resumes the story told in my previous book, and fulfills my longtime desire to see someone—eventually, me—give the black social gospel tradition its due recognition. The founding of the black social gospel in the late nineteenth and early twentieth centuries was a prolonged affair of forerunners and founders comprising four different ideological perspectives. This book is about something later and more specific—the mid-twentieth-century black church leaders who embraced the full-orbed, modern, progressive, justice-oriented, internationalist social gospel from the beginning of their careers and fulfilled it. They did not break their nation of white supremacy or other forms of oppression connected to it. But they inspired and led America's greatest liberation movement.

This book is distinctly personal for me because it converges on the figure that propelled me into social justice activism and Christian ministry and then into an academic career. I came of age during the climactic years of the civil rights movement. Martin Luther King Jr. seized my attention before I understood much of anything about politics or religion, and his contributions to the black freedom and anti–Vietnam War movements anchored my worldview when I entered college. In my twenties and early thirties I worked as a solidarity activist and Episcopal pastor; in my mid-thirties I became an academic; today I have the same touchstone with which I began: the peacemaking and justice-making way of Jesus, as exemplified by King.

In my early career I wrote books on post-Kantian idealism, Social Democratic politics, and Christian Socialism, and I puzzled over why early black Christian Socialists such as Reverdy C. Ransom and George W. Woodbey were completely forgotten. Why were there no books on the convictions that linked Ransom,

Woodbey, and W. E. B. Du Bois to King? That was the wellspring of what became my interest in the broader black social gospel tradition. My friend and role model from the mid-1970s on, Michael Harrington, had worked with King and Bayard Rustin, and I was a sponge for Mike's stories about King's personality, movement leadership, and worldview. The King scholarship of that period did not capture the person that Mike described. More important, neither did it convey the southern black Baptist sources of King's genius, partly because it relied on King's seminary-oriented account of his story.

The revisionist King scholarship of the late 1980s and early 1990s corrected the latter deficiency, yielding richer accounts of King's development and character. But it also yielded books that downgraded King's graduate education and intellectualism in order to play up his early formation and/or explain his personal flaws. Meanwhile I tried to fill the gaps in my knowledge about King's black social gospel forerunners and mentors. By 1995 I had a strong conviction that scholarship on the black freedom movements, progressive Christianity, and U.S. American history wrongly overlooked the very existence of the black social gospel tradition, let alone its immense importance. I sprinkled this conviction into various books and cheered as numerous scholars—especially black religious historians—advanced similar arguments. This book is immeasurably richer for having waited for the illuminating works of Victor Anderson, John J. Ansbro, Sarah Azaransky, Garth Baker-Fletcher, Lewis V. Baldwin, Wallace D. Best, Edward J. Blum, Taylor Branch, Rufus Burrow Jr., Anthea Butler, Clayborne Carson, Lawrence E. Carter Sr., David L. Chappell, James Cone, Keri Day, Quinton Dixie, Michael Eric Dyson, Peter Eisenstadt, Adam Fairclough, Juan Floyd-Thomas, Walter Fluker, David Garrow, Cheryl Townsend Gilkes, Eddie Glaude, Paul Harvey, Obery M. Hendricks Jr., Evelyn Brooks Higginbotham, Thomas F. Jackson, Randal Jelks, Robin D. G. Kelley, David Levering Lewis, Richard Lischer, Charles Marsh, Richard McKinney, Keith D. Miller, Aldon D. Morris, Peter Paris, Anthony Pinn, Albert J. Raboteau, Barbara Ransby, Jonathan Rieder, Barbara Dianne Savage, Nico Slate, Emilie Townes, Eboni Marshall Turman, Jonathan Walton, Cornel West, Preston Williams, Zachery Williams, and others.

To accentuate that the black social gospel was a public enterprise carried out by politically engaged church leaders and intellectuals, I have relied as much as possible on lectures, sermons, and published writings as source material. The black social gospel was emphatically public and political, and thus so is this book. Black social gospel leaders worked hard at building communities of resistance, they operated in the intertwined spheres of religious communities and movement politics, and they focused on racial justice. They had various theologies and ideologies but forged coalitions based on their pragmatic, modernist, unapologetically political commitment to racial justice. They anticipated what came to be called postcolonial theory but in a liberationist mode and without esoteric jargon. Though long denied the status of being a tradition, they forged an enormously important one.

This book, like much of my work, combines social ethics, theology, philosophy, politics, and intellectual history. But it does not range into social history, because I drew the line long ago at handling five fields. We need, very much, a social history of the black social gospel. It would lift up the rich communities of social outreach activists that sustained the black social gospel at the grassroots institutional level and made it possible for figures like King and Adam Clayton Powell Jr. to become famous. A social history of the black social gospel would be suffused with the women who ran the mission societies in most black congregations and the many others who kept institutions like Abyssinian Church alive and thriving. It would delve into the thirty-five-thousand black congregations where the NAACP actually existed across the country, overcoming the usual focus on how a New York City–headquartered organization marched through the federal courts. I hope, by providing a history of the black social gospel focused on public intellectualism and arguments about social justice politics and theology, to encourage others to take up the social history approach to this subject that we need.

I am deeply grateful to friends who have read or heard parts of the present work and helped me with it: Victor Anderson, Sarah Azaransky, Lawrence E. Carter Sr., James Cone, Juan Floyd-Thomas, Obery M. Hendricks Jr., Kipton Jensen, William Stacy Johnson, Michael Lerner, Robin Lovin, Dan McKanan, Rosemary Bray McNatt, Mark Morrison-Reed, Peter Paris, Peter Schmitthenner, Mark Lewis Taylor, Eboni Marshall Turman, Jonathan Walton, and Cornel West. Other friends were supportive in their customary fashion: Randy Auxier, Mary Boys, John B. Cobb Jr., Richard Cook, Mark Douglas, Marvin Ellison, Christopher Evans, Stacey Floyd-Thomas, Walter Fluker, James A. Forbes Jr., Pete Gathje, Eric Gregory, Walter Gulick, Roger Haight, Peter Heltzel, David Hempton, Michael Hogue, Joe Hough, Christian Iosso, Jennifer Jesse, James F. Jones Jr., Serene Jones, Catherine Keller, Nicole Kirk, Paul Knitter, Christopher Latiolais, Timothy Light, James McLachlan, Christopher Morse, Robert C. Neville, Romeo Phillips, Anthony Pinn, Wayne Proudfoot, Larry Rasmussen, Jan Rehmann, Joerg Rieger, David Robb, Don Shriver, Josef Sorett, Ronald Stone, Mark C. Taylor, John Thatamanil, Emilie Townes, Janet Walton, Sharon Welch, and Andrea White.

My three years of commuting to Harvard Divinity School as I wrote this book yielded special debts of gratitude to four teaching fellows: Aaron Goldman,

Kythe Heller, Filipe Maia, and Heather McLetchie-Leader. Many thanks to the students at Union Theological Seminary and Columbia University who helped me vet the manuscript before I was ready to let go of it: Requithelia Allen, Nathan Brockman, Ashley Chambers, James Dyer, Katrina Forman, Hannah Gallo, Asher Harris, Derrick Jordan, Theodore Kerr, Elijah McDavid, Rashad McPherson, William Meredith, Wesley Morris, Phoebe Myhrum, Janine Myrick, Yazmine Nichols, James Perry, Quantez Pressley, Deforest Raphael, Aaron Stauffer, Stanley Talbert, Jordan Tarwater, Robert Thompson, Joseph Tolbert, Sara Wolcott, and Ruth Ann Wooden.

As always I am grateful to my doctoral advisees for the distinct privilege of being their friend and learning with them. Some have graduated: Malinda Berry, Chloe Breyer, Ian Doescher, David Orr, Keun-Joo Christine Pae, Charlene Sinclair, Joe Strife, Eboni Marshall Turman, Rima Vesely-Flad, Colleen Wessel-McCoy, Demian Wheeler, and Jason Wyman. Others are en route: Nkosi Anderson, Jeremy Kirk, Kelly Maeshiro, Anthony Jermaine Ross-Allam, Isaac Sharp, Aaron Stauffer, and Todd Willison. Special thanks go to Isaac Sharp, who helped me assemble the photo gallery, and to Don Fehr, my literary agent.

For the rights of access to materials in special collections I am grateful to the Moorland-Spingarn Research Center at Howard University, Washington, DC; the Schomburg Center for Research in Black Culture, New York Public Library, in New York City; the Rauschenbusch Family Papers, American Baptist-Samuel Colgate Historical Society, Rochester, NY; the NAACP Papers, Library of Congress, Washington, DC; the Martin Luther King Jr. Center Papers, Center for Nonviolent Social Change, Atlanta, GA; Houghton Library of Harvard University in Cambridge; the Pauli Murray Papers, Schlesinger Library, Radcliffe Institute for Advanced Study, Harvard University; and the Martin Luther King, Jr. International Chapel at Morehouse College, Atlanta, GA. For daily access to materials not in special collections, and for unfailing courtesy and support, I am grateful to the staff of Burke Library of Columbia University. I am grateful for permission to adapt material from my books *The Making of American Liberal Theology: Idealism, Realism, and Modernity* (Louisville: Westminster John Knox Press, 2001); *The Making of American Liberal Theology: Crisis, Irony, and Postmodernity* (Louisville: Westminster John Knox Press, 2005); and *Social Ethics in the Making: Interpreting an American Tradition* (Oxford: Wiley-Blackwell, 2009).

Many thanks to my editors at Yale University Press for their superb work, especially executive editor Jennifer Banks, production editor Susan Laity, assistant editor Heather Gold, and copyeditor Lawrence Kenney. And thanks to my proofreader Fred Kameny and my longtime indexer Diana Witt for another excellent index.

Mordecai Johnson
(Library of Congress, Prints and
Photographs Division, Photograph
by Harris & Ewing)

Benjamin E. Mays
(Courtesy of Kenan
Research Center at
the Atlanta History
Center, Photograph
by Joe McTyre)

Howard Thurman
(Courtesy of BU
Photography Services,
Boston University)

Adam Clayton Powell Jr.
(Library of Congress, Prints
and Photographs Division,
Photograph by James J.
Kriegsman)

Pauli Murray
(Courtesy of North Carolina
Collection, University of
North Carolina Library at
Chapel Hill)

Martin Luther King Jr.
(Library of Congress, Prints
and Photographs Division,
Photograph by Marion S.
Trikosko)

Breaking White Supremacy

ACHIEVING THE BLACK SOCIAL GOSPEL

The phase of the black freedom movement usually called "the civil rights movement" — 1955 to 1968 — was incomparably beautiful and searing in modern U.S. American history. It abounded with noble visions, resounded with magnificent rhetoric, and ended in nightmarish despair. It put on global display the ravages of racism and racial caste in the United States. It rebelled against a century of racial abuse that followed upon 246 years of chattel slavery. It sang and preached and marched for a better world. It won a few legislative victories and had a profound impact on U.S. American society but failed to break white supremacy. The symbol of the movement, Martin Luther King Jr., became a global icon by assailing his country's racial prejudice, condemning its economic injustice, opposing its war in Vietnam, standing with the poor and oppressed, expounding a vision of liberation, and being assassinated for doing so. King soared so high that he tends to overwhelm anything associated with him. Yet the tradition that best describes him and other leaders of the civil rights movement has been strangely overlooked.

This is a book about the heyday and legacy of the black social gospel, a tradition with a shimmering heyday, a martyred central figure, and an ongoing legacy. Long before King burst upon the national scene in December 1955 there was an African American tradition of social gospel Christianity that preached social justice politics in the same way that King later personified. During King's lifetime he epitomized what it meant to apply the prophetic spirit of the black social gospel to modern society. He became, like Mohandas Gandhi, a global symbol of nonviolent resistance to oppression. After he was gone he left an incomparable legacy and an immense void. King's legacy is too colossal to fit into any single theological or ideological tradition, but the black social gospel he espoused remains as relevant today, as a form of liberation theology, as it was fifty years ago or a century ago.

Historically the black social gospel was rooted in abolitionist black religion and the teaching of the Bible that God favors the poor and oppressed. It emerged from the ravages of the transatlantic slave trade, the birth of African American Christianity, and the legacy of the abolitionist tradition, addressing the crisis of a new era. What did abolitionist religion mean after slavery and Reconstruction had passed? How should Christians respond to the mania of racial terrorism and oppression that terminated Reconstruction and instituted new forms of abuse? Four ideological traditions of black social Christianity arose in response to these questions, out of which a full-fledged, progressive, protest-oriented social gospel emerged. The black social gospel played a role in the civil rights organizations of the late nineteenth and early twentieth centuries, giving ballast to the National Association for the Advancement of Colored People (NAACP). Then it provided the neo-abolitionist theology of social justice that King and other freedom movement leaders spoke and sang.

But very few books even refer to the black social gospel, and until now there were no books that dealt with this tradition as a whole. My previous book, *The New Abolition: W. E. B. Du Bois and the Black Social Gospel*, described the founding of the black social gospel during the Progressive era and the influence of W. E. B. Du Bois upon it. This religious and social movement advocated protest activism within reluctant religious communities and helped to create an alternative public sphere of excluded voices. *The New Abolition* ended just as King's models of social justice ministry entered the story. *Breaking White Supremacy* describes the black social gospel luminaries who influenced King and the figures of King's generation who led the civil rights movement. Three theologians from the former group are featured: Howard University president Mordecai Wyatt Johnson, Morehouse College president Benjamin E. Mays, and mystical prophet Howard Thurman, plus King's Baptist role models George Kelsey, Vernon Johns, Martin Luther King Sr., and J. Pius Barbour. *Breaking White Supremacy* also gives featured attention to pastor/politician Adam Clayton Powell Jr. and to lawyer/theologian Pauli Murray. In the King generation the key players besides King are the Southern Christian Leadership Conference (SCLC) and Student Nonviolent Coordinating Committee (SNCC) leaders who shared King's Gandhian social gospel worldview: James Lawson, Andrew Young, James Bevel, C. T. Vivian, John Lewis, and Bernard Lafayette. The book also discusses King's SCLC colleagues Ralph Abernathy and Wyatt Tee Walker as well as numerous figures who were not social gospel ministers, especially Bayard Rustin, A. Philip Randolph, Ella Baker, Malcolm X, James Farmer, Diane Nash, Glenn

Smiley, A. J. Muste, Fannie Lou Hamer, Stokely Carmichael, and Stanley Levison, plus the roles played by Howard University, Morehouse College, the African Methodist Episcopal (AME) and National Baptist Convention (NBC) denominations, and the National Council of Churches.[1]

The founders of the black social gospel had key affinities with their some-time allies in the white social gospel and Progressive movements. They conceived the federal government as an indispensable guarantor of constitutional rights and principles of justice; they espoused typical Progressive beliefs about equality, politics, and social progress; and they wrestled with modern challenges to religious belief. But black social gospel leaders addressed these things very differently from white progressives, for racial oppression trumped everything in the African American context *and* refigured how other problems were experienced. Here the belief in a divine ground of human selfhood powered struggles for black self-determination and campaigns of resistance to white oppression.

The New Abolition delineated four ideological streams of black social Christianity and a specific black social gospel that emerged mostly from the third and fourth streams. The first group identified with Booker T. Washington and his program of political accommodation and economic uplift. The second group espoused the nationalist conviction that African Americans needed their own nation. The third group advocated protest activism for racial justice, strongly opposing Washington. The fourth group implored against factional division, calling for a fusion of pro-Washington realism and selective anti-Washington protest militancy. All four of these factions existed before Du Bois emerged as the intellectual leader of the protest tradition and influenced black social gospel ministers such as Reverdy C. Ransom and Richard R. Wright Jr. The full-fledged black social gospel stood for social justice religion and modern critical consciousness. It combined an emphasis on black dignity and person-hood with protest activism for racial justice, a comprehensive social justice agenda, an insistence that authentic Christian faith is incompatible with racial prejudice, an emphasis on the social ethical teaching of Jesus, and an acceptance of modern scholarship and social consciousness—my operative definition of the black social gospel.

This tradition of social justice religion, until recently, was wrongly neglected, which made King incomprehensible. King did not come from nowhere. The founders had much at stake in claiming that black churches should support social justice politics and social gospel theology. Many of them would not have been forgotten had scholars not ignored the black social gospel for decades. When the black social gospel is recognized as an important tradition, certain long-regnant conventions about black religious history no longer hold up. *The New Abolition* countered several of them. Supposedly the early black social gospel had only a few proponents. Supposedly it was a mere imitation of white social Christianity and did not produce significant public intellectuals. Supposedly it had little influence, so it was not an important tradition or perhaps not a tradition at all. Supposedly it was a species of something best left for dead—Progressive-era idealism—which theologian Reinhold Niebuhr shredded in the 1930s and liberation theology finished off in the 1970s.

On the contrary, the early black social gospel had numerous proponents. It was a self-standing tradition with its own identity and integrity, one which produced public intellectuals. It had a tremendous influence by providing the theology of social justice that the civil rights movement espoused. And it remains important as a wellspring of progressive Christianity, liberation theology, postcolonial criticism, and every form of Christianity that appeals to the witness of the civil rights movement.

This argument sets me against the landmark renderings of black religious history by Joseph R. Washington Jr. and Gayraud Wilmore, even though my constructive position is close to that of Wilmore. Washington, in *Black Religion* (1964), contended that black Protestantism in America was a folk religion based on the affirmation of black equality and freedom. Black church religion, according to Washington, lacked any theological grounding in the Protestant Reformation or the integral unity of the Bible, having sprouted as a folk tradition protest against racism. King, in this telling, exacerbated the problem of the black church. King leveraged the protest origin of black Protestantism and the love ethic of the New Testament to advance a twentieth-century justice movement, mostly in the language of the social gospel, which Washington described as a progressive white folk religion—a semi-Christian retreat from the real thing. Real Christianity, Washington said, stood on the indissoluble unity of Hebrew Scripture and the New Testament in blood redemption. In essence King refashioned the folk religion of the black church by assigning novel causes to it, charging that white churches betrayed the ethical principles of Christian faith shared by white and black Christians. In his subsequent book *The Politics of God* (1967) Washington was less disapproving of black church social activism, but he still insisted that King and the black church had a meager theological basis and that King substituted Gandhian nonviolence for Christian theology, which yielded King's purportedly disastrous opposition to the Vietnam War, "a violent distortion of the mission of the Negro." God, Washington pleaded, surely did not call black Christians "to redeem mankind from war, nationalism, pride, and other human weaknesses."[2]

Wilmore, in *Black Religion and Black Radicalism* (1973), had a very different agenda that soon fused with Washington's account in many renderings of black religious history. To Wilmore, what mattered was the radical tradition in black religion that sometimes operated within formal religious communities and sometimes did not. Black religious radicalism, according to Wilmore, had three defining features: It sought liberation from white domination, commended respect for Africa, and used protest and agitation in the struggle for liberation. It was less political and ideological than other forms of radical politics because it perceived the deeply pathological character of white racism and white society. The radical tradition fought against white supremacy, refusing to sing the liberal song of racial integration. It was usually nationalist or separatist, but however that sorted out, the radical tradition was always marked by a fervent racial pride and a refusal to be denigrated.[3]

These accounts had great influence in the fields of religious history, theology, and black studies. They were powerfully descriptive and explanatory, providing discursive frames for analyses of black religion and politics. Often they were folded together, despite the contrasts between Washington's traditionalism and Wilmore's liberationism. They fused readily because each made a case for dismissing the black social gospel, and each censured the social gospel for accommodating liberalism and modernity. To Washington, the social gospel and the black church had the same problem—a deficient theological basis. Thus it did not help when black church leaders adopted a social gospel theology of social justice and modern critical consciousness. To fuse black church Protestantism to the social gospel usually meant that doctrines got downgraded even further in black churches. Wilmore agreed that black Christianity lacked theological self-consciousness, a judgment that gave ballast to the liberation theology movement in the 1970s. But his chief critique of the black social gospel was social ethical, not theological, and it was dismissive. According to Wilmore, the black church produced nobody in the early twentieth century meriting more than a sentence or two. Ransom and Alexander Walters got a two-sentence mention for trying and failing, and Adam Clayton Powell Sr. got a one-sentence mention as a prototype of social welfare ministry.[4]

I share Wilmore's liberationist theological perspective and I do not believe that the black social gospel outstripped the older and ongoing tradition of black radicalism that Wilmore described. But *The New Abolition* made a case for taking the black social gospel much more seriously than Wilmore did, partly on the ground that some of its key figures belonged to the radical tradition. The black social gospel founders were ministers and journalists, including many who were both. They had limited success, they did not take over the churches,

and they provided only modest ballast for the NAACP. But they started something new. They fought to abolish Jim Crow, lynching, and economic injustice.
They established that progressive theology could be combined with social
justice politics in a black church context. They built up black Christian
communities and urged them to welcome the migrant stranger. They refuted
the racist culture that demeaned their human dignity and equality. And they
legitimized what they started, sometimes winning a bishop's chair or the
denominational publication or national acclaim as a scholar or church leader.
The founders gave way to a generation of social gospel ministers who refused to
give up on the black churches, even as a rising tide of black intellectuals
contended that black churches were hopelessly self-centered, provincial,
insular, anti-intellectual, and conservative.

Black social gospel leaders of the 1920s and 1930s had to negotiate harsh
criticism of the black church by leading experts on this subject, especially Du
Bois and historians Carter Woodson, E. Franklin Frazier, and Rayford Logan.
Du Bois and Woodson had lovers' quarrels with the black church, while Frazier
and Logan were more deeply averse to religion per se, but in both cases social
gospel leaders countered that Christian faith, critical rationality, and civil rights
advocacy went together or at least needed to do so, exactly as Du Bois and
Woodson said they should. Johnson, Mays, Thurman, and others drew on their
training in white universities and seminaries to make this argument, inevitably
raising the question whether white academic criticism of any kind belonged in
the black church.

White religious leaders took for granted their responsibility and ability to
address audiences in the church, academy, and general public. They had a
custodial relationship to U.S. American society as presumed guardians of the
nation's morality. Even stalwarts of the anti-imperial, Socialist wing of the white
social gospel—Harry Ward, George Coe, Vida Scudder, and Kirby Page—
sought to Christianize U.S. American society and culture. This presumption
reigned in white Protestant ethics long after American Catholics produced
their own tradition of social Christianity and long after Reinhold Niebuhr
ended the reign of social gospel idealism in the leading seminaries and divinity
schools.

The black intellectuals who were trained in Progressive-era theology and
sociology could not assume access to the academy or general public, and some
had uneasy relationships with their religious communities. They earned degrees
from elite universities that gave no thought to hiring them as professors. Their
expertise about black American life was of little interest to the white public, and
their expertise about anything else was of no interest to the white public. The

black social gospel was largely confined to black church contexts on this account. But that did not prevent it from producing intellectual leaders who addressed the general public and built up a black counterpublic. The intellectuals of the black social gospel movement got their academic bearings by fusing sociology, social ethics, and social gospel theology, in the manner taught at the University of Chicago, Union Theological Seminary, Boston University, Harvard University, Rochester Theological Seminary, Oberlin College, Morehouse College, Howard University, and other bellwether institutions. They brought the social ethical teaching of Jesus and the black church into everything they did. They believed in the power of the new social sciences to refute the racist culture of denigration. They struggled to legitimize social gospel theology in the black denominations to which most of them belonged. And they believed that social science combined with prophetic religion had a chance to build a commonwealth of freedom in American society and the world—a trope that numerous black religious scholars have emphasized in recovering aspects of the black social gospel, notably Calvin S. Morris, Walter E. Fluker, Wallace D. Best, Barbara Dianne Savage, Lawrence Edward Carter Sr., Anthony Pinn, Quinton H. Dixie, and Juan M. Floyd-Thomas.[5]

The New Abolition ended with an excursus on the perils of preaching the cross of Jesus to oppressed black Americans and the fact that nearly every black church nevertheless preached, prayed, testified, and sang the cross of Jesus. Jesus was a friend of oppressed black Americans who knew about their suffering. Jesus achieved salvation for "the least of these" through his solidarity with them, even unto death. Black American Christians, like Jesus, did not deserve to suffer. But keeping faith in Jesus was the one thing black American Christians possessed that white America could not control or take from them. To black Christians, merely knowing that Jesus suffered as they did gave them faith that God was with them, even if they ended up, like Jesus, tortured to death on a tree. The early black social gospel ministers, especially Ransom and Powell Senior, had the requisite imagination to see redemption in the cross *and* to refrain from explaining it in a theory. They let the spiritual power of the cross do its work without enveloping it in a required doctrine. The next generation of black social gospel leaders had this starting point, an inheritance of the churches in which Johnson, Mays, Thurman, Powell Junior, King, and Murray were shaped.

They also shared with Ransom and Powell Senior a fascination with the revolt against British colonialism in India led by Gandhi. From the beginning of the noncooperation campaign launched by Gandhi and the Indian National Congress Party in December 1920, leading black newspapers and ministers heralded the breakthrough importance of Gandhi and his strategy of nonviolent resistance. Parallels between Indian and black American oppression were noted and dissected. Differences between the Indian and U.S. American contexts were vigorously debated. In the early going, black American intellectuals did not say this was a reciprocal relationship, as they did not realize that Booker T. Washington had importantly influenced Gandhi's thinking about racism, caste, and education. Later they fathomed that Gandhi drew upon their struggle and identified with them. For thirty years "the Gandhi issue" meant primarily one thing to leading black journalists and social gospel ministers: "We need a Gandhi."

Gandhi had come from a Hindu merchant caste family in coastal Gujarat, western India, in the princely state of Porbandar, in the Kathiawar Agency of the British Indian Empire. His father was chief minister of Porbandar state. Gandhi grew up vague and shy and a mediocre student, although his family sent him to London for law school anyway, in 1888. In London he met some Theosophists who sparked an interest in Hindu–Buddhist interfaith religion, and for two years he floundered as a lawyer in India, opting for Natal, South Africa, in 1893, at the age of twenty-four. Gandhi started to become Gandhi in Natal, organizing opposition to South Africa's treatment of Indians. It began on his journey to Natal, during which he was shocked at being treated as a denigrated racial minority. Gandhi's early campaign protested that Indians deserved to be treated better than native Africans, on the same level as white South Africans. He took white supremacy for granted, counting South Africa's mostly wealthy Indian Muslims and its mostly poor indentured Indian Hindus as white.[6]

From these unlikely and ambiguous beginnings Gandhi became the world's foremost opponent of British imperialism and white supremacy, though his non-opposition to the caste system blinkered his opposition to white supremacy. Gandhi won concessions for Indians and blacks in South Africa, returned to India triumphantly in 1915, and led India's struggle for independence from 1915 to 1947. During World War I Gandhi recruited soldiers for the British viceroy and moved up the ranks of the Congress Party. He broadened his base by supporting the Muslim Khilafat movement in 1919, which protested the eclipse of the caliph after the dismemberment of the Ottoman Empire. In March 1919 Gandhi and the Congress Party launched a nationwide civil disobedience campaign against the Rowlatt Bills curtailing civil liberties. The following month British troops massacred hundreds of unarmed demonstrators in Amritsar. The following year Gandhi assumed leadership of the Congress Party, and in December he launched the noncooperation movement. By 1922 twenty thousand anticolonial protestors had been thrown into jail, and Gandhi was sentenced to six years in prison.

The spectacle of unarmed people of color revolting against the world's mightiest empire touched the hearts and minds of black Americans. Du Bois and Marcus Garvey, in *Crisis* and the *Negro World*, gave extensive early coverage to the Indian freedom struggle. *Crisis*, published by the NAACP, played up Gandhi's saintly character and nonviolent philosophy. Already in July 1921 white social gospel minister and NAACP activist John Haynes Holmes described Gandhi as a modern Christ figure, which Du Bois cited approvingly. Three months later Ransom declared in *AME Church Review* that Gandhi was an "Indian Messiah and Saint" whose brilliant use of nonviolent civil disobedience "paralyzed the British power in India." Du Bois and Ransom described the African American and Indian liberation struggles as contributions to a global struggle by people of color against imperialism and white supremacy. Du Bois, putting it colorfully in 1932, declared, "There is today in the world but one living maker of miracles and that is Mahatma Gandhi. He stops eating, and three hundred million Indians, together with the British Empire, hold their breath until they can talk sense. All America sees in Gandhi a joke, but the joke is on America."[7]

Having put it that personally, Du Bois seemed to sanction the customary editorial pleas of the *Pittsburgh Courier*, *Chicago Defender*, *Norfolk Journal and Guide*, and other newspapers and journals: Where is our Gandhi? The *Courier* put it plaintively in February 1931 in an editorial titled "If We Had a Ghandi." Black Americans needed a catalyzing savior figure like Gandhi, the *Courier* implored: "But where, oh where, in these United States of America is there a man who could win the plaudits and approval of his colored brethren? If we had a Ghandi in this country—or, better yet, if we had the following of a Ghandi in this country—we might liberate ourselves from some of the ills of which we complain." The *Chicago Defender* agreed: "What we need in America is a Gandhi who will fight the cause of the oppressed. One who, like Gandhi, can divorce himself from the greed for gold, one who can appreciate the misery of the oppressed and respond in spirit to their needs and requirements."[8]

Every such call for a Gandhi savior evoked cheers but also caveats and rejoinders. India was different from the United States. Gandhi was different from any conceivable black American equivalent. India had traditions of holy men fasting and sacrificing for a cause. Too much focus on moral heroes was disabling. Gandhi spoke for India's entire working class, a far cry from the African American situation. Gandhi rebelled against colonialism and untouchability, not the Indian caste system, but Jim Crow was like the caste system. Black Americans had more to lose by opting for civil disobedience because blacks were a small minority in the United States, and they had real economic gains to lose.

Du Bois was America's leading proponent of global solidarity for nonwhite peoples. He did more than anyone to inform African Americans about Gandhi's campaigns and importance, and he did it with colorful, quotable zingers. Yet Du Bois was also a leading exponent of every objection just summarized. To Du Bois, nothing came close to "magnificent India" in revealing to the world "the inner rottenness of European imperialism." He lionized Gandhi repeatedly as the apostle of an almost miraculous anticolonial revolution. He treasured him as the world's leading enemy of white supremacy. But Gandhi-like civil disobedience, Du Bois judged, would not work for black Americans, who needed to stick with agitation and publicity, "still our trump cards."[9]

Black social gospel ministers of the thirties and forties were schooled in this debate over the meaning of the Gandhian revolution and the applicability of the Gandhi example. Some agreed with Du Bois about colored cosmopolitanism and the limits of Gandhi's approach in the United States. Some were the opposite, spurning black internationalism while pining for a Gandhi-like rebel. All agreed with Du Bois that Gandhi was a singularly compelling and instructive figure regardless of how one came out on global solidarity or the situation in the United States, and all agreed with Du Bois that the protest/social justice tradition in black politics needed to prevail. Johnson folded a strong pro-Gandhi section into his stump speeches in 1930 and delivered it tirelessly for the next thirty years. Mays, Thurman, Channing Tobias, and William Stuart Nelson had personal encounters with Gandhi in India that shaped their activism and teaching. All were important influences on King before and after December 1, 1955.

Johnson was a role model for Mays and Thurman before he influenced King. Born to former slaves in 1890, Johnson grew up in Paris, Tennessee, and excelled as a student at Atlanta Baptist College, later renamed Morehouse College. He was sufficiently brilliant that John Hope promptly appointed him to the Morehouse faculty after he graduated. Later Johnson earned degrees at the University of Chicago, Rochester Theological Seminary, and Harvard Divinity School and became a scintillating preacher and speaker on the lecture circuit. In 1926 he moved from a Baptist pastorate in Charleston, West Virginia, to the presidency of Howard University. Johnson built Howard into a powerhouse of black scholarship, adding Mays, Thurman, and many others to the faculty. In particular he built up the School of Law, which contributed mightily to the NAACP's march through the courts.

Johnson espoused liberal theology, Socialist economics, anticolonial internationalism, civil rights progressivism, anti-anti-Communism, and Gandhian revolutionary nonviolence. One of his trademark lectures on Gandhi made a riveting impression on King. But Johnson was consumed by Howard University and embattled there. Many Howard professors looked down on ministers, claiming that Johnson ran the university in classic tyrannical preacher fashion. Some choked on his politics too, as did many alums and outsiders. He won little credit for launching a tradition of anticolonial criticism at Howard long before postcolonial theory bloomed as an academic perspective. Johnson prevailed over his critics, guiding Howard until his retirement in 1960. He had a sparkling career on the lecture circuit that was a model for King of social justice activism and preaching. But Johnson's long embattlement at Howard disqualified him from the role that fell to King.

Johnson and Mays were schoolmasters in the formidable, ambitious, disciplinarian tradition of their mentor, John Hope. Both were Baptists who came up through YMCA ecumenism. Both lifted historic black schools to new distinction, training generations of civil rights and social gospel leaders. Both were extroverted theologians. Both acknowledged the complicity of Christianity in American slavery and imperialism and the perils of internalizing Christian colonialism. Both had a global vision and an overriding conviction that black American Christians had to focus on the immediate struggle for justice in the United States. And both were quintessential social gospel progressives, upholding a theology of racial and social justice politics, Gandhian resistance strategy, and anticolonial internationalism. Johnson was only four years older than Mays, although he seemed older for a while because he brought Mays to Howard.

Mays was born in South Carolina in 1894, he grew up viciously repressed and excluded, he clawed his way to an education anyway, and he earned a Ph.D. at the University of Chicago Divinity School. Then he served as dean of the School of Religion at Howard, forming a social gospel trio with Johnson and Thurman that lifted the university and attracted students to it. Then he gave two generations of African Americans a model of dignified antiracist rebellion as president of Morehouse College. Mays exemplified the black social gospel and defended it. He pushed and prodded black churches to embrace social gospel progressivism, he was a leader in the national and world ecumenical movements, he pushed and prodded the liberal Protestant establishment to deal with racial justice, and he mentored King for twenty years. At bottom he was a moralist and a race man. The idea that he lacked a robust theology, however, would have struck Mays as very strange. By his lights, he had a powerful theology that stuck to what mattered. Like Johnson, Mays emphasized in classic social gospel fashion the kingdom of God, the social ethical teaching of Jesus, the sin of individuals and society, the way of the cross, the Christian commitment to social justice, and the providential grace of God. His ecumenical theology eschewed useless and distracting doctrinal speculation, sustaining the hope of the kingdom come.

The trio of Johnson, Mays, and Thurman established an extraordinary tradition of black internationalism and Gandhian nonviolence at Howard. Nearly every trope of later postcolonial theory—especially colonial framing, cultural hybridity, liminality, overcoming colonial presumptions and internalized self-images, and interrogating Christian complicity in imperialism and slavery—was anticipated in the school of black globalism that Johnson, Mays, Thurman, and Nelson built at Howard and that Murray refashioned in her later career. Here my approach is to address the issues raised in postcolonial criticism by showing how black social gospel theologians talked about dispossession, Africa, Christian complicity, faith, and universality. Thurman and Murray grappled most intently with these issues, but all of the Howard theologians and most of the black social gospel figures featured in this book wrestled with what was saving, and what not, in Christianity. It was possible to take very seriously the terrible Christian contribution to racism and imperialism while drawing deeply from the wellspring of black American Christianity; in fact, the black social gospel theologians said it was imperative to do so. To Johnson, Mays, and Thurman, the path to Gandhian internationalism ran through Protestant missionary societies, especially the YMCA and its youth activist offspring, the Student Christian Movement. For Mays and Thurman it also included meetings with Gandhi himself. Thurman was far more ready than Mays to cut Gandhi some slack for failing to oppose India's caste system. On the other hand, Thurman's tour in India, Ceylon, and Burma on behalf of liberationist Christianity cut him more deeply than Mays felt on a similar ecumenical Christian venture. Thurman balked at representing American Christianity in India, and, upon doing so anyway, he had a soul-shaking experience that clarified, to him, what mattered: the "religion of Jesus," which folded into Thurman's mystical pacifist predisposition to true-believing Gandhianism.[10]

In the late 1930s and early 1940s Thurman was supposed to be the answer to the Gandhi question. He heard it constantly on the lecture circuit, where he was a star performer. Thurman became a pastor, a professor, a chapel dean, a social gospel leader, a Quaker-influenced mystic and pacifist, a pathbreaking advocate of racial integration, a postcolonial prophet, an advisor to movement leaders, a prolific author, and a spiritual influence on King. He had his greatest influence on the civil rights movement during the early 1940s, on the lecture circuit. Then he became a sage and author, exerting a different kind of influence. Then his influence grew after he was gone.

Thurman had the usual Deep South childhood experience of never imagining that a friendly relationship with a white person was possible. The Klan controlled politics in his hometown, Daytona Beach, and the entire state of Florida had only three public high schools for black children. To Johnson and Mays, the YMCA was very important on the way up. For Thurman it was transformational, an incomparable influence and vehicle. Thurman attended his first Kings Mountain Student Conference in the summer of 1917, as a high school sophomore. The following year he heard Johnson give a bravura speech at the annual YMCA conference in Kings Mountain, North Carolina. Listening to Johnson, Thurman found a model of who he wanted to be. But Thurman decided in the 1940s that political movement leadership was not for him, a decision that dismayed many followers.

A. Philip Randolph, in the 1940s, was the one who emerged. The son of an AME Church minister in Jacksonville, Florida, Randolph moved to New York City in 1911, briefly attended City College, heard Socialist icon Eugene Debs and Harlem Socialist leader Hubert H. Harrison speak numerous times, and joined the Socialist Party in 1916. From the beginning he was a compelling speaker, attracting soapbox crowds in Harlem. In 1917 Randolph and Chandler Owen founded a Socialist monthly magazine, the *Messenger*, helped by a Socialist Party subsidy. The magazine had a dramatic run of rhetorical fireworks, ideological battles, brilliant editorializing, government harassment, and boastful name changes. Originally the *Messenger* called itself *The Only Radical Negro Magazine in America*. In 1920 the header changed to *The Only Radical Magazine Published by Negroes*. Four years and three name changes later it became *The World's Greatest Negro Monthly*.[11]

Meanwhile Randolph ran for state offices on the Socialist Party ticket and took up trade union organizing. He founded or cofounded six union organizations that failed, notably the National Brotherhood of Workers of America in 1919, briefly the nation's largest black union. The latter venture had some success with dockworkers but dissolved in 1921 under pressure from the American Federation of Labor. In 1925 Randolph made a breakthrough, founding the first union for employees of the Pullman Company, the Brotherhood of Sleeping Car Porters. The porters' union coped with ruthless opposition and firings until 1934, when the Railway Labor Act granted organizing rights to porters under federal law. Randolph emerged as the nation's foremost civil rights leader, urging that Gandhi's campaign against British occupation in India offered a model resistance strategy for African Americans. In 1941 Randolph and other civil rights leaders organized the March on Washington Movement, proposing to shut down Washington, DC, as a protest against segregation, lynching, and racial discrimination in war industries and the military. President Franklin Roosevelt responded reluctantly on June 25 with Executive Order 8802, banning employment discrimination in federal agencies involved with the defense industry. This was a half-victory in its time, as Roosevelt's order did not ban racial discrimination in the military or anywhere else. It was subsequently amended and expanded several times, notably by Title VII of the 1964 Civil Rights Act. But Randolph suspended the proposed march, and six months later Japan attacked Pearl Harbor. The moment passed for a civil rights movement that seized the nation's attention.

By then Adam Clayton Powell Jr. had emerged as a rival to Randolph's standing and influence. Powell's life overlapped the public career of the black social gospel and was intertwined with it. His father, Adam Clayton Powell Sr., epitomized the Du Bois–and–Washington wing of the black social gospel as the longtime pastor of Abyssinian Baptist Church in Harlem. In the 1930s Powell Junior assisted his father at Abyssinian and became a prominent community leader in Harlem, crusading for jobs and affordable housing. He forged alliances with nationalist, social gospel, Communist, unionist, liberal, and other activist groups, demonstrating what was possible for New York left constituencies that pulled together. In 1938 he succeeded his father as pastor at Abyssinian, preaching social gospel progressivism. The following year he organized a successful picket at the New York World's Fair offices in the Empire State Building, winning jobs for African Americans, which won him national acclaim. Two years later he won election to the New York City Council, and in 1944 he became New York State's first black representative in the U.S. Congress and the first from any northern state besides Illinois since Reconstruction.

Powell ended business as usual in the U.S. House of Representatives. Stubbornly, proudly, defiantly, by himself, sometimes gleefully, he forced the House to deal with racial segregation, week after week. He blasted segregation and challenged segregationists to defend their policies. He condemned racist language on the House floor, defied segregationists in his party, and goaded liberals to take a stand against racial tyranny. Often Powell hosted black constituents in the House's segregated restaurant. He was a joyous warrior who irked his enemies by enjoying the battle and his life. He added "Powell Amendments" to bills proposing federal expenditures, denying federal funds to segregated jurisdictions. The Powell defunding strategy was engrafted in Title VI of the Civil Rights Act of 1964, and Powell steered much of the Great Society legislation through his congressional committee. For most of his career Powell was the only nationally prominent black politician, period. He had a vivid theological imagination, a liberal theology steeped in romanticism, a global perspective, and a devoted following at Abyssinian Church. But Powell clashed with King and other civil rights leaders, deeply offending King in 1960 with a salacious threat that severed King's alliance with Bayard Rustin for three years. When Rustin, King, and Randolph pulled off the historic March on Washington in 1963, they kept Powell off the speakers' platform, and Powell's congressional career ended badly in 1971. He was charismatic and arrogant, righteous and corrupt, and religious and cynical. He mystified allies and enemies with his contradictions. Among black social gospel leaders, only King accomplished more than Powell, but Powell damaged his own legacy, and he learned belatedly that his Harlem constituents had tired of him.

The person who tried hardest to play the Gandhi role was James Farmer. When lightning struck in Montgomery, Farmer had been trying for fourteen years to spark a civil rights revolution with exactly the Gandhian tactics King subsequently employed, working with the same movement professionals who joined King. He had also married a white woman, Lula Peterson, refusing to concede how that would play out in movement politics. Farmer studied in the late 1930s under Thurman and Mays at Howard, where his father, James Farmer Sr., taught theology. In 1941, while working as an organizer for the pacifist Fellowship of Reconciliation (FOR), Farmer tried to convert FOR to Gandhi-style agitation against racial segregation. The following year he cofounded what became, after a couple of name changes, the Congress of Racial Equality (CORE), a scrappy, scattered, interracial offshoot of FOR. Both organizations were tiny left-wing groups with little chance of scaling up. Both had an international perspective and a critique of white colonialism, especially CORE. In addition, Farmer worked with trade unions that gave low priority to racial justice.

Farmer tried but failed to win for his organizations some of the spotlight that fell on Randolph. He and Randolph never quite worked together, although each had something the other lacked, and Farmer cut himself off from churches not belonging to his left-wing orbit. Farmer, Randolph, Du Bois, and many others were shocked when America's Gandhi turned out to be a young Baptist minister lacking any movement experience. Years later Farmer recalled, "We knew what we were doing, but no one else did." CORE, to him, seemed like a flea gnawing on the ear of an elephant. Not only did CORE's numerous sit-ins and pickets fail to bring the beast to its knees. It was hard to pretend that the beast even noticed.[12]

Direct action had one breakthrough half-victory before the *Brown* decision and Montgomery, far from CORE's northern base. In 1953 black Americans organized a boycott against segregated buses in Baton Rouge, Louisiana. It began with a petition asking the City Council to permit African Americans to be seated on a first-come-first-served basis. The council passed an ordinance granting such permission, on the condition that blacks fill the bus from the back to the front, while whites proceeded from the front. That was unacceptable to city bus drivers, who went on strike. The state attorney general agreed that the ordinance violated Louisiana's segregation laws, and local blacks responded by forming a coalition of churches, the United Defense League (UDL), spearheaded by Baptist pastor T. J. Jemison, to boycott the bus system. Previous protests in Baton Rouge had been organized by the NAACP and were aimed at achieving court victories. The UDL boycott was a direct action campaign mobilizing black Americans through local congregations. It struck for six days, winning a partial victory that set aside two front seats for whites and the long rear seat for blacks, with all remaining seats filled on a first-come-first-served basis.[13]

The Baton Rouge boycott established that mass action to challenge racial segregation could work in the Deep South. This was a victory for the entire black community of Baton Rouge, not merely a court victory for middle-class blacks desiring racial integration. Middle-class black Americans could drive their own cars, but working-class blacks had to ride the buses. At the time, Jemison's father was president of the five-million-member National Baptist Convention (NBC), and Jemison himself served as the NBC's national secretary. News of the victory in Baton Rouge spread through the NBC network, reaching two Baptist ministers in Montgomery, Alabama: Martin Luther King Jr. and Ralph Abernathy.

That was the only success story for direct action that Montgomery boycott leaders cited when they struck in 1955. The chief enemy of racial oppression in the United States was the NAACP, a legal juggernaut centered in New York but convening in thirty thousand black churches across the nation. The NAACP organized protest actions and fought court battles across the country on behalf of civil rights. It had many ministerial leaders at the local level; it pressed hard to desegregate public schools, chipping away at *Plessy v Ferguson;* and every time the NAACP won a case, it showed that white oppression was not invincible. In 1950–1952 the NAACP launched an all-out assault on public school segregation, filing suits in South Carolina, Virginia, Kansas, Delaware, and the District of Columbia that yielded, from the Kansas suit, the 1954 Supreme Court case *Brown v. Board of Education of Topeka.* The court's unanimous verdict in *Brown* overthrew the *Plessy* principle legitimizing "separate but equal" public schools for blacks and whites. It also overshadowed Baton Rouge, casting a national spotlight on the NAACP, which set up the organization for a furious backlash—opening the door to an upsurge of direct mass action.

The NAACP had moved into the South in 1918, when James Weldon Johnson joined the organization and spearheaded its expansion. From 1918 to 1950 the organization bravely grew across the South in the face of brutal, mostly local, largely uncoordinated campaigns of terror and repression. In the early 1950s, alarmed that the NAACP was pushing to desegregate public schools, the white power structure in the South escalated its attacks. After the *Brown* decision the power structure united to destroy the NAACP. Georgia governor Herman Talmadge and South Carolina governor James F. Byrnes vowed to defy the *Brown* verdict. President Eisenhower declined to enforce it, which encouraged southern defiance. Congress evaded the issue, and state governments throughout the South mounted systematic assaults on the NAACP, passing laws designed to disrupt or abolish it. Louisiana and Texas issued injunctions halting NAACP operations. Florida investigated the NAACP for Communist subversion. South Carolina barred teachers from belonging to the NAACP. Alabama completely outlawed the NAACP. From 1955 to 1958 the NAACP lost 246 branches as a consequence of government repression. NAACP leaders reasoned that unlawful protests were out of play for them, since the main business of the NAACP was to restore the rule of law, especially Fourteenth and Fifteenth Amendment rights. That created an opening for protest activists who were willing to break unjust laws. Some were longtime NAACP activists far removed from courtroom wrangling.[14]

Rosa Parks, Pullman porter E. D. Nixon, and Alabama State professor Jo Ann Robinson were among them. Nixon and Robinson had pined for a test case and waited for the right one. They got a perfect one when Parks, a department store seamstress and NAACP activist, kept her bus seat in Montgomery. Farmer marveled that black activists set off a nervy strike in the cradle of the Confederacy. But he disbelieved that any Deep South community had the will or skills to hold out against white supremacy. Farmer stuck to that view throughout, and long after the Montgomery boycott. He believed that Montgomery broke through only because it had an electrifying leader that the media flocked to cover.

I take a strong view of King's importance and indispensability, while contending that the black freedom movement lifted him to prominence, not the other way around. King came from a black social gospel tradition that slowly kindled the civil rights movement explosion of the 1950s. My discussions of Johnson, Mays, Thurman, Powell, and the entire movement of figures that led to King are geared to work up to King, who stands at the center of the book's narrative in the company of his SCLC coworkers and early SNCC allies. I believe that King's formation in the southern black Baptist church and his graduate education at northern theological institutions were both important to his identity, thinking, and career. Any reading that minimizes one or the other misconstrues King, which is what happens when scholars fail to credit the black social gospel that enabled King to play his unique mediating role. King soared to fame on the wings of a movement that he championed with distinct brilliance. He succeeded because he uniquely bridged the disparities between black and white church communities, between middle-class blacks and white liberals, between black nationalists and black conservatives, between church communities and the academy, and, above all, between the northern and southern civil rights movements.

He was the product of a black church family and congregation that espoused the social gospel in a broad sense of the category and prepared him for his singular role. King was nurtured in the piety and idioms of an urban, middle-class, black Baptist family and congregation. He deeply absorbed the evangelical piety and social concerns preached by his father. He got a more intellectual version of both things when he studied at Morehouse College, a distinctly social gospel institution, where Mays, Kelsey, sociologist Walter Chivers, and others influenced him. In seminary King adopted a Socialist version of social gospel theology and a personalist version of post-Kantian idealistic philosophy, and he acquired a conflicted attraction to Gandhian nonviolence. My reading emphasizes King's long-standing commitments to democratic Socialism, personalist theological liberalism, and Gandhian nonviolence. Above all, I stress that King got increasingly radical and angry as a consequence of failing to break white supremacy—a structure of power based on privilege. King spurned his access to the establishment in order to stand with the poor and oppressed, struggling against intertwined forms of racial, social, economic, cultural, and imperial oppression.

On social gospel Socialism, Walter Rauschenbusch was the foremost intellectual influence on King, and it mattered greatly to King that Johnson, Mays, Thurman, and Barbour adhered to Rauschenbusch's perspective in this area. On personalism, King's doctoral advisor Harold DeWolf was his chief mentor, although King knew much about personalist thought before he met DeWolf. On Gandhian nonviolence, King was vague and uncertain until Montgomery erupted and Rustin rushed to Montgomery. King had a full-fledged Socialist-personalist-pacifist model in his dean at Boston University, Walter Mueller, but, more importantly, when King entered the ministry he had models of everything he cared about in Johnson, Mays, Thurman, and Barbour. If they could blend black church religion, modern intellectualism, anticolonial internationalism, and social justice politics, so could he; in fact, he was called to do so. The best social gospel theologians were Socialists, which King took for granted from seminary onward. Personalism fit black church preaching and the social gospel like no other philosophy, which lured King to Boston University. Moreover, all his role models treasured Gandhi.

King stuck to these commitments throughout his career, in changing configurations. He had to camouflage what he believed about economic justice, until the so-called later King stopped doing so. He liked that he had a philosophical foundation, a variant of post-Kantian idealism, although he acquired critics who thought it quaint that he wanted one. He was predisposed to nonviolence by temperament and his education at Morehouse and two seminaries, though he was ambiguous about it until he became a movement leader. Afterward he embraced Gandhian nonviolence as a strategy and a spiritual–ethical way of life, while accepting some of Niebuhr's critiques of both. King got more radical every year not from repudiating what he believed previously but from failing to break his nation's addiction to white supremacy, economic injustice, and empire.

When King told the story of his intellectual development, he emphasized the white theologians and philosophers he read in seminary. He took for granted his nurture in the black church, which yielded accounts of his life and thought that obscured his cultural and religious formation. It took a great deal of scholarly deconstruction to correct the misleading account King provided in playing to white audiences. The black church was home and bread to King. He was steeped in its belief in a personal God of judgment, grace, and miracles, a gospel of redemption and sanctification, and a strong insistence that the gospel has a social dimension. He learned that he was "somebody" prized by a personal God, no matter what white society said. He learned how to read and move crowds by studying black preachers. The revisionist scholarship on King that started in the 1980s rightly reclaimed the role of the black church in King's life and work, and it laid the groundwork for the scholarship of the 1990s that wrestled with King's sexual behavior and faulty citation practices. However, even some of the best King scholars—notably David J. Garrow, Keith D. Miller, and David Levering Lewis—brokered these issues by wrongly contending that King took a cavalier attitude toward the theology he studied in seminary. This claim that King only pretended to care about his graduate education diminished his intellectual seriousness and achievements, and it encouraged others to pile on against liberal theology and personalism, dismissing both as not worth studying anyway.[15]

Repeatedly liberal theology was described in stereotypical terms as a perfectionist religious humanism that didn't believe in sin, and personalist philosophy got similar treatment as a thinly philosophical version of liberal theology. Homiletics scholar Richard Lischer, for example, in his otherwise outstanding rendering of King's preaching artistry, dismissed King's debts to liberal theology and personalism with flat stereotypes on both counts. Contrary to Lischer and numerous others, the liberal theologians King studied in seminary—notably William Newton Clarke, William Adams Brown, and Rauschenbusch—were long, strong, and vivid on the ravages of personal and collective evil. So were the personalist theologians under whom King studied. The theologians King studied practically battered their readers with descriptions of sin as badness, depravity, selfishness, and collective evil. King's teachers, especially DeWolf, reinforced this emphasis. DeWolf taught that liberal theology went to seed whenever it propagated humanistic substitutes for the language of sin and redemption. But you have to actually read these thinkers to know what they said, and too many scholars have settled for stereotypes.[16]

Lischer says that "personalism was devoid of the soul of religion" and it lacked any capacity to nurture a common life. King would have been incredulous at reading that Muelder, DeWolf, and S. Paul Schilling knew nothing of the soul of religion and somehow lacked a social ethic too. Muelder exemplified the fusion of vibrant personal faith and social justice passion that King admired and emulated. Theologically and ethically, King was so close to DeWolf that he channeled DeWolf's signature arguments throughout his career. Schilling wrote searching, vulnerable, spiritually powerful works on redemptive suffering and the ethical demands of the gospel. It would be hard to find anywhere three theologians less deserving of the ridicule that has been heaped upon them by scholars seeking to minimize King's graduate education and to belittle his teachers. King buttressed his black church faith with a personalist theological variant of the modern West's richest intellectual tradition, post-Kantian idealism. He was highly self-conscious and strategic about why he did so and how it worked for him.[17]

Mays, Kelsey, Johnson, and Barbour modeled for King why he needed the intellectualism that his graduate education provided. Then King studied under DeWolf and wrote a dense dissertation on why personality matters. His dissertation subjects, the theologians Paul Tillich and Henry Nelson Wieman, identified personality with limited human personality, which God transcended. King countered that personality as such means self-consciousness and self-direction. Applied to God, the idea of personality implies no limitation. More important, the idea that God is good requires the presupposition that God is personal. No theology, King believed, is better than the philosophy underlying it, and the best philosophy for theology upholds a quantitative pluralism in recognizing the manifold realities of sense experience, and a qualitative monism in affirming that reality has a unifying ground in God's being.

This fusion of black church faith and liberal personalist theology was King's mainstay in a turbulent world. He said so on numerous occasions, acknowledging that for him the crisis of belief was personal, cultural, social, and political. He gave highest place to his belief in a personal God and the infinite value of human personality. If the worth of personality was the ultimate value in life, racism was distinctly evil. Evil is precisely that which degrades and annihilates personality. King drew sufficient self-confidence from his theological undergirding that he expounded it to all manner of audiences in all manner of settings. It was not just church-talk to him, and his intellectualizing was not just to impress white intellectuals, although he worked hard at reaching white audiences.

The social gospel mattered to King because it was inherently social, it held fast to the gospel belief in salvation, and it was unabashedly political, a call to transform the structures of society in the direction of social justice. I give ample attention to King's theological beliefs and arguments, as I do with Johnson, Mays, Thurman, Powell, Murray, and others. But the social gospel acquired its name by proposing to change society, making society a subject of redemption. It was political without apology, building up a social justice movement. It took on the ravages of racism, militarism, empire, and injustice in the name of the gospel imperative to help the poor and afflicted and to break the chains of oppression. The social gospel grew out of the abolitionist movements of the black and white Christian communities, and, like abolitionism, it marshaled Christian arguments for a cause that had little support in the history of Christianity. The churches blessed slavery for centuries before abolitionism arose in the nineteenth century. The abolitionists had to buck that record when they claimed that slavery was anti-Christian. Their descendants in the radical wings of black and white social Christianity had a similar problem when they claimed a gospel warrant for theologies of social justice and abolishing white supremacy. To King, it mattered greatly that he had forerunners in this work and that a movement for it was building, however hard it was to see in the America of his seminary years.

Cornel West, delineating the principal intellectual and existential sources that shaped King, aptly cites four, in order of importance: prophetic black church Christianity, prophetic liberal Christianity, prophetic Gandhian nonviolence, and prophetic American civil religion. King heard the gospel and committed himself to it in the only institution owned by black Americans. His training in liberal Christianity provided intellectual and social ethical ballast for his religious faith. His commitment to Gandhian resistance provided a method for his racial justice activism and an extra-Christian language for the way of nonviolence. His belief in the U.S. American ideals of democracy, freedom, and equality enabled him to call the nation to fulfill these ideals. West rightly says that King embodied "the best of American Christendom" by synthesizing these sources.[18]

But this project was not unique to King, for it defines precisely what the black social gospel had become before King emerged. King stood in a tradition of black social gospel founders and mentors who heard the prophetic gospel in the black church, who appropriated social gospel liberalism, who engaged Gandhi as soon as the Gandhian revolution began in India, and who called America to stop betraying its vaunted ideals.

There are many ways to tell the story of the black freedom movement in King's era, and mine bears the limitations of its focus on black social gospel ministers who led the political struggle for racial justice and doubled as public intellectuals. Nearly all were male, southern, and Baptist. Ida B. Wells-Barnett and Nannie Burroughs were major figures in my previous book, in which I also gave extensive attention to the National Association of Colored Women. In the present book Ella Baker, Diane Nash, and Fannie Lou Hamer are important figures, and Pauli Murray is one of the six major social gospel intellectuals featured. But Murray was an outsider to the SCLC story that stands at the center of the book, and Baker, Nash, and Hamer were organizers, not religious intellectuals. Baker's exclusion from a leadership role in SCLC symbolizes exactly the clerical-gender problem at issue. Baker kept the SCLC going during its tenuous early years. The preachers who marginalized her—beginning with King—said that the SCLC needed to be a fire alarm operation of high voltage male preachers. Baker never agreed and thus ended up as a mentor to SNCC, which went on to replicate the male domination story, now with few ministers. Nash stood out as an indispensable leader of the sit-in and Freedom Ride movements, yet even during her moment of national renown she was pushed out of the way at spotlight time by male headliners who swooped into town. We need a social history of the black social gospel that highlights the work of local congregations and organizations. This book focuses on King, his role models and movement forerunners, and the SCLC—a tradition of prophetic ministers of unsurpassed historic importance.

Murray was further removed than Nash and Baker from the movement spotlight, despite her many years of knocking at the door. Being female, gay, queer, and Episcopalian disqualified Murray from a movement leadership role, even though she was also brilliant, accomplished, prolific, and a highly energetic activist. Very late in her career Murray became a feminist icon and an Episcopal priest, which drew attention to her many years of struggling in obscurity. She made original contributions to feminist legal theory and was an early contributor to the cultural studies movement. She anticipated the signature intellectual developments of the succeeding generation—queer theory, intersectional criticism, postcolonial theory, and critical race theory. She was a founder of feminist liberation theology who was already too postmodern and intersectional to endorse binary formulations of liberation theology. Thus she anticipated, in certain respects, womanist theology and ethics, although she is more accurately described as a black feminist than as a proto-womanist. Like Thurman and King, though differently from both, Murray is more relevant today than ever because her version of black social gospel Christianity radiated convictions that were ahead of her time and that remain high on the agenda of theology, ethics, and political theology. In her time, however, she barely got to her career as a theologian and priest. Neither were possibilities previously, while she tried other things, and then she was surprised to discover that she had been on a Christian spiritual journey all along.

This is a story about church leaders who embraced the social gospel of William Simmons, Reverdy Ransom, Ida Wells-Barnett, Alexander Walters, Nannie Burroughs, Adam Clayton Powell Sr., and Richard Wright Jr. and raised the demand for racial justice to a new level of public agency. They became important public intellectuals in the process, paving the way for America's greatest liberation movement, which was led by a succeeding generation of church leaders much like themselves. I am therefore making a continuity argument about an overlooked tradition, but always in a way that distinguishes the broad social gospel from the specific one that led to King and yielded radical protest activism. For all that Daddy King influenced his son at home, at church, and by sending him to Morehouse, neither Daddy King nor any of his buddies would have kept the bus strike going in Montgomery or struck hard in Birmingham or opposed the Vietnam War or spurned President Johnson or moved the struggle to Chicago or called a Poor People's Campaign of marchers to Washington, DC. The King movement must be continually renarrated, refashioned to what happened and why it fell far short of Martin's Dream of a decent society, let alone the Beloved Community.

PROPHETIC SUFFERING AND BLACK INTERNATIONALISM

The black social gospel leaders who succeeded Reverdy Ransom and Adam Clayton Powell Sr. were long on dignity, graduate degrees, simmering anger, and platform eloquence. They came to political activism and public intellectualism through the door of educational achievement. They graduated from prestigious white universities but had no chance of teaching in them. They got to be prominent by excelling at something familiar to black Americans—ascending through education and speaking prowess—and something unimaginable to most black Americans—compelling the attention and respect of sizable white audiences.

Many of them studied or taught at Howard University, where the exemplar of extroverted social gospel prophecy, Mordecai Johnson, presided. Johnson spent his entire career in the spotlight but wrote almost nothing. He turned Howard into a powerhouse, and suffered for it. He was one of the first to call for a fusion of social gospel theology and Gandhian anticolonial internationalism, which he established as a tradition at Howard. It had a rich harvest.

BECOMING MORDECAI W. JOHNSON

Mordecai Wyatt Johnson was named Wyatt Mordecai Johnson at birth, in December 1890 in Paris, Tennessee. He bore the first name of his father, Wyatt J. Johnson, but reversed his first and middle names in 1907, as a college freshman. Securing his identity was a factor, as was his desire for self-made distance from an emotionally distant father. Johnson loved the name Mordecai, however, long before and after he passed through his coming of age. For as long as he could remember, he treasured the biblical story of Mordecai plotting with Queen Esther to save the exiled Jews in Susa, the capital city of the Persian

Empire, from being slaughtered. The biblical Mordecai belonged to a people despised and enslaved by the Medes and Persians, playing a heroic role on behalf of his oppressed kin. Johnson took delight in his mother's story that she gave him this name because she believed that he, too, had a special mission in life.[1]

Wyatt J. Johnson was a stern taskmaster, handing out punishment with a leather strap. He worked in a succession of mills and seldom spoke, except on Sunday mornings, when he preached Baptist evangelical religion. Up to forty years of slavery in middle Tennessee, under several slavers, hardened Wyatt Johnson's character. He endured harsh treatment and conditions, seeing families ripped apart by slave trading. His body was stunted from abuse but strong and muscled from a lifetime of hard work. He served with his master in the Confederate army, incurring battle wounds that afflicted him for the rest of his life. He burned deeply over the outrages he saw and suffered, surviving by becoming steely, disciplined, and stoical. Just before the Civil War, Wyatt Johnson converted to Christianity. After the war he moved to the Memphis area, took up independent farming, felt called to preach, and moved to Henry County. He willed himself to literacy so he could read the Bible. He switched to millwork for many years and subsequently worked for twenty years at the Paris Lumber Company, leading a lumberyard crew.

The Johnson family lived in a small house set between two sets of railroad tracks that merged in the factory district of Paris. Wyatt Johnson had a strict regime. He rose at four o'clock, performed chores for an hour, took a long bath, climbed to the attic for an hour of prayer, and ate breakfast with his family before heading to the mill, where he planed for twelve hours per day, six days per week. Suppers were long and silent, with formal prayers. On Sundays he sat on the front porch after breakfast, read the Bible until he found a sermon text, ruminated for two or three hours, and headed to church. He founded a Baptist church in Cottage Grove, Tennessee, and later took over a congregation in Paris, Mt. Zion Baptist. Wyatt Johnson never preached for more than thirty minutes, in defiance of local custom, but he was said to preach with fierce authority. To Mordecai, Wyatt Johnson was severe, forbidding, old, and remote, pretty much in that order. Wyatt drove his son hard, dispensing swift punishment for lapses in obedience. Mordecai told his friend and biographer Richard I. McKinney that Wyatt Johnson's "greatest ability was generally applied from the rear." When Mordecai did something commendable, Wyatt said nothing— his version of praise. Mordecai was a college student before he could hold a conversation with his father. It took him forty years to comprehend why his father was so severe and why he should appreciate having had such a father.[2]

Wyatt Johnson had married a fellow slave, Nellie Biass, shortly before the Civil War and raised three children with her. She died in 1885; three years later Wyatt married Carolyn Freeman, a kindly, winsome, mixed-race woman with whom Wyatt had one child, Mordecai. Carolyn Freeman Johnson, who went by "Callie" to friends, was dramatically different from her husband. Thirty years younger than Wyatt, she was warm, generous, and nurturing, and emoted easily. She worked as a domestic, enjoyed music, and cultivated flowerbeds. Above all, she adored her son. Carolyn Johnson sacrificed her needs to provide whatever Mordecai needed and filled him with her dreams for him. Throughout his life Mordecai Johnson expounded lyrically on the tender wonders of mother love.[3]

Sickly as a youth but secure in mother love and his ability, Johnson was prone to prankishness, which annoyed Wyatt Johnson, and gifted with a near photographic memory, which made him a whiz at school, almost to his detriment. He memorized long passages of literature and wowed his public school teachers. One of Johnson's teachers, Benjamin Sampson, had been fired as a school principal in Memphis for allowing a student to write an essay on lynching. Sampson drilled Johnson on public speaking and debate, teaching him to direct his words and gestures to one person in the audience—winning over the crowd by persuading one individual. Johnson's self-confidence soared under Sampson's instruction, calling himself a "debate shark." Paris had no education for blacks beyond elementary school, so the Johnsons sent Mordecai to Roger Williams University in Nashville, an American Baptist Home Mission Society institution, where John Hope had recently taught and Samuel H. Archer had recently joined the faculty.

Hope was a native of Augusta, Georgia, and an 1894 graduate of Brown University. He taught at Roger Williams from 1894 to 1898 before moving to Atlanta Baptist College for Men in Atlanta, opting for a career at historically black schools. After the Civil War white northern missionary associations established forty-six black institutions of higher learning; another sixteen were founded by states. Hope's career as an educator was linked closely, for over thirty years, to Archer, his eventual successor as president of Morehouse College. Archer got his schooling at Peabody Public School in Petersburg, Virginia, the Wayland Normal Academy in Washington, DC, and Colgate University in Hamilton, New York. He had graduated from Colgate in 1902 and had recently joined the faculty at Roger Williams, teaching mathematics, when Johnson got there. Archer had a gift for befriending and inspiring the young men he taught; it helped that he coached football. Students called him, fondly, "Big Boy," and were devoted to him. Johnson was a prime example, one of many for whom Archer stood as a model of black manhood.[4]

In 1905, during Johnson's third year, a fire destroyed the campus of Roger Williams. Johnson transferred to Howe Institute, a new school in the Memphis Baptist Bible and Normal Institute. Archer moved to Atlanta Baptist College, joining Hope. Johnson left Howe after one semester, following Archer to Atlanta Baptist. Johnson's best friend, Robert Woodson, had already registered as a first-year college student, and Johnson's parents were determined to obtain a good education for him. Fortunately Johnson's advisor persuaded him to enroll as a junior in the (high school) academy program, discounting his recent record. Johnson was not ready for college, having coasted on superior ability. Benjamin Brawley, a respected English scholar at Atlanta Baptist College, delivered the news to Johnson that he did not write, read, or speak as well as he thought. Johnson, chastened and grateful, let Brawley teach him how to wield the English language. He also coped with loneliness, as Johnson had trouble making friends and he found Nashville and Memphis frightening. His mother had doted on him and his father had driven him constantly; being without both, in big-city schools, left him feeling lost.[5]

At the turn of the twentieth century, most black colleges still had white presidents—clerical descendants of the white northern missionary founders. The white presidents, being paternalistic and prizing their jobs, insisted that they were still needed, as did their boards of trustees. Atlanta Baptist College provided a better model in 1906, when George Sale retired as president and the trustees appointed Hope as acting president, just as Johnson entered the college as a sixteen-year-old freshman.

Hope was a voluntary Negro, a blond-haired, blue-eyed, light-colored black man who could have passed for white almost anywhere, or, if he chose, for an honorary white man in the northern white academy. His father, James Hope, was born in Scotland, immigrated to New York in the early nineteenth century, and became a prominent businessman in Augusta. Georgia law prohibited James Hope from marrying his light-colored African American partner, Mary Frances Butts, but the two lived openly as husband and wife in Augusta until James Hope's death in 1876.

John Hope was eight years old when his father died. He retained his status in Augusta's black elite mostly on the strength of his mother's pre–Civil War heritage as a free black in Hancock County, Georgia, and in 1886 he enrolled at Worcester Academy in Worcester, Massachusetts—a prep school stepping-stone to his education at Brown. In 1897 Hope married Lugenia Burns, subsequently a prominent social activist. The following year, upon moving to Atlanta, Hope met Booker T. Washington and W. E. B. Du Bois, eventually befriending both, especially Du Bois. These friendships symbolized Hope's long-running dual career as the president of a black college in the South and a national civil rights leader, two things that combined perilously, with constant tension requiring diplomatic skill and nerve.[6]

Hope's background in Georgia as the son of an unmarried biracial couple helped to steel him for his career as a race leader in the South committed to civil rights, black education, the social gospel, and the black community. Atlanta Baptist students felt the historic significance of his appointment, at first worrying that his "acting" title reflected a lack of commitment to him. They resolved to help Hope succeed, by behaving well. Johnson, newly thriving with self-confidence and a social life, took the pledge to help Hope but found it impossible to give up pranks. Some nights he blasted fellow dormitory residents awake by rolling Civil War cannonballs down the stairwell. Hope wrote a plaintive letter to Wyatt Johnson, warning that his son teetered on expulsion. Wyatt Johnson reprimanded Mordecai, told Hope he should have no further trouble, and added that if any further incident occurred, throw him out.[7]

Johnson needed to rebel, but he also wanted Hope, Archer, and Brawley to respect him. He buckled down, won top honors in the academy, and won a scholarship to the college, where he played quarterback on the football team and compiled an outstanding academic record. Archer in mathematics, Brawley in English, Hope in philosophy, and Matthew W. Bullock in geology and social science encouraged Johnson to pursue an academic career. He let them down again by playing cards in his room, an infraction meriting expulsion at Atlanta Baptist College. Hope and other college officials did not want to lose their best student. They realized that Carolyn Johnson's life revolved around Mordecai and that she would be crushed if they expelled him. So they suspended Johnson, sending him to Chicago to live secretly with a relative, keeping the secret from Wyatt Johnson. Upon serving his suspension Johnson returned to the college, won high honors, and graduated in 1911.

Hope was the gold standard disciplinarian among black college presidents of his generation. He ran the college with an iron hand, consulted minimally on hiring and policy decisions, and treated students with measured, autocratic, paternal care. Howard Thurman later recalled that students respected Hope more than they liked him, respecting him greatly. Hope found a favorite in Johnson, enthusing at his brilliance and seeing much of himself in Johnson — enough to appoint him to the faculty as soon as he graduated. Johnson was not quite as "voluntary" as Hope, but he was sufficiently light-colored that he could have passed as racially indeterminate in much of the country. Johnson began as Brawley's sabbatical replacement, later taught economics, and coached the debate team. In 1913 the college changed its name to Morehouse, and Johnson commemorated the occasion by writing a new school song. Since degrees from Morehouse and other black institutions were unaccredited, ambitious graduates often "validated" their degrees by studying for a fifth undergraduate year at a prestigious white university. The University of Chicago swelled its summer enrollments every year by this means. Johnson opted for validation at Chicago, despite being warned by friends that the university was a stronghold of atheism and Socialism.

His friends were adamant: Chicago was a terrible school. Merely being there might destroy his faith, and if he persisted in going he had to avoid the course on evolution ("It will ruin your religion") and the course on Socialism ("You will just be ruined in every way"). Johnson, upon registering, told sociologist and graduate school dean Albion Small that he wasn't sure what his third course should be: "But the course in evolution and the course in socialism—I want them right away." He thrived in both, fusing evolutionary theory and Socialism to his religious worldview, in line with the social gospel. For the rest of his life Johnson regaled audiences with this story, supplying the moral: Christians should never fear the best of modern learning.[8]

He had no experience of feeling threatened or injured by modern knowledge. Johnson moved smoothly from his father's literalistic orthodoxy to the intellectual religion modeled by his teachers, especially Hope. In Johnson's experience education was liberalizing and empowering, and he wanted as much as he could get. A decade earlier Hope had studied at the University of Chicago Divinity School during the summers, absorbing liberal theology and the social gospel. To Johnson, Chicago-style social gospel liberalism was not to be feared, no matter what church conservatives said. Liberal theology was simply the adjustment that theology had to make to accommodate modern biology, social science, and historical criticism. Positively, the church needed to respect intellectual freedom and be willing to follow the evidence. Negatively, the church needed to avoid a self-inflicted crisis of intellectual credibility. Chicago strengthened Johnson's intellectual predispositions and enhanced his intellectual self-esteem, even as he reeled from an emotional crisis.

It was not an experience of being wounded by racism. Johnson resented white Atlanta's relentless hostility toward black Americans, but he was bustling and extroverted, with a deep reserve of self-confidence, taking pride in not letting racists get to him. His crisis was a broken heart. Johnson had a sweetheart from his high school years, Alice Clinton Woodson, whom he met while managing a café in Memphis during summer break. The Woodson family belonged to the elite of black Memphis. They were descendants of Thomas Jefferson through his relationship with his slave Sally Hemings, and several

members of the Woodson family had a role in founding Wilberforce University
in 1856. Alice Woodson's father, Benjamin F. Woodson, an attorney and
contractor in Memphis, was a graduate of Wilberforce, and her mother, Alice
Allen Woodson, was a member of Fisk University's first class in 1866, having
come from a long line of free blacks who migrated from North Carolina to
Ohio. Alice Clinton Woodson belonged to the upscale Primrose Club, which
afforded her opportunities to socialize with Johnson. She was fourteen, he was
seventeen, they had one summer together, and Johnson loved her for the rest of
his life.[9]

Alice Clinton Woodson went to Howard University, where she lived with her
uncle, Howard trustee Jesse E. Moorland, secretary of the Colored Men's
Department of the YMCA International Committee. Then she transferred to
her mother's alma mater, Fisk, while maintaining a romance with Johnson.
There were many letters, several visits, and numerous professions of love, and in
May 1912 they agreed to announce their engagement. Johnson traveled triumphantly to Nashville to formally propose. He climbed the steps of Jubilee Hall,
asked the dormitory matron for permission to see Alice, and was told that Alice
was "out with her Meherry boyfriend." (Meherry Medical College was nearby.)
In fact, Alice was waiting for Johnson in her room, but he did not question the
matron's report. Johnson stewed for a while in the lobby, stunned and hurt,
before asking the matron to tell Alice, "Tell her I was here." Alice, after a long,
anxious wait, finally approached the matron, who claimed no one had come for
her. Johnson returned to Atlanta, writing to Alice that she had crushed him with
her duplicity and rudeness. She replied that the duplicity and rudeness belonged
to him; now he was even lying about having come to Fisk to see her. Each no
longer believed the other's profession of love, and both were offended at being
accused of duplicity. Somehow they never considered that there might be a
simpler explanation. Johnson resolved to move forward without her.[10]

In that mood he lost his beloved mother and decided what to do with his life.
Carolyn Johnson died in the fall of 1912. Mordecai spent several nights grieving
and brooding, seated on an easy-chair rocker that Carolyn had given him,
thinking about his life from death backward. His mother had poured herself out
for him, but what would become of her efforts? Johnson later recalled, "Always,
I started with my death. Before, I had looked forward, now I looked back. If I
were lying dead, as I had seen my mother lie, what in life would be worthwhile?
What, of the many things that I had done, would justify my existence? What
would have meaning?"[11]

A few nights into this brooding he had a vision: "I was lying on my deathbed
in a rough cabin, quite alone. The place was very still. Then, silently, the door

opened and people came in, poorly dressed, plain people, who moved in line past my bed. And as they passed, each had something to say in affection and gratitude. I had helped one who was in trouble. I had comforted another. I had given wise counsel to a third. I saw the line distinctly, coming in and passing out, while I lay there, dying, on the coarse bed." To Johnson, this vision was both revelatory and a confirmation of a message long instilled in him: "I knew that I had found the meaning of life. It was service, service to the poor and afflicted. And I felt that I could best render this service by leaving my scholastic work and entering the ministry."[12]

He needed to live up to his mother's dreams and the name she gave him. Johnson had a special, holy, ethical calling, like Mordecai. He dared not rest content with teaching history and economics to college students. His friends were incredulous: Why throw away an expensive education and a promising academic career for a church pulpit? Anyone could be a minister. Johnson replied that a true religious calling was not something to denigrate. His education would make him a better minister, and if he had a religious calling, he needed to go to seminary. One friend was persistent, deriding him: "The shining hero goes pious; God's glamor boy." Du Bois, hearing the story, had a similar reaction: "Another good man gone." The vehemence of Johnson's friends gave him pause. Were they right? Would it be a waste of his ability and education to go into ministry? Johnson weighed pros and cons for several weeks before deciding that his friends were not right, at least not in his case. He did not experience his call to ministry as settling for something beneath him. This was his best chance to do something noble and important.[13]

The best Baptist seminary that he knew of, by reputation, was Newton Theological Institution in Newton Centre, Massachusetts. Founded in 1825, Newton had a distinguished history and faculty. Like all American Baptist institutions, Newton traced its origins to Roger Williams, a Puritan pastor who arrived in Boston from England in 1631, got in trouble with colonial authorities, and founded the first American Baptist congregation in 1639. American Baptists took pride that Williams advocated religious tolerance, separation of church and state, and decent treatment of Native Americans. In 1900, however, the premier Baptist seminary stopped admitting African American students to avoid offending prospective white students from the South. No one had told Johnson, so he applied and was denied admission. Later the same thing happened to Benjamin Mays (in 1920) and Howard Thurman (in 1923). Newton kept rejecting black applicants until 1926.[14]

In that case, there had to be a better Baptist seminary than Newton. Johnson stewed over his options, finally applying to Rochester Theological Seminary, where Walter Rauschenbusch championed the social gospel and taught church history. Rochester had an annual quota of two black American admits, so the dormitory math was simple: one room each year. During the period that he applied to Rochester, Johnson noticed a striking beauty in his history class at Morehouse, Anna Ethelyn Gardner, a student from nearby Spelman Seminary (later Spelman College). Anna Gardner came from the same cultured Augusta community that produced John Hope, YMCA leader Channing Tobias, and NAACP executive secretary Walter White. She had grown up next door to Lucy Laney, the founder of a renowned school, the Lucy Laney Normal and Industrial Institute, which Gardner attended in her youth. Johnson had graduated from college two years previously and was only two years older than Gardner. Since Morehouse forbade romantic relationships between teachers and students, Johnson proceeded carefully, avoiding appearances of courtship. Gardner possessed the qualities he prized in women: dazzling attractiveness, refinement, intelligence, kindness, and quiet reserve. She and Johnson became friends, waiting until she graduated in 1914 to start a romance, on cooler romantic terms than he had risked last time.

In September 1913 he enrolled at Rochester Seminary and thrilled at studying under Rauschenbusch. Rochester Seminary was still quite conservative, as campus patriarch Augustus Hopkins Strong, a prominent evangelical theologian, had served as president for forty years until retiring in 1912. In 1907 Rauschenbusch published an electrifying manifesto for social gospel Socialism, *Christianity and the Social Crisis.* He half expected to be fired, especially for a radical chapter titled "What To Do." But the book became a supercharger for an ascending social gospel movement, making Rauschenbusch famous. Rochester Seminary gradually liberalized while basking in his success. Rauschenbusch taught that justice-oriented prophetic faith is the beating heart of Scripture, the prophetic spirit rose from the dead in the social ethical teaching of Jesus, and Christianity is supposed to transform society in the kingdom-bringing spirit of Jesus. Though Christianity usually obscured the revolutionary spirit of the gospel, it was not too late for the church to adopt the way and spirit of Jesus.[15]

Rauschenbusch believed the rise of corporate capitalism marked a crisis for American civilization but also an opportunity to recover the lost kingdom ideal of Jesus. *Christianity and the Social Crisis* called for a radical democratic politics of the cooperative commonwealth. The book was skillfully fashioned and perfectly timed. It went through thirteen printings in five years and set a new standard for political theology. It built upon works by American social gospelers Washington Gladden, Josiah Strong, Richard Ely, Shailer Mathews, and Francis Greenwood Peabody, but nothing like Rauschenbusch's stunning conflation of historical, theological, and political arguments had been seen previously.

Rauschenbusch later recalled that he crammed everything he knew into *Christianity and the Social Crisis*, so he thought he was done with this subject. What was left to say? He took a sabbatical in Germany and hoped not to get fired. "But meanwhile the social awakening of our nation set in like an equinoctial gale in March, and when I came home, I found myself caught in the tail of the storm." Now he was famous and besieged with lecture invitations, which required more writing. He recalled that until about 1900 he and a handful of ministers shouted in the wilderness: "It was always a happy surprise when we found a new man who had seen the light." He and his friends "used to form a kind of flying wedge" to support any newcomer who "attacked a ministers' conference with the Social Gospel." But now the social gospel was sweeping the ministers' conferences. A third Great Awakening was occurring, one that recovered the social spirit and kingdom goal of Jesus. In 1908 thirty-two Protestant denominations founded the Federal Council of Churches, promptly issuing a Social Creed of the Churches that was straight out of the social gospel. It called for "equal rights and complete justice for all men," the abolition of child labor, a living wage in every industry, and eleven other points mostly pertaining to the rights of workers.[16]

To his surprise, Rauschenbusch had two more big books in his head: *Christianizing the Social Order*, published in 1912, and *A Theology of the Social Gospel*, published in 1917, plus three shorter books. *Christianizing the Social Order* brimmed with progressive optimism and idealism. It urged that the crucial thing was the spirit and direction of Jesus's religion, not the dogmas he retained from his background. In Rauschenbusch's telling, the Protestant Reformation recovered Pauline doctrine but not the spirit of Jesus. Luther and Calvin had little feeling for the kingdom, theologically they were authoritarians, and they had precious little democratic spirit. It took modern social idealism and historical criticism to recover Jesus and his kingdom. The Reformation worked back to Paul; modern theology worked back to Jesus *and* adopted the master concept of modern thought, evolution, which helped Christians understand the world as the reign of God toward which all creation was moving. In 1912, before World War I savaged his optimism, Rauschenbusch stressed that history is God's workshop, the unfolding of an immanent divine purpose that works toward the commonwealth of spiritual freedom and righteousness.

Even at the high tide of the social gospel, *Christianizing the Social Order* was a provocative title. Rauschenbusch assured readers that he had no theocratic hankerings. The social gospel was not about putting Christ's name in the Constitution or breaching the American wall between church and state. It wanted social and cultural transformation, not a state religion. To Christianize society was to bring it into harmony with the ethical values of Christ. These values were not exclusive to Christ or Christianity, Rauschenbusch stressed. They were universal, shared by all people of good will, defining the universal content of good will: freedom, sacrificial love, compassion, community, justice, equality. So Rauschenbusch used "Christianize," "moralize," "humanize," and "democratize" as interchangeable terms. A bad society made good people do bad things; a good society compelled even bad people to be cooperative and democratic. Until the modern age most families and churches were decidedly bad, being reactionary and coercive. Both were despotic in ways that reinforced each other, condemning women to subservience. According to Rauschenbusch, the democratizing spirit of the modern age changed this picture. The churches lost their temporal power, they learned that coercion has the same relation to true religion that rape has to love, and feminism was abolishing patriarchal autocracy. The churches did not welcome their salvation, he noted; they had to be converted to the good against their will; and many of them were still determined to oppress women.[17]

Like most social gospelers, Rauschenbusch was a good enough Victorian to be conflicted about women's rights because he wanted wives and mothers to stay home and take care of their families. He implored his audiences not to erode the (late Victorian) middle-class ideal of family life in the name of individual progress for women. What made the middle-class family *ideal* was precisely that it allowed women not to work outside the home. Capitalism emptied the home of its nurturing wives and mothers. Christian Socialism was the wholesome alternative. It lifted women to the equality they deserved while supporting the family as the key to a healthy society.[18]

The U.S. American economic system, by contrast, was completely unregenerate. To Rauschenbusch, the root of the problem was systemic, not personal. It was the predatory logic of capitalism, which was inimical to Christianity, although theologians timidly avoided the subject. In Catholicism the dominant power was the dogmatic mythology of a priestly class; in Protestantism it was the financial and cultural power of the capitalist class. Rauschenbusch countered that the tests of Christian morality applied to every sphere, including economics: Did a given system reward cooperation and the common good or selfishness and will-to-power? Did it call people to the good or tempt them downward?

Capitalism, Rauschenbusch insisted, was essentially corrupting. Anticipating Harvard sociologist Daniel Bell's "cultural contradictions of capitalism" thesis by sixty years, Rauschenbusch argued that capitalism sapped its own foundations by degrading the cultural capital on which America's economic success depended. It commodified every profession it touched, turned impressionable people into small-minded consumers, and extended to every sector of society: "'Commercializing a profession' always means degrading it. Of the learned professions the Law is farthest gone. The most lucrative practice is the service of corporations, and they need the lawyer to protect their interests against the claims of the public."[19]

To Rauschenbusch, the problem was structural—the autocratic power unrestrained by democratic checks that capitalism gave to owners and managers. The root of the problem was that workers had no property rights under capitalism. In the political sphere an American worker was a rights-bearing citizen, but in the economic sphere the same worker could give forty years of labor to a factory and still possess no more rights over property than a medieval serf. Workers labored on industrial property that was too expensive for them to own but which was financed by the savings and labor of working people. The solution was to democratize the processes of production and investment: "Political democracy without economic democracy is an uncashed promissory note, a pot without the roast, a form without substance. But in so far as democracy has become effective, it has quickened everything it has touched." Democracy was needed in the economic sphere for the same reasons it was needed everywhere else. It promoted freedom and equality, it legitimated the necessary exercise of authority, and it served as a brake on the domination of privileged classes.[20]

Johnson deeply absorbed Rauschenbusch's theology and Socialist politics, while witnessing Rauschenbusch's painfully belated attempts to address racial justice. The early Rauschenbusch was strangely silent about racism, which caused religious scholars to claim wrongly, for decades, that the white social gospel ignored racial justice issues. Rauschenbusch knew few African Americans personally and realized that he had no moral authority on this subject. Moreover, in his early career at Rochester Seminary he ran the German department, catering to a conservative German American constituency that was hostile to racial justice and the social gospel. The later Rauschenbusch, during the period Johnson studied under him, confessed that he had been silent about racism because it seemed overwhelmingly tragic to him. America's racial pathology refuted his idealism, being too depressing to mix into his buoyant books on the forward march of the kingdom of God.[21]

In *Christianizing the Social Order* Rauschenbusch finally managed to say that the spirit of Jesus "smites race pride and prejudice in the face in the name of humanity." In his last book, *A Theology for the Social Gospel*, Rauschenbusch described racial lynching as the ultimate example of social evil. Traditional Christianity overlooked the transmission of evil through social traditions and institutions, he argued. It was at the social level that oppression, perversity, racism, and ethnic feuds were transmitted from one generation to the next: "When negroes are hunted from a Northern city like beasts, or when a Southern city degrades the whole nation by turning the savage inhumanity of a mob into a public festivity, we are continuing to sin because our fathers created the conditions of sin by the African slave trade and by the unearned wealth they gathered from slave labor for generations."[22]

Johnson wholly embraced Rauschenbusch's teaching that true Christianity inspired movements for social justice and a determined opposition to the "kingdom of evil." The latter notion was not a throwback to the kingdom of evil spirits headed by Satan. The kingdom of evil was social, historical, destructive, and solidaristic, not devil mythology, mere ignorance, or disjointed events. All people were bound together in the condition of bearing the yoke of evil and suffering, but only the social gospel made theological sense of this truism. Rauschenbusch, in Johnson's eyes, exemplified the ideal of confident, missionary, modern, radical Christianity. Historical criticism yielded the social gospel Jesus, and the social gospel made Christianity relevant to modern life. For each of his three years at Rochester Johnson earned the highest grades in his class, graduating in 1916 as class valedictorian. He wrote to Hope of his achievements and ambitions, enthusing in 1914, "Religion is going to be a great factor in the new adjustment. There never was such a reformation as we are now on the verge of. This religion reemphasized with new aspects to suit the modern needs will bring forth great moral and spiritual engineers. God grant that I may be one of these among my own people!"[23]

Students at Rochester did not receive the bachelor of divinity degree at graduation, as the seminary required a thesis for the degree, and one had to graduate before writing the thesis. Thus Johnson did not receive his degree until 1920, when he submitted a thesis on the twelfth-century Order of Knights Templar. By then he was a star speaker on the ecumenical lecture circuit and a seasoned pastor at First Baptist Church of Charleston, West Virginia. Hope tried repeatedly to lure Johnson back to the Morehouse faculty, but Johnson had already taught at Morehouse and had gone to seminary to prepare for church ministry and/or a national ministry. He got a taste of the latter possibility during his student days at Rochester, speaking at YMCA conferences. Rochester Seminary president Clarence Barbour boosted Johnson's speaking career, as did Hope and Jesse Moorland. It helped that Moorland was Alice Woodson's uncle and had met Johnson in her home during Johnson's high school days; by then all parties knew about the Fisk matron.

Johnson was a gifted speaker: eloquent, lucid, engaging, and intellectually commanding, with a formidable physical and emotional presence. Early on he developed the ability to speak without a manuscript, using only a brief outline. Upon graduating from Rochester he succeeded Max Yergan as student secretary of the YMCA's International Committee. Yergan had moved on to YMCA work in India, and Johnson spoke for the YMCA on national and international tours. On Christmas day in 1916 he squeezed a wedding into his speaking schedule, marrying Anna Ethelyn Gardner in Augusta; she had taught at Alabama A&M College while waiting for a marriage proposal. Johnson enjoyed his YMCA work but resigned in the spring of 1917 after YMCA officials relegated blacks to separate dining and sleeping facilities at a national conference in Atlantic City, New Jersey. He would not speak for an organization that capitulated to segregation. If the YMCA ditched Christianity and decency as soon as it confronted local racism, Johnson was better off ministering in a church. He had planned to take a congregation sooner or later anyway. Thus he chose First Baptist Church, Charleston, among several offers, just as Woodrow Wilson intervened in World War I.

SOCIAL GOSPEL MINISTRY

Ordained clergy were exempt from military service, which was fine with Johnson. Most white social gospel leaders had campaigned against intervening until Wilson did so. Most black church ministers had stayed out of the argument, treating it as white people's business. Johnson had witnessed Rauschenbusch's torment when war broke out in 1914 and the abuse he took for refusing to favor England over Germany. Then the United States intervened in April 1917, and Rauschenbusch was pilloried for refusing to join the prowar stampede. Johnson, beginning his ministry at Charleston in September 1917, played it safe, like most social gospelers, joining the prowar swing. He reasoned that the war offered an opportunity for black Americans to show they were patriots, ready to fight for their country and American democratic ideals. Wilson had tried to keep America out of the war, but now America needed to make the world safe for democracy, exactly as Wilson said, fighting for idealistic Christian objectives.[24]

Charleston, in 1917, had an African American population of five thousand and a total population of thirty-five thousand. It was the state capital of a state admitted to the Union in 1863 after the western counties of Virginia seceded, mostly over the politics and economics of slavery. West Virginians felt mistreated by the government of Virginia and cheated of job opportunities in eastern counties where the slave system predominated. A half-century later the consuming issue in coal mining West Virginia was the fight between labor and capital, which was sufficiently violent to require periodic interventions by the National

Guard. First Baptist was the city's leading black congregation. It was incorporated in 1868 and included much of Charleston's black professional class. Johnson thrived there from the beginning, making friends and attracting new members. His gregarious personality and growing family—Carolyn Elizabeth Johnson was born two months after the family moved to Charleston—drew Johnson quickly into the local community.

Though he supported the war, Johnson blistered the government for abusing black soldiers, citing Du Bois's articles in *Crisis*. Though he sought to be a peacemaker in the West Virginia class struggle, Johnson did not hide his politics. At Rochester Seminary he had absorbed Rauschenbusch's interest in cooperative ownership, studying the history of the cooperative movement. Johnson focused on the Rochdale Cooperative network in England, founded in 1837, which practiced one-vote-per-member worker ownership, service at cost, and religious nondiscrimination. Shortly after he arrived in Charleston, Johnson organized a worker-owned grocery enterprise, the Rochdale Cash Grocery Cooperative, drawing mostly on members of his congregation. This venture lasted only a few years, but it raised consciousness in Charleston's black community about business skills and economic cooperation. Johnson preached that acquiring competence in this area was indispensable. Black Americans had to learn about economic forces that shaped and governed their lives. They had to develop habits of economic cooperation that resisted the predatory logic of capitalism. And they had to fight for their rights in politics and society.

Johnson followed through on the latter imperative by founding a chapter of the NAACP, which grew to one thousand members. This was during the period that James Weldon Johnson joined the NAACP national staff and pushed the organization into black communities in the South, though Johnson interacted mostly with executive secretary Walter White. NAACP activism was direct, palpable, often reactive, and, especially in the South, perilous. "Stand up for your rights" had a mostly straightforward meaning in the context of NAACP activism: organize against segregation, racism, and lynching. Charleston's black community needed only a catalyzing figure to spur civil rights activism, creating one of the NAACP's strongest southern chapters.[25]

Johnson brought the same commanding style and self-confidence to the pulpit that made him a spellbinder on the lecture circuit. His sermons were strong, thoughtful, challenging, and long, often disputing tame readings of the Bible. He had three central themes, urging that they worked together: the "brotherhood of man," the necessity of Christian unity, and the Christian mission to build the kingdom of God. Every Johnson sermon and speech had a riff on at least one of these themes: "There must be a great united movement of the Christian churches given to the realistic purpose of transforming the real world, with its green grass and its fallible human beings and its injuriously working social institutions, into the Kingdom of God on Earth. If the church is to live there must be a Christian movement to give reverence to human personality, a movement to use all the forces of modern knowledge and technology to build a social order which will raise and enlarge the life of every human being."[26]

He liked asking rhetorical questions, and answering them. Why should people still care about Jesus, nineteen centuries later? Johnson did not appeal to a creedal statement about Jesus's divinity or resurrection—a conversation-stopper about what mattered. Jesus still mattered because he drew near to people, he made them "acutely conscious of their needs," and he filled them with hope that "somehow they might overcome their troubles and their blindnesses and their weaknesses and see and be new creatures." Jesus talked about the same obsessions that afflicted Americans, Johnson said: "Some boys are trampling over their mothers, are wounding the hearts of their sisters and brothers, and are doing things that will make us sorry as long as we live." Jesus preached against one kind of greed yielding another, a familiar spectacle: "We think that because we have more smoke coming out of our smokestacks and more express going down the road and more railroad trains running than anybody else that we have got the proudest civilization on earth and have made all the great advances in the world." But think of China, Johnson admonished. China's civilization went back six thousand years, and the courtesy existing between a Chinese daughter and her mother "is something we Americans can hardly dream of." When Americans, with all their cars and money, visited Chinese in their homes, they saw "dignity and beauty and loveliness" that Americans found unfathomable. Every day, before heading for work, Chinese men bowed down and vowed to live in honor, dignity, and purity. Jesus was still working on Americans to become that civilized, Johnson suggested. So far the Chinese were far ahead.[27]

In Jesus's time, Johnson said, most people followed the crowd and looked out for themselves. That was still the norm, as most people rationalized that nothing was more natural than selfish conformity. Self-sacrifice for the sake of a moral good was definitely unnatural. Johnson had in mind opponents of the League of Nations: "Jesus met that type in his day. He came with a message of salvation for his people, but they followed the majority. And one of the saddest things in the world is to stand up and see a great man like Woodrow Wilson, with a mind fifty years ahead of his generation, having to submit to the puny votes of a group of men who have no conception of what he is thinking about and no conception of his vision for the salvation of the people." In Johnson's telling, the greatest presidents—Wilson, Theodore Roosevelt, and Abraham Lincoln—got to be great by transcending the mediocrity and conventionality of their contemporaries.[28]

Johnson reiterated what he did not do. He did not answer his real-world question with a theological doctrine: "For years and years, the disciples of Jesus have been holding up to the young men the theological Christ: the pre-existent Son of God who came down in trails of glory and was born at Bethlehem and endowed with miraculous power of overcoming all things before him and ascended into heaven." This story about a theological Christ descended from heaven was a distraction from the religion of Christ, Johnson contended: "I am preaching the spirit of the love of God that walked in the consciousness of a man like you and me." The love divine in Jesus was more real than any doctrine: "And, bless you, when you have looked into his face, you will never be satisfied in this world anymore until you learn that God is love." There were too many denominations, Johnson lamented, they prattled too much about churches and otherworldly beliefs, and they alienated "the hungry minds of young people" who wanted something spiritual and real. This was not only an American problem. Johnson knew Christian missionaries in Japan facing the same challenge. They were told: "If you come with the spirit of Jesus, we will listen to you; but if you come talking of your racial superiority and materialistic civilization, stay at home. We want to see Jesus; we want to see him; we don't want to see you."[29]

Johnson was fond of saying that every living thing has a compulsion to give itself away. Every living thing gathers into itself the potencies of the past and projects whatever has passed through it into the living things of the future. Only human beings tried to impede this process, taking everything from the past while often putting nothing into it. Yet human beings were God's highest creation. Johnson put it sharply: "This generation in which we live is filled with young women and young men who have no intention whatever of gathering up the potencies of life in themselves and projecting them into the future. This generation is full of childless homes that are not childless by accident but childless by intention." Only a selfish age, lacking gratitude and grace, aspired to create childless homes, and every married couple that elected to have no children rudely insulted their mothers. Johnson allowed that some mothers were short on caring and responsibility. Nevertheless, no mother deserved to have children who wanted no children. No one would exist if all women were that selfish: "Have you ever thought, my beloved, have you ever just sat down and thought what your mother put into your life?" How could anyone think it through and then choose selfish ingratitude?[30]

Selfishness and ingratitude were intertwined forms of bondage. Johnson said that black Americans, despite their grievances, owed gratitude to white America for many things. Black Americans lived in a prosperous nation offering more liberty and opportunity than any nation on earth. That story began with "a handful of pilgrims" yearning for religious freedom. They "gave us a government of the people for the people and by the people." Undermining his point with a ludicrous exaggeration, Johnson exhorted, "We have received it all. Freely we have received." In other contexts Johnson emphasized what had not been received; in the pulpit he charged that too many African Americans fixed on a victim story that made them selfish, ungrateful, and stuck in victimization. He declared that God wanted much more from them: "A selfish human being is a monstrosity, is a monstrosity. Any human being who lives for himself and himself only is a monstrous creature. The very foundation of his life is the basest of all human qualities—ingratitude. For a man to be selfish in such a world as this, he must shut his eyes and his mind and his heart to all the great things that he has received from the human race." A selfish human being, Johnson chided, was lower than a pig that grunted gratefully for a heaping of slop. The worst were educated people that turned selfish after benefiting from expensive schooling: "Above all, an educated Negro—my God, what a monstrosity!" Virtually every educated person of African descent was a beneficiary of the sacrifices of others. Anyone fitting this description that snarled with ingratitude was "a base ingrate and scoundrel." Moreover, every such person was bound to become miserable and a failure because selfish people were never satisfied with anything.[31]

Johnson grieved for poor black communities that nurtured, and routinely lost, their brightest youth. He blistered the "selfish ingrates" who split shortly after taking all that a humble community could give. One of the world's "greatest tragedies" was that most highly educated black Americans lived in three cities: "As soon as one of us Negroes gets sufficient education here, we run off to New York or Boston or Chicago, where we won't have to offer anything." Johnson reserved his harshest condemnations for selfish takers: "They are the basest ingrates that God ever brought from the bowels of the earth. We may talk about the Negro race growing big and powerful, but unless God Almighty exercises more mercy toward this race than he has ever exercised toward any race in the world, we will produce the biggest bunch of base ingrates that ever cluttered up God's green earth." The teaching and religion of Jesus centered on the kingdom of God, Johnson said, but mere talking about the kingdom was pointless; one had to open one's heart to the humbling, self-sacrificial spirit of the kingdom.[32]

Johnson emphatically took Rauschenbusch's view of the social consequences of sin and the pointlessness of substitutionary atonement theory. The consequences of sin were terribly real and social, which substitutionary theologies did nothing to mitigate. Substitutionary doctrine said that Christ's death on the cross was necessary to satisfy God's wrath or the conditions of God's moral order, but neither version of this doctrine was actually saving. Orthodoxy made God the problem, treating God's wrath or honor as the problem standing in the way of every individual's salvation. The actual problem, however, was every person's bondage to selfishness. It was subjective in the sense of existing in every person's subjectivity. It was objective only in the consequences of sinning: the ravages that sin inflicted on individuals and society. Johnson likened sin to a stream of pollution that harmed and killed. A serious theology of salvation did not fix on appeasing God's wrath or satisfying the conditions of God's honor. Salvation was not saving if it did not abolish sin and its ravages.

It started with sexual immorality, Johnson said. Orphanages and hospitals overflowed with children who never got a chance in life because they had immoral parents. Johnson admonished his congregation to think about the children: "Wherever in any particular community sexual license is turned loose and the sin of adultery is made light of, that community is soon filled with disease." He mourned that U.S. American society no longer allowed anyone past preadolescence to be sexually innocent. To the ancient Greeks, dancing was innocent and delightful, a thing of beauty. In Europe Johnson saw folk dances that reminded him of the Greeks: clean, beautiful, and lacking any suggestion of lewdness. Later he saw the same thing in Arizona, watching Native Americans dance: "They had the most delightful joy." But he never saw dancing like that in Charleston or any U.S. American city. Dance, in places rife with promiscuity and sexual innuendo, always turned dancing into something dirty, "a sign of the degradation of the modern civilized life."[33]

From there he moved to the founding of slavery, stressing that African traders played a central role in creating the slave trade. In the Charleston pulpit Johnson put it sharply, exhorting congregants never to forget that "black captains went into the heart of Africa and chained us and brought us to the coast to sell us." Evil came in all colors, even in this area. Back in Georgia and Virginia, Johnson said, the first North American slavers were lazy and only normally bad, not extraordinarily vicious. They had crops to tend, the sun was hot, and Native Americans refused to work for them, so they enslaved Africans, rationalizing that Africans weren't human anyway. Two hundred forty-six years of slavery hardened this lazy, ignorant rationalization into an evil taken-for-granted dogma. It was recited so assiduously that sixty years after slavery was abolished, white Americans still believed it: "In this country, in some ways the most enlightened country in the world, we have the most diabolical crime in the universe of burning and lynching of human beings—all growing from the laziness and moral laxity of a group of human beings who wanted to get crops without putting forth the energy to raise those crops."[34]

Black Baptists, Johnson reasoned, had special expertise about white prejudice because they were connected to white Baptists who dominated the South. He shook his head over the Southern Baptist Convention sending huge missionary expeditions to China while spending nothing to help black Americans go to school: "Those little black children right down there by their doors are worse off than tens of thousands in China and yet not a single soul goes out and plans a Sunday School. Not a single soul goes out and builds a little schoolhouse." Revivals were not much better. White Baptists loved their revivals, they preached about loving Jesus and doing God's will, they insulted blacks routinely, and they excluded blacks from attending. Sometimes they had second thoughts about exclusion, so near the end of the revival they would invite blacks to attend, on Jim Crow terms. Johnson observed, "It appears that they think you can actually invite a human being to hear the gospel of Jesus Christ and insult him at the same time, and he won't see the insult but will receive the invitation."[35]

Salvation had to address the kingdom of evil, Johnson insisted; otherwise it was not saving. Jesus sacrificed his life to stop human beings from polluting the human race: "The reason Jesus allowed himself to be crucified upon the cross and hanged up there where you and I could see him is he knew that the salvation of the whole human race was bound up with the actions of the individual." The more power or influence any individual possessed, the greater capacity he or she held to harm the entire human race. The point of good religion was to build the kingdom and thwart the spread of evil, as in Jesus's plea, "The Kingdom of God is at hand, repent." Johnson offered a colorful paraphrase: "Don't squirt the polluted venom of your sins into my face and destroy my life before I am born." He could not understand why people spurned this plea to turn away from sin: "I don't see how it cannot appeal to a man unless he is a brute. I don't see how. I don't see how, I don't see how, I don't see how."[36]

Johnson understood why people said that religion and business belonged to separate realms. They went to church; the minister talked about things sacred and idealistic; only rarely did they hear something that applied to their weekday life; and they reasoned that if they were going to be religious, religion had to be about private, spiritual things unrelated to making a living. Or, their jobs were draining and dispiriting, and they wanted church to be an uplifting experience having nothing to do with their jobs. In either case they did not come to church expecting to hear anything about business or economics.

Johnson sympathized but countered that separating religion from work was not even possible, much less desirable. The person that puzzled at the sermon on Sunday was the same person that clerked at a department store, dug ditches, or waited tables. One could not be a saint in religion and a scoundrel in business, or the reverse. Johnson loved Epictetus, a slave, on this theme, and Paul. Epictetus said that the way to one's soul, which is mysterious, is through one's body, which is plainly evident and not mysterious. Paul said that the body is the temple of the Holy Spirit. Johnson said it was more important to be religious at work than at church, for people spent more time at work. Moreover, the church betrayed Jesus Christ if it reduced religion to private faith or status quo religion. Nobody remembered the three hundred prophets of ancient Israel who blessed the status quo. The prophets that mattered were Amos, Hosea, Micah, and others who told the princes, kings, priests, and false prophets, "You are all liars if you think God wants anything but justice, righteousness, and mercy."[37]

This message, in Johnson's telling, prefigured the saying of Jesus about needing to hate one's father, mother, wife, children, brethren, and self (Luke 14:26). Jesus was not a little off: "My friends, Jesus means this thing. He is not crazy. He is in a perfectly balanced state of mind, and he is a man who loves his mother." Jesus wanted only followers "who would follow him for the sake of goodness and goodness alone," fulfilling the hard demands of prophetic religion. Jesus talked only about the will of God and God's kingdom, and he countenanced no objections about the will of somebody's mother. The church subsequently favored the story about a preexistent Son of God descending "from a superhuman heaven," but this true story got in the way of remembering what Jesus cared about. The Jesus of history called people to die for the sake of righteousness. The church, however, smoothed that over: "And so we have got to be a flabby church." Johnson choked on the funerals he had to preach for people who kept their church membership intact for a dollar per year and gave no further thought to Jesus. Often there were testimonials about the person's deep Christian faith. Johnson snapped that if these testimonials made it to heaven, they were surely burned in an ashcan outside the gate of glory. The Protestant churches became flabby by requiring little or nothing of people. Roman Catholicism at least compelled Catholics to do things, albeit things that trivialized the gospel: go to Mass, obey the priests and bishops, and say the rosary: "So today we are living in a corrupt age of the church."[38]

Corruption and respectability went together, Johnson warned. The more pride Christians took in their respectable status, the more they corrupted themselves and the church. Johnson told his congregation that back in the heyday of First Baptist Church, no member tried to buy respectability. First Baptist had taken a steep fall since then, like many congregations, all the while getting more and more respectable. Respectable congregations resented hearing such things, so ministers usually spared them. Johnson declared that he was not one of those ministers. The church did not need to be respected by polite society. It did not need large numbers or lots of money, and it could do without leaders holding advanced degrees. Moreover, Jesus took no interest in being complimented. Jesus cared only about the willingness of his followers to give up everything for the sake of the kingdom. To be a true Christian was to put Christ above everything, including one's mother or race. Johnson put it personally, declaring that he felt a deeper "affinity of spirit" with Albert Schweitzer, running a mission hospital in Africa, than he felt with black Americans who put race above everything. Racial pride and love were very important, Johnson assured congregants. He believed deeply that Christianity and the "doctrine of race love" belonged together. But the love of race had to be subordinated, along with one's mother, to the love of Christ.[39]

Johnson's early preaching and ministry put him on the path to a national ministry. He tripled the size of his congregation, overhauled its financial system, and raised unprecedented sums for mission work. One year he raised $14,000 for mission work. In addition to leading Charleston's NAACP chapter, he gave speeches across the state on racial and economic justice and took special pride in making friends in mining towns. In four years he drove himself to nervous exhaustion, while yearning for more schooling. Rochester Seminary came through with a fellowship to finance a master's degree, but Johnson nervily asked Clarence Barbour if he could take it to Harvard Divinity School. The Rochester faculty consented, and Johnson enrolled in 1921 at Harvard, attracted by its prestige and liberal theology.

Harvard College, founded in 1636 to train Puritan Congregational ministers, by the late eighteenth century symbolized the liberal versus conservative divide in New England Congregationalism. Liberals called themselves liberal Christians, Arminians, or Unitarians and usually played down their non-Trinitarianism. Conservatives defended an embattled Calvinist orthodoxy and called their opponents Unitarians or heretics. Harvard's faculty was carefully balanced between these two factions, until 1805 and 1806, when the Hollis Chair and college presidency went, respectively, to two non-Trinitarian liberals, Henry Ware and Samuel Webber. Conservatives regrouped in Andover after they lost Harvard, founding Andover Seminary in 1808, and in 1816 Harvard established its own divinity school. Harvard Divinity School, though officially nondenominational from its founding, retained a Unitarian ethos through the nineteenth century. In the 1880s social gospel theologian Francis Greenwood Peabody established social ethics as a field of academic study at Harvard, teaching a mildly reformist version of the social gospel during his long career at the Divinity School and College, which ended in 1912. Johnson appreciated that Harvard supported the social gospel, but he was already an expert on the social gospel. He went to Harvard to study philosophy of religion.[40]

That did not quite happen, as Johnson befriended historian of religion George Foot Moore and theologian George La Piana. Moore was a Presbyterian minister from Chester, Pennsylvania, and a prolific scholar of Asian religions and the Hebrew Bible. He published a major work during the year that Johnson studied under him, *History of Religions: China, Japan, Egypt, Babylonia, Assyria, India, Persia, Greece, and Rome,* and students flocked to him, as he was a gifted teacher. Johnson studied world religions under Moore and also gravitated to Moore's friend La Piana, a figure in the controversy over Catholic Modernism. La Piana was born near Palermo, Sicily, ordained to the Roman Catholic priesthood in 1900, and grieved at the Vatican's condemnation of Modernist theology and biblical scholarship. In 1912, two years after the Vatican imposed an anti-Modernist oath on all Catholic clergy, La Piana earned a doctorate from the University of Palermo; the following year he moved to the United States, beginning his Harvard career in 1916. La Piana cheered the American social gospel for its social activism and liberal theology, and he wrote extensively about immigration, especially the experiences of Italians in the United States. He shared Johnson's belief that religious and political conservatism went together, harming vulnerable people twice over. Johnson treasured his friendships with Moore and La Piana. He reveled in the scholarly ethos of their world and could imagine himself as an academic holed up in Andover-Harvard Theological Library; he also prized La Piana as a fellow social gospel activist.[41]

Moore urged Johnson to stay at Harvard for a Ph.D., studying African religion. Johnson told Moore he had promised to return to his congregation; his ministerial calling had not changed. But Johnson's life turned a corner anyway, mostly as a consequence of his lecture touring and his invitation to address Harvard's 1922 commencement assembly. As commencement approached, Johnson brimmed with sentimental feeling over his godsend year at Harvard, the birth of his son Mordecai Wyatt Johnson Jr., and the death of Wyatt Johnson, who had lived somewhere near one hundred years. Eulogizing his father, Johnson observed that Wyatt Johnson was industrious, frugal, "of stern opinion and few words," and appreciated any kindness extended to him. Moreover, his life was a series of liberations. Abraham Lincoln freed Wyatt Johnson from slavery, the love of Christ freed him from sin, and he freed himself from illiteracy and economic dependency, earning the respect of black and white coworkers. Two months after the funeral Johnson spoke at Harvard's commencement, warning that black Americans were losing hope in American freedom.[42]

He went straight to the point, spurning prefatory banter. Ever since their emancipation from slavery, black Americans had lived on the strength of a simple but profound faith, believing in the "love and providence of a just and holy God," the principles of democracy and the "righteous purpose of the federal government," and the promise of eventual fair treatment. They sustained this faith through decades of hostility, mob violence, peonage, and disenfranchisement, believing they would win the esteem of whites and gain the rights and responsibilities of full citizenship if they grew in education and prosperity. But in recent years, Johnson warned, especially since the war, black Americans had lost much of this faith. They had rejoiced at the opportunity to serve their nation at war, even under segregated conditions. Their ministers had preached about saving the world for democracy, and some even prayed that the war would last long enough to change race relations in the United States. But as soon as the war ended, "the Negro's hopes were suddenly dashed to the ground." Blacks were treated as despicably as ever, returning black soldiers received no gratitude or respect, and lynching made a comeback, along with the Ku Klux Klan. Johnson remarked, "The swift succession and frank brutality of all this was more than the Negro people could bear. Their simple faith and hope broke down." Some resorted to armed rebellion, and many fell into broken despair.[43]

It was hard to believe in the righteous purpose of the federal government when the government did nothing to protect black Americans from racist savagery. Worse yet, "some of our young men are giving up the Christian religion, thinking that their fathers were fools to have believed it so long." Johnson noted that many in this group embraced atheistic Socialism, believing that blacks should seek their salvation by joining white revolutionaries in a struggle to smash the capitalist state. A larger group still believed in religion and democracy but not in white versions of either, and many in this group had converted to black nationalist politics, culture, and religion. Black nationalism, Johnson observed, was making a dramatic comeback in the United States. To nationalists, the distinction between the former slave states and the rest of white America had lost any meaning. They believed that "the creed of the former slave states is the tacit creed of the whole nation."[44]

These terrible problems were fully homegrown, Johnson admonished. Most black Americans did not belong to anti-American or antireligious radical movements of any kind, and most still believed in God and loved their country: "But they are completely disillusioned. They see themselves surrounded on every hand by a sentiment of antagonism that does not intend to be fair. They see themselves partly reduced to peonage, shut out from labor unions, forced to an inferior status before the courts, made subjects of public contempt, lynched and mobbed with impunity, and deprived of the ballot—their only means of social defense." In the former slave states, vicious hostility toward black Americans reigned supreme; everywhere else hostility was growing "by leaps and bounds." Johnson stressed that nothing compared to the "cry of pain and petition" of black Americans. No civilized nation in the world inflicted such pain on an oppressed race. Meanwhile, across the oceans on both sides of the United States, "the darker peoples of the earth are rising from their long sleep and are searching this Western world for light." Johnson still believed that Christianity and American liberal democracy—"our American faith"—offered the best and most light. But the actually existing United States betrayed both.[45]

The crowd affirmed its liberality by warmly applauding Johnson. Judge Julian Mack, a member of Harvard's Board of Overseers, rushed across the platform to meet Johnson, exclaiming that Harvard was no longer a progressive force in thought and society, but Johnson's speech had made him feel the spirit of "the great old Harvard." Mack added that Johnson would soon hear from his philanthropist friend Julius Rosenwald, a part-owner of Sears, Roebuck, who supported black schools. The following day Rosenwald invited Johnson by telegram to meet him in Scarsdale, New York, at the home of Rosenwald's son-in-law. Mack and Rosenwald urged Johnson to launch a national ministry funded by Rosenwald; Johnson's voice was too important to be confined to Charleston. Johnson was flattered and tempted but declined; he had promised to return to his congregation. Moreover, if he became a professional speaker and writer this early in his career, he would probably degenerate into a shallow propagandist, lacking spiritual depth and intellectual power. Mack, Rosenwald, and philanthropist Nathan Straus tried to dissuade Johnson but settled for the promise that down the road he would allow them to help him.[46]

First Baptist, Charleston, basked in the growing renown of its pastor. Some observers compared Johnson's Harvard speech to Booker T. Washington's Atlanta Exposition address. Johnson crammed his calendar with speaking engagements, preached at Howard University's annual religious week observances, and received an honorary doctor of divinity degree from Howard. Howard president J. Stanley Durkee tried to hire Johnson as a "full Baptist professor," pastor to Baptist students, and college preacher. Johnson, strongly tempted, did not like the sound of "Baptist professor" and demanded more than the $2,000 plus a house that Durkee offered. Durkee and Johnson stayed in close touch, befriending and respecting each other. Meanwhile in July 1923 Jesse Moorland retired from the YMCA and was sent off with a gala celebration; the roster of prominent speakers included John Hope, Richard R. Wright Jr., Howard University secretary-treasurer Emmett J. Scott, Tuskegee Institute principal Robert Moton, AME bishop John Gregg, Moorland's successor Channing H. Tobias, and Johnson. As the only young speaker on the program, Johnson gave notice that he was the one to watch.[47]

"THE CAPSTONE OF NEGRO EDUCATION"

Howard University, founded in 1867 by abolitionist missionaries and the U.S. Congress, was named after its chief founder and third president, Oliver O. Howard. In its early years the school was primarily a social center to feed and clothe the needy, provide a place to associate, and offer educational instruction. Oliver Howard epitomized its New England abolitionist ethos. A handsome, dashing, idealistic product of Maine, Howard was a war hero and general in the Civil War, in which he lost an arm. After the war he headed the Freedmen's Bureau and worked with the American Missionary Association to found a school open to all Americans. Like other founders of Howard University, Oliver Howard was active in the YMCA movement, a midcentury offshoot of Christian Socialism in England that became a wellspring of the social gospel and social work movements in the United States. The first YMCA in Washington, DC, was founded in 1852 by social Christian reformers who later founded Howard; Oliver Howard served as president of the university and the local YMCA simultaneously, from 1869 to 1873. The school grew into a high school in the 1870s and was funded by the Freedmen's Bureau until Congress abolished the bureau in 1872. The financial panic of 1873 wiped out much of the school's remaining financial support, especially from churches, and it nearly collapsed, barely hanging on. In 1879 Howard got its first appropriation from Congress, after which Howard presidents were judged primarily by their ability to win congressional appropriations and satisfy the U.S. Department of the Interior, under which the school operated. Every Howard president preceding Stanley Durkee was a white minister, except for Howard, who was not a minister.

Howard needed only two presidents between 1877 and 1903, but it needed three presidents and two acting presidents to get through the next fifteen years. The great president was William Weston Patton, a native of New York City and graduate of Union Theological Seminary whose father was a founder of Union. Patton had served as a Congregational pastor in Hartford, Connecticut, and played a leading role in the campaign to persuade President Lincoln to issue the Emancipation Proclamation. He served as Howard's president from 1877 to 1889, eloquently espoused equal rights, rescued the school from bankruptcy, and turned it into a college, all with distinction. His successor as Howard's president, Jeremiah E. Rankin, described Patton as "a man of exalted excellency of personal character, of broad and liberal mind, of high and varied culture, of clear and serious judgment, of great considerateness and sympathy, and of singular aptness for the important work he was called to do."[48]

Patton died on the day he resigned in 1889, giving way to Rankin, who kept the Patton renewal going until 1903, when Rankin died. Then the years of multiple presidencies and organizational controversy began. Rankin had built upon Howard's tradition of decentralized governance, working out a system that empowered three deans, Kelly Miller, George W. Cook, and Lewis Baxter Moore, to run their schools with minimal interference. In 1903, however, Howard's new president, Presbyterian minister John Gordon, tried to break the deans' control and lost, offering a preview of the Durkee presidency. Gordon lasted three years, amid charges that his usurpation of power was probably racist and certainly disrespectful. Howard historian Walter Dyson, usually slow to criticize, summarily judged, "President Gordon failed to comprehend the duties of the office and to respect the traditions of the founders."[49]

There were calls for a black president, and Howard's trustee board, which was 66 percent white, resolved to find a white minister with better interpersonal skills. That described Wilbur E. Thirkield, a Methodist minister and former president of Gammon Theological Seminary, an African American seminary in Atlanta. Thirkield was Howard's most successful president of the early twentieth century. He restored much of the power of the three deans, known as the Triumvirate. He cajoled $100,000 out of Congress for a new science building, an astounding achievement in 1910. He appointed additional faculty in subjects that had previously been covered by one chair per area, especially modern languages and social sciences. He was liked and appreciated by most of the Howard community, and, not coincidentally, he was the only Howard president during this period who knew many African Americans personally before he took the job.

But Thirkield resigned in 1912 upon being elected a bishop in the Methodist Episcopal Church. This time each member of the Triumvirate vied for the presidency. Miller, a mathematician and sociologist who introduced sociology to the Howard curriculum in 1895, had joined the faculty in 1890 and served as dean of the College of Arts and Sciences. Cook, a professor of English, civics, and commerce, had joined the faculty in 1881 and served as dean of the commercial department. Moore, a professor of Latin and pedagogy, had joined the faculty in 1895 and served as dean of Teachers College, an outgrowth of the pedagogy department. All were industrious, confident, ambitious, and accustomed to running their schools. Miller was a prolific public intellectual, active in the NAACP and numerous academic societies. Cook was almost singly responsible for developing Howard's commercial department out of the industrial department. Moore, whose wife, Sarah Tanner, was the daughter of AME bishop Benjamin Tanner and sister of the painter Henry O. Tanner, took pride in his diplomatic skill and later served for five years as the first African American on the executive committee of the American Missionary Association.[50]

By 1912 each believed his time had come to go higher. The board was ready to elevate any of them. Had any two of the Triumvirate given way, the other would have been president. But all three battled for a victory, and the board refused to choose among them, settling for another white minister, Stephen M. Newman. A product of Maine abolitionist Congregationalism and Bowdoin College, Newman had served for twenty-one years as pastor of First Congregational Church in Washington, DC, and served briefly as president of Eastern College in Virginia. He was friendly, agreeable, elderly, and in failing health, having resigned from Eastern for health reasons. On his watch the deans regained the rest of their power, although Newman helped the College of Arts and Sciences establish its first departments, founding a history department in 1913. The percentage of black faculty grew to two-thirds during Newman's administration, while he wrote lovely sonnets about his life's journey. Howard seemed to be on a good path, growing modestly, unless one believed the deans had become too powerful, as some trustees did. Howard rallied to the call for black officers in World War I, mobilizing a Student Army Training Camp, and when Newman retired in 1918 the usual call for a black president was muted. Thus the trustees appointed yet another white minister, Durkee, fatefully.[51]

Durkee hailed from Nova Scotia and Bates College and held a Ph.D. from Boston University. Before taking the Howard presidency he had served as pastor of South Congregational Church in Boston. Immediately he offended philosopher Alain Locke by rejecting Locke's proposal to teach a course on race relations. The following year Durkee clashed with historian Carter G. Woodson over his new course, "The Negro in American History." Durkee had hired Woodson to be head of the graduate faculty and dean of the School of Liberal Arts, so the course squeaked through on Woodson's short-lived authority. In both cases Durkee reaffirmed Howard's long-standing tradition of spurning black history. The university's biracial board dreaded black history as a provincial innovation, a subject lacking academic standing that would harm Howard's reputation. Durkee proved his mettle to the board by standing up to Locke and Woodson, believing that he and the board better understood what was good for Howard. He also instituted a sweeping reorganization of the colleges, believing that decentralization had gone too far at Howard. The professional schools had become virtually autonomous, and the deans, especially Miller, were like barons. In 1919 Durkee divided the college into junior and senior schools, demoting Miller to dean of the junior college, which angered Miller. Six years later Durkee abolished the junior college, eliminating Miller's role as a dean, which led to a fateful confrontation.

The study of history as a self-standing subject was a late development in U.S. American higher education. Until the 1880s Howard was like other American colleges in featuring a classical curriculum of Greek, Latin, and mathematics modeled on Oxford and Harvard. The United States had no German-style research university until Johns Hopkins University was founded in Baltimore in 1876. The research model conceived the university as a center of specialized research and graduate training. It exalted scientific method and knowledge, focusing on specialized research topics. This approach facilitated the rise of sociology, political science, psychology, and history as academic fields and, in 1884, the founding of the American Historical Association.[52]

Howard's first professor of history, William V. Tunnell, was schooled in the classical model at Howard, graduating in 1884 just before the classical model expired. Tunnell exemplified the transitional generation that taught history in a sweeping, dramatic, exhortatory fashion. He gave lively renderings of epic struggles, appealing to Renaissance ideals of character development and heroism. Among the emerging social sciences, history was especially suited for heroic narrative. In black colleges history became the chief site of vindicationist teaching—history as the vindication of black achievements, refuting racist stereotypes. Tunnell began teaching history at Howard in 1906, in the College of Arts and Sciences. As late as 1910 Howard had only three courses in history, all survey courses taught by Tunnell, who the following year added a seminar on Reconstruction. Howard's first research-oriented historian, Charles H. Wesley, joined the faculty in 1913, earned his doctorate at Harvard in 1925, and taught European history. Wesley was an AME minister and brilliant, marked with high expectations. He and Tunnell tried to make history an important subject, but it was scattered across three colleges, and the board said no to black history.[53]

The question of black studies at Howard went back to 1901, when the Howard board rejected Miller's proposal to subsidize the scholarship of the American Negro Academy. Negro anything smacked of provincialism to the board, especially a research agenda focused on black American history. In 1914 Miller persuaded Moorland to donate his huge private library on African American and African history to Howard, which later became the foundation of the university's Negro-Americana Museum. The following year, however, and the year after, the Howard board rejected the same proposals, respectively, from Locke and Woodson that both subsequently fought over with Durkee. Black consciousness was growing at Howard, and not only among progressives; Miller was conservative about feminism, authority, trade unions, capitalism, and blacks leaving the farms. In 1916 the entire faculty of Arts and Sciences declared that it wanted a course on black history, which set Durkee up for trouble, though his imperious style would have created trouble anyway.[54]

Locke wanted Howard to be known for studying and enriching black culture. A 1907 graduate of Harvard College, where he studied under philosopher Ralph Barton Perry, Locke was the first African American Rhodes Scholar. He joined the Howard faculty in 1912 to teach English and philosophy, enrolled in Harvard's doctoral program in philosophy in 1916, and graduated two years later, writing a dissertation on value theory. Returning to Howard in 1918, Locke expounded a black aesthetic combining a pragmatic conception of values and a critical appreciation of cultural pluralism. The primary responsibility of the artist, he argued, is to express one's individuality and thus convey something of potentially universal human value. Locke and Du Bois mostly agreed about pragmatism and value relativism. They clashed over Du Bois's view that black art should promote racial uplift, which Locke spurned as propaganda. In the early 1920s Locke became an important contributor to the Harlem Renaissance/"New Negro" movement celebrating black intellectualism and art. In 1925 he published a famous anthology, *The New Negro*—a few months after he got fired from Howard for constantly criticizing Durkee.[55]

Du Bois ripped Locke as an art-for-art's-sake dandy removed from the sociopolitical struggle, but to Durkee, Locke seemed unbearably political. It galled Locke to teach under a white president and a biracial board of trustees that did not share his vision of Howard as a mecca of black studies. Howard remained too much in the Booker mold, training black students for commercial success. Locke got fired for pressing the point and for charging that Durkee played favorites in paying Howard's mostly underpaid faculty. He embarrassed Durkee by organizing a faculty protest on pay inequity and attracting national publicity for it. Woodson met a similar fate more quickly. Woodson earned his doctorate in history at Harvard in 1912, taught at M Street high school in Washington, DC, and founded the Association for the Study of Negro Life and History in 1915, which sponsored conferences and published the *Journal of Negro History*. Though rebuffed in his first attempt to teach at Howard, Woodson had seemed to break through when Durkee hired him. Woodson was the first Howard faculty member to hold a Ph.D. in history. His breakthrough, however, was brief, as he and Durkee clashed, Durkee demanded that Woodson apologize for insulting him, Woodson refused, and he resigned/was fired. Woodson was scarred by this episode, refusing to accept another academic appointment, which diminished his career and Howard's. Historian Zachery Williams aptly laments that Woodson's "subsequent descent into isolation" might have been prevented had he or the American Negro Academy worked out an affiliation with Howard.[56]

Locke, Woodson, Brawley, and others implored Durkee to emphasize humanistic disciplines, especially black history, and pull back on religious talk. Durkee had not come to Howard to do that, yet he strengthened and expanded the university, even in black history. Durkee significantly increased Howard's black faculty, especially in history. He instituted a quarter system and centralized the university's governing structure, creating a council of administrative officers from all departments. He combined Howard's history professors from three schools into a single department housed in the School of Liberal Arts. The history curriculum soared from four courses to twenty-two, laying the foundation of a Howard stronghold. It also branched into black history, as Durkee added young historian William Leo Hansberry to the faculty in 1922.

Hansberry had studied briefly at Atlanta University, where he read Du Bois's book *The Negro* and found his calling. He transferred to Harvard and completed his undergraduate degree in 1921, just in time to help Howard branch into the study of African civilizations. Durkee declared at the opening convocation of October 1922, "The ignorant have ever declared that the racial group which we at Howard represent has no past history save that of ignorance and servitude. I am most happy to inform you that we bring to Howard this year, for the winter quarter, a young man who proves himself among the foremost investigators of the history of the race and will, therefore, conduct classes in that history showing great civilizations in the long past, built up and maintained by that race of which you are the proud representatives." New Negro consciousness had broken through even to Durkee, at least regarding Africa.[57]

Durkee got Howard through the wretched postwar years of antiblack repression and the first Red Scare. Congressional critics insinuated that Howard had Bolsheviks on the faculty; in 1920 Utah Republican senator Reed Smoot dramatically announced that Howard's library had a Communist book; Durkee denied the rumors and got rid of the offending pamphlet, *The Bolsheviks and the Soviets: Seventy-Six Questions and Answers on the Workingman's Government of Russia.* In 1924 Howard trustee Francis Grimké gave a scorching convocation address at the seminary criticizing the lack of Christianity in white American Christianity; Durkee begged a group of angry politicians led by South Carolina Democrat James F. Byrnes not to cut Howard's appropriation on account of one speech. Meanwhile Durkee raised enough money to build a new dining hall, greenhouse, and gymnasium and hired an accomplished treasurer/business manager, Emmett J. Scott, invariably described as suave. Durkee established sabbatical leaves for faculty, promoting faculty research, and he founded Howard University Press and *Howard Review*, backing up his constant urging that Howard should aim to be the premier black institution of higher education.[58]

For some faculty and alums, Durkee pressed uncomfortably hard on the latter point, as he was the first Howard president to emphasize that Howard was a black university. Hearing anyone say it was unsettling to some; hearing a white president say it was unsettling to integrationists who eschewed racial talk and to cultural nationalists who feared Durkee wanted Howard to be the best black example of a white university. By 1922 nine members of the forty-member American Negro Academy were Howard professors. Most were pleased that Howard would soon teach courses countering the white supremacist picture of Africa's supposedly worthless past, but all believed that courses on ancient African history marked a mere beginning.

Durkee's biggest problem, however, was not his ideological vision for Howard. He got into trouble mainly by centralizing the administration and running roughshod over colleagues, students, and alums. Stories of brusque treatment abounded, and in May 1925 the campus erupted in a student strike. The Monday chapel service was a site of grievance, for two reasons. At chapel, students had to sing "popular songs, plantation melodies, army songs and so forth," which many resented, especially when white visitors showed up wanting to hear a favorite spiritual. Students also believed that chapel should not be compulsory in the first place, as Howard was not some kind of church. Tensions escalated when Durkee fired Locke, mathematician Alonzo Brown, accounting instructor Orlando C. Thornton, and French professor Metz T. P. Lochard and proposed to assign Miller to public relations. Above all, students protested against compulsory Reserve Officers' Training Corps (ROTC) classes, specifically a new rule allowing the university to expel any student who cut more than twenty ROTC and/or physical education classes in a quarter. Howard students had put up with compulsory ROTC as long as there was no consequence for cutting class. Under the new rule five students were expelled on May 5 for amassing twenty absences that quarter. The faculty voted immediately to repeal the expulsions, but students struck the following day anyway, earning a rebuke from the professors, who added that no retribution would occur if students returned to class. That assurance eventually ended an eight-day strike, and the twenty-cut rule was not enforced.[59]

The strike provided crowning evidence that Durkee had to go. George Frazier Miller, a Brooklyn Episcopal rector and social gospel Socialist, served as president of Howard's General Alumni Association. Under Miller's energetic leadership the alumni council charged that Durkee was an autocratic disaster. Alumnus G. David Houston, writing under the pseudonym Alumnus, peppered the *Baltimore Afro-American* from April 1925 to July 1926 with weekly attacks on Durkee. In July 1925 Houston declared, "It is somewhat queer that Dr. Durkee would want to remain when there is no reasonable hope of his succeeding. It must be clear to a person of blunter discernment than his that he has lost the confidence of the people whom he is supposed to serve. Success is not possible. His removal to another field is the only proper course open to him." Meanwhile the Alumni Association took official action, charging that Durkee enacted misguided educational policies, ignored traditional administrative procedures, drove away valued professors, behaved in a dictatorial manner, assigned a secretary to the Alumni Association, personally insulted at least one professor (Thomas W. Turner) and one dean (Kelly Miller), hired new professors instead of raising faculty salaries, and secretly moonlighted for a segregated institution in Boston (Curry School of Expression).[60]

The board called forty-seven professors to assess these charges. Most strongly supported Durkee, five said that at least some of the charges were true, a few preferred not to answer, and Cook testified that he neither supported nor opposed Durkee. The leaders of the anti-Durkee five were Miller, Wesley, and Tunnell. Wesley said Durkee had a vindictive streak and was better suited for the pulpit than for Howard University. Tunnell lauded Durkee for achieving "very large substantial" increases in the university's financial and physical resources but judged that he was too autocratic to relate to students, ordinary people, and some professors. Miller said Durkee was a vindictive disaster who knew nothing about education and had once called him a "contemptible puppy." Durkee replied that Miller told him, "I have a notion to smash your face."[61]

On December 10, 1925, the board exonerated Durkee on all charges, noting that Howard had gotten bigger and stronger under him. The board sang Durkee's praises, and he seemed to have prevailed. But Durkee bristled at being criticized, he longed for wider praise than he got, and he was not willing to suffer further for Howard University. The Alumni Association kept protesting, and Durkee gave up. He may have realized belatedly that it was awfully late for Howard to have a white president, let alone a bullying one. He definitely realized that he was unwilling to absorb more criticism. His usefulness was used up. He told Johnson that if he were not a praying man, "I think I would have a long time ago gone insane here. In all my life, I have never been so much misunderstood as at Howard University." In March 1926 Durkee accepted a call to Henry Ward Beecher's storied former congregation, Plymouth Congregational Church, Brooklyn, announcing his resignation from Howard. Publicly, Durkee was brief and vague. Privately, he felt sorry for himself, telling a friend, "I did the things that had to be done, which no one else would do. I knew great opposition would develop, I knew that those who could not see would fight. I did hope that I might be spared to put Howard University into the class of one of the greatest American universities. Our colored people would not permit that, so I turned away to a greater task—which is the task here at old Plymouth Church."[62]

Now the same board that supported Durkee had to find a successor. Du Bois said the next Howard president had to be "a colored man" because "no one of the white men best fitted will feel like stepping into Dr. Durkee's shoes." On March 25, 1926, Howard's board voted unanimously in favor of that sentiment, although some meant only that they were predisposed to favor a black candidate. As it was, the discussion focused entirely on African American candidates. Some insiders favored Moorland, but he was a trustee, close to Durkee, and lacked a college degree. Moorland urged the board to consider Johnson, and Mack wrote several letters to the board strongly urging them to hire Johnson. Miller and Cook had support in the Howard community (Moore had resigned in 1920), but both had opponents from the recent factionalism. Emmett Scott headed the nomination committee. In April, Scott and several committee members met with Johnson, who said that Howard needed a black president and he did not want to be considered because Howard had better candidates: Wesley and graduate school dean Dwight Oliver Wendell Holmes. The group promised to respect Johnson's request to be left alone and considered other candidates.[63]

On June 8, 1926, the Howard board unanimously selected John A. Gregg, an AME bishop serving in Cape Town, South Africa. Johnson was elated by the announcement, as was the *New York Age*, which praised Howard for its historic decision. But the trustees knew that Gregg was a long shot to accept, as he had already told them he was not interested in the job. A veteran of the Spanish-American War and former missionary to South Africa, Gregg had run Edward Waters College from 1913 to 1920 and Wilberforce University from 1920 to 1924. Then he was elected bishop. From Cape Town he informed the board that he was still committed to being a bishop and still had no desire to take on Howard University.[64]

The trustees received this reply at a meeting on June 30. Scott's committee had met several times to select a back-up candidate but voted five to one against naming anyone. It recommended that Howard's Executive Committee should run the university for a few months while the board mulled its options. The dissenting member of the nominating committee, Washington, DC, physician Michel Dumas, countered that the board should not wait: There were several people worth considering, and the best was Mordecai Johnson. Harvard historian Albert Bushnell Hart, Du Bois's former teacher, asked the board to adopt the majority recommendation; by the 1920s Hart sported a white, flowing beard and was known for absentmindedly taking the wrong hat after board meetings.

Dumas persisted for an immediate selection, which the group surprisingly approved. Two candidates were promptly nominated: Johnson and Wesley. The trustees loved Johnson, and some had misgivings about Wesley for skewering Durkee. On June 14 Scott had informed Johnson he was likely to be drafted without being asked to be a candidate. On June 23, the day Johnson sailed to Europe on a Sherwood Eddy tour, Johnson met with the nominating committee and gave his permission to be nominated. The board briefly discussed Johnson versus Wesley and chose Johnson, offering $7,000 per year and a house. Eighteen members of the board were present, eleven were African Americans, and the fact that the board made its decision so quickly was raised repeatedly against Johnson for years to come.[65]

Most of the public reaction was positive; much of it was elated. Johnson was well known at Howard and highly regarded by students, alums, and trustees. Many considered him the ideal person to head the "capstone of Negro education." Howard alumnus Neval H. Thomas enthused, "I am glad to have lived to see this day, the realization of a youthful dream. Since my first entrance into her classic walls to sit at the feet of white and black alike, I have longed to see a Negro man or woman vested with leadership, and living in the beautiful vine clad mansion of the President. That day is here and we must appreciate it. We must get behind the new president with unanimous support, giving him unselfish advice free from personal ambitions for appointments, promotions, or patronage dictation." Some were skeptical or disapproving. A few longtime supporters of the university were not ready for a black president. Some protested that Johnson had never run a university, was only thirty-five years old, and lacked an earned doctorate. His doctorate was an honorary doctor of divinity, awarded by Howard in 1923. Basically he was a social gospel minister with a lecture circuit following. How could that qualify him to lead Howard University? Johnson's supporters replied that he succeeded at everything he undertook and was connected to the white Protestant establishment. He was a fixture in YMCA and Baptist circles, and his white philanthropic boosters would not let him down.[66]

Johnson was traveling with the Sherwood Eddy party when the announcement went out. Eddy, the international secretary of the YMCA, was a prominent white social gospel activist and founding chair of the Fellowship for a Christian Social Order (FCSO), closely affiliated with the pacifist Fellowship of Reconciliation (FOR). He was an important figure to Johnson, having plugged Johnson into Eddy's ecumenical activist network and arranged speaking tours for him. For many years Eddy was the YMCA's chief evangelist in Asia; during World War I he and his personal secretary, Disciples of Christ pastor Kirby Page, organized YMCA missions at Allied war camps. The latter experience turned both men into pacifist Socialists. If militarism and predatory economics caused World War I, as they believed, Christian social ethics needed to be antiwar, anticapitalist, and anti-imperialist. In 1921 they founded the FCSO as a vehicle of their antimilitaristic Socialism.

Eddy's novel idea was the leftist travel tour. Instead of taking American tour groups to the usual European landmarks and watering holes, each summer he and Page took approximately ninety ministers, educators, social workers, and activists to conferences and activist sites organized in cooperation with European political leaders, trade unions, and activist groups. Formally it was called "the American seminar," but everyone called it "the Sherwood Eddy party." The FCSO also sponsored conferences in the United States, retreats, summer outings, and special programs. Eddy and Page were straightforward about their purpose: to advance the cooperative and nonviolent way of Christ as an alternative to capitalism, militarism, and empire. From 1921 to 1939 the FCSO summer tours exercised an important influence over the dreams of progressive Protestant leaders. To Eddy and Page, Johnson was a breakthrough figure: a young black Christian leader who could help them evangelize for racial justice and Christian Socialism. Eddy had ambitious plans for Johnson, hoping to enlist Johnson as a partner in his national and international social evangelism campaigns. He urged Johnson to turn down Howard and stay with the tour, moving next to Russia and China.

Johnson found this offer more tempting than Rosenwald's. Eddy was an esteemed Christian activist with a vast global network, and Johnson was a full-bore internationalist for whom the entire world was a theater of religious and social ethical concern. No African American had ever been offered the global ecumenical venue that Eddy beseeched him to accept. But Johnson had made his decision by the time the Howard offer arrived by cable at the Collège de France in Paris. He was a race man with high ambitions for Howard and for himself. The Howard presidency better fit his sense of being called to a great mission, he had a social gospel conception of what it would mean, and he was thinking already of how Rosenwald might help him at Howard.[67]

SERVING, SUFFERING, BUILDING

He did not come to Howard merely to cope and survive. Johnson came to build an educational showcase that played a vital role in transforming American society. He came to ramp up Howard's academic base and infuse its religious culture with the social gospel. He appreciated the upsurge of New Negro/ Harlem Renaissance black consciousness and artistic expression; New Negro cultural nationalism had a role to play in renewing black America. But Johnson believed that the best parts of the New Negro movement were already institutionalized in black life, in churches that preached the social gospel. If numerous Howard professors scoffed at this belief and him, he would have to persuade them.

More important, Johnson knew the faculty was deeply polarized. Harsh things had been said during Durkee's tenure, bruised feelings abounded, and a Howard degree commanded little respect. The university had two hundred faculty and twenty-two hundred students spread over eight schools and colleges, none of which were accredited. The faculty stars were Wesley, Benjamin Brawley, and biologist Ernest E. Just. The university had an annual operating budget of $700,000, its physical plant was worth less than $2 million, and many buildings were decaying. Moreover, Washington, DC, was nothing like the bustling metropolis it later became. Washington was a segregated federal colony, unremittingly denigrating to the black professors in its midst.

Many years later, on the rare occasions that Johnson reflected on his early years at Howard, he emphasized the faculty factionalism and his willingness to suffer. In his unpublished memoir he recalled that he tried to reconcile the factions by refusing to take sides between them. He knew the situation was "dangerously confused and distressing" and that "I would be called upon to suffer—to what extent, I did not know." In his telling, Howard professors pulled him aside, derided each other across factional lines, and he refused to take the bait. They would rail against each other, and he would caution against factions, gossip, and intrigue. In a speech in 1953, when Johnson still had seven years to go at Howard, he put it bluntly: "This was the most dangerous period in the life of Howard University. The most perilous thing that has ever happened in this institution, as touching academic freedom, existed at that time, namely, formation of blocs of power in the faculty itself. For twenty years these internal blocs of power nearly ruined Howard University. The reason I came here to accept the presidency was the feeling that arose out of a sense of strong duty that the time had come for somebody who knew how to suffer to come here and solve the problem growing out of the existence of these internal blocs of power."[68]

Being smart, energetic, and ambitious would not be nearly enough. To heal the faculty, Howard needed a sacrificial black president who was willing and able to suffer for the university. Johnson judged that everyone at Howard felt insecure, so the faculty turned everything into a faction fight. His role model and best friend, Hope, had shown him how to be a president: command respect, respect others, encourage high achievement, rule with authority, and accept whatever abuse came with being strong. In the early going Johnson vowed to give the faculty more say than Durkee had allowed on appointment matters and policy, but that promise proved to be short-lived. He also vowed to make the faculty and staff more secure in their rights and standing, which he did, though his dominating style made it seem otherwise to many.

His inaugural address proclaimed that Howard was "a monument to the capacity of the Negro" and a school of noteworthy accomplishments in botany, zoology, law, sociology, and history. To serve the needs of black Americans, however, the university had to ramp up dramatically. America, Johnson observed, had 1 black physician for every 3,300 black Americans—among white Americans the ratio was 1 to 450—so Howard's medical school had to be strengthened immediately. The same thing was true of the nation's only bona fide African American law school, which was mostly a night school. Black Americans desperately needed Howard to train more lawyers, Johnson urged. The greatest need of all was in education, where Johnson pledged to train many more teachers that served "because they love the people." He singled out one other school, religion, long the poor stepchild at Howard and not really a school. Here the university needed a major upgrade because "the simple, unsophisticated, mystical religion of the Negro cannot continue to endure unless it is reinterpreted over and over to him by men who have a fundamental and far-reaching understanding of the significance of religion in its relation to the complexities of modern civilized life."[69]

Oliver Howard had founded Howard's theological department during his presidency in 1872. Local ministers were invited to a Bible study meeting two evenings per week, and twenty showed up. Most could barely read English, but all demanded to learn Greek, struggling for weeks to learn a bit of Greek. Howard himself came to class on occasion and organized the new department, winning support from the American Missionary Association and individual congregations. The seminary was a boon to Howard's identity and development.

It provided a religious glow, trained students for ministry, and strengthened Howard's relationships with its church-based philanthropic network. For many years some Howard professors in other schools were paid from the seminary budget, as it received more contributions than any department. Still, from 1879 to 1926 the university received more than $4 million from the federal government, while the seminary was disqualified from federal funds except in a few areas. Like the law school, the theological department never lacked able teachers, despite being poorly paid. But it attracted weaker students than the law school, and for over thirty years its basic curriculum was Bible study.[70]

From 1905 to 1918 only sixty-six Howard students earned bachelor of divinity degrees. Moreover, from 1917 onward the seminary was led by a spiritual hold-over from Howard's AMA heritage, David Butler Pratt, who was happy to keep the department as it was—a missionary enterprise steeped in the ethos of New England social Christianity. That was doubly problematic. The seminary remained less academic than other departments and schools, and it did not meet the vocational needs of its primary constituency: entrepreneurial ministers who preached in black folk idioms. The theological department was historically and structurally enmeshed in its own mediocrity. Johnson announced that big changes were coming, although he added diplomatically that the groundwork for a "great nonsectarian school" already existed. Howard needed a full-fledged graduate school of religion that taught and produced modern theological scholarship. Specifically, it needed to seek the truth "about the meaning of life without bias," deliver students "from superstition and from uncharitable sectarianism," and launch them into "constructive service to the common good."[71]

Many Howard professors took no interest in that dream. They cheered, however, Johnson's pledge to transform the university into a bastion of African American history, culture, and art: "Howard University should be the place where the undeveloped heritage of art in the soul of the Negro may be cultivated, a place where his music, his histrionic talents, and his instinctive kindliness of disposition may be brought up to its fullest self-consciousness and competency." Johnson wanted Howard to be known for its creative, strong, race-proud, and high-achieving students and faculty. He wanted Howard to help white Americans overcome their fears of black Americans, "but I want the original blackness there, and I want that blackness to be unashamed and unafraid." That day was far off, he acknowledged, but the success already achieved at Howard made him hopeful for the future. Making a rhetorical run that glossed Philippians 2:6–8, Johnson declared that "noble white men" had founded Howard University: "They humbled themselves, took upon themselves the form of servants, and made themselves obedient to the needs of slaves. They lived with us, ate with us, and suffered ostracism and humiliation with us so that by their personal contact with us they might teach us the truth and the truth might set us free."[72]

Johnson stressed what that did not mean. The white founders did not aim merely "to train Negro men and women for practical life." They sought to train educational leaders with whom they worked "on a basis of uncondescending equality in the whole enterprise of Negro education." Johnson was against low-expectations Bookerism, nationalist separatism, condescending equality, and spurning of white support. Idealizing Howard's white founders would help him to succeed; plus, Johnson fervently believed his preaching on this theme, and he was like Hope and NAACP leader White in believing that his light color and voluntary racial identity authorized him to speak across the color line. The country that Howard's founders sought to create "has not yet been attained," Johnson acknowledged, but he was optimistic: "I am encouraged for my country and my hopes are stimulated by a great inspiration."[73]

Howard University had reached a tipping point when Johnson delivered this inaugural address on June 10, 1927. Since the university lacked a guaranteed appropriation, every year it had to appeal for a new one. In 1924 Michigan Republican Representative Louis C. Cramton introduced the first congressional bill proposing a guaranteed appropriation; two years later, on the day after Johnson was named president, New York Republican Daniel A. Reed resubmitted Cramton's bill. Johnson befriended Cramton and lobbied aggressively for guaranteed appropriations at higher levels. He argued that the federal government had a moral responsibility to provide opportunities for black Americans, who lived mostly in the South, where only Howard provided comprehensive professional schooling. Lacking a guarantee, Howard would find it perilous to do long-range planning. Meanwhile Johnson inherited a half-completed capital campaign on the verge of losing its challenge grant from the Rockefeller-funded General Education Board. Johnson had twenty days to raise $125,000 by the June 30 deadline. He completed the capital campaign by leaning on Rosenwald and Howard alums; then he won a huge victory in Congress. In 1926 Howard's federal appropriation was $218,000. Two years later it nearly tripled, to $580,000, and was guaranteed. By 1930 it had doubled again, to $1,249,000. The following year it peaked at $1,760,000, a sensational run that lifted the entire university before the Depression forced painful adjustments.[74]

To most of Howard's faculty and community, Johnson was a colossal success. Many of his admirers passed beyond admiration to reverence, assenting when Johnson said he felt called by God to lead Howard. In the early going Johnson made a reconciliation move, welcoming Locke to the faculty in 1928. He spent much of his federal windfall on the faculty, hiring economist Abram L. Harris Jr. in 1927, political scientist Ralph Bunche in 1928, literature scholar Sterling A. Brown in 1929, theologian Howard Thurman in 1932, sociologist E. Franklin Frazier in 1934, theologian Benjamin E. Mays in 1934, medical researcher Charles R. Drew in 1935, religion scholar James Farmer Sr. and historian Rayford Logan in 1938, historian Merz Tate in 1942, and historian John Hope Franklin in 1947. Nothing remotely like this black intellectual powerhouse had ever been assembled. Johnson told everyone he wanted the best scholars he could find. He hired Harris, Bunche, and Mays when they were still working on their doctorates, and he stuck to his hire-the-stars strategy long after many of them turned against him. A few of Johnson's critics were temperamentally confrontational and acerbic, matching powers of will with him, notably Harris, Frazier, Logan, and Ernest Just. According to them, Johnson's domineering persona was the problem. Logan later reflected, "The longer he remained in office, the more determined he was to assert his will."[75]

Johnson, however, was very strong-willed from the beginning. He fired dental school dean Arnold Donawa for seeking autonomy for the dental school, charging Donawa with insubordination. He stripped James A. Cobb of his leadership position as vice dean of the law school, incurring campus drama. He established a budget system and demanded that every department operate within it, evoking angry protests. He eliminated long-standing disparities between the incomes of administrators and faculty. He clashed with Just over Just's single-minded devotion to biological research over teaching. He clashed with linguist and English department head Lorenzo Turner, causing Turner to leave Howard in 1928. Most dramatically to some, Johnson abolished the football team's dining privileges. Most important to Johnson, he fell out with Scott, each accusing the other of egotism and incompetence, which forced the board to take sides, siding with Scott.

The early protests against Johnson were intense and dramatic, decrying his strong-armed style, especially his stringent control of income and expenses. Then the Depression kicked in, Congress slashed Howard's appropriation by two-thirds, and the protests grew louder. In his early presidency Johnson consulted with professors, but soon he decided that faculty consent was either impossible to get or not worth the trouble. Professors often lacked common sense, he judged, and some were prone to grandstanding, not solving problems. If Howard was to survive the Depression without lapsing into mediocrity, he had to be a strong leader who defended the university's interests, no matter what critics said. Durkee had waited four years to be elected to the board, but Johnson got on the board in his first year, where he marshaled support for his policies. In the early going students defended Johnson's bullish style and faculty critics hung a nickname on him, the Messiah. Logan, later struggling to be objective, recalled that the Howard community divided between those who idolized Johnson and those who disliked him; there was little middle ground concerning Johnson. But Logan said everyone agreed that Johnson had a Messiah complex.[76]

Johnson's grandest ambitions fixed on the law school and the religion school. Early in his presidency he asked Supreme Court justice Louis D. Brandeis what he should do with the law school. Brandeis advised him to aim high, ditch the night school, hire a few high-achieving taskmasters, and train lawyers to develop racial discrimination cases capable of making it to the Supreme Court. Johnson found a zealous champion of this strategy in Charles Hamilton Houston, who had begun teaching at Howard in 1924 on a part-time basis while partnering with his father in a private law firm. Houston grew up in Washington, DC, and graduated from Amherst in 1915 as class valedictorian. He was a protégé of Felix Frankfurter, Joseph H. Beale, and Roscoe Pound at Harvard Law School, and at Howard he was the epitome of a taskmaster, flunking most students. Howard's law graduates fell by more than half in the early 1930s, reaching an all-time low of seven in 1934. The Depression was the major cause, but the shift to rigor also played a role. Houston's protégé Thurgood Marshall entered in 1930 with a class of thirty students and graduated three years later with seven classmates. Houston told them there were two kinds of lawyers: social engineers and parasites. If they were not in law school to defend underprivileged people and change society or were not smart enough to do so, find another career.[77]

Johnson pushed hard to qualify the law school for accreditation, working closely with law school dean Fenton W. Booth, a judge in the U.S. Court of Claims, and the Association of American Law Schools. He opened a day school in 1928, persuaded Booth to work overtime for the law school for a year, removed Cobb as vice dean, and promoted Houston to vice dean in 1929 after Booth was appointed to the U.S. Court of Appeals. By 1930 the night school had been abolished. The following year Howard Law School was partially accredited by the American Bar Association and the American Association of Law Schools and was fully accredited in 1935.

Houston was the driving force. Years later his successor, William H. Hastie, recalled of the period 1929–1935, "In those few years he carried the institution from the status of an unaccredited and little known—though undoubtedly useful—institution to a fully accredited nationally known and respected law school taking its place with the ranking schools of the nation." In 1935 Houston moved to the NAACP, where he served as special counsel for five years. From

1930 until his death in 1950 he played a leading role in nearly every civil rights case argued before the Supreme Court, laying the groundwork for *Brown v. Board of Education*. Hastie, a Harvard graduate in the Houston mold and former governor of the Virgin Islands, amplified Houston's legacy at Howard, training the nation's leading civil rights lawyers, several of whom became federal judges. Johnson took special pride in the law school, calling it "my law school." Faculty noticed that he referred to no other school in this way, although Johnson took pride in overhauling the entire university.[78]

Many Howard departments boasted high-achieving faculty. Charles Thompson, recruited to head the College of Education, in 1932 founded the *Journal of Negro Education*, which became a national treasure, a bulwark against segregation in education and society. Sterling A. Brown became a prominent literary critic, community leader, and New Deal advisor, working with the Federal Writers' Project. Percy Julian chaired the chemistry department from 1927 to 1929 and became a pioneer in the chemical synthesis of medicinal drugs from plants. Ralph Bunche made his early renown by attacking the New Deal from the left, served during World War II in the Office of Strategic Services and the State Department, served as an advisor to the U.S. delegation that cofounded the United Nations in 1945, and won the Nobel Peace Prize in 1950 for his diplomatic work as principal secretary of the UN Palestine Commission. E. Franklin Frazier amplified the important role of sociology at Howard and later wrote major works on the black family, the black middle class, and the black church. Abram Harris wrote influential works on race and economics, criticizing black entrepreneurs in his book *The Negro as Capitalist* for avoiding interracial markets. Four members of the Howard faculty—Bunche, Logan, Hastie, and political scientist Harold O. Lewis—played significant roles in FDR's Black Cabinet. Logan worked for Inter-American Affairs, Hastie advised the secretary of war, and Lewis and Bunche worked in the Office of Strategic Services. At the time Johnson lured John Hope Franklin to Howard in 1947, Franklin teetered on academic stardom; his classic textbook on African American history, *From Slavery to Freedom*, was published that year.[79]

But Johnson's extraordinary success at building up Howard University did not save him from more than a decade of blistering, caustic, fire-the-president opposition, as critics wrote off his fund-raising and favorable press. Scott, Miller, Cobb, and Donowa were ringleaders of the anti-Johnson opposition among current or former administrators; Harris, Bunche, Just, Locke, Frazier, Julian, and Lewis led the early anti-Johnson faction on the faculty, and Logan later joined them. In a few cases there were special circumstances. Just contended that his grant from the Rosenwald Fund was for him, not the biology department, contrary to Johnson and the Rosenwald Fund. Johnson clashed with Just until his death in 1941, always urging him to stop neglecting his students and department. Johnson's firing of Julian stirred little campus reaction, as Julian left in the wake of a sexual scandal involving his affair with the wife of a Howard colleague; he later became a wealthy businessman from his patents. Donowa's firing was a straightforward policy conflict complicated by a charge of insubordination, and the meaning of Cobb's demotion was too obvious not to be publicly humiliating: the law school was too important for him to remain dean.[80]

Johnson's conflict with Scott was distinctly frustrating and damaging to Johnson. According to Johnson, Scott's financial reports were sloppy and unreliable, and he looked down on Johnson. According to Scott, Johnson was incompetent and looked down on everyone, even Scott. Johnson complained to the board that he never knew what he was dealing with financially because Scott only pretended—with characteristic self-assurance—to have matters in hand. For five years the board stiffed Johnson, adoring Scott. Johnson asked for a budget officer to do most of Scott's job, but the board rejected that too. Scott and Cobb, holing up at a local social club, ripped Johnson repeatedly, regaling Logan and other guests. Logan later recounted that Scott flashed his famously sophisticated wit in such settings, and Cobb made similar points with blunt simplicity.[81]

Logan strangely screened out the politics in favoring Scott over Johnson. Scott was a holdover from the Durkee years, and before that, Booker T. Washington, having been Washington's chief aide from 1897 to 1915. Washington versus Du Bois hung in the air whenever Scott criticized Johnson for being too aggressive or Johnson criticized Scott for thwarting him. By 1931 Johnson was engulfed in fire-the-president demands and overwrought by his dispute with Scott. He withstood the former attacks with dignity, refusing to fire back. The battle with Scott, however, got to him. Johnson told Rosenwald Fund executive Edwin R. Embree that he had to resign; it was pointless to keep fighting with a subordinate who held the board's favor. Embree persuaded Johnson not to resign and probably lobbied the board, which slowly, reluctantly swung to Johnson's side. By the mid-1930s Johnson had the upper hand over Scott, but Scott held on until 1938, when he reached the compulsory retirement age of sixty-five. Scott demanded to continue as Howard's secretary, asserting that after nineteen years of service to the university he was not a "supplicant for decent treatment." He had a right not to be pushed aside. Johnson prevailed over Scott by an eleven-to-ten board vote and was finally rid of his nemesis, although Scott insisted until the end that he was not Johnson's enemy: he was the mediator between factions that idolized and hated Johnson.[82]

Johnson's fallout with Scott and his demotion of Cobb reverberated through the faculty, as Scott and Cobb had many friends. Miller stoked the anti-Johnson reaction, resenting his own diminished role at Howard and nearly everything about Johnson, especially his radicalism. Some cried foul whenever Johnson made news with a zinger about capitalism. Many complained that Johnson gave too many road lectures, made strident statements that embarrassed the university, and was incorrigible about capitalism, which threatened Howard's federal support. An anonymous "Special Reporter" for the *Afro-American* attacked Johnson every week on these points: "It is neither a secret nor an insinuation that the president of Howard University has had no intensive training for his position. His selection to such a position was a terrible slap at the trained educator. It was sheer folly to expect such a novice to begin a career with the most intricate and expensive type of machinery." Insiders believed that "Special Reporter" was Miller, or his scribe, since every article contained knowing put-downs sounding like Miller. Week after week the *Afro-American* said Johnson was unqualified, undisciplined, radical, dictatorial, obnoxious, and a preacher, not a serious educator. Embree defended Johnson from these attacks but tweaked him with a title, the Lord High Chancellor. Embree's colleagues at the Rosenwald Fund asked Tuskegee principal Robert Moton if Johnson had lost control at Howard; Moton replied that Johnson was a great president and Christian leader, albeit one prone to radical pronouncements, and certain officials at Howard were "much more concerned to discredit President Johnson than to advance the interests of the University."[83]

Certain officials at Howard went to extraordinary lengths to defame Johnson, warning government officials that Howard had a pro-Communist president. Miller descended to that level, urging Maryland senator Millard E. Tydings to orchestrate an Interior Department investigation of Johnson's Communist views and influence at Howard. Cobb similarly implored politicians and federal officers to investigate Communist subversion by Howard's president. Some faculty and alums joined the anti-Johnson stampede out of fear that his radical politics jeopardized Howard's standing and existence. By December 1930 the furor was so intense that Embree asked Johnson to take a six-week vacation at Embree's expense, to decompress. Johnson replied that Howard could not afford for him to take a vacation. The furor escalated in the spring, even as Johnson added sixteen professors to the liberal arts faculty. The board announced that a special meeting would be held to consider the charges against Johnson. Students protested in Johnson's favor, threatening to strike if he were fired or reprimanded; some carried placards saying, "Johnson for Howard, Howard for Johnson." Rallies for and against Johnson were held across the city, and telegrams poured in from both sides. Indiana Republican congressman William Robert Wood declared that the U.S. government had no business giving money to a Communist college president and Johnson had to go. That roiled the Howard community, as Wood chaired the House Appropriations Committee and had a record of supporting the university.[84]

The Benevolent and Protective Order of Elks played a colorful role in the controversy. Grand Exalted Ruler J. Finley Wilson and Elk commissioner of education William C. Hueston were leading supporters of Johnson, while Elks legal advisor Perry W. Howard countered that Johnson was "temperamentally unfit" to be president. The anti-Johnson forces had self-fulfilling prophecy going for them: first they raised a ruckus against Johnson; then they blamed him for causing turmoil. Wilson and Hueston refused to play that game. Addressing a mammoth pro-Johnson rally at Metropolitan Baptist Church, they inveighed against white paternalists and "Uncle Toms" who conspired against strong black leaders. Hueston, a U.S. Post Office solicitor, declared that Johnson caught hell mainly because certain officials at Howard pedaled lies about him to "big white men." Wilson followed Hueston with a quotable stemwinder that entered Howard lore: "We have been facing a crisis for twenty-five years. Everytime we get somewhere, some mean white man or some Jim Crow Negro is ready to pull us down. When you find these back door Negroes, these rank Uncle Toms who attempt to discuss the name of Dr. Johnson, whose shoe lace they are not worthy of touching, attempting to destroy our hero, our master, I am calling upon you to defeat these low men, these mad dogs, politically, fraternally, religiously and in every other way." Black Americans, Wilson urged, wanted and deserved political equality and social equality, exactly as Johnson said. Since Johnson could not say that his opponents were racists and Uncle Toms, Wilson was happy to do it for him.[85]

The board met in April, listened to speeches pro and con, and voted unanimously in support of Johnson, commending him for "a vision and a quality of leadership which cannot be excelled." Johnson's loyalty to the United States, the board said, was not seriously debatable, even though many questioned his patriotism. The trustees studiously avoided an accusatory tone, but their endorsement angered Johnson's opponents anyway, who kept protesting. In 1932 Mississippi Democrat Robert S. Hall introduced a resolution in the House of Representatives claiming that Johnson set off "continuous tumultuous" conditions at Howard by treating officials and faculty in an "arrogant and overbearing" manner and paying off his toadies. Hall advanced no evidence for the latter charge; he merely recycled what informers told him. In 1933 North Carolina Democrat Alfred Lee Bulwinkle charged on the floor of Congress that Howard's president wanted to replace religion with Communism:

"This man, whom the Government of the United States through a board of trustees has placed in charge of a college for the Negro race, and which is costing the Government of the United States a million dollars for next year, advocates doing away with all religions, because he says both the Protestant and the Catholic religions have fallen down, and that communism is the religion for America in the future."[86]

That was not what Johnson said about Communism, but his critics were averse to nuanced distinctions in this area. The previous week, in a baccalaureate sermon, Johnson said what he always said: Communism was based on admirable moral commitments, and the Soviet Union was doing a better job than the United States of helping poor people avert starvation and destitution. One did not have to be a Communist to recognize that the Communist movement had some commendable features: "The way to meet this new movement is not to persecute those who believe in it, or merely to focus attention upon the errors and perversities which may appear therein, but to beget on our own soil and in a manner consistent with the religious and political beliefs of our fathers, a movement which sets forth objectives no less splendid and which can arouse the wholehearted allegiance of our citizens." Johnson's opponents seized on this pronouncement, claiming vindication; they also demanded that the federal government investigate Johnson and Howard. Cobb implored government officials in 1933 and the Dies Committee in 1938 to pursue Johnson, which they did, in both cases fanning conspiracies that the Roosevelt administration and its Howard University beneficiaries were pro-Communist.[87]

Federal investigators pored over documents at Howard, searching for evidence of Communist indoctrination and subversion. Mostly they focused on gatherings at which Johnson and Howard professors had spoken. They found nothing, but Johnson was hauled before Congress anyway, where he declared,

> I am not a communist. I am always on my guard against any dogmatic panacea for the settlement of the complex difficulties which confront us in the modern world. On the other hand, I am not in accord with those who believe that the best way to deal with communism is to persecute those who believe in it. And I am not of the opinion that patriotism requires any thoughtful man to subscribe to the doctrine that there is nothing good in the Russian experiment. The determination of the leaders of this movement to make use of modern scientific and technical resources to emancipate the masses of people from poverty and its ills, including the disease of acquisitiveness, is a commanding undertaking which no modern nation can ignore. The enthusiasm and devotion with which they give themselves to their major purpose is suggestive of the kind of idealism which religion has always felt to be precious.[88]

Never one to cower anyway, Johnson took his investigation as a moral opportunity. Since the baccalaureate sermon had landed him before a congressional
committee, he quoted it pointedly, especially the section on how America
should "meet this new movement." For the next twenty years it was cited repeatedly against him. The House Committee to Investigate Un-American Activities
(HUAC, later renamed the Committee on Un-American Activities) was
founded in 1934 to investigate fascist influence in the United States.
Massachusetts Democrat John McCormack and New York Republican Samuel
Dickstein chaired HUAC until 1937, when Texas Democrat Martin Dies
replaced McCormack as cochair. Dies contended that Communists controlled
the New Deal. Like many southern Democrats, he warned that the expansion
of federal power threatened southern segregation and that New Deal agencies
such as the National Labor Relations Board, Federal Theater, and Writers'
Project were tools of Communist recruitment and subversion. Under Dies's
leadership, HUAC mostly pursued Democratic officials, notably Michigan
governor Frank Murphy, who was targeted for his close alliance with FDR and
his refusal to crush a sit-down strike at a General Motors plant in Flint. Many
black newspapers struggled to take seriously HUAC's ostensible agenda, noting
that Dies did not condemn lynching as un-American. Illinois Republican Oscar
De Priest, however, the first black American to win election to Congress in the
twentieth century, warned that Dies's strategy jeopardized every gain for civil
rights that blacks had attained in the twentieth century. "Un-Americanism" was
the new ruse to put down black Americans.[89]

White and other NAACP officials took De Priest's warning with some trepidation, aiming to avoid trouble with HUAC. Johnson took the view that he had
nothing to hide and would not be cowed. He had a strong viewpoint, as usual;
he welcomed any opportunity to express it clearly; and he was a passionate
believer in intellectual freedom and freedom of speech. In 1935 Johnson told a
visiting delegation of the House Appropriations Committee that if he had to
choose between losing Howard's federal appropriation and surrendering the
right of academic freedom, he would forgo the appropriation without hesitation. In reality Johnson was always more cagey and political than his pronouncements suggested, but his pronouncements appalled Howard's cautious
supporters. Illinois Representative Arthur Mitchell, at the time the only black
member of Congress, reproved Johnson for exaggerating. Miller blasted
Johnson for "the glib recital and fervid declamation of an eighteenth century
Libertarian." According to Miller, Johnson rudely thumbed his nose at Mitchell
and the entire Congress and thus jeopardized the university: "Your judgment
was as miserable as your courage was admirable—but in a college president,

discretion is the better part of valor." To Miller, this episode was like most of his encounters with Johnson, a sad confirmation that Johnson dragged Howard University to the political left, in defiance of those who preceded him and loved the old Howard.[90]

But Johnson also had fierce critics who did not begrudge him his politics, and some were beneficiaries of his stout defense of their intellectual freedom. Next to Johnson, Bunche was Howard's leading target of anti-Communists during the 1930s and early 1940s. In the late 1940s Bunche surpassed Johnson in this department, and it got worse for Bunche after he left Howard in 1950 to concentrate on his work for the United Nations. Through the many years of accusation Johnson adamantly defended Bunche's intellectual freedom and integrity, even though, on Saturday nights, Bunche hosted gatherings of social science faculty in his home, where the animating theme was fire-the-president.

The mainstays of the Saturday gatherings were Harris, Frazier, Lewis, and Bunche; often there were two or three others. To this group, the ruckus over Johnson's politics was a sideshow. The real problem was that Johnson was "a Psalm-singing S.O.B.," as Just put it. To the Bunche group, Johnson was a disaster on four counts: he was a preacher, a messianic tyrant, and a nonacademic, and he enlisted the trustees against anyone who opposed him. The Bunche group rued that Johnson ran Howard in classic authoritarian Baptist preacher fashion, but Howard was not a Baptist church. Harris and Frazier ridiculed Johnson for presuming to advise them on what they should write, and Just despised Johnson for making him share Rosenwald money with colleagues who could not have won it on their own. To some of the faculty stars, Johnson was not an intellectual peer, and he could not run a university either. He won his position by dazzling impressionable church audiences, not because he deserved it. Harris, Frazier, Just, and Locke castigated Johnson as bitterly as Miller and Cobb. Had Johnson deferred to his faculty critics, they might have found a way to tolerate him, as Howard professors had long indulged the mediocre white ministers who preceded Durkee. But Johnson seemed to believe he deserved his position, he was smarter than everyone else, and he was doing a great job. Frazier had a psychological explanation for Johnson's forceful and ostensibly clueless manner: it "masked a deep incompetence in piloting a modern university."[91]

The last major campaign to fire Johnson gathered steam in 1937. The General Alumni Association played the leading role; this time many students turned against him too, and the usual faculty and former administrative opponents weighed in. Scott and Cobb were still on the payroll, which helped to incite national press attention. Students protested that Johnson raised tuition and room costs. Faculty critics charged that he got more dictatorial each year. Some accused him of spending an Interior Department allocation for the library on a new chemistry building. Just, struggling with serious illness, told the board meeting of April 1938 that Howard owed him $25,000 of back salary. He explained that Durkee had agreed to pay him a full year's salary for a half-year of work, but Johnson reneged on the deal. It galled Just that Johnson bragged about having a distinguished biologist on the faculty and yet granted him no special treatment. Now Just was willing to settle for the back salary owed him and a lump sum of $15,000 for retirement: "After thirty-one years of continuous service to Howard University, I wish to retire in order to preserve what health is left in me and maintain my sanity which suffered in these last few years in servitude under the present administration."[92]

The alumni group pushed harder than ever, making a last-ditch effort to get rid of Johnson. It struck hard at the Charter Day celebration of March 2, 1938, the university's annual banner event. Alumni leader Eugene Davidson produced a special issue of the *Howard University Alumni Journal* titled "The Case Against President Mordecai W. Johnson," accusing Johnson of "hate, ill will, and malice" plus "uncivil, inconsiderate, discourteous and indecent conduct," which yielded "the present internal turmoil, bickering, strife, and unrest." There were many charges: Johnson misspent Public Works Administration allocations; he announced Lucy Slowe's successor as dean of women while Slowe lay on her deathbed; he paid his favorites more than his critics; his "petty and personal vindictiveness" drove away Donawa, Booth, Holmes, and Turner; his "personal vindictiveness" against architect Albert Cassell delayed the construction of men's dormitories; and he strong-armed Interior Secretary Harold Ickes into whitewashing all of it: "As an administrator he is the worst imaginable and as an educator he is an ignoramus." Turner, Miller, and Cobb wrote vitriolic attacks on Johnson. Turner had begun his seminal studies of Gullah language and culture as a linguist at Fisk University. Miller had retired in 1934 at the age of seventy-one, setting a precedent that Scott believed should apply to him. Cobb and Davidson, on March 23, 1938, urged a Senate subcommittee on appropriations to explore malfeasance at Howard; to Cobb, the April board meeting was a do-or-die occasion.[93]

Johnson was a master of inside hardball, but in public he was gracious and stoical. Even in private, according to friends, he rarely said an unkind word about anyone. Johnson told Benjamin Mays that he expected the truth to win out concerning his presidency, and he told his friend John Q. Taylor King, "People have reasons for doing things, and sometimes we are not the best judges of other people's reasons." In 1938 Johnson offered a rare word of public self-defense, noting that Howard had 8,000 living alumni and only 253 were in the Alumni Association. This organization employed tactics "almost equivalent to gangsters" and was not very representative, Johnson observed. Investigations into the charges against him were conducted. The Committee on Instruction and Research ruled that he had not mistreated Just and there was no basis for the back salary demand. Johnson was cleared of all charges of malfeasance, and he survived the years of accusation.[94]

Howard and Johnson had powerful friends in and near the Roosevelt administration and New Deal Congress. Eleanor Roosevelt was a staunch ally of Howard, second only to Ickes. She visited the campus often, kept her husband apprised of the situation at Howard, and lobbied Congress and the Roosevelt administration strenuously on the university's behalf, all of which made her, in Zachery Williams's description, "the major policy broker between Howard and the federal government." FDR's Black Cabinet, headed by Mary McLeod Bethune, similarly lobbied hard for Howard, as did the NAACP and the National Council of Negro Women. In the 1930s Howard built a new College of Medicine, three dormitories for women, a chemistry building, a classroom building, a library, a power plant, and a men's dormitory, together costing over $5 million. Ickes was central to the building projects and the university as a whole, and he was Johnson's chief defender.[95]

Ickes was a former NAACP official in Chicago with a long background in the Progressive Party. In 1935, speaking at an Interior Department dinner on behalf of Howard, Ickes declared, "I am for President Johnson. He is doing an excellent job under very difficult conditions. He is deserving of our gratitude." Critics told Ickes that Johnson was "a quite terrible man" bent on tearing Howard down. Ickes replied that Johnson was an outstanding president who roared for intellectual freedom and was guilty of no wrongdoing: "I think that we ought to be grateful that Howard University has a president of the caliber of Mordecai Johnson. I bespeak for him your devoted and unqualified support." In March 1938, facing another sack-the-president firestorm, Johnson asked Ickes to give the Charter Day address. Ickes said the same thing as before, this time defusing a controversy over a federal probe of Howard's treasurer, Virginius Johnston, and dashing the hopes of Johnson's opponents. The following month Howard's board terminated the services of Scott and Cobb, and Johnson's life turned a corner.[96]

The majority of Howard's professors supported Johnson through his years of accusation, but they were quiet about it. Walter Dyson, who taught history at Howard during the Durkee and Johnson administrations, was pro-Durkee and very pro-Johnson, contending that both elevated the university by taking on entrenched interests. Howard had three great presidents, Dyson judged: Oliver Howard founded and inspired the early school; William Patton saved the school and renewed it; and Mordecai Johnson lifted the school to historic importance. But Dyson and most of his colleagues avoided the fray during the many years of anti-Johnson accusation. The chief exception was Mays, followed by Thurman. Mays and Thurman were essential to Johnson's aspirations for Howard and his enjoyment of the job. Thurman had idolized Johnson since his coming-of-age years, and Johnson had sought to hire Thurman as soon as he got to Howard. In 1932 Thurman joined the faculty, later recalling, "I was caught up in Mordecai Johnson's vision to create the first real community of black scholars, to build an authentic university in America primarily dedicated to black youth." Mays shared that excitement and vision, joining the faculty two years later.[97]

INTERNATIONALISM AND VINDICATION

First, Johnson turned the theological department into a School of Religion, a job he completed in 1932. Then he hired Thurman, telling the Howard community that his young friend was "an extraordinary personality." Bringing Thurman to Howard reminded Johnson that the beating he took was worth it, and why. Johnson viewed Thurman in the way Hope viewed Johnson: as a younger version of himself. Johnson and Thurman were deep-spirited, brilliant, charismatic social gospelers, though Thurman was mystical, plus uncomfortable with the demands of social justice leadership. Johnson counted on Thurman to change the spiritual culture at Howard. Once Thurman arrived, Johnson had a spiritual partner in his work. Then Pratt retired in 1934, and Johnson asked Mays to run the School of Religion. Mays had completed his course work at the University of Chicago but not his doctoral dissertation when he joined the Howard faculty. He and Johnson were friends; they shared a network of black church and ecumenical activist friends; and Mays was deeply committed to helping Johnson succeed.[98]

For the rest of his life Mays put the latter point emphatically: "I am basically a 'race' man. I believe in the black man's ability, and my heart leaps with joy when a Negro performs well in any field. For me it was imperative that the first Negro president of Howard University be an unqualified and triumphant success." Mays recalled that when Howard needed a new president in 1926, "few of us" believed that able black candidates existed. When Howard hired Johnson, most of Mays's friends believed the school made a mistake. Mays told them to consider Booker T. Washington, who built Tuskegee Institute out of nothing, and Hope, who ran Morehouse College. They replied that no black man would be able to get money out of Congress. Mays ruefully recalled, "All too many Negroes saw no good at all for Howard University in the election of Mordecai Johnson as president."[99]

That was always the trump issue for Mays, but he also believed that Johnson was a colossal success and deserving of far better treatment than he got. "It was no prize that had been handed to Mordecai Johnson," Mays noted. Miller and perhaps two or three others conferred some prestige on Howard, "but by no stretch of rhetoric could it be called an outstanding institution. It was a puny thing." Johnson changed this picture dramatically, accomplishing "wonders for Howard." Mays stressed that in Johnson's first fourteen years he tripled Howard's financial take from Congress from the previous forty-seven years: "These figures prove that Negroes could and did get big money from the government, and, moreover, that those few who in 1926 expressed confidence in Negro leadership at Howard University have been vindicated a thousandfold." Mays came to Howard believing that Johnson was already a smashing success, no matter what his critics said, and there was more to accomplish, especially because religion lagged behind: "I had watched Howard's growth during Johnson's first eight years there; and I was eager to help him build a great university by making the School of Religion a first-rate institution."[100]

Mays gave six years to this mission and grew in admiration for Johnson. The storm of accusation puzzled and angered Mays, even though much of it came from Mays's friends: "I never really knew why a few people hated the man so intensely." According to Mays, the anti-Johnson faction never gave him a sensible explanation of why it campaigned to get rid of Johnson: "The only reasons I ever heard expressed were, 'He is dogmatic!' 'Dishonest!' 'A liar!' " None of these accusations was even remotely true, Mays insisted. Johnson was modern and progressive intellectually and a man of honor and integrity. He had a commanding style, but that was a good thing. Mays claimed that Johnson did not even realize he was reviled. His proof was that Johnson never talked about it. In the succeeding paragraph, however, Mays described vicious attacks on Johnson that became too public not to notice. The *Afro-American*, skewering Johnson every week with "bitter, vindictive diatribes," obviously relied on inside information. Some insider falsely told government investigators that Johnson used government material to build a home in West Virginia. The Alumni Association observed Founders Day by smearing Johnson with invective and fabrications. Mays remarked, "No gossip was too petty or mean, no charge too preposterous or damaging; but against his would-be character assassins Mordecai Johnson never tried to defend himself, either on the platform or in the press. He never fired from the faculty persons known to be his enemies."[101]

Mays kept it vague and categorical to avoid arguments about specific explosive things. Johnson, Mays, and Thurman wanted churches to catch up to the NAACP and Urban League as vehicles for social change, joining the political struggle for equality. Moreover, the NAACP and Urban League increasingly came under fire from the same Howard professors that looked down on ministers. Frazier ripped the black establishment—eventually in a famous book—as a bourgeois class lacking actual capitalists. Bunche, Harris, and others similarly charged that civil rights organizations were middle-class, self-satisfied, provincial, and slow, relying too much on wealthy white donors and putting too many ministers out front. The next civil rights movement had to be based on economic justice and, whenever possible, new interracial alliances based on shared working-class interests. This emphasis on economic justice and interracial solidarity was fine with Johnson, Mays, and Thurman, but they refused to write off the black churches or the work of struggling bourgeois civil rights organizations. They wanted to be allies with Frazier and Bunche, which proved to be difficult when Frazier and Bunche pilloried Johnson for being a typical Baptist preacher. Mays bit his tongue when his colleagues sneered at ministers. Sometimes he retorted that Howard became a great university mainly because of the "magnificent leadership" of a minister.[102]

Mays built up the School of Religion's faculty, curriculum, library, and enrollment; Thurman enthralled overflow crowds on the lecture circuit and at Howard's Andrew Rankin Memorial Chapel, where he served as chapel dean; and Johnson expanded his public audiences in the church, academy, and society. The three Morehouse Men formed a social gospel troika that changed the image of religion on Howard's campus, advocating Gandhian nonviolence. Johnson came early to this cause, thrilling at Gandhi's noncooperation campaign in the 1920s. Like Ransom and Powell Senior, Johnson viewed Gandhi as a modern Christ figure wrongly denigrated by white Americans. Gandhi's loincloth was not something to be sneered at; in 1930 Johnson declared that black college graduates should demonstrate their solidarity with poor blacks by wearing the "cheapest variety of homemade overalls." Black Americans had much to learn from Gandhi, Johnson continued: "Gandhi is conducting today the most significant religious movement in the world, in his endeavor to inject religion into questions of economics and politics." For the next thirty years Johnson lionized Gandhi as the epitome of true religion. At Howard the social gospel trio set off a campus buzz about social justice religion and the relevance of Gandhi to the U.S. American situation. Thurman's chapel talks stirred excitement and intellectual energy that reverberated across campus. The School of Religion began to attract better students, boosting its intellectual reputation.

Johnson's secular critics had mixed feelings about this development, but their respect for Mays and Thurman helped Johnson survive the 1930s.[103]

The New Deal was very good for Howard. At the Seventeenth Annual Charter Day ceremony in 1941 Johnson was praised for six things: he transformed the university's physical landscape, placed Howard on a strong financial basis, strengthened its faculty, established security and tenure for professors, maintained high academic standards, and applied the standards to all departments. In 1930 Johnson raised private funds to renovate Carnegie Library, providing a new home for the School of Religion. In 1938 Founders Library was completed. Three years later Johnson unveiled a ten-year program involving fourteen new building projects. By then Mays had departed for Morehouse and Thurman was restless for a new adventure, but both stayed in touch with Johnson. In Thurman's case there were mixed feelings; for Mays there was no ambiguity: Johnson was a strong, noble, exemplary, astoundingly successful leader, a role model in every way.[104]

In 1943 Howard's federal appropriation topped $1 million for the first time since 1933. The building surge kept Johnson closer to home than usual, just as white institutions began to compete with black colleges for black faculty stars. Harris and Bunche were bellwether examples of the brain drain that began in the 1940s, though of different kinds. Johnson incurred no blame for losing Bunche to the United Nations. Losing Harris, however, fell entirely on Johnson. In 1945 the University of Chicago lured Harris with a lowball offer he did not want to take. Harris had published articles for the *Journal of Political Economy*, edited by Chicago economist Frank Knight, and became friends with Knight. He asked Johnson for a salary hike, hoping Johnson would negotiate with him. Money was not the issue for Harris. He wanted respect and appreciation from Johnson, which he did not get. Johnson took the Chicago offer as a chance to get rid of Harris. He chided Harris for greedily taking the money from a white university, which enraged Harris, who wrote to Locke, "My disgust with the place is just about as great as yours." He was glad to leave Howard: "Good riddance by no means expresses the Administration alone."[105]

Harris already had a strong case of market reverence before he joined the Chicago faculty. Then he became more reverential, in Chicago School fashion, and stopped writing about racial justice issues. Johnson took his lumps for losing Harris, believing that Harris's later conservatism vindicated him for chasing away Harris. In 1943 Johnson established a history chair for William Leo Hansberry, confirming Howard's commitment to African history, and in 1947 he shrewdly lured John Hope Franklin from North Carolina College just as Franklin's *From Slavery to Freedom* was published (he lost Franklin to

Brooklyn College in 1956). Franklin had scholarly intelligence and intellectual courage of a high order, things that Johnson prized. Johnson worked hard at keeping his faculty stars, establishing a merit pay system that rewarded some of his harshest critics. Locke and Frazier were the first to be paid more than anyone else, $6,000. In 1948 Johnson added Brown, Bunche, Logan, and psychologist Francis Sumner to the top tier.[106]

The law school bore a special burden at Howard, and in the 1940s Johnson pined for a super-achiever of Houston's caliber. World War II was hard on the law school. There were twenty-one graduates in 1940 and fourteen in 1941, but the numbers for the war years, successively, were seven, six, seven, and three. Some became important civil rights leaders and lawyers. Robert Lee Carter, class of 1940, served for many years as legal counsel of the NAACP, and Pauli Murray was one of seven in 1944. But the law school struggled to get through the war years, and Hastie resigned as dean in 1946. Longtime law professors Bernard Jefferson and Leon Ransom expected to be the next dean, but Johnson bypassed both, naming George M. Johnson (no relation) to the deanship. Jefferson and Ransom resigned in protest. In years past the campus would have erupted: the law school was losing its core faculty just as enrollments soared after the war. Mordecai Johnson solved the crisis by appointing university secretary James M. Nabrit Jr. to the law school, where he became a legendary figure at Howard, training the postwar generation of lawyers. Nabrit served as dean of the law school from 1958 to 1960 and succeeded Johnson as president in 1960.[107]

On the road Johnson talked constantly about race; a speech was a wasted opportunity if he said nothing about racial justice. After the United States intervened in World War II Johnson protested that white Americans somehow condemned Nazi racism without noticing that their own racism was very Nazi-like: "To advance into the struggle naively relying upon the might of our economic and military resources, without attending to the repair of this disease at the root of our evil, is to flirt with Destiny at the risk of the most precious cause in the world. I call upon you to bring about a halt and a healing of this disease while there is yet time."[108]

In 1947 he spoke at the inauguration of Charles S. Johnson as president of Fisk University. As always on these occasions Johnson began with the founding of black colleges after the Civil War and the kenotic idealism of white missionaries who "humbled themselves and came here and made themselves obedient to the needs of slaves and the children of slaves." These missionaries, Johnson declared, saw something in black Americans that white southerners did not see: "Underneath our rude personalities, bruised and aborted by the slave system, there was the unrevealed and essential dignity of human nature endowed by its

Creator with unlimited possibilities." Johnson loved to recall that the mission-aries "lived with us, ate with us, slept in the same dormitories with us, [and] suffered ostracism and humiliation with us." A missionary teacher would ask, "Mr. Johnson, will you read?" Johnson stressed that no white person in the South called any black person "Mr." This simple question, with its "reverent courtesy," opened out to something truly radical—real democracy. Democracy was not in the Declaration of Independence or the Constitution. It resided in the souls of men and women dedicated to freedom and equality for all people. It was "the highest friendship that we have known," the creation of an egali-tarian social order built upon human dignity. To love anything less than the radical project of democracy, Johnson declared, was to betray one's humanity.[109]

At Fisk, Johnson pivoted to the peril and promise of postwar America. He believed that segregation was collapsing from its own degeneracy: "I predict that within this decade that system will be abandoned in principle, that it will be breached in fact and irreparably, and that from this decade on it will be in inevitable retreat." Many black schools would fade away when segregation ended, Johnson acknowledged, but all black schools would be better off. The sheer force of huge graduating classes would demolish segregation in higher education. Johnson noted that record numbers of students were attending college, including 78,000 African Americans. Many blacks planned to study medicine, but in the South they were excluded from enrolling anywhere except Howard and Meharry. Already in 1947 Howard had 1,351 applicants for 70 School of Medicine slots. That was just the beginning, Johnson said; in three years it would feel like a tidal wave, and the new graduates were sure to demand their rights. Black graduates would bang on the doors of every professional and graduate school supported by public funds: "They are going to say, 'Let us in there. We have got to come in there. We have a right to be in there, and we must come in.'"[110]

Lawsuits were sure to multiply, and the white South was sure to defend segregation in the schools, courts, and streets. Undoubtedly, Johnson said, there would be much wailing about "separate but equal." But this time white south-erners would be forced to learn "the true expense of segregation." Johnson expected an uptick in public funding for black institutions in medicine, engi-neering, and law, which would not last: "I predict they will not do it, because they cannot do it. And I predict that the Walls of Jericho will fall." On second thought, Johnson said this was not much of a prediction because the walls were already falling. The Roman Catholic Church, after "three hundred years of reflection," had begun to oppose racial discrimination, specifically in the Catholic dioceses of Washington, DC, and Missouri. That put southern

Protestants in a squeeze between Communists who crossed the color line "to establish brotherhood" and Roman Catholics who tried to learn how. The soul of white Protestantism was at stake, Johnson contended. White southern Protestants would either disavow their racism or lose their moral standing. Johnson feared that white Baptists might fail the test "because the local preacher is isolated." He believed that white Methodists would not fail because Methodists had bishops and the holiness theology of John Wesley.[111]

To Johnson, Communism was a challenge, not a threat. Communists cared about the poor and afflicted, and they were miles ahead of U.S. American political parties on racial justice. The Communist movement, for all its faults and disasters, took seriously that the acid test of a decent society was how it treated its poor. For that reason Johnson refused to condemn Communism, as though Americans stood on higher moral ground: "We must answer the question of whether the man who is on top of America can be trusted, unequivocally, to come in contact with the man who is on the bottom and to love him with persistence and strength enough to lift him to security and brotherhood. America knows she has got to do this. She knows that there must be no pussyfooting, and that she has got to do it now or her candlestick is going to be taken away from her and her own God is going to transfer the moral center of gravity to this universe clear out of the Western Hemisphere."[112]

Charles S. Johnson, the center of attention on this occasion, maintained a stony blank gaze as Johnson spoke, right hand fixed to jaw. E. C. Peters, white president of Paine College in Augusta, Georgia, and W. C. Jackson, white chancellor of the women's college at the University of North Carolina, were easier to read: tense and unhappy. Harvie Branscomb, white chancellor of Vanderbilt University, fidgeted uneasily through Johnson's speech. Later, when Branscomb spoke, he commended every speaker except Johnson. Johnson had not come to Fisk to say innocuous things offending no one—he never did, even on ceremonial occasions at Howard. A reporter for the *Afro-American* noted that Johnson stared straight at Peters and Charles Johnson as he spoke, reading and measuring both, perhaps trying to evoke a reaction. The crowd gave Johnson a strong ovation, but the applause from the platform was tepid and strained. On the platform, the most offensive part of Johnson's address was his prediction about segregation falling in the South.[113]

The ravages of racism harmed whites as well as blacks. Johnson's usual riff on this theme mentioned that slavery dehumanized the owner class, but he stressed something else: that slavery impoverished millions of whites in the South by depriving them of work and opportunity. Johnson confessed that it took him a long time to say this because he was thirty years old before he believed it: "The first thirty years of my life were spent in irritation and a vastly rising bitterness." He had to meet many poor whites before it sunk in: they were products of grinding poverty and lack of opportunity. Johnson reminded his audiences that slavery existed for two and a half centuries alongside miserable conditions for the vast majority of whites. Millions of poor whites "never had anything approximating economic and political liberty—to say nothing of human kindness—until the emancipation of the Negro. This we must keep in mind if we want to understand the terribleness of slavery."[114]

The new slavery of peonage was much like the old one. Blacks had it worst as tenant farmers, but they had plenty of company in the hopelessness of scratching for survival on farms that buried them in debt. Many African Americans sang the nationalist song of economic separatism; Johnson countered that poor blacks—like poor whites—had no chance of succeeding separately. The commercial chain stores, backed by big organizations and wealth, moved wherever they wanted, crushing separatist efforts by underselling competitors. Johnson urged that as long as poor whites feared blacks as a class, they held the power to repress blacks economically and politically while stunting themselves in the process. He pressed the distinction between fear and hate: "I do not believe that in his heart the poor white man normally hates the Negro. He has been taught to hate the Negro because his leaders have never so governed the economic life of the South as to give him a normal chance to live and think like a normal man." Johnson told the Woman's Auxiliary of the Episcopal Church that their beloved nation had a vicious system of racial caste much like India's, and their church did little to oppose it: "The Negro has not found that Christian white people in general make an exception to this rule of practice."[115]

In August 1947 India won its freedom, and a massive bloodletting between Hindus and Muslims broke out. Five months later Gandhi was assassinated, slain by a member of a Hindu supremacist organization, the Hindu Mahasabha. Johnson followed events in India closely, conferring with William Stuart Nelson, who had extensive contacts there. In 1949 the Indian government invited Johnson to address the interfaith World Pacifist Meeting in India, where Johnson lingered for forty days. He savored India's independence and conversed with Gandhian movement leaders, just before India officially became a republic on January 26, 1950. This experience became a staple of Johnson's stump speeches, folded into his broadside against Cold War militarism. At Howard's fall convocation of 1953 he blasted Secretary of State John Foster Dulles for fueling anti-Soviet hysteria: "We have reached the climax of hate. We now see what the Scriptures of the world have always said—that they who take up the sword shall die by it." The world, Johnson exhorted, needed desperately to turn from "the calculation of brutality and deception." It was not too late for the United States to be a force for world peace and cooperation. In India a single Spirit-filled man had brought the brutal British Empire to its knees, "the greatest example of successful international negotiation that this world has ever seen." Johnson called the United States to "rise from the spirit of violence, into the great statesmanship that Gandhi has set before us."[116]

Johnson tried to believe that his country might be a force for a just world order, and he did believe that a breakthrough for racial justice was coming in the United States. To be ready for it, he urged, black leaders needed to believe it was coming, even as another Red Scare created special problems for African Americans. Cold War ideology and anti-Communist "containment" strategy arose in the late 1940s, conceiving the entire planet as a battleground between Communist totalitarianism and Western democracy. In 1947 HUAC launched hearings aimed at exposing Communists in the entertainment industry; the following year it pursued a sensational espionage case against former State Department official Alger Hiss. The Hiss case went to trial in 1949, just as Communist forces overthrew the government in China, which yielded accusations that the Truman administration lost China. In February 1950 Wisconsin Republican senator Joseph McCarthy charged that the State Department employed 205 Communists. Four months later North Korean troops invaded South Korea, setting off the Korean War, just before the Senate Foreign Relations Committee discredited McCarthy's claims. McCarthy kept accusing, aided by two forms of war psychology—the Cold War and the U.S./United Nations intervention in Korea. McCarthy said that the State Department, Central Intelligence Agency, Truman staff, U.S. Army, and numerous American universities and professional organizations teemed with Communists. That went on for four years, until the Senate censured McCarthy in 1954 for smearing countless individuals and harming the government, notably the army. But McCarthy was just an extreme example of the Cold War hysteria gripping Washington, DC, and the nation.[117]

Howard was especially vulnerable to the new Red Scare because Howard belonged to the U.S. Civil Service. "McCarthyism," already a term by 1950, battered the Howard community, as the Federal Security Agency targeted twenty-five professors for suspected subversion. Johnson defended them forcefully, inadvertently becoming an expert on the slippery politics of Communism-on-campus. This story had five stages. The Red Scare of the early 1920s had passed when Johnson took over at Howard, so he focused on federal funding and internal problems. He later recalled, "When I first came to Howard

University, this institution was in turmoil." Professors felt insecure in their work and standing, the campus was polarized by rival factions on the faculty, and "nearly every problem in the institution fell on the president's desk." Johnson vowed to make Howard professors secure in their jobs and intellectual freedom, although he soon stopped consulting them about how to run the university. By his reckoning it took him ten years to establish that every professor was free not to adhere to the party line of a power bloc or an administrator. Likewise he defended the rights of students and staff; on occasion Johnson had to tell faculty and administrators that students had a right to express negative opinions about them.[118]

Stage two began in the late 1930s, when Howard established its first labor union for faculty and staff. Johnson flushed with disappointment and conflicted feelings. It was sad that Howard wanted a union, but Johnson was pro-union. He could not be pro-union if he opposed one at Howard. He told himself that no decent union would want more for Howard employees than he did, so there was nothing to regret. But the union alienated its members by operating as a dictatorship, and it folded. Fifteen years later Johnson learned it was a Communist union—his first brush, albeit unknowingly, with Communism-on-campus. Subsequently Howard established a CIO union; on one occasion Johnson had to admonish congressional members of the Appropriations Committee that Howard students had a right to invite Communist leader James W. Ford to speak at a forum. At the time, American Communists ran openly for office like candidates of other parties; for Johnson, these became the good old days. Years later he boasted that he lost only one vote on the Appropriations Committee for permitting an actual Communist to speak at Howard.

Stage three began after World War II ended. The government vowed to root out Communists from the government, and Johnson cultivated a trusting relationship with Federal Security Agency administrator Paul MacNutt. One by one Johnson and MacNutt pored over MacNutt's list of twenty-five suspected faculty Communists. None belonged to the Communist Party itself, Johnson stressed, and it was not illegal to join a front organization. Moreover, he said, the government needed to understand something about black professors. They belonged to a vulnerable minority, the issue of racial injustice was "always on their minds," they had precious few allies, and when Communist front groups offered to be their friends it was hard to say no. Johnson and MacNutt had the same back-and-forth twenty-five times. MacNutt exonerated twenty-three of the suspects, and the other two were eventually absolved after lengthy proceedings.[119]

Meanwhile Johnson implored HUAC members to see that it was truly un-American to scour faculty syllabi for incriminating Communist content.

America had much to learn from England in this area, he contended. The Brits understood that a healthy government could tolerate "a whole lot of thinking about violence and a whole lot of talking about violence." Actually trying to overthrow the government was one thing and hanging out with mere talkers was something else. It was wrong to strip anyone of rights merely for joining the Communist Party: "The notion is preposterous that we can preserve democracy by batting every man on the head who has the idea that there are certain circumstances under which the government ought to be overthrown. It is impossible to legislate out of existence one of the alternatives that confront every honorable man when he is trying to reform an injurious situation and cannot get if reformed by due process. It just naturally occurs to him that he has got to change that process some way or other, even if he has to overthrow it."[120]

Stage four arrived at Howard after the government learned that Communists had infiltrated numerous American trade unions, including the CIO-UAW to which Howard's union belonged. That surprised Johnson because Howard's CIO Union Ten had behaved honorably. He hated having to cancel Howard's contract with the union, and some Howard faculty hated it more. But the faculty closed ranks in support of Johnson, concurring that he had no choice. The federal government had legitimate reasons to drive Communist organizations out of trade unions, and Howard's federal appropriation was gone if Howard retained a Communist-dominated union.

Stage five came fast upon stage four, as federal courts ruled that the Communist Party actively conspired to overthrow the U.S. government. Now Congress decreed that no part of Howard's appropriation was to be paid to anyone belonging to any group advocating the overthrow of the U.S. government by force. Howard, being part of the government, lacked any legal ground for defying the congressional ban, and Johnson pledged to comply. He consoled himself that no one would have to be fired, since all twenty-five of Howard's suspects had been exonerated. Johnson declared in 1953, "The government of the United States is within its own proper rights in being very greatly concerned about the existence of the Communist Party in this country." It was no longer debatable whether the Communist Party USA took instructions from Moscow to subvert and overthrow the U.S. government, so the U.S. government had to target the Communist Party.[121]

Thwarting the Communist Party was one thing, however; discriminating against individuals belonging to it was something else. Johnson protested that Congress betrayed Americanism by lumping these things together. Congress had no business hunting for individual Communists and depriving them of their rights. If HUAC continued on this path, "that inquiry may possibly destroy the most precious thing in the whole American higher education, namely academic freedom." Johnson reasoned that many Communists were Communists on ideological grounds and some were actively engaged in espionage and subversion. Sorting out one from the other, he urged, was a job for the FBI, not the Congress. Johnson was naïve and sadly wrong about FBI director J. Edgar Hoover, "one of the ablest, most restrained, and decent men" ever to serve in the U.S. government. In Johnson's view, when the FBI found that a Communist professor had not engaged in subversion, it was the university's call whether it wanted to employ the professor. Universities had to be able to conduct such inquiries "without such a blustering, blundering indictment of the whole faculty and the whole cause of education as is now going on at the hands of this committee."[122]

Putting it strongly, Johnson said that to accuse a person of being a Communist and then deprive that person of the right to self-defense was "to commit murder upon him." No congressional committee had any business doing that. He exhorted educators to stir up some courage: "It would be better that our American institutions lose the last dollar than that we should turn our faculties into a group of frightened sheep, afraid to think independently, and afraid to go out to dinner for fear they may accidentally sit down by somebody who is a member of the Communist Party. We cannot run American universities that way. We cannot carry on the process of democracy that way. Democracy will die unless, in these citadels of thought, men are at liberty to examine every area of thought and every institution on its merits in relation to the objective criteria of the mind, both intellectual and ethical, and to teach the students to think independently and to think dangerously."[123]

Johnson cautioned that Caesar was a great investigator. Caesar hunted down Christians, locked them up, and fed them to the lions. He pursued them so aggressively that they had to go underground. But Christians multiplied anyway, and the empire's repressive force was no match for them. Johnson likened modern Communists to the ancient Christians in preaching a message of hope to the poor, and he likened much of modern Christianity to the Roman Empire. Modern Italy exemplified both sides of the problem. The Roman papal magisterium, Johnson said, resembled the Roman Empire, not the early church: "They are in complete control of institutional thought and no subversion is possible theoretically." Yet Italy had two million Communists, every one a protester against poverty, exploitation, ancient estates still existing, and repressive violence. Italy was a breeding ground for Communism. Johnson observed that when human beings were aggrieved "it makes little difference what is the name of the organization through which they are to function." Oppressed people gave their allegiance to anything offering the hope of deliverance from oppression: "Italy can have all the FBI it pleases and survey all the universities. Unless it changes these basically hurtful economic conditions, Communism will some day take over Italy."[124]

He was more hopeful about racial justice, contending that big changes were coming. On January 10, 1954, Johnson told an Emancipation Day gathering in Baltimore that the very existence of a biracial gathering in Baltimore proved something important: "We have passed through a great dark period in the South. We are through it and are in another period." He noted that he no longer spoke differently when whites were in the audience because whites needed to hear from blacks an unfettered message of protest. Admittedly, black Americans held little political power, holding only the power of moral persuasion: "But the obligation to persuade is upon us today as if God Himself had made us an assignment. We ought to be as near as we can, as clear as we can, about what it is that we want." Blacks needed to believe and say "that we are commanded by the Eternal God to work for the complete elimination of segregation in every institution of the public life." And southern whites needed "to take an entirely new attitude toward us as individual human beings."[125]

The South, Johnson said, had no experience of democracy and almost no experience of Christianity. Preserving a one-party dictatorship based on racism had nothing to do with democracy. Moreover, Christianity was founded on "the sacred and inviolable worth of every human individual." Anyone who opposed that principle was not a Christian. Alongside stern remarks of this sort, especially near the end of a long talk, Johnson often sprinkled cheeky ones. He was fond of saying that the Lord told him to speak, but not for how long. In Baltimore he answered a question about racial intermarriage by declaring that he believed in it because there was only one race, the human race. As for him, he happened to be married to the world's most beautiful woman, but if she were to dump him there were ten black women "I'd like to speak to privately." On second thought, having been to India and seen its stunning women, he upped the list to one hundred.[126]

To Johnson, America's greatest president since Lincoln was obvious: Harry Truman, the only president to advocate equality of opportunity for blacks. In 1947 Truman's Presidential Committee on Civil Rights called for the elimination of racial segregation. The following year Truman endorsed the committee's report, called for an end to racial discrimination in federal hiring practices, and issued an executive order to end segregation in the military. Johnson wanted Truman to run for reelection in 1952 but did not blame him for walking away. Truman "risked his political life and lost it," Johnson said. If his achievements were meager, it had to be said that no other president since Lincoln had risked or accomplished nearly as much for racial justice.[127]

Johnson was a controversial leader at Howard throughout his presidency, and he never won over the Alumni Association. An undercurrent of resentment and negative lore made him easy to write off after he was gone, and he got unsympathetic treatment in books about several Howard scholars. But Johnson's dictatorial bullying was no worse than that of other high-powered university presidents of his type. He fired only a handful of top administrators and did not clean house at the next level down. He overrode the turf interests of faculty and administrators, as strong presidents usually do, and he provoked the sensitive egos of certain professors, sometimes to his credit. His biographer, Richard McKinney, noted that some Howard professors were unaccustomed to being challenged: "Some teachers at Howard held themselves in lofty esteem and did not like challenges to their egos." To the end of his presidency Johnson's preachy oratory and air of importance evoked eye rolling from Howard professors. Some accepted him only after he prevailed over Scott and Miller, and still found him hard to take. Logan explained, "He increasingly seemed to consider himself 'the indispensable man.' " But even Logan described the 1950s at Howard as "the golden years" and acknowledged, after Johnson retired, that he was one of the great university presidents of the twentieth century.[128]

Johnson ran the university effectively, and he had generally friendly relationships with students and faculty. The campus, by the golden years, was transformed, resembling Thomas Jefferson's University of Virginia, as Cassell favored Jefferson's classical symmetry. The majestic upper quad featured Founders Library (modeled on Independence Hall in Philadelphia) and Frederick Douglass Memorial Hall among other new buildings, all designed in Washington Victorian style. In the 1950s there were new buildings for the schools and departments of biology, law, education, engineering and architecture, dentistry, and pharmacy, and the administration—symbols of Johnson's success. Howard founded an African Studies program in 1954 and its first doctoral programs in 1955 (chemistry) and 1958 (physics). Johnson took special pride in Howard's relationship to the *Brown* decision of 1954, lauding Houston and Marshall for breaking through against school segregation. Marshall, at the time, was director of the NAACP's Legal Defense and Education Fund and later served on the U.S. Supreme Court. Howard law classes mostly chipped away at *Plessy v. Ferguson*, but the frontal assault on segregation that prevailed in the *Brown* decision also came out of Howard Law School: racism subverted the original intent of the Fourteenth Amendment, "separate but equal" was not equal, and the purpose of segregation was to perpetuate a racial caste system.[129]

Next to Howard's contribution to the *Brown* decision, Johnson took special pride in upgrading the School of Religion, where Thurman, Mays, and William

Stuart Nelson took up Johnson's commitment to Gandhian resistance. Nelson was born in 1895 in Paris, Kentucky, and served in the army during World War I. He earned his undergraduate degree at Yale in 1924 and joined the Howard faculty in 1925, teaching religion. In 1931 Nelson took over the presidency of Shaw University, in 1936 he took over the presidency of Dillard University, and in 1940 he returned to Howard, succeeding Mays as dean. Nelson's commitment to Gandhian nonviolence was deep and long-standing. He became an authority on Gandhian *satyagraha*, toured India in 1946–1947, organized Quaker services in Calcutta, held meetings with Gandhi, and organized interfaith dialogues. Though some Howard faculty continued to scoff at the School of Religion—Logan insisted it "remained in the doldrums" under Mays and Nelson—the school played an important role in identifying Howard with civil rights activism, the social gospel, and postcolonial internationalism.[130]

Nelson founded Howard's influential *Journal of Religious Thought* and served the university in numerous faculty and administrative capacities, eventually as vice president of special projects. In the spring of 1950 he and Johnson gave signature speeches on Gandhian nonviolence. Johnson spoke at Fellowship House in Philadelphia shortly after returning from India. He explained that Gandhi forged soul force—satyagraha, the power of love and truth combined—into a vehicle of radical social transformation. Young Martin Luther King Jr. was in the audience and was electrified; he later described the speech as a turning point. Nelson, speaking at Rankin Chapel, offered a capsule version of his message about the exemplary importance of Gandhi: "In leading India into her freedom, he demonstrated that first, the oppressed must never cease to seek his freedom; second, he must seek his freedom in such a manner as to preserve his own soul; and third, he must seek his freedom in a manner that will lift to a higher moral and spiritual plane the oppressor from whom he wrests his freedom."[131]

Movement leaders must be willing to stick with a message, expounding variations on the same message repeatedly. Johnson was emphatically a message speaker, sticking to the same tropes and themes throughout his career. He spoke twice a year at Rankin Chapel and always at the university and School of Religion convocations, to overflow audiences. In 1940 he gave the Rauschenbusch Lectures at Colgate Rochester Seminary, an annual four-lecture series that usually produced a published book. Johnson spoke about the global significance of American Christianity but never produced a manuscript, despite promising one. He had never written a book or written out his lectures, and he probably realized after giving the Rauschenbusch Lectures that he did not want a published version of stories and arguments that he used every week. Routinely he began with a tribute to the northern missionaries who founded the black colleges, blasted segregation as a vile abuse of black Americans, and asserted that the United States was unfit for world leadership as long as it practiced segregation. Often he added that the colonizing powers of Europe "ruthlessly conquered more territory" and abused more people than any comparable empire. In 1957, warming to the latter theme, he added a proposal: if the United States truly opposed colonialism, it should stop supporting European nations that practiced it.[132]

Two years later he put it more diplomatically at the First Atlantic Congress of the North Atlantic Treaty Organization (NATO) in London. Johnson attended the congress as a delegate, board member, and plenary speaker. He started with the missionary founders of black colleges, "the noblest and best element in the Western world." He pressed NATO dignitaries to emulate the missionary founders, who championed "the inherent dignity and immeasurable possibilities of the human individual." And he stressed that most human beings were not white or European, which set up a blunt version of his argument about Communism.[133]

Johnson noted that European Social Democracy derived from the Second Socialist International, and the Communist movement derived from the Third Socialist International. Social Democracy was liberal and democratic, and Communism was neither, so Johnson was a radical Social Democrat. But he grieved that even the best European tradition—Social Democracy—had a track record of caring only about organizing white workers, while Communists appealed to Africans and Asians. Communists, despite lacking a metaphysical worldview remotely comparable to Christianity, had something precious: "They have radical, universal ethics in their relationship to the black and brown and yellow peoples of the world." The Communist movement organized workers of every color everywhere, and in less than forty years it captured one-third of the world's population. Johnson admonished that harping on the deficiencies of Communism would not defeat Russian or Chinese Communism, and losing India would tip the global balance in favor of Communism: "We are up against a great antagonist with a great passion, with an immense achievement as a result of that passion, and with a profound faith that he is getting ready to turn the corner that leads to our graveyard." On second thought, he put it more sharply: Communists believed the West was digging its own grave by denigrating most of the world's people, and they were right about that.[134]

Rightly conceived, Johnson implored, NATO had a religious mission and a political mission, and both were anticolonial. The religious mission was to recover the biblical belief that all human beings are bearers of God-given dignity and equality. Johnson called out delegates from England, France, and

Germany because these nations gave birth to Christian Socialism, especially "you great Germans, who have meditated upon socialism long before the idea was born among the Russians." All Christian Socialists understood what he meant, Johnson said, because Christian Socialism was based on the doctrine of God-given dignity and equality. Second, NATO needed to carry out "the Eternal's veto on the colonial system" by abolishing every vestige of colonialism in Africa. Johnson also meant colonialism wherever it existed, but he urged NATO to start with Africa because NATO would have no anti-imperial credibility anywhere if it did not acquire credibility in Africa: "We have got to listen to the cries of those 100 million black Africans who are crying out against political domination, economic exploitation, segregation, and humiliation as if we were listening to the words of our children."[135]

The young ministers who founded SCLC in 1957 often felt slighted by northern civil rights leaders of Johnson's generation. Johnson was a notable exception, lauding King and SCLC profusely and reaching out in solidarity. In 1957 Johnson conferred an honorary doctorate on King at Howard's commencement, as did Chicago Theological Seminary, Morehouse College, and Kentucky State University. Johnson declared, "You have led your people on a victorious pathway seldom tried in human life. You have shown them how to mobilize the fullest powers of their souls for effective resistance to evil and how to overcome humiliation and abuse without violence and without hatred in deed or in words. . . . The example of your leadership has given hope to those who suffer from oppression all over the former slave states and those who suffer from humiliation all over the world."[136]

Then Johnson tried to lure King to Howard as dean of the School of Religion. King, leaning toward yes in June 1957, conjectured that his activist work in the South might be finished within a year. A month later he told Johnson that abolishing segregation would take longer, so he needed to decline: "Please know that I regret this very deeply. This has been one of the most difficult decisions that I have had to make in my brief career." Johnson replied that he admired King enormously and supported his decision: "There are indeed vast possibilities of a non-violent, non-cooperative approach to the solution of the race problem in the South; and this undertaking is challenging beyond measure. Intellectually and spiritually, you are fitted for the work; and I believe that God will give you all the strength which is needed day by day to go forward with it."[137]

A year later Johnson made the same offer and got the same reply. Then he retired, with surprising contentment. Normally strapping and buoyant, Johnson confessed at the NATO congress that he had grown tired. In 1955 he had reached the customary retirement age of sixty-five, but no one expected him to retire. Five years later he was ready. On his way out in June 1960 the Howard board hailed Johnson for "his magnificent leadership, his great accomplishments, and his inspiring example." Mays declared that he knew Johnson from close acquaintance as a person of enormous integrity and good will: "He has given the university and the nation a courageous leadership. Few university Presidents would have had the character and the ability to speak the prophetic word in criticism of the social and political ills of our times as he." Johnson's glittering retirement dinner at the Sheraton Park Hotel in November 1960 was cochaired by Eleanor Roosevelt, attended by Supreme Court justice Felix Frankfurter and twelve hundred others, and adorned with tributes; Johnson's favorite came from president-elect John F. Kennedy: "You have truly been one of the outstanding leaders in American education in this century."[138]

He planned to spend a year "just thinking," do a bit of public speaking, and write about his career at Howard: "I want to think about America and the Negro's role in our great country. I want to think about America and the West and their relations with the Soviet Union. I also want to think about the underdeveloped and oppressed people of the world, and how we can bring them to a decent standard of living and the right for them to determine their own futures. And even after this period of thinking, who knows, I might embark upon a new career."[139]

Johnson rested and thought for a year before asking Howard for his files, so he could start writing. The university board had promised him in 1960 that he would have access to university files. Now the university told him the files were missing; no one could find them. That was unbelievable, but Johnson did not press the issue. The files belonged to Howard, and he would not make a fuss that made his successor and former legal advisor, Nabrit, look bad. Mays implored him to write something, but Johnson produced only a fragment. Disappointed and puzzled, Johnson let go of his plan to tell his story. Howard's trustees and administrators worried about lawsuits likely to arise from a published account of the Johnson years, especially one relying on board minutes. Any account that named names and/or took a side would stir acrimony or something worse. In 1962 Howard commissioned Logan and Sterling Brown to write its official centennial history, providing access to files that the administration denied to Johnson. But Nabrit's staff worried about Logan, too, which led to years of wrangling, censorship, and anguish for Logan. Thirty years later McKinney still had to make do without the presidential files; Howard was zealous in keeping its secrets.[140]

Meanwhile Johnson settled into a surprisingly leisurely retirement, centered on his family: his wife, Anna Ethelyn; daughter Carolyn, a housewife; son Mordecai Junior, a dentist; son Archer, a psychiatrist; son William, an engineer;

and daughter Anna, a public service professional. Johnson regaled his grand-children with stories of his visits to Panama, Ethiopia, and Liberia, where he was showered with high national honors, and of his tours of India, Sierra Leone, Monrovia, Ghana, Syria, Lebanon, Jordan, and Israel. He told his daughters, sons, and grandchildren that their mission in life was to build the kingdom of God, and he was a demanding enforcer of family order. Johnson ran his house-hold with the same domineering spirit he used to run Howard University, ever-more the son of Wyatt Johnson and protégé of John Hope. But his powerful will and tendency to sermonize were leavened by warmth and humor.[141]

He accepted occasional speaking engagements, served for three years on the District of Columbia school board, and helped King raise money for the Gandhi Society. But Johnson did not try to stay in the limelight or seek a new career. His last move was unexpectedly personal. In 1969 his beloved wife of fifty-three years died, and Johnson grieved Anna's loss for several months, feeling sad, nostalgic, exhausted, and finished. He lived, uncharacteristically, in the past, comforted by memories, which yielded a surprising turn. A few months after Anna's death Johnson gave a speech in Memphis, reuniting with an old friend from Memphis, Fred Hutchins. The two men reminisced about their years at Howe Institute and the Primrose Club. Johnson, remembering Hutchins's friendship with Alice Woodson, asked him, "By the way, whatever happened to that very pretty little girl, 'Sweet Alice,' I was supposed to marry?" Hutchins replied that she was a widow, owned a prosperous funeral parlor, and lived in Austin, Texas. He also had her address and telephone number. Johnson said, "Give it to me right now."[142]

Johnson had not seen or heard from Alice Woodson King since their fateful parting in 1912. She had married a physician, John Q. Taylor, in 1916. Johnson had learned through friends that Alice married a Meharry graduate, which seemed to confirm his original misconception. Later he and Alice Woodson Taylor learned through friends that the Fisk matron had caused their breakup, but contacting each other seemed pointless and dishonorable by then. Taylor served in World War I, was gassed in France, and suffered ill health until his death in 1931, leaving Woodson Taylor with three children. She married an insurance salesman, Charles King, who opened a funeral parlor in Austin. He died in 1941, and Woodson King took over the business, expanding it with the help of her children John Q. Taylor King and Edwina King. Woodson King told her children the story of her first love, adding that he became quite famous as the president of Howard University. In the 1950s John made his way to Howard, introducing himself to Johnson, who greeted him warmly; Johnson cleared his calendar to learn about John and his mother.

But propriety ruled out any contact between Johnson and Woodson King until both were widowed, and he had her phone number. Johnson called her promptly, on a day when John King—then president of Huston-Tillotson College in Austin—happened to be visiting his mother. King waved "good-bye" after the conversation had exceeded thirty minutes, and a romance was renewed. Johnson was eighty years old and Woodson King was seventy-eight. All his sons and daughters were happy for him, pleased that his ebullience returned. Johnson told a Howard acquaintance, "And she has never loved any man but me!" Alice Woodson Johnson probably wanted him to keep that secret to himself, but many who disliked Mordecai Johnson and many who revered him agreed that he was short on tact.[143]

Johnson had six happy years of marriage with his first love before dying in 1976. His funeral took place at Rankin Chapel, where Howard president James E. Cheek spoke, a recorded tribute from Thurman was played, and Mays gave the eulogy. There were many editorial tributes. The best emphasized Johnson's achievements at Howard and his legacy as a globally minded national civil rights leader. The *Washington Evening Star* said that Howard was merely "an educational gesture" when Johnson took over, and it became "a mature and vigorous institution" under his leadership. Moreover, Johnson was brave and forceful in advocating racial justice: "There was in his philosophy no passivity, no acceptance of the image to which racism and ignorance consigned generations of Black Americans. Rather, Dr. Johnson challenged, fought tenaciously, and at risk, for the ideals of racial equality."[144]

Howard's newspaper, *Hilltop*, similarly stressed Johnson's heroic strength: "Dr. Johnson was a scholar among scholars, a president among presidents, a man among men—but even more important, he was his own man. He was not slow to criticize slovenly standards, racism, imperialism, or any species of intolerance or injustice. He held up to withering scrutiny black as well as white leadership in civic, religious, and economic life." The *Washington Post* similarly lauded Johnson's two-track legacy as a college president and national social justice leader. Johnson's "vision, determination, and administrative skills" turned a weak, unaccredited college into "a recognized center of learning," the *Post* observed. He transformed the entire university, "which at times involved bitter struggles just to keep Howard alive." The *Post* added that this achievement alone would have been enough to earn Johnson "worldwide recognition" as an educator, but the "full measure of his greatness" involved something more important: "Mordecai Johnson's most important contribution to America and to the Negro was that he provided the climate in which were forged the instruments that overthrew Jim Crow."[145]

That was exactly right. In his lifetime Johnson got plenty of attention for lifting Howard to prominence and helping to change American society. Afterward he got little attention aside from books in which he was described as being controversial in a not-good way. The faculty that liked and appreciated Johnson did not say enough to counter the image of him conveyed by prolific faculty that disliked him. He rated few mentions in works on King and the civil rights movement, and the official history of his career at Howard—Logan's *Howard University*—spoke through clenched teeth and summaries of board minutes. Logan knew more than he tried to say. He aimed for objectivity and comprehensiveness, but Brown contributed almost nothing to the book, Logan's wife died, Logan grieved and struggled, and he had to battle Howard's censors, an awful experience in his telling. He quit the book as a protest against the censorship, which caused Nabrit to relent; Logan eventually completed, more or less, the book he had meant to write. It conveyed his New Negro cultural nationalism and his low view of religious intellectuals. It muzzled Logan's repugnance for the new language of blackness spoken by the Black Power movement. And it conveyed dislike and grudging respect for Howard's dominant figure.[46]

Johnson deserved to be better remembered. Very few black leaders of the 1930s and 1940s reached interracial audiences, regardless of the message. Johnson enthralled large interracial audiences while proclaiming that racism "is our most dangerous enemy, for it is a disease at the very root of our democratic life." Embree justly ranked Johnson with Charles Eliot, who transformed Harvard, and William Rainey Harper, who founded the University of Chicago, as an educational giant. But Johnson had a greater legacy than his record as Howard's greatest president: his powerful racial justice advocacy, which offered a model for Mays, Thurman, and King. They saw Johnson command the attention and respect of white audiences that did not want to hear about the racist sickness of Western civilization but took it from him anyway. Mays, Thurman, and King saw in Johnson a model of radical Christian prophecy that scaled up.[47]

3

Moral Politics and the Soul
of the World

The black social gospel was a complex phenomenon from its beginning. It was a form of social Christianity that imagined what a new abolitionism needed to be under the conditions of modern social consciousness and racial segregation. Most of it powerfully identified with U.S. Americanism despite its variable strains of black nationalism, especially cultural nationalism. Black social gospel theology featured evangelical and modernist tropes, a politics of racial justice opening out to a comprehensive politics of social justice, and, usually, an aspiration to forge alliances with white progressives on both counts.

On all these counts the early black social Christian leaders, being pioneers, held little hope of becoming prophets with honor in their time, either within or outside black churches. Reverdy Ransom's fellow AME ministers drove him out of Chicago and Boston for advocating social gospel theology and social justice politics. Ida Wells-Barnett tried and failed to build a national anti-lynching movement. George Washington Woodbey preached Christian Socialism with eloquence, energy, and distinction, to little effect. Ransom and Richard R. Wright Jr. became slight exceptions by eventually making bishop, as did Adam Clayton Powell Sr. by becoming a nationally renowned pastor. But even they were embattled in their denominational contexts and had only slight success in crossing racial lines.

The social gospel leaders who came of age in the 1920s represented something new in both respects. By the time Johnson, Mays, and Thurman came along, social Christianity had won a respectable following in black churches, winning legitimacy status. Moreover, the idea of reaching sizable white audiences with a racial justice message was no longer impossible. For Johnson, Mays, and Thurman it happened after they endured harsh upbringings in the

Deep South, earned graduate degrees in the North, and made connections with ecumenical organizations. To Mays and Thurman, Johnson was the exemplar of social gospel possibility. Thurman got to be Thurman by trying, on the way up, to be like Johnson, while Mays provided a model for King by following Johnson's example.

All three were scarred by growing up under southern racial tyranny, but Mays and Thurman had more to overcome, especially Mays, which made his story more dramatic. Mays had a breakthrough college experience he could not have attained in the South, or almost anywhere, period. But he returned to the South for his entire career, where he believed the chief struggle against racial caste had to be waged. "I am a Southerner," he would say. "I have elected to live in the South." There the "last of the great schoolmasters" shaped thousands of Morehouse Men and urged the most heavily churched section of the country to take up the struggle.[1]

BORN TO REBEL: BENJAMIN ELIJAH MAYS

Benjamin Elijah Mays did his greatest work without realizing it, by influencing young Martin Luther King Jr. He played a similar role for many others who helped King wage nonviolent war against white supremacy. Mays was born in the town of Ninety Six, South Carolina, in 1894, one year before South Carolina stripped blacks of the right to vote and two years before the U.S. Supreme Court ruled that racial segregation was legal. Until 1946, when Georgia's white primary system was declared unconstitutional, Mays was completely disenfranchised. His earliest childhood memory was of watching his father bow down to a lynch mob associated with the infamous Phoenix Riot in 1898—a form of mob terrorism by Ben Tillman operatives aimed at eliminating the last vestige of black political agency in South Carolina. For the rest of his life Mays felt the pain of lacking a home: "The experiences I had in my most impressionable years, hearing and seeing the mob, observing the way my people were treated, noting the way in which they responded to this treatment, never having developed any white friends in the county, and living all my early years in a rented house—all this left me with a feeling of alienation from the county of my birth."[2]

This alienation extended to his family background, which Mays mostly eschewed. He knew only a few details about his family and took no interest in the cultural legacy of West and West Central Africa across South Carolina, even though his mother's worship practices contained echoes of the circle dance and the shout. Both of his parents, S. Hezekiah Mays and Louvenia Carter Mays, were born into slavery, in 1856 and 1862. As a child Hezekiah Mays drank milk with his hands, fed from a plantation trough by the wife of his slavemaster. The wife's son taught him to read, illegally, and thus Hezekiah was able to pass the gift of literacy to his eight children. Hezekiah and Louvenia Mays were cotton farmers who owned their own mules and usually rented forty or sixty acres. When Benjamin Mays told the story of his life he stressed that his parents "never went to school a day in their lives" and that only two of their eight children were schooled beyond the fifth grade; he was the baby. Louvenia Mays, a devout Baptist, encouraged her gifted youngest child to get as much education as possible, but her husband disapproved of formal schooling, and he was both kindly and abusive to her. Sometimes he beat her after getting drunk. "All too many times we children had to hold him to keep him from hurting Mother," Mays later recalled. "He would take out his knife and threaten to cut her." At the age of twelve, "repelled and disgusted by my father's indulgence in these habits," Benjamin Mays vowed to his mother never to smoke, chew tobacco, or drink alcohol. He also resolved to get as much education as possible.[3]

The prevailing rule in Mays's home was, "Stay out of trouble with white people!" Mays noted that blacks often got into trouble no matter how they acted; those who cringed and kowtowed took just as many beatings as those who kept their dignity: "Hundreds of innocent Negroes were insulted, cheated, beaten, even lynched for the sole reason that they had incurred the displeasure of some white man." As a youth Mays lived in constant fear of being lynched. He avoided white people assiduously, recoiling at the servility that many blacks displayed toward whites. Many nights Mays trembled in his bed as white mobs rampaged through his neighborhood. Having a white friend was unthinkable to him.[4]

On one occasion a white physician slapped Mays across the face as they walked past the local post office. The physician accused him of "trying to look too good." Walking while black, especially with dignity, was an offense against Jim Crow in Ninety Six. Mays later put it bluntly: "I was black and a black man had no rights which he, Wallace Payne, was bound to admit, let alone respect." Mays grew up so deeply alienated from white southerners that in later life he was shocked when he received accolades from white newspapers and civic groups. Long after he was revered as a historic figure, he could write, "I have lived in constant fear of the mob and lynching." He also recalled of the world into which he grew up that "the wings of ambition were crushed at birth. Negroes accepted their role without overt complaint. They were not expected to aspire to noble things, and it is safe to say that 99.8 percent of them never did."[5]

Religion was a refuge for him and a bond between Mays and his mother. He later recalled that God was "very real" to his mother: "So, I caught her spirit and relied heavily on God and prayer. I needed to rely on something. I was the youngest of eight and no one before me had finished elementary school." Louvenia Mays was a loving spirit who had "genuine affection" for some white people, whereas "Father had no such affection." Hezekiah Mays's favorite story, often told, was about him beating up two white men simultaneously: "This story was his pride and joy." Mays figured that he got his religious spirit from his mother and his disbelief in black inferiority from his father. On the first Sunday of every month the Mays family attended a nearby Baptist congregation, Mount Olive, using the family mules. On week two they attended the Baptist congregation to which they belonged, Old Mount Zion, to hear James F. Marshall preach. The mules had a longer trip on week two, as Mount Zion was four miles from Mays's home; on the other Sundays, Marshall had other congregations to serve. On weeks three and four Hezekiah Mays stayed at home while his family walked four miles to Mount Zion and then back.[6]

Mays later recalled that Marshall was honest, sincere, biblically literate, and an important figure in Greenwood County. He moaned and emoted, getting people to shout. He was "highly otherworldly, emphasizing the joys of heaven and the damnation of hell." His funerals usually packed the house, and Marshall did not fudge, assigning the deceased to heaven or hell with straightforward certainty. For the rest of his life Mays was ambivalent about compensatory religion. He acknowledged that his neighbors probably would not have survived their oppression "without this kind of religion." Marshall's version of the gospel, Mays explained, was "primarily an opiate to enable them to endure and survive the oppressive conditions under which they lived at the hands of the white people in the community." Religious historian Randal Maurice Jelks, in his excellent biography of Mays, adds that Marshall was "a first-rate ecclesial politician" who navigated treacherous cultural terrain in which country pastors were considered threats to Jim Crow.[7]

Marshall allowed no talk against whites or lynching in his church, and he stayed on good terms with a local white Methodist minister, despite preaching that only Baptists went to heaven. Mays had two breakthroughs in church. The first occurred on Children's Day when he was nine. He recited part of the Sermon on the Mount and got a huge ovation, evoking predictions that he would go far in life. Marshall took a special interest in Mays from that day, as did the congregation, which boosted his self-esteem: "They gave me encouragement, the thing I most needed." Four years later Mays responded to an altar call and was born again, receiving baptism the following week. He later recalled that one Sunday morning he had an indescribable feeling, came forward for the altar call, and cried a little: "I felt lifted up and it was a new kind of feeling.

I was a boy and did not understand what had happened, but there was something within me that I had never known before and I felt a little excited and happy and very safe." Thirteen years later, upon enrolling at the University of Chicago Divinity School in 1921, Mays chose to be ordained in Chicago instead of at Mount Zion, which offended Marshall. Marshall never forgave him. To Mays, this outcome was an honest mutual acknowledgment that he had little in common, theologically, with "my fifth grade educated pastor."[8]

Education was the story of Mays's life. He refused to be denied an education, which opened a door. He prayed constantly, always for the same thing: that God would remove the obstacles to his education. "I was a frustrated child. . . . Many a day, I worked in the field and cried." Like most black children in his area, Mays had to help his father in the cotton field, which left little time for school—never more than four months per year—in a context where little opportunity existed anyway. The law allowed sharecroppers and tenant farmers to force their sons to provide free labor as field hands until they reached the age of majority. Hezekiah Mays was hardworking and productive, secondary education seemed pointless to him, and his children were afraid of him. He believed that preaching and farming were the only viable and decent occupations for a black man, and neither required more than an elementary education. Thus his youngest child had to plead for the right to study. Mays later reflected, "I had an insatiable desire to get an education. I wanted to be somebody."[9]

In 1909, when Mays was fifteen, Marshall persuaded Hezekiah Mays to let Mays study at a Baptist school twenty-four miles away, in McCormick, still on the agricultural cycle. Two years of four-month cycles got Mays through the seventh grade, which Marshall and, for a while, Louvenia Mays considered a crowning achievement. Mays defied his father and pastor by insisting he was not finished with school. Hezekiah Mays, realizing that Mays would not be denied, angrily threw a ten-dollar bill at him and waved him off. At the age of seventeen Mays enrolled at South Carolina State College, a black institution in Orangeburg formerly named the Colored Normal Industrial Mechanical College, where he was placed in the eighth grade.

Being taught by African American graduates of Benedict College, Lincoln University, Fisk University, and Oberlin College was life-changing for Mays. It countered the message of inferiority he received from white America. It gave him models of educational achievement and heightened his determination to excel academically. He later recalled, "The inspiration which I received at State College was and is of incalculable value." For two years Mays grudgingly went home at the end of February to help with the planting, and his father grudgingly helped him pay for school. Mays could feel his dream slipping away each time he returned home. In 1913, at the age of nineteen, he rebelled, refusing to interrupt his studies. Mays declared that he was staying in Orangeburg to complete the full term, his father objected angrily, Mays held his ground, and his father threatened to send the sheriff after him. Had Hezekiah Mays carried out his threat, Mays would have been forced to return home. Instead his father renounced him, and Mays was on his own.[10]

For a while he cleaned campus outhouses to survive financially. In the summers he worked for the Pullman Company as a porter, making enough money to put graduation within reach. Mays excelled at State College, ranking at the top of his class. According to him, he would have ranked high with much less effort, as most of his classmates majored in partying and did not pretend to study. State College could not afford to fail any students that could afford to be there, and they knew it. Mays looked past his classmates, living for the praise of his teachers, especially mathematics professor Nelson C. Nix, who implored students not to fall behind the whites at Clemson and the University of South Carolina. Nix had studied for a summer at the University of Chicago, an academic paradise in his telling. Mays vowed that someday he would study at the University of Chicago. Although Mays had no social life to speak of at State College, he found a love interest, Ellen Harvin, who agreed not to marry until he had finished college. In 1916, at the age of twenty-one, he graduated from high school. Mays figured he would have graduated at fourteen if not for involuntary farming. He bitterly regretted "those lost years," although Mays later reconciled with his father, who apologized for not having known better. Louvenia Mays attended her son's high school graduation and rejoiced.[11]

In 1900, when Mays started school, South Carolina spent $6.50 per white child in education and $1.50 per black child. By 1915 the figures were $24 and $3. Mays felt the difference when he applied to colleges, sending inquiries to Brown University and Dartmouth. The catalogues frightened him, so he applied to a northern prep school that rejected him with a sort-of apology: The school would lose its southern students if it accepted him. Reluctantly Mays settled for Virginia Union College in Richmond, Virginia, for a year. He burned for a chance to study at a northern college "where I could compete with whites." He befriended a mathematics professor, Roland Wingfield, and a chemistry professor, Charles Hadley, who supported his ambition; both had graduated from Bates College in Lewiston, Maine. Mays had a good year at Virginia Union, adjusting to the school's racially mixed faculty. He found a handful of classmates that he considered "worthy competitors," and it surprised him that Virginia Union had white professors who cared about black students. He met Virginians who considered themselves northerners, which seemed comical to Mays. He went to a segregated theater and vowed never to do it again. In the spring of 1917 Woodrow Wilson issued his call to save the world for democracy, but Mays was nonplussed, having no experience of democracy in America. He gave fleeting consideration to the black officer camp in Des Moines and opted for Bates College, where Wingfield and Hadley had arranged his admission.[12]

Bates College was a breakthrough experience of achievement and transformation for Mays. He felt he had entered a better world in which emancipating self-discoveries could occur. The school was theologically liberal, proud of its abolitionist heritage, and determined to preserve its Baptist identity. By the fall of 1917 it was a coeducational college with daily chapel services and a classical liberal arts curriculum supplemented by an increasing emphasis on the social sciences. Mays dragged a lifetime of denigration to Bates, stalked by self-doubt that he would survive at a white college, determined to prove otherwise, and warned by friends that he would freeze in frigid Maine. He was welcomed with friendly sincerity, which astonished him: "The weather was cold but the hearts at Bates were warm," he later recalled. "How different a world it was from any I had known before! The teachers and students were friendly and kind. I was treated as a person, as a human being, respected for what I was." He had to adjust to previously unimaginable social interactions: "We met and mingled as peers, not as 'superior' and 'inferior.' This was a new experience for me. I was getting another view of the white man—a radically different view. They were not all my enemies." For the first time in his life he "felt at home in the universe."[13]

Bates had a handful of African American students, who helped Mays identify the local bigots, but there were only a few, and his classmates stood up for him in the only racist incident he experienced on campus, a slur by a white student waiter. The town was equally friendly and welcoming, although children stared confusedly at Mays, and he had one night in Lewiston that felt threatening. Mays and his black classmates saw Hollywood's racist blockbuster *Birth of a Nation*, which evoked racist shouts in the audience. Walking back to campus that night, Mays and his friends worried for their safety. Otherwise, "I spent three wonderful years at Bates."[14]

In the early going Mays earned a D grade and a few Cs that marred what became a sparkling academic record, but even in the early going he felt relieved at realizing that top of the class success was within reach: "It did not take me long to discover that Yankee superiority was as mythical as Negro inferiority." Mays won the sophomore declamation prize, joined a host of student organizations, became one of two blacks on the football team, and made many white friends, although he noted pointedly that none were southerners. In his junior year he began to earn mostly As with some Bs. By his senior year he was president of the

Forum Club, the Phil-Hellenic Club, and the Debating Council; he represented Bates in the Northfield YMCA Conference; and he was selected Class
Day Orator by his classmates. In 1920 he graduated with honors; ten years later
the college enrolled him in its Phi Beta Kappa chapter. Fifty years after he
graduated Mays felt a twinge of self-consciousness at recounting his grades at
Bates but overcame it. These grades had been "tremendously important" to him,
making his subsequent career possible, so how could he not mention them?
"Bates College did not 'emancipate' me; it did the far greater service of making
it possible for me to emancipate myself, to accept with dignity my own worth as
a free man. Small wonder that I love Bates College!"[15]

The bedrock of Mays's faith—all people are brothers and sisters under the
fatherly rule of God—he got from the black church and Louvenia Mays. That
faith and his ambition carried him to Bates, where he readily accepted biblical
criticism as conveyed in the Department of Biblical Literature and Religion.
Herbert Purinton, a friend of University of Chicago religious historian Shirley
Jackson Case, taught Mays the rudiments of historical criticism. In religion
classes Mays also read social gospel theology, relating it to the Jesus-like witness
of Socialist Party leader Eugene Debs. Debs roared for Socialist equality, and
on September 14, 1918, he was sentenced to prison for violating the Espionage
Law, having made antiwar speeches. He declared before his sentencing, "While
there is a lower class, I am in it, while there is a criminal element, I am of it, and
while there is a soul in prison, I am not free." This statement enthralled Mays,
catching Debs's heroic masculine bravado. A meek and mild Jesus was not for
Mays; he had seen too many meek black Christians. The social gospel was
about struggling for justice, especially for the downtrodden. Debs had much to
teach Christians about that. Mays later explained, "Eugene Debs inspired me
greatly. To me, Eugene Debs has shaped my sensitivity for the poor, the diseased
and those who have given their lives for the good of those sick and poor, the
great and the small, the high and the low."[16]

The usual story of liberal theology causing an initial crisis of faith did not
occur to Mays. Biblical criticism seemed reasonable to him, and he loved the
social gospel. Bates College thoroughly prepared him for more of both at seminary. Purinton advised Mays to apply to Newton Theological Seminary and the
University of Chicago Divinity School, not realizing that Newton did not take
black students. A Newton admissions officer told Mays he had no chance of
being admitted; Purinton responded that Chicago was better anyway. Shortly
after he graduated from Bates, Mays married Ellen Harvin and might have
taken an attractive Baptist pulpit had one been open to him. But Mays was a
rural southerner with no standing in urban Baptist circles, where ministers

guarded their following and groomed their sons to succeed them. Moving to Chicago in 1920, Mays enrolled at the Divinity School and hooked on at Olivet Baptist Church, assisting National Baptist Convention president Lacey Kirk Williams.

The Divinity School taught theology from a naturalistic, empirical, pragmatic, and historicist perspective. Every Chicago theologian had his own version of empirical theology, but all exalted scientific method, opposed supernaturalism, treated ideas as instruments enabling useful action, and took for granted that all meanings and values are historical. Shailer Mathews was the Divinity School's longtime dean and intellectual exemplar. Along with Shirley Jackson Case, Mathews developed a sociological form of history of religions method, emphasizing the concept of a culturally formative "social mind" and the discontinuities between modern and premodern Christianity. Modern theology, to be modern, had to pass stringent tests of intellectual credibility established by the worldview and methods of modern science. Mays did most of his course work with Mathews and Case. He later recalled that despite his "extremely conservative" background "the ultramodern views of the University of Chicago scholars did not upset my faith. What they taught made sense to me." It made sense to him that all doctrines have a story, religious thinking is rightly concerned with understanding the story behind the canonical narratives of Scripture, and religious meanings are always layered within relative, culturally conditioned historical forms.[17]

Though Mays enjoyed his course work at the Divinity School, his social existence was another story. Jim Crow was pervasive in Chicago, the city had exploded in race riots in 1919, and Mays was chagrined to have to deal with white southerners again. Even at the Divinity School white southerners and a few northern students tried to enforce Jim Crow in the cafeteria. They fled from any table at which a black student sat down to eat. Sometimes they moved two or three times to avoid the unbearable affront of sharing a meal with a black person. Mays pressed the issue by sitting near the offended types. He also made a point of greeting icy professors, making them deal with him. At Bates his professors were friendly on campus and downtown; at Chicago Mays had two professors who never greeted him. Mays and his black friends made a special project of one of these professors, greeting him profusely, tipping their hats, and calling him by name, forcing him to acknowledge their existence. Years later Mays recalled that although the university was surely "interesting and stimulating," it was not the progressive heaven that Nix had painted.[18]

Near the end of his first year at Chicago Mays got an unexpected visit from John Hope, who recruited faculty on his fund-raising trips. Mays was flattered to be sought out. Hope asked him to teach mathematics at Morehouse for the coming academic year, and Mays tallied the plus side: He would earn a teaching salary, Ellen would return to her former teaching position at Morris College, and Hope was nationally prominent and connected. Being favored by Hope might pay off for decades. Expecting to teach for a year at Morehouse and return to the Divinity School, Mays decided that his master's degree could wait. Instead he taught for three years, sidetracked by the first of several "temptations" and "detours" that put off his academic plans.[19]

Morehouse had no history that was not tied up with what became the black social gospel, a point stressed by a later Morehouse dean, Lawrence Edward Carter Sr. Moving to Morehouse returned Mays to the humiliation of riding segregated train coaches, drinking from segregated fountains, and being addressed as "boy," all of which cut him deeper than ever. He recoiled at Atlanta's intense, unavoidable, volatile racism, finding it even worse than expected, as Mays had little experience of the urban South. His childhood was rural and grim, he spent his year in Richmond almost entirely on campus, and the racism in Chicago was "not too bad." The scale of Atlanta's bigotry was a shock to him: "It was in Atlanta that I was to find that the cruel tentacles of race prejudice reached out to invade and distort every aspect of Southern life." Atlanta, the national headquarters of the reorganized Ku Klux Klan, lacked a single public high school for blacks, forcing black colleges to provide high school instruction. Black soldiers returning from World War I were harshly put down, ratcheting up racial tension across the city. To Mays, southern society as a whole appeared to stand for the proposition "*Anything* to be offensive."[20]

Mays joined a reform organization, the Atlanta Commission on Interracial Cooperation, one of the first organizations in the South to bring blacks and whites together to oppose racism. Led by Methodist minister Will Alexander, it organized church opposition to the Klan, tracked and publicized Klan terrorism, called for a congressional investigation of the Klan, and campaigned against lynching, all without opposing segregation or violating Jim Crow rules. Alexander, Mays, and Hope, besides bowing to political reality, tried to avoid being lynched. Sneaking and hiding were necessary whether the group met in a white church, as it sometimes did, or one of the local black colleges — Atlanta University, Morehouse, Morris Brown, Spelman, Gammon Theological Seminary, and Clark College. The commission was the chief activist vehicle for members who belonged to it and the NAACP.

Meanwhile Mays taught Morehouse's first course in calculus and, on the side, preached on Sundays at Shiloh Baptist Church, a small congregation near Morehouse where he was ordained in January 1922. Politically and socially

Morehouse walked a tightrope, refusing to teach or exemplify submission but also refraining from challenging the system. Morehouse told students never to believe they were inferior in any way. It taught that virtue and academic achievement would help blacks succeed in racist America, and it carefully avoided trouble with white people. Years later Mays reflected, "Perhaps Morehouse could and should have done more," but it planted "good seeds" in many young men. Mays taught debate in addition to mathematics. In 1923 one of his debate students was Howard Thurman, with whom he began a fifty-year friendship. That year Mays suffered what must have been a devastating tragedy: "Ellen, my first wife, while still teaching in South Carolina, died early in 1923 after an operation in an Atlanta hospital."[21]

Ellen Harvin Mays had devoted herself to Mays ever since he was a bookish, impoverished country striver at South Carolina State College. She supported his dream and waited for him after he moved to Virginia and Maine. Afterward Mays resolutely refrained from speaking of her. In several autobiographical reflections he said nothing about her, and his memoir offered one sentence about her death, tucked between his account of coaching Thurman in debate and preaching at Shiloh Church. The silence spoke loudly; Mays must have grieved deeply for Ellen, unable to say so.

Near the end of his time at Morehouse, Mays met Mordecai Johnson, then serving as a pastor in Charleston. Hope invited Johnson to speak at Morehouse's chapel service. Mays later recalled, "I shall never forget that address. He spoke to us and challenged us so eloquently, that we were led to believe that this man was called of God to do his work. I can see Mordecai years later, walking across the Howard campus, walking with a sense of dignity and freedom. Strangers on the campus had to know he was the President. Surely God called Mordecai Wyatt Johnson to expound the social gospel and to make Howard University a truly great university." Johnson's powerful speech enthralled Mays and stayed in his head. Mays had found a model for his life and career. In every way, Johnson was the gold standard to Mays, showing what was possible. It was evidently possible for a black minister to sway audiences with commanding renderings of social gospel theology and racial justice righteousness, for Johnson did it every week, and he was only four years older than Mays.[22]

In 1924 Mays belatedly resumed his graduate studies at Chicago, where whites still ran from blacks in the cafeteria, most restaurants refused to serve blacks, and relations between African Americans and Asian Americans were equally tense. Attending an academic forum, Mays heard a white graduate student in sociology from Texas, W. O. Brown, say that white Americans invented segregation to justify their exploitation of blacks. Mays was stunned. Befriending a white southerner had been unthinkable to him, even though Alexander took greater risks in the racial cauldron of Atlanta. Mays and Alexander were mere acquaintances; Brown became the realized impossibility for Mays, a white southern friend. Meanwhile Mays took courses with Mathews, Henry Nelson Wieman, and Edwin Aubrey, writing a thesis titled "Pagan Survivals in Christianity" that bore the stamp of his teachers. Christianity's cultural environment, Mays argued, shaped the kind of religion it became, as Christianity absorbed numerous pagan thought forms and customs: "Those who deny it think that Christianity is too noble, too sacred to be associated with heathenism. They take the attitude that everything pagan is bad and should be rejected, and that everything Christian is good, and should be accepted." Mays countered that conventional orthodoxies "do not conform with the facts, and are not in accord with sound reasoning."[23]

"Pagan Survivals in Christianity" identified Christian motifs deriving from or influenced by pagan sources. The miraculous birth of a god figure appears in Hindu, Buddhist, Chinese, Egyptian, Greek, and Roman sources. The deification of a savior god has Greek and Roman prototypes, a point stressed by Case. The death and resurrection of a savior god and the immortality of the soul play strong roles in Hellenistic mystery cults and philosophy. Without denying the formative role of Hebrew Scripture and tradition in Christianity, he contended that Christianity survived and flourished because it absorbed vital elements of its pagan background into a dynamic new religion—especially a philosophical conception of spiritual deity and the idea of immortality—and because it took advantage of the existence of a universal empire and a growing cosmopolitan ethos. To decipher the pagan aspects of Christianity was not to negate Christian faith, he cautioned. Baptism had a heathen origin, which did not make it less Christian: "It simply means that Christianity was inevitably bound up with the environmental forces of the Roman world; that it is an evolutionary movement; and must be modified, as all movements are, by its environment."[24]

He was charting his own course. Mays's eighty-nine-page thesis made a heavy draft on Chicago school liberalism, notwithstanding that Chicago liberalism was alien to the folk culture of black churches and the church-based culture of many black colleges. It had gained barely a toehold in black Baptist colleges through a handful of academics. Mays was keenly aware of the cultural variables and undaunted by them. Throughout his career he spoke in declarative phrases: "it is crystal clear," "the truth is," and especially, "the fact is," but also, "I could be wrong" and "I am not wise enough to say. . . ." He had little taste and no time for ironical spinning about anything that mattered. In person Mays was buoyant and charismatic; his close friend and protégé Samuel Du Bois

Cook aptly remarked, "He was an impressive figure who had magic about him." There were no laugh lines, however, in Mays's prolific writings and speeches, except for an occasional resort to wry sarcasm. Dignity, wisdom, moral serious- ness, humility, directness, passion for justice—these were his trademarks. By his lights there were always important moral and factual truths to be faced and expressed. Servility to ignorance, prejudice, or injustice was never to be tolerated. He was fond of saying that no person is free who backs away from the truth.[25]

A second detour took him back to South Carolina State College in 1925, where Mays met sociology instructor Sadie Gray. Gray had earned her under- graduate degree at the University of Chicago and was currently enrolled in Chicago's graduate program in social work. She belonged to the Colored Methodist Episcopal Church and spent the summer of 1926, like Mays, taking courses at Chicago. The couple married at the end of the summer, petitioning for a waiver from state law and, secondarily, from college policy. State College had a policy against faculty marriages, which was redundant since state law required women to give up their academic careers if they married. Sadie Gray Mays needed a job to keep her mortgaged family homestead.

The newlyweds, upon Sadie's losing her job at State College, reluctantly moved to Tampa, Florida, where he served as executive secretary of the Tampa Urban League and she worked for the Tampa Family Service Association. This was another detour for Mays, a dismal one, except for some treasured friend- ships. He burned with frustration at the temporizing demands of Urban League work in a segregated state. Though Mays got to work for the rights of blacks, his position made him a semiofficial liaison between black and white Tampa. He felt the contradiction deeply, seething inwardly against the evils of segregation while working to reform it. Mays scored a few small victories and headed back to Atlanta in 1928, this time to serve as national student secretary of the YMCA.[26]

But working for the YMCA was a lot like working for the Urban League. Mays wanted to love the YMCA, which cultivated black leaders like no other interra- cial organization. Ralph W. Bullock, William Craver, J. H. McGrew, James Moreland, and Channing Tobias were prominent among them. At Lincoln Academy in Kings Mountain, North Carolina, the YMCA conducted national conferences, encouraging young black men to imagine themselves as civic and religious leaders. Historian Nina Mjagkij observes that these conferences served as "sanctuaries that preserved African-American manhood," preparing young males for leadership roles. Mays took Johnson's path, giving speeches to students at YMCA forums across the South. He gave Johnson-like talks about working hard and living honorably, but he repeated Johnson's experience of being repulsed by the YMCA's timidity. Everywhere the organization proceeded cautiously, adhering to prevailing local standards of segregation. Mays later wrote scathingly, "The sky would have fallen, the world collapsed" had the YMCA sent a black representative to a white college. Making a career in that milieu was out of the question for Mays; his YMCA job left a bitter mark. Years later he still fumed: "Surely the leadership of the YMCA must have felt a furtive blush of shame to label their segregated God 'Christian!'"[27]

THE BLACK CHURCH, THE CHICAGO SCHOOL,
AND THE GOD OF BLACK AMERICANS

Mays kept saying he wanted to earn a doctorate at Chicago, but he kept taking jobs that put off his dream. In 1930 he took another detour, one which got him through the early Depression. The Institute of Social and Religious Research (ISRR), founded in 1921 and financed (by 1934) on $3 million of John D. Rockefeller Jr.'s money, funded research on religious congregations, missions, religious education, and race relations. In the 1920s the ISRR funded two pioneering works dealing with the black church: *The Education of Negro Ministers* (1925) by William A. Daniel and *The U.S. Looks at Its Churches* (1930) by C. Luther Fry. In 1927 it also paid Carter Woodson and his Association for the Study of Negro Life and History to produce a more ambitious study of black churches. Woodson gave the job to Charles Wesley and Lorenzo Greene but found their work seriously inadequate. He tried to get E. Franklin Frazier to take over but Frazier didn't want the job, so Woodson, with anguish, had to return the grant money to the ISRR.[28]

This episode caught the attention of John R. Mott, Channing Tobias, and Mays. Mott was president of the YMCA's World Committee and president of the ISRR board, and Tobias was the YMCA's senior secretary of interracial services. Both knew Mays from his YMCA work. Tobias urged Mays to make a proposal, and Mott supported Mays's proposal to team with Christian Methodist Episcopal minister Joseph W. Nicholson. Mays assured Tobias and Mott that he and Nicholson would succeed where Wesley and Greene had failed. In 1930 they launched what became a fourteen-month study, collecting data on 609 churches in twelve urban areas and 185 churches in rural areas. The cities were Atlanta, Baltimore, Birmingham, Charleston, Chicago, Cincinnati, Detroit, Houston, Memphis, New Orleans, Philadelphia, and Richmond.

By the spring of 1931 Mays was ready to speak about his findings. A seminar at Yale Divinity School provided the occasion, featuring panelists A. Philip Randolph, Federal Council of Churches official George Edmund Haynes,

Congregational pastor Henry H. Proctor, and YMCA Executive Secretary of
Colored Student Work Frank T. Wilson. Randolph, at the time, was struggling
to hold together the Brotherhood of Sleeping Car Porters. He lamented that
most black ministers had little to say about industrialization and did not support
union organizing. The church had to change, Randolph implored; above all,
it needed to buck up the "practically shattered" porters and other black unionists: "They need spirit or will to go back into the fight." Mays countered that
organizing black female domestic workers was even more important, something Randolph played down as impossible. Otherwise Mays agreed that
the black church had a crisis of leadership: "In the main, the church remains
rather conservative and does not courageously grapple with basic wrongs
inherent in our social and economic order." The black church, Mays suggested,
had too many ministers and too few of high quality. Moreover, some highly
educated ministers opted for teaching or social work over ministry, a tragedy for
the churches. That was a preview of *The Negro's Church* (1933), by Mays and
Nicholson.[29]

They called their book "a rather dark picture." The black church was
born in a "strange and somewhat hostile environment," Mays and Nicholson
observed. Founded at Silver Bluff, South Carolina, in 1773, it had no history not
bound up with slavery and racism, and its weaknesses reflected white America's
denigration of black people. The authors moved quickly to 1933, showing in
grim detail that most black churches were poorly financed and deeply in debt,
most black neighborhoods had too many churches, most black ministers were
poorly trained academically, and the prevailing theology of the black church,
"except in rare instances, is static, non-progressive, and fails to challenge the
loyalty of many of the most critically-minded Negroes."[30]

Mays never doubted that enlightened leadership was the key to the advancement of African Americans. He knew what had worked for him, and he was too
seared by his own experience of Deep South poverty and oppression to harbor
romantic ideas about the poor and oppressed. *The Negro's Church* insisted
that the black church needed educated pastors and an educated theology more
than it needed anything else. Eighty percent of ministers in black churches
did not hold a college degree, over 90 percent of ministers in rural areas had
not advanced beyond high school, and less than one-fourth of black ministers
in urban areas held a seminary degree. The undereducated minister, the
authors judged, was usually a preacher but not a real pastor, and he preached
an emotional religion of otherworldly salvation: "The Negro churchgoer has
been consistently reminded of the otherworldly aspect of religion and life." By
their count, more than three-fourths of the sermons in urban churches were

"other-worldly and unpracticable" and less than one-fourth were constructive. In rural areas black preaching was nearly always otherworldly. Mays and Nicholson provided extensive excerpts of typical black preaching, which they criticized for its lack of rationality, commenting dryly, "It is hardly possible that fifty-four sermons, with fifty-four different texts, could all logically end on the idea of heaven." A higher standard of discourse was sorely needed: "It is a conviction of the writers that preachers often underestimate the intelligence of their audience and fail to give men and women of little formal training credit for being able to appreciate and follow a logical constructive discourse. It is a further conviction that ministers frequently try to hide their own nakedness, their lack of preparation, when they resort to a type of preaching that seems to be designed to 'shout' the people."[31]

Pointedly the authors allowed that it "could hardly have been otherwise." The grotesque oppression of African Americans throughout American history produced impoverished churches clinging mainly to the hope of heaven. But Mays and Nicholson ended their work on a hopeful and appreciative note. Shortcomings had to be faced, but black churches were culturally and emotion- ally indispensable to African American life. The churches helped an oppressed people cope with oppression; they offered emotional consolation and spiritual hope; they functioned as all-purpose community centers; and they were the only institutions that black Americans owned and controlled. Above all, the churches offered recognition and affirmation to individuals: "The opportunity found in the Negro church to be recognized, and to be 'somebody,' has stimulated pride and preserved the self-respect of many Negroes who would have been entirely beaten down by life, possibly completely submerged." In the everyday world, most black Americans were made to feel their lives counted for nothing, "but in the church on X street, *she* is Mrs. Johnson, the Church Clerk; and *he* is Mr. Jones, the Chairman of the Deacon Board."[32]

There was one thing more. Mays and Nicholson modestly noted, in their closing pages, that the black church was a genuinely democratic fellowship. It was one of the few institutions in American society that welcomed people of all races. It treated whites and Asian Americans with respect, and it opened its pulpits to visiting white ministers even though African Americans were not welcome in white churches. The authors concluded, "The Negro church generally practices love and tolerance toward all races and abides by these ideals in its practice."[33]

The Negro's Church filled a gaping sociological and religious need. It had no rival in its time, and for thirty years it ruled the field of black church studies. Walter White hailed the book as an overdue assessment of the strengths and weaknesses of an enormously important American institution, "an important achievement." Thurman described the book as an "indispensable handbook" presenting a "rather disinterested interpretation" of a "pathetic picture." He explained: "The churches seem to be lacking in almost everything except in vitality. What a criminal indictment they are to the American white man's religion in whose midst they were established and subsequently developed!" Eight years previously Thurman had a memorable encounter with a Nigerian Muslim who commented incredulously on inter-Christian racism. Thurman ended his review of *The Negro's Church* by appropriating the Nigerian's comment: "Loud must ring the laugh of Allah in his Mohammedan heaven as he beholds the spectacle of the First Baptist Church (Colored) and First Baptist Church (White)." Mays and Nicholson ignored black churches in the Holiness/Pentecostal traditions, and some reviewers noted that the authors criticized black church theology from a liberal standpoint that held a marginal place in black American Christianity. But the book outstripped everything in the field as a description of the non-Holiness black churches, and it said plainly, with regret, that biblical criticism and social gospel theology had only a marginal existence in black churches.[34]

Mays had returned to Chicago to complete his doctorate when the book was published in February 1933. He reveled in having authored a book that his teachers had to read to be current in their field. At the same time, his teachers and local company had no trouble seeing their reflection in the book, as Mays was a Chicago School academic in almost every sense of the category. Robert Ezra Park, a seminal figure in Chicago School sociology, was a major influence on Mays's thinking. Park had worked as Booker Washington's secretary and ghostwriter prior to his career as a Chicago professor, and at Chicago he mentored two of Mays's contemporaries, E. Franklin Frazier and Charles Johnson. Park taught that oppressed people needed effective organizations to resist and overcome the social structures of domination that governed their lives. He believed that black churches were too dependent on emotional appeals and spontaneity to provide the kind of leadership for social change that was needed. His alliance with Washington gave him unusual moral authority for a white academic, but his argument gave ballast to the critiques of black social gospel leaders. Mays believed that Park was essentially correct, which enabled Mays and Park to give ballast to each other, launching a Park-style field of study—sociology of black religion—to which Frazier and Johnson subsequently made distinguished contributions.[35]

The Divinity division of the Chicago School emphasized social structure and social process, both linked with the social gospel. Case and Mathews contended that empires produced imperial deities, feudal societies produced feudal deities, and modern societies had to figure out what sort of God went with democracy, science, biblical criticism, and the social gospel. The Chicago School tried to make theology as scientific as possible, restricting God-language to the concreteness of empirical method and description. "God" was an expression of ideals, an analogical expression for an idealized concept of the universe. Mathews, the key figure in this group until Wieman joined the faculty in 1927, conceived God as an instrumental pattern, a name for the personality-evolving reality of the cosmos. Mathews eschewed metaphysical discussion about whether the universe is pluralistic or monistic or whether God is finite or infinite. God, Mathews reasoned, is an empirically knowable process in which the potencies of ultimate reality find expression in emergent reality, especially human consciousness. In a democratic and scientific age, Christian theism had to leave behind the (political) patterns of biblical and classical Christian thought, which conceived God as a sovereign ruler and religion as transcendentalized politics. The pattern of modern naturalistic theism had to be biological, on the model of an organism seeking development through its relationships with its environment. Religion is cooperation with the universe and its evolution, although process is not identical with progress since there is such a thing as devolution.[36]

Wieman took less interest than Mathews in history, and he was more emphatic that God has an objective reality. In Wieman's view liberal theology had become too sentimental. It shrank from defending God's existence, and it tried to make itself attractive by appealing to social concerns. That strategy was a loser; it drove the strong and intelligent people away from religion. After Wieman joined the Chicago faculty he assured students and colleagues that he supported the social gospel. Nonetheless, theology had to become toughminded again. Religion was pointless without God, but science negated traditional ways of conceiving God's existence. Wieman argued that whatever else the word "God" may mean, at bottom it designates the "Something" upon which human life and the flourishing of the good are dependent. It cannot be doubted that such a Something exists. If there is a human good, it must have a source. The fact that human life happens proves the reality of the Something of supreme value on which life depends. Wieman made that the object of theology. He conceived God as a structured event and theology as the analysis of the total event of religious experience.[37]

These were the distinguishing marks of Chicago School theology during the third cycle of Mays's studies there, 1932 to 1935. During his previous studies at the Divinity School in the early and mid-1920s his teachers debated the limits of their religious naturalism. Intrigued that relativity physicist Alfred North Whitehead was said to be a genius, they tried to understand his organic meta-physical theism but failed. They asked the only American expert on Whitehead—Wieman—to give a lecture on Whitehead's thought. Wieman convinced the Chicago theologians that Whitehead was a thinker of great importance; they responded by adding Wieman to the faculty. In 1929, however, Whitehead published his system, *Process and Reality,* and Wieman had second thoughts about Whitehead. The system was too metaphysical, logically deducing concepts from concepts.

Whitehead taught that duration is actual and factual, events constitute the ultimate fact beyond which there can be nothing else, everything that is or can be pertains to events, and objects are aspects of events. Events are not occur-rences that happen to things or that things experience. Events are the funda-mental things, the immanent movement of creativity itself. Wieman retained these ideas more than he acknowledged, contending that he tracked the flow of experience instead of endorsing Whitehead's metaphysical system. Wieman's theology of creative process rested on Whitehead's doctrine that duration is real; moreover, Wieman's distinction between "creativity" and "the creative event" was an echo of Whitehead's distinction between the primordial and consequent natures of God. But Wieman told his students that Whitehead overreached in the manner of all great speculative system-builders. As a meta-physical theorist, Whitehead was in a class with Plato, Leibniz, and Hegel. In a scientific age, theology needed to stick closer to empirical facts. That sounded good to Mays, who had a Chicago School idea for a dissertation that no scholar at Chicago or anywhere had attempted: a book on the black American experi-ence of God.[38]

Wieman taught Mays about philosophical theology, Whitehead, and his own version of empirical theology, which stripped academic theology clean of senti-mentality. Mays got a gentler version of empirical theology from his doctoral advisor, theologian Edwin A. Aubrey, and he drew upon two sources that had sustained him for the past decade. One he cited repeatedly throughout his career: Walter Rauschenbusch. Mays embraced wholeheartedly Rauschenbusch's teaching that the church is supposed to be a revolutionary Christ-following movement that transforms society into the kingdom of God. In the 1920s Mays memorized numerous Rauschenbusch quotes that he dispensed for the rest of his career.[39]

The other crucial source, Carter Woodson, Mays never acknowledged aside from obligatory reference citations. Woodson was the major pioneer of Mays's field. His *History of the Negro Church* appeared when Mays began his graduate studies at Chicago, and his Association for the Study of Negro Life and History published the mainstay of black historiography, the *Journal of Negro History*. Woodson's cry-of-the-heart book of 1933, *The Mis-Education of the Negro*, issued Mays-like polemics against sectarian, dogmatic, otherworldly black sermons, adding that seminary-credentialed ministers were often just as bad, mouthing "merely memorized words and phrases, which meant little to him and nothing to those who heard his discourse." Though Mays owed sizable debts to Woodson, to him Woodson was a rival, not a friend or ally. Woodson was known for looking down on ministers, he wrote a blistering review of Mays's second book, and Mays got his first book contract because Woodson had to return the ISRR money. Mays was scathing about ministers, too, but always out of love for the church and his ambitions for it. Woodson's sympathy was sometimes hard to detect. He ridiculed one minister for going on about "John Knox Orthodox" as though "Orthodox" was Knox's last name, and sometimes Woodson crossed the line into invective, such as: "Almost anybody of the lowest type may get into the Negro ministry." Although Mays had his reasons for not giving credit to Woodson, credit was due for mapping out much of the terrain Mays covered.[40]

Meanwhile Mays's teachers at Chicago worried that he had already exhausted the subject of American black Christianity. What was left to say after he published *The Negro's Church*? Mays told them not to worry; he had barely touched what most interested him: the history of black American ideas of God. With the help of Howard University librarian Dorothy Parker, who supplied Mays with a treasure trove of sources, he wrote a dissertation titled *The Negro's God as Reflected in His Literature*. The book version, published in 1938, declared at the outset, "The aim of the author is to tell America what the Negro thinks of God." No one, Mays noted, had ever published a book on the idea of God in black American literature, "as strange as it may seem." His interpretation rested on two sets of distinctions and a three-epoch scheme. The first era began in 1760 with the poetry of Jupiter Hammon and ended with the end of the Civil War. The second era stretched from Reconstruction to the dawn of World War I in 1914. The third era ran from the war to 1937. Mays framed his argument by distinguishing between "classical" and "mass" literature and between "constructive" and "compensatory" views of God and religion.[41]

In his telling, classical literature consisted of novels, poetry, slave narratives, formal speeches, biography, academic discourses, and the like, while mass literature included African American sermons, Sunday School literature, and the spirituals. Mays's second distinction was even more weighted with his personal convictions, although he claimed for it "a high degree of objectivity." He described compensatory religion as partial, anthropomorphic, vengeful, highly emotional, supernaturalist, and virtually defined by its "shallow pragmatism," while constructive religion was oriented to the struggle for social emancipation and justice. In some forms constructive religion was universal in scope "but inclusive of the needs of the Negro." In other forms it was concerned primarily with the social and economic needs of African Americans. In both cases it emphasized that African Americans were entitled to the same rights as other groups.[42]

The Negro's God was an example of Park-style sociology of knowledge. Like his Divinity School teachers, Mays prized the social scientific approach to religion as the best way to understand religion and the best way to help religion build a better society. Like Mathews in particular, Mays argued that all ideas of God are constructs reflecting and produced by particular social circumstances. Before the Civil War, African Americans generally conceived God as being involved in their struggle for emancipation. During Reconstruction, the Gilded Age, and the aftermath of *Plessy v. Ferguson* black writers and composers conceived God as being involved in their continuing struggle against racism and segregation. After World War I the focus of God-language shifted to the experience of disillusionment after the Great Migration led to new forms of misery in northern cities. Mays's social situation pervaded the text, sometimes explicitly. He was loyal to the black church and sharply critical of it. He appreciated the survival ministry of traditional churches but warned that it stood in the way of successful black assimilation into American society. He sprinkled the book with recollections of his background in southern compensatory religion, which reminded readers that he came from and was still committed to the tradition he analyzed.

To Mays, the spirituals belonged almost entirely to the compensatory category, emphasizing miracles, the spectacular, consolation, and the consoling belief that God punishes the wicked: "In the midst of the most stifling circumstances, this belief in God has given the Negro masses emotional poise and balance; it has enabled them to cling on to life though poor, miserable, and dying, looking to God and expecting Him, through miraculous and spectacular means, to deliver them from their plight. The idea has made Negroes feel good; it has made life endurable for them; and it has caused them to go to church on Sunday and shout and sing and pray." Compensatory religion is good therapy, he acknowledged; it is also a mixed blessing: "This idea of God had telling effects upon the Negroes in my home community. It kept them submissive, humble, and obedient. It enabled them to keep on keeping on. And it is still effective in 1937."[43]

Mays allowed that some spirituals broke through to another kind of religion. "Go Down, Moses" was a prime example, as were "Oh, Freedom" and "No

More, No More, No More Auction Block for Me." These hymns of African American Christianity rebelled against oppression without seeking relief in a heavenly afterlife. They reflected the black American practice of correlating American and Egyptian slavery. Black Americans were God's suffering people in America just as the Hebrews suffered as slaves in Egypt. Mays gave a similar accounting of black preaching before and during Reconstruction, most of which fell into the compensatory category, with notable exceptions that he quoted generously. Presbyterian abolitionist Henry Highland Garnet and AME bishop Daniel A. Payne were prominent among the exceptions. In Mays's account, classical black American literature before Reconstruction represented something of an antidote to the otherworldly character of black religion. African American writers such as Frances Ellen Watkins Harper and Frederick Douglass took their ideas of God from black religion, but they were selective in doing so, emphasizing that God is just, God is love, and God takes the side of the righteous and oppressed.[44]

The Negro's God covered more material than its binary distinctions could handle. On the whole, Mays found that between Reconstruction and World War I black religion was mainly compensatory, while classical literature leaned toward constructive action, but he devoted ample space to countercurrents on both sides, and his categories often blurred to the point of seeming arbitrary. He relegated preachers as a class to the mass category, ignored the irony that some mass literature was as profound and sublime as anything in the classical category, and treated prophetic ministers as exceptions to the mass disinterest in social gospel religion. At the same time, he importantly emphasized that even the most otherworldly forms of traditional black religion were not detached from the struggles of African Americans against slavery, racism, and segregation. Compensatory religion represented one kind of response to the conditions of oppression. It enabled a denigrated people to survive their mistreatment, kept alive the true values of the gospel in a situation of domination and repression, and proclaimed hope for a new day under the shadow of God's hand.

According to Mays, the great disillusionment after World War I spawned two crosscurrents of reaction. One was the rise of the black social gospel in the activism and preaching of Francis Grimké, Alexander Walters, and other latter-day proponents of prophetic religion. The masses resisted prophetic religion, Mays noted, but some black pastors interpreted God and salvation along social gospel lines. The other reaction, one taken increasingly by black artists and cultural critics, dropped God altogether.

Mays described option one by recycling a long section from *The Negro's Church* on the meaning of "thy kingdom come." An unnamed pastor remarked that American Christians routinely prayed, "Thy Kingdom come," but they didn't really want the kingdom to come at all, for the kingdom has to do with emancipating and lifting up the condition of the oppressed. If the kingdom were to come to America, America would have to get rid of its selfish economic system, its "prostituted conception of nationalism," and its "distorted notion of race superiority." The minister built up to a sweeping conclusion: "If this kind of Kingdom should come to the earth, no race would want to keep another race down. Our military forces would not be in Nicaragua; they would not be in Haiti. We would gladly help the Philippines to independence and without condescension and without patronage. India would be free and Africa would not be exploited. All forms of segregation and discrimination such as those that exist in the United States in the expenditure of public funds, in travel, in politics, and those that operate against us in social and economic areas would all disappear if the Kingdom of God should come."[45]

That was Mays's kind of religion: "It does not encourage one to wait for justice in the other world. It does not dissipate itself in mere feeling." The kingdom of God in social gospel teaching was antiracist, antiwar, universal, and social ethical, Mays explained. It nurtured a desire for peace, it cared about the "physical, mental, and spiritual growth of every child," it advocated economic justice, and it cultivated personal maturity: "It tends to give one poise and balance to struggle for social righteousness here on the earth."[46]

Meanwhile he worried that African American intellectuals were turning against God. Young poets like Countee Cullen and Langston Hughes said that black Americans needed to give up the God illusion. Novelist and composer James Weldon Johnson and cultural critic George Schuyler gave up the God idea for themselves while allowing that God was still compensatory for poor blacks. Mays acknowledged that Du Bois sometimes conveyed powerful spiritual feeling, but intellectually Du Bois had apparently become some kind of deist. To Hughes, Mays noted, Communism had become a substitute faith—a novel development in black American history, for blacks had always sustained their faith in God no matter how much they suffered.[47]

Mays believed that the minority advocating a prophetic, educated, social Christianity needed to grow dramatically and soon, replacing the ministerial majority that made the church look feeble. Otherwise black atheism was sure to grow. Black Americans in general, he argued, held to three dominant convictions concerning God. They insisted that God was impartial and universal: "The Negro will not accept the idea of a partial God." They believed that things would eventually work out for black Americans because God was just: "God is on the side of the right. This being true, the Negro cannot lose." And they often expressed frustration, doubt, dissatisfaction, and cynicism, despite insisting that God was impartial, universal, and just. The recent surge of black atheism, Mays argued, instead of holding together the three planks of black religion, made a religion out of protest and cynicism.[48]

Woodson, reviewing *The Negro's God*, admonished that Mays dwelt too much on elite black literature and did not show that black Americans conceived God differently than white Americans. Mays somehow did not ask whether blacks and whites held differing beliefs about God. Although Mays wrote many words, he did not come up with much. Woodson explained: "In a sense, therefore, the American Negro's conception of God is still that of those around him rather than any special contribution which he has made himself." This critique lumped Mays into the line of "educated Negroes" that Woodson panned in *The Mis-Education of the Negro*. Black America, Woodson argued, needed intellectual leaders who thought through their own experience and concepts. Mays gave the appearance of pursuing this agenda, so Woodson felt compelled to say that he failed. Mays was still an example of the problem, failing to venture a constructive argument or even raise the crucial question.[49]

This line of critique had a rich legacy, decades later, in the black theology movement. From the beginning of the liberationist turn in the late 1960s, the charge was made that black social Christianity depended on white social gospel ideas about biblical interpretation, theology, and intellectual credibility. Early black liberation theology centered this argument on King and subsequently went through a complex history of contention and reconsideration. In Woodson's case this critique already mixed a legitimate point with a dose of unfairness. *The Negro's God* had serious methodological and organizational problems, but it did not lack reflection on the issue that Woodson pressed. Mays did not claim that black Americans had developed a distinctive concept of God. He did not even say that black intellectuals who rejected God needed a better concept of God or needed to read better theology. He said that black Americans fashioned their ideas of God out of their struggles for survival and freedom. He said they persistently described God as impartial and just, "no respecter of persons." And he said they were too oppressed in America to have the luxury of developing philosophical concepts of God.

Mays put it bluntly: "The Negro is not interested in any fine theological or philosophical discussions about God." *The Negro's God* had not set out to prove otherwise. Mays did not believe that the importance of his subject depended upon proving otherwise. Neither did he believe that sophisticated theology was the answer to the problem of black atheism, although he desperately wanted a higher level of discourse on Sunday morning. These were separate issues for Mays. The black church had some and needed many more ministers who preached about the kingdom of God and the struggle for social justice. It did not need ministers who worried about Kant or Whitehead. It did not need a stronger dose of Reformation theology or seventeenth-century confessional orthodoxy. Mays observed that black ministers, progressive or otherwise, did not describe God as "personality-producing activity" (Mathews) or the "source of growing good" (Wieman) or even the neo-Reformation "Wholly Other" source of revelation (Karl Barth). Neither did they worry about intellectual conflicts between religion and science. They worried about "the chasm that exists between the actual and the ideal." Their ideas of God were "chiseled out of the very fabric of the social struggle."[50]

Until World War I, Mays argued, black Americans believed as fervently as white progressives that the world was getting better; the Progressive movement's gains were promising for black progress. Then the march of progress and hope stopped cold. The war that was fought for noble ideals ended with the betrayal of these ideals. Black Americans returned from serving their country and were told to resume their servile station in life. They migrated to northern cities and were treated despicably, while the Klan staged a comeback. Under these circumstances, Mays observed, "it is not surprising to find frustration, doubt, cynicism, and denial of God's existence in the writings of Negroes during this post-war period." The great disillusionment drove some into prophetic religion and others into atheism, but both groups felt deeply that things had gotten worse in their time.[51]

Had Mays been less fixated on describing his massive research base, he might have developed a stronger constructive theology of his own. Jelks justly contends that Mays "missed an opportunity to construct a positive theology. His understanding of theological modernism was too narrowly focused and bound by his desire to make a manly theology that presumably fought against domination." *The Negro's God,* however, emphatically fought against domination, anticipating liberation theology by thirty years by privileging black experience and emphasizing the prophetic aspects of biblical testimony. Moreover, Mays had a compelling reason to restrain his own constructive theologizing: "The Negro's life has been too unstable, too precarious, too uncertain, and his needs have been too great for him to become sufficiently objective to theologize or philosophize about God."[52]

Mays wanted black seminaries to be incubators of the prophetic and intellectually proficient theology that the churches needed. But he grieved that black seminaries and theology departments were the least progressive institutions in

African American life. He wanted promising students to have a real choice between studying at a white or black seminary. But he told them to go to Chicago, Union, Harvard, Boston University, Drew, Oberlin, Colgate-Rochester, or Yale, declaring, "Negro seminaries are, for the most part, so inferior in quality that Negro students are forced to take their religious training outside of Negro seminaries."[53]

To Mays, everything was at stake in changing this situation. Black higher education as a whole suffered from want and neglect, and theological schools were the most wanting and neglected of all. Most church-related black colleges had theology departments staffed by faculty with little graduate training who taught religion from the perspective of their denomination. Fisk College was Congregationalist, Virginia Union and Morehouse were Baptist, Gammon Theological Seminary was Methodist, and Johnson C. Smith in Charlotte, North Carolina, was Presbyterian. None had the requisite faculty to offer professional training at the graduate level. Mays might have jeopardized his career options by being so blunt about the situation. Instead he got two job offers shortly after he finished his doctoral course work in 1934.

Fisk University called first, in the early summer, and Mays agreed to teach religion at Fisk. Later that summer Mordecai Johnson asked Mays to come to Howard, and Mays begged off at Fisk. Johnson and Mays agreed to drop the bachelor of theology degree, accepting only college graduates to the School of Religion. Years later Mays recalled that when he arrived at Howard the seminary was housed in "a shabby frame building," its library holdings were "grossly inadequate," and it needed prestige desperately, lacking any. As far as he could tell, the seminary's heritage going back to Reconstruction "added no luster to its reputation."[54]

Mediocrity had ruled at the School of Religion, undergirded by a muddled modernist curriculum. Mays swiftly established that the new School of Religion was about social gospel religion, intellectual distinction, racial justice, and preparing students for prophetic ministries. His courses featured books by Rauschenbusch and Mathews, fusing liberal theology and social ethics. On Mays's watch the school hired James Farmer Sr. to teach Greek, New Testament, and biblical criticism. Many students reeled from this curriculum, finding it contrary to their upbringing and threatening to their faith. Farmer's son James Farmer Jr. studied at Howard under Mays and Thurman, later recalling that most of his classmates had a hard time, having come to seminary with "a devout and dogmatic Sunday School theology." Some were "devastated" by biblical criticism, even though every Howard theologian combined critical rigor with a "very devout" spirit.[55]

Farmer was not like them: "I loved the social gospel of Walter Rauschenbusch and was enthralled with the study of Christian ethics, but I was not sure what I believed about God." In his telling, the School of Religion had "an air of pious devotion" to which he already felt a worldly half-aversion, though he placed Thurman's Gandhian religion of nonviolence in a different category. Farmer caught Mays, Thurman, and Johnson in the buoyant heyday of their Gandhian advocacy. Forging links with the Gandhi movement was inspiring and enlarging, imagining a colored cosmopolitanism that overthrew white supremacy and imperialism with the power of nonviolent soul force. Johnson lauded Gandhi on the lecture circuit, and Thurman conveyed his admiration of Gandhi to students, especially Farmer. For Mays and Thurman, as for Johnson, the path to Gandhian internationalism ran through Protestant missionary societies, especially the YMCA and its youth activist offspring, the Student Christian Movement. For Mays and Thurman, it also included meetings with Gandhi, and for Thurman, a mystical pacifist predisposition much like Gandhi's.[56]

THE MYSTIC WAY AND THE RELIGION OF JESUS: HOWARD THURMAN

Howard Thurman was a product of the southern black church and a classmate of Martin Luther King Sr. In his early career he became a pastor, professor, social gospel leader, and Quaker-influenced mystic and pacifist. Later he became an ecumenical leader of racial integration, a chapel dean, an advisor to movement leaders, a prolific author, and a spiritual influence on Martin Luther King Jr. He may also have become a saint. He played his most direct role as a civil rights leader in the 1930s and early 1940s, as a star on the lecture circuit. Then he became a sage and author, exerting a different kind of influence. Then his influence grew after he was gone.

He was born in 1899 to Saul and Alice Thurman, probably in West Palm Beach, Florida, and grew up in the Waycross section of Daytona. Thurman's father was a large, gentle, reflective, dignified track laborer for the Florida East Coast Railroad. Saul Thurman did not care for church. On Sundays he sat on his porch and read; one of his favorite authors was freethinking agnostic Robert Ingersoll. He died of pneumonia when Thurman was seven years old. Alice Thurman, deeply devout and shy, and her mother, Nancy Ambrose, equally devout with a forceful personality, tried to arrange a church funeral, at first unsuccessfully. The deacons and pastor of Mount Bethel Baptist Church refused to bury anyone who died out of Christ. Thurman's grandmother got the deacons to back down, but she and Alice had to enlist a traveling evangelist to perform the funeral, who preached Saul Thurman to hell, describing him as an evil reprobate who deserved to burn for eternity. To the evangelist, it was an evangelistic opportunity not to squander. To young Howard Thurman, the funeral was an occasion of traumatizing violence. Repeatedly he asked Alice to assure him that the evangelist had not known his father. Riding home from the cemetery, Thurman vowed he would have nothing to do with the church when he grew up.[57]

Avoiding Christianity as a youth was not an option for Thurman, as he was devoted to his mother and grandmother, and the church became a refuge in his lonely, awkward youth. For the rest of his life, however, Thurman was averse to authority religion, fear-based religion, and evangelism. In later life he recalled feeling haunted, upon feeling called to ministry, "that somehow I was violating my father's memory by taking leadership responsibility in an institution that had done violence to his spirit." Alice Thurman supported her three children by cooking and cleaning for white people; meanwhile Thurman's grandmother took chief responsibility for him. Alice Ambrose had been enslaved on a plantation near Madison, Florida, and one of Thurman's regular chores was to read the Bible to her. Though illiterate, she knew the Bible well and was especially fond of the devotional Psalms, Isaiah, and Gospels. Pointedly she never asked him to read from Paul's epistles, except 1 Corinthians 13. In later years she explained to Thurman that during her youth the slavers recited Paul's statements about slavery, and she vowed that if freedom ever came to her she would have no further dealings with the apostle Paul.[58]

Daytona, in Thurman's early youth, was not as harshly racist as most of the Deep South. The town was founded in 1876; it grew in the 1880s with the growth of the citrus industry; it attracted wealthy northern migrants; its beach sections (Daytona Beach and Sea Breeze) attracted tourists; black Americans shared in its civic and political life; and the railroad aided the citrus business. By 1910 over half the town's population of thirty-five hundred was African American, including the founder of a recently established (1904) training school for girls, Mary McLeod Bethune. Thurman admired Bethune, a family friend, witnessing her speeches on temperance and education to racially mixed audiences at her school. He also watched Daytona become a more typical Deep South town, as white southerners moved there for jobs and brought the full vengeance of Jim Crow with them. "Colored" and "white" signs went up when Thurman was a toddler. Blacks were allowed to work in the tourist areas but not to linger after dark. For a while they were allowed to use the beaches, but that was terminated. Thurman later recalled that blacks lived in the Waycross, Midway, and Newtown sections of Daytona, "surrounded by a white world. . . .

Thus, white and black worlds were separated by a wall of quiet hostility and overt suspicion."[59]

A friendly relationship with a white person was unthinkable, the Klan controlled politics in Daytona Beach, and the entire state of Florida had only three public high schools for black children. Thurman later recalled, "There are few things more devastating than to have it burned into you that you do not count and that no provisions are made for the literal protection of your person. The threat of violence is ever present, and there is no way to determine precisely when it may come crushing down upon you." In his experience the only whites who treated blacks as fellow human beings were the rich northern families that wintered in Daytona, especially the Rockefellers and Gambles. The only local black public school, in Newton, went only through seventh grade; Thurman's principal tutored him privately when he reached eighth grade.[60]

Meanwhile he cultivated a mystical ocean spirituality much like that of another introverted loner, Unitarian founder William Ellery Channing. Thurman loved the vast expanse of sea and sky and its calm. He watched the stars etch their brightness on the "face of the darkened canopy of the heavens" and felt that he, the sea, the sand, the stars, and all else were one lung through which all life breathed. He was part of a "vast rhythm" enveloping all things, and all of it was part of him. The ocean at night gave Thurman "a sense of timeliness, of existing beyond the reach of the ebb and flow of circumstances. Death would be a minor thing." He loved especially the storms that swarmed up the Florida coast, enthralled by the power of annual autumn hurricanes. Thurman exulted in his connection to natural powers that laid waste to human constructions: "The boundaries of self did not hold me. Unafraid, I was held by the storm's embrace." In later life the memory of his identification with the storms gave him "a certain overriding immunity" from inner pain and outward evil: "I felt rooted in life, in nature, in existence."[61]

Self-conscious, pigeon-toed, overweight, with protruding front teeth, and usually chosen last in playground games, Thurman took consolation in intellectual achievement. Admitted to Florida Baptist Academy in Jacksonville, a hundred miles north of Daytona, Thurman caught a break at the railway station from a black stranger who paid his luggage fare—an experience of grace he savored for the rest of his life. He caught a second break from James Gamble, a part-owner of Procter and Gamble Company, who subsidized Thurman's education on a monthly basis. Thurman excelled in high school and developed into a youth leader, serving as president of the school's YMCA branch. The YMCA was transformational for Thurman. He attended his first Kings Mountain

Student Conference in the summer of 1917, as a high school sophomore. The following year he forged lasting friendships with YMCA international secretary Channing Tobias and YMCA field-worker Max Yergan, and he heard Johnson give a bravura speech. Listening to Johnson, Thurman found a model of who he wanted to be. He appealed for Johnson's attention in a letter of raw feeling.[62]

Thurman told Johnson that he had let Johnson "slip into my heart and occupy the place of a precious friend." Admiring Johnson's eloquence, he thrilled at realizing that Johnson cared: "I wanted to know you and wanted you to know me; I longed for a cheering word from a man like you; I yearned to tell you my hopes, ambitions, and discouragements." But "Mitchell of Morehouse" monopolized Johnson's time at the conference, and the opportunity passed. Thurman begged for a second chance: "Listen while I tell to you my soul." He told his story of poverty, deprivation, losing his father, earning straight As, leaving home for high school, and eating one meal per day. Next year he would graduate, and he was not unwilling to fight in the war, for which "young men are being snatched daily." Thurman assured Johnson that he was patriotic, believing that America fought for democracy: "But my friend Rev. Johnson, my people need me. . . . Please take a personal interest in me and guide me and God will reward you, for you are God's trustee." He closed on a plaintive note, confessing that he felt discouraged in his decision to become a minister: "Sometimes I think nobody cares but thank God, Jesus does, mother does, and I believe you do."[63]

Johnson replied graciously, thanking Thurman "heartily" for his letter and urging him to attend college and seminary instead of taking a shortcut such as adding a "shallow course in theology" to his high school diploma. There was no substitute for advanced academic training, and ministry could be combined with it: "Many young men pastor churches while they are doing their theological work. I did that in Rochester. Prepare! Prepare! This is the one and only word for you." Johnson added that Thurman should not worry about the military draft. He was three years removed from draft age, and by then the war might be over. Even if he had to fight, that would be good too: "You will have the joy of giving your country a superior type of service such as college men can give, and you will return from the war prepared to take your place again in the higher college classes with an early prospect of being one among the few well trained thinkers and leaders who will have the destiny of our people in their keeping." Later that summer Thurman's school moved to Saint Augustine, changing its name to Florida Normal and Industrial Institute, while he represented the school at Howard University's student army training corps, sponsored by the U.S. government. Students were trained to qualify as sergeants upon being drafted into the army. Thurman spent his senior year of high school drilling students for war, forcing him to study in the wee hours, which drove him to exhaustion. But he graduated as valedictorian and won a scholarship to Morehouse.[64]

Thurman did not chafe at Morehouse's strict regime of no drinking, no smoking, no dancing, no card playing, and no fraternizing with Spelman College females without a chaperone. This was his chance to change his life. He respected Hope enormously; to Thurman, Hope's scholarly, decorous weekly chapel talks formed the centerpiece of a Morehouse education. Morehouse required every student to compose and deliver an oration every year at a chapel service, which helped to produce self-confident Morehouse Men. Thurman excelled at Morehouse, winning contests and debate prizes, the class presidency, and top of the class standing. He thrived under Hope's paternalistic rule, encouraged that Hope addressed Morehouse students as "young gentlemen" amid Atlanta's brutal atmosphere. From Mays Thurman acquired an interest in philosophy and learned how to debate. From Frazier, he got a lesson in humility. Thurman returned from a summer course at Columbia University a bit full of himself, impressed by his performance in Columbia philosopher E. A. Burtt's course "Reflective Thinking." Basically the course was an introduction to skeptical inquiry in the mode of John Dewey's pragmatism. Thurman judged that black colleges like Morehouse were woefully short on critical inquiry, a view he expressed volubly upon returning to Morehouse. He thought his aggressive classroom behavior made him a model student. Frazier took a different view, prohibiting Thurman from saying another word in his class. Even the word "present" at roll call was forbidden; Frazier had heard all that he could bear from Thurman. Thurman, however, earned an A in the course, and later he got along with Frazier at Howard, with nothing said about their classroom relationship at Morehouse.[65]

The YMCA became even more important to Thurman in college. He was president of the campus YMCA at Morehouse and spoke frequently on the YMCA and YWCA lecture circuits. His primary institutional home was the Student Christian Movement, a fusion of YMCA and YWCA activists. Then he joined the other major activist organization to evolve out of the ecumenical missionary society orbit: the Fellowship of Reconciliation (FOR). The American branch of FOR, founded in Garden City, New York, in 1915, stood for pacifist opposition to war and imperialism, generally from an anticapitalist standpoint. Joining FOR was singularly significant for Thurman: "I found a place to stand in my own spirit—a place so profoundly affirming that *I* was strengthened by a sense of immunity to the assaults of the white world of Atlanta, Georgia."[66]

He had a sense of holding a secret by bonding with black and white Christian pacifists, Socialists, and civil rights activists. Thurman's politics at Morehouse, a blend of Dewey-style pragmatic Socialism and anti-imperial Christian pacifism, were clearer than his theology. The Morehouse yearbook of 1923 listed him among three pacifists in his graduating class and (probably) among fourteen Socialists. As for his theology, the yearbook affirmed more vaguely that Thurman was "our ideal of a minister, one who will furnish us with a rational and practical Christianity." Mays later recalled that Thurman was already quite mystical during his Morehouse years, "so much so that I am inclined to think that he was considered queer by some of the students and professors." They liked him nonetheless. Mays recalled that he "possessed a mind and an integrity of character which they were forced to respect."[67]

Thurman had not read much theology before he made his next move, to Rochester Theological Seminary. Though he was following in Johnson's path politically, theologically, and academically, he spurned the offer from Hope that Johnson had taken: faculty status at Morehouse and undergraduate validation at Chicago. Thurman was in a hurry to get where he was going, and he had some Mays-like anxiety about how he would do in a predominantly white environment. Summer courses at Chicago would not provide a sufficient answer. He applied to Newton Seminary, which was still barring black students. He settled for Johnson's alma mater, which was still admitting two black students per year. Thurman caught a whiff of self-congratulatory white supremacy in his acceptance letter, which belabored his great privilege in being admitted. Then he made the riskiest move of his life by plunging into a white world.

"I was living for the first time in a totally white world," he later recalled. "The impact of this fact alone was staggering." Every Rochester Seminary professor was white, male, and old, and they addressed students as "mister." Everything at the seminary felt formal and reserved compared to the buoyancy of Morehouse. Thurman took refuge in the library, a place of innumerable marvels and delights to him. At last he had access to a library exceeding his capacity to read every book. Eventually he realized that his classmates did not know more than he did and were less motivated, although they held the advantage of not being strangers: "Whether they were gifted intellectually, or mediocre, the fact remained that this world belonged to them."[68]

The YMCA and Student Christian Movement had extensive networks in the Northeast, providing numerous speaking engagements for Thurman, which Klan operatives closely monitored. Thurman urged audiences that they could not live in the Spirit of Christ if they were indifferent to racial oppression or contributors to it. On one occasion he had to walk past a row of menacing unhooded Klansmen to enter a church. At the same time, Thurman developed friendships with two white classmates—Red Matthews and Dave Voss—that altered his moral landscape. It had never occurred to him that he shared the same religion as his white classmates or might pray with them. In his words, "It had not ever occurred to me that my magnetic field of ethical awareness applied to other than my own people." Thurman had not expected to share his dreams or fears with white people. After it happened, he began to consider that people of different races owed moral responsibilities to each other in a shared world.[69]

Intellectually, two influences stood out for him during his seminary years. The first was systematic theologian George Cross, a Chicago-trained theological liberal and neo-Kantian taskmaster. Thurman measured his intellectual progress by his ability to argue with Cross, who often ripped apart his arguments. In a paper for Cross on conceptions of God, Thurman argued that theology fused objective description and subjective experience. This paper lifted verbatim statements from an article by C. A. Richardson and a book by Charles Allen Dinsmore as Thurman's own work, without acknowledgment. The editors of the superbly edited papers of Thurman, headed by Walter Earl Fluker, caught the problem in the first volume of their work in 2009. Although Cross missed Thurman's plagiarism in this paper, the two had a frank and admiring relationship. In their last meeting Cross turned philosophical, advising Thurman not to waste his time on superficial books. If he could read more than fifteen pages of a book in an hour, it was not worth reading. The trick was to study for the long term, reading books that made a difference for ten or twenty years.[70]

Somewhat in that vein, Thurman had an awkward moment with Cross near the end of his senior year. Cross told Thurman he had "superior gifts" and probably the ability to make "an original contribution to the spiritual life of the times." He appreciated that Thurman felt called "to put all the weight of your mind and spirit at the disposal of the struggle of your own people for full citizenship." However, Cross urged Thurman to aim higher. All social problems were transitory in nature, he reasoned. It would be a terrible waste if Thurman limited his creative energy to struggling against racism: "Give yourself to the timeless issues of the human spirit." Thurman was stunned speechless. Cross retreated momentarily, acknowledging that perhaps he had no right to speak in this way, as he did not know what it was like to be in Thurman's situation. But he pressed on, promising Thurman to make arrangements for him to study with the right doctoral advisor in Europe. Thurman never learned who it was, as Cross fell ill and died. Thurman was left with the ambiguous memory of a powerful, caring teacher "who did not know that a man and his black skin must face the 'timeless issues of the human spirit' together."[71]

The second influence was white South African novelist Olive Schreiner. In 1925, while attending a Student Christian Movement retreat in Pawling, New York, Thurman heard a story written by Schreiner read aloud, about a hunter who broke the bars of a cage to set free beautiful wild birds. Schreiner's story overwhelmed Thurman like nothing he had ever heard. It seemed to him that his entire life had been a preparation for this riveting illumination of the deep natural unity of all things. Thurman's nature mysticism had been a guilty secret, something he could not cognize, much less express to others. Schreiner's romantic spiritual sensibility and gorgeous writing resonated powerfully with Thurman. He became an expert on her work, learning that Schreiner had written an early feminist novel, *The Story of an African Farm* (1885); an attack on British imperialism in South Africa, *Trooper Peter Halket of Mashonaland* (1897); a feminist treatise on labor, *Women and Labor* (1911); and a first volume of allegories, *Dreams* (1891); plus more volumes of allegories.[72]

She had the gift of radical imagination, writing works of feminist daring and rebellion, and she expressed Thurman's conviction that helping the afflicted and belonging to the universe went together. Yet Schreiner was pathetically commonplace on racism. She said little about the oppression of native Africans, and her books had occasional racist slurs. Thurman later observed that Schreiner was not a proud racist like Cecil Rhodes or a messianic racist like the Boers, but she belonged sufficiently to her "exploiting and colonizing community" to be shabby on this subject. In seminary, and for years to come, Thurman struggled to absorb the paradox. How could Schreiner's vibrant humanity break down on something so momentous? How could he have a racist soul mate? Thurman wished he could have met Schreiner, who died in South Africa in 1920. But he would not leave her behind. Schreiner rebelled against the oppression she knew personally, and her brilliant romantic vitalism enabled Thurman to recognize his own.[73]

In that mood Thurman wrote a master's thesis on sexual morality, by far the most daring thing he ever wrote on this topic. Thurman scholars Quinton H. Dixie and Peter Eisenstadt put it concisely: "Thurman knew oppression when he saw it, and Thurman became a feminist." It helped to have been raised by a grandmother with a strong personality, but many had strong women in their lives without becoming feminists. Schreiner convinced Thurman that women were put down in ways that resembled his own oppression. His thesis focused on the ethics of premarital sex, informed by three things: academic literature on the history of sexual morality; the rebellion of Thurman's generation against what he called "Mrs. Grundy's position," an orthodoxy much derided at YMCA youth conferences; and the feminist liberationism of Schreiner and her friend Havelock Ellis.[74]

Thurman took a grand tour of his subject, explicitly historicizing it. He began with East African tribes lacking any concept of the ostensible moral problem in question, swept through the ancient Hebrews, Muslims, Greeks, and Christians, surveyed historic Christianity, and ended with a disapproving summary of the regnant American orthodoxy: Premarital chastity was the ideal for women and "winked at" by men; plus women of low status were given a pass. Church and society, Thurman observed, worked together to enforce this orthodoxy, mainly to drive respectable women into marriage and motherhood. Women had a place and a role, both subordinate to men, especially if they wanted the approval of church and society. Until very recently, Thurman noted, American men excluded all women from voting, and they were still determined to repress women through the sexual code: "At no point has the domination of men been more disastrous than in the conventional attitude toward pre-marital unchastity."[75]

Thurman reported that young people of the 1920s ridiculed the governing orthodoxy when they gathered, even at church conferences. Drawing on religious education theorist George A. Coe, Thurman judged that young people were alienated from the world of their parents for social and cultural reasons that folded together. Young people lived in a society in which women's roles had changed significantly, women increasingly worked in industrial jobs, industrial civilization bred alienation and sick souls, and mechanization created a chasm between work and leisure. People hated their mechanized jobs, so they needed an enjoyable release. In addition, public school students learned about evolution and democracy, but at Sunday school they were taught creation and authority, which made religion look ridiculous. The church made everything worse by convincing young people that Christianity loathed sex. Thurman countered that good religion did not view sexual desire as "the great destroyer of the Spirit." Sexual desire was an expression of the loving and unifying Spirit of God. It affirmed, as good and harmonizing, the desire lovers held for each other: "When through constant and intimate association with one another there has grown up between two individuals a true fellowship, then there is brought to the sexual act a funded experience of rich contact and association. Under such experience the sexual act becomes the highest compliment that the two individuals of different sex can pay to each other." He added one sentence about what that did not mean: "When it is indulged in on any other basis it becomes a violation."[76]

This was a seminary thesis, and Rochester Seminary was not ready for the romantic pansexualism of Havelock Ellis, an advocate of open marriage. Thurman quoted Ellis selectively, stopping short of free love apologetics or any reference to Ellis's controversial marriage to feminist writer Edith Lees. But he ended with a tribute to Schreiner: "May we dare believe with Olive Schreiner that the history of sex with its great power and its beauty of holiness is still in its infancy."[77]

Thurman was living his subject at the time, engaged to a social worker, Katie Kelley, whom he had met when she was a student at the Atlanta School of Social Work. Kelley ran a tuberculosis clinic in Morristown, New Jersey, while Thurman studied at Rochester, and the couple married a month after his graduation. Despite his "infancy" rhetoric and his moral passion about it, Thurman never ventured again into the subject matter of his master's thesis. He never wrote again about sexuality, premarital or otherwise, or about feminism or the lives of women, apart from side remarks, or about his conversations with young people, despite speaking constantly to students during his long career as a chapel dean and pastor. These subjects, after Thurman entered the ministry, went into a private file for him, sublimated into topics he wrote about constantly: the indispensability of interpersonal dialogue and the spiritual basis of physicality. Dixie and Eisenstadt rightly observe that Cross, despite saying it in a patronizing way, identified a sensitive issue for Thurman. He wanted to speak and write about spiritual matters that he conceived as universal, and he had to address the matters of race. How to do one without violating the other was a puzzle to him. Thurman wrestled with that issue throughout his career.[78]

Fresh out of seminary, he and Kelley moved to Oberlin, Ohio, where Thurman gave two years to Mount Zion Baptist Church. He hoped to continue his studies at Oberlin School of Theology, but that desire faded. He preached didactic sermons about modern theology and biblical criticism, sharing the riches of his learning, which some of his college-town congregants appreciated and others emphatically did not. Averse to evangelism, Thurman came early to a signature theme. He undertook mission work to share and receive, not just to give: "I go because he has something for me that I must have if I am to be what I ought to be." For better and for worse, Thurman reasoned, "I am tied by the fact of the source of life to all the rest of the people of the world." This yearning for spiritual connection lured Thurman to a deeper recognition of his mystical wellspring. He fed his growing spiritual hunger by practicing contemplative prayer and meditation. At first he separated his spiritual hunger from his job, preaching didactic sermons out of his head, but gradually it occurred to him that his congregants had similar spiritual needs: "As I began to acquiesce to the demands of the spirit within, I found no need to differentiate human need, theirs and my own. I became more and more a part of the life of my people and discovered that at last I was able to pray in public as if I were alone in the quiet of my own room. The door between their questing spirits and my own became a swinging door."[79]

The feeling deepened in Thurman that he was called to help people recognize their spiritual unity in the love of God. A visitor from China, after weeks of attending services, introduced himself, telling Thurman that when he closed his eyes in Thurman's church he was back in his Buddhist temple experiencing the renewal of his spirit. This remark was a breakthrough for Thurman: "I knew then what I had only sensed before. The barriers were crumbling. I was breaking new ground. Yet, it would be many years before I would fully understand the nature of the breakthrough."[80]

Thurman was uneasy about giving himself to a form of spirituality in which he had little training. Where was he going? What language should he use? One day, while making an early exit from a religious education convention that bored him, he noticed a book table near the exit. He bought a little book by Quaker mystic Rufus Jones, *Finding the Trail of Life*, for ten cents, sat on the church step, and read the entire book. Thurman was enthralled; he had found his spiritual mentor: "When I finished I knew that if this man were alive, I wanted to study with him."[81]

Rufus Jones was the apostle of mysticism in American liberal Protestantism. A prolific spiritual writer and philosopher at Haverford College, he was the product of an intense Quaker upbringing in Maine, an undergraduate education at Haverford College, an early career as a popular Quaker writer and lecturer, and a half-completed graduate education at Harvard in philosophy. Raised by three strong-willed women and an emotionally distant father, Jones idolized his Aunt Peace, who radiated spiritual serenity. As a college student, reading Emerson, Jones discovered the word "mysticism," recognizing that it named the kind of religion in which he had been raised. Reading George Fox, the founder of the Society of Friends, Jones discovered that his seemingly strange dogmatic sect belonged to a great spiritual tradition of mystical faith. The Society of Friends was supposed to be a catalyzing religious movement of a mystical type, inaugurating a universal religion of the Spirit. Jones devoted his career to exemplifying and explicating what that meant, writing books about the inner light of the Spirit and its redemptive, peacemaking, justice-making work.[82]

Finding the Trail of Life happened to be autobiographical, but many of Jones's books had an autobiographical slant, as he believed that the only real starting point for religion or theology was in personal experience. Repeatedly he urged that religions of external authority are soul-deadening: "The moment a religion becomes a system of thought or a crystallized truth, its service to the world is over, it can no longer feed living souls, for it offers only a stone where bread is asked." True religion always begins with a manifestation, "a revelation of God and the soul's answer to it." The way of true religion is the way of spiritual immediacy and practical authentication; it asks only to be tested by direct experience. We are called to test the beauty and power of God's Spirit in the world. Steeped in post-Kantian idealism even before he studied with Josiah Royce at Harvard, Jones played up that his brand of liberal mystical religion folded seamlessly into the modern West's richest philosophical tradition: "It is in harmony with all the great leaders of modern philosophy, notably Descartes, Kant, Fichte, and Hegel, all of whom build their systems on the immediate testimony of self-consciousness."[83]

A bit later, after studying at Harvard and beginning his academic career at Haverford, Jones delineated more carefully his relationship to Kant. With Kant he argued that it is futile to look for God through logic or empirical reasoning. Against Kant he argued that the existence of conscience depends on the existence of God, not the other way around. We must look for things where they belong, Jones argued. We do not look through a microscope to find love, sympathy, goodness, or patience. These realities are "facts of personal life" belonging to the realm of spirit. Similarly, in looking for God "we must include under the knowledge-process our entire capacity for dealing with reality." God must be sought where God *could* be found, in the spiritual realm where spirit manifests itself. Since God is not less personal than we are, all attempts to find God apart from the personal life are doomed to fail.[84]

There is a door that opens to the Holy of Holies, Jones taught. Science cannot open it, but the door is accessible to every conscious person by asking the questions of one's subjectivity and discerning the movement of God's Spirit. Social science, to Jones, was more useful for theology than natural science because society is an essential condition of self-consciousness and personality. There can be no self without many selves; self-consciousness is a possibility for each self only in a world in which self-consciousness already exists. Personality involves interrelation at every stage of its development. Thus religious thinking needs social science, but only to a point, for the formative role of society is limited. The social influence is not creative, and it does not confer personality. Personality, although achieved within social relationships, must be won by something more fundamental to the self than its embodiment or its process of socialization. The self's realization of spiritual being—personality—can be won only by a self's will to be. Until this personal force asserts itself, society can do nothing to make a person. A self is created by its struggle to attain something personal that is not yet one's own. Jones explained, "There must be presented to consciousness a better state of existence than has yet been realized. It must appeal to consciousness, furthermore, as a condition which would satisfy if it were put in the place of the actual present state." The ideals of consciousness propel and direct, passing into life, making a self what it becomes. Nobody's experience can be a substitute for one's own, and the more we comprehend that God is essentially self-revealing Spirit, "the less it is possible for us to stop *satis-fied* with a record." Revelation is not a thing that anybody comes to possess. It is the flame that kindles seekers to pursue God's presence and grace.[85]

Thurman wrote to Jones, asking to study with him on a special arrangement. A semester spent with Rufus Jones would be worth more to him than the doctorate he had previously wanted: "I sensed somehow that if I were to devote full time to the requirements of a doctoral program, academic strictures would gradually usurp the energy I wanted so desperately to nourish the inner regions of my spirit." Numerous obstacles stood in the way of getting to Haverford. Katie was seriously ill with tuberculosis, and the couple had a baby daughter. Thurman had a full-time job, he needed to provide for his family, he would need financing for his studies at Haverford, and Haverford (like most Quaker colleges) did not accept black students. Swiftly Thurman solved these problems. He resigned from Mount Zion church, turned down Johnson's offer to teach at Howard, accepted a joint appointment at Morehouse and Spelman, which placed Katie near her family, obtained a fellowship from the National Council for Research in Higher Education, and got Jones to arrange his admittance. In the spring semester of 1929 he became Jones's daily companion. Thurman attended Jones's lectures, joined a seminar for local philosophers on Meister Eckhart—"exciting and stimulating beyond anything I had known before"—and took part in Quaker meetings. He later recalled, "These were seminal times. Rufus was utterly informal and his discussions ranged over the broad expanse of his thought and experience." Gently, never with any pushing, Jones invited Thurman to a life of mystically inspired faith, teaching, ministry, and social activism.[86]

Jones was not the kind of mystic that blurred moral distinctions by naming everything "God." He opposed dualistic theologies that drove God out of the world and pantheistic theologies that negated God's capacity for transcendence. Thurman welcomed this approach and appreciated that Jones was deeply committed to antiwar and anti-imperial activism; Jones played a leading role in founding the American Friends Service Committee. In most respects Thurman found a model in Jones: "My study at Haverford was a crucial experience, a watershed from which flowed much of the thought and endeavor to which I was to commit the rest of my working life." But it puzzled him that they never talked about race. Jones apparently believed that race should not matter and therefore it should not be discussed. Thurman, to his surprise, caught something of this attitude: "I felt that somehow he transcended race; I did so, too, temporarily." It was a new experience for Thurman, and a relief, not to have to think about being black. But Jones's apparent racial blindness was confounding. Was it really possible to disregard race in racist America? Even if Jones somehow carried out the ideal of race-blind liberalism, how could he ignore the brutal reality of racism that all black Americans had to endure?[87]

This aspect of Jones's witness remained an enigma to Thurman. For ten years Thurman rarely wrote or spoke about mysticism, even as he taught courses on it at Morehouse and Howard. It took him that long to speak confidently about interreligious experiences of God and the mystical way of knowing. Upon coming out, he sprinkled his writings with quotes from Jones and moved further away from Christian categories than Jones found to be necessary or desirable. Thurman treasured Jones's gift of sharing his spiritual experience in a personal way that caused no embarrassment; he possessed the same gift in abundance. But Jones's failure to deal with racial oppression left a chasm between Thurman and his spiritual mentor.

Having turned down Howard University and returned to Atlanta so Thurman could have a semester with Jones, Thurman suffered the consequences. He felt battered by the relentless racism of Atlanta. He later recalled that the racial climate in Atlanta was "so oppressive and affected us so intimately" that it was impossible for him not to consider the parallels between the oppression of black Americans and the suffering of Jesus. Adding significantly to his distress was his tense relationship with Florence Read, Spelman's formidable president. Thurman clashed with Read over her patronizing treatment of students and, indirectly, her refusal to acknowledge that the era of white presidents leading black colleges had passed. In 1928, responding to the recent fate of the spirituals, Thurman made a case for memory and renewal, urging Spelman students not to disparage their heritage. In 1930 he lost his beloved Katie, who died after a long battle with tuberculosis. For two years Thurman stopped writing letters, grieving silently. Then he said yes to Johnson and moved to Howard, marrying a YMCA national secretary, Sue Bailey, just before he left.[88]

The argument about the spirituals absorbed Thurman for the rest of his life. In the 1920s students at black colleges refused to sing the spirituals, especially for the entertainment of white donors. Thurman had witnessed this transformation at Morehouse, where his classmates enraged Hope by refusing to serenade the all-white General Education Board, a major source of funding for Morehouse. Hope excoriated the students, who replied, in Thurman's telling,

"We refuse to sing our songs to delight and amuse white people. The songs are ours and a part of the source of our own inspiration transmitted to us by our forefathers." Two years later this issue played a role in the student strike at Howard that led to Durkee's resignation. There the mood was hotter, as students disparaged the slave songs as emblems of servility.[89]

Thurman knew what it felt like to sing for the endearment of white donors, and he did not blame the students for shutting down. But he hated that students and intellectuals increasingly put down the spirituals as something beneath them. At Spelman Thurman gave chapel sermons lauding the religious genius of the antebellum slave songs. Unlike later exponents of this tradition of retrieval, he did not say that the songs exemplified a distinctly African American spirituality or that they conveyed political expectations. Thurman did not believe the spirituals contained African retentions or that anything important was at stake in believing it. He took the Frazier side of the later-famous Frazier versus Melville Herskovits debate, contending that the spirituals were cries of a ravaged people stripped of all cultural resources. This was precisely what made the spirituals so profound, Thurman argued. The slave songs showed that even in a seemingly hopeless situation, religious experience provided a wellspring of hope. Even people stripped of everything were not lost or hopeless; on the contrary, they created and sang universal sacred wisdom.[90]

In that case, the spirituals were still relevant, containing clues to how black Americans might survive and transform the structures of white violence that oppressed them. Thurman's commitment to nonviolence was personal and racial before it involved beliefs about militarism, nation-states, and warfare. Christian nonviolence answered the question of how he should live in a society that violently threatened his existence. He put it cogently in December 1928 in an article for the pacifist Socialist magazine *World Tomorrow*. Building on George Coe's analysis of relaxation in *The Psychology of Religion*, Thurman argued that being committed to nonviolence meant different things in the white and black communities. White pacifism was about relaxing the will of white Americans to dominate blacks. Black pacifism was about relaxing sufficiently to enable creativity.[91]

In America the tension of the dominant group was severe. Thurman had a fantasy of white Americans, by some miracle, relaxing their will to dominate blacks. If it ever happened, he wrote, the consequences would be revolutionary. White Americans would discover a different basis of security. To white Americans, the will to dominate and the will to live were fused together. Thus they described black Americans as a burden, a menace, and worse, all cloaked in (anti-Christian) Christianity. Fear engendered tension, Thurman observed, and tension engendered oppression. To white Americans, the Christian will to love was impossible without letting go of the desperate need to dominate. Thurman said it started with individuals before it became social: "There must be individual creative experimentation along with the actual harnessing of social forces to that end." Black Americans, on the other hand, saw education as the way to salvation. Salvation, to blacks, was to become at home in the world and to experience the possibility of creative living. Education was not saving if it enabled only a few to live creatively, Thurman cautioned. Moreover, just as white Americans had to sever the will to live from the will to dominate, black Americans had to separate the will to live from "the will to hate the man who makes living such precarious business." Thurman told black readers they could not be free if they hated their white oppressors: "When there is relaxation, then the way is clear for the operation of the will to share joyfully in the common life—the will to love healingly and creatively."[92]

This essay gave ballast to Devere Allen's announcement that a "new pacifism" had arisen in America. Allen, a movement activist and longtime editor of *World Tomorrow*, published a reader titled *Pacifism in the Modern World* (1929). In his telling, the new pacifist movement was anti-imperialist, antiracist, anticapitalist, antiretributive punishment, and anti-everything that thwarted fellowship and love. It took inspiration from Gandhi's anticolonial campaign in India and rejected the casual white supremacy of earlier pacifist movements. It was devoted to the "art of life," leaving no place for the arts or machinery of killing: "Pacifism touches all of life with a new beauty and lets loose in society a leavening ideal profoundly in contrast with our contemporary economic and social structure." The book had twenty contributors, notably Thurman, Rufus Jones, Rabindranath Tagore, Paul Jones, Reinhold Niebuhr, and A. J. Muste. Tagore was a famous Bengali poet and polymath; Paul Jones was an Episcopal bishop and FOR leader; Niebuhr was in the final phase of his pacifist period; Muste was getting started as a leading revolutionary pacifist. Thurman was breaking into company that no black religious intellectual had experienced. By the time he joined the faculty at Howard he was accustomed to hearing himself introduced as the idol of the social Christian movement and as "Howard Thurman the Great."[93]

Johnson had pined for Thurman's presence and genius as soon as he took the Howard presidency. By the time Thurman arrived, he and Johnson fretted over the Du Bois/Bunche/Frazier contention that black churches were hopelessly conservative and black reformers too comfortable with their bourgeois mentality and status. Thurman kept giving speeches about racial uplift through education and respectability, but with a troubled conscience. He did not want to be left behind as an apologist for a self-congratulatory ideology, and he did not want churches to become irrelevant to the struggle for equality. It was not too late for progressive Christians to transform the churches. Churches had a crucial role to play in the very neo-Marxist strategies Du Bois and others talked about. At Morehouse Thurman had recoiled whenever Frazier berated the futility and backwardness of black America's devotion to religion. Joining Bunche and Frazier at Howard, Thurman sought to inspire a new black American Christianity that overthrew its many-sided provincialism. He had been working on that for two years at Howard when the Student Christian Movement invited him to head up a delegation of black American Christians to India, Ceylon, and Burma.

This invitation started with Augustine Ralla Ram, executive secretary of the Student Christian Movement of India, Ceylon, and Burma. Ralla Ram was a Brahmin convert to Christianity, a minister in the (Presbyterian/Congregational) United Church of Northern India, a theological liberal, an Indian nationalist, and a friend and associate of Gandhi. He spoke on the World Student Christian Federation circuit, where he told audiences that Gandhi's ideals and spirit were identical to those of Christ. Ralla Ram decorated his church in the bright colors of Hindu temples and openly acknowledged that Christianity, in India, was the oppressor's religion. Thus he had a difficult task in speaking for Christianity. He proposed to bring a delegation of black American Christians to India to show that some Christians had nothing to do with Western imperialism.[94]

Thurman's friends in the Student Christian Movement welcomed this proposal. In the 1920s nearly every American Protestant denomination fought over modernism versus fundamentalism, focusing on three questions: What should the church say about biblical infallibility and millennial eschatology? Which theology should prevail in the seminaries? And which theology should control the mission board? Some of the worst blowouts occurred between social gospel progressives and conservative evangelicals over the mission boards. The World Student Christian Federation, a forerunner of the World Council of Churches, was a leading player in the latter debate, pressing for a social gospel conception of Christian missions. All six of the Student Christian Movement leaders that selected the black American Christian delegation to India were veteran leaders of the YMCA or YWCA, and two were African Americans: Frank Wilson and Marion Cuthbert. For this group, the India Committee, there was no question about who should head the delegation: Thurman. The questions were whether Thurman would go and who should go with him.[95]

Thurman, upon being invited, was determined not to go. He felt keenly the absurdity of his representing organized American Christianity in South Asia, and he did not want to spend day after day explaining that he opposed conversion-focused proselytism. Moreover, the prospect of a lengthy separation from Sue Bailey Thurman repelled him. The India Committee said the right things on all three counts: The point was to make an anti-imperial Christian witness, this would not be an evangelistic enterprise, and Bailey Thurman would be a member of the delegation. Thurman and Bailey Thurman, pledging to make the trip, waited for the two remaining members to be named, which turned messy and prolonged. Mays, Wilson, and YWCA official Celestine Smith were among the final candidates. Eventually Virginia Methodist pastor Edward Carroll was chosen, agreeably to Thurman; a few months later Carroll's wife, Phenola, was added, angering Thurman. Phenola Carroll, unlike Bailey Thurman, was not qualified for public speaking, which heightened the workload of the others, especially Thurman, and made Bailey Thurman's appointment look like nepotism, unjustly. The delegation left New York in September 1935. Thurman deposited his daughters, Anne (age three) and Olive (age seven), with his sister Madaline in Geneva, and the delegation arrived in Ceylon exactly a month after departing New York.[96]

The pace was grueling and unrelenting, in punishing heat, and the issue of evangelistic expectations dogged Thurman at every turn. The group had 265 speaking events in 140 days in addition to innumerable panel discussions, interviews, and receptions. There were also choir lessons for groups wanting to sing the spirituals. Thurman spoke 135 times; Bailey Thurman spoke 69 times and accommodated the demand for musical performances; Edward Carroll and Phenola Carroll spoke 65 and 23 times. Thurman struggled to talk all day long, one way or another, plus handle correspondence and keep track of expenses. In his journal he reminded himself that this was basically a goodwill mission and an opportunity to make friends. He talked about the spirituals, black education, "The Faith of the American Negro," black achievements, peace, and "The Tragedy of Dull-Mindedness." Bailey Thurman spoke about black women, women's organizations, and "Internationalism in the Beloved Community." The spectacle of black Americans touring South Asia with a Christian message attracted audiences wherever the group went, often in a way that disappointed local missionaries. Thurman tired of explaining that he had not come to proselytize anybody. Sometimes he had to fend off ministers and missionaries who turned the worship service into an evangelistic occasion. It didn't help that E. Stanley Jones, a famous Methodist Episcopal missionary to upper-caste Indians and a friend of Gandhi, hailed the group's coming to South Asia as a historic opportunity to save souls.[97]

Very early in the tour, shortly after speaking at a college of law in Colombo, Ceylon, Thurman had a confrontation in a post-lecture discussion that helped him clarify what he needed to say about Jesus, Christianity, and Western civilization. A young lawyer asked him bluntly, "What are you doing here?" The lawyer rehearsed pertinent facts: Christians enslaved Africans in the United States for three hundred years; the slaves were freed by economic forces, not Christian idealism; and white Christians went on to oppress and terrorize blacks. "In light of all this, I think that for a young intelligent Negro such as you to be over here in the name of a Christian enterprise is for you to be a traitor to all the darker peoples of the earth. Such I consider you to be. Will you please account for yourself and your very unfortunate position?"[98]

Thurman caught his breath, thanked the lawyer for his frankness, and explained that he had not come to Ceylon to "bolster up a declining or disgraced Christian faith in your midst" or convert anybody to Christianity. Neither was he there to be an exemplar of what Christianity did for black Americans: "I am Christian because I think that the religion of Jesus in its true genius offers me very many ways out of the world's disorders. But I make a careful distinction between Christianity and the religion of Jesus." The churches worshipped power just like institutions that made no pretense of following Jesus, Thurman acknowledged: "I am dead against most of the institutional religion with which I am acquainted. I belong to a small minority of Christians who believe that society has to be completely reorganized in a very definite egalitarian sense if life is to be made livable for the most of mankind." Thurman concluded that the religion of Jesus repudiated the evils underlying imperialism and racism.[99]

According to Thurman, the lawyer was much relieved by this answer. To Thurman, the answer became a turning point to an interreligious spirituality that let go of privileged claims for Christianity. There was already a suggestion of this turn in his journal account of a conversation with a Buddhist hostel warden in Colombo, which Thurman repeated four decades later in his memoir. In Thurman's telling, the warden told him he disliked that Buddhist students attended Christian schools in Ceylon. The warden's reason, however, was not that Christian schools converted Buddhists to Christianity. He would have accepted that outcome, as he believed there was not much difference between the two religions anyway. What distressed the warden was that Christian schools produced drifters and relativists who ended up with no religion. Thurman surprised himself by not sharing the warden's lament. He heard himself say that a good education helped a person realize "what he is in root and essence already." A Christian school succeeded if it helped students confirm what they were already inwardly—Christians, Buddhists, drifters, whatever. This reply, Thurman later reflected, "had been moving in and out of my horizon like a fleeting ghost through all the years, an elusive insight." Upon saying it aloud, he began to worry less about shoring up even his favorite religious institutions. The speaking tour pulled him in this direction, as Thurman was asked constantly if Christianity was powerless before the color bar. If Christianity was not powerless, why was the racial situation so terrible in America? And if Christianity was powerless, why bother to put a good face on it in South Asia? Thurman stuck with his "religion of Jesus" answer and tried not to be defensive about it.[100]

In India, Thurman had an awkward meeting with Tagore and a sublime meeting with Kshiti Mohann Sen. Tagore, a Pirali Brahmin and Bengali polymath from Calcutta, was a revered figure in India. He wrote lyrical poetry, modernized Bengali art by introducing new prose and verse forms, and won the Nobel Prize in Literature in 1913, the first non-Westerner to do so. Tagore combined a fiercely nationalist opposition to British colonialism with a humanistic internationalism and universalism, epitomizing the Bengal Renaissance. Thurman's group journeyed to Tagore's university and ashram Santiniketan, where Tagore spent an hour with the two Thurmans, more or less. Tagore had trouble focusing, seeming to be in a dialogue with himself. Thurman later recalled, "I felt his mind was going through cycles as if we were not even present. Then he would swing back from that orbit, settle in, take us into account, and sweep out." Sen, on the other hand, connected intimately with Thurman. Sen taught Sanskrit at Santiniketan, and in a morning get-together he and Thurman bantered about Hinduism, Buddhism, and Christianity. In a second meeting that afternoon, Thurman later recalled, "I had the most primary, naked fusing of total religious experience with another human being of which I have ever been capable." He felt united with Sen on a spiritual ground unmarked by cultural or linguistic difference, confirming Thurman's belief that mystical experience was the wellspring of all religions—a pure experience of a nameless and formless divine reality: "This was a watershed experience of my life. We had become a part of each other even as we remained essentially individual."[101]

Near the end of the tour Thurman's group met belatedly with Gandhi at Bardoli, a small town near Bombay. A plan to spend Christmas vacation with Gandhi at his ashram at Wardha had been canceled when Gandhi fell ill with hypertension. A plan to meet in Delhi in early February had been canceled when all four members of Thurman's party fell ill with exhaustion. Later that month Gandhi offered to meet the group in Bombay; Thurman came instead to him in Bardoli, where the Congress Party had an encampment. Gandhi greeted the group warmly outside his bungalow tent and peppered them with questions about African American history, discrimination, religion, and

education. Bailey Thurman asked the first question of Gandhi, inquiring why
he excluded native Africans from his campaign in South Africa. Had he opted
for candor, Gandhi might have explained that during his early career he held
the customary white supremacism of his caste and acquired a keener grasp of
white racism and a higher view of blacks only after battling South African bigotry
and studying the career of Booker T. Washington. Gandhi admired Washington
immensely. Throughout his career he drew inspiration from Washington's
cagey, eloquent campaign for black advancement in the United States and his
emphasis on the dignity of labor. Gandhi believed that Washington's social
gospel religion was crucial to Washington's success, both personally and socially.
With Thurman's group he cut to a formula answer, replying that including
native Africans would have put them in danger because they did not understand
ahimsa (nonviolence). Gandhi and Thurman moved on to Islam, agreeing that
Islam had a better record than Christianity or Hinduism on racial equality,
though Thurman noted that Hindus were generally friendlier to him than
Muslims.[102]

The conversation swung back to ahimsa. Thurman asked if nonviolence was
a form of direct action; Gandhi replied, "It is not one form, it is the only form."
Nonviolence was meaningless without direct action: "It is the greatest and the
activest force in the world. One cannot be passively nonviolent. In fact 'nonviolence' is a term I had to coin in order to bring out the root meaning of Ahimsa."
Nonviolence was not a negative force, Gandhi asserted, even though the term
began with the negative particle 'non.' It was a self-acting force "more positive
than electricity and more powerful than even ether." Gandhi allowed that
violent strife and bloodshed permeated everyday existence. However, a great
seer, "ages ago," penetrated to the heart of truth itself: "It is not through strife
and violence, but through nonviolence that man can fulfill his destiny and his
duty to his fellow creatures." Gandhi's great seer was Jesus, via Leo Tolstoy's
book *The Kingdom of God Is Within You.* He probably judged that explaining
the Jainist root of "ahimsa" would be a distraction. The apostle Paul, Gandhi
added, in his "beautiful" statement in 1 Corinthians 13, caught most of the
Christian meaning of love, although not quite all of it: "Ahimsa includes the
whole creation, and not only human." Moreover, "love" in English bore other
meanings than the Pauline definition, so Gandhi felt compelled to coin the
term "nonviolence": "But it does not, as I have told you, express a negative
force, but a force superior to all the forces put together. One person who can
express Ahimsa in life exercises a force superior to all the forces of brutality."[103]

Thurman fastened on the "one person" claim. Did Gandhi really mean that
any individual could achieve it? Yes, if there were any exclusiveness about it,

Gandhi would not believe in it. Any idea of possession was foreign to ahimsa? Yes, Gandhi replied, "it possesses nothing, therefore it possesses everything." So was it possible for a single human being to hold off the violence of the world? This question cut two ways, Gandhi said. Was Thurman asking about the capacity of one Indian to hold off the oppression of three hundred million Indians or about the capacity of a single individual not to be contaminated by the violence of the world? Thurman replied that he had both concerns, but the greater question was the former one. Gandhi affirmed that he took the radical position. Any person who could not protect millions of others from the violence of the world was "not a true representative of Ahimsa." Nonviolence was about converting violent adversaries to nonviolence. If one failed to convert a single adversary or millions of them, one did not express ahimsa in its fullness. Did that mean, Thurman asked, that ahimsa overrode all other forces in life? Gandhi said yes, because ahimsa was "the only true force in life."[104]

Gandhi's in-house reporter, Mahadev Desai, noted that Thurman was "absolutely absorbed" in this part of the discussion. Thurman asked Gandhi how his group should train individuals and communities in nonviolence. Gandhi replied, "There is no royal road, except through living the creed in your life which must be a living sermon." One had to study and persevere, cleansing oneself of all impurities. Gandhi analogized that it took a lifetime to master chemistry or biology: "How many lifetimes may be needed for mastering the greatest spiritual force that mankind has known?" Since it would take several lifetimes to master nonviolence, Thurman should not worry about it. But since this was "the only permanent thing in life" and thus the only thing that really mattered, "whatever effort you bestow on mastering it is well spent. Seek ye first the Kingdom of Heaven and everything else shall be added to you. The Kingdom of Heaven is Ahimsa."[105]

Bailey Thurman, realizing that her husband and Gandhi would stay on this plane if indulged, broke in with a practical question: "How am I to act, supposing my own brother was lynched before my very eyes?" Gandhi told her, "There is such a thing as self-immolation." If a group lynched her brother, she should not "wish ill" to the lynchers or cooperate with them or cooperate with blacks who tolerated the lynchers: "That is the self-immolation I mean. I have often in my life resorted to the plan." Gandhi cautioned that his famous starvation strikes would have meant nothing if he had carried them out mechanically: "One's faith must remain undimmed whilst life ebbs out minute by minute. But I am a very poor specimen of the practice of nonviolence, and my answer may not convince you. But I am striving very hard, and even if I do not succeed fully in this life, my faith will not diminish."[106]

It was hard to focus on ordinary things after this fantastical standard had been established. Thurman's group swallowed Gandhi's reply respectfully, realizing it worked for him and he was undoubtedly sincere in it. Surprisingly, Thurman's group did not raise the issue of caste, but Gandhi brought it up in reply to a question about why his movement had failed thus far to expel the British. Gandhi said the masses lacked sufficient vitality to sustain a liberation campaign based on ahimsa for two reasons: They were poor and hungry, and they lacked self-respect. Thurman smiled knowingly at the reference to self-respect, but Gandhi cut him off: He did not mean what he figured Thurman was thinking. The Indian masses did not lack self-respect because they were colonized. They lacked self-respect because the Hindu system of untouchability degraded them.

"They are the scavengers, the worthless," Gandhi explained. A Hindu temple was considered contaminated if the shadow of an untouchable fell upon it. To counter this stupendously repressive force, Gandhi started with personal gestures, adopting an outcast into his family and describing every outcast as a Harijan, a child of God: "I became the spearhead of a movement for the building of a new self-respect, a fresh self-image for the untouchables in Indian society." Thurman later reflected, "He was striking close to home with this." As it was, their time together ended, and Gandhi asked the group to sing "Were You There When They Crucified My Lord?" "I feel that this song gets to the root of the experience of the entire human race under the spread of the healing wings of suffering." Bailey Thurman and the group complied, and they implored Gandhi to visit the United States as their guest. Bailey Thurman clarified: "We want you not for White America, but for the Negroes; we have many a problem that cries for solution, and we need you badly." Gandhi said he would come only if he thought he could make a contribution to the struggle for racial justice in America, and he would have no right to try until the struggle had been won in India. Thurman noted there were striking parallels between the Negro spirituals and everything Gandhi had just said. This comment evoked Gandhi's parting words to the group, immortalized by citation: "Well, if it comes true it may be through the Negroes that the unadulterated message of nonviolence will be delivered to the world."[107]

According to Thurman, this prophetic statement occurred early in the conversation, not at the end, and Gandhi ended by declaring that in India the greatest enemy of Jesus Christ was the Christian religion, "Christianity as it is practiced, as it has been identified with Western culture, with Western civilization and colonialism. This is the greatest enemy that Jesus Christ has in my country—not Hinduism, or Buddhism, or any of the indigenous religions—but

Christianity itself." In both versions of the "unadulterated message" story, however, the message was virtually identical, and it reverberated for years to come with retelling. Returning to the States in April 1936, Bailey Thurman lectured extensively about India, while Thurman resumed his normal routine of teaching, preaching, writing, and lecturing, now as dean of Rankin Chapel. He told a faculty gathering at Howard that the racial situations in India and the United States were more alike than different; elsewhere he enthused that his new position gave him a connection to the university as a whole. Princeton and Chicago originated the position of chapel dean, both in 1928. At Rankin Chapel Thurman perfected his distinctly dramatic, lofty, poetic, deep-voiced preaching style, featuring long pauses and abstract topics. Farmer heard Thurman preach many times: "When Thurman occupied the university pulpit, Rankin Memorial Chapel was packed. Though few but theologians and philosophers comprehended what he was saying, everyone else thought if only they *had* understood it would have been wonderful, so mesmerizing was his resonant voice and so captivating was the artistry of his delivery. Those who did grasp the meaning of his sermons were even more ecstatic."[108]

Thurman taught in a similar fashion, bringing his spiritual sensibility into the classroom and prodding students to discover their passion. At Morehouse and Spelman he had already dispensed with textbooks, drawing students into winding discussions of particularity, universality, eternity, temporality, relativity, and other concepts. At Howard, Thurman's reflective style of classroom performance contributed to his growing mystique. Mays noted that Thurman invited students to ponder fundamental problems such as the one and the many and the relation of finite and infinite. Whenever Thurman spoke, Mays said, "people knew that a free person was speaking." Farmer said most students were bewildered by Thurman's classes, which fed a growing perception on campus that he was a religious genius. Until Thurman and Mays came to Howard, Farmer recalled, faculty leaders openly derided their religious colleagues. Then it became harder for critics to say that "religious intellectual" was an oxymoron. It helped that Thurman endorsed Bunche's attack on the early New Deal and Mays documented much of the customary neo-Marxist critique of the black church. Thurman and Mays symbolized the ambition of the black social gospel to make an impact in the church *and* the public *and* the academy, gaining influence as it expanded.[109]

Most of the time Thurman did not write or speak directly about the struggle for racial justice. In the first place, he was averse to didacticism on any topic, especially this one. Moreover, invitations from white organizations to talk about race struck him as patronizing, since he preferred to discuss religious experience and was adamant about it. On occasion Thurman made a half-exception, usually for black audiences, although he always protested that there were better speakers for a speech about race, politics, or both. He discussed his experiences in India with a similar reserve. In 1938, writing about India's caste system, Thurman declared, "I do not know enough about India to determine whether caste is good or bad for that land." On first blush, he acknowledged, the caste system seemed awful, "but this is a superficial and uncritical judgment." Wading deeper into this subject was not his business, Gandhi's nonopposition to caste was a factor, and Thurman felt no obligation to adjudicate criticism of Gandhi on this point. To Thurman, however, as to Gandhi, the humanity of the untouchables was another matter: "I think that untouchability is a very very terrible thing because it destroys every vestige of self-respect on the part of the outcast." Thurman commended Gandhi "with all my heart" for campaigning against the outcast system. He wanted to believe that Christianity might help to abolish untouchability, but as long as Christianity did almost nothing to abolish racism in the West, "it seems to me sacrilegious for it to boast about its power to redeem the untouchables from their desperate lot."[110]

Two years later the Chicago Roundtable of the National Conference on Christians and Jews caught Thurman in the latter mood. Speaking to a large interreligious gathering, he granted a rare full-exception to his reserve about racial politics. The surprise doubled as Thurman echoed Frazier's argument in *The Negro Family in Chicago*, declaring, "The Negro in the northern city is not a citizen and his position is a perpetual threat and constant disgrace to democracy." The Great Migration left many African Americans worse off, Thurman said. In the premigration South, blacks were oppressed and terrorized, but they never starved, they had a home, and they had the "status of a person," albeit on Jim Crow terms. In the North, black migrants were "forced to be marginal dwellers," struggling constantly for "crass, elemental, physical survival." Losing every shred of community and security cost them nearly every vestige of personhood. Migrant blacks lived in crowded tenements where they were victimized by disease, crime, and exploitation, and threatened with starvation: "The housing problem of Negroes in cities smells to high heaven; this is beyond debate!" Thurman reflected that when most blacks lived in the South, some northern churches were "kindly disposed" to them. When blacks moved to the North, they stopped being lovable to established northern white and black churches.[111]

On the other hand, migrant blacks found more democracy in northern cities than they experienced in the South. Generally speaking, Thurman observed, black Americans were not citizens, as they were denied responsibility, social agency, and a sense of the future. Yet there were places here and there in the North where black Americans got a taste of a better future. This was the only hope for blacks in America, Thurman urged. American democracy had to be reinvented to include the African American as a full citizen: "He must be given responsibility and the incentive to exercise a free initiative if life ultimately is to be sane and secure for us all."[112]

Thurman rarely talked like that, however. He chafed at the crudeness of political advocacy, even during his lecture circuit years. Afterward he got more so, which caused critics to accuse him of abdicating his ethical responsibility. Thurman prized the social justice activism of others, and he encouraged friends and allies who gave themselves to it. In 1936 his friend Ralph Harlow, chaplain at Smith College, ran for Congress on the Socialist Party ticket. Thurman commended Harlow for carrying out his religious convictions in the political realm: "I only wish that I myself were located in a community where that sort of activity would be possible for me." But Thurman could not picture himself as a Socialist activist, a nearly nonexistent option in black America. He lacked the temperament to be the Gandhi of black America, although black newspapers entreated him to try. And he had no desire to carry on as Johnson and Mays did, giving stump speeches about the evils of white supremacism.[113]

His mystical wellspring had claimed him early in life. It claimed more of him after he found a language for it and exemplars of it. For a while he aimed for greater social ethical balance than Jones exemplified, but Thurman's devotion to spirituality claimed him more and more wholly. Increasingly he lectured about mysticism itself, developing Jones's signature idea of affirmative mysticism. Like Jones, Thurman cautioned against ascetical types of mysticism, contending for a worldly, affirmative, personalistic mysticism that made an ethical difference in society. He never thought of himself as having abandoned the struggle for social justice, and he never did. Spiritual enlightenment and social justice went together, and needed to.[114]

But in the late 1930s Thurman became restless, dissatisfied with his life and work. It was no longer enough to inspire students and lecture audiences. He felt stifled at having spent almost his entire career in black institutions. He received tempting job feelers, over which he lingered, tellingly. And he had a falling out with Johnson that made Howard less of a home to him.

First, Johnson refused to provide financial support for Thurman's sabbatical leave in South Asia, a financial blow that Thurman struggled for years to overcome. It galled Thurman to be victimized by Johnson's legendary tightfisted rule. His admiration of Johnson grew strained, and on one occasion Johnson admonished a faculty gathering that Howard University was not to be "used as a basis of operations." Thurman told colleagues the remark was directed at him, purportedly for using the university as a platform for his lecture career. That tweaked Thurman's moral pride, in a public way. Characteristically, Thurman did not talk about his eroded relationship with Johnson, and he remained a family favorite, visiting Johnson in his home and sustaining their friendship. By the end of the 1930s, however, Thurman was looking for an exit from Howard. Then he turned down the presidency of Morehouse College, and Mays accepted it.[115]

"THE LAST OF THE GREAT SCHOOLMASTERS"

In the early going Johnson was the instigator of Howard's Gandhian internationalist turn, and Thurman joined him in it, extending their shared YMCA ecumenism. Mays played a mostly supportive role until 1937, when the world opened to him. That year Channing Tobias helped Mays break into the world ecumenical movement by arranging for him to be a delegate at the YMCA's World Conference in Mysore, India. Later that year Mays served as a delegate to the Oxford Conference on Church, Community, and State at the University of Oxford, a stepping-stone to the World Council of Churches. In Mysore Mays and Tobias had a ninety-minute meeting with Gandhi, who told them nonviolence was three-fourths invisible and always practiced in absolute love. Nonviolence was not just for individuals. It could be practiced on a mass scale, and caring about the adversary was essential to nonviolence. Any nonviolent campaign that turned violent had to be called off immediately because violence was always self-defeating. Any resort to violence carried violence into the outcome. Moreover, Gandhi urged, nonviolent resistance was not contemptuous of law; the resister showed respect for law by accepting the legal consequences of disobeying an unjust law. Mays later recalled that the latter part of Gandhi's teaching struck him deeply; if not for his encounter with Gandhi, he might not have appreciated King's program after King became prominent.[116]

The Indian caste system appalled Mays, who found it much worse than American segregation. He judged that caste prejudice and exclusion did more to retard India than two centuries of British rule. Gandhi, however, told Mays and Tobias that the caste system was merely too rigid, not intrinsically evil. Every society had a division of labor, sorting out priests, teachers, politicians, soldiers, merchants, and farmers. India's system calcified to the point that no caste cared about anybody outside its group, which was a travesty. But the idea of the caste system was evil only at the bottom—the untouchables. So he cast his lot with the untouchables.[117]

This was Gandhi's customary line on caste, which he pressed against Bhimrao Ramji Ambedkar and other leading Indian opponents of the caste system. In the 1920s Gandhi carefully avoided the issues of inter-dining and intermarriage between castes, either for or against, and in 1930 Gandhi's close friend and ally the Anglican cleric Charles Andrews confirmed that Gandhi refused to give his consent to inter-dining and intermarriage. This position got into Andrews's condensed version of Gandhi's autobiography, *Mahatma Gandhi's Ideas*, causing distress in India and the United States. Gandhi realized he was coming off badly to some of his own followers, so in 1934 he told the *Baltimore Afro-American*, "Prohibition against other people eating in public restaurants and hotels and prohibition of marriage between colored people and white people I hold to be a negation of civilization." The caste system was "an offspring of untouchability," he declared. As such, it was "a most harmful institution. Either it has to go or Hinduism will die." Mays hoped for something in that vein, a clear condemnation of caste prejudice and exclusion. Instead Gandhi went back to waffling about caste apart from untouchability and Mays did not press the point in their meeting. Mays was scathing about the evils of caste after he returned to the States, Gandhi's team omitted the exchange about caste in its version of the conversation with Mays and Tobias, and Gandhi subsequently returned to saying that prohibitions against inter-dining and inter-marriage had to go.[118]

Shortly after Mays met with Gandhi, the headmaster of a school for untouchables asked Mays to speak at his school. Mays hesitated. There were thirteen U.S. American delegates at the Mysore conference, so why pick him? The headmaster wanted an African American speaker. So why not ask Tobias? Tobias, came the answer, had a light complexion. Still not quite getting the point, Mays spoke at the school, where the headmaster introduced him as an untouchable from the United States who had proven how far a person could rise despite being a member of a despised class. Mays was stunned and insulted by this introduction. It took him several weeks to absorb that the label applied to him almost exactly. He had been treated for most of his life as a member of an impossibly contemptible class.[119]

The Mysore conference roundly condemned racial discrimination, which Mays appreciated, although he shuddered to hear European delegates complain about "the Jewish problem." European persecution of Jews caused the so-called Jewish problem, propelling persecuted Jews to Palestine, where they drove out the native population. Mays warned, "There is great danger, even if less cruel and inhuman, that the Jews will do to the Arabs in Palestine what the Germans are doing to Jews in Germany." Upon returning from Mysore he wrote a flurry of articles—six for the *Norfolk Journal and Guide* and a major article for the *Journal of Negro Education* with a Du Boisian title, "The Color Line Around the World." Mays emphasized the threats of war and destruction in Europe and Asia, admitting it was hard not to be pessimistic about the world situation. However, there was one brilliant sign of hope: the Gandhi phenomenon.[120]

Mays described Gandhi's philosophy and why it mattered, explaining that Gandhian nonviolence was active and protest-oriented, resting on four cardinal principles expounded by three main sources. The principles were ahimsa, love, fearlessness, and truth, and the sources were Hindu Scripture, Jesus, and Tolstoy. The principles were ancient, even eternal, forming the bedrock of ancient religious traditions, yet Gandhi was "the first man to try the non-violent method on the mass level." Thus it was rightly called Gandhian nonviolence. Mays stressed that Gandhi was a hero to the Indian people, as he "has gone a long way towards making the Indian people proud of their race and proud of their great history." India's newfound pride in its racial and cultural identity showed through in revivals of native dress and local languages, Mays said. This alone would have qualified Gandhi for exalted status, his anticolonial politics notwithstanding: "A leader who teaches his people to love their native culture and who teaches them not to be ashamed of their heritage will take his place among the immortals."[121]

Gandhi taught fearlessness and exemplified it, inspiring even untouchables to cast out fear. He deeply understood and exemplified the power of sacrifice, inspiring millions to similarly claim their power through sacrifice. Mays moved swiftly and bluntly to the point: "The Negro people have much to learn from the Indians. The Indians have learned what we have not learned. They have learned how to sacrifice for a principle. They have learned how to sacrifice position, prestige, economic security and even life itself for what they consider a righteous and respectable cause. Thousands of them in recent times have gone to jail for their cause. Thousands of them have died for their cause."[122]

Elsewhere Mays said the same thing more elaborately, after promising "just a word about Mahatma Gandhi." The world was too close to Gandhi to appraise him adequately, Mays allowed. The outcome of Gandhi's campaign was unknown in 1937, and an Indian republic could only be imagined. Still, Mays felt certain that future historians would say, " 'He did more than any other man to dispel fear from the Indian mind and more than any other to make Indians proud to be Indians.' " Mays added, "That the non-violence campaign was a failure, no one has a right to say. All the evidence is not yet in. Time alone will write the final verdict. But the fact that Gandhi and his non-violent campaign have given the Indian masses a new conception of courage, no man can honestly deny. To discipline people to face death, to die, to go to jail for the cause without fear and without resorting to violence is an achievement of the first magnitude. And when an oppressed race ceases to be afraid, it is free. The cardinal principles of nonviolence are love and fearlessness."[123]

Mays relayed what Indian leaders told him at Mysore. Before Gandhi came along, "the average Indian was very much afraid of a Britisher. Many Indians would run and hide when a British officer appeared." After Gandhi came along, ordinary Indians stopped cowering and running. A missionary told Mays that Gandhi made the Indian masses proud of their language, creating in them "a respect for their culture and has instilled in them a feeling that, 'It's great to be an Indian!' " One did not have to wait for political outcomes and the distance of time to weigh the historical significance of Gandhi's achievement at this level, Mays contended. Gandhi was already an eternal figure for unleashing so much cultural pride.[124]

These articles stirred significant interest and comment. The *Norfolk Journal and Guide* published commentary for weeks, adding editorially that Mays was spot-on about African Americans needing to learn from Gandhi's example: "Death, intense suffering, self-denial, imprisonment—these hold no terror for the little brown man of Asia." The paper stressed that Gandhi's power was fundamentally spiritual, "where values are weighed in the scale of a community of interest rather than in the light of fleeting materialism." It piled on against current black American leaders, noting there were "no real Negro leaders in jail, none in exile, none upon whose head there is a price." This had to change, the editors pleaded; Mays was right on all counts, especially about sacrificial suffering: "People who have not learned how to suffer, how to subordinate self, how to be humble and charitable, can not appraise spiritual values, can not walk and talk with God and commune with his fellowmen and serve humanity. Until then, such people are doomed to oppression and poverty and servitude."[125]

The back and forth over Mays's prescription was still ensuing when he headed to the Oxford Conference on Life and Work in July. Organized by Scottish YMCA missionary and ecumenist J. H. Oldham, the Oxford conference built upon decades of international ecumenism and was a milestone in founding the World Council of Churches. Its chief forerunners were the Stockholm conference of 1925, led by Swedish Lutheran archbishop Nathan Söderblom, and the founding of the World Student Christian Federation in 1905, symbolized at Oxford by John R. Mott's role as presiding chair. Echoes of the Stockholm conference were strong at Oxford, but theology had changed. Early ecumenism spoke a language of interfaith dialogue and social gospel idealism that still resonated at Stockholm despite the ravages of World War I. To most delegates at Stockholm, the Barthian theologies coming out of Germany and Switzerland seemed strange, backward, despairing, otherworldly, and irrational. Ecumenical theology was northern European, liberal, and consumed with world peace. It contended that reason and faith went together, historical criticism made sense of the Bible, confessional traditions could be liberalized, and theology had to accommodate modern science and culture. Above all, it sought to build a global cosmopolitan peace backed by international law and the League of Nations. Barthian theology was a throwback to the Reformation emphasis on the wrath and grace of a transcendent God and the authority of Scripture. It spoke to the crisis of disillusionment caused by World War I, albeit strangely. By 1937, however, the crisis had worsened, there were many varieties of neo-Reformation theology, and some were very influential. Reinhold Niebuhr and Swiss Barthian theologian Emil Brunner made forceful speeches at the Oxford conference, and even England had Barthian theologians.[126]

Mays's teacher Edwin Aubrey shared the Chicago School's opposition to neo-Reformation dialecticism, but he recognized that it preached and sang to generations scarred by World War I, the Great Depression, and soon World War II. Aubrey tracked the flow of theological contention at Oxford with a critical ear. Many speakers, he noted, wrongly identified the church with the clergy, the headline speakers got too much time, and almost no women were present at Oxford and hardly any laity. There were no Roman Catholics or German Lutherans either. Niebuhr, in Aubrey's rendering, brandished his "unique brand of satire and penetrating paradox," plunging the audience "into despair down the torrent of his oratory." Then Niebuhr turned ministerial, assuring his audience that "the times of human despair are the creative epochs of the human spirit." Aubrey did not share Niebuhr's immense fondness for paradox, but he appreciated that Niebuhr's dramatic reliance on it spoke to the troubled mood of the time. Niebuhr said the ultimate question is not whether life has a meaning. The ultimate question is whether life's meaning is tragic: "Christianity is a faith which takes us through tragedy to beyond tragedy, by way of the cross to a victory in the cross."[127]

Aubrey dwelt on the irony that Oxford, like all ecumenical conferences of its kind, had no chance of agreeing on the nature and ministry of the church, as the idea of ecumenical conferences was to gather leaders of competing confessional traditions. A major session on the significance of the church featured an Orthodox canon lawyer, a Presbyterian missionary in China, and an American Baptist social gospel minister. The Orthodox theologian, Zankov of Sofia, described the church as a "divine-human house of unity," not a human institution, which filled the world with God's love awaiting Christ's second coming.

The missionary, William Daton, said the task of the church was to show that in Christ there was neither Aryan nor Semite. The social gospeler, Justin Wroe Nixon, said the church was a social institution bearing witness to a divine moral order of love, requiring a world-embracing fellowship. Aubrey rendered a blunt judgment: "This menu was calculated to produce ecclesiological indigestion."[128]

Ecumenism worked better in the social ethical arena, and Oxford was no exception, even with Barthians on hand to say that doctrine was more important. Although Aubrey played up in-house battles over competing theologies, the Oxford conference convened primarily for one reason, which Aubrey obscured: Ecumenical Christian leaders felt compelled to say something about the frightening rise of fascist movements in Germany, Austria, Spain, and Italy before these movements devoured Europe. Speakers described fascism as a form of political religion embraced by people lacking any compelling meaning or purpose in their lives. Fascism was very bad religion, filling the void left by declining state churches. The Oxford conference called for a renewal of strong, assertive Christian conviction as a bulwark against ascending anti-liberal, anti-Christian, antihuman fanaticisms. Specifically it condemned nationalistic chauvinism, racial bigotry, mistreatment of racial and ethnic minorities, and deification of the state. There was such a thing as legitimate love of one's homeland, the ecumenists said, just as there was such a thing as morally legitimate pride in one's racial identity. But nationalistic egotism was irredeemably evil and so was racial animosity. The ecumenists exhorted congregations "to show greater concern for the outcasts, the underprivileged, and the persecuted," undertaking "new, daring social experiments" on behalf of oppressed people and human solidarity. They declared that in Christian homes, congregations, and communities "there can be no place for discriminations of race or color." Aubrey looked forward to hearing the latter statement read in segregated American churches.[129]

Mays took no interest in the jousting over Barthian theologies, confessional theologies, and old-line ecumenism that he endured at Oxford. Thus he wrote nothing about any of it. To him, Oxford mattered because it forcefully condemned nationalistic idolatry and racial bigotry as irredeemably repugnant and anti-Christian. The ecumenical movement was becoming what it needed to be. Still, Mays rued the irony that international ecumenism pulled together just in time to be powerless to stop Germany, Italy, and Japan from plunging the world into war. He acknowledged that the fight between Communists and fascists in Spain would continue no matter what the ecumenical movement said about it. Even if the churches confessed their sins, the world would continue on its destructive path, and the churches didn't confess their sins anyway, except at the elite ecumenical level. Mays sensed that the way of the cross was about to become newly real to many Christians: "When the church truly repents, let us not deceive ourselves, it will be a *suffering* church."[130]

In 1938 Samuel H. Archer resigned as president of Morehouse and college officials pressed Thurman to take the job, but he begged off. Morehouse had declined drastically, and Thurman did not want to spend the rest of his career struggling to save a college, even his own. In 1929 Morehouse entered a formal affiliation with Atlanta University and Spelman College, which mostly benefitted Atlanta University and Spelman College. The Depression hit Morehouse hard; in 1933 Morehouse ceded its financial control to the university. By the time Morehouse trustees asked Mays to take the presidency, Morehouse was teetering on junior college status.

Between 1930 and 1940 the Atlanta University faculty increased by 220 percent, Spelman increased by 78 percent, and Morehouse decreased by 16 percent. Morehouse offered its presidency to Mays in May 1940, just as Winston Churchill took power in England. Both events made front-page news in Atlanta, three weeks before Mays accepted. He insisted on thinking it over, which was not easy to do after the offer made page one. There was some backlash that the Morehouse presidency should not go to a University of Chicago liberal. Morehouse alumnus D. D. Crawford, a Baptist minister, warned that Mays was "a notorious modernist. . . . He is a scientific Christian, not a religious one." If Mays took over, he would force upon the college "what they call a liberal religion." But only a few talked like that publicly, and Mays agreed to try to save Morehouse.[131]

There was something special about Morehouse. Mays had felt it when he taught there—the pride and poise of the Morehouse Man cultivated by John Hope. This factor loomed large in Mays's decision to return, although he soon puzzled that Morehouse pride did not generate much financial support from alumni. The college's endowment barely exceeded $1 million when Mays got there. Then Morehouse barely stayed in business during the war years, averaging 350 students per year, with a low of 272 in 1943–1944. Mays endured the war years by scrounging for back payments from graduated students, earning him a nickname that stuck, "Buck Benny." He instituted an early admission program for high school seniors that kept enrollment from collapsing, which brought fifteen-year-old Martin Luther King Jr. to Morehouse in 1944.[132]

Mays had friends in the FOR orbit that opposed mobilizing for war, notably Farmer and Bayard Rustin, but he supported America's intervention in World War II without hesitation, declaring in 1942, "Nothing interferes with our united effort to win the war." Black Americans were loyal Americans, he argued, and it was imperative for the causes of freedom, democracy, and racial justice that the fascist powers be defeated. On his trips to conference sites Mays had briefly visited Japan and Germany, where he reeled at the openly virulent racism of both societies. The United States was far more promising than that, he told audiences. Black Americans had a right to expect that fighting for their country would yield some respect and gratitude. This time, it had to be different. If black Americans served their country in another war, they had to be granted the overdue "fruits of democracy." Mays urged church leaders to say it clearly and persistently: "As long as the Gospel of Christ is preached in America and as long as we have a Constitution that guarantees equality of opportunity to all of its citizens and a supreme court to interpret the spirit of that Constitution, the Negro can accept whatever responsibility his country lays upon him."[133]

Mays presided with a regal dignity that became legendary in the Morehouse community. He improved the college's fiscal situation and raised its educational standards, welcoming a surge of students after the war, although he increased the endowment only modestly. Every Tuesday morning he spoke in chapel, usually on moral responsibility and the good society, often warning that African Americans were in danger of "forsaking and even belittling" the religious faith that sustained their ancestors. Theologically he preached a gospel-centered version of liberal theology, proclaiming that Christian light revealed "a spiritual and ethical order which governs nature and human relationships. But Christian light is not enough. We need the power of God unto salvation."[134]

Dignity and elegance fit together in Mays's case. He honed his elegance determinedly, dressing in impeccably tailored suits and colorful ties, sometimes favoring bowties. Russell Adams, a Morehouse alumnus, recalled that Mays "always dressed *Gentlemen's Quarterly* style, usually some version of pin-stripe gray suit accentuating his height and lack of body fat. He was camera ready." To two generations of Morehouse Men, Mays set the standard for how college presidents should look and how they should present themselves. The Mays effect was amplified by the contrast between his stylish bearing and the stories he told about his deprived youth. On one occasion Mays introduced one of his brothers to an audience at the college auditorium, saying his brother had sacrificed to help Mays stay in school. Adams recalled, "I remember going back to my room, Graves Hall, Room 452, and crying without restraint at the sheer nobility of the gesture."[135]

In 1944 the Federal Council of Churches elected Mays as its vice president, a breakthrough yielding a windfall of honors and publicity for Mays and a welcome spotlight on Morehouse. *Time* magazine informed readers that Mays was a "religious liberal" and a "quiet, earnest" spokesman for "education and patience as cures for racial discrimination." *Time* knew that Mays was closer to

Du Bois than to Washington, but it cast him in the Booker tradition anyway, puckishly adding that Mays was so tolerant "he has never once tried to proselytize his Methodist wife." Mays understood that assurances of this sort from the white establishment opened doors for him. He tried to raise money for Morehouse from the old Tuskegee network and Atlanta's business class, with little success. He found a secret revenue stream in *Gone With the Wind* author Margaret Mitchell, which must have given him heartburn. Meanwhile he accepted a deluge of honorary doctorates and led the fight for racial justice advocacy at the highest levels of the national and world ecumenical movements. His federal council vice presidency began at the 1944 assembly in Pittsburgh, where Methodist bishop G. Bromley Oxnam became president. In 1948 Mays participated in the founding convention of the World Council of Churches as a representative of the National Baptist Convention, USA, and from 1948 to 1954 he served on the Central Committee of the World Council of Churches.[136]

With steely persistence Mays used his standing in these organizations to press for racial justice. He had Johnson's attitude about doing so: not doing so was ethically unthinkable. Mays showed up to give a witness and to make a difference, always determined to advance the cause. Repeatedly he protested that racial discrimination was America's original sin and it remained America's greatest evil. Racial segregation was "a wicked thing" because it penalized a person "for being what God has made him and for conditions over which he has no control. Of all the sins, this is the greatest." It amazed him when people said that segregation could not be abolished by legislation. What were they talking about? Segregation was established by legislation and only legislation would get rid of it: "If men can legislate evil they can and should legislate good. The Christian must choose the weapons that he will use to advance the Kingdom of God."[137]

The color line intruded everywhere, turning Mays's life into a crusade against racism, in which he implored that race should not matter. Complete integration and the abolition of the color line were the only morally legitimate goals for a Christian to pursue in this area. The Bible gives no sanction whatsoever to racial discrimination, Mays stressed. Early Christianity wrestled with the exclusionary import of Jewish law for Christians, but the early church's debates over Judaizing versus Hellenizing had nothing to do with discrimination on the basis of race, and ultimately the universalist character of Jesus's message prevailed in early Christian practice: "From the beginning of his teaching, Jesus proclaimed a religion that was super-racial, super-national, super-cultural, and super-class. To deny the universalism in the gospel of Christ is to deny the very genius of the movement." This genius, Mays argued, is symbolized in Christian Scripture by the founding of the church at Pentecost, when people of fifteen nations drew together out of love for Jesus: "It is crystal clear that the Christian community began in what one might call an amalgamation of the spirit."[138]

Christianity never claimed that Christ belongs to some races more than others—until the modern era. Mays stressed that racist betrayal belongs exclusively to modern Christianity. He put it provocatively in a speech to the Second Assembly of the World Council of Churches in 1954, in Evanston, Illinois: "It is the modern church that again crucifies the body of Christ on a racial cross. Race and color did not count in the early existence of the Protestant church. It was when modern Western imperialism began to explore and exploit the colored peoples of Africa, Asia and America that the beginning of segregation and discrimination based on color and race was initiated. It was then that color was associated with 'inferiority' and white with 'superiority.' "[139]

Mays took pride in the World Council of Churches' condemnations of racial prejudice, and he took special pride, with two regrets, in the role he played in the Federal Council of Churches (which reorganized as the National Council of Churches in 1950). Will Alexander chaired a federal council commission on race on which Mays served from 1943 to 1946. Back in Atlanta, Alexander's Commission on Interracial Cooperation still did not oppose segregation, but Alexander guided the federal council to a historic repudiation of Jim Crow. The commission debated how far it should take social equality. Mays pushed for no exceptions, advocating the right to love romantically across racial lines. The most intimate right, however, was still the hardest one to demand. The commission supported interracial marriage until the penultimate draft of its resolution was presented to the federal council in 1946, when all references to it were eliminated. In his memoir Mays did not mention this issue, choosing not to besmirch the 1946 condemnation of segregation, the American ecumenical movement's finest moment to that point: "The Federal Council of the Churches of Christ in America hereby renounces the pattern of segregation in race relations as unnecessary and undesirable and a violation of the gospel of love and human brotherhood. Having taken this action, the Federal Council requests its constituent communion to do likewise. As proof of their sincerity in this renunciation, they will work for a non-segregated church and a non-segregated society."[140]

Mays coauthored this historic statement, which brought together the black and white Protestant establishments. Like many black Baptist leaders, only more so, Mays took advantage of the American Baptist Convention's policy of permitting dual memberships; his memberships in the National Baptist Convention and American Baptist Convention strengthened his hand as a player in the ecumenical movement. But Mays deeply regretted that statements by church leaders had little effect and that congregations in the white and black denominations triggered little activism at the local level. He said it repeatedly and angrily: The power of courage was lacking. American Christianity at the elite level issued declarations against racial injustice, but aside from a smattering of congregations little change took place at the local level. Mays focused on two groups: white ministers who feared getting fired and black ministers who feared that eliminating segregation would diminish their congregations. He implored both groups to stir up some courage: "Segregation is the great scandal in the church, especially in the United States and South Africa. We have plenty of light on the subject, but like Pilate of old we lack the power to act on the light we have." In America, he judged, as in South Africa, "social custom makes cowards of most Christians and I fear of the majority of ministers."[141]

In 1950, thirty-two years after Rauschenbusch died and eighteen years after Reinhold Niebuhr blasted the social gospel in *Moral Man and Immoral Society*, Mays accentuated his enduring commitment to the social gospel by publishing a Rauschenbusch reader. It was too soon to let go of Rauschenbusch and his dream of a cooperative commonwealth, Mays believed. Niebuhr had rightly overthrown the genteel optimism of social gospel liberalism, but Rauschenbusch powerfully emphasized sin and the kingdom of evil. The social gospel would have been nothing without its emphasis on social sin. More important, to Mays, Rauschenbusch roared for the transformation of social structures to achieve a radical, fully realized democracy. Whatever might have been wrong with the social gospel during its heyday, it rightly tried to democratize American society, politics, and economics. Dismissing that project as an idealistic overreach was not an option for the black social gospel. The democratizing work of the social gospel had barely begun and was still the point. Thus Mays continued to employ the terms "Christianize" and "democratize" interchangeably, in Rauschenbusch's fashion. American society needed to replace its modicum of Christianity and democracy with the real things. Realists counseled that social change occurred slowly and civil rights proponents had to be patient. Mays replied defiantly that profound social changes were possible within a single generation: "If Germany through brutal means can build a kingdom of evil in one decade and if Russia, through brutal processes, construct a new order in two decades, we can democratize and Christianize America in one generation."[142]

This issue, along with the Cold War, consumed Mays's attention in the late 1940s and 1950s. He wrote a weekly column, "My View," in the nationally syndicated *Pittsburgh Courier*, persistently denouncing segregation and Cold War militarism. Niebuhr, though a supporter of racial integration, told civil rights advocates to proceed slowly, advising Democratic presidential candidate Adlai Stevenson to play down the integration issue. In the late 1940s he also became a leading Cold War apologist. Mays disputed Niebuhr vehemently on both issues, protesting that most of the world's people were poor, nonwhite, and exploited by colonial powers. Telling them to choose sides in the Cold War was repugnant. Moreover, Communists were prominent in civil rights activism; the FBI routinely tagged white civil rights activists as Communists. In 1949 Mays signed a public letter asking President Truman to negotiate with the Soviet Union instead of forming NATO. Repeatedly he blasted anti-Communist extremism, defending the rights of people who got in trouble for criticizing the U.S. government and/or sympathizing with the Communist Party, such as singer and actor Paul Robeson.[143]

Since Mays had never flirted with Communist ideology, he felt he had nothing to prove in this area. He could oppose Cold War militancy without fearing McCarthy-like probes into his past. He believed in democracy and freedom, things that Communists and anti-Communist extremists put at risk. Trying to imagine a different postwar world, Mays thought back to his meeting with Gandhi. More than ever Mays appreciated Gandhi's insistence that nonviolence requires a special valor. Violence is always self-defeating, nonviolence breaks the vicious spiral of hatred and revenge, and nonviolent activists had to be fearless. Reflecting on these maxims in the post–World War II context, Mays became more deeply convinced that Gandhian nonviolence was the right path: "If one refuses to use violence out of fear, it is not only not nonviolence but the person is a coward. It would be nobler to use violence and fight it out to the death than to practice the non-use of force because of fear."[144]

Meanwhile Mays closely tracked the *Brown* case. It started with the NAACP chapter of Topeka, Kansas, and its named plaintiff, welder and part-time pastor Oliver Brown, in a class action suit filed in 1951. Thirteen plaintiffs in the Topeka case appealed to the local school district to reverse its policy of racial segregation, and the district court ruled in favor of the Board of Education, citing *Plessy v. Ferguson*. By 1953 the *Brown* case lumped five cases sponsored by the NAACP in Kansas, South Carolina, Virginia, Washington, DC, and Delaware, a historic challenge to *Plessy*. The Supreme Court heard the case in 1953 but put aside the issue, chiefly because the majority wanted a unanimous verdict and Chief Justice Fred Vinson stood in the way. Vinson died in September, President Eisenhower appointed Earl Warren as chief justice, and the *Brown* decision came down on May 17, 1954. Mays anticipated the ruling with a hopeful attitude. A favorable decision would be enormously important, he wrote. He tried to be optimistic that it would be accepted, writing in February 1954, "I suppose I have more faith in my native South than most Southerners. If the United States Supreme Court rules against segregation in public schools, I believe the Southern people will meet the challenge with dignity, poise, and calm."[145]

That was emphatically not to be. The court overthrew *Plessy* by nine to zero, White Citizens' Councils sprang up throughout the South, and political leaders defied the Supreme Court. Mays urged that a precious moment had arrived, one lacking precedent for African Americans since Reconstruction. Now was the moment for blacks to stand up for their personal dignity. Mays stressed that *Brown* applied to interstate transportation, not only to schools. To carry out the *Brown* decision, black Americans had to demand their rights on trains and buses: "I know that many Negroes are afraid to protest. Some lack poise and cannot protest without blowing up; others are like the blind mule. But those who are blessed with the ability to raise questions calmly without emotional display should protest more." He did not expect grand drama or a social explosion: "I am not fighting to be with anybody. I just want to be human and be allowed to walk the earth with dignity."[146]

He did not see the explosion coming, but the tipping point had already been reached, yielding the eruption that made King famous. Mays supported and praised King as soon as it happened, helping him withstand the world-historical drama that overtook his life. Mays felt he had given himself more and more fully to his ideals. Now he watched his greatest accomplishment bear fruit, not having realized what it had been. For all his achievements elsewhere, Mays had done his greatest work in the Morehouse chapel, from 1944 to 1948. King's father, Daddy King, was a member of Morehouse's Board of Trustees, and King was young and unready for college, so he got extra attention from Mays. Every Tuesday King absorbed Mays's chapel addresses, often taking notes. Mays was a spellbinder, always speaking in a high style while rocking back and forth, which hypnotized his audiences. He once told Lawrence Carter that he unconsciously picked up the rocking technique while studying black preachers for *The Negro's Church*. King would linger afterward to discuss what Mays had said. Always he was respectful; sometimes he had a probing question to ask; sometimes he dared to disagree. A friendship developed between the president and student; Mays later recalled it was strengthened "by visits in his home and by fairly frequent informal chats on the campus and in my office."[147]

King admired Mays's blend of dignity, scholarship, racial pride, theological liberalism, and passion for social justice. From an early age King knew that gospel religion, civil rights militancy, public intellectualism, and social justice activism could fold together, because he knew Mays. By the time King graduated in 1948 at the age of nineteen, he wanted to be like Mays. Seven years later, when movement leadership was thrust upon him and his life exploded, King had to instantly come up with the persona of a mature, seasoned, centered, movement leader. He pulled it off by imitating Mays. For the rest of his life King called Mays his spiritual mentor.

LOOKING FOR THE AMERICAN GANDHI

For thirty years "We need a Gandhi" was a staple of the black protest tradition, declared and debated in the *Pittsburgh Courier, Chicago Defender, Crisis,* and other venues. If Gandhi could bring the British Empire to its knees with nonviolent civil disobedience, why couldn't African Americans do something similar in America? James Farmer, cofounding the Congress of Racial Equality (CORE) in April 1942, took the question very seriously and personally. But Farmer was barely employed by FOR and in no position to achieve Gandhi status. For nearly twenty years, until King shot into prominence, the person journalists, intellectuals, and activists usually nominated for the American Gandhi role was Thurman, if only he would step up to it.[148]

The *Pittsburgh Courier* put it bluntly in August 1942. Thurman had muted his pacifist voice after America entered the war, which was fine with the *Courier,* since blacks had enough trouble without opposing the war and Thurman was indispensable to the cause of civil rights. The *Courier* noted that Thurman was famous on the activist lecture circuit but not well known to the general public. He was a mystic, but not lacking "a practical turn of mind," especially about politics. He had a Gandhi-like brilliance, with Gandhi-like spiritual qualities. In short, Thurman was "one of the few black men in this country around whom a great, conscious movement of Negroes could be built, not unlike the great Indian movement with which Gandhi and [Congress Party leader Jawaharlal] Nehru are associated."[149]

But Thurman disappointed the many who held movement ambitions for him. He heard it through the 1940s and early 1950s, when the tone was usually plaintive or demanding. He heard it after the civil rights movement erupted, when the tone was often accusatory. Some said he retreated to self-indulgent mysticism. Some said he dishonored African American experience by dwelling on the unity of human experience. Then the civil rights movement took off, and Thurman was accused of sitting on the sidelines while black Americans put their bodies on the line for justice.

He had a favorite story on this theme, which he told to *Ebony* senior editor Lerone Bennett. In Thurman's telling, Reinhold Niebuhr had barely mentioned Thurman's name at a speaking engagement at Howard when a student in the audience interrupted to say, "I'm glad you mentioned that man. He is the great betrayer of us all. We were sure that he had the makings of a Moses and then he turned mystic on us." Cultural critic Benita Eisler, reviewing Thurman's autobiography, was similarly scathing: "Not since the Abolitionist movement had so many American clergymen moved down from their pulpits and into the trenches of social protest and reform. One wants to know, simply, why Thurman felt so little impulse to join them." In 1978, reflecting on his life, Thurman gave a capsule version of his usual reply: "I have never considered myself any kind of leader. I'm not a movement man. It's not my way. I work at giving witness in the external aspect of my life to my experience of the truth. That's my way—the way the grain in my wood moves." Thurman's most renowned saying was a variation on this theme: "Don't ask what the world needs. Ask what makes you come alive, and go do it. Because what the world needs is people who have come alive."[150]

He did not play an active role in the civil rights eruption of the 1950s for the same reasons that he held back before it. He was not a movement person. He was temperamentally reserved and a loner, he disliked politics and political strategizing, and his spirituality had a decidedly inward pull. Thurman, however, created leadership expectations in the first place by lecturing constantly. He hit the lecture circuit extremely hard in the mid-1930s. In the late 1930s he spoke even more, cramming his calendar with commitments. Sometimes he spoke several times per day in different cities. He spent so much time lecturing that Johnson worried he had veered out of control.

Thurman relied on trains, having never learned to drive. He shared with Johnson a rare ease in speaking to white audiences and a gift for doing it. Johnson, like King, used different styles with black and white audiences, although in his later career Johnson worked at reducing the difference. Thurman was the same everywhere. He did not employ different rhetorical styles with black and white audiences. He used the same allusive, eloquent, elevated, dense, poetic, and intimate style wherever he spoke. He had a gift for making listeners feel he was speaking directly to them, and he loved to give speeches. Thurman needed a lot of time to himself, and thus he craved the down time he experienced on trains, where he pored over train schedules.

The more his reputation grew, the more he was asked to address white audiences about race. Nearly always he said no. Sometimes he explained that he was not a propagandist or sociologist. To Thurman, it was pointless to scold whites about racism, and winning the sympathy or pity of a white audience was even worse. Prone to mood swings and depression, he fought off both during the war years. In 1940 A. J. Muste asked Thurman to serve as a vice-chair of FOR. Thurman stewed for ten days before accepting: "I know that war is not only futile but is thoroughly and completely evil and diabolical." He added that he felt obligated to help black Americans serving in the military. Thus "what my duty is as a Christian is sometimes very obscure." After America intervened Thurman registered for the draft as a conscientious objector and retained his membership in FOR but never publicly opposed the war.[151]

Like Mays, Thurman made a major contribution to the civil rights movement by doing his day job, teaching students at Howard, notably Farmer. He also made a major contribution on the lecture circuit, but Thurman gave that up in 1944 to launch a new kind of Christian ministry. For years he dreamed of a progressive interracial Christianity espousing a universal religion of Spirit, nonviolence, and what was then called "inter-culturalism." Writing a book about it would not have been enough. As it was, Thurman still had not published a book in 1944, and he had tired of Howard. The dream was to launch an interracial community based on Thurman's kind of religion. The closest approximation to it was Fellowship Church in Philadelphia, an interracial group sponsored by the Society of Friends meeting once per month, where Thurman sometimes preached. He promised to become the group's minister if it developed into an every-week religious community. But that didn't happen, and in October 1943 Muste told Thurman that a Gandhian cooperative in San Francisco led by their mutual friend Muriel Lester was seeking to build an interracial religious congregation at a building owned by the Presbyterian Church.

Muriel Lester was a white English pacifist and social reformer who worked for the International FOR and accompanied Gandhi on his anti-untouchability tour in 1934. Her autobiographical book *It Occurred to Me* (1937) was an antiwar classic, and her group in San Francisco had already selected a white co-pastor when Muste contacted Thurman. Alfred Fisk, a white Socialist Presbyterian minister and philosophy professor, agreed to serve as co-pastor. Now the group wanted a black co-pastor for what became the Church for the Fellowship of All Peoples, otherwise called Fellowship Church.[152]

Thurman and Fisk conferred, and Thurman took a leave of absence to pursue his dream. Johnson, Mays, Bailey Thurman, and others close to Thurman were distraught, hoping he would get over it. At Rankin Chapel Thurman preached to crowds numbering up to five hundred. Fellowship Church, holding its first service in December 1943, before Thurman got there, drew a crowd of sixty-six. It averaged about forty the following year, even after Thurman got there in July. How could that be a good move? Thurman replied that building some-thing new that he believed in meant everything to him. He threw himself wholly into Fellowship Church, severed its Presbyterian connection in 1945 to ensure its interracial standing, and resigned from Howard in 1946, shortly before Fisk resigned as co-pastor. Thurman reveled in combining aspects of liturgical, Quaker, liberal Protestant, and black church traditions. He built a meditation room containing a statue of the Buddha, a painting of Gandhi (by Thurman), and sacred texts of Hindu, Buddhist, Muslim, and other faiths. He thrived in church ministry, greatly reducing his outside lecturing; by the early 1950s Fellowship Church had an average weekly attendance of two hundred.[153]

To Thurman, the religion of Jesus and the inward presence of God's illumi-nating Spirit were enough. Though inclined to emphasize his positive religion, he believed that organized Christianity misrepresented Jesus and thus betrayed the hope of the disinherited. Jesus was the exemplar and medium of God's love and spiritual power, and Christianity did not own Jesus. Cutting back on the lecture circuit gave Thurman more time to write, an ambition he had repressed during his years of enthralling lecture crowds. His first book was his master-piece, *Jesus and the Disinherited* (1949). It had gestated for twenty years, growing out of a course Thurman taught at Spelman on the life of Jesus. His purpose was to explicate "the significance of the religion of Jesus to people who stand with their backs against the wall." Like the gospel, Thurman had a special concern for the poor and oppressed. He also sought to rescue readers from bad forms of Christianity: "For years it has been a part of my own quest so to under-stand the religion of Jesus that interest in his way of life could be developed and sustained by intelligent men and women who were at the same time deeply victimized by the Christian Church's betrayal of his faith."[154]

Thurman took little interest in formal theology and no interest in theological orthodoxy. He put it bluntly: "I belong to a generation that finds very little that is meaningful or intelligent in the teachings of the Church concerning Jesus Christ." For example, traditional atonement theory was not saving for oppressed people: "I do not ignore the theological and metaphysical interpretation of the Christian doctrine of salvation. But the underprivileged everywhere have long since abandoned any hope that this type of salvation deals with the crucial issues by which their days are turned into despair without consolation." Thurman wanted nothing to do with the kind of Christianity that espoused "essentially an other-worldly religion."[155]

Yet the spirit of Jesus was precious to him, "so perfect a flower from the brooding spirit of God." Christianity is true as the religion of Jesus and the claiming of God's inward spiritual presence, Thurman contended. The blending of the ethical and spiritual in Christianity is intrinsic to its true character. Thurman emphasized the ethic of "love your enemies" and thus, for African Americans, the ethical and spiritual imperative of finding a way to love their white oppressors.[156]

Thurman looked hate in the eye. He noted that hate burned hotter at some times than others, but "in season and out of season," oppressed people were always intimately acquainted with hate as its victims. In wartime, he wrote, hatred is always in season. Hate becomes respectable as an effect of war psychology and propaganda, "even though it has to masquerade often under the guise of patriotism." Thurman noted that hostility toward blacks and other nonwhite groups spiked after America entered World War II, "especially in trains and other public conveyances." Shortly after Japan attacked Pearl Harbor, a Chicago taxi driver exclaimed to Thurman, "Who do they think they are? Those little yellow dogs think they can do that to white men and get away with it!" The uninhibited language was revealing to Thurman. War hatred apparently eliminated normal restraints on common bigotry. Racism was commonplace all the time, but war gave social license and even a patina of respectability to racist feelings that usually stayed beneath the surface.[157]

His memoir, reflecting on the ravages of racism, told a story about his mother, Alice, who came to live with her son in San Francisco near the end of her life. The Church for the Fellowship of All Peoples was bewildering to her. She could not fathom and did not like its race-mixing. She trusted her son and tried to be gracious to his guests, but it greatly disturbed her to have to deal with whites in his home and church. In her last days, confined to Stanford Hospital, Alice begged Thurman to take her home. She was terrified at being surrounded by "Buckra," as she called white people: "The first chance they get, you don't know what they will do to you. I'm scared to go to sleep at night, and you just have to take me out of this place." Thurman took his mother to his home to die in peace.[158]

Jesus and the Disinherited told a similar story about younger victims of racial violence. Seated in a Jim Crow car at a railway station in Texas, Thurman overheard a teenaged black girl fantasize about two younger white girls who were skating toward the train. The black girl told a friend she would love to see the white girls fall and splatter their brains across the pavement. Thurman shook with sadness and fright: "I looked at them. Through what torture chambers had they come—torture chambers that had so attacked the grounds of humanness in them that there was nothing capable of calling forth any appreciation or understanding of white persons?"[159]

Jesus and the Disinherited had chapters on Jesus, fear, deception, hate, and love. The chapter on love circled back to the opening chapter on the religion of

Jesus: "The religion of Jesus says to the disinherited, 'Love your enemy. Take the initiative in seeking ways by which you can have the experience of a common sharing of mutual worth and value. It may be hazardous, but you must do it.' " Thurman acknowledged that racial oppression made it very difficult for blacks to view whites as belonging to a common humanity with them: "The fact that a particular individual is white, and therefore may be regarded in some overall sense as the racial enemy, must be faced; and opportunity must be provided, found, or created for freeing such an individual from his 'white necessity.' "[160]

Hatred met by hatred will never free the oppressor from his or her bondage to sin. Thurman urged that only the enemy-loving spirit exemplified by Jesus could do that. *Jesus and the Disinherited* was slow to find an audience, but it found one after the civil rights movement got rolling, providing inspiration for King and many others. Many readers, including King, read the book for clues about how they should appropriate Niebuhrian criticism. Thurman and Reinhold Niebuhr were friends, sharing social justice commitments and an easy camaraderie, and Thurman appreciated Niebuhr's attacks on the moral-istic sanctimony of the Protestant establishment. But Niebuhr ridiculed liberal ministers for conflating the way of Jesus with the way of Gandhi. According to Niebuhr, Jesus taught a vertical ethic of love perfectionism that was heedless of pragmatic consequences and had nothing to do with solving sociopolitical problems. Jesus did not teach that returning evil with the truth-force of love would save the world. Moreover, Gandhian resistance was always coercive, despite what Gandhians said, which in some ways made it less worthy of respect than the self-interested forms generated by power politics. Thurman struggled with these aspects of Niebuhr's critique. He appreciated that Niebuhr advised black Americans to use the boycott and sit-in method, and he accepted that it was coercive; Thurman was not trying to win a prize for moral innocence. He rejected Niebuhr's thesis, however, that the love ethic made Jesus's teaching irrelevant to the problems of politics and society. Thurman believed in the transformative moral power of love divine in every realm of society. The point of social ethics was to apply the love ethic everywhere, including the social realm, unleashing the saving force of regenerated unselfishness.[161]

Thurman insisted that the difference between holding due regard for the well-being of others and lacking it is central to everything else in Christian ethics. He cited Anglican moral theologian Kenneth Kirk on this theme, contending that only unselfish service to others is redeeming or serves any morally worthy cause: "Disinterested service is a kind of service in which the person served is not a means to some end in which he does not share and participate directly." The religion of Jesus, Thurman argued, does not call people to base their actions toward others on their personal or material interests. It calls people to relieve human suffering out of love for others and to build structures of social justice so all people may be freed from the shackles of hatred, torment, oppression, and selfishness. Thurman taught that it helps to be mystical; otherwise the full import of spiritual transformation cannot be grasped: "It is in this latter sense that we come upon the mandatory *raison d'etre* of the mystic's interest in social change and in social action." Mysticism is about the unity of all things—the realization that all life is one. Human beings are meant to participate in the transformation of all being into the summum bonum, the vision of God: "The mystic is forced to deal with social relations because, in his effort to achieve the good, he finds that he must be responsive to human need by which he is surrounded, particularly the kind of human need in which sufferers are victims of circumstances over which, as individuals, they have no control."[162]

Thurman's later books were mystical in that vein, evincing an interreligious spirituality lacking the gritty particularity of *Jesus and the Disinherited*. His first book had stewed in him for twenty years. His later books reflected his later inter-religious turn while still invoking the religion of Jesus. He reasoned that some people come to God through nature, others find their way to God through the witness of Spirit-filled people, and whoever seeks God "with all of his heart will someday on his way meet Jesus." Like Jones, Thurman taught that the way of Jesus is the way of true religion: living in God's presence "with renewed minds and chastened spirits." Also like Jones, but more emphatically, Thurman opened the door to a religion of spirit dispensing with any need to make this confession. To idealize only the spiritual life and religion of Jesus was to cut loose from having to believe anything in particular about Jesus to know God fully. To Thurman, as to Jones, the touchstone was the experience of divinity that produces moral fruit; Jesus was an exemplar of this spiritual ideal. What mattered was "to focus the mind and the heart upon God as the Eternal Source and Goal of Life."[163]

Everything rested upon the existence and recognition of the Spirit of God as "the unifying principle of all life." The mission of the church is to be an exemplar of Spirit-filled community and build the commonwealth of God. To know the inner presence of God's Spirit is to know one's spiritual unity with all creatures and creation, as Jesus showed: "To be in unity with the Spirit is to be in unity with one's fellows." It followed that alienation from other people is alienation from God's Spirit: "When I have lost harmony with another, my whole life is thrown out of tune. For the sake of my unity with God, I keep working on my relations with my fellows. This is ever the insistence of all ethical religion."[164]

Thurman preached this gospel at Fellowship Church until 1953. He wanted the congregation to be a model for inclusive and progressive religion and a catalyst for an interracial church movement. He made an impressive beginning toward the former goal, although Fellowship Church was predominately middle-class, with a white majority. Thurman kept saying the congregation needed to reach beyond its middle-class base, but it never did, and it did not catalyze a national interracial church movement, although it spawned a few West Coast interracial congregations. Cities became even more segregated in the 1950s, with blacks and whites living at greater distances from each other. White ministers who made an issue of racial justice were often fired, and others tried and failed to integrate their congregations. Thurman's Fellowship Church stood out for trying, in his case on a postconfessional model. White Protestant congregations usually did not see why they should outgrow their ethnic families of origin. Even when they saw the need, they made weak or clueless attempts to do it. Moreover, black congregations were not willing to give up what they had to pursue a Thurman-like interracial dream.

Thurman and Mays believed that segregated black churches were obstacles to the civil rights movement and that racial justice, in the churches, began with abolishing the color line. They also believed that racially segregated congregations would not last. Both said it forcefully, condemning segregation in the churches as a betrayal of the gospel. After Montgomery propelled black churches into the movement Mays insisted there would be no black churches or white churches by the end of the century. Racial integration would abolish segregated Christianity. This vision of the integrated church brought out Mays's lyrical voice. The process of desegregation, he claimed in 1964, was unstoppable: "So the churches will have no choice; they will follow. Powerful laymen, supporting their minister in his desire to live as well as preach the gospel, will free his hands. The guilt that besets the minister's conscience because he preaches what he cannot practice will be washed away, and there will be peace in his soul."[165]

That was just the beginning; real integration was the payoff: "Within his heart every church member will feel better, for his conscience will no longer trouble him. Negroes will worship in and join white churches. White people will worship in and join Negro churches. How many? It doesn't matter! God's people will be free to worship God anywhere they choose." In the South, Mays envisioned, black ministers would be invited to speak to white Christians, just as white pastors had long been welcome to preach in black churches. Some congregations would have black and white co-pastors. "In that day Negro and white Christians will worship together, sing together, pray together, share each other's joys and sorrows. And none shall be afraid. We will then know that our greatest fears are fears of things that never happen. And God will bless us."[166]

That was Thurman's goal and expectation at Fellowship Church. Like Mays, he averred that the rich and redemptive history of the black church had to be sustained, in some way, in the integrated church that was coming. This assurance was vague and parenthetical, always overshadowed by Thurman's insistence that the next Christianity had to be interracial, interreligious, multicultural, and universalistic. In 1959, six years after he left Fellowship Church to become dean of Marsh Chapel at Boston University, Thurman published a book about Fellowship Church, *Footprints of a Dream.* He ended the book by calling for "a common meeting place in which there would be no Negro church and no white church, but the church of God—that is the task we must work to finish."[167]

But Thurman and Mays were wrong about the political agency of black churches and wrong about the imminent triumph of racially integrated Christianity. Though only a minority of black congregations joined the civil rights struggle in the 1950s, the ones that did made the revolution possible. Congregations from black denominations that were said to be too provincial, otherworldly, and inward-looking to change society rallied to the cause of racial justice. Johnson, Mays, and Thurman took justified pride in having started something. Sometimes they registered grateful surprise at what they had wrought. Usually they were gracious about being surpassed. All three were thrilled by King's ascendance and their connections to him. Mays said modestly that King "did as much for me, if not more, than I did for him." Though Mays was a pillar of the black establishment in Atlanta that wanted no SCLC disruption in Atlanta, he played a crucial role in legitimizing King in Atlanta, where SCLC was headquartered.[168]

Thurman finished his career as a chapel dean and professor of spiritual disciplines at Boston University, where he had a hugely successful ministry, drawing overflow crowds to Marsh Chapel, and where he befriended King during King's doctoral studies. His sermons expounded a mystical vision of spiritual unity and an ethical-spiritual commitment to nonviolence, urging that all forms of violence, oppression, and prejudice offend against the divine good. Thurman repeated Jones's maxim that the best kind of prayer is prayed out of sheer love and enjoyment of God, which Thurman called "the overflowing of the heart as an act of grace toward God." To awaken to the unifying divine presence within is to be held in graceful adoration. Thurman explained, "It is the sheer joy in thanksgiving that God is God and the soul is privileged and blessed with the overwhelming consciousness of this." Remarking on Jones's influence on him, Thurman recalled, "He gave to me confidence in the insight that the religion of the inner life could deal with the empirical experience of man without retreating from the demands of such experience."[169]

True religion is grounded in the mystical experience of God's presence, and it makes no compromise with violence or oppression. Religious truth is never conferred by outside authority, for religions are true only to the extent that they teach and practice universal love. Contrary to Niebuhr, who used the word "perfectionist" as an epithet, Thurman insisted that the perfectionist principle defines true religion. The very point of true religion is to be transformed by love divine. It is natural to kill one's enemies, but true religion is a call to transformed existence: "The insistence here is that the individual is enjoined to move from the natural impulse to the level of deliberate intent. One has to bring to the center of his focus a desire to love even one's enemy."[170]

Though Niebuhr said that Christian Gandhians were naïve, sentimental, and usually stupid, he did not name Thurman, and not only on account of friendship. To Niebuhr, shredding white social gospel idealism was morally imperative in the 1930s because it promoted pacifism in the mainline churches and thus stood in the way of justice and security. But Niebuhr said that Gandhian methods were aptly suited to help black Americans make gains for justice in their distinct situation. He put it hopefully, with a patronizing streak, in 1932, suggesting that the "aggressiveness of the new and young Negro" might be fused with the "patience and forbearance of the old Negro" to strip the "former of its vindictiveness and the latter of its lethargy."[171]

Moreover, the sentimentality issue played out very differently. Niebuhr excoriated white idealists as sentimental types, but Thurman knew the ravages of hatred and violence more intimately than Niebuhr, which Niebuhr realized. Thurman, despite respecting Niebuhr greatly, judged that Niebuhr ruled out the most important thing: the possibility of spiritual transformation. Thurman conceded no exceptions to the universality of the good. The hope of the disinherited is to be included in the flourishing of democracy and the saving work of God's Spirit. If moral truth is not universal, it is neither moral nor true. The disinherited, while coping with their oppression, needed to claim their rights without reproducing the world's mendacity and hatred.

Thurman and Mays had a similar experience of giving themselves more fully to their ideals with age, and they said the same thing about how it happened: They grew in their sense of the presence of God. They would not have believed that the good prevails had they not believed that a really existing God wills the good. Mays warned that whenever human beings violate God's moral laws they suffer for it: "Every effort that men have made to build a nation or a civilization on injustice and exploitation has led to the fall of that nation or civilization." Thurman put it positively: "The disinherited will know for themselves that there is a Spirit at work in life and in the hearts of men which is committed to overcoming the world. It is universal, knowing no age, no race, no culture, and no condition of men."[172]

King echoed these words in his sensational close to the speech that launched him as a movement leader, on December 4, 1955. He had heard Thurman speak many times. He had consulted with Thurman about his career options and considered taking over at Fellowship Church. He pored over Thurman's books, especially *Jesus and the Disinherited* and *Footprints of a Dream.* In his early ministry King quoted or borrowed from Thurman numerous times, notably in his sermons "A Religion of Doing," "Overcoming an Inferiority Complex," and "Living Under the Tensions of Modern Life." After King broke through in Montgomery Thurman advised him behind the scenes, usually about self-care or leadership. On the road, campaigning to break white supremacy, King carried a copy of *Jesus and the Disinherited.* American Christianity has no greater legacy than what King got from Thurman and Mays.[173]

4

PROTEST POLITICS AND POWER POLITICS

The eruption of social activist black Christianity was hard to see coming. Those who dedicated themselves to it and laid the groundwork for it did not see it coming; Mordecai Johnson was an exception. The most visible sign of its possibility, Adam Clayton Powell Jr., contributed more to the black social gospel vision of justice than any figure of the 1940s and early 1950s. To say it more expansively, for twenty years he did more for the cause of civil rights than anyone, and he remained a major player after he was surpassed. But he had trouble welcoming the movement that came, and he had a troubled legacy on other counts.

Powell was born into the black social gospel, grew up amid its development, succeeded his father at Abyssinian Baptist Church, and took the path of electoral politics. He was handed a powerful platform by his father and made the most of it, surpassing nearly every social gospel leader as a public figure. He became a brilliant protest leader and an accomplished congressional lawmaker—two things that no one else of his time combined. Powell spent his entire life in the limelight, and he struggled with the contradictions of his privilege and marginalization, though he gave the appearance of never struggling with anything.

As a preacher Powell understood the power of story, especially his own. As a raconteur he loved drama and hyperbole, so many of his stories were exaggerated, and some were completely made up. Powell's fictionalizing played a role in the troubled side of his legacy, and he was habitually unreflective about things he did not want to think about. But he was keenly perceptive about human beings. He understood what he owed to his remarkable father, the many women in his life, and Abyssinian Church. Throughout his career Powell made poignant asides about growing up as the son of America's most famous black preacher, and he assured audiences that he and his father had the same "first love": Abyssinian Baptist Church.

Adam Clayton Powell Sr., however, was married to Abyssinian Church. Powell noted that his father spurned opportunities to pursue other career options, sticking with his bride and first love and giving himself to it. Powell Senior was accomplished, charismatic, vain, extroverted, righteous, and joyous. To grow up in his family was to experience "the sheer joy of living that he possessed, the secret of which we were struggling to find."[1]

The secret, Powell believed, was the kingdom of God. Powell Senior believed that the mere act of seeking the kingdom brought all things needed to the seeker. Certainly that was his experience. Powell Senior survived desperate poverty after the Civil War to become a beloved minister and civil rights leader. Very little about his family background is certain, but he was born to Sally Dunning, a free woman with African, Choctaw, and German heritages, near the end of the Civil War. She was given refuge during her pregnancy by a former slave of Virginia planter Llewellyn Powell, Anthony Dunn. Dunn had a letter "P" branded on his back, he took in many homeless people, he served as a church deacon, and in 1867 he married Dunning and accepted the role of stepfather to Powell Senior.[2]

Powell Senior had little to say about his mother and stepfather, and what he told his son and daughter for many years, out of love for all concerned, was not true: that Anthony Dunn was their grandfather. Powell learned the truth about Dunn, a man he met only once, only after Dunn's death. To Powell, however, Dunn became the key to the meaning of his life. Dunn, a human being branded in the manner of cattle, gave refuge to a woman bearing the child of the very slaver who had owned and burned him. Dunn was a Jesus figure "who forgave while the wound of the flesh and the wound of memory were yet warm." When Powell preached about the way of Jesus, he thought of Dunn suffering, forgiving, and giving refuge. Often he told the story of meeting Dunn at the age of ten, standing on a chair to trace down his back "that P of seared human flesh." When Powell described kingdom religion, he thought of his step-grandfather and father: "I am another witness that when a man seeks a kingdom on earth and puts that trust into his life, loves the people of the earth, friend and foe, black and white, the beautiful and the ugly, even if in that loving he sometimes is unable to have the time to love an individual, then 'All things will be added unto him.'"[3]

Adam Clayton Powell Jr. was a complicated case in everything he espoused and took up. He was both enabled and brought down by his immense self-confidence, charm, arrogance, brilliance, and loner style. And his legacy is enormous.

INHERITING THE BLACK SOCIAL GOSPEL

Powell was born in New Haven, Connecticut, in 1908, six months before his family moved to Abyssinian Church in New York City, at the time located on Fortieth Street in midtown Manhattan. Powell's mother, Mattie, was quiet, shy, elegant, refined, and of mixed black and German descent on both sides of her family; his sister, Blanche, ten years older than Powell, had blue eyes and blond hair; and both women doted on him. They pampered Powell, curled his blond hair, dressed him in Little Lord Fauntleroy suits and gondolier hats, and often dressed him as a girl, confusing passersby. Powell later recalled, "Between the two of them I was spoiled, utterly and completely. . . . Women have always spoiled me." A longtime family servant, Josephine, plus a bevy of Abyssinian churchwomen, added to the spoiling. Powell Senior railed against the coddling of his only son, but he was outnumbered at home and usually not there. At the age of nearly six, Powell fell ill with a lung ailment. For six years he was carried from place to place, requiring constant care, which heightened feminine pampering. Restricted from playing with fellow children, he had to overcome a sissy image when he tried. By the time he regained his health, his family lived in a new neighborhood in a new era of Harlem's history, where Powell rebelled from churchy Powell family moralism.[4]

In the early 1900s Harlem was completely white, and much of it was designed for the upper middle class, brimming with rows of elegant brownstone homes designed by Stanford White. Eighth Avenue in Harlem was Irish, Lenox Avenue and most of central Harlem were Jewish, Fifth Avenue was Scandinavian, and East Harlem was Italian. The wealthiest man in America, William Waldorf Astor, heir to the fortune of financier John Jacob Astor, erected an apartment complex on Seventh Avenue for the colossal sum of $500,000. A real estate boom fed on itself and the coming subway. Speculation soared on the expectation that property values in Harlem would double or triple as soon as the subway extended there. The bubble burst in 1905, threatening real estate investors with financial ruin. Some compensated by renting homes to blacks at high prices. Others merely threatened to rent to African Americans, extorting high rental income in neighborhoods determined to remain white. Others invented "blockbusting," placing blacks in white neighborhoods to set off white flight and buying up the homes of fleeing whites at bargain prices.

Powell Senior, alert to this drama, saw no reason not to take advantage. In 1911 he began to urge Abyssinian Church to move to Harlem, where blacks were moving. By 1915 the Great Migration was surging and approximately fifty thousand blacks had moved into Harlem's twenty-three blocks. For a dozen years

Powell Senior gave the same sermon about moving to Harlem, which the congregation resisted. Abyssinian had already made an expensive move from Greenwich Village to midtown Manhattan and was chastened by the experience. Powell grew up watching the conflict between Abyssinian's old guard of "divine aristocrats," who treasured their "decadent splendor," and his father, who "dreamed of the day when the church would be a social gospel institution." In 1912 Powell Senior applied his Harlem sermon to himself by purchasing a beautiful home on 136th Street, assessed at $17,000, for $6,000. A few years later he sold it for $15,000 and bought a palatial home on 134th Street, where his son grew accustomed to mammoth bathrooms and having too many rooms to use.[5]

Powell had a happy childhood, illness notwithstanding. He loved his magnificent homes in Harlem and could not bear, in later life, going near them, as his beloved childhood neighborhood had become "a place of squalor." Harlem was still mostly white when he got there, and he stressed that he grew up in a white world, although Harlem changed dramatically during his growing up. Marcus Garvey moved to Harlem in 1916, planting his headquarters next door to the Powell family. Garvey's back-to-Africa movement electrified Harlem and frightened Abyssinian's old guard deacons, who cited it as further reason not to move to Harlem. Powell Senior did not get his way until 1923, moving Abyssinian to West 138th Street. As a youth Powell watched Garvey parades from his family's roof, enthralled at their colorful pageantry. Powell Senior, however, got rough treatment in the streets from Garveyites, which heightened his protective impulses for his wife and children. Powell had little contact with the Garvey movement, and he grew up with little sense of his racial identity, a topic rarely discussed at home.[6]

One of his favorite stories described his discovery of racial consciousness. According to Powell, he first became aware of racism at the age of twelve, when his mother sent him to a bakery or his father sent him to get a newspaper—the story varied on details. On his way Powell was confronted by a group of black youths demanding to know his race. This was a new question for Powell. He looked at his skin, decided he was white, and got beaten up. The next night his mother sent him to Eighth Avenue, where a group of Irish kids beat him up for apparently being black. In some versions Powell said he provided the incriminating answer, "colored," chastened by his beating of the night before. Later that week he encountered another group of blacks demanding to know his race. This time he offered that he was "mixed," which incurred another beating, as the youths thought he said, "Mick."[7]

Powell Senior and Mattie Powell avoided race talk at home to protect their children from emotional injury, a common tack of middle-class black families.

Powell was grateful for his gentle upbringing, but he stressed that the neighborhood dispelled his innocence. The turf war between blacks and Irish taught him there was such a thing as racial bigotry. To get to Public School Five, Powell had to cross Eighth Avenue, something he dared not try by himself. Every weekday morning he walked six blocks north to join a group of non-Irish students before venturing across. The Irish toughs were always in place to beat up anyone who tried to cross alone, and they were especially abusive to blacks and Jews. To Powell, claiming his blackness became a survival necessity, even as his parents insisted that race should not matter. Powell said his introduction to racism convinced him that racial marking of any kind was deeply wrong. His encounter with racism in Harlem "sowed the seeds of my belief that it's not the color of your skin but the way you think that makes you what you are."[8]

But race was going to matter no matter what Powell or his father believed. White renters and homeowners fled Harlem, accepting huge financial losses to keep away from blacks. Midtown blacks migrated to Harlem and struggled to accommodate newcomers from the West Indies and U.S. American South. Garvey built a mass movement by renewing the black nationalist dream of a black empire in Africa. Powell, meanwhile, floundered at Townsend Harris prep school and City College of New York. He partied more than he studied at Townsend Harris, from which he barely graduated in 1925. He partied harder at City College, failing three classes in his first semester. In his account and that of friends, Powell's sexual magnetism engulfed him in welcome company. One friend recalled, "The girls never gave him much time for studies." Another added, "Adam loved the girls even in his mid-teens. But he didn't chase girls any harder than they chased him. The girls just loved his savoir faire." In later life Powell sometimes let on that Powell Senior was not quite as morally strict as his image. Powell Senior drank gin in secret while sermonizing against alcohol, and he put up with Powell's playboy mentality. But during his adolescence Powell rebelled wholeheartedly from Powell Senior morality. He indulged himself, defied his parents, ran through girlfriends, and found a refuge in the company of his sister, whom he still adored.[9]

Blanche worked on Wall Street, passing for white. Powell Senior was famously stylish, and Powell became even more so. In later life Powell routinely replied, when asked if he was not a man of the cloth, "Silk!" But Powell attributed his fashion sense more to Blanche than to his father. He admired that Blanche dumped cotton stockings, brocades, broadcloth and high collars for silk stockings, shimmery chiffons, and georgettes. She also cut her long hair, wounding Mattie Powell. Blanche married twice and had a child. Powell relied on her big-sister affection and indulgence, bringing his girlfriends and booze to her apartment, away from disapproving parents. Normally, three Fs in one semester would yield expulsion from City College. Powell Senior, however, was a friend of the president, whom he begged for a second chance. Powell got a second chance and kept partying, until tragedy struck: Blanche suffered a ruptured appendix and died, partly as a consequence of inept medical treatment. Powell was devastated. Blanche was the great love of his life; he loved her as a brother and was in love with her. Everything else paled by comparison. He failed all five of his classes and was dismissed from City College.

Powell Senior burned with shame that his son had flunked out, but Powell shrugged off the flunking and spurned his father: "That was the end of college, of church, and of faith! My sister was dead. And I just didn't give a damn!" He fell into despair, rejecting his father's world of Bible, prayer, preaching, and church life: "I began to hate, mistrust. God was a myth, the Bible a jungle of lies. The church was a fraud, my father the leading perpetrator, my mother a stupid rubber stamp. The smiling good people of the church were grinning fools." In that mood he surprised himself by letting his mother reenter his life. Mattie Powell, on Sunday afternoons, showed up unannounced at the homes of Abyssinian members who had missed church that morning. Usually they were ill, as she suspected. She nursed them and cooked, sometimes cleaning their houses too. She had nursed her son for six years when his life was endangered. Now she returned to save him again, remembering that Powell Senior had gone through a similar phase in his youth, which Powell still did not know about. Powell, at first, was bored and put off by his mother, but she persisted and he had nowhere to go. A longtime family friend figured out what the next move needed to be. Charlie Porter told Powell Senior and Mattie that they were too holy to help their son grow up. Powell needed to get away from them, and Porter knew where he should go, to Colgate University.[10]

Colgate was Baptist and remote, in upstate New York. It had one black student and one thousand white students, but most important, in Porter's calculus, it had no female students. Powell was not a candidate for a scholarship and never got one. Mattie Powell always had money, paying for his schooling. Powell believed that her money came from her connection to the Schaefer Brewing Company, although evidence is lacking, and it is undoubtedly true, as Powell told friends, that his parents gave him a whopping sum of pin money, although the amount he cited, $1,000, was incredible. Powell Senior renewed his friendship with Colgate's president, George Barton Cutten, who said nothing about Powell's race. That fall Colgate enrolled four new black students. All except Powell were athletes, but he passed for white, living in a dormitory reserved for whites. There he had a roaring good time until students discovered he was black. Powell planted the seeds of his outing by pledging to a fraternity and telling classmates that his father was a renowned minister in New York. Both actions led students to Abyssinian Church, as the fraternity checked out his family background and others heard Powell Senior preach at Abyssinian.[11]

Powell's roommate, Howard Patterson, erupted upon hearing this information. He demanded a new roommate and was promptly granted one by embarrassed college officials. Colgate's four black students had heard that somebody was passing for white; they resented Powell when it turned out to be him. The fraternity dropped Powell, many students shunned him, and Powell apologized to two black students, Ray Vaughn and Daniel Crosby, asking for their friendship. Both were football players, and Vaughn was struggling with German. Powell tried briefly to join the football team, and he helped Vaughn with German, which won over Vaughn and eventually Crosby. (Years later, media profiles described Powell as a star in football and track at Colgate, though he never competed in either sport.) Powell got himself into Alpha Phi Alpha, a national black fraternity, and bonded with Colgate's black students, which eased tension for him everywhere on campus. He became popular by lighting up parties and bringing Colgate students to New York City, where Powell dated showgirls. He also used his weekend trips to New York to resupply his bootlegging operation. In his last year at Colgate Powell began dating nightclub singer and dancer Isabel Washington. Powell was sufficiently light-colored to get into the Cotton Club, where he mixed readily with black performers and the mostly white customers.[12]

When Powell told the story of his crisis at Colgate, he obscured his role, did not mention the fraternity, reduced the campus reaction to his roommate's reaction, did not mention his apologies to black students, and made it a story about Powell Senior. According to Powell, he thoroughly enjoyed Colgate until Powell Senior gave a powerful sermon at Colgate about racial justice, saying things that "no one but he would dare say." In this telling, Powell Senior outed his son by blasting racism from Colgate's pulpit. Patterson suddenly realized that Powell was black, ending their friendship. Powell later recalled, "This was the first time in my life that deep discrimination had touched me directly. It came as a tremendous shock to me." It shocked him because he and Patterson were buddies and Colgate capitulated to Patterson's demand for a new roommate. Powell Senior's powerful sermon, Powell wrote, should not have set off this reaction—ignoring that this was really a story about racial identity, passing, and deceit. Powell never again overtly crossed the color line. Sometimes he let racist whites believe what they wanted, as when he worked as a summer bellhop at the Equinox Hotel in Vermont. But that was different, Powell reasoned, as he had no obligation to convey his racial identity to Negrophobes at a snotty hotel.

Powell Senior made him work a summer job, and Powell indulged his father's need to believe that lugging a few suitcases would build his character.[13]

Powell thrived at Colgate, attaining respectable grades and cutting a large, stylish, gregarious image on campus. He wore three-piece suits and silk ties, and his charisma was already fully developed. He bought a Model A Ford and introduced his black classmates to Harlem nightlife, securing dates for them with performers. He brought home his closest white friend, Howard Armstrong, to whom Powell Senior declared that being light-colored was a great advantage to him and his son, making them attractive to women of various racial hues. Powell majored in premed at Colgate, aiming for Harvard Medical School. He glowed at vindicating his mother's faith in him and took pride that Powell Senior regained respect for him. He swelled his bank account by bootlegging to gullible Colgate students "at fantastic prices," giving thanks for Prohibition. Near the end of his college experience he had a spiritual experience that brought him home, in his telling, to the family religion. According to Powell, it was a mystical moment, at two o'clock in the morning in February 1930, as he gazed out the window of his dormitory, Andrews Hall, bordering a golf course. He peered at the snow glistening on a fairway by the light of the moon and heard a voice, "something like my father's, but softer, and yet more insistent." The voice asked, "Whom shall I send? Who will go for me?"[14]

The next morning Powell told his parents by telephone that he intended to enter the ministry. Powell Senior babbled incoherently with joy and shock, and Mattie Powell, equally shocked, sobbed repeatedly, "God bless you, sonny boy." Two months later Powell's trial sermon at Abyssinian attracted his usual gang of bootleggers, gamblers, and nightclub performers, "all the fantastic array of acquaintances I had accumulated through the years." They came to laugh and party, incredulous at the thought of Powell preaching. He said they knew him as a gambler and heavy drinker "who had slept with more women than anyone could count." What could he possibly preach about? Powell's answer riffed on a popular billboard ad, "I'd walk a mile for a Camel." He asked how many gathered would walk a few feet for Jesus. Thirty-seven came forward to join Abyssinian, and the congregation granted Powell a license to preach.[15]

Thirty-three years later Vaughn told the rest of the story. Vaughn had often accompanied Powell to Manhattan on weekends and stayed with the Powell family. One night Powell Senior summoned Vaughn to the living room, declaring that he wanted Powell to succeed him. Would Vaughn please persuade Powell to aim for the ministry—specifically, at Abyssinian? Vaughn agreed to try, telling Powell it was crazy to spurn something that was "all set up for him." He was not going to find a better opportunity than what his father wanted to give him. This may have been a revelation to Powell, who attested that his father never encouraged him "in the slightest" to become a minister, although many acquaintances found that unbelievable. According to Vaughn, Powell's mystical moment occurred shortly after he and Vaughn had their discussion.[16]

Powell Senior gave his son a staff position and sent him to Europe and Palestine for four months as a graduation present. He had an ambition for the trip, to break Powell of his attachment to Isabel Washington. Powell Senior's romantic cosmopolitanism did not extend to nightclub singers, in this case a divorcée with a son. Washington had grown up in Savannah and moved to Harlem to enter show business. She hung around stage doors, seized her first break, and rode it to singing and dancing acclaim at the Cotton Club. Recently she had made it to Broadway, performing in *Singing the Blues* and *Harlem*. Powell Senior shuddered at her immodest publicity photos, a nonstarter for a minister's wife. He probably said so to his friend Henry Sloane Coffin, president of Union Theological Seminary, where Powell enrolled in the fall of 1930. Coffin brought up the Washington issue shortly after classes began, which helped to abort Powell's seminary training.

Powell had trouble finding time for class, so he sent Abyssinian secretaries to take notes for him, which offended Coffin. In a course on prayer Coffin gave Powell an F on a prayer, telling him it "had no value." Powell dropped out of Union, dismissing Coffin as a "reactionary." Who was Coffin to judge Isabel Washington or Powell's conversations with God? Meanwhile Powell Senior had a nervous breakdown, and Powell took over as acting minister for three months. By the time Powell Senior recovered, Powell had launched a relief ministry at Abyssinian, and in the fall of 1931 he enrolled at Teachers College, Columbia University, to study religious education. These were golden years for Teachers College, a graduate school in education. Powell heard philosopher John Dewey, education theorist George Counts, and anthropologist Margaret Mead lecture on the role of education in achieving social progress. He liked that Teachers College studied all major religions, not just Christianity. Holding a graduate school understanding of religion was better than being schooled in seminary theology. As for preaching social gospel religion, Powell had a lifetime of training in that, having stood next to Powell Senior as he preached. Powell did not need Union Theological Seminary to grade his sermons or prayers.[17]

Until he became a minister, at the outset of the Depression, Powell had never identified with poor blacks or given much thought to them. He lived in a penthouse, drove his father's Packard around Manhattan, hung out with a fast crowd, and had a guaranteed job. His family vacationed at Bar Harbor, Maine, and exclusive resorts in Canada. He later recalled that when he began his career he "had no feeling or sensitivity for the suffering around me." He was not very political either, as his father was still a progressive Republican in 1930, defending Herbert Hoover and Prohibition. All of that changed swiftly. Tammany Hall, the Irish-led network of ward bosses in New York City and state, dominated New York politics by providing patronage and welfare relief in exchange for political support. For forty years Progressive movements had blasted Tammany and other political machines for corruption and graft, calling for clean government. Near the end of the 1920s Tammany was still riding high, boasting a popular mayor, Jimmy Walker, and a recent U.S. presidential nominee, New York governor Al Smith. The ravages of the Depression, however, gave ballast to the Progressive indictment that machine governments were corrupt and undemocratic. New York governor Franklin D. Roosevelt, New York City Board of Aldermen president Joseph McKee, Harlem populist Republican Fiorello La Guardia, and Harlem Socialist Republican Vito Marcantonio became prominent in and through the fight against Tammany rule. Black Harlem had no standing politically because Harlem's Jewish and Italian districts were carefully carved across and around central Harlem. Tammany was contemptuous of black and Hispanic Harlemites, who were reduced to begging favors from La Guardia and Marcantonio until black Harlem got its due. Powell came perfectly in time to make it happen.[18]

He started by helping to inaugurate public relief in New York City, although he later claimed it started with the Harlem Hospital campaign, mistaking the chronology. In October 1930 Powell joined the staff at Abyssinian as business manager. New York City had no public aid agencies, and the programs that existed were tied to Tammany and/or local congregations. Two bankers with a social conscience, Seward Prosser and Harvey Gibson, created the Emergency Work Bureau to provide workfare jobs and relief. Prosser headed the bureau, securing money from Rockefeller philanthropies, which he sent to Abyssinian. Every Saturday an armored truck delivered between $2,000 and $3,000 to Powell, who paid people to scrub and paint and teach adult education classes. Powell soon added a food pantry in the church basement, helped by a donation from Powell Senior. He bought discounted food from city grocers and fed the needy, assisted by Abyssinian churchwomen. He added a clothing program and bantered with the crowd each day, building a reputation as an up-and-comer.

His political breakthrough came in 1933, the same year Powell married Washington and New York City held a historic mayoral election. Only one New York City hospital, Harlem, took black patients, and it was notorious for its overcrowded conditions and terrible care; locals called it "the butcher shop." Harlem Hospital reeled from Harlem's high rates of poverty, syphilis (nine times higher than white Manhattan), and tuberculosis. It segregated black nurses, and in 1933 the hospital fired all five of its black physicians. One was Conrad Vincent, who enlisted Powell to organize a protest campaign. Powell organized a sensational campaign, opening the doors of Abyssinian to protesters, who told heartrending stories of abuse and neglect at Harlem Hospital. He also discovered his gift for rally speaking. Powell had spellbinder talent plus a knack for making aggrieved listeners feel he was angrier than they were. He excoriated the hospital and Tammany Hall, demanding the resignation of hospital commissioner J. G. William Greeff. He vowed to register ten thousand voters to defeat Tammany in the upcoming mayoral election. He posed with the five doctors on the steps of City Hall, dramatizing that black Harlem had a young new leader.

No black minister had ever taken the fight downtown, rallying Harlemites against Tammany misrule and the blacks on Tammany's payroll. Tammany was newly vulnerable, as Roosevelt appointed a reformer judge, Samuel Seabury, to investigate Tammany corruption. Seabury dug for two years, helped by youthful, idealistic lawyers working for no pay. They exposed a stunningly corrupt regime of shakedowns, no-show jobs, tax dodges, illegal building permits, and judges on the take. Walker resigned in 1932, and McKee took over as acting mayor, pending a special election. Tammany's candidate, John O'Brien, a surrogate court justice, won the special election of 1932 but still faced a regular municipal election in the fall of 1933. Powell bull-rushed a Board of Estimate meeting at City Hall after his group of protesters was denied a hearing. McKee persuaded O'Brien to let Powell speak, and, in Powell's telling, the masses triumphed and "the new black emerged in New York." In later versions he claimed that the doctors were reinstated. Actually the doctors were not reinstated, and the crisis at Harlem Hospital went on for years, but Tammany pushed out Greeff, and Powell had broken through. He won the attention of Bronx Democratic boss Edward Flynn (a Roosevelt operative) and McKee, and he had his first taste of the power of mass protest politics.[19]

New York City politics, already legendarily complex, became more so as Tammany staggered. FDR won the presidency in 1932 and sought to replace O'Brien with a reform candidate. He and Flynn wanted McKee to run against O'Brien, but McKee returned to banking. Republicans had similar problems in New York City, needing to ally with independents and Roosevelt Democrats to have a chance against the Tammany candidate. They settled on La Guardia, a Republican former U.S. congressman from Italian Harlem who had offended his party in 1924 by supporting the Progressive Party in the national election. La Guardia had a gregarious personality and a national reputation as a prolabor populist, but in 1932 he lost his congressional seat after urging voters in a neighboring district to support a black candidate, Hubert Delaney. In 1928 La Guardia ran unsuccessfully for mayor against Walker and returned to Congress. Now he ran for mayor as the candidate of the Fusion Party, an alliance of Republicans, independents, and reformers.

La Guardia blasted Tammany operatives as thugs and punks to their faces, and he was a greater threat than O'Brien to win black support. Belatedly Flynn convinced McKee to change his mind about running, now as the candidate of the Recovery Party. Reform Democrats in New York could not let La Guardia claim the mantle of progressive reform. That would be a disaster for New York reform Democrats shortly after winning the White House; moreover, reform leaders felt that La Guardia was crude and volatile. Barely two months before the election, McKee launched his maverick candidacy. Railroad magnate Averell Harriman supported McKee, as did lawyer Samuel Leibowitz, stalwart defender of the Scottsboro defendants. Powell joined them, officially as chair of McKee's Harlem operation, but he promptly changed his title with typical Powell bravado, dubbing himself chair of the entire campaign. McKee finished a respectable second, losing by 250,000 votes to La Guardia and beating O'Brien. Powell outshone McKee on the campaign trail, where he gave the impression of being the candidate.

Powell Senior cheered his son's political breakthrough, thrilled that Abyssinian became a force in New York politics. In March he conferred another blessing that was much harder to give, by presiding at Powell's marriage to Washington. Powell and Powell Senior had fought for years over Washington, often in her presence, sometimes in public. Powell Senior threatened to disown him, and Powell told him to go ahead; he and his bride would barnstorm the country together as a speaking and singing duo. Finally the old man gave up, at age sixty-eight. He desperately wanted Powell to succeed him at Abyssinian, even if he had to swallow a showgirl daughter-in-law. Washington was Catholic, so she had to be baptized as a Baptist. Powell Senior dunked her so hard that she feared he was trying to drown her. Later she said, "I came up fighting and I thought, 'Oh my goodness, this old man is going to get rid of me now.'" The wedding occurred on March 8, 1933, two days after FDR closed the nation's banks. It occasioned four stag parties for Powell and drew over two thousand guests, though Powell tried to hold back on extravagance. The meaning of the wedding was obvious to Abyssinian's old guard of deacons: Powell had won, he was stronger than his father, and there was probably no stopping him now.[20]

Two years later Powell Senior tried to retire, but the deacons would not stand for it. They were not ready for him to leave or for Powell to take over. They did not like Isabel Powell, even though she gave up her career and became an active member of Abyssinian. They knew that Powell still picked up women at nightclubs and parties. Above all, the deacons were deeply attached to Powell Senior. Finally the old man got his way in 1937. The church had sixteen hundred members when he started; twenty-nine years later it had fourteen thousand members and a national reputation. The transition took place on November 21, at a gala service covered by *Life* magazine. Powell Senior delivered a charge to his son, summarizing his mission theology: "Preach with all the power of your soul, body, and mind the old-time simple Gospel because it is a fountain for the unclean, food for the hungry, drink for the thirsty, clothing for the naked, strength for the weak, a solace for the sorrowing, medicine for the sick and eternal life for the dying." Abyssinian never lacked skeptics who worried that Powell Senior, "not the Lord," called Powell to preach. Will Haygood, in his superb biography of Powell, *King of the Cats*, leaned on Abyssinian stalwart Olivia Stokes for tart quotes on this subject. Powell, however, stressed that he preached much like his father. Both were social gospel liberals in the pulpit, but Powell erased the already blurry line between social activism and political activism.[21]

Powell Senior was fond of saying that he built up Abyssinian Church, while his son's ministry was to interpret Abyssinian's mission. That was fine with Powell: "I intended to fashion that church into a mighty weapon, keen-edged and sharp-pointed." Abyssinians loved church, but God and the masses were elsewhere: "I intended to move the people out of the church to where God was—along the avenues and up the byways where hundreds of thousands were languishing in hopeless squalor." The old guard fought Powell tenaciously. The two Powells preached a similar social gospel, but the "old hard-shell" deacons caught the crucial difference between them, which Powell acknowledged: "My father was a radical and a prophet—I am a radical and a fighter."[22]

Powell Senior dragged Abyssinian into social gospel activism and liberal theology but in a way that kept the churchy ethos of old Abyssinian in place. He railed against ministers that talked only of heaven and hell, but heaven was important to him and the social gospel was not an alternative to preaching about eternal life. Heaven was an aspect of kingdom of God religion. Powell eschewed his father's both/and version of social gospel preaching. The needed reform in Christian preaching was not to add social relevance to an otherworldly hope, he argued. It was to repudiate otherworldliness as a distraction from the kingdom preached by Jesus: "This is my personal credo: There is no heaven or hell in the sense that they are places to which one goes after death. The heaven or hell to which ones goes is right here in the span of years that we spend in this body on this earth. That is the life I believe in."[23]

All people are sinners, Powell preached. All are prone to selfishness that holds them in spiritual bondage, and the only cure for this condition is to know God. Knowing *about* anything is not saving for anyone. Powell implored Abyssinians not to let doctrines, creeds, or theology get in the way of experiencing the divine. Theological arguments did not bring anyone closer to God, and the only good reason to join a church is to experience God. Powell had a romantic, idealistic concept of God: "All the beauty and truth and goodness in the world." Good religion, he taught, looks for the beauty in all things, believing that all things come from the divine creator of beauty. It operates like a chain reaction, moving from the perception of beauty to the truth that makes one free to be good. Secondhand religion is a pointless distraction or, worse, an obstacle to knowing God. One cannot acquire awareness of God through any thing or any other person. Powell rejected all versions of substitutionary atonement, denying that divine goodness or salvation is attained by "something that someone else purchased through a cross two thousand years ago." To be freed from the bondage of sin, one must know God personally, which purges the believer of hatred, vengeance, and selfishness: "This is why I view askance the average white man's religion; and in this religion of his I include not just his church but the whole priesthood of believers and of preachers, his institutions of theological learning and his outer projection of his religion into community and world life."[24]

Powell was too urbanized to feel the oceanic mysticism that Thurman shared with Unitarian founder William Ellery Channing, but Powell was very much like the liberal romantic Channing on sin, religion, the divine indwelling, and salvation. In both cases there were debts to German idealism in play, although Powell absorbed most of his Germanic influence through music and culture, and he preached from the Jefferson Bible. Channing held fast to the early Enlightenment insistence on the unity of the Bible, spurning the Jefferson Bible. God was rational, unified, and perfectly good and so was the Bible. Powell sided with Jefferson on the crude superstition of the Bible. Describing the gospel he preached at Abyssinian, Powell declared, "We do not believe in the Bible as the word of God. It is too filled with contradictions. We believe in the Thomas Jefferson Bible. Carefully, that brilliant Founding Father cut from the New Testament only those words that Jesus spoke. Then in logical and chronological order, he put them together until he had created a new Bible, a new Bible of old words, only the words of Jesus himself. This is the Bible from which I preach."[25]

Powell preached on the Prophets, too, and he appreciated the "lyrical witness of Paul," but only the words of Jesus as recorded in the gospels deserved to be called the Word of God: "I reject all else, even the other words of Matthew, Mark, Luke and John; and all of the Bible from Genesis to Revelations must be measured in terms of the words of Jesus Christ alone." God is truth, which is absolute, Powell reasoned. The aim of religion is to be imbued with God's absolute goodness and beauty, like Jesus. Jesus revealed God by loving God completely and loving his neighbor as himself. But much of the Bible is a far cry from absolute truth. To espouse or defend God's absolute truth by promulgating a doctrine about the Bible or anything else or by making a claim about something that supposedly happened in history is ridiculous. Powell urged that good religion is not confining and does not traffic in relative or superficial things. All versions of Christian orthodoxy are human constructions smacking of human fallibility and pretension. When Powell warmed to this subject he stressed that Abyssinian became theologically liberal through Powell Senior, not him, and his father got more liberal in his later career, letting go of doctrinal support structures of the "outer man." Powell, however, did not wrestle with scriptural texts in the manner of his father, and his father's churchly style of ministry felt cramped to him.[26]

SUCCESSION AND ELECTION

Powell was twenty-nine years old when he succeeded his father. By then he was a seasoned protest activist with a consuming passion, "Jobs for Negroes." The Depression ravaged Harlem, eliminating even menial labor jobs. Unemployment rates reaching 70 percent in some areas wreaked a devastating human toll and cast a spotlight on the exclusion of blacks from Harlem businesses. The mostly Jewish immigrants to Central Harlem who built businesses on 125th Street were not inclined to relinquish them after they moved to Long Island and the Bronx. They held on to their businesses, sending relatives and friends to work in them. Blacks lived above the stores and down the block from the stores. They bought things in the stores but had no jobs in them, which became intolerable during the Depression. The protest campaigns against employment discrimination kicked off in 1934. Nationalist, liberal, anti-Semitic, and Communist groups organized pickets, as did groups lacking a discernible ideology. Powell supported all of them, holding rallies at Abyssinian. He burnished his reputation as a civil rights militant but sowed distrust among groups demanding to know where he stood ideologically. Powell's answer—he was a pragmatic, united front radical—smacked of opportunism to many allies. Ideologically, Powell believed in uniting all the groups that pushed for democracy and freedom. He favored the church-based Citizens' League for Fair Play but eagerly supported any group that agitated for racial and economic justice. Powell got his political education in the streets, walking picket lines for groups demanding, "Don't Buy Where You Can't Work."

In 1934 a New York State Supreme Court verdict shut down the "Don't Buy" pickets, ruling that community groups lacked the legal status of organized labor unions. Similar campaigns affiliated with the Washington, DC–based New Negro Alliance (NNA) were shut down in other cities. The NNA, founded in 1933 and led by Belford Lawson Jr., John Davis, and M. Franklin Thorne, became the leading organizational advocate of economic boycotts and other direct action protests to combat racial discrimination. It filed suit against the Washington, DC–based Sanitary Grocery Company, a large retail chain operating in many black neighborhoods that refused to hire African Americans in any capacity. Lawson took the case to the U.S. Supreme Court, which ruled on *New Negro Alliance v. Sanitary Grocery Company* in March 1938. The court said that boycotts opposing racial discrimination were legal and that community group pickets were protected by the Norris–La Guardia labor act: "Those having a direct or indirect interest in the matters of employment have the freedom to take action against discrimination and peacefully persuade others."[27]

This verdict was a godsend for direct action activism. Powell and St. James Presbyterian Church pastor William Lloyd Imes seized upon it, founding the Greater New York Coordinating Committee for Employment (GNYCC) to oppose employment discrimination. Imes, a Union Theological Seminary graduate and future president of Knoxville College, made a good partner, as Powell later recalled: "I was young and he was mature. I was a radical and so was he, but his radicalism was tempered by thoughtfulness. I was impetuous and impatient, as was Imes, but he paused to reason." Powell and Imes gathered a wide-ranging coalition: Harlem Communist leader James W. Ford; Garvey stalwart Captain A. L. King; independent black nationalists Arthur Reid and Ira Kemp; moderate social gospeler Elizabeth Ross Haynes; and black Cuban progressive Arnold Johnson. The social gospel cochairs wanted the widest possible coalition and did not apologize for working with Communists. They appreciated the contributions of Communists to racial and economic justice. Randolph and Baptist minister John H. Johnson founded a rival organization, Harlem Job Committee, blasting Powell for his alliance with Communists and for refusing to focus on public utilities. Powell countered that Communists were admirable allies and there was no reason for his group to restrict itself to the hardest problem, the utilities. He cut his teeth politically in a legendarily volatile, factional, and accusatory environment. Powell was a happy warrior who usually let criticism roll off him. His friend Roi Ottley noted that Powell enjoyed himself so thoroughly that some had trouble recognizing his sincerity. Political scientist Charles V. Hamilton, putting it more dourly, noted that the "back-biting and sniping" atmosphere in which Powell was groomed fatefully became "part of his own political life-style."[28]

The GNYCC struck hard. Powell later recalled, "We set out to blitzkrieg One Hundred Twenty-Fifth Street. We made it a disgrace for any black to cross a picket line." There were pickets six days per week for several hours a day at up to ten stores at a time. The pickets stirred Harlem and shook the business owners. It helped that the Harlem Labor Union, a radical nationalist group, scared white proprietors and gave no hint of compromising. Powell conducted strategy meetings, spoke at rallies, and enticed Duke Ellington and other celebrities to march with him. He announced rallies on two days' notice that drew up to 7,000 participants. The GNYCC never conducted a membership campaign: "We always acted on the assumption that all Harlem belonged." After a few stores relented and hired black workers the bandwagon crowd began to show up: "Cautious but well-meaning folks had waited to see how we would make out. They joined, and we welcomed them." From a handful of movement leaders in a living room, the GNYCC morphed into an organization of 207 organizations comprising 170,000 members.[29]

All the early victories involved small businesses. The utility companies proved harder to crack. In April 1938 Consolidated Edison Light Company became the first big entity to break, hiring four black workers. Con Ed, however, had a history of employing low-level black workers, so Powell knew he had not really broken through. He courted press attention and celebrated victories shrewdly, sometimes exaggerating a victory. Powell cheered that white activists increasingly joined the pickets. Most came from church social action groups and the Communist Party. Some came from secular progressive groups, although Powell lamented that few came from the Socialist Party. American Socialists, white and black, were unwilling to touch anything that involved working with Communists. To Powell, it was sad to watch the Socialists become tiny and irrelevant through division and purism: "Both the black and the white socialist would rather see the black continue as a second-serf than cooperate with any movement in which communists were involved, regardless of how insignificant the role the communists played."[30]

Powell treasured FDR, whom he called "Father Franklin," for pulling one-third of the nation through the Depression. He had generally warm feelings for New York governor Herbert Lehman, especially in 1941 when Lehman won the fight for a congressional district in central Harlem, and he often made up with La Guardia after blasting him. But in 1939 Powell gave heartburn to all three by picketing the New York World's Fair. The fair's slogan, "Building the World of Tomorrow," took on a sinister cast after fair officials declined to employ blacks for anything above menial labor. The GNYCC moved downtown to fair headquarters at the Empire State Building. Pickets took place every day throughout the day, condemning a world lacking black workers. For the first time protesters won significant support from what Powell called "the intellectuals, mulattoes, and the few remaining upper-class blacks." Powell eventually moderated his demands, settling for a targeted strategy favored by the NAACP that yielded few actual jobs. But even that relative failure burnished his reputation as a lightning rod who knew when to pull back: "The new black sure was something!"[31]

He surprised his critics in the NAACP—friends of Powell Senior—by showing personal discipline, refusing to let merchants buy him off. NAACP leaders Walter White and Roy Wilkins never liked or trusted Powell, resenting his caustic gibes at "the Big Negroes." But they learned to work with him selectively, acknowledging his achievements. Nationalists proved harder to impress in some areas, objecting that the pickets yielded jobs mostly for light-colored women. Powell played a careful hand in dealing with this problem, treating it as an obstacle to racial unity. In June 1938 he spoke at Shaw University's commencement and excoriated black leaders, factionalism, and Talented Tenth conceits: "The hour for Negroes to move ahead has long since struck. We've got too many Uncle Toms among our leaders. We've got to streamline our race and come to realize that mass action is the most powerful force on earth." It would not happen, Powell admonished, as long as light-colored blacks ranked themselves higher than darker blacks: "Prejudices within our own race are doing us more harm than many outside discriminations. Because of the differences in the color of our skins and because a few of us can trace our ancestry back a few generations, we refuse to follow and all want to be leaders. In most cases, if we move our family tree six inches, we find ourselves either in a cotton patch or among mangrove trees. What we need is a closely knit, militant race with a new leadership."[32]

He flew higher and higher, during the same period that Randolph's March on Washington coalition pressured FDR to issue Executive Order 8802 prohibiting racial discrimination in the defense industry. Powell was a member of Randolph's steering committee. In the spring of 1941 Powell latched onto a Harlem Labor Union campaign against the New York City Omnibus Corporation and Fifth Avenue Coach Company. The bus issue was deeply personal in Harlem, a source of daily humiliation and frustration. Powell's GNYCC leaders merged with the Harlem Labor Union but were ignored by bus company officials. The protests grew into thousands of picketers in Harlem, with no breakthrough. Powell coped with the usual tensions: Nationalists emphasized race, unionists emphasized worker rights, and Communists emphasized worker solidarity. Finally the coalition announced it would begin picketing in midtown Manhattan, and bus officials asked for a meeting. Powell had to eat some crow, wrangling for compromises that contradicted his rally speeches. Three-way negotiations carried on through the summer among the bus companies, the Transport Workers Union, and Powell's group. In the fall he announced that at least thirty-two blacks would be hired as drivers and mechanics. Powell was jubilant and not shy about touting his indispensable role in leading a fractious coalition. He organized a thrilling reception for the first black bus drivers who rolled through Harlem. To Harlem, winning the bus boycott was akin to winning World War II. By then Powell had made a major career move.

The boycott was risky because failure seemed likely, and Powell was already contemplating a political career when he agreed to lead it. Ordinary social gospel activism was one thing, even on Powell's scale. Using the church as a basis for a political career was something else. Powell was ready to cross the line, but his political options were very limited, and he had no money for a political campaign. The state assembly held no lure for him, as that meant living in Albany and dealing with rural issues. He could run for Congress, but that was hopeless without Tammany support, as long as black Harlem had no district of its own. Powell set his sights on the New York City Council, an institution proud of its ethnic diversity and system of proportional representation despite lacking a single African American.

The crucial thing was to cross the line at Abyssinian. Powell did not bother to tell Randolph or Wilkins he was thinking of running for city council, nor did he tell Harlem's district leaders, as they were Tammany operatives. The power brokers could learn the news after Abyssinian heard it; what mattered was Abyssinian's support. One Sunday Powell was atypically subdued in the pulpit, laboring through his sermon. Some thought he must be ill. He seemed to finish, quietly. Then he walked to the edge of the rostrum, creating a sense of intimacy, and announced that he had decided to plunge into electoral politics. It took a few seconds for the congregation to absorb this information. There were murmurs and a few amens, the talking got louder, it built up to a roar of approval, and the roaring went on for twenty minutes. Abyssinian was ready to cross the line with its minister. Decades of social gospel exhortation and draining, miserable exclusion and invisibility had led to this moment. Abyssinians had cheered Powell Senior as he told them to be faithful, productive, and courageous, keeping their eyes on Jesus and supporting the NAACP. They fretted that Powell lacked his father's spiritual sincerity but took pride that he stirred Harlem to act, making Abyssinian a player in New York politics, a bigger world than black

Harlem's six square miles. Black Harlem needed a machine of its own, and Abyssinian was the place for it.[33]

Powell knew from his pickets and rallies that anti-Semitic feeling was growing in Harlem, and he needed money. He believed he understood why anti-Semitism was growing. Black nationalism evoked strong racialist emotions, the Depression caused immense suffering, and Jews owned most Harlem businesses. Many picketers, he noted, walked with a chip on their shoulder: "Anyone who did not hate a white man and want to kill him was considered an Uncle Tom or handkerchief-head. Black nationalism came to the forefront. It was radicalism of the most vicious type. Predicated upon 'down with all whites,' it was directed against the corner merchant in the form of anti-Semitism. Children spawned in these resentful homes roamed the streets as mobsters." Powell expected movement politics to be rough and hyperbolic, and he had a high threshold for rally polemics. But he grieved at the Jew-hating rhetoric he heard. He spent much of his time countering it, imploring that anti-Semitic bigotry and antiblack bigotry were similarly poisonous. And he had a well-connected new friend who worried about the same thing: Maurice Rosenblatt.[34]

Rosenblatt was a magazine researcher for the Amalgamated Labor Union and a Zionist activist. He absorbed Progressive activism in the mid-1930s as a student at the University of Wisconsin; he believed that Zionism and left-wing politics were natural allies; he wanted black and Jewish leaders to work together more effectively; and thus he founded the New York City Coordinating Committee for Democratic Action. The group had a twofold agenda: to mobilize Americans against Nazi racism and to promote fair treatment for blacks in Harlem. Rosenblatt persuaded Randolph, Imes, Rabbi Jerome Rosenbloom, and Rabbi David De Sola Pool to join the new organization. But Powell was his prize ally.

Rosenblatt worried that Jewish Americans naively believed they were liked and appreciated by black Americans. Black respect for Jews was declining sharply, he warned. It had to be earned anew, and not by pleading defensively that Jews helped to found the NAACP and Urban League. Powell was the key to Rosenblatt's strategy. Rosenblatt was intense, idealistic, extroverted, a bit starstruck by Powell, and zealous for a Jewish homeland in Palestine. He believed that David Ben-Gurion was selling out Zionism in his negotiations with the British government and that Jewish freedom had to be won by armed struggle in Palestine. He raised money for the two underground organizations waging terror campaigns in Palestine, Stern Group and Irgun. Powell worked with Irgun through Rosenblatt. Shortly after Hitler invaded Russia in July 1941, Powell addressed a Rosenblatt rally for Irgun at Madison Square Garden. Dramatically he held up a hundred-dollar bill, asking, "If a black man will give a hundred dollars for freedom, what will you Jews do?" The crowd responded by donating nearly $150,000.[35]

The payoff came swiftly. According to Powell, he and Rosenblatt climbed into a taxicab that night to visit four of Rosenblatt's friends, who promptly provided Powell's entire campaign fund: $1,200. Actually it took a few weeks to raise the money, from many donors, and Powell often accompanied Rosenblatt on fund-raising trips. He relied on Rosenblatt to finance his entire campaign. Powell told this story frankly for the rest of his career, describing Irgun as "an underground terrorist organization in Palestine." On the campaign trail he stressed his American patriotism and his opposition to fascism. Powell took for granted that he could not win a citywide election if other black candidates siphoned votes from him. The American Labor Party (founded by Social Democrats formerly belonging to the Socialist Party) nominated Max Yergan, Republicans nominated Channing Tobias, and Tammany selected a black district captain, Herman Stoute. Powell ran as an independent endorsed by the United City Party and City Fusion, and he persuaded Yergan and Tobias to withdraw from the race. In the end there were ninety-nine candidates, and Powell won La Guardia's endorsement. Downtown newspapers ignored Powell, dismissing his candidacy; Abyssinian backed him energetically, and he won a seat by placing third, stunning Manhattan's political establishment. Powell and Rosenblatt took victory laps at clubs and parties, where Rosenblatt noticed that Powell mesmerized women with his bad boy charm. To Rosenblatt, it seemed a potent gift for a politician.[36]

America entered World War II the following month, and Powell shrewdly took a third way between war boosting and antiwar criticism. America was right to fight fascism, he argued, but this war had to work out differently for black Americans than the previous ones; otherwise there would be riots and rebellion. White newspapers did not convey this message appropriately, and Powell felt that black newspapers were not much better. The *Amsterdam News*, in particular, fell woefully short, notwithstanding that Powell wrote a column for it. So he founded his own newspaper, the *People's Voice*. Financed by Jewish entrepreneur Mo Gail, who owned the Savoy Ballroom in Harlem, the weekly tabloid allowed Powell to reach and build his following directly. It operated on 125th Street across from the Apollo Theatre, and Powell plunged into it gleefully, conducting job interviews at Abyssinian. Staff members described him as supremely self-confident, commanding, and ebullient. Powell, in their telling, overwhelmed his staff and infused it with his idealism.

Black newspapers bristled at Powell's criticism and associates, stressing that the tabloid's financiers were white. *Amsterdam News* described Powell as an "ambitious mercenary colored political newcomer" and the forthcoming tabloid as an example of white capital "simply seeking to further exploit the race." Powell countered that he and Savoy Ballroom manager Charles Buchanan owned the paper and that Harlem needed better journalism. His inaugural issue, published on February 14, 1942 (Frederick Douglass's birthday), described the *People's Voice* as a "working class paper" that was "one hundred percent owned and operated by Negroes." The masthead boasted, "Largest Negro Tabloid in the World," letting pass that it was the only one. Powell called for massive government investment in housing and schools, abolition of racial discrimination, and "a just quota of jobs in all city, state and federal agencies." Later he lauded Gandhi's struggle for independence in India, condemned the U.S. government's confinement of Japanese Americans to prison camps, and criticized the prosecution of Communist Party leader Earl Browder on a passport violation. Repeatedly Powell linked the war against fascism to the war against segregation: "We are demanding a share in carrying this cross of world conflict, and just as strongly as we demand that, we demand a share of the crown of victory." Many Americans, he charged, were not real Americans because they believed that American democracy did not apply to all Americans: "It is just as important to see that these people and their brand of Americanism be crushed as it is to recapture Singapore."[37]

Every week the paper featured lengthy accounts of Powell's speeches and activities, lauding his accomplishments. Occasionally an unsigned editorial went overboard in praising the editor's brilliance. At its peak the *People's Voice* reached fifty thousand copies per week and boosted Powell's influence. His staff defended it zealously; for them it was a crusade and a rare journalistic opportunity. Paul Robeson, Langston Hughes, and Richard Wright wrote occasionally for the paper, and Ollie Harrington supplied popular cartoons. There were also numerous photographs of acclaimed jazz pianist Hazel Scott. Scott's stylish performances and stunning beauty would have been reason enough for the paper to pay attention to her, but Powell's interest cut deeper.

Hazel Scott was nineteen years old and a supper club celebrity when Powell met her in 1939 during the World's Fair protest. Born in Trinidad and raised in New York, she had been a child prodigy, joining her mother's jazz band at the age of five and enrolling at Juilliard at eight. As a youth she sang and played piano and trumpet in her mother's band. At sixteen she had her own radio show; at eighteen she made her Broadway debut in *Sing Out the News*. When Powell met her she was a featured performer at the downtown and uptown branches of Café Society, "swinging the classics" with jazzy renditions of classical music. Scott performed at the World's Fair; she was sensuous and worldly, having grown up in nightclubs, and she liked Powell's politics. She followed him in her limousine after rallies, shyly at first. After America entered World War II she spoke at rallies in support of the war and was seen increasingly in Powell's company. Powell often heard her perform in Greenwich Village, sometimes in the company of his wife. His friends could see where this was going, although Isabel Powell was shocked when it happened.[38]

Isabel became less interesting to Powell shortly after she gave up her career to devote herself to him, although she blamed his political turn. She later recalled, "I didn't like his entering politics at all. I said you sell your integrity. In the pulpit he was his own boss. But in politics you cannot be your own man. I believe this was the beginning of my downfall." His version was colder: "One day I caught up with her and then passed her. She loved me completely and utterly, yet I grew and she stood still." Besides outgrowing Isabel, Powell felt confined by the city council. He kept his pledge to "raise a ruckus," protesting against racial discrimination in city hospitals. He pressed the council to rename Harlem streets after historic black figures. He had an on-again, off-again relationship with La Guardia, mostly off. Each was wary of the other, and Powell accused La Guardia of ignoring black protest organizations. La Guardia did not deserve his favorable reputation among black Americans, Powell charged. In fact, he was "one of the most pathetic figures on the current American scene. Never has a public figure disintegrated so thoroughly as has Fiorello La Guardia." La Guardia approved an apartment development (Stuyvesant Town) owned by Metropolitan Life Insurance that excluded blacks from renting, and Powell furiously called for his impeachment. But city politics was mostly about borough rivalries over sewage budgets and streetlights, and Powell pined for a larger stage.[39]

The idea that black Harlem should have its own district in the U.S. Congress had kicked around Harlem, Albany, and Washington, DC, since the mid-1920s. The 1940 census showed that redistricting was overdue in New York, giving ballast to calls for a black Harlem district. Harlem political leader Herbert Bruce lobbied Lehman, hoping to represent the new district. Lehman pressed the Republican-controlled state assembly and senate for congressional and state redistricting plans, declaring he would not "countenance any attempt longer to withhold from any locality its just representation." Plans were drafted and scuttled for eighteen months, Republicans and Tammany opposed reapportionment, and in April 1942 the state senate voted against it. Powell blasted the vote as "a direct insult to the Negro people," vowing to organize a third party if reapportionment failed. The state legislature seemed hopelessly deadlocked until word came that Congress might intervene if the state failed to get something done. That scared Republicans into dealing with Lehman, who won a congressional district for central Harlem, the twenty-second, to be filled in the 1944 elections.[40]

Amsterdam News urged Randolph to run for the seat, but he was devoted to the Brotherhood of Sleeping Car Porters. Bruce was keen to run, but he had a rocky relationship with Tammany, which opened the door for Powell to make amends with Tammany. Powell quietly negotiated with Tammany operative Clarence Neal while a coalition of black activist groups organized a freedom rally at Madison Square Garden. Over twenty thousand participants packed the Garden on June 16, 1942, representing various groups and ideologies. The organizers bridged their differences by agreeing to honor Randolph. Many did not trust Powell or want him to speak, but he wrangled a speaking invitation. At the Garden Randolph graciously allowed others to speak before him. The speeches ran long; then Powell came forward and talked about protest, pickets, himself, and the lack of protest politics in New York before he got there. The crowd could feel this speech was heading somewhere. Powell built up the drama, shushed the timekeeper, and shocked the crowd: He would run for Harlem's seat. Black Americans needed a national voice in the nation's capital. The Garden exploded with jubilation. The cheering went on and on, rapturously loud. Randolph never got to speak, and his aides—notably Bayard Rustin—fumed that Powell had hijacked their event.[41]

His election was never in doubt, as Powell brashly entered all three party primaries, winning the endorsements of the Democratic, Republican, and American Labor parties. Tammany endorsed him, and Abyssinian women worked zealously for him. The congregation as a whole took a few months longer to go political, then rushed into the campaign, pledging $10,000 to it. The only candidate to provide even mentionable opposition, attorney Sara Pelham Speaks, had no political experience. Speaks and Bruce—the latter bitter at Tammany's betrayal—charged that Powell had Communist sympathies and backers. Powell's customary retort played well in Harlem: Communists stood out in caring about black Americans. Even the Harlem riot of July 1943 played to his advantage, as Powell called it an explosion against economic misery, not a "race riot," which confirmed the necessity of resorting to politics, not to violence.

Powell worked hard to secure his landslide victory in the Democratic primary and his comfortable Republican victory. Afterward he and Isabel Powell headed to their summer home at Oak Bluffs in Martha's Vineyard for a rest, where

Powell told her she would not be coming to Washington with him. Isabel was devastated, gasping for breath. At first she was too stunned to say anything. Then she pleaded. How could he throw her away after eleven years of marriage? Powell said nothing about Scott. Isabel asked what she should do about love and sex. Powell coldly advised her to try celibacy. He was done with her and needed to smooth the way for Scott to join him in Washington. The news stunned Abyssinian, too, although Isabel did not find the comfort and sympathy she expected there. Many had never liked her; some resented her for clinging to a light-colored clique; and nearly all backed their minister, as Powell expected. Isabel sued for divorce and received a generous settlement. In her suit she grieved that Powell "tossed me aside because of his infatuation for this nightclub performer." She held a torch for Powell for the rest of her life and never remarried. Powell saw her only once, at the funeral of prizefighter Canada Lee. He said nothing to her, later recalling, "Time had taken its toll on both of us."[42]

Powell felt keenly the lack of a militant, comprehensive, self-affirming black leadership at the national level. Black nationalists affirmed their blackness, but their world was too small. Congress had one black member in 1943, Chicago Democrat William L. Dawson, but he was a standard Chicago machine Negro. In September and October 1944, heading into a general election in which he had no opposition, Powell wrote a book titled *Marching Blacks*. The very title provoked the fears and anxieties of white readers and what Powell called "the average Negro." Blackness had not yet come of age, but Powell presented himself as a herald of its coming. He spoke the book into a Dictaphone while making a few speeches for the Roosevelt-Truman ticket, swallowing his disappointment that FDR dropped Powell's friend Henry Wallace from the vice presidency in pursuit of border state support. Needing to make no speeches for himself, Powell had time for a two-hundred-page book on the march of blackness. He made five arguments: A second Civil War began in America on December 7, 1941. This war pitted "the new black and new white man" against racist-fascistic Americans in the struggle for a genuine democracy. The new black had tried to emerge during World War I but would not be denied this time. Nonviolent mass activism was the key to winning Civil War II. Southern blacks should leave the South. And the white man had one last chance to avert a global race war.

There was no meaningful difference, Powell contended, between Nazi anti-Jewish racism and American antiblack racism, yet black Americans were told to swallow the latter while risking their lives to fight Hitler. Black Americans were completely done with being put down. They were already at war for their freedom in America, even as white Americans focused on the war against fascism: "The new black has come forward. He has taken this war seriously, refusing to let it remain a white man's war." Powell worked both ends of a liberationist argument, emphasizing the newness of the moment *and* three centuries of struggle for freedom. Blacks had always resisted their oppression, and they came out of World War I saying they were done with being put down. But oppression continued, and the Depression drove blacks to new depths of despair: "There in that terrible hour of complete loneliness, abject poverty, and black misery, the new black was born." Powell stressed that he witnessed the birth: "The black has discovered the technique of direct nonviolent social action. His resentment is keen, but it is disciplined. His indignation is great, but it is directed." American democracy had to win the war at home; otherwise the war abroad was pointless. Marching blacks were "going up Freedom Road," and they had to win if America was not to descend into fascism.[43]

On his way to the U.S. Congress Powell told a story of "last shall be first" reversal. In the old racial caste system house blacks "secretly copied" the white upper class, "openly copied" the white middle class, and had "nothing but utter contempt" for the white lower class. Field blacks, on the other hand, were jealous of house blacks, obeyed the white upper class "except for occasional revolts," and despised the white lower class. This picture had changed completely, Powell said. In 1944 house blacks strove to ingratiate themselves with the black masses, and the black masses strove to reach an accord with the white masses. Powell contended knowingly that it was still possible for an upper-class black or white individual to be accepted by the black or white masses. But the old order was completely upended: "Today the field black is in the ascendancy and he means to stay there."

He stressed that he learned this lesson in the streets. Powell spoke to crowds that recoiled viscerally at his light color, educated diction, and stylish clothing. Every time he cut a deal he was accused of selling out poor, dark, vulnerable people he did not represent. For all his bristling egotism—Harrington called him "a fantastic ego person. . . . He considered himself about the best person in the world"—Powell had the requisite humility to be vulnerable, absorbing personal criticism at his own rallies, which helped him win supporters. In private he called himself a "yellow Negro" and occasionally urged light-colored friends that he and they needed to prove their blackness. In *Marching Blacks* he set the bar high in grading his success: "The men who would bridge the gap between the light and the dark must be acceptable to the West Indian and the native-born, the religious fold and the non-religious. In other words, they would have to be radicals whom conservatives could follow."[44]

According to Powell, Booker T. Washington was "a sincere but subsidized black nationalist" who retarded black progress for all but a small black bourgeoisie: "He sanctioned Jim Crow and kept the South safe for white dominance." Du Bois was the greatest black leader, believing in "the complete integration of the black man in American life," although Du Bois did not prevent the NAACP from lapsing into middle-class reformism. Garvey was the third important black leader and the least understood. Powell grieved that even in Harlem people remembered only the early Garvey: "At the outset of his career he distrusted light blacks and bitterly hated all whites. He combined all the black's former attitudes—escape from reality, religious fervor, sorrow songs, wove them together in a dazzling pattern, and cried out to the submerged blacks, 'Any black is better than every white.'" Nobody, Powell said, compared to Garvey in conveying to the black masses a sense of racial pride. Moreover, in later life Garvey changed his program, adopting "the philosophy of Du Bois—stay in America and fight until you are integrated into every part of American life." Powell told audiences that Garvey deserved to be better remembered and that nationalists perpetuated a wrongly narrow version of his legacy.[45]

Marching Blacks had a similar word about Communism, explaining that black Americans did not fear it, rarely subscribed to it, and appreciated Communists. Until 1943, Powell noted, there were no more than five hundred card-carrying Communists in Harlem, coalition activism notwithstanding. In 1943 that number tripled, for two reasons: black Communist activist Benjamin Davis Jr. was elected to the city council, and the Communist Party renounced its Leninist ideology and tactics, reorganizing as the Communist Political Association. Powell stressed that red-baiting simply did not exist in black communities, aside from a few old-line black Socialists. African Americans appreciated that Communists fought "vigorously, courageously, and persistently for the rights of black people." He put it more strongly in a sentence often quoted: "Today there is no group in America, including the Christian church, that practices racial brotherhood one tenth as much as the Communist Party."[46]

Swedish sociologist Gunnar Myrdal, in *An American Dilemma*, contended that white fears and black grievances about race were inverted. White Americans feared racial intermarriage above everything else, followed by fear of personal and social equality, fear of joint use of schools and other public places, fear of equal voting, fear of equal standing in law courts, and fear of equal economic opportunity. For black Americans the list of racial grievances was exactly reversed. Blacks cared most about economic opportunity, next about legal justice, next about voting, and so on. The right to intermarry was a distant last. Myrdal said there was at least some ground for optimism in the fact that blacks did not want what whites most feared. The American dilemma was that white Americans had an admirable creed they dared not practice, out of fear and loathing of black Americans. Powell judged that Myrdal was right on all counts but cautioned that the gap between social equality and intermarriage was steep for blacks. African Americans cared greatly about social equality and not at all about intermarriage. He and his father, Powell noted, ministered to "the largest liberal church in the world's largest and most liberal city." In thirty-five years they performed two thousand weddings; only fourteen were interracial. That was a tiny number, Powell stressed, and, unlike the social equality issue, intermarriage was a purely individual matter.[47]

Powell had two prescriptions, which did not fit well together. (1) Every black community needed to form a direct action protest organization. (2) But the South was hopelessly racist and oppressive, so blacks needed to leave the South. He did not quite mean *all* southern blacks. Some were happy, somehow, being slaves, so they should stay. Some reaped benefits from exploiting fellow blacks, so they deserved to stay: "But to the vast millions who have been suckled with the milk of freedom from the depths of black bosoms—let them leave! Turn their backs on Egyptland!" Powell had no patience with people who said the North was no better. The North had "no lynching and no poll tax" plus decent schools and hospitals. Basically he wanted African Americans to converge on a few northern cities, where they exercised democratic power and avoided rural whites. Blacks in Florida, Georgia, South Carolina, North Carolina, and Virginia should move to New York and Philadelphia, "with Boston catching the overflow." He envisioned one million going to New York in the first wave. Blacks in Alabama, Arkansas, Louisiana, Mississippi, Kentucky, and Tennessee would move to Detroit and Chicago and some to Cleveland. Blacks in the Southwest would move mainly to Los Angeles and San Diego, with a select overflow heading to San Francisco and Seattle. The three worst states needed to be evacuated first, he urged—Mississippi, Georgia, and Texas. These were the states with the most lynchings. Powell looked forward to the end of the war, when hundreds of thousands of black soldiers received separation pay. He urged them to invest none of it in the South: "Whatever money the government has given them, they must use it to bring their families north."[48]

He didn't really care if that sounded harsh. The South of the "Lost Cause" and *Gone with the Wind* had never existed, "except as a thin scum." He looked forward to joining Congress but recoiled at the prospect of hearing Mississippi House Democrat John Rankin and Mississippi Senate Democrat Theodore Bilbo spew their "rotten filth" about black inferiority. Powell stressed that blacks had nothing to lose by marching north: "As soon as you cross the Mason-Dixon

line you sense squalor, poverty, disease, and hopelessness in the very air." This
was a "song of bitterness," he allowed, but also a song of hope: "My bitterness
will not be sweetened until my hopes are realized. My hopes can only be realized when ten million blacks hit the road to freedom."[49]

Three things in white America gave ballast to this hope. First was the ethical
potential of Christianity. "The fundamental postulate of Christianity is equality
and brotherhood," Powell wrote. "We have perverted this glorious doctrine to
exclude interracial love." There was always the hope that white Christians
would learn from black churches how to practice the gospel. Powell Senior
preached this sermon many times; Powell called it "Christianizing religion."
The second thing was more real: the exemplary unionism of the Congress of
Industrial Organizations (CIO). Founded by John L. Lewis in 1935, the CIO
opposed the old craft unionism of the American Federation of Labor (AFL),
supported industrial unionism and the New Deal, and condemned the racism
of the AFL. Powell treasured the CIO for fighting race hatred "with all of the
power it could muster." Economic justice for African Americans had been off
the table when blacks were excluded from unions. Cheering the ascension
of the CIO, Powell looked forward to a "showdown fight" between it and AFL,
one that would drive racist AFL leaders out of unionism.[50]

Number three was that white liberals were a growing tribe. Powell did not
mean only his usual white activist allies. He meant that decent, moderate
whites increasingly got it. Mordecai Johnson's buddy at the Rosenwald Fund,
Edwin Embree, was the best example. Embree never walked a picket line, but
he understood the politics of the color line better than almost anybody Powell
knew. Powell let Embree speak for him in expressing his concluding point:

> The rise of the black Americans is a part of the general upsurge of colored
> peoples the world over. . . . Having material power, it was natural for us to
> suppose we were superior to all people in every way. . . . The balance was
> radically shifted during the periods of the First and Second World Wars. We
> do not yet see the shift that is taking place. Again there is a cultural lag, a
> delay between changes and our adaptation to them. . . . The white man of
> the Western world is offered his last chance for equal status in world soci-
> ety. . . . If the Western white man persists in trying to run the show, in exploit-
> ing the whole earth, in treating the hundreds of millions of his neighbors as
> inferiors, then the fresh might of the billion and half nonwhite, non-Western
> people may in a surging rebellion smash him into nonentity.[51]

Marching Blacks was a trove of quotable zingers that Powell heard for and
against him for the rest of his career. Many reviewers deprecated Powell's factual

errors and breathless prose, although he never claimed to be a stylish writer. He wrote as he talked, and *Marching Blacks* was meant to be his introduction to a national audience. Dial Press, however, needed over a year to produce the book, by which time Powell had made a nervy, aggressive, and unpredictable splash in Congress. Most reviewers went straight for the chapter on leaving the South, passing lightly over the rest. Some noted that another migration surge was already under way and that northern cities were struggling to cope. Some quoted Powell against himself. If Harlem was a cesspool of overcrowded poverty, as Powell argued in part 2, how could he say that hundreds of thousands more should move to Harlem?

The *People's Voice* pressed that question. Ben Richardson was an assistant minister at Abyssinian, Powell's speechwriter, and a reviewer for *People's Voice*. But he had not written *Marching Blacks*, and he grieved that Powell ruined the book with a misguided late chapter. He tried to say it gently, given his tricky situation: "I say this in great kindness, the suggestion that Negroes in the South come North in these days of crisis, ill housing, unemployment, labor-capital struggle, and racial tensions, is an invitation to catastrophe for millions of the oppressed." Powell replied sadly that white liberals were "way ahead of so-called Negro liberals" like Richardson; moreover, too many reviewers did not face up to their own admonitions. The migration surge was, indeed, already happening, so parlor arguments about whether it was a good thing held little worth. What mattered was how white and black Americans reacted, especially in the North.[52]

RESORTING TO POLITICS

No one remotely like Powell had ever joined the U.S. Congress. He put it sharply, calling himself "the First Bad Nigger in Congress." On other occasions he put it more prosaically, calling himself an irritant that rubbed until something gave—the image that Hamilton used to describe Powell's congressional career. Committee chairs dominated Congress, and one became a committee chair through seniority. That yielded a Congress dominated by southern segregationist committee chairs. One became somebody in Congress by keeping one's head down, toiling quietly on committees, building up seniority, and building up social capital with colleagues. The only part of this prescription that Powell applied to himself was getting reelected. House Speaker Sam Rayburn welcomed Powell by cautioning him not to throw bombs, and Powell replied that he had one in each hand. Rayburn laughed uproariously; he could appreciate having another big personality in the House.[53]

Politically, Powell was a liberal Democrat affiliated with the Eleanor Roosevelt and Henry Wallace wing of the Democratic Party, but he spent his early career putting the squeeze on liberal Democrats, and his only close ally in Congress, Marcantonio, did not survive the McCarthy purge. In Powell's first months he supported bills for an anti-lynching amendment, rights for District of Columbia residents, and naturalization for Native Americans. All were crushed by the same coalition of conservative Republicans and southern Democrats that tried to gut the Fair Employment Practices Commission (FEPC) for combating discrimination in industry during wartime. Two months into Powell's congressional career FDR died, and Powell joined the national mourning, conducting an emotional memorial service at Abyssinian. Ten days later Mattie Powell died, and Powell bruised some feelings at Abyssinian by attending her funeral hand in hand with Scott. Two weeks later his divorce came through, and two months after that he married Scott; his years of fending off rumors about her were mercifully over.

Scott did not need to be loved at Abyssinian and did not try very hard to make friends there. She was not a Baptist and took no interest in becoming one, although she attended services when she was in New York. Many disliked her proud bearing, celebrity, and salty language. Some grieved the lack of a successor to Mattie Powell. Rose Stokes told Haygood, "Hazel was pretty, but nasty . . . sexy and loud." To most Abyssinians, however, and to vast numbers beyond its walls the Powell–Scott marriage was a romantic, dazzling celebrity union—a celebration of each other. Powell and Scott lit up nightclubs and Broadway openings, providing grist for society pages. They bantered engagingly about political causes they shared and enticed other celebrities to step out politically. They shuttled from their Long Island beach home to Hazel's New York suburban home to apartments in Harlem and Washington, DC. Powell enjoyed making friends in Scott's world of jazz musicians. He took delight that she had her own career, which morphed to solo concert touring and big money. He opined that most wives of ministers got overly involved in their husband's business, which was not good for the wife, the church, the marriage, or the husband. In 1946 Scott gave birth to a son—Adam III, nicknamed "Skipper"—and the baby's arrival was treated in Harlem like a royal birth. When bigots slighted Scott on the road, they had to deal with Powell shortly afterward. His first big controversy centered on his new wife and the wife of the new president.[54]

Scott was twenty-five when she married Powell and heavily traveled, but she had never played Washington, DC. Powell had an idea for her debut: Constitution Hall, the venerable homage to the Revolutionary War draped in images of George Washington and Thomas Jefferson. Scott's agent tried to book the hall through the Daughters of the American Revolution (DAR), the organization of privileged white women that controlled bookings under a congressional charter. Every player in this story knew that the DAR did not allow blacks to perform at Constitution Hall, as the DAR had famously refused opera singer Marian Anderson in 1939. Everyone knew how the Anderson episode played out: A controversy erupted; the DAR stuck to its refusal; Eleanor Roosevelt resigned from the DAR; and Harold Ickes arranged for Anderson to perform on the Washington Mall on Easter Sunday. The DAR told Scott she could not sing at Constitution Hall, and Powell sent a telegram to President Truman, whom he had never met. Truman wired back that he could do nothing because the DAR was a private outfit. Had this been a replay, Bess Truman would have to resign from the DAR. But the president's wife liked her DAR tea parties, which echoed her southern upbringing. She attended the next one at the Sulgrave Club, and Powell called reporters from a phone booth, declaring that Bess Truman had become "the last lady of the land," not the nation's first lady. The first lady was still Eleanor Roosevelt.[55]

Harry Truman was infuriated by this unbelievable attack on his wife. "That damn nigger preacher," he snapped to aides. Truman was devoted to Bess Truman, who did not like Washington, DC. She spent a lot of time in Missouri, and he wrote to her almost daily when she was there. The story went national, introducing millions to the new black congressman. Powell's nemesis in the House, John Rankin, told reporters it was obviously a Communist plot. Segregationist papers howled about Powell's affront to decency. Powell stoked the controversy by pressing the real indecency: Black American soldiers were returning from war only to learn that black Americans still could not perform at Constitution Hall. Many northern Democrats implored Powell to ease up on Truman; alienating a Democratic president would not be good for Harlem. Powell told Abyssinians he was apparently risking his political future by not easing up. They thanked him for standing proud; the DAR had affronted every black American who strove to be somebody. Powell took heart that New York's two U.S. Senators, Robert Wagner and James Mead, supported him publicly, as did several major newspapers. But he noticed that few other northern Democrats defended him, which confirmed his feeling about how he should proceed. Powell went after his supposed allies, and he never made up with Truman, who stiffed Powell on patronage.[56]

Dawson got streams of patronage, but he could not eat in the congressional dining room or stay in a nearby hotel. Powell vowed not to play like Dawson. Powell ate wherever he wanted, and he hounded Rankin in the House chamber by moving as many times as necessary to sit next to him. He also objected to

Rankin's rants employing the N-word on the House floor, disrupting the House's complicity of silence about racist slurs. If speaking for the dignity of all black Americans meant that Powell had to sacrifice patronage for Harlem or embarrass colleagues who indulged Rankin, he was willing. He later recalled, "There was only one thing I could do—hammer relentlessly, continually crying aloud even if in a wilderness, and force open, by sheer muscle power, every closed door. Once inside, I had to pierce the consciences of men so that somewhere someone would have to answer; somewhere something would have to be done." The tool he used to that end was called the Powell Amendment.[57]

The Powell Amendment was a throwback to the abolitionist Tallmadge Amendments, first employed by New York Republican Congressman James Tallmadge Jr. in 1819 to permit Missouri to enter the Union only as a free state. The idea was so long forgotten outside the NAACP that Powell's colleagues thought he invented it; hence the name. Attachable to any bill, the Powell Amendment prohibited federal funds under the act in question from going to any state or school that practiced segregation. Segregationists hated and loved it, depending on circumstances, and it usually put liberals on the hook. Every time Powell thought there was an opportunity to pass a bill containing the amendment or to defeat a bad bill by employing it, he introduced the Powell Amendment. Liberals were forced to choose between their commitment to civil rights and something else they cared about, especially federal funding for schools. Federal aid to education could not pass without southern votes, so the Powell Amendment doomed school aid bills through the Truman and Eisenhower years.[58]

Powell first deployed it in February 1946, attaching the amendment to the National School Lunch Act. The free lunch program built on a succession of New Deal programs and had broad support. Powell rebuffed pleas from all sides to withdraw the amendment, counting on the bill's popularity. If Congress killed the school lunch program at its founding, working-class voters would blame their own representatives, not Powell. The amendment passed by 258 to 109, and Powell had a huge, instructive victory, albeit one that deprived poor southern schoolchildren of a guaranteed lunch.

That was the high point of his first term in office. Powell got his only competitive race for the next twenty years in the next election, from black Republican minister Grant Reynolds, who got his chance through Republican New York governor Thomas Dewey. Reynolds nosed out Powell in the Republican primary, and it appeared that Powell would have to campaign. Reynolds blasted New Deal welfare programs, and Powell ignored him. Reynolds won support from Randolph, boxer Joe Louis, author Zora Neale Hurston, and actress Fannie

Brice, but Powell still declined to campaign. Reynolds pleaded for a debate, and Powell sent Marcantonio in his place. Isabel Powell told Reynolds she had a no-show job on Powell's staff, but Reynolds declined to go there. Tammany stuck with Powell, as did the American Labor Party through Marcantonio, and Powell waited until the final week of the general election to campaign. He had Reynolds's army medical record, a gift from someone in the War Department, which suggested that Reynolds was mentally ill. That was absurd, but it crushed Reynolds's momentum, and Powell got no more election fights for two decades.[59]

The Cold War came, and Powell made adjustments. He had pro-Communist writers at the *People's Voice* that made him vulnerable: Doxey Wilkerson, Max Yergan, Marvel Cooke, and Ben Davis. Powell fired Wilkerson for being openly Communist. Yergan and Cooke resigned under pressure, though Yergan soon flipped to anti-Communism; Cooke believed the newsroom had a spy. By 1947 the paper no longer interested or helped Powell, so he severed ties with it. Later that year he had a heart attack, which slowed him briefly. Truman fired his commerce secretary, Wallace, for opposing the Cold War, and everyone expected Powell to endorse Wallace's Progressive Party candidacy in the 1948 presidential campaign.

But Powell was serious about repairing his image on Communism and breaking free of his lefty allies, and it mattered to him that Wallace had no chance of winning. Wallace was a latecomer to racial justice politics, having caused no trouble for FDR in this area when he worked for him. As a liberated Progressive, however, Wallace blasted racism, segregation, and the Cold War, he called for the nationalization of banks and railroads, and he stayed in black-owned hotels. Marcantonio worked hard for Wallace, but Powell endorsed nobody until eight days before the election. Endorsing Dewey was a possibility for him, as Dewey had a good record on civil rights and was widely expected to win. But Dewey ran a frontrunner campaign of platitudes: "Our future lies before us" . . . "Agriculture is important" . . . "Our rivers are full of fish." Truman countered with a feisty campaign defending the New Deal and his advocacy of civil rights and anti-Communism, closing a huge gap in the polls. Powell could deal with Republicans who were not bad on civil rights. Dewey's New York, in particular, had a tradition of Republican racial liberalism, and in 1948 Nelson Rockefeller was an up-and-comer in New York Republican politics. In the bigger picture, however, Republicans were the bad party. They controlled both houses of Congress in 1948 and stood in the way of making the FEPC permanent. So Powell belatedly supported the one major candidate he really disliked, Truman. The following week the candidate he liked, Wallace, finished fourth behind Dixiecrat Strom Thurmond.[60]

By 1948 Powell was the indispensable ally of the NAACP in Congress, notwithstanding that Wilkins and other NAACP leaders held him in medium low regard. Powell took the lead in fighting for a permanent FEPC, he employed the Powell Amendment shrewdly, and he sponsored the NAACP's amendment to the Taft-Hartley Act prohibiting trade unions from practicing discrimination. In January 1950 the NAACP sponsored a major civil rights conference in Washington, DC, the biggest ever convened to that point. The agenda was to mobilize support for Truman's program in Congress — comprehensive civil rights legislation and a permanent FEPC. The House Rules Committee blocked civil rights measures from coming to the floor, and the Senate stood ready to filibuster anything that came through. Over fifty organizations allied with the NAACP to break the congressional logjam, led by Americans for Democratic Action (ADA), the CIO, AFL, National Council of Negro Woman, Negro Elks, and numerous church groups. This was an emphatically mainstream coalition, excluding left-wing speakers and organizations long important to the civil rights movement. Davis, Wallace, Marcantonio, and Paul Robeson were not invited to speak. The Southern Negro Youth Congress had expired in 1948, and eleven pro-Communist trade unions were expelled from the CIO in 1949–1950. All were excluded as untouchable, as Wilkins explained in the *New Leader*: "It is a non-partisan, non-left movement, rejecting the persistent proffers of 'cooperation' and 'assistance' made by individuals and organizations long identified as apologists for communist doctrine and Soviet foreign policies."[61]

The NAACP treasured its mainstream status, it rejoiced at having a friend in the White House, and it struggled to accommodate the many groups seeking to support the movement. Wilkins later recalled that after World War II "the main problem we had at the NAACP was coping with success and booming growth." New members joined across the country. The war accelerated migration, urbanization, and industrialization, which nationalized civil rights issues and enhanced black voting power. Every speaker at the mobilization conference understood that the agenda was to help Truman take the fight to Congress. Every speaker except Powell followed the script, daring to be on-message and slightly boring. Powell was hot and demanding. He defied the premise that Truman was an ally, and he challenged the organizers to prove their militancy. Truman, Powell thundered, needed to press House leaders immediately to bring FEPC to the floor. Otherwise Truman had lied to the American people. The organizers needed to demand immediately that Truman do so. Otherwise they were sellouts too. Many delegates cheered while conference leaders sat stricken and appalled. Instead of building support for Truman and his program, Powell was making Truman and them look bad. They fumed as Powell repositioned himself. He had left behind his pro-Communist friends but not his proclivity for radical independence. He belonged to the respectable main-stream but at its militant edge, where he stood out.[62]

This adjustment came just in time to get Powell through the McCarthy hysteria. He put the Powell Amendment on hold after America entered the Korean War in 1950. Later that year he spurned the American Labor Party endorsement, bowing to the new Tammany boss, Carmine DeSapio, who revived Tammany in the early 1950s. In 1951, two years after Davis lost his city council seat, Davis blasted Powell for adopting "a line of surrender to the warmongering oppressors of the Negro people." Powell did not merely sell out and betray his friends, Davis said. He became a perfect foil of the Wall Street masters: "Wall Street needs a radical-sounding orator who can dress up the 'white supremacy' war program so that it sounds like a militant struggle for Negro rights. That's Rep. Powell." Powell welcomed criticism of this kind for its protec-tive value. His congressional status helped him with the FBI, but the FBI tracked down Scott's involvement with unions linked to Communism, and Powell advised her to testify voluntarily to HUAC. On September 22, 1950, Scott did so, skillfully. She had never been a Communist. She had dropped her association with groups that turned out to be Communist. She believed that Communists should be ousted from unions, through orderly procedures. She would help to oust them. And she eloquently asked HUAC not to smear innocent people: "We should not be written off by the vicious slanders of little and petty men. . . . We will be much more useful to America if we do not enter this battle covered with the mud of slander and the filth of scandal."[63]

That became Powell's message too. Marcantonio served East Harlem for eight terms in Congress, representing an increasingly Puerto Rican district while holding together New York's fractious left coalitions. He spoke Spanish and Italian fluently, battled for civil rights legislation throughout his career, and stuck to his independent Socialism. He was wildly popular and respected, often winning three party nominations. But the twin upsurge of anti-communism and Tammany overtook Marcantonio. He got in trouble for supporting Wallace and opposing the Korean War, and in 1950 Tammany ran a stridently prowar Democrat against him, James Donovan. Marcantonio lost his seat and an era ended. Upon taking down Marcantonio, DeSapio vowed to turn Powell into a regular Democrat. He had reasons for thinking it was possible. Powell had cut his ties to his leftist past; he lived in White Plains, not Harlem; he wanted more influence in Congress, which required team play; and DeSapio briefly restored much of Tammany's former clout. Powell had to figure out how to preserve the two things he cared most about—his status as "Mr. Civil Rights" and his independence—in a new political environment.

The McCarthy hysteria consumed Truman's administration and extinguished his desire to be president. He won more battles than it felt like, building a postwar order and a Cold War establishment. But by 1951 Truman just wanted to go home. Both parties convened in Chicago the following year, and both produced weak platforms on civil rights. Democrats probably would have nominated war hero Dwight D. Eisenhower for president had he turned out to be a Democrat. Tennessee senator Estes Kefauver won most of the primaries, but the northern party bosses did not want him, and Kefauver was too liberal for most southern Democrats. Powell supported Averell Harriman, who never caught fire. At the convention the party bosses settled on Illinois governor Adlai Stevenson II, who mesmerized the convention with a flowery speech about campaigning truthfully and governing with wisdom. Stevenson reached for ticket balance by selecting Alabama senator John Sparkman as his running mate. Powell spent the convention fuming at the weak platform, the inordinate attention given to Dawson, and Stevenson's victory over Harriman. The entire proceeding was a setback from the 1948 convention, where young Minneapolis mayor Hubert H. Humphrey challenged Democrats to adopt a strong civil rights platform and the convention did so with noisy passion, conflict, and Dixiecrats stalking out. Four years later the convention aimed for conflict-averse blandness. Then Stevenson named Sparkman, and Powell erupted, bolting the convention with a wave of his hand, storming out with a flock of black delegates. Party regulars and Randolph were aghast at Powell's tantrum and bad judgment; surely he had ruined his reputation.

That was completely wrong. Powell cared what the maids and parking attendants thought, not the party bosses. He went home to New York and excoriated the party for nominating a symbol of Deep South segregation. He waited for Stevenson to come to him, which happened at the end of August. Stevenson asked Powell what it would take to win his active support. Powell said it would take money and a campaign staff. Stevenson agreed, and Powell campaigned for him, although he took a September break in England, as he and Scott had become borderline Europhiles. Later they became emphatic Europhiles.[64]

Stevenson won nine states, none outside the South, and Powell recalculated his approach. Republicans held the presidency and slight majorities in both houses of Congress, and Richard Nixon had ridden McCarthy-style anti-Communism into the vice presidency. The heady days of imagining the next New Deal were over. And it had galled Powell to be frozen out of Truman's White House. Eisenhower was tremendously popular, long on genial dignity, and conservative on almost everything Powell cared about. Powell reasoned that attacking Eisenhower for opposing civil rights would not work. Americans were thrilled to have an affable war hero Republican in the White House. To move civil rights forward Powell had to treat Eisenhower the opposite of how he had treated Truman. Instead of pressuring and attacking, he claimed to believe that Eisenhower supported the civil rights agenda. The problem was that certain Eisenhower officials did not share the president's feelings or program, so they had to be exposed.

Eisenhower had a popular view about "the race problem." He hated even to use these words because they made the problem worse. There was no legislative cure for the race problem, he said. Only education and the growth of goodwill on all sides would overcome it. In 1948 Eisenhower urged Congress not to integrate the army below the platoon level, where soldiers lived together in barracks. It was unwise to use the force of law to force integration. Eisenhower opposed making the FEPC permanent at the national level; at best, this was an issue for states. He supported voting rights but opposed everything smacking of enforced "social mingling." Eisenhower's support of voting rights, however, was vague and verbal, and on social equality he was sympathetic to southern feelings. When pressed on the latter subject he was not above pedestrian bigotry, assuring that he would not want a Negro to court his daughter. The NAACP worked on Eisenhower with no illusion that he was secretly a racial liberal. Ironically, Powell's strategy of blaming Eisenhower's aides would not have worked had Powell not made friends in the administration.[65]

Eisenhower filled his administration with wealthy white businessmen and a token black, E. Frederick Morrow, a former CBS executive lacking an actual position. Morrow had to complain to get a job title, which became undesignated assistant to the president. Powell needled Morrow about having no job and refusing to deal with civil rights. Morrow felt diminished when people viewed him as a black man; Powell knew the type and took pity that the dark-colored Morrow could not claim his blackness. Powell had similar feelings about the new president and his white corporate minions. These people were bland, entitled, emotionally undeveloped, and unreflective about their privilege. But some were reachable, and three were more open to Powell than Truman officials had been. The key figure was Maxwell Rabb, Eisenhower's secretary to the cabinet, who had served as assistant to Massachusetts senator Henry Cabot Lodge. Powell also bonded with Attorney General Herbert Brownell, whom he knew from New York political circles, and he won over Eisenhower's top assistant, Sherman Adams. Rabb later told Haygood that Powell was impressive and "very charismatic," not the wild man of his stereotype: "He had a winning way."[66]

Black veterans returning from Korea got shabby treatment in still-segregated military hospitals. They wrote to Powell, who worked, at first, through normal channels to address the problem. In April 1953 Powell learned that Oveta Culp Hobby, secretary of the newly created Health, Education, and Welfare Department, was not carrying out the department's mandate to desegregate military bases. Hobby was a southern opponent of integration and the New Deal and Eisenhower's only female cabinet secretary. Powell wrote a page-one story for the *Washington Evening Star* accusing Hobby and Secretary of the Navy Robert Anderson of insubordination to America's commander in chief, whom Powell described as a man of "decent instincts and strong moral character." He ended with a nervy sermon about Eisenhower's moral duties to the free world and asked for a personal reply from the president. Eisenhower was livid that Powell ambushed him publicly without warning. He told Adams to do something, and Adams dispatched Rabb to Powell's office. There a friendship was born. Rabb told Powell this administration would not make promises to blacks. However, he had something to offer Powell: insider status. If Powell was willing to work behind the scenes he could be a player in the Eisenhower White House.[67]

Powell agreed immediately. Three days later Eisenhower sent a telegram to Powell thanking him for his kind words and assuring him that he intended to eliminate segregation in federal institutions: "We have not taken and we shall not take a single backward step. There must be no second class citizenship in this country." Powell was overjoyed that Rabb had sealed the deal with Eisenhower. He wrote an effusive, jubilant, absurdly exaggerated reply to Eisenhower, enthusing that his telegram was "a Magna Carta for minorities and a second Emancipation Proclamation." This was remarkable praise for a telegrammed pledge to obey an existing federal law. Powell wanted very much to be a player in the White House, and he was willing to keep his end of the deal. He would report something to Rabb, who would get something done, all with no aspersions on Eisenhower's commitment to civil rights. Powell would stroll into Adams's office and explain the political angles at work. Adams, a self-described country boy lacking Powell's freewheeling brilliance, came to rely on these visits. Years later Adams told Haygood, "I guess you could say we leaned on Powell quite a lot. Powell, at those early stages, was a political asset, and we treated him as such." Powell was "an expert at political chicanery, and not in a bad sense," Adams added. "He was about the smoothest guy I ever saw. I always felt he had an intuition about how to act."[68]

Quiet, gradual desegregation was the way to go, to the extent that the law required, exactly as Eisenhower said when he was forced to say something.

Segregation fell away on military bases and almost nowhere else, except Washington, DC. The surprise was that Powell became so central to this strategy. He sprinkled his sermons and speeches with praise for Eisenhower, often letting on that he was tight with the president's men. In February 1954 Powell told a union rally in Chicago that Eisenhower had done more to restore black Americans to first-class citizenship than any president since Lincoln. Rabb, thrilled with this claim, asked Powell to say it to a really big audience, in *Reader's Digest*. Powell wrote an effusive draft that got more so after the *Brown* decision came down on May 17. The article appeared in October 1954, a few weeks before the midterm elections. Powell mentioned military desegregation, appointments of blacks to minor positions, desegregation initiatives in Washington, DC, and Eisenhower's appointment of Chief Justice Earl Warren to the Supreme Court. He did not mention that Eisenhower privately considered the *Brown* decision a colossal mistake that would seriously damage the cause of civil rights. Implying that Eisenhower agreed with him, Powell described *Brown* as "democracy's shining hour" and "communism's worst defeat." He was still a Democrat, he avowed: "I nevertheless believe that Dwight Eisenhower is proving to be the President of all the people and that, not Negroes only, but all the people will be better and America stronger because of it."[69]

These overblown plaudits for Eisenhower seriously annoyed all Democrats compelled to campaign for their election. Powell spent much of the year in Europe, where he didn't have to hear about it. Democrats narrowly took back Congress anyway in a historic election, winning an eight-seat majority in the House and a two-seat majority in the Senate. It proved to be historic because Democrats held the Senate until 1980 and the House until 1994. Powell, happy for his party, still poured on praise for "the daring leadership of President Eisenhower." In December 1954, preaching at Abyssinian, where some faithful had never stopped voting Republican, Powell declared that each form of discrimination was linked to every other and all were going down: "The abolition of segregation in the public school system of America is more than a national problem, more than a racial problem, more than a political problem, more even than a problem of the Constitution. It is a moral problem which will directly shape the ethical future of the entire world." The following month Powell announced that he would attach the Powell Amendment to all new legislation in education. Years later, still rationalizing his role in the Eisenhower administration, Powell reflected, "But something had happened to Eisenhower. Some influences had begun to pressure him into changing his views. Maybe it was the defeat that his appointees in the State Department had suffered because of the Bandung Conference."[70]

The Bandung Conference was the first formal gathering of what came to be called the Third World. It convened in the mountain resort West Java city of Bandung, Indonesia, in April 1955. Indonesian president Sukarno invited the United States to send an official representative. Powell made a speech on the House floor urging the administration to send an interracial delegation. Secretary of State John Foster Dulles had no interest in sending anyone, so Powell pleaded that at least he should go. Powell added that he was known throughout Africa, but that meant nothing to Dulles and the State Department. Rabb appealed to Eisenhower on Powell's behalf, but the answer was still no, even though Powell let on that he would go one way or another. He secured press credentials from a group of black publishers and sent himself, flying to Manila and Jakarta. Upon arriving in Bandung, Powell was snubbed by the American embassy but treated by his hosts as a dignitary along with Sukarno, China's Chou En-lai, Egypt's Gamal Abdel Nasser, India's Jawaharlal Nehru, and other leaders.

The Soviet Union sent no leaders, but *Pravda* reporters sought out Powell, expecting a propaganda windfall. Powell sorely disappointed them, reporting that blacks had made dramatic gains under American freedom and democracy. He noted that hotels and schools in Washington, DC, had been integrated, a Negro had been elected to a citywide office in Atlanta, Negroes held offices in Richmond and Norfolk, and Virginia had decided not to resist the *Brown* decision. Second-class citizenship was fading and on the way out, Powell claimed. The *New York Herald Tribune, New York Mirror, New York Times,* and *Minneapolis Tribune* gave the story front-page treatment, playing up that Powell defended the United States. The *Herald Tribune* headlined, "Powell Tells Asia About U.S. Negro; Red Newsmen Find Him off the 'Line.'" Many editorialized that Powell greatly helped his country despite representing nobody and having to pay his own way. Some black papers had a harder time congratulating Powell; the *Pittsburgh Courier* scoffed that he became a hero by recycling white America's mawkish pieties about itself. But even the *Courier* said it was a good thing for Powell to become so famous.[71]

In November 1955 he took his fame to Birmingham and Montgomery, Alabama, having heard that a protest movement was brewing in both places. In Birmingham two state troopers whisked Powell to the governor's mansion, where he had drinks and a pleasant off-the-record portico visit with Alabama governor James Folsom. Folsom was a swashbuckling populist who cared about the suffering of blacks and poor whites. He supported Wallace at the 1944 Democratic Convention; in 1946, running for governor, Folsom campaigned with a mop and bucket, vowing to clean up the capital. Powell took heart that Folsom's brand of populism had a following in Alabama. The following night

Powell spoke to the Alabama Education Association (a black teachers' organization), where he commended Folsom as "a big, open-hearted fella" who supported black advancement through education. Local Baptists were already criticizing Powell for drinking with Folsom, so Powell puckishly declared that if drinking with the governor could make things easier for black Americans, he was a confirmed alcoholic.[72]

Then he went to Montgomery. Gardner C. Taylor, pastor of the mammoth Concord Baptist Church in Brooklyn, organized a speaking engagement for Powell with the budding protest network in Montgomery, but Powell failed to show up. He did not know these southern Baptist ministers, except that they were southern and affiliated with the NAACP, two things that put off Powell. Whoever these people were, they spoke in the idioms of southern folk culture and religion. Actually, some of the Montgomery organizers were nervous about affiliating with the NAACP, which smacked of radicalism and northern professional activists, and others were leaders of southern NAACP chapters. But both groups made Powell uneasy. Southern churches, to Powell, had no important role to play in the civil rights struggle, and southern folk culture was decidedly backward. Moreover, the only NAACP official Powell respected was Clarence Mitchell, a lobbyist in Washington, DC, who fed him information from NAACP field reports. The rest were establishment plodders. Powell called Taylor to find out how big the crowd had been and how long it waited for him. Taylor said the crowd was huge and very excited to meet him. Powell reconsidered, and the Montgomery organizers gathered a second time. Powell encouraged them to go ahead with the bus plan. Recounting the bus strike in Harlem, he relished the memory of the maids who refused to ride buses into Manhattan. The organizers responded appreciatively, and Powell later claimed credit for explaining to King, Rustin, Rosa Parks, and E. D. Nixon how to run a boycott.[73]

At the time, however, Powell made news by deflecting attention from what he said. A reporter asked Powell about his Montgomery visit, and Powell said he had a swell time drinking with the governor. All hell broke loose for Folsom. Editorialists raged against him for race mixing, drinking with a notorious radical. Papers that had previously overlooked or chortled at Folsom's womanizing now berated him for amorous tendencies that he shared with the notorious Powell. Others piled on that Folsom took bribes. Folsom never won another election. In 1958 a vengeful segregationist, John Patterson, beat Folsom's protégé George Wallace, who was endorsed by the NAACP. Patterson aggressively persecuted King and civil rights leaders, and Wallace underwent a political conversion, denouncing Folsom for being "soft on the nigger question." In 1962 Wallace fatefully won the governor's chair in a race against Folsom.[74]

Back at Abyssinian, old-timers had long feared that Powell's political career would drag the congregation into corruption and scandal. Their fears were realized in 1954, a year after Powell Senior's death, when Powell's secretary Hattie Dodson was hauled before a New York grand jury for tax fraud. In the late 1940s Powell left Abyssinian mostly in the hands of Joe Ford, a former street hustler who had become a Tammany operative and Powell's link to Tammany. Ford had no spiritual link to the church, but he ran Powell's campaigns and Harlem office. Since the church was Powell's district headquarters, he needed a political loyalist to run the office and church. He later explained that he had no experience in practical politics when he started, so he relied on Ford. A self-trained accountant, Ford opened an income tax agency in the basement, with Powell's blessing. Ford drafted Dodson to work for the agency, and he ran a sloppy shop. Then he had a bitter falling out with Powell, in 1951. Three years later the IRS came after Dodson, backed by testimony from Ford that she had drawn a salary from Abyssinian and a salary from the government under different names and kicked back the government salary to Powell.[75]

Dodson did not testify at her trial in May 1956, but her grand jury statement provided her explanation of what happened. She had kept her government salary in a safe deposit box, wanting to surprise her husband someday with funds for a house. The government money added up to $9,000, she had managed to save little of it, and none went to Powell. Judge Irving R. Kaufman sentenced her to seven months in prison and a $1,000 fine, and her conviction caused deep pain at Abyssinian, as Dodson was beloved at the church and she loved Powell dearly. Three other employees at Abyssinian were convicted of similar crimes the same year—two for tax fraud and one for embezzlement of church funds. All had served on Powell's congressional staff and all served time in prison. All got in trouble through investigative probes aimed at Powell. Powell provided testimony in each case, denying any personal wrongdoing. He charged that Abyssinian came under special scrutiny because of his civil rights militancy, which was certainly true. But this charge was tricky for Powell during the very period that he crawled into bed with the Eisenhower administration. Many suspected that he got there to protect himself from being prosecuted. For the rest of his career he lived amid a swirl of innuendo and accusation. Hamilton observed, "Without question, he lived on the cusp of suspicious wrongdoing. Persons around him were going to jail, sometimes because of questionable but unproven financial dealings with him. And it was equally clear that virtually any political decision he took from then on would be subject, by friend or foe, to scrutiny for its relation to his personal problems."[76]

The white South defied the *Brown* decision and lashed out at the NAACP, the Montgomery boycott erupted, and the Deep South boiled over. On January 30, 1956, King's home was bombed, and Powell called for a National Day of Prayer to give moral support to besieged blacks in the South. That was too strident for Eisenhower's team. Morrow urged Adams and Rabb to let him go to Birmingham to speak with black leaders. He claimed they trusted him and did not trust Powell, the "flamboyant opportunist." In fact Morrow had no credibility with movement organizers and was not sent. Rabb chastised him for trying, telling Morrow that the new black leaders were surly, ungrateful troublemakers bent on causing an explosion. In March the FBI reported that 127 new anti-integration organizations had been founded since the *Brown* verdict. Eisenhower exhorted his aides to be calm and prudent. They had to stay neutral on the issue in Montgomery. Extremists on both sides were inciting violence and the federal government had to tamp it down.[77]

Since Powell was tight with Adams, Rabb, and Brownell, he knew that Eisenhower was willing to do very little for civil rights. On various occasions Powell lamented that the no-step-backward Eisenhower of 1953 somehow lapsed into the dodge-the-issue Eisenhower of 1956. In May 1956 Powell upstaged King, Randolph, Wilkins, and Eleanor Roosevelt at a rally in Madison Square Garden, where he chastised both political parties for dodging the issue and ridiculed Rustin for trying to hold him to a time limit. Powell kept needling both parties while Stevenson battled Kefauver for the Democratic presidential nomination. Kefauver, a New Deal liberal, reminded Democrats that he was cheated in 1952. He had conflicted feelings about racial integration, but in 1956 Kefauver said the federal government should intervene in southern communities to enforce the Constitution. Stevenson disagreed, telling a group of black Americans that integration could not be achieved by federal troops. In a much-quoted statement that defined the term "gradualism," he added, "We must proceed gradually, not upsetting habits or traditions that are older than the Republic." Liberals debated whether this position made Stevenson merely as bad as Eisenhower or worse. Black newspapers protested, and Stevenson groused, "Evidently what they want to hear about is civil rights, minorities, Israel, and little else, and certainly no vague futures." Sometimes he added that he disliked the Powell Amendment, a crude instrument that strangled federal aid to education. Powell and Wilkins replied that even the gradualist strategy could not be served by allowing southern states to build new Jim Crow schools. Stevenson blithely told Wilkins, "We must recognize that it is reason alone that will determine our rate of progress."[78]

The politics of race had changed since the 1952 election, which made Stevenson as averse as Eisenhower to talking about race. After Stevenson won the nomination he let the convention choose his running mate, realizing that he had offended many liberals. Liberals won a consolation prize—Kefauver instead of John F. Kennedy—but Powell skipped the convention, in Europe. The consolation prize did not impress him, and he wanted to support Eisenhower anyway. In early October Powell told Rabb he was ready to do it, if appropriately accommodated. Rabb was stunned and incredulous. Some civil rights leaders were reachable—King and Ralph Abernathy quietly voted for Eisenhower in 1956—and some were definitely not reachable: Randolph and Wilkins were staunchly anti-Republican. But Rabb had never dreamed that the only important black politician, a Democrat, would publicly campaign for Eisenhower. Rabb arranged a meeting on October 11, and Powell told the president he was eager to campaign for him. Eisenhower told Powell he would support a voting rights bill granting additional powers to the Justice Department and permitting civil suits over infringements of civil rights. He would also support a school aid bill that cut off funds to districts refusing to obey court orders. Upon announcing his plan to campaign for Eisenhower, Powell mistakenly said that Eisenhower promised to charge school officials with contempt of court when they refused desegregation orders. Eisenhower had carefully not crossed that line, so Powell had to retract point three.[79]

He worked hard for Eisenhower, campaigning in Baltimore, Cleveland, Toledo, Detroit, Chicago, St. Louis, Los Angeles, San Francisco, and New York. He was handsomely accommodated with a room at the Waldorf-Astoria Hotel, an apartment at Middletown Hotel, $50,000 cash, and a new organization on Park Avenue, Independent Democrats for Eisenhower (IDE). Powell may have received help with his tax investigation, as many charged, and may have been provided with sexual partners on the road, as IDE executive director Frederick Weaver reported. Scott had separated from Powell in 1955, mostly over his philandering and her drinking; she took a three-week engagement in Paris that stretched to three years. There were later versions of the IDE story in which Nixon provided help with Powell's tax problems and tire baron Harvey Firestone bankrolled Powell's campaign. Powell took pride in living in high style on his terms, and he did little to refute the growing lore about it. Eventually the lore caught up with him and overwhelmed his congressional career. But most of it was standard fare for celebrities and high-rolling operatives, and Eisenhower had ample support among blacks with or without Powell's influence; the *Pittsburgh Courier* remained resolutely Republican.[80]

Fallout came swiftly. Emphatically, Powell did not get the welcome-home treatment that Dixiecrats received after the 1948 election. House Democrats fired Powell's two patronage appointments on the ground that Democratic patronage was for Democrats. Powell was stripped of his seniority on the Committee on Education and Labor, a major blow. Eleanor Roosevelt terminated their friendship. Roosevelt oscillated between reform and regular Democrats, but she was a die-hard Democrat in any case and seethed at Powell's betrayal. She schemed with DeSapio to get rid of Powell. Republicans treated Powell rudely, too. New York Republican leaders spurned him, and Powell felt abused at the White House, although Eisenhower aides told a different story of not fathoming what he wanted from them. Powell wrote that Republican leaders "had used me and now wanted nothing more than perhaps to destroy me." They were done with him, except when they needed a favor. Powell had to beg the White House to pay his staff for overtime and unused vacations.[81]

Worst of all, IRS commissioner T. Coleman Andrews and attorney Roy Cohn pursued Powell for tax fraud. Andrews owed his IRS appointment to segregationist Virginia senator Robert Byrd, having run for president in 1956 as candidate of the far-right States Rights Party. Cohn was a former Joe McCarthy aide. *National Review* founder William F. Buckley Jr. made Powell his new project, McCarthyism having faded. Brownell thought there was nothing to the tax issue, but he did not want to fight with Andrews with a civil rights bill pending. Many rallied to Powell's defense on the Democratic Party issues, notably Wilkins, Gardner Taylor, ADA leader Joe Rauh, and the *Amsterdam News*. But almost no one defended Powell on the tax probe, which he noticed: "With everyone now against me, all seemed lost. Stripped of my seniority and patronage, with Republican leaders out to knife me, Carmine DeSapio whispering that a purge was coming, Mrs. Roosevelt becoming a blindly unreconstructed enemy, I felt like giving up. But the still, small voice bade me, 'Fight on!'"[82]

GOOD RELIGION AND WINNING POLITICS

Powell seemed to be fading just as the civil rights issue took off. Randolph and Wilkins had long believed that Powell was overly political and lacking a moral compass. Now they had a movement peer who agreed, King. Many insiders had favorite stories about Powell picking up beautiful women at clubs and political gatherings. Now his moral laxity was catching up with him. But to view Powell as a simple hypocrite was never right. He reveled openly in his nightclub lifestyle, he did not have a conservative idea of religion, and he never had a conservative religion to give up. Religion, for Powell, was about cultivating an experience of the divine mystery of life and fulfilling the prophetic demand for justice. He was a Christian because Christianity was supremely dialectical. It held together the idea of an unfathomable, transcendent, holy

mystery *and* the experience of historical, particular, kingdom-seeking incarnation. In the pulpit Powell noted various parallels between Christianity and other
world religions, stressing that several religions taught that God is a loving heavenly father. But the point of the comparison was always to confirm his commitment to seeing the world through a Christian lens.

"In God there is something eternal," symbolized as Father, Powell would
say. "In God there is something historic," the life of Jesus Christ. And in God
"there is something progressive," the forward-moving lure of the Holy Spirit.
Christianity is fundamentally the union of transcendence and immanence,
with a distinct moral trajectory: "In Christianity there is a distinctive and central
teaching concerning Jesus Christ as the unique incarnation of the Word of
God, preeminently manifested in the historic person, on the ground that his
moral character perfectly represents the character and purpose of the invisible
holy God." Powell prized the Bhagavad Gita for its offer of universal salvation
but criticized its teaching about caste. He praised Islam for repudiating "all
ideas of hereditary status and social superiority" but rejected its harsh attitude
toward infidels. He appreciated that Judaism, Islam, and Sikhism shared the
Christian belief "in the worship of one supreme cosmic power by all people"
but preached that only Christianity worships a God "who in His own character
is self-sacrificingly seeking the redemption of the world, who is historically
represented by a person of that same moral character." Only in Christianity
does a loving God suffer to save others. Christian monotheism, Powell taught,
thus "has the highest possible moral content, a holy, loving, heavenly Father
who actively seeks the welfare, trust, obedience, cooperation, and love of
all men."[83]

Powell appreciated that eight religions taught some form of the golden rule.
He stressed, however, that only Jesus expressed it "positively and universally,
not negatively as a warning to abstain from misbehavior." Only Jesus taught his
followers to love their enemies, and only Christianity taught that divine love
is the willingness to love all without exception to the point of self-sacrifice.
Salvation is precisely self-sacrificial love divine saving all without exceptions:
"Jesus is the only one who based this universal rule of human conduct upon the
character of universal conduct of God Himself: 'Love your enemies, bless them
that curse you, do good to them that hate you.'" Powell told Abyssinians that too
many churches focused on trivial things or distorted the radical message of the
gospel. Bad religion does not save; it reinforces ignorance, selfishness, bigotry,
and fear. Christianity, though not the only good religion, is by far the best religion, although much of Christianity is terrible: "Christianity alone teaches that
all human society has a sacred moral character, and that every individual, every

nation, should be brought lovingly into the comprehensive brotherhood of humanity under the universal thought 'whosoever will come after me, let him deny himself, and take up his cross, and follow me' (Mark 8:34)."[84]

Powell did not start with sin and work up to salvation, although he allowed that that is how salvation works. In preaching the gospel, he started with the divine creator and savior of all things before getting to things from which people needed to be saved. Every religion is a salvation strategy, he taught. Buddhism focuses on emotional suffering and suppresses individuality. Hinduism seeks salvation through union with God, teaching that evil is illusory. Islam says that evil is arbitrary—"the only evil in the world are the non-Muslims." Confucianism says that human beings are inherently good—"there is not much evil in the world." Taoism says that evil is real but should be ignored. Powell shook his head at religious asceticism wherever he found it, countering with John 10:10: "I am come that they might have life, and have it more abundantly." Christian salvation is about the flourishing of personality, Powell preached. It is worldly, spiritual, life-affirming, and social, and it builds upon liberation from bondage: "Christianity says that evil is a terrible and widespread fact in life. Each individual is directly responsible for choosing evil rather than good. The fundamental evil is any selfish use of our God-given free will, with its resultant injury to our personality. All individuals are liable to evil and actually do sin against God, against other persons and against their own best self. But, thanks be unto God, salvation is available to all—women as well as men, the lowest class as well as the highest, the believers and nonbelievers."[85]

Powell had the classic social gospel ambition of changing society with the moral power of the gospel. The aim was to Christianize society, not to politicize religion. In other words, "We are not putting politics in the church, we are putting religion into politics." He had seven guiding principles for this work. First, the church is above all a spiritual fellowship dependent on God, but, second, the church needed to "lay more stress upon the participation in politics as a religious vocation." Third, the church had to preach nonviolence; otherwise it was not Christian. Fourth, the church needed to rally nonpartisan political activism on any issue "where the principle of respect for personality is at stake—child labor, sharecroppers, civil rights, housing, public health, the rights of workers." Fifth, the church in its social witness needed to subordinate the power of the state to the individual Christian conscience. Sixth, every congregation should be an exemplary democratic fellowship, "a nucleus from which a new democracy can be built." Seventh, reason and revelation go together in guiding the church's activism: "Without reason there is no knowledge of how to act in civic affairs. Without revelation one sees little to ask for."[86]

Powell told Abyssinians they were right to struggle for equality but cautioned that freedom "is always more important." God created human beings to be free and to take responsibility for their freedom to care for others: "He did not beget the human race so that men could get a little fun out of life. He did not put His Son on the cross so that we could have a picnic. He is after something that He risked death to get. He wants strong men. He wants the kind of character that can withstand the acids of time, the kind of spirit that is immortal because it has become indestructible. He wants men stable and sturdy, holy men with moral heroism."[87]

By the late 1950s that was an exhortation to himself. Powell warred against smallness and conformism, imploring his congregants to think big. Meanwhile he refused to be pushed aside while King's star ascended. Ghana celebrated its independence in February 1957, and the State Department and House Democratic leadership excluded Powell from representing the United States. Powell had to finagle an invitation as a member of King's party, just after King founded the Southern Christian Leadership Conference (SCLC) and was invited to the celebration by incoming prime minister Kwame Nkrumah. In the spring, King, Rustin, and Randolph organized a national civil rights march on Washington, DC, dragging Wilkins along. Powell warned the White House that King was planning an anti-Eisenhower march and vowed to do whatever he could to stop it. He settled for helping to tone down the Prayer Pilgrimage for Freedom, which was carefully not called a protest march. Thirty thousand people gathered at the Lincoln Memorial on May 17 to hear ten speakers plus a bevy of musical performers including Sammy Davis Jr., Mahalia Jackson, and Harry Belafonte. At Randolph's request, the program had a religious tone and eschewed applause and thus began slowly. Mordecai Johnson revved up the crowd, calling the *Brown* decision a second Emancipation Proclamation. Wilkins gave an eloquent sermon about not giving in to distress or despair, while a military helicopter buzzed overhead, drowning him out. The quiet feeling dispersed with Jackson's powerful singing of "I've Been 'Buked; I've Been Scorned," and Powell got the audience roaring by declaring that black Americans were getting more from a dead Republican (Lincoln) than from living Democrats and Republicans. Powell gave way to an interracial choir from Philadelphia, setting the stage for King, who ended the program with his first address to a national audience, "Give Us the Ballot." Afterward the *Amsterdam News* said that King was obviously the new Number One, and Wilkins blasted the paper for snubbing the NAACP and sowing division among black leaders.[88]

Three months later the Senate passed a stripped-down version of the Civil Rights Act of 1957. The NAACP and ADA pushed it through, working with

Nixon and Senate Majority Leader Lyndon Johnson, with little input from Powell. King cultivated a personal relationship with Nixon, who advocated voting rights protections that Johnson dropped on the way to wheedling a bill through the Senate. Johnson deleted a provision empowering the Justice Department to enforce school desegregation, and he supported a trade union demand guaranteeing state officials the right to a jury trial when they were accused of violating voting rights. The jury trial provision, in effect, nullified the House bill's defense of voting rights, since no southern jury would convict a state official of violating the voting rights of blacks. Johnson told liberals that nothing stronger than his bill would get through the Senate, and he told southern Democrats that his bill was as weak as possible. Eisenhower and Nixon bitterly swallowed the loss on voting rights, as did Wilkins, King, and Powell. Although Powell was not asked to round up votes for the bill, he lauded its passage, unlike King, who stressed its weakness.

In September Arkansas governor Orval Faubus ordered the National Guard to prevent nine African American students from enrolling at Central High School in Little Rock. Federal courts ruled against Faubus, and the National Guard briefly enforced school integration, but Faubus withdrew the troops, exposing black students to a large, hostile white mob. That forced Eisenhower to send one thousand U.S. Army troops to Little Rock, very reluctantly. He claimed he was not forcing integration; he was putting down an insurrection. Powell implored Eisenhower officials to put a better face on it. He had a specific face in mind, his own, urging Rabb to send him on a worldwide speaking tour to publicize America's racial progress. Powell wanted the U.S. Information Agency to sponsor the tour. Rabb liked the idea but didn't trust Powell. In December the Little Rock crisis faded, and Rabb and Adams decided there was no need to risk a Powell speaking tour controversy.

Powell warned that more Little Rocks were coming and Eisenhower needed to be more assertive about civil rights. That marked the end of Powell's usefulness to Eisenhower. For months Powell had urged Eisenhower to hold a White House conference on civil rights, and in June 1958 the White House belatedly held a very small one, without Powell. White House aides wanted only two civil rights leaders at the meeting, King and Randolph. King said that excluding Wilkins was a nonstarter for him, so the White House added Wilkins and Urban League president Lester Granger. Eisenhower aide Rocco Siciliano, prepping the president, advised him to avoid the words "patience" and "tolerance." That confused Eisenhower; why should he avoid such good English words? Siciliano explained that civil rights leaders were touchy in this area and it wasn't worth setting them off. At the meeting Granger said that Eisenhower's calls for patience made life difficult for Urban League moderates and that black Americans were angrier than ever. This news baffled and disappointed Eisenhower. If black Americans, he said, were angrier than ever after his administration did so much for them, he probably should not push forward. Attorney General William P. Rogers echoed that view. Meanwhile Powell, chagrined at being excluded, tried to save face by announcing that he had decided which blacks to invite. Nobody bought that; years later Powell spun it differently: "And so, the meeting I had fought to arrange was held without my presence. I could only conclude that the Administration feared that I would take too militant a stand. If so, the fear was justified."[89]

Perhaps so, but Powell had spent the past five years promoting Eisenhower. The White House made a cold-eyed judgment about who mattered. The action had moved elsewhere, Powell was in legal trouble, and he always brought his self-dramatizing ego, of which the White House had tired. Back in New York, DeSapio made a similar judgment about Powell, vowing to punish him for betraying the Democratic Party. DeSapio wanted to run Thurgood Marshall against Powell in the 1958 primary, but Marshall, still working for the NAACP, was not interested. DeSapio settled for city councilman and *Life* editor Earl Brown, whom Powell derided as a "hat-in-the-hand-Negro." Powell crushed Brown by a three-to-one margin, delivering a staggering blow to Tammany from which it never recovered. DeSapio's machine unraveled after he failed to humiliate Powell.[90]

Though Eisenhower tried to get voting rights into the civil rights bill, he did almost nothing else to improve black registration in the South. His administration did not study the problem seriously until John Doar joined the Justice Department in 1960; Doar later served in the Kennedy administration as assistant attorney general for civil rights. The NAACP and Tuskegee Civic Association (TCA) produced hard data on the problem, taking a disciplined teamwork approach that detailed outlandish registration exams and the like. Powell, however, offended voting rights activists by disdaining research and teamwork. In June 1959 Powell proposed a voting rights bill (HR 7957) that went nowhere; he didn't even speak for it. Hamilton, at the time a TCA official and instructor at Tuskegee Institute, admonished Powell about working with others and floating legislation prematurely. Powell dismissed him airily. Civil rights activists charged that Powell failed to pass legislation partly because he could not be bothered to work with others; thus he had little real influence. But that changed dramatically with one election.[91]

Powell did not like John Kennedy; no civil rights leader did. Kennedy voted against the Civil Rights Act of 1957, and he courted Dixiecrat support. He had no gut-level passion for social justice, he was soft on McCarthyism, and being Roman Catholic did not help him at Abyssinian Church. Kennedy reminded Powell of the feckless Stevenson, except Kennedy was worse. For president in 1960, Powell supported Minnesota senator Hubert Humphrey, Michigan governor G. Mennen Williams, and Missouri senator Stuart Symington. All were fighting liberals who cared about racial justice. Jackie Robinson, a Republican for Humphrey, was ready to vote for Nixon if it came down to Nixon versus Kennedy or Lyndon Johnson. Powell could not bear the thought of Nixon as president. Nixon as McCarthy witch-hunter and craven opportunist outweighed whatever credit he had earned on voting rights.

By July 1960 the only liberal with a chance was Symington, and he had little chance. Kennedy had swept the primaries, Johnson had party bosses in his corner, and some Democratic stalwarts wanted Stevenson to get a third chance. Powell mounted the pulpit at Abyssinian to make a risky, breathtaking case for Johnson. He allowed that Johnson mutilated the civil rights bill of 1957; still, he whipped it through the Senate, it would not have passed without him, and he did it as a Texas southerner. Johnson had a ruthless tenacity that Powell respected and the movement needed. If it came down to Kennedy versus Johnson, Powell said, there was no contest. Abyssinians had to support Johnson, and to get there they had to work on themselves. Powell declared, "Any Negro who automatically dismisses Lyndon Johnson because of the accident of birth automatically qualifies himself as an immature captive Negro, and a captive of his own prejudices." He put it more strongly: "This is a test of your own Christianity and if you rise to the heights you will be putting the reactionary segregationists of the South squarely on the spot so that all Americans, Northerners and Southerners, will know that they alone are the immature people. Let us not be captives of our own prejudices."[92]

Building up to the Democratic Convention in Los Angeles, Powell enjoyed his undeniable resurgence. He had humbled Tammany and returned to the party on his terms. He had refuted everyone who said he was politically dead. The Democratic nominee, whoever it turned out to be, would need Powell to swing black votes away from Nixon. In March Powell had beaten the federal tax case against him. The federal government charged that Powell falsely claimed deductions from Scott's 1951 tax return and their joint return of 1952 and understated his income for 1952. The trial yielded a dizzying swirl of stories about money wired to replace money spent in Paris, Monte Carlo, and Rome, befuddling jurors who tried to imagine Powell's lifestyle. Much of the trial hinged on whether Powell was on official government business when he accompanied Scott to European locales. Super-lawyer Edward Bennett Williams defended

Powell brilliantly; Hattie Dodson took the stand to say, repeatedly, that she could not remember; and a hung jury deadlocked on the only charge not dismissed by the judge, regarding Powell's 1951 return.

On his way to Los Angeles, Powell aggressively reclaimed his importance in national Democratic and civil rights politics. Basically he demanded that the civil rights movement run through the Democratic Party and, specifically, him. Students had ignited sit-in wildfire in Nashville, Greensboro, and far beyond, flooding the movement with youthful protesters willing to get arrested. They worked on King to commit to civil disobedience. Older movement leaders welcomed the surge while waiting anxiously for King's trial in Montgomery for tax fraud. They expected King to be convicted and sent to prison, but on May 28 King was acquitted, near miraculously, by an Alabama jury. Immediately King and Randolph planned demonstrations at both party conventions. It was hard to say where the movement was going or if it tilted toward the Democratic Party. To Powell, the flip side was equally relevant. Regular Democrats needed him more than ever. If Democrats were to be the party of civil rights or even aspire to that status, Powell was indispensable. King, Randolph, and Rustin laid plans for what they called a "March on the Convention Movement for Freedom Now." They had platform demands for both party conventions backed by pick-eters, and Rustin claimed that the NAACP supported the pickets.

That was a blunder, evoking Wilkins's wrath. Wilkins had not agreed to any specific plan, and he was outraged that Rustin misrepresented him. Wilkins was angry anyway because he resented King's celebrity, and now a youth move-ment evolving out of SCLC openly derided NAACP stodginess. The Student Nonviolent Coordinating Committee (SNCC), trained by Methodist pastor James Lawson and veteran organizer Ella Baker, was founded on April 15, 1960. Lawson derided the NAACP as a stodgy vehicle of the black bourgeoisie, offending Wilkins. Who was Lawson, a mere youth organizer in Nashville, to sneer at the NAACP? Then Rustin pulled a fast one, and Wilkins erupted. He fired off an angry, accusatory letter to Randolph, who waited eight days to reply. Wilkins took his complaint to Powell, who seized the moment. On June 18 King spoke to the National Sunday School Congress in Buffalo. The next day Powell told the Sunday School Congress that King and Randolph had bullied Wilkins. Moreover, Powell said, this had become a pattern. King and Randolph thought they were above other civil rights leaders and relied too much on two advisors, Rustin and Stanley Levison, who were outright Socialists. Powell posed as an apostle of unity, albeit by red-baiting Rustin and Levison. King and Randolph, Powell said, had good intentions, but they had to work better with others; other-wise the movement would be hopelessly splintered.[93]

The *Pittsburgh Courier* ran the story, which Rustin and Randolph shrugged off. Powell was always angling to make himself the center of attention. Randolph chuckled at the suggestion that he was a Socialist because of Levison's influence over him. King, however, was stung by Powell's attack, and said so. Powell retreated, telling King the *Courier* misquoted him. King went to Rio de Janeiro for the Baptist World Alliance, believing the episode was over, but in Rio he received a stunning message from Powell through an emissary, Ann Arnold Hastings. Powell demanded that King cancel the pickets at the Democratic Convention. If King refused to cancel, Powell would announce at a press conference that King was sexually involved with Rustin.[94]

This totally fabricated threat horrified King. He tried to call Randolph in New York, but Rustin picked up the phone; Randolph was out of the office. Mortified and panic-stricken, King conveyed the message to Rustin. The two men tried to gauge if Powell would do it. They had never trusted Powell, but this was fantastically over the top. Finally Rustin reached Randolph, who surmised that Powell was desperate to shore up his standing with party regulars who would vote on Powell's chairmanship of Education and Labor. Randolph told Rustin to tell King they had to carry out the conventions project. They could not control what Powell did, and if King canceled the picket, Randolph would have to explain that King did so at Powell's insistence.

That was reverse blackmail, leaving King stranded with no guarantee that Powell would not smear him anyway. Rustin agreed with Randolph, but King hesitated. Rustin, hoping to force King's hand, offered to resign his position with King and SCLC. King did not reject the offer, which wounded Rustin. The SCLC board had never wanted Rustin, and it chafed at King's reliance on him. Rustin was gay, a former Communist, and not a Baptist, and his fund-raising ad for King's tax defense had triggered crippling lawsuits against SCLC. The board was already screaming to fire Rustin when Powell shrewdly blackmailed King on Rustin's vulnerability points. Rustin later recalled, "Martin had one very major defect. He did not like contention with people who were supposed to be friends. . . . He sort of folded on in-fighting." Rustin announced his resignation, declaring that Powell had sought "to weaken, if not destroy, the march on the conventions for his own obvious political reasons." The convention demonstrations went on without Rustin but garnered little attention. The July protests in Los Angeles were small, the subsequent Republican demonstrations in Chicago were bigger, and in both cases there was a march, a rally, and all-day picketing. King walked several shifts on the picket lines. SNCC won some breakthrough attention at both conventions, but even with King's celebrity the pickets needed NAACP backing to make an impact, which did not occur.[95]

The NAACP stuck to its favored mode, holding rallies at both conventions. In Los Angeles Kennedy was roundly booed upon entering an NAACP rally. He won a few grudging claps with a game performance, but the crowd saved its acclaim for Humphrey, who declared that he would rather stand up for civil rights than win any election at any level. After the candidates departed Powell gave a barnburner speech about retaking the White House and fulfilling American democracy. He rocked the house with acidic jibes at white conservative cluelessness, bringing King, Randolph, and Wilkins to their feet. Then the pickets went up, and Powell skipped out along with Wilkins. The following day Kennedy racked up a first-ballot victory, and Powell seethed with frustration. Black delegates across the convention shook their heads, crying out, "No, no, no." The scene unnerved the Kennedy team—people who thought their suave gentility entitled them to black votes. Robert Kennedy, Theodore Sorensen, Kenneth O'Donnell, Pierre Salinger, and Lawrence O'Brien guided the Kennedy team. They had no connections to black communities and had not campaigned for black support.

Belatedly they signed up civil rights lawyer and King advisor Harris Wofford and former *Chicago Defender* editor Louis Martin to acquire some low-ranking, quiet outreach to black communities. The Kennedy team disparaged white liberals like Wofford as idealists who cared too much about civil rights. Wofford had studied at Howard Law School, studied Gandhian nonviolence theory in India, served on Eisenhower's Civil Rights Commission, and reached out to King during the Montgomery boycott. Martin had run two newspapers owned by John H. Sengstacke, the *Michigan Chronicle* and *Chicago Defender*, and with Sengstacke he had cofounded the National Newspaper Publishers Association in 1940. Kennedy aides knew nothing of Martin's world and looked down on Wofford's Gandhi fixation, but now they needed blacks and white liberals. Powell relished that Kennedy needed him, especially after Johnson wrangled the vice presidential nomination from the Kennedy brothers. Now there was a southerner on the ticket. All Powell had to do was wait for Kennedy to come begging for help. Powell boarded a yacht in the Mediterranean and cruised for two months waiting for Kennedy to call.

Martin reached out to Jackie Robinson but failed. Robinson campaigned for Nixon, a disaster for northern Democrats. Powell aide Ray Jones told Martin and Kennedy staffer Sargent Shriver that Powell was eager to campaign for Kennedy, if sufficiently accommodated. He would need a limousine, hotel suites, and a cash advance of $300,000. He settled for $50,000 paid out in $5,000 chunks for each speech. Powell also agreed to delay the announcement of his impending divorce. He worked hard for Kennedy, speaking in thirty-four cities in fifteen states. The campaign devised a tag team approach in which Kennedy followed Powell or the other way around. Powell loved all of it—the huge crowds and furious pace and predictable questions. Day after day he defended Kennedy's religion and Johnson's place on the ticket and ridiculed Nixon. Nixon had once made a property sale forbidding resale to a black or Jewish buyer; Powell campaigned with a six-foot replica of the deed. In Harlem Kennedy and Powell ribbed each other good-naturedly and an overflow crowd ate it up. Kennedy promised to abolish racial discrimination in federally subsidized housing with an executive order. He emoted that Africa had no children named Marx or Lenin, but there were plenty named George Washington, and there might be a couple named Adam Clayton Powell. This drew a playful "Careful, Jack" from Powell that the crowd enjoyed.[96]

Kennedy won an election squeaker by two-tenths of 1 percent, lifted by two brief phone calls that almost did not occur. Near the end of the campaign King was maliciously imprisoned in Georgia on a misdemeanor, and Wofford secretly persuaded JFK to make a sympathetic call to Coretta Scott King. Robert Kennedy was enraged when he learned what Wofford had done, but on second thought RFK called the Georgia judge to free MLK from prison and danger. These two calls reverberated through black churches and newspapers, changing the image of the Kennedy brothers. The Kennedy team tapped into something it knew almost nothing about. Wofford and Martin spread the word about the calls, chiefly through the Gardner Taylor wing of the National Baptist Convention, and Daddy King dramatically announced his switch to Kennedy.

JFK would not have been elected had Wofford and Shriver not defied Kennedy's kitchen cabinet, persuading JFK to risk a brief gesture of decency by telephone. In 1956 blacks supported Eisenhower by a 20-point margin. Four years later blacks supported Kennedy by a 40-point margin, and Kennedy won by 118,000 votes. This extraordinary swing accounted for more votes than Kennedy's victory margins in Michigan, New Jersey, Pennsylvania, Illinois, North Carolina, and South Carolina. The black vote decided the election, to the astonishment of both parties. Kennedy had done almost nothing to deserve it, but he had two low-ranking staffers who knew something about black America, and he had Powell. Kennedy's debt to Powell was so obvious that Powell uncharacteristically refrained from touting it publicly, letting others say it. Many said that JFK was beholden to black voters and Powell. Kennedy disliked the talk about his debt to black voters, which set off immediate retrenchment, but he was happy to repay Powell.[97]

Powell was flying higher than ever. The civil rights movement soon flowed through the Democratic Party in very much the manner that he prescribed. No civil rights leader symbolized this transformation as much as Powell. But he also came out of the 1960 election with self-inflicted wounds, having crossed an unforgivable line with movement leaders. King and Rustin never overcame the tensions that the Powell episode created in their relationships with each other. Randolph shucked it off, long accustomed to dealing with Powell. He took for granted that with Powell, one had to take the bad with the good. To Rustin and King, the episode cut more deeply, showing Rustin that King would not stand up for him and showing both that Powell would say anything to win a fight.

The coming of the Kennedy presidency coincided with Powell's accession to the chair of the Education and Labor Committee, which was a very big deal. Politics in Washington, DC, was still the domain of southern committee chairs. In 1960 the House had twenty-one committees and southerners headed fifteen. In the Senate there were sixteen committees and ten southern chairs. Graham Barden, a North Carolina reactionary, had ruled the Education and Labor Committee. Now he retired, and Powell was next in line, if his seniority was recognized. AFL-CIO chief George Meany urged Democrats to block Powell, but Teamsters president James Hoffa and United Mine Workers president John L. Lewis backed Powell, and he acquired a powerful position.

Powell's divorce came through in November 1960, and the following month he quietly married a young woman he had met in Puerto Rico, Yvette Flores Diago. Governor Luis Muñoz Marín introduced Powell to the winsome, twenty-nine-year-old Flores during one of his visits to San Juan. Powell liked to say that his interest in Puerto Rico began with his Puerto Rican constituency in Harlem, which was 10 percent by 1960. Flores, however, came from the island's tiny, wealthy, politically connected elite that rarely moved to Harlem. Few people in Washington knew of her existence when Flores joined Powell's staff as a secretary in 1960. After their wedding Powell raised her pay grade to the highest level, $13,000. But Flores had come from a lush island world of servants, vistas, and easygoing Spanish gentility. Washington seemed harsh to her, and Powell wanted her to stay in Puerto Rico anyway. So she returned to their beach home and gave birth in 1962 to a son, Adamcito, while remaining on the payroll.

On the week after Kennedy's inauguration two celebrity gatherings made a statement about the coming of civil rights. On January 27 Frank Sinatra and Sammy Davis Jr. staged a five-hour tribute to King at Carnegie Hall, with help from other entertainment stars in their orbit, notably Dean Martin, Count Basie, Tony Bennett, and Nipsey Russell. The gala raised $50,000 for the SCLC and confirmed that King had soared past other civil rights leaders as a national figure. Two nights later Powell's friends and foes convened at the Hotel Commodore in New York to celebrate his ascension to the chair of Education and Labor. This gathering was short on Hollywood celebrities but long on Washington powerbrokers. Randolph served as master of ceremonies. Two incoming cabinet officials attended, Health, Education, and Welfare secretary Abraham Ribicoff and Labor secretary Arthur Goldberg. Eleanor Roosevelt sent warm greetings, while declining to come. One hundred fifty labor officials came, as did eleven congressional members of Education and Labor, and Davis provided entertainment. Powell emoted that the people lifted him to power, not unions, but unions and the people needed to lift America together. He was eager to begin a new chapter of American history.[98]

He commanded attention from the outset of the Kennedy administration. Kennedy reached out to Powell, offering friendship and a political partnership, both of which Powell treasured. Powell hired a large staff, announcing that Education and Labor would sponsor vast new research on social legislation. For eight years Education and Labor had done almost nothing. That changed immediately as Powell called for new research on poverty, education, and juvenile delinquency. He more than tripled the committee's budget to $600,000 and abolished do-nothing subcommittees. In April he gave Kennedy a huge gift by pledging to withhold the Powell Amendment from school aid legislation. Powell pitched this decision as his contribution to helping America keep up with the Russians in education at all levels. On the same day, April 14, Attorney General Robert F. Kennedy dropped the remaining charge against Powell in the tax case. NAACP officials fretted about how that looked, but Powell was finally in the clear legally, except for Esther James.[99]

JFK and Powell, in the early going, had a similar reading of the politics of the moment. The country was changing but Congress looked much the same. The votes were there for big things on education and poverty, so Powell teamed with Ribicoff and Goldberg in pursuing an activist agenda. The votes for new civil rights bills were not there, so JFK relied on executive decrees. Kennedy wanted very much not to lose the white southern votes he had just regained for Democrats after two dismal Stevenson campaigns, so he walked a careful line on racial politics. He said so just before he took office, announcing that he would not seek new civil rights legislation or challenge the filibuster rule in the Senate. After taking office he waited two years to issue a narrow executive order on housing, which excluded all existing housing and all new housing not owned or financed directly by the federal government.

Powell accepted JFK's judgment that a failed civil rights bill would only hurt civil rights. Doable gestures from the top would do more good while the protest movements built pressure from below. Although Kennedy disliked being in debt to black voters, and his aides refused to acknowledge what they owed to Wofford,

Kennedy grasped that his party had an opportunity to seal a historic realignment. He and his aides vowed to learn more about the black Americans who had swung the election. JFK appointed blacks to judgeships and high administration positions. He supported efforts to register black voters, backing the new Voter Education Project housed in Atlanta's Southern Regional Council. In 1962 he airlifted army troops into a riot at the University of Mississippi to facilitate James Meredith's entrance as a student. Kennedy invited civil rights leaders to the White House and bantered with them affably, something Eisenhower never managed. JFK liked Wilkins especially, who appreciated his new access, and Wilkins mostly appreciated Robert Kennedy's work on the Meredith case, which the NAACP carried for two years to the doorstep of Ole Miss.

But even Wilkins burned with chagrin as Kennedy aides spelled out the congressional math to him. Wilkins and King urged JFK to issue a Second Emancipation Proclamation eliminating segregation and discrimination in all areas of public life. King said it to Kennedy in the Lincoln Room at the White House. He pressed Kennedy to do it on the one hundredth anniversary of the proclamation or the Day of Jubilee, which came and went in September 1962 and January 1963, with no sequel. King called for it again, dramatically, in May 1963, at Birmingham. On the level of principle Kennedy appeared to sympathize. On the level of doing it he stalled and prevaricated. The time had not come; America was not ready; there would be hell to pay socially and politically. Wilkins had heard that from FDR and Truman: "It was the same rationale we had been hearing for twenty-five years." It was maddening. Now a supposedly friendly president wanted nothing to do with civil rights legislation and balked on executive action, and even the Powell Amendment was gone in education, eliminated by the very arguments that liberals had used against it under Truman and Eisenhower. Wilkins experienced Kennedy's first two years, especially 1962, as a nadir of frustration. Freedom Riders were jailed and beaten in Mississippi, imploring King to catch up with them, while the NAACP was stuck with a cautious president and its own lumbering slog through the courts. Meanwhile SNCC derided Wilkins for expecting deliverance from Kennedy.[100]

Powell spent two years stewing over this quandary and deflecting it. The *New York Times* editorialized that giving Education and Labor to Powell would be a disaster because Powell was a racist with a "miserable record as a legislator," and he was gone half the time. Liberal columnist Murray Kempton predicted that Powell would do "a terrible job, because he is a lazy, careless, and selfish man." But Powell did an outstanding job, albeit without improving his attendance record. He hired zealous staffers and encouraged them. He played the game, signing his letters to Kennedy, "your friend and supporter." He began with a huge achievement, steering Kennedy's minimum wage hike to passage, which raised the minimum wage from $1.00 to $1.25. Powell tried to include waiters, maids, and laundry workers in the bill but was rebuffed, so he accepted defeat and a historic victory, promptly introducing legislation to include hotel, restaurant, and laundry workers under the new law, which failed. There were smaller bills promoting mine safety, compensation for dockworkers, youth programs, and a special education program, and a major bill on manpower training and development, all of which passed. In Kennedy's first congressional session he achieved more success with Powell's committee than any other, winning congressional victories on nineteen of twenty-six requests, despite losing all but one labor vote.[101]

Powell was enthralled at becoming an insider and racking up congressional victories. His enemies had to stop taunting him for lacking congressional achievements. He socialized with Kennedy, told friends the president was deeply kind, and did not let on whatever he knew about JFK's sexual promiscuity. Powell enjoyed saying that Kennedy surprised him. But Powell prized his image as America's foremost protest leader, which he was no longer. He snapped at reporters who asked him about King's ascendance. He watched with envy as SNCC won influence and media notice. He hurt himself by responding arrogantly to a libel charge and conviction that plagued him for years. He damaged his reputation in August 1962 by taking a lavish European junket in the company of two female aides. And he marveled at Malcolm X's huge crowds in Harlem, recognizing that Malcolm's ferocious critiques of black leaders had vast appeal in his congressional district. Powell spent a lot of time thinking about how he should respond to the increasingly fractious politics of racial justice.

The libel nightmare grew from a seemingly minor episode. Until the late 1950s Powell indulged the numbers racket in Harlem. He was not above cracking wise about a lucky-sounding hymn number during church services. But in the late 1950s the mob decided it no longer needed black employees in Harlem. Powell lashed back, naming numbers runners. He gave a speech on the House floor in March 1960 naming Esther James as a bagwoman. He repeated the speech on television, claiming that James collected bribes from Harlem gamblers and numbers racketeers for the police. It was great theater, and dangerous; Powell hired a bodyguard. James had a criminal record, but she was a sixty-six-year-old widow of a railroad porter, she cleaned houses for a living, and she took offense at Powell's accusation, suing him for $1 million. The trial began on April 3, 1963, just as SCLC struck in Birmingham. Powell and King had the same lawyer, Clarence Jones, a high-rolling California entertainment attorney who was personally close to King. Jones was interrogating a witness when he received a whispered message that Powell would not be attending his own trial. The news staggered Jones, who failed to explain his client's absence. Jones demolished James's public image as a churchly matron, but she was a plucky witness, testifying that she supplied information about gamblers to the police. James was awarded a libel judgment of $211,000, and Powell refused to pay. James and her scrappy lawyer, Raymond Rubin, proved to be tenacious, pursuing Powell for eight years. Eventually eighty judges in ten different courts were called upon to rule on whether the House of Representatives could expel a member for standing in contempt of a court order to pay Mrs. James. By then it mattered very much that Powell had a lot of enemies.

He made some enemies by responding sympathetically to Malcolm and the Black Power movement. Some speculated that Malcolm might run for Powell's seat in Congress, and Powell worried that he might do so, whether or not the Nation of Islam continued to shun electoral politics. Malcolm taunted King and other ministers that Moses never told the Hebrews to worship the god of their Egyptian slavers or to integrate with them. The language of black power, long spoken in the nationalist tradition, resounded in Malcolm's electrifying speeches. Powell recognized its feeling and logic from his direct action days. It was self-denigrating for blacks to plead for racial integration, especially when the organizations devoted to this agenda included white leaders. Powell, sensing that the new black radicalism was getting somewhere, felt compelled to respond to it. He might have blasted Kennedy for going slow, but that would accomplish nothing except wreck his standing in the administration. He decided to blast his friends in the NAACP, the very people he had defended against the convention pickets of 1960.

Powell came out swinging just as King headed for Birmingham, Alabama. Powell told Kennedy aide Lawrence O'Brien that black Americans were angry and could not be controlled: "I'm not going to watch the parade pass me by. I'm gonna lead it." He told a rally at a Baptist church in Washington, DC, "The white man has given the Negro just about all he intends to give him. From now on we will win only what we fight for. Now this may sound like black nationalism—and maybe it is." A few days later he spoke at a massive rally in Harlem, alongside Malcolm. Powell launched a blistering attack on the NAACP and National Urban League: "I don't agree with some of the things Malcolm X preaches and he doesn't agree with some of the things I preach. But one of the things I am very close to agreeing almost completely with is Malcolm X's analysis of our present Negro organizations." These organizations, Powell noted, had white leaders sprinkled among the black leaders. Jewish, Italian, Irish, and Polish organizations felt no need to diversify their leadership, yet somehow the civil rights organizations thought they needed whites at every level. Moreover, white NAACP board members opposed the Powell Amendment without being asked to leave the NAACP. Powell called for black enterprises, black schools, and bloc voting. If that sounded like black nationalism, "What is wrong with that? Why is it that racism and nationalism are only dirty words when applied to Negro people?"[102]

Powell's nationalist turn sparked a media furor while Bull Connor's water jets and police dogs attacked demonstrators in Birmingham. Much of the backlash against Powell centered on his apparent contention that blacks should boycott the NAACP until it dumped its white board members, although Powell later pulled back from demanding a boycott. The back and forth informed a vast white national audience that there was such a thing as black nationalism, to which Powell had converted. Wilkins lambasted Powell's attack on the NAACP, issuing a scorching twelve-page pamphlet titled *Adam . . . Where Art Thou?* There were four pages of NAACP achievements followed by four pages of black newspaper editorials describing Powell as irrational, vindictive, an embarrassment, and a racist. There was a reprinted article by Jackie Robinson accusing Powell of harming black Americans and betraying his leadership position by denigrating the NAACP. On the lecture trail people waved the pamphlet in Powell's face, demanding a response. He replied that he was getting old, so he didn't really care what people said, but in recent weeks he had gone back to saying things he had said twenty years earlier. If people were interested in black radicalism, they should read a book titled *Marching Blacks.*[103]

In March 1963 Powell and Malcolm spoke at a rally in Harlem for the Mississippi Relief Committee, where Powell invited Malcolm to speak at Abyssinian on June 23. The two men bantered respectfully at Abyssinian, driving up tensions there, as many members did not like where this was going. The following week Robinson spoke at Abyssinian, and Powell called in that he could not make it to New York. The following month *Newsweek* asked Malcolm what he thought of black leaders, and he dismissed nearly all of them. All from Wilkins to King to Benjamin Davis were "Uncle Toms and sell-outs." The single exception was Powell. Malcolm wanted to say "no comment" about Powell, but *Newsweek* reporter Claude Lewis pressed for more, so Malcolm added, "Adam is a pretty unsteady character. If I give you my opinion now, it may be altogether different by tomorrow. He's one of the few men who can't be placed because he rolls with the punches." Malcolm liked what he heard Powell say the previous week: "The only way the Negro is going to gain his freedom is to fight for it!" That was the right song, Malcolm said, "but he may be singing a different tune tomorrow. One thing, though, he's no Uncle Tom." Powell must have felt, reading this interview, that he had played his hand very well. He had a leading role in the power structure and yet outflanked King and SNCC to the left.[104]

Meanwhile thousands of Birmingham schoolchildren transformed the civil rights movement. King was reeling from a sputtering campaign in Albany, Georgia, when he risked everything in Birmingham. The protests started slowly on April 3 and went on gamely for four weeks. They exploded into a game-changer on May 2 when former SNCC cofounder and new King associate James Bevel flooded the streets with very young protesters. Birmingham made America look bad to the world, a crucial point for Kennedy. Near the end, King and Kennedy needed each other to prevent Birmingham from spiraling into a bloodbath, and King swallowed a weak settlement. JFK hated the demonstrations in the first place, but he and King agreed that preventing a bloodbath trumped everything by May 10. Birmingham dramatized what blacks were up against in Alabama, and it caught the eye of the nation like nothing before.

After Birmingham a thousand demonstrations erupted across the nation. SCLC helped out in Savannah, Georgia; Danville, Virginia; Williamston, North Carolina; Gadsden, Alabama; and many other places, often with dismal results. Unlike SNCC, which made long-term commitments to a few towns and cultivated relationships, SCLC was a fire alarm outfit, rushing wherever it could. King soared to superstar status in the summer of 1963, drawing enormous crowds. SCLC fund-raising skyrocketed too, although Kennedy forced King to drop his chief advisor, Levison, and SCLC's New York director and fund-raising guru, Jack O'Dell. At the FBI it was an article of faith that Levison and O'Dell were Soviet agents, and King depended wholly on Levison. FBI director J. Edgar Hoover did not tolerate dissent from his certainties on this subject, which opened the door to a phone-tapping spree authorized by Hoover and Robert Kennedy. Birmingham also lifted Alabama governor George Wallace to his first taste of national attention. Wallace excoriated the Birmingham protests and settlement and dramatically opposed the entrance of two black students, Vivian Malone and James Hood, to the University of Alabama.

JFK, confronting a political minefield, tangled infighting between the FBI and Justice Department, and—to him—the real danger of being fatally burned by King's Communist associates, more or less embraced his inner liberal. Kennedy tied himself to King and a new civil rights bill, with trepidation and hedging in both cases. He cared about civil rights, but, above all, JFK was desperate to get black protesters off the streets. Birmingham convinced him that his administration had to get behind stronger federal civil rights laws; otherwise places like Birmingham, Danville, Williamston, and Jackson were going to explode.

On June 11, 1963, Kennedy provided one of the golden moments of U.S. American history by proposing the Civil Rights Act of 1964. He announced in a televised address that National Guard troops were helping two black students enroll at Alabama and that he had made a decision about new civil rights legislation. He had made the decision a few days previously, having discussed it with Robert Kennedy immediately after Birmingham. But JFK did not decide until June 11 to make an address about it. Eloquently he cast civil rights primarily as a moral issue, not a legal issue:

> One hundred years of delay have passed since President Lincoln freed the slaves, yet their heirs, their grandsons, are not fully free. They are not yet freed from the bonds of injustice. They are not yet freed from social and economic oppression. And this Nation, for all its hopes and all its boasts, will not be fully free until all its citizens are free.
>
> It ought to be possible for American consumers of any color to receive equal service in places of public accommodation, such as hotels and restaurants and theaters and retail stores, without being forced to resort to demonstrations in the street, and it ought to be possible for American citizens of any color to register and to vote in a free election without interference or fear of reprisal.
>
> It ought to be possible, in short, for every American to enjoy the privileges of being American without regard to his race or his color. In short, every American ought to have the right to be treated as he would wish to be treated, as one would wish his children to be treated. But this is not the case.
>
> We preach freedom around the world, and we mean it, and we cherish our freedom here at home, but are we to say to the world, and much more importantly, to each other that this is the land of the free except for the Negroes; that we have no second-class citizens except Negroes; that we have no class or caste system, no ghettoes, no master race except with respect to Negroes?
>
> Now the time has come for this Nation to fulfill its promise. The events in Birmingham and elsewhere have so increased the cries for equality that no city or State or legislative body can prudently choose to ignore them. . . . A great change is at hand, and our task, our obligation, is to make that revolution, that change, peaceful and constructive for all. Those who do nothing are inviting shame, as well as violence. Those who act boldly are recognizing right, as well as reality.[105]

Sorensen had two hours to write the historic Civil Rights Address, using input from JFK and Louis Martin. Kennedy riffed on Sorensen's text throughout the address, adding moral and rhetorical flourishes that he and Sorensen usually eschewed. Civil rights leaders were denied even a moment to enjoy the occasion, as one of the movement's bravest heroes, Jackson, Mississippi, NAACP leader Medgar Evers, was gunned down that night on his doorstep. King hailed the speech in deep sorrow, calling it the "most sweeping and forthright" ever delivered by an American president on civil rights. Powell told an NAACP labor banquet in Philadelphia that he liked it, too, having stayed up half the night writing it with Sorensen. In Powell's telling, he provided the thoughts and Sorensen fashioned them into a speech. This was completely made up; Powell had nothing to do with drafting the speech. The White House called him on it, admonishing that he would not go down in history as the coauthor. Powell said he was misquoted; he had referred only to the president's legislation going through his committee. The White House replied that reporters had a tape recording of his speech. Powell said that tape recorders had lots of knobs that turned on and off, so they should not be trusted. His invention got ample play in southern newspapers, requiring White House aides to say that Sorensen did write it and that Powell, to their knowledge, did not claim otherwise.[106]

This episode evoked unhappy memories for King, Randolph, and Rustin as they organized the March on Washington for Jobs and Freedom of August 28, 1963. They did not want Powell on the podium, as he was too likely to be self-dramatizing and off-message. In the early going they operated secretly, not wanting Kennedy aides, Powell, or the NAACP to get in the way. Randolph had proposed a march in October focused on jobs, but in early June King turned it into a colossal August march focused on civil rights. King and Randolph realized it would fail without the NAACP, so in mid-June they cut Wilkins into the planning, who wanted Randolph to run it, who in turn bargained for Rustin as his lieutenant. Thus Rustin organized the march of the century and enjoyed telling Powell that no government official would be allowed to speak, including him. For Powell it was a bitter fall from the Prayer Pilgrimage for Freedom, when he was too big to be excluded by Randolph, King, and Rustin. Now he was handed a ceremonial role, leading the congressional delegation to reserved seats. There Powell heard speeches by Randolph, Wilkins, National Council of Churches general secretary Eugene Carson Blake, SNCC chair John Lewis, United Auto Workers leader Walter Reuther, CORE chair Floyd McKissick (substituting for arrested CORE director James Farmer), National Urban League director Whitney Young Jr., and King, among others. The others included no women either. Instead, the movement's female leaders were represented by a collective "Tribute to Women," and a few, including Rosa Parks and Diane Nash Bevel, were introduced for bows.[107]

The buildup alone was historic and immense. Many pundits warned that such an enormous gathering of up to three hundred thousand people would turn violent. Wilkins shocked insiders by swallowing his resentment of King and linking arms with him. King and Wilkins made harmonious appearances together on television, urging supporters of civil rights to come to DC for the greatest march ever. The march crowned King as the leader of a great moral crusade, and it left Powell feeling deflated. Powell shared some of Malcolm's feeling that it was better called "the Farce on Washington." Novelist James Baldwin was similarly bitter at being excluded, but Baldwin represented no organization, and his literary "fire next time" individuality was not what Randolph and King wanted on this day. To Powell, the idea that he should listen to a parade of others on this subject was ridiculous.

Moreover, Powell's spat with James had morphed into a nightmare. He stuck to his refusal to pay her, telling his lawyer, "Don't give the bitch a dime." To prevent courts from seizing his assets, Powell hid money in dummy corporations outside New York and refused to be questioned about doing so, so the courts issued contempt citations against him. The first citation was civil and the next one was criminal, after which Powell could not enter New York City, except on Sundays. That was very hard to take. Powell told friends he was sick of it. If only Kennedy would send him to London or Paris as an ambassador, he would go in a heartbeat. But the president was assassinated in November, and Powell told his bereaved congregation, "Weep not for Jack Kennedy. Weep for America. Weep for a land that does things to people because they are black. Weep for a state that can bomb seven churches in one day."[108]

Powell believed that right-wing Texas oilmen killed the president and that the same gang later engineered the assassination of Robert Kennedy. The idea that Lee Harvey Oswald gunned down the president with no prodding or assistance struck Powell, for the rest of his days, as bitterly laughable. Powell joined the national mourning for Kennedy that spoke in whispers and moved in slow motion. It covered the fallen president with a moral, unifying, healing glow he had never attained in life. At the time Kennedy was killed, the civil rights bill was bogged down and going nowhere. He had urged civil rights leaders to wait until after the November 1964 election. Then Kennedy was slain, and Johnson urged the nation to pass the civil rights bill as a fitting eulogy. Kennedy won posthumous credit for a moral revolution he had only partially, halfheartedly, and belatedly supported. Powell, like many others, grieved for Kennedy to the point of not accepting that he was dead. He later recalled it took him a year to shed a tear or to realize Kennedy was truly gone: "The night it finally struck me I was almost hysterical for the entire night."[109]

By then he was deeply involved in building Johnson's Great Society, which Powell considered a mere carrying out of Kennedy's New Frontier. Powell was never close to Johnson, who never invited him to the White House for a social occasion. All his business with Johnson was business. Johnson lacked Kennedy's smooth affability with civil rights leaders and his comfortable self-confidence. The first time King visited the Johnson White House, the new president nervously refused to be photographed with him. Civil rights leaders grasped early on that Johnson's White House would feel less welcoming, even as Johnson worked with them more earnestly. But Powell did not need to be friends with Johnson, and he reminded audiences that he had backed Johnson in lonely defiance of northern prejudices. Johnson was keenly mindful of that. He had come to Washington in 1937, he had a gut-level New Deal passion about poverty, and he appreciated what Powell had done for him. Early in the Kennedy administration Johnson had sunk into depression, feeling denigrated and excluded. Then the resurgent civil rights movement woke him up. Johnson told friends the movement liberated him; it helped that he faced no more Senate elections in Texas. This development had annoyed Kennedy aides, who did not need Johnson crowing about civil rights; they needed him to help them win Texas, Louisiana, and Georgia again. Now Johnson held the White House, he viewed Powell as an important ally, and he counted on Powell's bulldozer qualities.

Shortly after assuming the presidency Johnson announced his commitment to sign a huge antipoverty bill. The Economic Opportunity Act of 1964 had sections on job training and employment, public health, welfare, urban renewal, and local community action that might have been parceled out to various committees, but that would have been slow, and Johnson was in a hurry. Powell got the whole package, delegating most of the grunt work to a subcommittee. He conducted hearings at a furious pace, summarily dismissed conservative critics, and produced a bill in two months. In August it became law, creating the Office of Economic Opportunity (OEO), Community Action, Head Start, and Upward Bound plus numerous work-study and jobs programs. The Economic Opportunity Act opened entire communities to government assistance. It created new categories of social investment and placed blacks and whites side by side across the nation in Job Corps programs. Johnson lauded Powell for ramming the bill through the House, and Powell, thoroughly enjoying the experience, called Johnson "the greatest living pro in the field of politics."[110]

That pulled Powell away from the legislative process that produced the Civil Rights Act of 1964. The Leadership Conference on Civil Rights, a liberal lobbying coalition led by Clarence Mitchell and ADA chair Joe Rauh, led the fight for passage of the Civil Rights Act. Liberals evoked the memory of a fallen president in carrying forward Kennedy's civil rights bill, and it became law on July 2, 1964. The Civil Rights Act outlawed discrimination in public places and employment and created the Equal Employment Opportunity Commission and the Community Relations Service. Title Six incorporated the Powell Amendment, authorizing the federal government to terminate financial support to any agency practicing racial discrimination. Johnson, upon signing the act into law, asserted that Americans were capable of understanding their nation's tragic racial legacy "without rancor or hatred," but it had to stop: "Our Constitution, the foundation of our Republic, forbids it. The principles of our freedom forbid it. Morality forbids it. And the law I will sign tonight forbids it."[111]

This historic legislative achievement was Powell's greatest legacy, fulfilling nineteen years of advocacy in Congress. He took bows on the road for it, appreciating the applause, and he did not exaggerate his role in the legislative process, which was weirdly minimal. He was not asked to play an active role in the hectic closing weeks of the struggle, and he did not say he should have been asked. By then Powell accepted that King and Wilkins got more credit, and he had his eye on things to come.

He worked hard for Johnson's presidential campaign and skipped his own, not minding when Johnson polled significantly better than he did in Harlem. Powell enjoyed working the same cities he had pitched for Kennedy. Except for CORE and SNCC, the civil rights movement took a break from demonstrating in the fall of 1964 to avoid hurting Johnson. Summer riots and a gathering white backlash convinced civil rights leaders to abandon any pretense of nonpartisanship. Harlem, Philadelphia, Chicago, and other cities erupted in July and August, fanning backlash forces that lifted Barry Goldwater to the Republican nomination for president and made George Wallace a national figure. King decried the Goldwater ascendancy as Nazi-like. After Johnson won a landslide victory King gathered the executive staff of SCLC to ponder where they should strike for the right to vote.

Two years of brave and assiduous work by SNCC had nudged black registration in Mississippi from 5 percent to not quite 7 percent. In Alabama 20 percent of blacks were registered, but in Selma, Alabama, where blacks were the majority population, they had 1 percent of the registered voters. King chose to strike in Selma because it was the worst place he could find. The only reason not to choose Selma was that SNCC was already there. The historic protests in Selma began on January 2, 1965; King was arrested on February 1; and on March 7 the great march from Selma to Montgomery commenced. Eight days later, addressing a joint session of Congress, Johnson called Congress to enact a strong voting rights bill.[112]

Johnson had committed to voting rights legislation in January but told King it would take a year. Selma was King's answer that he and the movement were finished with waiting. Meanwhile Johnson's landslide election turned 1965 into the career highlight of every liberal Democrat in Congress. Agenda items left over from the dismal end of the Truman administration barreled through Congress. A huge bill supporting elementary and secondary education passed in April after Powell pushed it through the House. Johnson signed it in the one-room schoolhouse in Stonewall, Texas, where his schooling began, thanking Powell and Oregon senator Wayne Morse effusively. In November there were eight more pieces of Great Society legislation to sign, most of which went through Powell's committee. Six years later, in a sprawling memoir filled with names, Johnson mentioned Powell only once, recalling that Powell held the education bill hostage for a while to get maximum funding for it. Johnson had trouble giving credit to an ally he always had to worry about.[113]

Powell took pride in every program that helped working-class and middle-class citizens get an education, find a job, and attain a secure retirement. He was happy to help the middle class and happy to help the working class climb into the middle class. He took it personally when antipoverty programs were poorly managed, blasting Shriver's OEO for ignoring mayors and bungling the war on poverty. By the end of 1965 Powell worried that early screw-ups, a growing political backlash, and the costs of fighting in Vietnam would cripple the war on poverty before it made much headway. He was a vocal opponent of allowing that to happen, contributing to the "guns or butter" debates of 1966. Powell called for butter and tried not to get entangled in the early politics of the Vietnam War.

The Civil Rights Act had direct bearing on segregated schools in the South and little bearing on de facto segregation in northern public schools. In 1966 Powell became the lightning rod in Congress on the latter issue. Northern school segregation, he implored, was every bit as "destructive of the human spirit and intellect" as the southern version that the Civil Rights Act addressed. The time had come to throw off the "blinders of hypocrisy" on this subject. Black children subjected to poorly funded, all-black schools in northern cities were deprived of the education they deserved, despite what the Civil Rights Act did not say. Powell proposed, in HR 13079, to create a federal program offering grants to local school districts to desegregate racially imbalanced schools. He argued that it should be possible to eliminate de facto school segregation in four years, after which federal funding would be cut off for noncompliant school districts. The Civil Rights Act would not have passed had northern politicians been compelled to deal with their own school segregation, so segregation remained. Powell did not advocate busing or other specific strategies to desegregate northern schools, issues that inflamed Congress after he was gone. But he started the discussion: "We cannot wait for the Departments of Justice or Health, Education and Welfare to develop any courageous consistency and make up their minds that Negro children in New York, Chicago, Los Angeles, Washington, DC, and most northern cities are the innocent victims of a hand-me-down school system."[114]

That was in March 1966—near the end of Powell's effectiveness in Congress and very near the change from "Negro" to "black" in language usage. References to "black power" began with Richard Wright's 1954 book, *Black Power*. SNCC had a slogan in Birmingham: "Black power for black people"; and on May 9, 1966, Stokely Carmichael replaced John Lewis as head of SNCC at a raucous meeting that dramatically changed the organization. Twenty days later Powell declared in a baccalaureate address at Howard University, "To demand these God-given human rights is to seek black power, audacious power—the power to build black institutions of splendid achievement." The following week James Meredith, conducting a solo March Against Fear from Memphis, Tennessee, to Jackson, Mississippi, was shot and wounded, and civil rights leaders converged on Memphis to complete Meredith's march. SNCC staffer Willie Ricks riled up small gatherings by referring to "black power," which intrigued Carmichael. In Greenwood, Mississippi, Carmichael tried out the phrase and electrified the crowd: "We been sayin' 'Freedom Now' for six years and we ain't got nothin'. What we gonna start sayin' now is *Black Power!*"[115]

Black Power swept like fire through American cities that summer. It repudiated "love your enemies" and redemptive suffering. It expelled white activists from SNCC. It famously chanted, "Burn, baby, burn," and it scared the hell out of white America and the deacons of Abyssinian Church. The deacons did not like reading that their pastor was somehow affiliated with what he called "this new breed of cats." Associate pastor David Licorish held the congregation together and was loyal to Powell, waiting his turn. Meanwhile Abyssinian's new part-time minister, Wyatt Tee Walker, won the hearts of many members. Walker was a riveting preacher, fresh from his years of running SCLC's Atlanta office, 1960 to 1964. He was brilliant, domineering, and egocentric, having ruled and lifted the SCLC during its glory run, until the staff rebelled against him and the board tired of him. Walker was in transition in 1965, directing a publishing house in New York. Many Abyssinians pictured him as the ideal successor to Powell. Some winced that Walker preached too many sermons on sexual morality from Powell's pulpit, but Walker was long on talent and ambition, he wanted a big church of his own, and he proudly wore the mantle of King. Powell fired him abruptly, giving no reason. The deacons objected, and Powell threatened to split the church. The deacons backed down, and Powell announced that he would convene a Labor Day conference on Black Power at his office on Capitol Hill. Two months later King arrived for a preaching engagement at Abyssinian with Walker in tow, planning to tell the congregation that he loved and admired Walker, contrary to rumors spread by Powell. Powell cut him off in the robe room and told Walker to wait outside. Powell and King made a show of unity, just after King solemnly told Walker, "Adam is going to hell."[116]

The Labor Day conference was sweet revenge for being frozen out of the March on Washington. Powell invited Wilkins and King to come to his conference to learn about Black Power. Carmichael urged King to come, who declined. Labor Day came and Powell enjoyed the discomfort of the Capitol police. One conference participant told him he was too light-colored to be a Black Power leader. Powell was long practiced at swatting that one away: "Black is the way you think, not the way you look." The meeting sparked much commentary, and Powell followed up at Abyssinian, explaining to anxious congregants what he meant by Black Power. He did not speak for Carmichael, "that fiery young radical" who used the phrase to spark rebellions in American cities: "I can only speak for Adam Clayton Powell. And in so doing, I only remind millions of black people of my thirty-six years of commitment to the cause of freedom for the black man."[117]

He was not a newcomer to black radicalism, he had a track record of accomplishments, and he welcomed the young militants. To Powell, black power was not antiwhite; it "incorporates everybody who wishes to work together, vote together and worship together." It was not white supremacy in reverse because it made no moral judgment on the humanity of others: "Black power simply reaffirms the integrity, dignity and self-respect of black people." It was not about burning cities and killing white people, although Powell said it did mean that to some, "those who would run through the streets drunk with the 'wine of violence,' shouting 'black power' in a purposeless scorched-earth orgy." Powell had already seen more riots than he could stand. He pleaded for no more in Harlem, or anywhere. Instead of lighting the sky with Molotov cocktails, black power needed to register millions of new voters. Instead of throwing firebombs, black power needed to "fire up our energies to build more black-owned businesses in our communities."[118]

The Watts neighborhood of Los Angeles had exploded the previous year—six days of rioting just after the Voting Rights Act was signed. Powell admonished that only two businesses had returned "to that charred community." What good was that? What sense did it make for blacks to burn their own homes and businesses while "hysterically screaming, 'Get Whitey!'" Powell shook his head at young people lacking souls and *Time* magazine asking if God was dead: "God is not dead. People are dead—dead to an awareness of God and his wondrous love for all mankind." He pulled out a book, *Riots and Ruins*, by Powell Senior and began to read. It was written in the despairing aftermath of the riots of 1943. Powell shook his head that entire chapters could have been written that week: "My father is talking about conditions which still exist today—1966! He does not use the terms 'black power' and 'white backlash,' but these concepts are implicit in his thinking."[119]

Just as Powell was like his father, he could see himself in the young radicals. They were like him when he was their age, and they were useful to him in deflating King. The previous year King had wanted to bring his southern crusade to Harlem, and Powell frostily told him to stay where he belonged: "You're dealing with more sophisticated Negroes up here." Now Powell delivered a stunning judgment about the King movement: "We have indulged ourselves in the past five years in a magnificent exercise of near futility with our marches, our sit-ins, our demonstrations, our picketing and now our rebellions." He stressed futility, not near futility. The King movement won a few victories, Powell allowed, but it changed very few minds and did nothing at all to change "the economic servitude of the black masses."[120]

Thus he was unequivocally an advocate of Black Power, a new name for an old ideal: "Black people themselves must exercise a massive responsibility for their fate. Black people themselves must assume control and direction of their destiny." First and foremost, black power was Godly power, incorporating God in one's life and community. Second, it was black pride, "the cry of an in-gathering for all black people to be proud of their black culture, their black roots." Third, it was black initiative, mobilizing the energies of millions to create something powerful. Fourth, it was black productivity, vastly expanding the sector of black-owned businesses. Fifth, it was black responsibility, taking moral responsibility for the fate of black communities. Powell took for granted that white Americans needed to find a way to join hands with Godly, self-respecting, productive, socially minded blacks. He cited his conclusion to *Marching Blacks:* The black man did not want the day of victory to be attained through violence and bloodshed, but he would not be denied the victory, whether in the wrong way or the right way.[121]

Powell was reinventing himself *and* claiming he never changed. Nobody was like him. He could work closely with three successive presidents and still outflank SCLC and SNCC. Malcolm had struggled to figure him out: "It's hard to tell which direction Congressman Powell moves in. He moves in one direction one minute and another direction another minute." Powell, in 1963, had replied that Harlem didn't need Malcolm because Harlem had Powell, but perhaps Malcolm could move to Washington, DC, where leadership was needed. The following year Malcolm announced his break from the Nation of Islam and struggled with reinvention issues of his own. He founded a mosque and a secular Pan-African organization, converting to Sunni Islam. Powell took credit for this transformation. Malcolm, "a dear friend of mine," did not understand Christianity, Powell recalled: "I also taught Malcolm that his concepts of Muslimism were incorrect, and I urged him to go to the Arab countries and if possible to Mecca to find out what Islam really was." Powell admired Malcolm's subsequent conversion and grieved that it led to his assassination. He stressed that his adjustments did not compare to Malcolm's conversions to two forms of Islam. Powell had always been a radical Christian, and he remained one, while keeping with the demands of the times.[122]

Back on Capitol Hill resentment mounted and his defenders shrank. By the fall of 1966 Powell was bleeding politically, wounded by years of scuttlebutt about his personal life and federally financed junkets. The White House started going around him to get things done, treating him as a political liability, which encouraged enemies to go after him. Powell contributed to the falling out by charging that the antipoverty programs were rife with opportunism, fraud, and mismanagement. He cared about poverty too much not to be offended when programs worked poorly. Powell charged that the Urban League shook down the government for more than it deserved or could handle, and Shriver was in over his head. Since Powell's committee funded OEO he felt entitled to say publicly that Shriver was doing a bad job. To liberal Democrats and Johnson aides, however, Powell's criticism hurt the antipoverty effort, strengthening conservatives who opposed antipoverty programs. White House aides and House Democratic leaders urged each other to avoid Powell, as he could not be trusted not to blindside his allies.

This was a replay of Powell's relationships with civil rights leaders, and a new chapter of that story, as Powell skewered Whitney Young for wasting government money and killed James Farmer's national literacy campaign. In 1964 Johnson asked Farmer what he should do next, and Farmer proposed a literacy program. The need was enormous, he said; plus, thousands of activists were eager to do something meaningful besides protesting and going to jail. Johnson liked the idea, and CORE submitted a formal proposal in October. By then Johnson had cooled toward Farmer because Farmer did not go "all the way with

LBJ," as the slogan went. CORE existed to cause trouble, which it kept doing through the election campaign. Johnson took it personally, but Shriver told Farmer not to worry, the proposal was still in play. It stayed in play through 1965, and on Christmas day the *Washington Post* reported on page one that the literacy project had been approved and Farmer would be resigning from CORE to lead it. Both items were news to Farmer, but he was happy, albeit briefly. Conservatives wailed that Farmer opposed the white establishment, not illiteracy; now the government was funding social revolution. Farmer stopped getting calls from Shriver. He tried to contact Shriver and Powell, without success. Then he learned that somebody high up had killed the program. There would be no literacy campaign; meanwhile Farmer felt obligated to resign from CORE. Randolph asked Johnson what happened, who replied that he liked the program; it was Powell who killed it. Powell told King a different story. Johnson had turned against the program, and Powell went along. King was incredulous. Since when did Powell do whatever Johnson wanted? Powell coughed up the real story: "Oh, well, they're going to give me something I need very much; in fact, something I've got to have."[123]

Powell did not tell King what it was, but Farmer learned from journalist Simeon Booker it was to relieve Powell of the "bagwoman libel case." Powell needed Johnson to lean on New York mayor Bob Wagner to lean on the judge that levied the judgment against Powell. For a week Farmer was skeptical of this explanation, until he heard that Powell's judgment had been dramatically reduced. Then he believed it, not realizing that Powell's lawyer Henry Williams had doggedly appealed the judgment for years, finally whittling the fine down to $46,000. A few years later, after Powell had been expelled from Congress, Powell apologized to Farmer through his successor at CORE, McKissick: "They were supposed to give me something for doing it, but they didn't. They just gave me the business."[124]

Powell's downfall began on February 5, 1963, when Delaware Republican senator John J. Williams scolded him on the Senate floor for taking an over-the-top lavish tour of Europe in the company of two young women at government expense. Powell was a disgrace to Congress and something had to be done about it. Wayne Morse protested that Williams violated the Senate's rule against attacking the character of a colleague. Williams countered that actually he held back, having said nothing about Powell's no-show job for his wife or his chronic absenteeism. Now these things were on the table too. Powell pushed back, believing that many colleagues did not want a debate about how much they could spend abroad or how many votes they could miss. He drew from the same counterpart funds available to other government officials at U.S.

embassies—foreign currencies earned by the United States through aid programs that could not be spent outside the country of origin. He believed that "travel is a very broadening kind of education." He knew of no member in the House or Senate who did not travel on counterpart funds provided by the State Department. He had gone to Europe to study employment opportunities for women in Common Market nations. His two travel companions were members of his staff, helping him do his job, and the same thing was true of his wife in Puerto Rico, who answered his mail from Spanish-speaking constituents. A reporter asked if counterpart funds were set up for nightclubs; Powell said it would be strange to visit Paris and never leave Notre Dame. And he had seen other members of Congress in the same clubs.[125]

For a while this counterattack held Powell's enemies at bay. There was no real news in Williams's speech, except that he dramatically broke the Senate's prohibition on personal attacks. Columnist Drew Pearson broke the junket story before the tour ended, detailing Powell's trail of high-end hotels and night-clubs in London, Paris, Venice, Rome, and Greece in the company of two young women. The flap over Pearson's story had caused Powell to cut short the tour and fly home to Puerto Rico to his distraught wife and infant son. One of the companions, Corinne Huff, a former Miss Universe runner-up and former Miss Ohio, was Powell's current romantic partner. A reporter asked Yvette Flores Powell about the tour, and she replied plaintively, "What can I do?" Powell told her he was not involved with Huff; two years later he chose Huff and Bimini over his third marriage and Puerto Rico.[126]

These stories began to define Powell more than anything else. Pearson wrote in 1966 that Powell's top concerns were fishing and women, perhaps not in that order. Powell oscillated between flaunting his lifestyle and admonishing reporters to find something that mattered to write about. The problem was obvious to him: Jealousy is always unattractive, and it was doubly difficult for many to see a black man live a fantasy life. Powell unnerved his colleagues and scared them. He admired very few of them; Morse and Symington were the foremost exceptions. The rest struck him as fearful types sadly lacking courage or even genuine self-confidence. Political leaders should be happy warriors like him, Powell believed. Instead most were timid souls, easily fright-ened. They were especially frightened of sex. Sex had always come easily to Powell. He enjoyed it and wore it lightly. He realized that sex scared his colleagues, making them do foolish things, and made them jealous of him. Haygood reported that when Powell ran into congressional colleagues at risqué clubs in Europe, he gave them a nod and let them be. They were mortified, and he understood.[127]

All of that fed their desire to get rid of him. More important, many congressional Republicans and Democrats hotly resented Powell's claim that he spent State Department money no differently than they did. Ohio House Democrat Wayne Hays, whom Powell once encountered at the Lido in Paris, was put in charge of investigating Powell. His committee dredged up familiar tabloid fodder and some new information about staff vacations to Puerto Rico and Powell's new refuge, Bimini, but no smoking gun. Powell seethed through the process, objecting that he was not the only member of Congress to take expensive trips, so why was he the only one investigated? In November 1966 Harlem defied the clamor against Powell by giving him his largest victory margin ever, 74 percent. Powell spent December in Bimini, the Bahamian island closest to Miami, where his life revolved around deep-sea fishing, the End of the World bar, and Huff. The following month *Newsweek* asked in a cover story, "Must Adam Leave Eden?" House Speaker John McCormack, an elderly Massachusetts Democrat, tallied likely votes and realized he had a serious problem. Though Democrats held a sixty-one seats majority in the House, Powell stood in danger of being refused his seat. Congress had not unseated an elected representative since 1921 (and before that, 1919), when Milwaukee Socialist Victor Berger was excluded for opposing World War I. Now McCormack faced an insurrection against Powell on his watch.[128]

McCormack hatched a two-part strategy: strip Powell of his committee chair to save his seat. Hopefully this would persuade representatives demanding his expulsion to settle for humiliating and denuding him. Powell did not realize, returning from Bimini, that his situation was this bad. He waved off reporters asking if he was worried. What a stupid question! He breezed into his office, greeting his assistant Chuck Stone, "What's up, baby?" Stone tried to get his attention: "What's up? You're gonna lose your seat, that's what!" Two hours later Powell sat in stunned disbelief as House Democrats took Education and Labor from him. He had worked for sixteen years to attain power in Congress, which he lost in an hour. The next day was worse, as the House voted on refusing to seat him, pending an investigation. Powell wrote a slightly contrite speech but grew angry at hearing himself described as an embarrassment. By the time he spoke he was defiant. "My beloved colleagues," he began sarcastically. All of them had skeletons in their closets, so how did they presume to judge him? The vote against him was brutal, 364 to 64. According to the Constitution, the people decide who serves in Congress, and there are three qualifications for serving in the House: citizenship, state residency, and being at least twenty-five years old. According to the Ninetieth Congress, however, Congress decided who served in Congress, making up its own disqualifiers along the way.[129]

McCormack tabbed Brooklyn Democrat Emmanuel Celler to head the nine-member bipartisan committee that investigated Powell. Several Powell aides felt the glare of the spotlight. It turned out that Powell lacked a residence in Harlem and listed his longtime aide Odell Clark's apartment as his residence. Stone acknowledged that he improperly used Labor and Education funds to buy airline tickets, which Powell signed. Powell told the committee he was ready to name others that misused funds, but Celler cut him off, and Powell refused to answer questions about his case. Powell told Huff and Flores Powell to say nothing, which played out differently. Huff spurned a subpoena and took exile in Bimini, falling into depression. Flores Powell testified that she received only four paychecks during her six years on the payroll; the rest went into Powell's account; and for two years she did no work for her top-grade position. Her testimony hurt Powell badly, although the Celler committee found no secret bank account or the like. Powell glared at the House liberals who tried to minimize the damage; this was not a legitimate process, so he would not pretend to cooperate. The committee proposed a $40,000 fine and cancellation of Powell's seniority.

But that did not satisfy the wrath of the majority. This was a chance to banish Powell, not merely humiliate him, ridding the House of its only powerful black man. The House rejected the committee's recommendation and took a vote for expulsion, which passed overwhelmingly by 307 to 116. The sheer vindictiveness of the majority blew away all appeals to reasonableness and proportionality. If Powell could be unseated for "peccadilloes of middling gravity," as the *Detroit News* aptly put it, what was to stop any majority from throwing out whomever it loathed from the other party? The white majority that expelled Powell did not take the question seriously because Powell was not like anyone else in the House.[130]

Civil rights leaders were slow and guarded in defending Powell. Wilkins dryly remarked that he and other civil rights leaders lost no sleep over Powell's problems. After Powell was unseated, Wilkins, King, Randolph, Rustin, and Young issued a joint statement focused solely on the double standard issue. They recognized that Powell, like other members of Congress, had shortcomings: "We ask only that Mr. Powell be judged by standards equally applied to all Congressmen." That was it for the civil rights establishment, except for Randolph, who could not believe that civil rights leaders settled for a single bland press release. Randolph called for rallies across the nation to protest Powell's expulsion. But very few occurred anywhere. The biggest one, at Abyssinian, drew forty-five hundred protesters, small by Abyssinian standards. Licorish winced that much of the crowd consisted of angry young nationalists he never saw on Sundays. On the day Powell was unseated, Carmichael spoke at a protest gathering on Capitol Hill, unaccompanied by established civil rights leaders; he told the crowd to focus its anger on Johnson and the Democratic Party. Harlem, at least, remained loyal to Powell, defending him from double standard injustice and voting for him at the next opportunity. The *New York Times* advised Harlemites to move on. Powell, the *Times* assured readers, was not a victim of racism and had exploited for years the fear of whites of being called racist. Now he was overdue to rectify his legal problems before he deserved to represent Harlem.[131]

Powell's ridicule of black leaders caught up with him. He tagged King as "Martin Loser King," Young as "Whitey Young," and Wilkins as "Roy Weak Knees." They, in turn, did the minimum for him when he got in trouble. Powell retreated to Bimini, and for a while a smattering of Black Power activists came to see him. But they had things to do, and he had a career to revive. New York governor Nelson Rockefeller called a special election in April 1967 to fill Powell's vacant seat; Powell won it without leaving Bimini, by a seven-to-one margin. Harlem would not be told by the Ninetieth Congress to elect someone else. Needing income, Powell recorded an album of sermons titled *Keep the Faith, Baby!* He knew the "baby" part grated on the political class, so he said it constantly. The album helped Powell pay off the Esther James judgment, but his contempt of court citation was still in play, and he grew bored on his island refuge. In January 1968 he returned to the United States to reclaim his life and his right to be in Congress.[132]

He returned as a flat-out Black Power radical, telling students at UCLA, UC-San Diego, UC-Berkeley, and Stanford that King was a milquetoast has-been and they should listen to Carmichael and H. Rap Brown. Powell drew huge crowds and adulation, which he had expected to energize him. Instead he wilted from exhaustion. He canceled the rest of his speaking tour, telling himself he must have grown soft from a year of fishing and drinking. Powell sent his lawyer Henry Williams, still working solo above the Apollo Theatre, to cut a deal with a New York judge allowing him to return to Harlem. On March 22, 1968, Powell returned for a quick arrest and release. Word spread instantly that he had come home. He strolled down 125th Street and drew a surging crowd. He mounted a ladder and gave a speech excoriating American racism, Harlem's co-opted leaders, and King. He spoke to an overflow crowd at Abyssinian the following Sunday, where church members exulted at seeing him but recoiled at Powell's entourage, replete with revolutionary garb. Abyssinian regulars uneasily took in Powell's message that they had "Judases" among them and the future belonged to young black militants. Powell resumed his interrupted speaking tour in Florida and North Carolina. On April 4 he was scheduled to speak at Duke University in Durham, North Carolina, but suffered a mild seizure and was rushed to a hospital. There he learned that King had been assassinated. Powell feared for his own life, believing there was a conspiracy to assassinate black leaders. He returned to Bimini, and three weeks later he had surgery for prostate cancer in Miami.[133]

There was drama still to come and two abrupt endings. In January 1969 Michigan House Republican Gerald Ford led an effort to keep Powell unseated in Congress, but Harlem had gone two years without representation and the House faced a possible repudiation by the Supreme Court. Celler called for Powell to be seated without punishment, which was voted down. Celler tried again, seating with punishment—a whopping $25,000 fine and no seniority— and it passed, by 261 to 160. Powell was back as a freshman member of the Ninety-first Congress, reduced to a staff of Odell Clark and two secretaries. On April 21 the Supreme Court heard arguments in *Powell v. McCormack*. Powell's ad hoc band of activist lawyers—Arthur Kinoy, Jean Camper Cahn, Herbert Reid, William Kunstler, and Frank Reeves—took on a powerful New York firm (Cravath, Swain & Moore) that defended what House Democrats and Republicans had done to Powell. The defense contended that the case was moot since Powell now held a seat in Congress; moreover, his expulsion had nothing to do with race. Kinoy countered that Congress had no right to ignore the Constitution. The Warren Court asked more questions about race than the defense lawyers expected, and on June 16 the court ruled by seven to one that the House had violated the Constitution by inventing qualifications for Powell not specified in Article One.[134]

Vindication from the Supreme Court was hard to top, especially as Warren's majority opinion chastised the House for dangerously misusing its power. But Powell could not rally himself to celebrate when his lawyers arrived in Bimini. He was ill with cancer of the lymph glands and distressed at receiving no back pay or compensation. Ford condemned the Warren Court for another repugnant decision related to civil rights, demanding that the Justice Department investigate Powell. Powell returned to Congress but felt lonely and useless. He had a few moments, mostly speaking at antiwar rallies. At Howard University he ripped the faculty for being stuck in the past and ripped the administration for having no leaders. On other occasions he got similar treatment from young audiences demanding to know why he was still in the Democratic Party and devoted to the Kennedys. The latter reaction diminished the lure of the road for Powell. In the fall of 1969 he returned to Bimini, where he learned that Hull had left him for Powell's boat driver and taken her share of his dwindling assets.

Then Charlie Rangel came to plead that Powell's constituents needed him to do his job.

Powell had no telephone in Bimini, and he fished nearly every day. To contact him, one had to leave a message at a hotel, and he rarely responded. Rangel had long idolized Powell. In the early 1960s Rangel served as an assistant U.S. attorney under Robert Kennedy, and in 1966 he was elected as Central Harlem's representative to the New York State Assembly. Governor Rockefeller asked Rangel to nudge Powell, and he tried, telling Powell that people needed him back home. Rangel added that Floyd McKissick and Jesse Gray were planning to run for Powell's seat in 1970. Powell waved off this information dismissively, so Rangel added that he might run too. Powell patted Rangel on the cheek, replying, "Do what you have to do, baby." Rangel felt patronized and belittled in front of his wife. Then Powell stuck him with the bill for thirty partygoers, and Rangel decided to run for Congress. Powell rallied to the challenge, returning to Harlem to campaign for his seat. He refused to debate Rangel, relying on stump speeches about all he had done for Harlemites. But lately he had abandoned them, and they were done with that. Rangel stunningly beat Powell in a primary squeaker, by 203 votes. Powell demanded a recount, and the victory margin shrank to 150 votes. Had Powell been well, he undoubtedly would have formed a third party to get on the November ballot. But he pined for Bimini and was fading, which allowed him to let go of Abyssinian too.[135]

David Licorish had waited for his turn at Abyssinian. For twenty-eight years he had given strong, loyal, pious service to the church, often not knowing on Sunday morning whether he would be preaching that day. Licorish was West Indian, divorced, and not a public figure. It was long unclear which of these factors weighed most against him, as Powell failed to tab a successor. In the end Powell told the deacon board that Licorish fell short on leadership and public standing, and the deacons agreed. Abyssinian reached out to a friend and former associate of King's, Samuel DeWitt Proctor, who had served as a regional director of OEO under Shriver. Proctor turned down Abyssinian twice before saying yes, taking over after Powell died in 1972.[136]

Proctor was perfectly suited for Abyssinian, and he carried on the Abyssinian tradition of social gospel liberalism. Proctor had first met Powell in 1941 when he was a student at Virginia Union University and Powell gave a speech there. Proctor later told Haygood that Powell astonished the students. They were from small towns in the South and had never imagined a black man speaking so boldly. But in personal conversation Powell turned aloof, not revealing anything; Proctor found it strange. The next day, planning to escort Powell to the train station, Proctor found that Powell had already left; he had no time for a student still hoping for some personal time. Many years later, after Proctor succeeded Powell at Abyssinian, Proctor recalled his first impression, especially its accuracy. He knew many congregants who said they never had a personal conversation with Powell. Proctor reflected that his life and Powell's had been intertwined for many years, yet he had never been in Powell's home. In fact he didn't know where it was.[137]

Roi Ottley was one of the few who knew Powell well, having grown up with him. In 1943 Ottley's book *New World A-Coming* prepared a national audience for the coming of his friend. Powell was something new, Ottley explained: a light-colored black man who aspired to be a leader of Negroes and working-class whites. Women at Abyssinian called him "Mr. Jesus," which, to Ottley, was the key to everything about Powell. Women swelled Abyssinian to overflowing whenever Powell preached, and they called the church every week to learn if he would be in the pulpit that Sunday. "No more contradictory character exists in Negro life," Ottley wrote. Powell was messianic and careerist, spiritual and carnal, charming and withholding. More specifically, "he is an incredible combination of showman, black parson, and Tammany Hall. He is at once a salvationist and a politician, an economic messiah and a super-opportunist, an important mass leader and a light-hearted playboy." Powell, according to Ottley, was a "young man on horseback—with a love for pleasure, quest for power, and unusual capacity for work." He had ample flaws on a personal level, but his "weaknesses as a man are his virtues as a public figure."[138]

Powell cited this portrait with delight and lived up to it. He seemed in danger of dying alone when Hull left him, but he found a last love, Mississippi native Darlene Expose, who took care of him at the end. Very near the end Powell dragged himself to a speech at Florida State University in Tallahassee, where he saw that he could still move a crowd. Scanning the audience, he spotted his former lawyer from the Education and Labor Committee, Michael Schwartz. The two men got to a rooftop bar at the Holiday Inn, started drinking, and relived their days of glory when they passed dozens of bills that transformed the American social landscape. They talked about issues, personalities, conflicts, and victories. Powell had once sent Schwartz to Florida to investigate racial discrimination in unions, so they relived that adventure. The reminiscing went on and on, ebullient and boisterous. As the night wore on, Schwartz kept expecting the conversation to turn toward Powell's expulsion, punishment, financial loss, romantic loss, election defeat, and/or cancer. It never happened. Powell remained in high spirits, and they shut the place down. Schwartz told Haygood, "One thing about Adam, you never knew when he was suffering."[139]

He died on April 4, 1972, at Jackson Memorial Hospital in Miami, exactly four years after King. Inevitably there were complications with the women in Powell's life. Yvette Flores came to Jackson with Powell's son Adamcito, but Expose tried to stop her from seeing Powell. Expose said that Powell had married her in the Bahamas, and Flores said that she and Powell had never been legally divorced. Powell undoubtedly told Expose that Flores hurt him. Corrine Huff came to Jackson and suffered a nervous collapse when told that he was dying. Shortly before he died Powell lauded Huff—"the first soul sister to be in the Miss Universe contest"—for caring for him "when everyone had turned their backs upon me." Hazel Scott came to Jackson and spent a day with Powell; they had remained friends, partly through their son, Adam III. Isabel Powell did not come to Miami, but she came to the funeral at Abyssinian and confirmed that she had never stopped loving him.[140]

Inevitably there were obituary comparisons to King, nearly always to Powell's disfavor. It seemed never to register with Powell that he trashed his own legacy by threatening to smear King and Rustin. Powell routinely dismissed this incident as typical political hardball. All were sinners, so he did not expect anyone to be good. Politics was about power, so people inevitably did bad things in striving for political success. Political players who paraded their goodness were either deluded or hypocrites. Powell did not have to read Reinhold Niebuhr to exceed Niebuhr's propensity for realism, bordering on cynicism, on this subject. For Powell, however, what remained was a hard-edged version of social gospel activism.

Like Niebuhr and King, Powell was deeply political in the ordinary sense of power politics. He did not apologize for injecting his ministry into the political struggle for justice. The moral right, in politics, was never an abstract moral ideal; it was whatever served the cause of justice in a particular situation. Unlike Niebuhr and King, however, Powell held office and made himself an expert in passing laws. Every year in London he attended the international convention of the World Parliamentarians for World Government, where he studied ways of passing legislation. He rose to the rank of vice president in this organization. Powell would not have passed nearly fifty bills in Congress had he not been a world-class parliamentarian. To him, it made no sense to be a lawmaker and not become an expert in lawmaking. After Powell steered the National Defense Education Act to passage in 1966 Morse wrote to him, "In all my 20 years in the Senate I have never seen a chairman of a conference committee do as effective a job as you did in handling the NDEA bill through conference."[141]

He veered all over the map politically, he was prone to skip important votes, even on the poll tax, and he was not given to reflection about his motives or choices. When pressed on these points Powell routinely dismissed them out of hand, reinforcing his reputation for arrogance and being a bad colleague. He seemed never to take seriously what he could have been. The question came up in every phase of Powell's career. As a minister and civil rights leader, shouldn't he have aimed higher? Didn't he have a moral responsibility to show others the way and avoid harming the movement? Powell gave the same reply throughout his career: Why should he have to be better than other people? He was for equality, not moral heroism.

This reply nearly always got a laugh, and it usually won for Powell the reprieve that he sought for cheating on his wives, making his congressional aides falsify airline tickets, and the like. But it cut him off from normal account-ability in relationships near and far. It put the people closest to him in danger, landing Hattie Dodson in prison and stranding Corinne Huff in exile. Powell was too selfish to notice the pain he inflicted on people that he used, especially women. He cut off Flores and refused to see their son after he took up with Huff, yet he was shocked and angry when Flores testified to the Celler committee. Contrary to what Powell said, his consuming self-regard did not make him a stronger leader than King or Randolph. It made him someone less worthy of trust, undermining his own criticism of the racial double standard. Powell diminished his standing in history by rationalizing that he should not have to be more ethical than the run-of-the-mill congressmen he despised. Even a tiny dose of moral humility would have left him standing considerably higher, closer to the level of his achievements, where almost no one surpassed him.

As a protest leader, Powell ranked with Randolph and King. As a politician, no black American compared to him. In combining these fields of action, no one came close to him. It became hard to remember that Powell climbed so high, because he refused the moral responsibility that came with the struggle.

5

REDEEMING THE SOUL OF AMERICA

Martin Luther King Jr. was twenty-six years old when lightning struck in Montgomery, Alabama, on December 1, 1955. He had been a pastor for slightly more than a year, and his activist record was very recent and extremely short. Had King lived anywhere else, someone else would have had to emerge. But had King lived anywhere else, lightning would not have struck in Montgomery.

Ralph Abernathy was a faithful sidekick of King's but not a candidate for movement leader. Bayard Rustin and James Farmer were protest leaders long before King emerged, but both were activists in northern leftist organizations and very different from the southern black Baptist preachers who created the Southern Christian Leadership Conference (SCLC). King built a movement vehicle around himself that was shot through with a defining irony: SCLC was dominated by southern ministers with big personalities who could imagine themselves as Number One, yet they deferred to King.

Abernathy and Fred Shuttlesworth stayed with King and deferred to him throughout his entire career while stewing over personal rivalries with him. Wyatt Tee Walker was the same age as King, a better writer and organizer, a commanding speaker, and boastful about his abilities. James Lawson was the same age as King, too, and a stronger influence on the young firebrands who created the Student Nonviolent Coordinating Committee (SNCC)—James Bevel, Diane Nash (Bevel), Bernard Lafayette, Marion Barry, and John Lewis. SNCC protested constantly that SCLC was founded on the large egos of male ministers and their ironic willingness to glorify King. Legendary organizer Ella Baker made this objection before SNCC existed and was snubbed by SCLC leaders for doing so. But the chaotically organized, ego-driven, hit-and-run SCLC was exactly what the movement needed to pull off Birmingham and Selma.

The movement held together because King distinctly combined charisma, humility, magnanimity, ambition, daring, a passion for justice, and, especially, poetic preaching brilliance. He was guilt-ridden about his exalted status but assiduous in protecting it. He subjected himself to danger and a punishing schedule while fearing that one or the other would kill him. He accepted harsh criticism from young SNCC activists and adjusted to it while guarding his preeminence. He did the same thing after Black Power nationalists challenged his standing, philosophy, and strategy. In both cases he became more radical in response, but in line with Socialist and anti-imperialist commitments that he held all along. The later King took the civil rights struggle to the North, came out against America's war in Vietnam, and campaigned against economic injustice. He got more and more angry and radical because America did not change very much.

He was deeply the product of a southern black Baptist clerical family. King's maternal grandfather, Alfred Daniel Williams, took over tiny, seventeen-member Ebenezer Baptist Church in Atlanta in 1894, moved his growing congregation several times on and around Auburn Avenue, and died of a heart attack in 1931, leaving a congregation of four hundred members. King's maternal grandmother, Alberta Williams, convinced Ebenezer to replace her husband with her son-in-law, Martin Luther King Sr., which left her intact as First Lady of the congregation. King's cultured mother, Alberta Williams King, did not want her husband to take Ebenezer, where she ranked below her mother, but he seized the opportunity. Martin Luther King Sr. was rough-hewn and strong-willed, having come from rural poverty, with minimal schooling, to claw his way to an education at Morehouse College. As a youth he was taunted by his classmates for smelling like the mules he tended. Then he endured snickering that he preached in his father-in-law's church and lived in his mother-in-law's house. Ebenezer was bankrupt when King Senior took over in January 1932, padlocked by a court order. But he built it into a thriving congregation that straddled the line between a class church and a mass church, emphatically in the emotional preaching style of a mass church. He raised his three children in middle-class privilege in the same hovering, raging, loving style with which he ruled Ebenezer.[1]

King Senior epitomized the authoritarian and entrepreneurial black Baptist preacher, aside from deferring to his mother-in-law and, at times, his wife. He raised money with bluster and daring, copying the techniques of local insurance salesmen and publishing member contributions. He resurrected Ebenezer so quickly that by the end of his first year he was Atlanta's highest-paid black pastor. In 1934 he toured Paris, Rome, Jerusalem, and Bethlehem on his way to the Baptist World Alliance Congress in Berlin. His name was Michael King, and his three children were named Christine, Michael Luther Jr. ("Little Mike"), and Alfred Daniel ("A.D."). Christine was sixteen months older than Little Mike, who was born in 1929, and he was seventeen months older than A.D. King Senior, enthralled at visiting the land of Martin Luther and consorting with Baptist leaders, returned home to a gala reception at Ebenezer. In a burst of emotion he honored the occasion by changing his name to Martin Luther King, adding that Little Mike would heretofore be named Martin Luther King Jr.

This is a concise rendering of a tangled story, as King Senior's parents had long disputed whether he should be called Michael or Martin, and he eventually honored the deathbed request of his father, who died in 1933, notwithstanding that he loved his mother and had been long estranged from his abusive father. Then King Senior passed a similar confusion onto his middle child. Family and friends continued to call the two Martin Luther Kings "Big Mike" and "Little Mike," which eventually morphed into "Daddy King" and "M.L."[2]

Daddy King, though pugnacious and domineering, always keeping the deacons in line, was also winsome, vibrant, and careful. He rebuked Jim Crow effrontery on the rare occasions that he failed to avoid white people, refusing to be addressed as "Boy." Being addressed by one's first name was also problematic in Jim Crow America, so black Americans often chose not to have one, opting for initials. Daddy King told his children to avoid whites; otherwise he did not talk about white people or racism. To him, segregation was evil, white racism was a mystery best left to God, and there was nothing else to talk about concerning race. In the pulpit and at home he oscillated between cajoling and yelling, tirelessly admonishing about how to behave. His famous son, not coincidentally, never barked at anyone until very near the end of his life. King Senior doted over his children and intimidated them. When King was thirteen his father whipped him in the backyard, vowing to make something of him even if he had to beat him to death. An older teenaged neighbor, Howard Baugh, guffawed at the scene, and Daddy King gave him a whipping, too.

Daddy King preached about a personal God of judgment, grace, and miracles, a gospel of sin and redemption, and a gospel never lacking a social dimension. He called himself a social gospel preacher and knew about modern theology by virtue of having studied under C. D. Hubert at Morehouse, but King Junior, upon acquiring the language for such distinctions, said that his father was a fundamentalist—a characterization he never retracted. Daddy King was fully a social gospel minister in the sense that the category mattered to him. He was practical and entrepreneurial, focused on growing his congregation. He was involved in civic affairs, had an acute social conscience, and disapproved of exclusively otherworldly preaching. By 1940 Ebenezer had one thousand members. Unlike his nearby rival at Wheat Street Baptist Church, William Holmes Borders, Daddy King had no seminary degree and did not give polished, erudite sermons. Borders built Wheat Street into Atlanta's leading black class church, boasting four thousand members, during the same period that Daddy King built up Ebenezer. But Daddy King cut a comparable figure in Atlanta as a leader of the Voters' League and stalwart of the NAACP, he became a pillar of Atlanta's black establishment, and he and Borders bridled at each other for forty years.[3]

King appreciated that he had a "real father," as he pointedly put it, and a nurturing mother. When he reflected on his youth he dwelt on his father's power and barely mentioned his mother, except to say that her loving care operated "behind the scene" and he relied upon it. This rendering obscured that King got his deep and enabling sense of being "Somebody" of inestimable worth primarily from his mother. As a youth he was sensitive, bright, expressive, friendly, guilt-ridden, and depressive, twice attempting suicide at the age of twelve by throwing himself from a second-story window. Both attempts focused on his beloved maternal grandmother, a regal presence in his home and the person he loved above all others. The first time, King thought that A.D. had accidentally killed her. The second time, Alberta Williams died of a heart attack just after giving a Women's Day speech at Mount Olive Baptist Church. Convulsed with grief, King could not imagine living without her. He also blamed himself, having stolen away to watch a parade and thus missed her speech. For several days, after he flung himself through the window again, he sobbed uncontrollably. King's immense capacity for guilt puzzled his father, who did not operate on a guilt basis. Daddy King later recalled that his middle child was unusually bookish, and he took corporal punishment stoically, never crying at a whipping. Others noted that for all his guilty tendencies, King played like a normal kid and seemed happy. He had huge appetites for food and fun and acquired a nickname, "Tweedie," for his love of dandyish outfits. King's first autobiographical reflection, at the age of twenty-one, took a sunny view of his abilities: "I have always been somewhat precocious, both physically and mentally. My I.Q. stands somewhat above the average. So it seems from a hereditary point of view nature was very kind to me."[4]

He was grateful for growing up middle class in a supportive family. King learned how to handle his overbearing father, unlike A.D., who wilted under the pressure and never won Daddy King's approval. King's superficial descriptions of his mother, however, masked two things. Alberta King's nurturing care instilled in him his profound sense of personal worth, and she ruled her household in strong-willed fashion, which made him averse to female leaders for the rest of his life. Andrew Young, who knew King's secrets and mediated his rocky relationships with female activists, said that King avoided assertive women because he had a conflicted history with his controlling mother. King, however, described an affectionate family upbringing that sheltered him from the worst of Jim Crow brutality without sparing him of being seared by it. He hated whites as soon as he learned that whites hated blacks—in his remembrance from the age of six onward. He witnessed police brutality against African Americans and saw the Klan beat African Americans in broad daylight on city streets. He loathed segregation, asking his parents incredulous questions about it. He hated "the oppressive and barbarous acts that grew out" of segregation, later recalling in *Stride Toward Freedom*, "All of these things had done something to my growing personality." King's early memoir, written while he was studying at Crozer Theological Seminary, put it poignantly, recalling that his parents "would always tell me that I should not hate the white." Instead he had a Christian duty to love white people. That made it a religious issue, King noted, which raised an excruciating question: "How could I love a race of people who hated me?"[5]

The feeling in that question peaked in King's early teens, at Booker T. Washington High School, where he skipped the ninth and twelfth grades. One night King's debate team had to stand in the aisle of a bus returning to Atlanta from Valdosta, Georgia, and he seethed with rage, the angriest he ever felt. Later he took a summer job on a Connecticut tobacco farm and was astonished at how differently he felt in the North. The veil of denigration and threat seemed to disappear, leaving King exhilarated, until he returned to Atlanta. Then he reeled at feeling constantly denigrated and threatened. In King's telling, he struggled not to presume that all southern whites were hatefully racist, and after he returned from Connecticut he briefly imagined himself as a civil rights activist. But the latter thought was fleeting, and King studied hard to qualify for early admission to Morehouse College. Benjamin Mays had two reasons for establishing an early admission program: Segregated high schools failed to challenge or support their gifted students, and Morehouse teetered on bankruptcy because of World War II. Thus King entered Morehouse in September 1944, at the age of fifteen.[6]

He was too young and unfocused to be there, and he rarely missed a party. King later estimated that when he began at Morehouse he read at an eighth-grade level. Thus he was a mediocre student, earning eighteen Cs, twenty Bs, and a single A. But Daddy King made the right call in sending King to Morehouse, and he got his way about why it mattered. Morehouse was one mile from the King home; Daddy King reasoned that living at home would prevent M.L. from feeling overwhelmed at college. Furthermore, four years at home would prepare him for a ministerial career, never mind that King already felt overdosed on the family religion. Daddy King's emotional preaching employed most of the whooper arsenal of cajoling, bellowing, and screeching, minus moaning. Sometimes he "walked the benches," throwing himself into the congregation without warning, stepping over swooning worshippers. He addressed the congregation as a child in need of admonition, and he embarrassed his middle child. Daddy King kept Ebenezer in a state of unease and agitation by screeching at unpredictable moments when the content bore little relation to the shouting. He threw himself around the sanctuary and down the aisle, and he sprinkled his sermons with unfiltered remarks about how congregants looked that day. Ebenezer found most of it enthralling; M.L. found much of it excruciating. Sometimes he snuck away to hear Borders, whose church on Auburn Avenue (formerly Wheat Street) was one block west of Ebenezer. King sought to emulate Borders's use of sophisticated language, though not as a minister.[7]

He was adamant that he did not want to be a pastor. King's conversion at the age of five had been a vague affair, having merely followed his sister when she responded to an altar call from a guest evangelist at Ebenezer. He struggled to believe that he would see Mama Williams again, and for years he doubted that any soul was raised to eternal life. At Morehouse King hung out with an older friend, Walter McCall, who derided piety and dogma. On Sundays they occasionally slipped into the balcony of Wheat Street to study Borders. On Tuesdays King absorbed the intellectual, ethically oriented, theologically liberal sermons that Mays gave at chapel, which unknowingly gave him a model. King absorbed the cult of Mays and the cliquish mystique of Morehouse Manhood. At Morehouse he experienced his first probing discussions of race, especially in sociology courses, and he studied enough to pass. King aimed for a medical career but washed out with two Cs in biology under Mary Reddick. He switched to a major in sociology under Walter Chivers, anticipating law school. He caught his first whiff of fascination with Hegel in a philosophy course under Samuel Williams, although King earned a C. His life turned a corner in his junior year, in a surprising place, theologian George D. Kelsey's course on the Bible.[8]

Kelsey was a graduate of Andover Newton and a doctoral candidate at Yale who began his teaching career at Morehouse in 1938; later he completed his doctorate in 1946. He specialized in Christian ethics and taught introductory courses on the Bible and philosophy of religion. Kelsey's lectures on biblical criticism caught King's attention. King took for granted that the Bible had to be taken literally and that a college course on the Bible would be something like advanced Sunday school. Kelsey's course was a revelation to him, stripping away the make-believe feeling of literalistic religion, instilling in King a new interest in theology. Later he recalled realizing that "behind the legends and myths of the Book were many profound truths which one could not escape." King earned his only A at Morehouse in Kelsey's class. He began to think about applying to seminary, motivated by his respect for Kelsey. If seminary was something like Kelsey's course, and Kelsey was respected in the Southern Baptist Convention, King had to reconsider the whole business about seminary and ministry. Daddy King wanted both of his sons to be ministers and to take advantage of his connections in the Baptist convention. Both eventually became pastors and assisted their father at Ebenezer, though on very different tracks. King later enthused that at Morehouse "the shackles of fundamentalism were removed from my body." Because of Mays, Kelsey, and other teachers, "when I came to Crozer, I could accept the liberal interpretation with relative ease."9

Daddy King believed that his son needed no further education. He wanted M.L. to join him at Ebenezer, in line to succeed him, where being a Morehouse graduate was fully sufficient. But King's models were Mays and Kelsey—and, harder to mention, Borders—so graduate study was imperative. J. Pius Barbour, a Baptist pastor and friend of Daddy King's, had graduated from Crozer Theological Seminary in Chester, Pennsylvania. Chester was an industrial city of thirty-six thousand, much of the town was off-limits to black Americans, and Barbour's large congregation, Calvary Baptist, was a fixture of the city's western section, where blacks lived, two miles from the Crozer campus. On Barbour's advice King applied to Crozer in 1948. Mays wrote an underwhelming recommendation, noting that King was hardly a brilliant student. Kelsey worked harder at helping him, writing that while King's academic record was "short of what may be called 'good,' " he was a late bloomer worth taking a risk for. Daddy King worried that Crozer was too white and liberal, but he paid the tuition and expenses anyway, consoling himself that Barbour was nearby.10

Crozer Seminary was struggling, with fewer than a hundred students, and it was decidedly liberal. It sponsored a leading journal, *Crozer Quarterly*, and was often called "the little University of Chicago Divinity School." In King's first year the seminary's president was Mays's former teacher at Chicago, Edwin Aubrey, who admitted a large freshman class in 1948 in hopes of saving the school. In King's second year the president was a reticent, slow-walking caretaker whom students called "Creeping Jesus." In King's third year the president was an able administrator, Sankey Blanton, who saved the school by raising money and moderating its liberal image. Hebrew Scripture scholar James B. Pritchard and New Testament scholar M. Scott Enslin gave first-year students a hard-edged introduction to biblical criticism. Pritchard told classes the Exodus narrative was highly exaggerated and Moses was probably legendary; Enslin taught that Albert Schweitzer was right about the apocalyptic Jesus and that traditional Christianity and the social gospel were both pitifully mistaken. Students joked that Pritchard demolished the biblical Moses in the first semester and Enslin finished off Jesus in the second.[11]

King flourished at Crozer, despite having only ten black classmates. During college he had met white students in Atlanta's Intercollegiate Council that didn't seem racist, which was a beginning. At Crozer he made his first white peer southern friends—Georgians DuPree Jordan and Francis Stewart—and welcomed Walter McCall as a classmate at midyear. King was acutely conscious of white stereotypes and being a minority. Determined to refute stereotypes, he studied hard, dressed snappily, always arrived on time, and risked a campus reputation for quiet humorlessness. Later he recalled having overcompensated, especially concerning humor. King told his mother, "I never go anywhere much but in these books." He found a breakthrough friend and teacher in theologian George Davis, with whom King took seven courses. Davis taught the canon of American liberal theology: Horace Bushnell's *The Vicarious Sacrifice*, William Newton Clarke's *Outline of Christian Theology*, William Adams Brown's *How to Think of Christ* and *Christian Theology in Outline*, Walter Rauschenbusch's *Christianity and the Social Crisis* and *A Theology of the Social Gospel*, Edgar Brightman's *Philosophy of Religion*, and other standard works. King studied Clarke's textbook with particular care, absorbing Clarke's evangelical liberalism. His papers for Davis rejected literalist interpretations of the virgin birth and resurrection of Christ, embraced Friedrich Schleiermacher's rendering of Christ's divinity, and affirmed that the kingdom of God "will be a society in which all men and women will be controlled by the eternal love of God." The true significance of the divinity of Christ, King wrote, "lies in the fact that his achievement is prophetic and promissory for every other true son of man who is willing to submit his will to the will and spirit of God." In a sermon outline for a preaching course King said that the social gospel was right in conceiving economic justice as an essential aspect of gospel teaching: "I am a profound advocate of the social gospel."[12]

Rauschenbusch's *Christianity and the Social Crisis* was foundational for King; in *Stride Toward Freedom* he called it "a book which left an indelible imprint on my thinking by giving me a theological basis for the social concern which had already grown up in me as a result of my early experience." Christian socialism, as described by Rauschenbusch, made sense to King and inspired him. It centered on the prophets and the teaching of Jesus, reclaimed the gospel for social justice activism, and pointed to systemic structures of oppression. King embraced Rauschenbusch's charge that American capitalism was exploitative and predatory, far from the vehicle of liberation celebrated by Daddy King. The early Rauschenbusch, however, was no pacifist, and neither was King. A. J. Muste came to Crozer during King's second year, stumping for radical Christian pacifism. King surprised his classmates by challenging Muste heatedly. Back home every household that King knew had guns, and he scoffed that allowing Fascism to conquer the world would not have been virtuous. Later he softened the memory, having acquired ghostwriting allies who admired Muste. In King's later telling, Muste impressed him without persuading him: "During this period I had about despaired of the power of love in solving social problems." Elsewhere he elaborated, "The 'turn the other cheek' philosophy and the 'love your enemies' philosophy are only valid, I thought, when individuals are in conflict with other individuals; when racial groups and nations are in conflict a more realistic approach is necessary." For a brief time King fell under the spell of Nietzsche, especially on the theme that life is about struggling for power and Christianity is hypocritical in its valorization of love. Then he felt mortified at being fascinated; Coretta Scott King later recalled that her husband held a special revulsion for Nietzsche.[13]

King's storied encounter with Mordecai Johnson occurred during his second year at Crozer, at Fellowship House in Philadelphia. Johnson, fresh from India, was in top form, lauding Gandhi's witness and legacy. Hearing it from Muste had brought out King's incredulity. Hearing it from a black social gospel leader enthralled King: "His message was so profound and electrifying that I left the meeting and bought a half-dozen books on Gandhi's life and works." According to King, he relinquished his belief that "love your enemies" applies only to individual relationships. He had regarded himself as a realist about the struggles between nations, classes, and racial groups, "but after reading Gandhi, I saw how utterly mistaken I was." King explained: "Gandhi was probably the first person in history to lift the love ethic of Jesus above mere interaction between individuals to a powerful and effective social force on a large scale. Love for Gandhi was a potent instrument for social and collective transformation. It was in this Gandhian emphasis on love and nonviolence that I discovered the method for social reform that I had been seeking."[14]

This entire rendering of King's intellectual development is problematic. In King's version of what happened, he came to Gandhi early and deeply, through Johnson, and he came to his social gospel theology by reading Rauschenbusch,

Hegel, and Niebuhr under the guidance of liberal seminary professors. In the mid-1980s Lewis V. Baldwin, David Garrow, James Cone, and Taylor Branch variously challenged this account of King's thought. Baldwin argued that King's published writings reliably reflected his views, but his account of his life and the many accounts subsequently based on it wrongly minimized the formative importance of his cultural background: "Many books and articles on King reflect a narrow, elitist, racist approach that assumes that the black church and the larger black community are not healthy and vital contexts for the origin of intellectual ideas regarding theology and social change. The consequence of that approach has been to abstract King's intellectual development from his social and religious roots—family, church, and the larger black community— and to treat it primarily as a product of white Western philosophy and theology." Garrow and Cone went further, stressing that King's books were largely ghost-written by Stanley Levison, Bayard Rustin, Al Duckett, Harris Wofford, and other King advisors. Garrow chided scholars for relying on the "least depend-able King texts" even as they knew that King relied on ghostwriters. Cone urged scholars to pause over the fact that the books bearing King's name were produced while he made 450 speeches and traveled 325,000 miles per year.[15]

This revisionist corrective acquired ballast from the subsequent discovery that King's writings contained unacknowledged borrowings that fictionalized his past and that much of his scholarly and published work contained extensive plagiarized sections. King scholars had long been aware of occasional unaccred-ited references in his writings, but in 1986 rhetoric theorist Keith D. Miller began publishing essays that revealed King's persistent pattern of borrowing unattributed passages in his sermons and writings. In January 1990 Miller's essay "Composing Martin Luther King, Jr." demonstrated that King's memoir chapter in *Stride Toward Freedom* used unattributed passages in ways that gave a misleading picture of his intellectual development.[16]

Miller's articles attracted little attention at first, but in November 1990 histo-rian Clayborne Carson, senior editor and director of the King Papers Project, revealed that King had extensively plagiarized more than forty of his seminary and graduate school papers, including his doctoral dissertation at Boston University. For years afterward Carson was engulfed in controversies that singed the reputations of King and his teachers. On the one hand, these revelations reinforced the new emphasis in King scholarship on the distinctly southern black church style of King's religious thinking and preaching. On the other hand, they inspired exaggerated claims about his lack of intellectual sincerity and accomplishment. Miller and Garrow deprecated King's graduate education, claiming it was not much of an education and King never really cared about academic theology anyway. Miller said that King dismissively threw off "his professors' strange, artificial tongue and their ivory-tower theological formalism." Garrow said that King went through the motions for professors requiring mere regurgitation. David Levering Lewis followed suit, declaring that the revelations about King's plagiarism shockingly refuted Lewis's biography of King: "Who he was simply escaped me." Now Lewis had a different picture: "A picture emerges of King the young graduate student tooling about Boston on dates in his green Chevrolet, cavalierly submitting essays and dissertation chapters that were mosaics of the works of others, and of smug professors willfully indulging a bright enough degree candidate who, his studies completed, would return to the South to serve his people." Richard Lischer said the real issue was that King struggled falteringly for much of his career to hold together black church evangelicalism (good) and white liberalism (mostly bad). In the crossfire of scholarly overreactions it became hard to say that King might have been complex and sincere all along while taking some shortcuts.[17]

It is wrong to say that King glided blithely through graduate school without caring about the theology he learned. King studied Rauschenbusch intently and dated his commitment to Christian socialism to doing so. He learned the liberal tradition through theologians—Rauschenbusch, William Newton Clarke, William Adams Brown, and Harold DeWolf—who took sin and evil very seriously, contrary to standard caricatures of these thinkers. All wrote profusely about sin as badness, pride, selfishness, perversity, and tyranny, and all expounded a prophetic social gospel rendering of the kingdom of God. King's papers demonstrated real intellectual engagement, source problems notwithstanding, and he struck everyone who knew him in Boston as a serious, engaged scholar. DeWolf pressed King to pursue an academic career in the North, contrary to Lewis. It is true, as Miller and Branch emphasized, that King did not name the books he read by or about Gandhi, and when King discussed the impact of Gandhian philosophy upon him he recycled unattributed passages from articles by Harris Wofford and William Stuart Nelson. Moreover, King's knowledge of Gandhi was patchy and thin when the Montgomery boycott began. When Rustin and Fellowship of Reconciliation (FOR) activist Glenn Smiley got to Montgomery and asked King how much he knew about Gandhian nonviolence, King did not say what he later claimed, that he had studied Gandhi intently for years. He told the Gandhian professional activists that he knew very little.[18]

These problems considerably complicate the telling of King's story, which becomes more tangled if one judges that King never became a true-believing Gandhian. Rustin and Smiley later exaggerated King's utter ignorance of Gandhi before they got to Montgomery, an exaggeration subsequently adopted by scholars who dismiss or overlook Kenneth Smith's recollection that King wrote a term paper on Gandhi for him at Crozer. The paper is lost, but Smith remembered that it drew upon Richard B. Gregg's primer on Gandhian philosophy, Charles F. Andrews's exposition of Gandhian ideas, and Gandhi's autobiography. The greater exaggeration, however, was the story that King and his ghostwriters told. Rustin, especially, helped King tell a story he knew to be off-kilter, which Rustin later called "a hoax." King learned most of his Gandhian theory and strategy from Smiley and Rustin, not from his seminary professors or his independent seminary reading. Furthermore, though King unfailingly insisted that he accepted Gandhian nonviolence as a spiritual way of life, not merely a Niebuhrian strat-agem of power, he adopted and surpassed the whittling tack of his American mentors, stripping Gandhianism of doctrinal encumbrances. King did not employ Gandhi's jargon or concepts or make hard-case arguments for absolute pacifism. From early in his movement career, he said he came to Gandhi through Jesus, not the other way around. King stewed critically over what that meant because he had Reinhold Niebuhr in his head from seminary onward. In the official King story, however, King was a true-believing Gandhian who came to Gandhi early.[19]

The kernel of truth in the "early" claim was that King first wrestled with Gandhi at Crozer, along with Niebuhr. His interest in Niebuhr spiked as soon as he thought seriously about Gandhi and nonviolence. In King's telling, he luxuriated briefly in social gospel idealism, was impressed by Niebuhr's slashing critiques of idealism and pacifism, and on reflection found Niebuhr more convincing about human nature than about the efficacy of pacifism: "My reading of the works of Reinhold Niebuhr made me aware of the complexity of human motives and the reality of sin on every level of man's existence. Moreover, I came to recognize the complexity of man's social involvement and the glaring reality of collective evil. I realized that liberalism had been all too sentimental concerning human nature and that it leaned toward a false idealism."[20]

It strains credulity that a black son of the South who had struggled not to hate white oppressors had to be convinced by Reinhold Niebuhr that idealistic versions of liberalism underestimated the ravages of human evil. In addition, King knew that Rauschenbusch and Clarke were grimly realistic about human evil. Still, Niebuhr may have helped King confront a deep truth of his own experience or at least given him language for it. King wrote, "The more I thought about human nature, the more I saw how our tragic inclination for sin causes us to use our minds to rationalize our actions." King treasured liberal theology for its resistance to dogmatism and its open-ended search for truth; on these counts, like Niebuhr, he was unambiguously a liberal. At the same time, he was persuaded by Niebuhr that reason is never innocent of the self-interested struggle for power and advantage: "Reason, devoid of the purifying power of faith, can never free itself from distortions and rationalizations."[21]

But King held fast to the possibility that reason can be purified by faith. As a product of black church piety, King could imagine losing faith in God, but Niebuhr's Lutheran/Reformed disbelief in redemption from sin in this life was not a theological possibility for him. From the beginning of his seminary ponderings about such things King worried that Niebuhr's fixation with sin and his polemics against (usually Methodist) sanctification undermined the struggle for racial justice. In later life he allowed that Niebuhr was more balanced and helpful than Karl Barth. King lauded Niebuhr for refuting liberal "false optimism" without lapsing "into the anti-rationalism of the continental theologian Karl Barth, or the semi-fundamentalism of other dialectical theologians." On other occasions, however, King lumped Niebuhr with overreacting Barthians: "If liberalism was too optimistic concerning human nature, neo-orthodoxy was too pessimistic. Not only on the question of man, but also on other vital issues, the revolt of neo-orthodoxy went too far." The neo-orthodox reaction in theology overplayed the themes of divine hiddenness and transcendence, falling into "antirationalism and semifundamentalism, stressing a narrow uncritical biblicism. This approach, I felt, was inadequate both for the church and for personal life."[22]

Niebuhr versus Gandhi on pacifism was equally absorbing to King. According to King, as a seminarian he already judged that Niebuhr misrepresented Gandhi's strategy as a species of naive trust in the power of love. King countered that Gandhi was never naive or passive:

> My study of Gandhi convinced me that pacifism is not nonresistance to evil, but nonviolent resistance to evil. Between the two positions, there is a world of difference. Gandhi resisted evil with as much vigor and power as the violent resister, but he resisted with love instead of hate. True pacifism is not unrealistic submission to evil power, as Niebuhr contends. It is rather a courageous confrontation of evil by the power of love, in the faith that it is better to be the recipient of violence than the inflicter of it, since the latter only multiplies the existence of violence and bitterness in the universe, while the former may develop a sense of shame in the opponent, and thereby bring about a transformation and change of heart.[23]

That was the language and certainty of King two years after lightning struck in Montgomery and he became friends with Rustin and Smiley, but it was also, as King knew, exactly what his former dean at Boston University, Walter Muelder, argued about Niebuhr and nonviolence. At Crozer and Boston University King knew just enough about Gandhian strategy to feel attracted to it. At the level of this feeling he struggled with the implications of Niebuhrian realism. According to his recollection, he sought to blend Gandhian/Christian pacifism with Niebuhr's realism: "I came to see the pacifist position not as sinless but as the lesser evil in the circumstances." Pacifists have no immunity from the tragic realities that cover nonpacifists in moral guilt, he acknowledged. There is no escape from guilt; the question is whether violent resistance to evil or nonviolent resistance to evil is the lesser evil.[24]

King's papers at Crozer were liberal and antiwar but decidedly chastened on both counts. In a paper for Davis he reflected, "At one time I find myself leaning toward a mild neo-orthodox view of man, and at other times I find myself leaning toward a liberal view of man." He had too much experience with the "vicious race problem" of the American South to believe in the essential goodness of human beings, yet his hope that racial injustice might be eradicated rested on his faith that even whites were capable of goodness. He had witnessed some progress toward racial justice in his lifetime, in which he saw "some noble possibilities in human nature." By training and temperament King leaned toward liberal optimism; moreover, he kept in mind that Davis was a white liberal: "My liberal leaning may root back to the great imprint that many liberal theologians have left upon me and to my ever present desire to be optimistic about human nature."[25]

King's genius, once it was called upon, was to personally unite disparate ideologies, theologies, and movements from the North and South and across racial lines, with inspiring power. At Crozer Seminary he acquired some of the skills he would need to play this role. Crozer was his first experience of integrated education, but Chester's segregated black community felt like home to King. Many Chester residents came from the South, and many knew King as a fun-loving extrovert who loved the spirituals, the blues, and southern food, laughed uproariously at his own dry humor, enjoyed sex lightheartedly, and took up beer drinking and smoking. Young female parishioners at Barbour's church flocked to King, especially after Barbour announced that King came from a wealthy family; King told his mother, "The girls are running me down." Most Crozer students held outside jobs to support their studies, as did all of Crozer's black students except King. King worked with his checkbook, as they put it, spending Daddy King's money and spreading cheer. Emma Anderson, who knew King from Barbour's congregation, recalled, "He would go from house to house looking for food and fun. He made you feel comfortable around

him. He was very easy to meet." On Sundays King ate breakfast and dinner with
Barbour's family and often preached at services. Then he gathered with Crozer
students in Barbour's parlor as Barbour held forth on preaching and life.[26]

Barbour was a prominent figure in the National Baptist Convention and
editor of *National Baptist Voice.* Theologically he combined the same influences that marked King, playing a crucial role in passing them to King. Barbour
was rooted in southern black Baptist religion, modernized by liberal theology
and historical criticism, and influenced by Brightman's personalism, Niebuhr's
realism, Rauschenbusch's socialism, and Henry Nelson Wieman's naturalistic
behaviorism, although Barbour was less defensive than King about Wieman's
naturalism. Barbour was fond of saying that his authority in religion was his
experience of God and that he was the deepest theologian in the Baptist
Church. He appropriated social gospel socialism negatively as a critique of
capitalist exploitation and positively as a vision of economic democracy.
Barbour organized his sermons in thesis-antithesis-synthesis fashion, sometimes
announcing in advance that he would "make a synthesis" between two things.
He expounded Brightman's theory of moral laws from the pulpit, excoriated
adulterous ministers—"They have harems!"—and blistered idealistic sentimentality, sometimes citing Niebuhr or Wieman on the latter theme. King's fascination with Wieman began in Barbour's living room and was reinforced at Crozer.
In his senior year King fell in love with a young white woman, Betty Moitz,
whose parents worked for the seminary as a building and grounds superintendent and a cook. Barbour admonished King that intermarriage would bring
terrible trouble. King's friends said the same thing while he persisted in the
relationship for six months. King insisted that love should not be denied, asking
Barbour to perform the wedding. Barbour refused with a long, fatherly lecture,
pleading with King not to ruin his ministerial career before it began. Reluctantly
King ended the relationship. According to Barbour it was more than reluctant:
The ending broke King's heart, and he never recovered.[27]

From early childhood King acquired the rhythms of language and feeling
that moved black worshippers. He loved the drama of the sermon, and he practiced in front of a mirror. He once vowed to his mother to get some big words, a
pledge that family lore immortalized. At Morehouse he hung on Mays's chapel
sermons, committing to memory Mays's catchphrases and favorite poems. King
adopted Mays's habit of listing heroic figures. He learned from Morehouse
speech instructor Louis Chandler to aim for clarity, unity, coherence, and
emphasis. At Crozer King majored in preaching, taking nine courses. Homiletics
professor Robert Keighton taught King the three *p*'s of classic oratory, proving,
painting, and persuasion, and stressed that a sermon should have a definite

structure. The ladder sermon climbed to a powerful conclusion with one increasingly compelling argument after another. The jewel sermon examined a single idea from a variety of angles. The skyrocket sermon started with a dramatic story and lesson yielding a shower of smaller lessons. King enthused at learning different ways to make his sermonizing artful and orderly. He hung on Barbour's artful wordplay, noting catchphrases such as "paralysis of analysis." He doodled melodious phrases into his notebooks while passing time in class, crafting sermon material. In Queens, New York, King's internship at a Baptist church did not impress the Reverend William E. Gardner, who found King aloof, arrogant, and snobbish plus only a middling preacher. In Barbour's pulpit he honed his skills and thrived, confident in his ability to draw and move a crowd.[28]

The question of what he should say theologically, however, was more vexing, holding implications for King's doctoral ambitions. In Crozer classrooms and in Barbour's living room King heard much about Chicago School naturalism versus Boston School personalism. Having enjoyed Crozer far beyond his expectations, King took guidance on graduate schools from Davis, who steered King toward Yale (his own school), Boston University, and Edinburgh University, in that order. Yale rejected King despite his stellar record at Crozer, not even waiting for Graduate Record Exam scores that would not have helped his candidacy. Crozer historian Raymond Bean urged King to aim for Boston University, where he had studied. Meanwhile King wrestled with Brightman's *Philosophy of Religion*, which confused, challenged, and inspired him. "I was amazed to find that the conception of God is so complex and one about which opinions differ so widely," King wrote, admitting that he was "quite confused" about what to believe. Then Boston University admitted him, and King's confusion became clarifying. He liked Brightman's liberal personalist emphasis that critically interpreted experience is the privileged source of religious knowledge. He welcomed the opportunity to study under Brightman, choosing Boston over Edinburgh and New England over Scotland: "How I long now for that religious experience which Dr. Brightman so cogently speaks of throughout his book. It seems to be an experience, the lack of which life becomes dull and meaningless. As I reflect on the matter, however, I do remember moments that I have been awe awakened; there have been times that I have been carried out of myself by something greater than myself and to that something I gave myself. Has this great something been God? Maybe after all I have been religious for a number of years, and am now only becoming aware of it." In that mood he enrolled at Boston University to become a theologian.[29]

Daddy King felt burned again. He wanted King to join him at Ebenezer, he worried that King's southern Baptist roots were thinning out, and he hated the

"Communist propaganda" that King brought into his home. Daddy King saw no reason why any Christian preacher needed to read anything by Marx or Lenin. For that matter, graduate education as a whole puffed up graduates with fancy verbiage, making them merely strange and conceited. But Daddy King could not deny that King had good models in Mays and Kelsey, so yet another degree was needed. It helped that King's Ebenezer background showed through in his sermons. Daddy King gave his son a new green Chevrolet for graduating from Crozer and kept financing his education, later recalling that he "was moving forward into a modern, advanced sort of ministry." King joined a generational flow of African Americans to Boston University. In the 1950s, under Muelder's leadership, the School of Theology awarded approximately half the religious studies doctorates earned by African Americans in the United States. The seminary's identification with the social gospel was a major factor; after 1953 Thurman's presence was another. Muelder later recalled, "Blacks said to me, 'We know where Boston University stands and the word gets around.' "[30]

King ventured carefully into urban, cosmopolitan Boston, sharing a Massachusetts Avenue apartment with former Morehouse classmate Philip Lenud. Highly motivated to impress his teachers, King kept an immaculate appearance, dressed in tailored suits, and cultivated the ponderous, detached, pipe-wielding air of a philosopher. He organized a discussion group called the Dialectical Society, providing a supportive environment for black students to discuss ideas. The group met once a week over a potluck supper, presenting formal papers. King kept it determinately philosophical, avoiding politics, race, piety, and emotion. He also fended off challenges to his leadership, employing his genial charm. Two African American students, George Thomas and Douglas Moore, disliked the avoidance of race and politics, but King had no political interests at the time, and his academic work absorbed him. Lenud later said, "He was just a born pacifist. People would just take advantage of him because he was so good-natured." Classmate Cornish Rogers added that King was a ringleader for southern black students, who tended to be uncomfortable with white acquaintances: "He was just a very amiable person, and he liked folks, he liked parties, and he was fairly well off because he had a good salary, and he lived in an apartment and not on campus as we did, and he had his own car and a closet with a lot of very expensive clothes in it. He was like a prince."[31]

Though King enjoyed himself in Boston, he never had an African American instructor or took a course in which a black author was assigned. Neither did he linger in perpetual doctoral student adolescence. To all he seemed a model graduate student, long on intellectual ambition and eager to move through his program. He took Brightman's course on the philosophy of religion, but

Brightman was ailing. King took five courses with L. Harold DeWolf and found a mentor. DeWolf, a Nebraskan and Brightman protégé, was kindly, direct, intellectually exacting, and eager to help students. He exuded a positive, liberal, warmly evangelical message, which attracted seminarians to him, especially African American students. In his first year King took three courses with DeWolf on systematic theology plus DeWolf's courses on personalist theory and New Testament theology. Having come for Brightman and philosophy, King got a pulpit-ready version of personalist theology and philosophy from a Brightman protégé.

Boston personalism was a variant of post-Kantian idealism. Founded by Boston University philosopher Borden Parker Bowne in the late nineteenth and early twentieth centuries, it blended Descartes, Leibniz, Berkeley, Kant, Schleiermacher, William James, and Göttingen philosopher Rudolf Lotze. In its second generation it also appropriated Hegel and the social gospel. With Descartes, Bowne taught that the existence of the soul is known immediately as the experience of consciousness, though Bowne rejected Descartes's absolute dualism of body and soul. From Leibniz, Bowne took the ideas of spiritual individualism and the essentially active nature of the soul. With Berkeley and Lotze, he argued that self-consciousness is the necessary presupposition of all thinking and the world of objects, although Bowne rejected Berkeley's immaterialism and Lotze's disbelief in free will and the immortality of the soul. With Schleiermacher, Bowne taught that the wellspring of religion is religious experience; with James, he valorized pragmatic experience as a test of truth, though Bowne eschewed James's antimetaphysical temper. From Kant he took the basic elements of his critically idealistic epistemology and ethical conception of the person, although Bowne sharply rejected Kant's unknowable "thing-in-itself" and Kant's exclusion of purpose from pure theoretical reason.[32]

The key to Bowne's system was the argument that personality—the self as a center of conscious experience—is the single reality that cannot be explained by anything else. Against the monism of his mentor, Lotze, Bowne affirmed the metaphysical reality of finite persons and the empirical experience of the world as real and plural. In its monist and pluralist versions alike, however, personal idealism was a theory of the transcendent reality of personal spirit and the organic unity of nature in spirit. Lotze and Bowne argued that natural science, being mechanistic, does not account for the reality and unity of consciousness. It is possible to move from mind to matter, but matter cannot be the ultimate or sufficient cause of mind. Bowne took experience as a whole as his datum, questioning how reality should be conceived on the basis of particular experiences as interpreted by thought. He told his classes that Kant dethroned the things of sense by demonstrating that the mind is active in producing experience; this was Kant's greatest and permanent contribution to philosophy. But Kant's epistemology relegated the category of purpose to practical and aesthetic reason, which disastrously overlooked that purpose is essential to all higher forms of thought. To Brightman, Kant was great mainly for paving the way to Hegel, who overcame the Platonic atemporalism of Western thought and restored metaphysics to its rightful exalted place in modern thought.

Boston personalism was emphatically a school in both senses of the term: a school of thought centered at a Methodist university. Brightman taught in the Philosophy Department and his friend Albert C. Knudson was a theologian at the School of Theology. Brightman and Knudson earned their doctorates under Bowne; Muelder, DeWolf, and Peter Bertocci earned their doctorates under Brightman; and Knudson and Muelder reinforced the school's identity as deans of the School of Theology. During its second generation there were Brightman versus Bowne and Knudson arguments over temporality, identity, and theodicy that saved Boston personalism from party-line insularity, and King got there just as the third generation of Muelder, DeWolf, and Bertocci came into its own. Though DeWolf was too evangelical to rely as heavily as Brightman and Muelder on philosophical arguments, he told his classes that theology needed a good philosophical undergirding, which struck the right balance for King.[33]

In the classroom DeWolf praised Bowne's originality and affirmed the primacy of personality as a metaphysical principle. DeWolf taught that Bowne's idealism was better than the impersonal absolute idealisms propounded by Hegelians and perhaps Hegel himself. Absolute idealism was metaphysically and epistemologically monist, which made it both strong and unacceptable. It was strong as an account of the unity of mind and unacceptable because it failed to account for error and evil. If error and evil are incomplete goods that are actually good when viewed in light of the whole—which is impossible—one might as well claim that good is incomplete evil. DeWolf persuaded King that personal idealism made greater sense because of its epistemological dualism. Personalist theory explained error and evil without attributing either to the Absolute, and it had a real doctrine of creation. King also embraced DeWolf's "double aspect" revision of an interactionist theory of mind-body relation, combining personalist and behaviorist ideas about the self. DeWolf argued that a person is an intrinsically conscious self in, of, and for itself, but as viewed by others a person is a system of processes. King found his reward in DeWolf's gospel-centered personalism, which he praised as "an important and brilliant" contribution to theology.[34]

In his second year King enrolled in Brightman's two-semester seminar on Hegel, but Brightman fell ill after the second class, and Bertocci took over the course; Brightman died shortly afterward. That left King stranded in the Philosophy Department without a doctoral advisor, so he made the obvious move to DeWolf and the School of Theology, taking three more courses with DeWolf. Through Bertocci, King absorbed Brightman's high regard for Hegelian idealism. He embraced Hegel's idea that "truth is the whole" and, with Brightmanian caveats, Hegel's dialectic. In a paper he explained that Hegel conceived Becoming as the dialectical passage of Being and Nothing into each other and that Hegel's triads simultaneously abolish and preserve, in the synthesis, the differences between the dialectical pairings of thesis and antithesis. For the rest of his life King called Hegel his favorite philosopher. King thought in triads yielding a synthesis, on occasion he commended Hegel's dialectic of master and slave, and he invoked Hegel's notion that Spirit uses the passions of partly unsuspecting individuals to fulfill its aims of self-consciousness and freedom.[35]

Philosophically, theologically, and socio-ethically King accepted and absorbed personalist thinking. Although he took no courses from Muelder, he studied and cited Muelder's social ethical writings, identifying with his Christian Socialist pacifism, which broadly influenced Boston personalism in the 1950s. King agreed with Muelder that Niebuhr's theological ethic was strongest as a critique of liberal perfectionist complacency and sentimentality. Niebuhr deserved immense credit for insisting that politics is about power and every ethical choice is shot through with moral ambiguities. But Niebuhr's ethic had a fatal flaw, King wrote, exactly as Muelder said: "There is one weakness in Niebuhr's ethical position which runs the whole gamut of his writings. This weakness lies in [the] inability of his system to deal adequately with the relative perfection which is the fact of the Christian life." To Niebuhr, the Pauline emphasis on spiritual regeneration simply did not fit into Christian realism, so he excluded it. King followed Muelder in objecting that Niebuhr simply dropped essential Christian questions of salvation. How do human beings develop spiritually? How does personality actualize Christian values? What is the significance of self-sacrificing love in human nature and history? King observed, "All these problems are left unsolved by Niebuhr. He fails to see that the availability of the divine *Agape* is an essential affirmation of the Christian religion." King sealed his case with a lengthy quote from Muelder that there is such a thing as redemptive energy that transcends individual and collective egotism.[36]

King had grown up on Daddy King's Pauline sermonizing that in Jesus Christ one becomes a new creature. Dropping the language of spiritual regeneration was not an option for King. Moreover, Muelder emphasized self-sacrificial love (*agape*), drawing on Anders Nygren's theological analysis of love. This conceptuality named and rationalized King's deep spiritual feeling; thus he invoked it for the rest of his life, often mystifying audiences that puzzled over why it mattered. On other doctrinal topics King was a down-the-line social gospel liberal in the manner of Davis, DeWolf, and, indirectly through DeWolf, Albert Knudson. Against the classical two-nature doctrine that a divine and a perfect human nature were united in the personality of Jesus, King repeated Knudson's objection that Chalcedonian Christology presupposed the static, abstract substantialism of Platonist philosophy. Any genuinely modern theology had to view reality as dynamic and concrete. Knudson theorized that the divine and human factors in Christ's personality were "simply different aspects" of one personality and that Christ's personality, like all others, was active, not a substance; King agreed that Jesus had one unitary personality, not two natures: "We must then think of Christ as a unitary being whose divinity consists not in any second nature or in a substantial unity with God, but in a unique and potent God-consciousness." Christ was uniquely bonded to God by spiritual purpose, not by substance.[37]

King followed Knudson and Bowne in contending that objectivist atonement theories are similarly wrong. The entire scheme of substitutionary atonement theory is "based on a false view of personality," he argued. Merit and guilt belong to individuals; they cannot be transferred from one person to another. Moreover, it is immoral to punish one person for the sins of another, and substitutionary atonement theory compounds its immorality by making God the obstacle to human redemption. "The real obstacle to man's redemption has always lain in man himself," King wrote, expounding a Bowne/Knudson theme. "It is from this standpoint, therefore, that the death of Christ is to be interpreted. Christ's death was not a ransom, or a penal substitute, or a penal example; rather it was a revelation of the sacrificial love of God intended to awaken an answering love in the hearts of men."[38]

He also took a liberal personalist line on reason, sin, and the church. Against the Barthian "deification of revelation," King insisted that revelation and reason are complementary and that, without reason, revelation "remains a bundle of nothing." Against Barthian and Niebuhrian claims about original sin and the essence of sin, King contended that there is no single essential sin, guilt and merit are inalienable in individuals, and sin happens whenever human beings misuse their free will. Against the Catholic doctrines of papal primacy and the infallibility of the church, King replied, "All of this strikes me as erroneous and unhistorical." Jesus may have organized the disciples, "but to say that Christ consciously organized the Church and made Peter the first Pope is [to] push the record to false proportions." Invoking DeWolf's distinction between the spiritual church and the organized church, King affirmed, "The true Church is the spiritual Church. If there are any claims to infallibility it is here. It is in the spiritual church that we witness the kingdom of God on earth."[39]

Many of King's papers at Boston University and Crozer Seminary contained extensive unattributed passages, such as his paper for DeWolf's seminar on systematic theology, which copied over twenty pages of Walter Marshall Horton's *Contemporary Continental Theology* while citing Horton's book only once. Somehow his teachers did not detect this practice, despite the fact that many of King's sources (such as Horton's book and Walter Stace's *The Philosophy of Hegel*) were well-known works. Some of King's papers were properly researched and referenced, and he escaped detection on others, probably because he was an excellent classroom student who espoused a consistent theological position. In several courses he dominated class discussions, conducting lengthy back-and-forth dialogues with the instructor, especially DeWolf.[40]

To some degree King's faulty citation practices reflected his boundary situation as a product of the oral culture of black church preaching, which prized repetition, imitation, call-and-response dynamics, and the rhetorical expression of religious authority through the preacher's gift for synthesizing the words of many voices. King grew up in a folk culture that viewed speech and ideas as communal property, but he knew that his graduate papers violated basic academic standards. Unfortunately, the same faulty practices that might have been rooted out of his scholarship had they been detected by a teacher were perpetuated in his dissertation, which copied extensive sections of others' works, including an article by Walter Marshall Horton, a review of Tillich's *Systematic Theology* by Raphael Demos, and, especially, a 1952 Boston University dissertation on Tillich by Jack Boozer. It copied more than fifty sentences from Boozer's dissertation, relied on this source throughout its discussion of Tillich, and followed the general structure of Boozer's work.[41]

As an academic text King's dissertation was seriously flawed, but that does not negate its value as an expression of the religious worldview that undergirded his ministry and activism. Although King took shortcuts in his academic work, the parts that he wrote were indistinguishable from the parts that he took from others. He had serious and defining intellectual and spiritual concerns. He wanted very much to be a religious intellectual like Mays, Kelsey, and Barbour. He had chewed over Tillich versus Wieman in Barbour's living room and Davis's classroom. He had pulled the Dialectical Society into his inner debate over the theologies of Tillich and Wieman, pressing the question of divine personality. To King, studying at the bastion of personalist thought renewed the question on a weekly basis: Did his teachers have a persuasive alternative to the differently impersonal theologies of Tillich and Wieman? If not, had he made a mistake in choosing Boston University? But if his teachers were wrong about the divine ground of human personality and dignity, what gospel should he preach?

King had all that at stake as he mulled his dissertation topic and courted a partner, Coretta Scott. The daughter of a prosperous storekeeper in Marion, Alabama, Scott had graduated from Antioch College and was studying voice at the New England Conservatory of Music. King almost blew his chance with her, which he got after complaining to an old friend from Atlanta, Mary Powell, that Boston women were cold compared to the warm, empathic, sensual girls he knew in the South. He was striking out with Boston women, which frustrated and puzzled him. Powell and Scott were classmates at the conservatory. Powell gave him Scott's phone number, while cautioning that Scott was reserved, too, plus she looked down on ministers. King, persisting in his Don Juan self-image, called Scott and cooed to her, "I am like Napoleon at Waterloo before your charms." That was absurd, Scott replied; he had never met her. King scrambled to recover, switching to his intellectual persona, which won a first date. Then he proposed on the first date, and many times afterward. Coretta's early impression was that King didn't look like much, but he had a radiant charm. She asked what would happen to her singing career; King told her they could be like Adam Powell and Hazel Scott. Daddy King smoldered while Coretta made her decision. He had a better spouse in mind for his son, an upscale Atlanta woman. Finally Scott said yes, Daddy King relented, and he performed the wedding service in June 1953 at her family garden in Marion. The following December King told Davis he still held "to the liberal position" that Davis and DeWolf taught him and was grateful to be steeped in their "warm evangelical liberalism." In April, with an approved dissertation topic in hand, King accepted a call to Dexter Avenue Baptist Church in Montgomery, Alabama.[42]

The dissertation analyzed and evaluated the theologies of Tillich and Wieman from a personalist perspective. It made no attempt whatsoever to relate King's theological convictions to his experience as a black American. Cone later observed incredulously that it was "as if the black experience in the white world had nothing to contribute to King's critique of Tillich and Wieman or any other thinker or idea in Euro-American history." King stuck to the view that he had urged upon the Dialectical Society: They needed to produce academic work making no mention of race, showing the academy they could do it. King and classmate Major Jones vowed to write dissertations belonging to the realm of race-transcending theory, where philosophical theologians supposedly dwelt. Tillich and Wieman, King observed, sought to establish God's existence ontologically, by definition, even though Wieman disavowed ontological speculation. More important, both refused the attribution of personality to God. Tillich overemphasized God's power and Wieman overemphasized God's goodness. To Tillich, God was the ground or power of being that cannot be denied unless one denies the reality of being itself. To Wieman, God was the "something of supreme value" that cannot be denied unless one denies the reality of the good. Citing Yale theologian D. C. Macintosh, King judged that both strategies sought to make the question of God's existence a dead issue by positing a God-idea of minimal qualities.[43]

The problem was the minimal qualities. Macintosh criticized Wieman for "subtracting so drastically and, it would seem, so permanently" from God's personal and active character. King agreed that Wieman (and Tillich) made the idea of God credible "by drastically subtracting from what God means." Personal idealism had better concepts of God and personality, King contended. Tillich and Wieman identified personality with limited human personality, reasoning that God transcends the limitations of personal existence. King countered that only human personalities are limited in the manner of creatures: "Personality as such involves no necessary limitation. It means simply self-consciousness and self-direction. The idea of personality is so consistent with the notion of the absolute that we must say with Bowne 'that complete and perfect personality can be found only in the Infinite and Absolute Being, as only in him can we find that complete and perfect selfhood and self-expression which is necessary to the fullness of personality.' "[44]

Applied to God, the idea of personality implies no limitation. Moreover, King contended, the idea of divine personality is the necessary presupposition of the idea that God is good. Wieman's emphasis on divine goodness was better than Tillich's emphasis on divine power, but Wieman's axiology had no theological foundation, and both theologians were wrong to accentuate one pole of God's being. Citing Knudson for support, King argued that God can be good only if God is personal. The reciprocal union of heart, will, and intellect described in Scripture "is possible only between personal beings. Only the personality of God makes possible the union of communion with him." Apart from the reality of freedom and intelligence, there is no such thing as goodness: "Only a personal being can be good." Wieman's theorizing about goodness and love was merely abstract, not genuinely ethical, for goodness and love are always attributes of personality.[45]

Personal idealism, by contrast, espoused a quantitative pluralism in recognizing the manifold realities of sense experience and a qualitative monism in affirming that reality has a unifying ground in God's being. That was the right balance, King argued: "Neither swallows the other. Such a view defends, on the one hand, individuality against the impersonalism and all-engulfing universalism of any type of ultimate monism. On the other hand, it vindicates the idea of a basal monism against the attacks of any ultimate pluralism." King accepted Kant's basic account of knowledge as an a priori synthetic activity of the mind. Human reason makes sense of the world by applying its a priori categories of understanding to phenomena perceived by the senses. No experience is intelligible apart from the categories of unity, plurality, totality, reality, negation, limitation, causality, and other rules of mind. But King was post-Kantian in rejecting Kant's restriction of pure reason to knowledge of phenomena. Experience, King believed, yields metaphysical clues about reality that deserve to be regarded as genuine knowledge. Mechanical causality yields only a low level of thought that cannot unify things and events. Kant relegated purpose to practical and aesthetic reason, leaving no role for purpose in pure reason. Every version of post-Kantian philosophy said that Kant had a truncated concept of pure reason; the personalist version stressed that there is no knowing without self-conscious intelligence. Intelligence is nothing without purpose. What matters is to uphold a personal worldview against the mechanistic wasteland of impersonalism.[46]

King entered the ministry confident in his theological and philosophical basis. It mattered to him greatly that he had one. He had studied two powerful theological minds that opposed his belief in divine personality and came out believing in it more than ever. He had exactly the experience his teachers commended: Grounding himself in a sophisticated philosophy had strengthened his religious convictions. The fact that King gave a misleading rendering of his story invited scholarly deconstruction after he was gone, which came with a vengeance. Academics derided his conviction that personal idealism gave him a strong intellectual foundation. As Miller explained, "Today almost no one prizes, studies, or even remembers Personalism for itself." Historian David L. Chappell said that personalist ideas did not really matter in King's work as a civil rights leader because King's personalist ideas did not differentiate him "from thousands of preachers nobody has ever heard of." Thus personalism should not be considered an important category in rendering King's significance.[47]

This scholarly fashion usually plays up Niebuhr's influence on King, which gets a crucial thing right. King was influenced by Niebuhr's theorizing about the unavoidability of coercive violence in all struggles for justice. Chappell and Branch say that King was Niebuhrian on this point all along, and Garrow says he turned that way after moral suasion failed in 1962. I believe that King was Niebuhrian on this point all along *and* that he remained dead serious about embracing Gandhian nonviolence as a way of life, not merely a tactic. He said so emphatically until the end, which Branch brushes off too dismissively. King did not believe he had to choose between nonviolence and recognizing that it was coercively violent. Moreover, debates over this point have wrongly pushed out of view King's understanding of what mattered to him theologically. He had distinct theological beliefs that undergirded and enabled him, exactly as he said. Post-Kantian idealism, the modern West's richest philosophical tradition, was never refuted or surpassed. It merely fell out of fashion. King rightly insisted that his belief in personality divine and human was his mainstay in a turbulent world. It mattered to him greatly that there was a modern, progressive, justice-oriented theological perspective that centered on his most cherished belief. This perspective blended black church religion, liberal theology, Christian philosophy, and racial justice and social justice militancy like nothing else: "This personal idealism remains today my basic philosophical position. Personalism's insistence that only personality—finite and infinite—is ultimately real strengthened me in two convictions: it gave me metaphysical and philosophical grounding for the idea of a personal God, and it gave me a metaphysical basis for the dignity and worth of all human personality."[48]

God is the personal ground of the infinite value of human personality. This two-sided credo had a negative corollary confirming King's deepest feeling: If the worth of personality is the ultimate value in life, America's racial caste system was an abhorrent evil. Evil is precisely that which degrades and negates personality. The purpose of Jim Crow was to humiliate, exclude, and degrade the personhood of African Americans, but King's family and church taught him he was "as good as anybody." No philosophy supported these convictions more powerfully than the one that King absorbed and embraced as a graduate student, just as he said, although what he said was only a sliver of what happened and what mattered.

The notion that King dumped his graduate school theology after he became a movement leader has a hard time accounting for the fact that he preached from the same barrel of sermons throughout his career. From the beginning he riffed on them differently in different contexts, constantly revising and improvising his stock sermons. Some were already staples for him when he arrived in Montgomery. By the end of his first year in Montgomery, almost the entire corpus existed. Each had set pieces that King inserted into other sermons as the occasion demanded or the Spirit moved him. Churchgoers and movement veterans would cheer as soon as he got rolling on one, much like a singer performing a medley of her hits. "I Have a Dream" was one of them three years before the March on Washington. "I've been to the mountaintop" was a staple from January 1957 onward, which he used whenever he was especially down or anxious. King's favorite sermon, "The Three Dimensions of a Complete Life," was already his favorite when he gave it as a trial sermon at Dexter Church. It won plaudits and the job at Montgomery. He gave it many times and every year afterward, notably at Purdue University in 1958, addressing the first National Conference on Christian Education of the newly formed United Church of Christ, and at St. Paul's Cathedral in London in 1964, on his way to accept the Nobel Peace Prize. He kept giving it until the end, which meant, for King, that he never stopped composing it.

VERNON JOHNS AND MONTGOMERY LIGHTNING

King told his friend and first biographer, Lawrence D. Reddick, that "ambivert" fit him best—a blend of extrovert and introvert. To Reddick, that was spot-on. King was outgoing, amiable, a big talker, and not a brooder, but he needed time to himself and his ample inner life, and he had "a touch of suspicion in his nature." Coretta King cut deeper by stressing that King was "a guilt-ridden man," far too guilt-driven to buy a big house or take care of himself. Reddick and Coretta agreed, however, that King was more playful and comical than the public ever saw, and he was two-sided about everything, not just himself. In his early career King swung back and forth between picturing himself as an academic or a pastor and in the North or South. He told friends he was better suited to the ministry than to scholarship, but he felt the lure of the academy, especially for the right offer. Daddy King, by his lights, had the perfect offer. King would come home to Ebenezer for his main job and teach at Morehouse on the side; Mays had already agreed. But King needed independence more than anything else. Shortly after he completed his doctoral residency requirements he received job offers from three northern colleges and job feelers from churches in New York, Massachusetts, and Michigan. Then First Baptist Church of Chattanooga, Tennessee, and Dexter Avenue Baptist Church emerged as possibilities. Daddy King was emphatically against Dexter, which had imperious deacons and frosty manners. "That's a *big* nigger's church," he warned. Dexter was in the market because Vernon Johns had worn out his welcome there and resigned one too many times.[49]

Vernon Johns was brilliant, earthy, eccentric, rough-hewn, and truculent, invisible to white America but a legend in black Baptist America. His Scottish maternal grandfather had maintained two families, one white and one black, and ended his days in prison as a convicted murderer. Johns was born in 1892 and grew up outside Farmville, Virginia, where his father, Willie Johns, was a farmer, peddler, and Baptist preacher. Johns adopted his father's threefold regime. He plowed and read simultaneously, reading voraciously. He learned Latin, Greek, Hebrew, and German, mostly on his own. He attended a Presbyterian mission school, Boydton Institute, and talked his way into Virginia Union University. He transferred to Virginia Theological Seminary, which expelled him for rebelliousness, and challenged Oberlin Theological Seminary to deal with him, where Johns absorbed liberal theology and graduated in 1918. The following summer he deepened his commitment to liberal theology and the social gospel by studying at the University of Chicago Divinity School. In the early 1920s Johns taught at Virginia Theological Seminary and ministered at Court Street Baptist Church in Lynchburg, acquiring a reputation for intellectual sermons studded with quotations from Plato, Aristotle, Shakespeare, Thomas Jefferson, Abraham Lincoln, and William James.[50]

Johns took offense at prevailing assumptions that a black preacher had to be some kind of fundamentalist. In the mid-1920s nearly every white mainline Protestant denomination battled over modernism versus fundamentalism, while Johns insisted that black churches were not exempt from the issue. He bridled that white publishers ignored Reverdy Ransom, Adam Clayton Powell Sr., Mordecai Johnson, and Howard Thurman, so stereotypes prevailed. In 1925 Johns urged Joseph Fort Newton, editor of the book series *Best Sermons*, to publish sermons by Johnson and Thurman, but *Best Sermons* remained lily-white for another year. The next year Johns submitted one of his sermons, "Transfigured Moments," and Newton published it grandly: "Mr. Johns is the first colored preacher to appear in *Best Sermons,* and it is both an honor and a joy to bid him welcome, alike for his race and his genius. . . . The sermon lifts us into a higher air, above the fogs of passion and prejudice, where the ages answer, antiphonally, telling us of the brotherhood of man in the life of God in Christ." Johns's sermon grappled with the Transfiguration story in Matthew, highlighting Peter's outburst that he, James, and John should build three tabernacles for Jesus, Moses, and Elijah. Johns described Peter as the rare type that dared to say what others felt but dared not say. Peter had a "blundering genius for expression" that Jesus prized; otherwise Jesus would not have made him the "foundation man" of the church and kingdom. Johns commended the way and "Personality" of Jesus in quintessential liberal fashion, emphasizing "the strength of a Personality, radiant with truth and love." Jesus was like Moses and Elijah in saving others through his radiance, "a glowing flame" that kindled spiritual power to change the world. Moreover, it mattered that Jesus, Peter, James, and John were "members of a despised race," leftovers from a conquered, ravaged nation: "Jesus kindled the consciousness of human brotherhood in the most self-conscious and provincial of all races."[51]

By the early 1930s Johns had a genius reputation comparable to those of Johnson and Thurman, which drew crowds the many times he preached at Howard University. But he rarely stayed anywhere for long. He had wanderlust in a big way, and he offended people wherever he took a job, so he had many stormy endings. Had he not had six children with his wife, Altona Trent Johns, Johns might have taken fewer jobs, as he preferred the lecture circuit and its ample travel. As it was, his schoolteacher wife often had to hold the family together while Johns hit the road; his favorite pastime was to read Keats or Byron on a trip through Alabama or Georgia. Johns was prickly and demanding, he ran roughshod over deacons whenever possible, he raged against Jim Crow, and he set a stringent example of resistance that he imposed on his family. He had a stormy four-year run as president of Virginia Seminary; then he lasted four years in Charleston, where he antagonized Johnson's former congregation, lambasting its bourgeois conceits. He circled back to Court Street Baptist Church in Lynchburg but clashed with the deacons and was ousted. In 1948 he seized his last chance to pastor a congregation, in Montgomery, where his wife joined the music faculty at Alabama State College. Altona Trent Jones, the daughter of a college president, pleaded with her husband to make nice with the physicians, dentists, professors, and teachers of Dexter Avenue Baptist Church. But white Montgomery enraged Johns on a daily basis, and he challenged his beaten down congregants to stop cowering. Montgomery, where Jefferson Davis became president of the Confederate States and the Confederate flag was first unfurled, was home to the Maxwell and Gunter Air Force bases, where racial integration was the law. White Montgomery, despite depending on the military, zealously upheld Jim Crow everywhere else.

For a while Dexter deacons took pride in Johns's sophisticated sermons and put up with his affronts to their self-respect. Dexter did not allow shouting, responsive "Amens," or other displays of emotion. For a while that was fine with Johns, as he preached social gospel religion, not rapture. But it galled him that Dexter spurned the spirituals and did not assert its self-respect where it really mattered. Johns protested that it was far from self-respecting to refuse to sing "Go Down, Moses." He invented an epithet for Dexter's icy formality, "spinksterinkdum." He ripped Dexter for esteeming status and prestige over work. Dexter leaders, Johns lamented, wrongly believed that farming, business, and waiting tables were beneath Dexter members. They considered labor demeaning; he said they perpetuated a self-sabotaging holdover from slavery. Johns defied the Dexter ethos by selling produce on the church lawn in his muddy farmer boots. He was higher and lower than everyone at Dexter. He called out criminals from the pulpit, playing judge and jury for a community that white Montgomery rarely policed, and his funeral sermons were sometimes scathing. Johns was too irascible for civic organizations, but he offered a model of individual militancy, which posed dangers for Dexter. One week he protested a lynching with a sermon titled, "It's Safe to Murder Negroes in Montgomery." Johns stressed that Jesus was lynched too. Another week his sermon courted special danger: "When the Rapist Is White."[52]

Johns loved to quote Teddy Roosevelt's lament that the Progressive Party meant well "but meant it feebly." That was exactly his complaint about most black churches. One Sunday he bellowed during a service, "Why do you sit there like bronze Buddhas?" He lasted four and a half years in Montgomery; near the end Johns upped the ante on provocation, ending his sermons by announcing bargain prices on potatoes and cabbage. The deacons did not like being insulted or endangered. Johns clashed with them constantly, he resigned five times to get his way, and the fifth time, to his surprise, Dexter voted to let him go. By then Altona Johns had moved to Virginia State College in Petersburg, and Johns defied Dexter one more time, for an entire year, refusing to leave the parsonage. The deacons turned off the lights, water, and heat, and Johns stayed defiantly while Dexter sought his successor.[53]

Though averse to polite chatter and ingratiating repartee, Johns had a sense of humor. He and the gregarious Ralph Abernathy had a friendship that was long on fellow-preacher joshing. Abernathy boasted that his congregation, First Baptist, was Montgomery's other bourgeois black church. When King came to Montgomery for his trial sermon at Dexter, Abernathy and Johns regaled him with puckish descriptions of the two congregations. In their telling, especially Abernathy's, one could mention Jesus in a sermon at First Baptist, but Dexter preferred to leave Jesus out of it. Dexter was eager to hear about Plato, although Johns added that no one at Dexter actually knew anything about Plato. Both congregations were cold as ice, they agreed, with more exaggeration, as Dexter considered First Baptist a shouting congregation. Johns indulged his friend's exaggeration that First Baptist was almost equally upscale and frosty. He and Abernathy conducted revivals together, and Abernathy worked for Johns as a street peddler. Abernathy took merry pride in being Johns's leading seller of women's lingerie; his prowess in this endeavor evoked much preacher chortling between them. Still, it was no laughing matter that Johns had been reduced to a freezing parsonage for the past year and was out of career options. Abernathy pulled King aside, lamenting that Johns was "a mess." The following morning Johns preached for Abernathy at First Baptist, and King won the job at Dexter with his most polished sermon.[54]

Throughout his career, from Montgomery to Memphis, King lugged musty tomes by nineteenth-century preachers with him. He pored over Victorian preachers intently, looking for sermon themes, exegetical clues, striking phrases, and inspiration. The brittle pages would break at the corners, leaving paper trails in King's hotel rooms. Long after King won the job at Dexter with his favorite sermon, "The Three Dimensions of a Complete Life," Abernathy teased him about his sermon research, the bulkiness and smell of his books, and the mess they made. "Three Dimensions" was based on a gem of nineteenth-century liberal New England preaching, "The Symmetry of Life," by Boston Episcopal bishop Phillips Brooks. King's first four paragraphs closely paraphrased Brooks without acknowledgment, at Dexter or later. Invoking the geometric perfection of the city of God as described in Revelation 21, Brooks and King analogized that the complete life, like a cube, possesses three dimensions of length, breadth, and height. The length of a life is its inner drive to achieve personal ends. The breadth of a life is its outward-moving care and concern for the well-being of others. The height of a life is its upward-moving desire for God.

Brooks elaborated a vision of humanity growing in consciousness, adapting to heredity and environment, and realizing its spiritual nature as a glorified collectivity infused by God. That was too Hegelian and foreign to black church experience, so King substituted Rabbi Joshua Liebman's popular rendering of self-love: one cannot love others without loving one's self. King rounded out his section on length with a set piece—the "street sweeper"—about taking pride in ordinary occupations. He rounded out the breadth theme by contending that the fates of white and black Americans were tied together. He rounded out the height theme by circling back to Brooks, urging congregants to reach up to God. King's height section featured a Platonic/personalist excursus on unseen realities, echoing every personal idealistic thinker from Bowne to Brightman to DeWolf: "You can never see my personality." Every self knows itself in immediate experience and knows other selves only through their effects. Every self is thus as formless and invisible as God, just like all the meanings by which we live and the motives that move us. In later versions King ramped up the sermon with references to contemporary black American life and took a shot at fashionable death-of-God theologies of the mid-1960s. But in every version, as in Brooks's sermon, there was only one reference to Jesus and no hint of an otherworldly biblical God reaching down to save human souls. Richard Lischer, plugging for evangelical preaching, criticized King for following Brooks in completely disregarding "the awesome splendor of the Bible's witness to God."[55]

One reason that King gave this sermon so many times and liked it so much was that it spoke reliably to the disparate audiences he addressed. Coretta King said it was her favorite King sermon, too. It was a thoroughly personalist sermon in general and specific senses, recycling trademark idioms and claims of the personalist tradition. The fact that King preached it repeatedly every year and on especially august occasions is a measure of his enduring debt to personal idealism. His favorite sermon drove to a credo that the good life is about the flourishing of personality, which is "something of a great triangle," creatively integrating personal, social, and ultimate concerns: "At one angle stands the individual person, at the other angle stand other persons, and at the top stands the Supreme, Infinite Person, God. These three must meet in every life if that life is to be complete."[56]

The King newlyweds debated whether they could stand to live again under southern racial caste. Coretta did not want to return to the South, let alone to the cradle of the Confederacy, fifty miles from her childhood home. King persuaded her to give Montgomery a chance, "at least for a few years." But DeWolf kept recommending King for academic positions, and Barbour, always colorfully opinionated, urged King shortly after he moved to Montgomery to keep looking: "I warn you. Don't get stuck there. Move on to a big metropolitan center in THE NORTH, or some town as ATLANTA. You will dry rot there. I feel sorry for you with all that learning. I wrote a two hundred-page thesis on RELIGION AND PHYSIOLOGICAL PSYCHOLOGY and with the exception of lectures to colleges have been unable to use ONE SINGLE IDEA in the Baptist Church. The country Negroes have swept into town and REDUCED the intellectual level of RELIGION. This is the day of Mass preachers except in certain spots. Hurry and get one."[57]

That reflected Barbour's disappointment and loneliness in Chester. His Crozer students joked about his blustery airs, but sympathetically, with a certain reverence, calling his living room "Barbour University." Barbour never got the recognition or perch he deserved, so he covered up by boasting, in raconteur style. He also had domestic advice for King: "You [and] Coretta are going to rue the day you have children. The Catholics are right. Preachers should be celibates." He liked Coretta, he said in a postscript, which was unusual since "I do not like preachers' wives . . . most of them are empty headed and butt in their husbands' business too much." By hand he scratched a second afterthought: "Tillich is all wet. There is no being-itself. 'Das Ding im Sich' is Non-Being! Kant proved that. Being-Itself is a meaningless abstraction. As Marx said."[58]

The chasm between King's nonactivist past and the movement leader he became tends to obscure the social justice ambitions he held when he moved to Montgomery. He had no glimmering of national movement leadership, but he did have a social gospel ministry in mind from the beginning, emphasizing racial justice. King came to Montgomery determined to be a civil rights activist and was ahead of other local ministers when he arrived. Johns was outspoken but not a candidate to lead anything. L. Roy Bennett led the Interdenominational Ministerial Alliance, but his windbag monologues evoked eye-rolling and faction fighting. On the night preceding his trial sermon King told Johns and Abernathy that he was committed to pressing the civil rights issue. Abernathy later recalled, "He was, he said, committed to the preaching of a social gospel that would awaken the Christian churches and mobilize them in the fight against segregation. He indicated that he had been working on plans to do just that and when the time came to do battle, he hoped the churches would be ready." Abernathy, pleased but surprised that the tweedy, intellectual King talked like this, asked how long the churches would need to make a move. King said it would take "at least several years." The churches had to prepare carefully for the breakthrough that was coming. This memory was surely filtered by the whirlwind that overtook King and Abernathy in December 1955, but it is not far off from King's early ministry; Abernathy insisted that King never really changed.[59]

King joined Montgomery NAACP shortly after arriving at Dexter. He preached his first sermon as Dexter's pastor in May 1954, spent most of the next four months writing his dissertation, and took up full-time ministry in September. He told the congregation that he—not them, the deacons, or trustees—was in charge. Leadership descended "from the pulpit to the pew" because ministers were ordained and authorized by God. King launched a flock of new committees, bestowing special importance on the Social and Political Action Committee, which recruited members for the NAACP. Rufus Lewis, a former football coach at Alabama State, and Jo Ann Robinson, an English professor at Alabama State, were active in it. King made voter registration a precondition for membership at Dexter, a nervy move that Johns never attempted. He gave a speech at a local NAACP gathering, which yielded an invitation to the presidency that he declined and an invitation to the executive committee that he accepted. The Dexter sanctuary remained quiet and almost half empty in King's first year, the only year he preached every week. The center of Dexter's life was Alabama State College, not Dexter. But King made a mark and unwittingly prepared himself and Dexter for the drama to come, crafting metaphorically rich sermons on which he relied for the rest of his life.[60]

In August 1955 Rosa L. Parks, a churchgoing Methodist seamstress and secretary of Montgomery NAACP, informed King that he had been named to the executive committee. Parks straddled the class divide in black Montgomery. She belonged to the working class but won respect and standing in the Women's Political Council, where college-educated professionals prized her professionalism and sterling character. December 1, 1955, was a Thursday. Parks finished her workday at Montgomery Fair department store, settled tiredly into a bus seat just behind the whites-only section, and refused to move when driver J. P. Blake told her to yield her seat to a white rider.

She had long resolved never to yield again but had not expected this to be the day. By refusing to move, Parks risked the frightful disgrace of criminal status and the wrath of white Montgomery. Pullman porter E. D. Nixon, Montgomery's leading civil rights activist, and lawyer Clifford Durr, an NAACP ally, bailed out Parks from jail. They discussed with Jo Ann Robinson and lawyer Fred Gray whether this was the case they had sought. They had a plan but had waited for an ideal case to come along. Nixon was a former president of Montgomery NAACP, and Robinson was president of the Women's Political Council. The previous March they had pulled back from a similar case involving a fifteen-year-old girl, Claudette Colvin, because she was pregnant and charged with resisting arrest. This tiny band of mostly female activists longed for a bus boycott. Now they agreed that their friend Parks offered a near perfect case and witness. By prosecuting Parks under a state segregation ordinance, Montgomery officials invited a federal court test of the Jim Crow laws. Nixon called Abernathy, then his own pastor, H. H. Hubbard, and then King, who had to think it over. King was number nineteen on the minister list when Nixon called him back, and he did not know Parks personally. Meanwhile the women's council blanketed black Montgomery with a call to boycott the buses the following Monday.[61]

Montgomery happened because Robinson and her female activist colleagues were already prepared to call for a bus boycott. But they were sure to be fired from Alabama State if they stepped out too far, and a boycott would need the ministers anyway, so Nixon rallied them, with mixed feelings. On Friday the ministers held a desultory meeting that Bennett monopolized. On Sunday the ministers urged congregants to stay off the buses, and Nixon shrewdly won a publicity windfall by tipping off the white *Montgomery Advertiser*. On Monday the buses were empty, Parks was convicted, and Nixon convened the ministers and activists, who founded the Montgomery Improvement Association (MIA). There was much discussion about keeping their names secret, until Nixon exploded: "You ministers have lived off these wash-women for the past hundred years and ain't never done nothing for them." He called them cowards, "little boys" wearing aprons. It was time for the aprons to come off, he chided: "If we're gonna be mens, now's the time to be mens." King arrived late just as Nixon was scorching the ministers. King bellowed that he was not a coward and did not appreciate being called one.[62]

History turned quickly. Somebody had to speak for this organization, and the ministers were not going to elect Nixon. Rufus Lewis nominated his pastor, who surprised many by accepting; King was elected as the only candidate. Being a newcomer, unscarred, respected, and singly willing to stick out his neck settled the issue. Discussion moved to that night's mass meeting. Someone noted that newspaper reporters would be present, which struck fear in the ministers. Nobody volunteered to speak, and Nixon erupted again: "Somebody in this thing has got to get faith. I am just ashamed of you." He implored the ministers to recognize that somebody besides King had to risk getting hurt: "If you preachers are not the leaders, then we have to pray that God will send us some more leaders." That shamed the ministers into forming a clergy committee headed by Abernathy. One very large question remained: Should they declare victory, after one day of boycotting, and call off the boycott? A long boycott that fizzled would be demoralizing. Finally the group decided to let the rally audience make that decision. King raced home to tell Coretta and plan his speech, for a rally scheduled to begin in forty minutes.[63]

Hurriedly he tried to write something down. King anxiously told himself that he had to be militant and moderate. His mind raced back and forth, and he chastised himself for squandering most of his twenty minutes. He settled on a three-layered appeal to self-respect, which would hopefully come to him in the pulpit. Meanwhile the "reprisal" issue nagged at him. The *Advertiser* said that Montgomery blacks were copying the economic reprisal tactics of the White Citizens' Councils. That was offensive in every way, yet there was something to it, which disturbed King. He had barely a few notes in hand when he headed to Holt Street Baptist Church, a large, barnlike church on the poor side of town. King had to park his car four blocks from the church because five thousand people were gathered outside. It took him fifteen minutes to get through the overflow crowd; by then he realized the boycott would not be ending that night. Some recognized King as the young pastor of the rich church; most did not know him. Inside, one thousand people were jammed into the sanctuary, singing "Onward, Christian Soldiers." There was another hymn, "Leaning on the Everlasting Arms," a prayer, a reading of Psalm 34, and King was on.[64]

Self-respect could be rendered militantly or moderately or, with special skill, both. King aimed for both by rooting his theme in the democratic traditions of America, the deep integrity of oppressed black Americans, and the teaching of Jesus. He began by declaring that all gathered were American citizens who loved American democracy. They were there because they loved democracy and because American democracy was grievously distorted. Negroes in America were humiliated and oppressed simply for being Negroes. "That's right!" the crowd shouted. He moved to Parks, lauding "the boundless outreach of her integrity" and her deep devotion to the teaching of Jesus. King was glad that Parks turned out to be the catalyst because nobody could deny her exemplary Christian integrity, which she shared with black Americans. He started a justice run: "And you know, my friends, there comes a time when people get tired of being trampled over by the iron feet of oppression."[65]

The crowd erupted in thundering applause. King kept the run going. People got tired of being "plunged across the abyss of humiliation" and driven into the "bleakness of nagging despair" and "pushed out of the glittering sunlight of life's July and left standing amid the piercing chill of an alpine November." Now the crowd exploded in frenzy. All black Americans, King continued, were tired of all that. Yet they did not advocate violence and never had. "Repeat that!" the crowd called. King stressed that Negro Americans were Christians who knew and followed the gospel: "We are Christian people. We believe in the Christian religion. We believe in the teachings of Jesus. The only weapon that we have in our hands this evening is the weapon of protest." He tacked back to the promise of American democracy, declaring that the "great glory of American democracy is the right to protest for right," which Montgomery blacks were exercising. All they wanted was the rights they already possessed under the American Constitution. The Klan and the White Citizens' Councils terrorized to oppress, while black Americans opposed oppression in the spirit of Jesus. There was no basis of comparison; how could anyone say otherwise?[66]

"There will be no crosses burned at any bus stops in Montgomery," King declared. No whites would be extracted from their homes and "taken out on some distant road and lynched for not cooperating." The Montgomery protest existed merely and entirely "to see right exist." That got him started on a second run about gaining justice. If they were wrong, so were the Supreme Court, the Constitution, Jesus, and God Almighty: "If we are wrong, justice is a lie. Love has no meaning. And we are determined here in Montgomery to work and fight until justice runs down like water and righteousness like a mighty stream." King moved from Amos to solidarity. "We must stick together," he exhorted. The movement needed unity and courage, two things that went together: "Don't let anybody frighten you. We are not afraid of what we are doing because we are doing it within the law." He risked a trade union analogy. When working people got "trampled over by capitalistic power," there was nothing wrong with pulling together to demand their rights. This was like that, except that black people had always been oppressed in America: "We, the disinherited of this land, we who have been oppressed so long, are tired of going through the long night of captivity. And now we are reaching out for the daybreak of freedom and justice and equality."[67]

The crowd erupted again at the stunning image of daybreak. King said he was nearly finished, although the crowd sensed a third run coming. He told the crowd to "keep God in the forefront" and never do anything that was not Christian. But it was not enough to talk about Christian love, for love was only one side of the Christian faith. The other side was justice, he said, "and justice is really love in calculation. Justice is love correcting that which revolts against love." Christians lived in the spirit of divine love and employed the tools of divine justice. King risked a Niebuhrian riff on what that meant: "Not only are we using the tools of persuasion, but we've come to see that we've got to use the tools of coercion." It was a process of education *and* political struggle, he urged. History would be written in Montgomery. If they pulled together, struggling for justice in the work of love, the history books would say of them, "There lived a race of people, a *black* people, 'fleecy locks and black complexion,' a people who had the moral courage to stand up for their rights. And thereby they injected a new meaning into the veins of history and of civilization."[68]

The crowd thought that King was mounting a climactic third justice run, now with a nationalist flourish, but he had run out of ideas and metaphors, so he ended weakly, asking the gathering to "think of these things." There was an awkward silence, King turned from the podium, and the crowd realized he was done, bursting into applause. King was thrilled and relieved at his movement debut. He had held together justice and love, which he called the balance between militancy and moderation. Soon he stopped calling the bus boycott a boycott because he did not like how that sounded or felt—a coercive economic squeeze smacking of vengeance. King adopted Henry David Thoreau's language for it, saying that black Americans would no longer lend their cooperation to an evil system.[69]

The Holt Street Address and the Thoreau language of systemic evil were both outsized for a movement that almost quit after one day and that strove for two months afterward merely for a gentler form of segregation. The MIA asked Montgomery officials to let blacks seat themselves from the rear forward and whites from the front backward, as in Mobile. MIA leaders believed the boycott would be over in a few days because their demand was so moderate. Since the MIA did not oppose segregation—a point that King stressed—the NAACP refused to endorse the MIA. But white Montgomery burned hot with Deep South post-*Brown* anger. Black Montgomery's modest bus proposal ran straight into the white majority's infuriated repugnance at the idea of integrated schools. Battle lines were drawn, and nothing was to be conceded. City and bus company officials refused to bend. White officials inflamed the situation repeatedly, hurting their own cause; they couldn't seem to help it. King was stunned that logic and fairness meant nothing to them; officials were too consumed with vengeance even to recognize their self-interests. A month after the boycott began, the *New York Times* finally carried a story about it. Montgomery's rabidly racist police commissioner, Clyde Sellers, excoriated the boycott leaders, ramping up the danger for them. By mid-January the early sprinkling of death threats against King and his family had become a downpour.

The phone rang day and night. Many callers savaged King and threatened him, and some threatened to kill Coretta and baby daughter Yolanda. People told King every day of hearing about plots to kill him. He later recalled that he had "sallied through" college, seminary, and graduate school on Daddy King's money and enjoyed his life. Then Parks kept her seat, and suddenly he was receiving forty threatening phone calls per day. Arrested for exceeding a speed limit by five miles per hour, King feared he would be lynched on the way to jail. The lonely terror he felt heading toward jail stuck with him for the rest of his life; meanwhile the pressures of speaking for a reviled and fractious movement tormented him. On January 27 he got a call, near midnight, that broke him: "Listen, nigger, we've taken all we want from you; before next week you'll be sorry you ever came to Montgomery." The caller vowed to "blow your brains out, and blow up your house" if he were not gone in three days. King tried to shuck it off and go to sleep, without success: "I had reached the saturation point." He went to the kitchen and made coffee, pondering fearfully what to do. He wanted to resign but didn't know how to do it without looking like a coward. He thought about his secure upbringing under a strong father. He thought about Coretta and Yolanda and the fact that his activism put their lives in danger. It occurred to him that Daddy King could not fix this problem; King had to do something that Daddy King often told him about—calling on the power within that made a way out of no way. Religion had to become real to him, he thought: "I had to know God for myself."[70]

King quietly confessed to God that he was weak, faltering, losing his nerve, and at the end of his powers: "I have nothing left. I've come to the point where I can't face it alone." He had barely uttered the words when he felt a surge of seemingly divine something he had never experienced previously. An inner voice spoke to him, saying, "Stand up for righteousness, stand up for truth; and I will be at your side forever." It was the voice of Jesus, King believed. One of King's favorite sermons, "Our God Is Able," subsequently told this story through the refrain of a favorite hymn, "Never Alone," recounting that Jesus told him to fight on: "He promised never to leave me, never to leave me alone. No never alone. No never alone. He promised never to leave me, never to leave me alone."[71]

The import of this experience is variously gauged. Reddick, who was close to King, did not mention it in his telling of the Montgomery story, and Reddick later raised the subject only defensively, against critics who lampooned King's appeal to a mystical encounter. King made no such appeal, Reddick said; he and King interpreted the experience as "a psychological release of the subconscious or unconscious mind," not as a mystical or supernatural revelation. This minimizing approach may have influenced David Levering Lewis, King's first critical biographer, who passed over the kitchen experience. Stephen Oates, writing in 1982—when insiders still refused to give interviews—gave a minimal exposition of King's telling without commenting on its meaning or significance. Taylor Branch described the kitchen experience briefly and modestly, like King, but David Garrow claimed it was the central event of King's life, a life-changer. Garrow felt compelled to explain how a shallow young man became a world-historical moral hero. After Garrow learned of King's plagiarism, which he found devastating, he heightened his emphasis on the kitchen experience. Lewis Baldwin said the experience trumped King's "liberal training" at Crozer and Boston, showing the greater importance of "the spiritual resonances of his heritage in the South." That was both true (for King) and misleading (regarding others), since many northern-trained liberal ministers had life-changing spiritual experiences that they expounded in their writings and sermons. Historian Nathan I. Huggins thought the kitchen occurrence was obviously a conversion experience, which is not right; King needed God to become real to him, not to be converted. Marshall Frady, taking what he took to be King's view, said that King's "kitchen epiphany" was apparently the source of his "almost galactic remoteness, as if the deepest center of him were lost in a secret communion with something far beyond the furors of the moment."[72]

Certainly, something like mystical belonging showed through in King's extraordinary peacemaking demeanor only three days after the kitchen episode. King was at a mass meeting on January 30 when he learned that his home had been bombed. He rushed home to find an angry crowd jeering Sellers and other police officials as they assessed the damage. Coretta and a friend had heard a noise on the front porch, which they fortunately did not investigate. A dynamite blast went off on the porch that brought neighbors running from many blocks away. King was frightened for his family but remarkably calm as he approached the house. The mood was angry and fed up; King believed it was verging on a violent eruption; he noticed that many of his neighbors had brought guns.

"Now let's not become panicky," King cautioned:

> If you have weapons, take them home; if you do not have them, please do not seek to get them. We cannot solve this problem through retaliatory violence. We must meet violence with nonviolence. Remember the words of Jesus: "He who lives by the sword will perish by the sword." We must love our white brothers no matter what they do to us. We must make them know that we love them. Jesus still cries out in words that echo across the centuries: "Love your enemies; bless them that curse you; pray for them that despitefully use you." This is what we must live by. We must meet hate with love. Remember, if I am stopped, this movement will not stop, because God is with the movement. Go home with this glowing faith and this radiant assurance.[73]

The crowd dispersed, and King's stature soared. Until the bombing nobody knew if the leadership question had been settled. At the mass meetings King spoke last as the official leader and best speaker, but Nixon already resented King for usurping him, and King stressed that he never sought to be a protest leader; he was merely there when the movement called. Two days after the bombing the MIA crossed its Rubicon in federal court by filing suit against Alabama's bus segregation laws. King and MIA lawyer Fred Gray stopped pretending that the issue was not the evil and illegality of segregation. Three weeks later a local grand jury indicted 115 MIA leaders for violating an anti-boycott law, and the national media rushed to Montgomery. King was in Nashville when the indictments came down; Daddy King implored him to come home to Atlanta, as Alabama was not worth sacrificing his life. Daddy King enlisted Mays and other Atlanta heavyweights to his side. King replied that he could not live with himself if he abandoned Montgomery; he would rather spend ten years in jail than forsake the Montgomery movement. He said it with such conviction that Mays changed his position and Daddy King backed down. The state went after King first, winning a guilty verdict on conspiracy to boycott, which catapulted King to national fame. "We are not bitter," King declared. "We are still preaching non-violence. We are still using the weapon of love. We are still using the method of passive resistance."[74]

That was the simple language of King's early movement speeches, but between the indictments of February 21 and the verdict of March 23 Rustin and Smiley made their way to Montgomery, befriended King, and provided grist for the conspiracy theory that white locals already believed: It could not be that black activists in Montgomery had mounted the boycott movement. New York radicals had to be running it.

In fact, the Montgomery protest was wholly homegrown until Rustin and Smiley arrived. Rustin represented a new, eclectic, union-based activist group, In Friendship, and Smiley represented FOR. In Friendship was founded in early 1956 to raise money for the Montgomery boycott and other racial justice protests in the South. It was led by Rustin, Farmer, Randolph, Ella Baker, Norman Thomas, Stanley Levison, Harry Emerson Fosdick, and labor chief Jerry Wurf and financed mostly by the Workers Defense League, American Jewish Council, and State, County, and Municipal Workers Union. The group used a donation from a War Resisters League supporter to send Rustin to Montgomery.

Any outsider would have provoked grumbling and accusation among local whites and blacks. As it was, Rustin was impossibly controversial and exotic in Montgomery. Bayard Rustin was an eloquent, selfless, intellectual, sometimes haughty Greenwich Village bohemian and minstrel activist with a criminal record for being gay and antiwar. Born in Chester, Pennsylvania, in 1910, he was raised by a Quaker grandmother and learned as a teenager that the woman he thought was his sister was his mother. Rustin dropped out of Wilberforce in 1934 and eked out a living as a singer in New York, performing with Josh White and Leadbelly. The Scottsboro sensation swept Rustin into the Young Communist League, but after Hitler invaded Russia in 1941 and the Communist Party dropped its pseudopacifist line, Rustin returned to Quakerism and worked for Randolph's March on Washington movement. He learned movement building through Randolph, joining the Socialist Party and FOR. As an FOR staffer he helped Farmer found CORE in 1942, and, like most FOR staffers, Rustin was imprisoned during World War II as a conscientious objector, serving three years in Lewisburg Penitentiary. After the war he learned Gandhian resistance strategy firsthand in India, returning to the United States in 1947. The following year he worked with Randolph to end segregation in the armed services, and in 1949 Rustin rode the CORE/FOR "Journey of Reconciliation" bus against segregation in North Carolina, which landed him on a chain gang. At the time of the Montgomery boycott Rustin was working for the War Resisters League, although he later remembered it as an FOR job.[75]

On Rustin's first day in Montgomery a hotel employee warned him that "Communist agitators and New Yorkers" were said to be running the boycott. On his second day he helped persuade MIA leaders to stage an almost-celebration of their arrests, in their Sunday church suits; he also recalculated what he should do in Montgomery. Instead of conducting formal training sessions on Gandhian strategy, as he had planned, Rustin worked organically with MIA leaders, reacting to situations as they unfolded. On his third day the MIA resolved to dispense with mass meetings and hold only prayer meetings, accenting the moral nature of the struggle. On his fifth day Rustin acquired a handbill distributed at a White Citizens' Council meeting: "We hold these truths to be self-evident: that all whites are created equal with certain rights; among these are life, liberty, and the pursuit of dead niggers. In every stage of the bus boycott we have been oppressed and degraded because of black, slimy, juicy, unbearably stinking niggers." White Montgomery, the handbill urged, had to exterminate "these black devils" with guns and knives; otherwise "we will soon wake up and find Reverend King in the White House."[76]

Rustin shuddered at wondering how much of white Montgomery that represented. King knew sympathetic whites in Montgomery who quietly commended him, but he also told Rustin that the White Citizens' Council was capable of serious violence leading to catastrophic violence. King added that black Montgomery was acquiring the spirit of true nonviolence; in six weeks' time "the whole Negro community will react nonviolently." This extraordinary prediction did not seem like an unrealistic boast to Rustin. He wrote in his diary, "I had a feeling that no force on earth can stop this movement. It has all the elements to touch the hearts of men." Rustin formed a movement partnership with King but lasted only a week in Montgomery, being too controversial to stay. He did not need to be told by anyone in New York or even Montgomery that he was radioactive in Montgomery. Rustin's sexuality evoked anxiety reactions even among activist allies, and he had a grand manner, which put off many as arrogance, though he was never self-aggrandizing. He would not stay if he could not help, and he was willing to help from afar. King quickly perceived that Rustin's reputation as a brilliant organizer was fully merited. Meanwhile Smiley arrived just before Rustin departed.[77]

Rustin's FOR friends feared from the beginning that he would attract harmful police and press attention. FOR executive secretary John Swomley and national chair Charles Lawrence warned Randolph that Rustin would become a spectacle, hurt King and the MIA, and destroy any possibility of MIA cooperation with northern organizations. Randolph heard the same thing from Nixon, so he gathered Thomas, Farmer, Swomley, Lawrence, and others into his office and reconsidered: Maybe they should clear out of Montgomery and let the MIA handle things on its own? Smiley, who had just arrived in Montgomery, opposed

Swomley on Rustin and opposed Randolph's reversal on Montgomery. Smiley admired Rustin enormously and wanted him to stay in Montgomery. He also believed that northern activist organizations had a crucial role to play in Montgomery, where the protest movement had almost petered out before King's home was bombed and the MIA leaders were indicted. Smiley brushed off Swomley's demand to stay away from Rustin, later explaining, "I don't forbid well." Rustin introduced Smiley to King, who promptly introduced Smiley to an MIA mass meeting on March 1.[78]

As a white, southern, hardcore Christian pacifist dispatched from New York FOR who idolized Rustin—"Bayard was my guru all this time"—Smiley was as foreign as Rustin at MIA meetings but less dangerous as a subject of controversy. He stuck out at MIA meetings, along with white Montgomery Lutheran pastor Robert Graetz. Smiley told Swomley of King, "He had Gandhi in mind when this thing started, he says." King wanted to do the right thing, Smiley wrote, but he was very young "and some of his close help is violent . . . The place is an arsenal. King sees the inconsistency, but not enough. He believes and yet he doesn't believe. . . . If he can *really* be won to a faith in non-violence there is no end to what he can do." The next day, fresh from a warm reception at an MIA meeting, Smiley wrote again to FOR leaders: "We can learn from their courage and plain earthy devices for building morale, etc., but they can learn more from us, for being so new at this, King runs out of ideas quickly and does the old things again and again. He wants help, and we can give it to him without attempting to run the movement or pretend we know it all."[79]

King smuggled Rustin to Birmingham, where he raised money for the MIA and linked King to Rustin's labor-Socialist-pacifist-liberal network in the North. Rustin ghosted King's first published article, "Our Struggle," which announced that "a new Negro" had been born in Montgomery, signaling a "revolutionary change in the Negro's evaluation of himself." The Montgomery movement, King/Rustin said, wielded a "new and powerful weapon—non-violent resistance" and demonstrated that "our church is becoming militant." Rustin sealed King's trust by writing for him in a voice that stressed moral arguments and sounded like him. Rustin perceived, and told King, that King represented a major turning point in the civil rights struggle. There had not been a major southern mass leader since Booker Washington. Now the action had swung back to the South.[80]

Meanwhile Smiley wrote statements for the MIA, advised King on local tactics, and conducted training sessions on nonviolent resistance. He and Rustin took delight that King eagerly took counsel from them. Rustin combined Quaker, Gandhian, and Marxist perspectives, and King prized his ethical-Quaker sensibility, even as almost everyone close to King distrusted Rustin.

Smiley and white northern Unitarian minister Homer Jack were the only insiders to commend King's reliance on Rustin. Besides his vast northern network and high-powered expertise Rustin was valuable to King in demanding little of him. The same factor soon drew King closely to Levison. King did not have to worry about Rustin's ego, as Rustin was unfailingly willing to forgo personal recognition. King counted on this virtue to the point of never mentioning Rustin in *Stride Toward Freedom*.

American Gandhianism was already a highly mediated tradition. Smiley, Rustin, Muste, Swomley, Farmer, and other FOR stalwarts had pared back Gandhianism to nonviolence, dropping Gandhi's doctrines about vegetarianism, celibacy, and the like. Like Thurman, they still used the Gandhian jargon of *satyagraha* and *ahimsa* but did not impose it on King, who embraced their ambition for him: to become the American Gandhi. King trusted his intuition about how to communicate the message of nonviolence to audiences that found Gandhian philosophy strange at best. The religion of Jesus, undeniably, had something to do with loving one's enemies. But King had to negotiate the seeming absurdity of a philosophy based on converting white oppressors through Christian love and self-sacrifice. His ongoing experience of assimilating Gandhian thought helped him couch the message in ways it could be heard. "Passive resistance" captured both sides of the message, he thought. Rustin and Smiley pressed him to expound the "cycle of violence" argument against retaliating against evil: Evil multiplied through the law of retaliation. Everything depended on holding fast to nonviolent deliverance from the cycle of violence.

White Montgomery's ferocious hostility crushed King's first secretary at the MIA. He replaced her with Maude Ballou, a devout, idealistic churchgoer who was so devoted to King that MIA insiders coined a nickname for him, "L.L.J." Ballou, they said, truly regarded King as the Little Lord Jesus. The NAACP came through, winning a federal district court verdict in June against bus segregation in Alabama, and in November the Supreme Court agreed. Wilkins never tired of saying afterward that King owed his only achievement to an NAACP rescue. On December 21, 1956, King and Smiley ceremoniously boarded Montgomery's first integrated bus. King told audiences across the country that Montgomery was merely an early wave: "The oppressed people of the world are rising up. They are revolting against colonialism, imperialism, and other systems of oppression." He took a break at Barbour's home, and Barbour reported that King struggled to fathom his sudden fame: "He wanders around in a daze asking himself, 'Why has God seen fit to catapult me into such a situation?'" Only God knew the answer to that, King and Barbour agreed.

King realized that the Holt Street Address would not have caused a sensation had he not been sensational, but he could not say that. He said the story was that Montgomery blacks turned out that night. But blacks had turned out thousands of times across the South without sparking anything. Why did lightning strike in Montgomery? King said that every rational explanation broke down at some point: "There is something about the protest that is suprarational; it cannot be explained without a divine dimension." One might, King observed, call it a principle of concretion, like Whitehead, or a process of integration, like Wieman, or something else: "Whatever the name, some extra-human force labors to create a harmony out of the discords of the universe."[81]

SCLC REDEMPTION

The band of preachers King gathered around himself at SCLC nearly always said that his preaching brilliance made him stand out. This was not easy for them to say because most of them were powerhouse preachers whose egos rested on their preaching prowess. A word they did not use but that fit him twice over was "magnanimous." King was almost superhumanly magnanimous. To follow Christ, he taught, is to accept hardship with grace, suffer mistreatment for the sake of others, and forgive oppressors without demonizing them. Often King drew on his graduate school theology to make the point, citing Anders Nygren and Paul Ramsey on the self-sacrificial character of divine love (agape), especially Nygren's emphasis that divine love is disinterested and Ramsey's ethical analysis of "enemy-neighbor" love.

But King rejected the Nygren/Ramsey contention that agape applies directly to God alone. Nygren and Ramsey conceived agape as the outpouring of God's gracious love on behalf of human subjects, enabling them to practice more qualified forms of altruism. To King, that smacked of theological exclusivism, shortchanging the infinite value of the human soul. King echoed Muelder and DeWolf when he expounded on this subject, which was often: "There must be a recognition of the sacredness of human personality. Deeply rooted in our political and religious heritage is the conviction that every man is an heir to a legacy of dignity and worth." Religiously and politically his theme was the universality of God's image in human souls. Human beings are divinely endowed with infinite value apart from any particular religious conviction that one may hold or any special grace that one may have received: "This innate worth referred to in the phrase *image of God* is universally shared in equal portion by all men."[82]

This creed was the bedrock of King's social activism. It was the basis of every "you are somebody" sermon that he heard growing up. It fused his black church faith and academic training, infused his willingness to preach theology at political rallies, and fused the SCLC preachers to each other. After the Montgomery boycott ended, Smiley and the FOR tried to kindle a new organization in the South that would be an FOR affiliate or an independent offshoot like CORE. Smiley and Homer Jack organized efforts toward this end in cooperation with King and other black leaders from Baton Rouge, Tallahassee, Birmingham, and Montgomery. King would have taken this path had Rustin, Baker, and Levison not developed an alternative with greater potential.

Ella Baker had grown up in North Carolina and absorbed her mother's missionary Baptist idealism, which emphasized quiet, selfless devotion. She graduated from Shaw University in 1927, moved to New York the same year, joined the Young Negroes Cooperative League in 1930, and joined the NAACP staff in 1940, first as a field secretary and later as director of branches. Racial justice organizing was her great passion. She had organized dozens of NAACP youth chapters in the South, she cofounded In Friendship to fight Jim Crow laws in the South, and she made many friends in and near the Communist Party, notably Levison. Stanley Levison was a New York lawyer and Roosevelt Democrat who became wealthy through Ford dealerships and real estate investments. He devoted his spare time to the American Jewish Congress and NAACP, meeting Baker in the NAACP, where she chaired the New York branch. To Levison and Baker, the strategic limitations of the NAACP were frustrating and obvious. Levison was a pro-Communist in the 1940s and early 1950s who probably raised money for the Communist Party in the early 1950s. Afterward he shrugged off his past, explaining that one could not be a New York intellectual of his generation without having Communist friends.[83]

Rustin, Baker, and Levison were determined to capitalize on the breakthrough in Montgomery. They envisioned a new organization that would kindle many Montgomerys. To succeed, they believed, the organization had to be led and constituted by southern blacks. CORE had already demonstrated the limitations of interracial Gandhian organizing. CORE struggled bravely and doggedly but failed to spark a mass movement. It was top-heavy with white middle-class intellectuals who gave an impression of patronizing sincerity and earnestness. Another version of CORE was not what the movement needed. Rustin, Baker, and Levison took for granted that their venture needed Randolph's backing, which would not be easy to get. Randolph had tired of lending his name to groups lacking money, he had joined In Friendship reluctantly, and he recoiled at northern activist presumption. He thought that southern protesters might do better by spurning all help from northern organizations. But King pleaded that the movement needed northern financial support and expertise. Randolph told Baker he would get behind a new initiative if it arose spontaneously from the South with a call from King or the Montgomery church leadership.[84]

King spent much of 1956 telling supporters like singer Harry Belafonte that he had no idea where the movement was headed and he needed help. Many were struck that off the platform King had a quiet, vulnerable, almost doe-like persona. His pacifism seemed to be temperamental, not merely philosophical or strategic, and he was disarmingly vulnerable in seeking help. After the mass arrests came down in Montgomery, however, King stood up to Wilkins, protesting that the NAACP enriched itself off the Montgomery movement. To Wilkins, that got it backward. Montgomery was an episode in the NAACP's long battle against segregation. The court battle was in its final stage and not to be jeopardized by new groups inflamed with visions of mass protest. Moreover, anything that groups like the MIA achieved would have to be won by the NAACP in court and undoubtedly paid for by the NAACP. It was hard for Wilkins not to regard King as a latecomer and usurper.

In December 1956 King told a celebrative gathering at Holt Street Church that the goal of the movement was to "awaken a sense of shame within the oppressor and challenge his false sense of superiority," not to defeat white oppressors: "The end is reconciliation; the end is redemption; the end is the creation of a beloved community." That month Rustin introduced King and Coretta to three of his closest white allies: Harris Wofford, Clare Wofford, and Stanley Levison. The group bantered in friendly fashion until someone said that white opponents might give the movement another boost by stupidly arresting King. Coretta King cut off the laughter, saying her nightmare was that King would be killed in jail. There was an awkward silence, which King broke by confessing that he would have run away had he seen the whirlwind coming. Now he had no choice, for "the choice leaves your own hands."[85]

On New Year's Day 1957 King, Fred Shuttlesworth, and Tallahassee minister C. K. Steele called for a conference on January 10 at Ebenezer Church, where sixty activists agreed to establish a "Southern Leadership Conference on Transportation and Nonviolent Integration." They urged Eisenhower to deliver a major speech in the South urging southerners to accept the *Brown* decision. A second gathering on February 14 at A. L. Davis's church in New Orleans voted to establish a permanent organization named the Southern Negro Leaders Conference. King was elected president, and the group repeated its appeal to Eisenhower. The following month King attended the founding of independent Ghana, where he had a cordial exchange with Richard Nixon. In August the new activist group held its first convention, in Montgomery, adopting a new name: the Southern Christian Leadership Conference. It also adopted a motto for the organization: To Redeem the Soul of America.

This was emphatically a black organization. Graetz was the only white invited to the initial gathering at Ebenezer, and SCLC subsequently named an entirely African American board. From the beginning the Christian integrationist theology of SCLC somewhat obscured that its organizational politics echoed Niagara Movement nationalism, dominated this time by southern ministers. At Ebenezer the founders called for mass action protests using nonviolent methods: "We must recognize in this new period that direct action is our most potent political weapon. We must understand that our refusal to accept Jim Crow in specific areas challenges the entire social, political and economic order that has kept us second class citizens since 1876." Nonviolence, they added, brought out the nobility in humble people and cohered with Christian principles. Moreover, the new organization was emphatically centered on the black church, the "most stable social institution" in black America. The founders were Baptist ministers, they were determined to capitalize on their access to the black masses, they sought to avoid the charges of being Communist and radical that plagued the NAACP, and thus they stressed that the new organization was Christian.[86]

Eight of the SCLC's founding nine officers were Baptist ministers: King, vice presidents C. K. Steele, A. L. Davis, and Samuel Williams, secretary T. J. Jemison, corresponding secretary Fred Shuttlesworth, treasurer Ralph Abernathy, and chaplain Kelly Miller Smith. Only the group's historian, Reddick, was not a minister; Reddick had a doctorate from the University of Chicago and was nineteen years older than King. All the founding officers were southerners and male, most were approximately thirty years old, and eight of the nine had a connection to Morehouse or Alabama State. The executive board contained sixteen additional members, thirteen of whom were ministers. Of the twenty-five founding board members, twenty-one were ministers, plus one professor, one dentist, one pharmacist, and one attorney, and of the original thirty-six formal leadership officers, thirty-two were ministers. Nearly all were Baptists, as clannishness kept them from reaching out to other denominations; the Methodist exceptions were S. S. Seay and Joseph Lowery. This was the gathering legacy of the black social gospel, especially the Baptist stream of William Simmons, Nannie Burroughs, Adam Clayton Powell Sr., Adam Clayton Powell Jr., Mordecai Johnson, J. Pius Barbour, William H. Borders, Vernon Johns, Howard Thurman, and Benjamin Mays. The SCLC ministers had role models for believing that ministers should be social justice activists. Many were NAACP stalwarts, and five of the founding executive officers were current or former NAACP presidents. They were committed to building something new, keenly grasping their advantage over the NAACP. White racists did not fear black preachers the way they loathed the NAACP. SCLC was designed to seize on this advantage and to avoid competition with the NAACP.[87]

Rustin, Levison, and Baker avoided conflicts with the NAACP by designing SCLC as an umbrella organization of local southern organizations, not a national organization with individual memberships. Local groups acquired affiliate status in SCLC by paying a yearly fee. This arrangement deprived the organization of an adequate financial base, but it spared individuals from feeling disloyal to the NAACP and it supported King's claim that no rivalry existed. Some affiliate groups were new organizations modeled on the MIA, notably Birmingham's Alabama Christian Movement for Human Rights, the Baton Rouge Christian Movement, and the Nashville Christian Leadership Council. Others were voter registration organizations or civic groups such as the United Christian Movement in Shreveport, Louisiana, and the SCLC's only nonsouthern affiliate, the Western Christian Leadership Conference in Los Angeles, a fund-raising operation. The very existence of a church-based, protest-oriented, movement organization of organizations fulfilled a social gospel dream, the rise of the black church as a movement entity. Lowery called it "the black church coming alive."[88]

SCLC had no chance of not suffering an immediate letdown, which King took personally. He felt responsible for spreading the Montgomery eruption. His speaking tours raised money for the MIA and SCLC but never enough, so he crammed his calendar with speaking engagements. The boycott gave way to in-fighting and personal attacks that wounded King deeply. Unprepared for a torrent of complaint, he often felt "deserted and alone," in Reddick's phrase. Every article about Montgomery focused on him, which angered Nixon and many others. Sometimes King had to be reeled back from making it worse; Levison admonished him that *Stride Toward Freedom* was much too King-centric. King felt guilty about his fame plus obligated to exploit it. Northern liberals showered him with awards and honors. Back home, wildly exaggerated things were said about his supposed buck raking, which yielded years of torment over unfounded accusations and formal charges. MIA secretary U. J. Fields contributed greatly to the turmoil, wrongly accusing King of misusing funds. Nonetheless, the success of the Montgomery boycott gave enormous ballast to the prestige of nonviolent resistance. Fear of white violence had pervaded black Montgomery before the boycott, but nonviolence proved to be disarming. Racist groups wreaked much less violence than they threatened, which emboldened the MIA. The success of nonviolent resistance in Montgomery significantly reduced the fear among black Americans of white officials and jails.[89]

King sought to capitalize on this liberation from fear, he worked closely with Rustin and Levison to build up the SCLC, and he put off SCLC board members who chafed at this arrangement. From the beginning the key players except Baker conceived SCLC as a King-centered operation that guarded King's back. Rustin and Levison influenced King's thinking, briefed him for meetings, arranged speaking engagements, ghosted his articles and books, handled the press, and linked him to their networks. Both derived leverage from having no official position in the organization, while SCLC's founding executive secretary, John Tilley, floundered ineffectively. Then Rustin and Levison persuaded King to hire Baker as the sole executive staffer.

Rustin, Levison, and Baker were veterans of the Old Left who fondly remembered how the CIO used strikes, boycotts, and marches to make gains for economic justice. They were also chastened by this history because the Old Left strategy of fusing antiracism with trade unions and Socialism failed in the 1930s and 1940s. Black southerners had to accept that their chief allies were northern liberals and leftists, not southern white workers. The three movement veterans were strategic in basing SCLC on the black church, notwithstanding that Levison was Jewish and Baker had a grassroots-female experience of the black church that made her averse to authoritarian preachers. Her religious upbringing had taught her to be quietly dignified, steely, and service-oriented. Heroic preachers were not her models, since she could not be one anyway. In the early going King seemed less conceited to Baker than other charismatic preachers, and she enthused that the MIA grew out of a mass protest, not a ministers' conference. The black church facilitated mass protests more effectively than the formal, democratic, membership-based NAACP. Like the MIA, SCLC was a movement first and an organization second. It embraced nonviolence and touted its political nonpartisanship, although Baker accepted nonviolence merely as a tactic, not as the faith it was for Rustin and King. NAACP chapters had to submit their membership lists to hostile state officials, a problem that SCLC eliminated by dispensing with individual members. SCLC leaders did not like King's reliance on the three movement veterans, but King was emphatic about needing them.

King took in stride that Rustin, Levison, and Baker had Old Left backgrounds. It was one of God's mysteries why so many Communists and so few white liberals had cared about black Americans. King could not alter the past. History being what it was, it was inevitable that his allies came with Old Left baggage. Moreover, he agreed with Rustin and Levison about things he rarely brought up at SCLC meetings. Rustin and Levison believed that black Americans would never be free as long as there were large numbers of poor and underprivileged whites. Capitalism itself, they said, played different roles in the struggles for racial justice North and South. In the North, blacks suffered primarily from the predatory nature of capitalism. In the South, blacks suffered primarily from the tyranny of racial caste, and capitalism was increasingly an ally in the struggle against racial tyranny because the capitalist class experienced the demands of racial caste as a needless waste. Thus the two struggles, South and North, had to be kept separate. These arguments cut little ice with southern ministers, who could not possibly take responsibility for the suffering of poor whites and who needed to say that SCLC was their movement regardless of what might be true about capitalism.[90]

The idea of the Prayer Pilgrimage for Freedom originated at SCLC's founding meeting in New Orleans. The *Brown* decision was approaching its third anniversary. Randolph had asked Eisenhower to meet with black leaders to discuss school integration, and the White House brushed him off. The fledgling SCLC vowed to organize a "mighty Prayer Pilgrimage to Washington" if Eisenhower did not respond. Rustin and Levison carried the idea forward, along with King and Randolph, conceiving it as an opportunity to dramatize that the movement now had two superstars, Wilkins and King. To pull it off, however, Rustin and Levison had to get Wilkins to support the event and secure the necessary permissions. Only the NAACP had the inside game to get the Lincoln Memorial. Wilkins reluctantly went along. He did not care for marches, but at least In Friendship respected him enough to ask. Wilkins figured, rightly, that he might incur favor with Eisenhower by vowing to keep things mild, peaceable, and focused on Congress, not Eisenhower.

Rustin and Levison expected fifty thousand and were disappointed to get thirty thousand. They urged Mordecai Johnson not to run overlong, and he ran less overlong than usual. They showcased the struggles in Birmingham, Tallahassee, New Orleans, and Atlanta by assigning speaking roles to Shuttlesworth, Steele, Davis, and Borders. They let Powell go next to last, risking that he might upstage King. Levison wrote the first draft of King's speech, and King practiced it on the road, honing the text with Rustin and Levison. Editorial smoothening went fine except for the key line. Rustin insisted that "Give us the ballot" was weak. He wanted King to say, "When we have achieved the ballot" or perhaps "We demand the ballot" because black Americans didn't want anything to be *given* to them. To Rustin, King's phrase fell "like a pile of dirt." King gave Rustin a vintage King gentle stare: "Well, Bayard, I don't mind your criticizing my ideas. But I don't like your criticizing my words, because I'm better at words than you are." Whether it sang was more important to King than a quibble about the message. That settled the issue, and King electrified the crowd with "Give us the ballot."[91]

The *Brown* decision came as a "joyous daybreak" to end the long night of forced segregation, King said. It should have abolished *Plessy* tyranny, but "all types of conniving methods" were still used against blacks, so democracy was still an aspiration in the United States, not a reality. One could not be a democratic citizen if one could not vote. King ran off six iterations of his title. "Give us the ballot and we will no longer have to worry the federal government about our basic rights. . . . Give us the ballot and we will fill our legislative halls with men of good will. . . . Give us the ballot and we will place judges on the benches of the South who will 'do justly and love mercy.' " The crowd picked up the refrain and chanted it back. King stressed that the South's defiance of *Brown* set off a "tragic breakdown of law and order." America desperately needed a president who restored the rule of law and defended the Constitution, and it desperately needed Congress to pass strong civil rights legislation. Instead, the executive branch was "all too silent and apathetic," Democrats capitulated to Dixiecrats, and Republicans capitulated to "right-wing, reactionary Northerners." Both political parties "betrayed the cause of justice."[92]

King implored liberals to defend true liberalism and implored white, southern moderates to find their courage. "There is a dire need today for a liberalism which is truly liberal," he declared. True liberalism was devoted to justice, standing up for the rights of oppressed minorities. It was not the callow individualism of so many so-called liberals, who respected every viewpoint without holding one: "We call for a liberalism from the North which will be thoroughly committed to the ideal of racial justice and will not be deterred by the propaganda and subtle words of those who say, 'Slow up for a while; you are pushing too fast.' " The North needed to grow its meager supply of fighting liberals, and the South needed to demand moderate leaders. King said there were more moderate whites in the South than hatefully racist whites. It seemed otherwise only because the party of bigotry was more aggressive and politically active: "There are in the white South more open-minded moderates than appear on the surface. These persons are silent today because of fear of social, political, and economic reprisals." King called for an upsurge of white moderate courage in the South that dared to lead "in this tense period of transition."[93]

He had words of counsel and hope. The civil rights movement had to stand for integration and democracy, and it had to be led by people of good will and deep conviction. "We must be sure that our hands are clean in the struggle," King urged. "We must never struggle with falsehood, hate or malice. Let us never become bitter." In other contexts he turned theological at this point; to this gathering he cautioned against black supremacist versions of black nationalism. "We proudly proclaim that three-fourths of the peoples of the world are colored," King declared. The black struggle for freedom in the United States was deeply linked to similar struggles in Asia and Africa. But solidarity had to be claimed and practiced "in the right spirit." Otherwise it turned into reverse bigotry: "We must not become victimized with a philosophy of 'black supremacy.' Our aim must never be to defeat or to humiliate the white man, but to win his friendship and understanding, and thereby create a society in which all men will be able to live together as brothers."[94]

King lauded the NAACP for marching through the courts, not mentioning that it fixated on legal battles only under Walter White (who died in 1955) and Wilkins. Wilkins and Thurgood Marshall denigrated activism that distracted from court battling. In the run-up to the Prayer Pilgrimage Marshall dismissed King as an "opportunist" and "rabble-rouser." King was more generous, praising the "marvelous achievements" of the NAACP: "Every person of good will is profoundly indebted to the NAACP for its noble work." Still, court victories were not enough; thus they were gathered at the Lincoln Memorial: "We must act in such a way as to make possible a coming-together of white people and colored people on the basis of a real harmony of interest and understanding. We must seek an integration based on mutual respect." King often ended by reciting the patriotic anthem "My Country, 'Tis of Thee." On this occasion he opted for the third verse of "Lift Every Voice and Sing," which James Weldon Johnson wrote in 1900 to honor Booker T. Washington's Lincoln Day visit to Johnson's segregated school in Jacksonville, Florida:

> Shadowed beneath thy hand, may we forever stand
> True to our God, true to our native land.[95]

This speech was too new and important for King not to have a manuscript, so he stuck to it closely, until he didn't. Rustin realized immediately that King was right about the cannon shots of "Give us the ballot." He marveled that King galvanized the crowd like nobody else and puzzled that he could not say why. So much of King's stump material was straight out of a schoolbook. The crowd cheered even when King strayed from his text with an aside he could not resist about *eros*, *filios*, and *agape*. How many times could he get away with a seminary excursus on three forms of Greek love? Rustin realized more than ever that King distinctly understood the musical power of words. He was a once-in-a-lifetime phenomenon, a verdict many journalists put more prosaically, declaring that King's commanding performance proved that Montgomery was no fluke. There were demurrals about the event's significance. The *Brown* anniversary date fell on a Friday, which drove down attendance. The *New York Times* and the *Nation* stressed the disappointing turnout. Harlem New York City council representative Earl Brown chided, "You can't exorcise the devil with prayer alone." Rustin, Levison, and Randolph did not say publicly what they said to each other: The event was a huge success because it put King onstage alongside Wilkins, where his star qualities showed through.[96]

That was the movement highlight of the late 1950s. Everything else was hard, grinding, and ambiguous by comparison. The bus issue was unique as a source of economic leverage for black southerners, so white officials desegregated city buses. Usually there was a one-day protest yielding the necessary arrests for a legal challenge that city officials welcomed. New Orleans, Baton Rouge, Memphis, Savannah, and Atlanta averted another Montgomery in this fashion, depriving the SCLC of its best shot at a Montgomery chain reaction. Shuttlesworth launched a bus boycott in Birmingham in October 1958, but it sputtered and failed. By then SCLC had moved to voter registration, putting off the dream of boycott wildfire, and SCLC leaders in key places dropped out. Jemison resigned as secretary, and Shuttlesworth took his place; Davis resigned as vice president, and Lowery took his place. Since King was in Montgomery, Shuttlesworth in Birmingham, and Lowery in Mobile it became hard to deny that SCLC was basically an Alabama operation, albeit headquartered in Atlanta.

Tilley lasted one year as executive secretary, and Baker replaced him in January 1958. She intended only to set up an office and launch a voter registration program, Crusade for Citizenship, as her appointment was temporary. But there was no organization without her, so Baker stayed for two years, singlehandedly holding it together. Fatefully, she found SCLC leaders to be arrogant and self-centered. In her telling, they looked down on women, wasted her time, habitually came late to meetings, and did not respect her. Her expertise seemed to count for nothing, nor did the fact that she was old enough to be their mother. King was habitually chauvinistic. Baker found him pompous, spoiled, condescending, and eager to be idolized. On one occasion she asked him why he condoned such hero worship; King replied it was what people wanted.

To Baker that was a pathetic answer. She believed that mass movements should be organized from the ground up, with a radically democratic ethos. Instead, SCLC was building a personality cult that impeded the movement from growing. Baker respected King enough to work with him; years later she denied King family accusations that she hated King. She had never despised King, but she very much disliked the kind of organization he fostered. The ministers expected Baker to wait on them and defer to them while they deferred to King. Baker's response, at the time and later, was blunt: "I have no respect for that." Septima Clark, the other woman besides Baker to serve on the SCLC's executive staff in the 1960s, had the same experience of chauvinistic treatment.

The word of a woman had no weight whatsoever, she said. SCLC ministers had a dramatic idea of activism centered on their heroics and supported by others consigned to underling roles.[97]

There were others who felt pushed aside by the ministers, excluded for not belonging to a clerical elite, notably Nixon: "I'm proud that I was part of it, even though so many people got famous out of it and I was still left here. And I'm still here servin' the people and the rest of 'em are gone." SCLC leaders, virtually to a person, told a different story of creating the very protest organization that Rustin and Baker originally proposed. They appreciated King's distinct ability and accepted that his word was the final authority. They never claimed to be grassroots organizers in Baker's mold. They were committed to a charismatic leadership model, they cultivated a chaotic style, and they did not even pay much attention to their affiliates. SCLC needed to be a hit-and-run operation led by ministerial firebrands who supported King. Wyatt Walker judged that Baker had the wrong personality and philosophy to "fit into the mold of a preacher organization." SCLC's leadership model was obvious, so why did she expect it to become something else? Steele put it positively: "Dr. King was the last word on everything. I don't remember any time that Dr. King made a proposal that we did not accept."[98]

SCLC's switch to voter registration seemed more doable than its original dream of boycott wildfire; meanwhile Wilkins smoldered at King and the new organization. Wilkins had four top-drawer complaints. He did not like having a personal rival, let alone a neophyte rival. He fumed that King and SCLC soaked up money that should have gone to the NAACP. He protested that SCLC cut into the NAACP's following and organizations in the South. And SCLC's very existence felt like an unjust reproach to Wilkins. Anything that hurt the NAACP in the South hurt the civil rights movement; moreover, SCLC had it both ways with the NAACP, taunting the organization for its conservatism while benefiting from southern repression of the supposedly radical NAACP. Wilkins thus forbade NAACP officials to join or work with SCLC. His operatives planted articles ridiculing King's identification with Gandhi and nonviolence. Privately King burned at feeling unfairly attacked. Publicly he turned the other cheek, claiming to feel no rivalry with Wilkins or the NAACP. It helped that King genuinely believed the two organizations complemented each other, although he evoked snickers inside SCLC for saying it.

In the early years of the movement, Wilkins was wrong about the money. SCLC lacked a professional fund-raising operation until 1962, so King exhausted himself keeping the organization alive. In public view King and Wilkins said nice things about each other and pledged to work together. Reddick claimed in

1959 that rumors about tensions between them were completely made up, as King and Wilkins "always got on famously together." In fact, Wilkins seethed against King to insiders, who told King, who tried to make nice.[99]

King's ascendancy was laced with irony. He became famous while the movement stalled and faded. Insiders routinely called it "the Movement," even as it floundered, and King's own denomination spurned him. Joseph H. Jackson, pastor of Chicago's mammoth Mount Olive Baptist Church, presided over the National Baptist Convention (NBC). Jackson dreaded King's fame, theology, and politics, fearing that King would try to wrest the presidency from him, although Daddy King implored Jackson not to worry about that. Nannie Burroughs, shortly after King had moved to Montgomery, invited him to address the Woman's Convention of the NBC, where King excoriated colonialism, imperialism, and segregation plus the church's role in buttressing all three: "We stand between the dying old and the emerging new. . . . The old order of ungodly exploitation and crushing domination is passing away." Jackson hated that kind of talk in his denomination, contending that King perverted the faith by politicizing it with left-wing shibboleths. According to Jackson, authentic black Baptist Christianity was otherworldly, separatist, and orthodox, and King's celebrity was a baleful creation of white liberals and backsliding black Christians. The white liberals were of no concern to Jackson, and the King-supporting black Christians were a disgrace. Jackson blasted King and SCLC, setting the world's largest black Baptist organization against the civil rights movement. King quietly supported Gardner Taylor's opposition to Jackson in the NBC, which climaxed in failure and schism in 1961, leading to the founding of the Progressive National Baptist Convention.[100]

King's defenders grew accustomed to saying that he was nothing like a radical: He was at home in the black church, he had gone to mainstream seminaries, and he was a bourgeois moderate in all things. In September 1958 a deranged woman stabbed King in the chest with a letter opener while he signed copies of *Stride Toward Freedom* at Blumstein's department store in Harlem. The wound nearly killed him. Reddick, commenting after King recovered, pressed two points. One, King was like Gandhi in being vulnerable to crazy people or nationalists harboring murderous ambitions. Two, King had nothing to do with Marxism or Communism: "Neither by experience nor reading is King a political radical. There is not a Marxist bone in his body. He accepts his society save where injustice and violence defile it. In the classic phrase, Martin Luther King is a bourgeois leader of the masses." *Time* magazine gave King a huge boost in this area, declaring that he was fully American and "no radical"— even his suits were conservative.[101]

Having founded SCLC in the same year that Du Bois joined the Communist Party, King felt compelled to stress the difference. He approved every line of Reddick's book, while bridling at what could not be said. Acknowledging that he was a democratic Socialist would not have gone well for King. Spelling out the Socialist worldview that he took from Rauschenbusch, Du Bois, Johnson, Randolph, Barbour, the early Niebuhr, Mays, Muelder, and Rustin would have yielded only turmoil and vilification. Every insider in the Randolph/Thomas/Farmer network was intimately acquainted with this problem and wanted King to finesse it. Since they were open about being Socialists, they were Red-baited constantly, especially by Communists who lied about their own politics and by reactionaries who equated social democracy with Stalinism.

Rustin and Michael Harrington were drinking buddies and Socialist comrades. A native of St. Louis and a brilliant speaker and writer, Harrington led the youth division (Young Socialist League) of Max Shachtman's International Socialist League. In 1956, during the Montgomery movement, Harrington introduced Rustin to his protégés, Brooklyn activists Tom Kahn and Rachelle Horowitz. Rustin and Kahn became lovers, and the following year Harrington met King for the first time, at the Prayer Pilgrimage. In 1958 the International Socialist League merged with the Socialist Party, which yielded a surge of Socialist activism in the civil rights movement spearheaded by Harrington. Harrington and Rustin, organizing in Harlem, were heckled as "Jewish Communists" who should go home. Both laughed off the tag, as both were neither plus adept at shucking off accusation; Harrington presumed that the hecklers were Garvey nationalists. To him, the civil rights movement was *the* Social Force of its time. Harrington pressed the upshot to Shachtman and other Old Left luminaries: King was the star of the next great social surge and all leftists had to get with it. At the Democratic Convention of 1960, after Powell's stunning threat against Rustin and King cut off Rustin from King and Levison, Harrington teamed with California entertainment lawyer Clarence Jones to organize a march of five thousand demonstrators, narrowly averting no-show failure. King impressed Harrington enormously: "I marveled that he had the emotional strength and maturity to keep his equilibrium given the fantastic pressures to which he was subjected."[102]

King told Harrington that he was leaning toward Kennedy; Harrington begged him to hold back. They turned to political philosophy, and Harrington gasped at realizing that King was a flat-out democratic Socialist. King had not merely been influenced by social gospel Socialism or his friendship with Rustin; his worldview was Socialist: "He understood that full civil rights for an exploited and hungry mass of black Americans constituted only a first step in the transformation of the intolerable conditions under which they lived." The conversation made Harrington anxious before it yielded a bit of ideological pride. This could not get out; it would ruin King if people knew how closely he agreed with Rustin, Randolph, Harrington, and Rauschenbusch. Harrington did not even want to hear King say it. Nonetheless, "it was a revelation to me that this warm and luminous man of the South had, in the course of a much more profound political and intellectual journey than mine, come to a view of America and the world that I largely shared."[103]

King's Socialist worldview was explicable from the mentors and intellectuals who influenced him, albeit something he could not talk about. Meanwhile the interesting question was how he got to be a Gandhian pacifist. King made no secret of his aspiration to be a good Gandhian. He noted that the Montgomery boycott required mass meetings every Monday and Thursday because nonviolent resistance was counterintuitive for most black Americans. He and Smiley had to explain Gandhian method repeatedly, stressing that it was "nonaggressive physically but strongly aggressive spiritually." When King told this story, he lauded the "sensitive and frail" Juliette Morgan for introducing the Gandhi comparison to white Montgomery in a newspaper letter and suffering condemnation for it. Always he said that Jesus furnished the "spirit and motivation" of the Montgomery rebellion while Gandhi provided the method. Violence is not redemptive and never leads to reconciliation, King urged. Unearned suffering, however, is redemptive or at least can be redemptive: "Suffering, the nonviolent resister realizes, has tremendous educational and transforming possibilities." Redemptive suffering was "infinitely more powerful" than the predatory law of the jungle for converting the hearts of oppressors, exactly as Gandhi said.[104]

King's climactic run on this subject paraphrased Gandhi with images ripped from African American history:

> We will match your capacity to inflict suffering with our capacity to endure suffering. We will meet your physical force with soul force. We will not hate you, but we cannot in all good conscience obey your unjust laws. Do to us what you will and we will still love you. Bomb our homes and threaten our children; send your hooded perpetrators of violence into our communities and drag us out on some wayside road, beating us and leaving us half dead, and we will still love you. But we will soon wear you down by our capacity to suffer. And in winning our freedom we will so appeal to your heart and conscience that we will win you in the process.

Reddick, asking how his friend got like this, said that King was always on the path despite hearing nothing like it "from his father or brother or schoolroom or playground or the way of life of his region or social order." King transcended his background long before he related Jesus to Gandhi or knew anything about Gandhi. Reddick played up the contrasts between King and Daddy King; King stood out because he was extraordinary, like Gandhi.[105]

Though Reddick idealized King, he also challenged him. Reddick was prickly, and he worried that King expected royal treatment and his own way. Merely preaching about nonviolence did not make King a good Gandhian, Reddick cautioned. It remained to be seen whether King would carry out "the discipline of meditation and restraint and the renunciation of worldly goods" that true nonviolence entailed or accept "the hard necessity of planning ahead and cooperatively sharing the tasks and rewards." Gandhi achieved revolutionary sainthood, and he did it by humbly enabling others; King was just getting started. Reddick challenged King to go to India to meet the homegrown Gandhian experts. In 1959 the American Friends Service Committee sent King, Coretta King, and Reddick to India as guests of Prime Minister Jawaharlal Nehru and the Gandhi Memorial Trust of India. On his way to India King spoke at the annual War Resisters League dinner in New York, declaring that "the colored peoples" of the world held the key, through nonviolence, to establishing "an alternative to war and destruction." In India King was welcomed warmly as a champion of oppressed people of color—"Virtually every door was open to us." He met with Nehru, President Rajendra Prasad (a stalwart Gandhian freedom fighter), and Vice President Sarvapalli Radhakrishnan (a renowned philosopher), remarking to Coretta that it was like meeting George Washington, Thomas Jefferson, and James Madison. He met Vinoba Bhave, a revered Gandhian who walked perpetually across the nation asking rich landowners for contributions to his Bhoodan movement, a land reform program benefiting landless peasants. King told a press conference that he traveled elsewhere as a tourist, "but to India I come as a pilgrim."[106]

Reporters asked King if nonviolence was a creed or a policy to him; he replied, "I have come to believe in it as a way of life." They asked if nonviolence included vegetarianism and if many African Americans were leftists. King said no to both questions. Vegetarianism, cloth spinning, and the like were disposable husk for him, and he estimated that "not more than one per cent" of black Americans subscribed to radical non-American ideologies. Nonviolent being and doing were what mattered. In India he gave true-believing speeches that nothing worked like nonviolence. King grieved at the contrast between India's vast poverty and its wealthy elite, later remarking sharply, "The bourgeoisie—white, black, or brown—behaves about the same the world over." In a meeting with Nehru, Reddick asked if India's policy of "reservations" for Dalits did not amount to reverse discrimination; Nehru replied that it barely began to atone for centuries of abuse. On King's last night in India, after a month of touring, he gave a radio broadcast urging India to take the lead in calling for global disarmament. The United States and Soviet Union, he lamented, "have not shown the faith and moral courage to do this." He wrote upon returning home, "I left India more convinced than ever before that nonviolent resistance is the most potent weapon available to oppressed people in their struggle for freedom." Six years later, refashioning his stump speech "The American Dream" as a sermon at Ebenezer, King recalled his India pilgrimage by telling the Mays story about being introduced as an untouchable at a Dalit school in Kerala, complete with the offended reaction and subsequent reconsideration. He seemed to forget that this happened to Mays, not to him.[107]

THE COMING OF THE YOUTH

King returned from India determined to carry out Gandhian nonviolence, while puzzling over what that would mean. He used the Institute on Nonviolent Resistance to Segregation to explore the answer, moving his annual summer gathering from Montgomery to Atlanta. In July 1959 the institute met at Spelman College. King, Rustin, Smiley, and James Lawson led workshops, and Walker joined the group as a session chair. King sat in the front row during Lawson's workshop, which became a practice for him at SCLC gatherings, sending a message: the workshops were essential to SCLC's work, and Lawson was a master teacher who would help the movement find its way.

King had met Lawson in February 1957 at Oberlin College, where Lawson was a graduate student in religious studies, and King gave three speeches at the invitation of Oberlin chaplain Harvey Cox. It took King only ten minutes of conversation at a luncheon to decide that the movement needed Lawson desperately and right away, not after Lawson earned a doctorate in theology at Yale, as he was planning. James Lawson was the son of a Methodist minister, James Lawson Sr., who fathered nine children in eight congregations in Massachusetts and New York before settling in Massillon, Ohio. Lawson was child number six, but the first boy. His father founded NAACP chapters wherever he moved, and he did not believe in nonviolence. Lawson's mother, Philane, was the pacifist influence in his life, quietly teaching her son that violence never solved anything. Philane Lawson moved to the United States from Jamaica in her late teens and sent five of her children to college, taking for granted that her brilliant first son would go to college despite the family's meager economic means. Lawson went to Baldwin-Wallace College in Berea,

Ohio, a United Methodist school that supported his commitment to Christian pacifism—until it didn't.[108]

A. J. Muste spoke at Baldwin-Wallace during Lawson's freshman year, 1947, and Lawson joined FOR, deeply drawn to Muste's kindness and religious faith. At the end of Lawson's junior year, North Korean forces crossed the thirty-eighth parallel and he spurned all three of the draft deferments available to him. Lawson wanted no privileged status for being a student or a conscientious objector. He also abhorred the ministerial deferment, which bought off Christian leaders who should have taken a stand against war. Imprisoned for draft evasion in 1951, Lawson won less support from his supposedly progressive Christian college than he expected. Like many FOR workers, Lawson treated his year in prison as an opportunity to witness to Christ, which the Methodist Church respected, sending him to India as a missionary in 1952. Lawson taught for three years at a Presbyterian college in Nagpur, Hislop College. He thoroughly enjoyed the experience, studied Gandhian nonviolence, and felt tempted to stay, shaking his head at Indian Christians who scorned Gandhi. Then Montgomery erupted and Lawson pined to come home. From the beginning he identified with King and sought to follow his path.

Lawson had barely begun his studies at Oberlin, preparing for doctoral study, when King came to Oberlin. To King, it was wonderfully serendipitous to meet someone so much like himself, imbued with Gandhian Christian convictions. Lawson also shared King's theological and philosophical interests, but King told him abruptly to put off such things. The movement needed him now. Lawson agreed to come, asking Muste where he should go. Muste considered Atlanta, but white Atlanta was extremely hostile and black Atlanta had a hidebound aristocracy. Nashville seemed more promising to Muste. Nashville had Fisk, Meharry, a slightly liberalizing Vanderbilt, and a black Baptist seminary, plus a revered civil rights leader, Baptist pastor Kelly Miller Smith. Muste sent Lawson to Nashville as FOR's southern field secretary, where Lawson formed a tag team with Smiley, teaching nonviolence workshops together. On Tuesday nights Lawson taught a workshop at Clark Memorial United Methodist Church, which Smiley ran when Lawson was out of town. On other nights Lawson and Smiley taught workshops together across the South.[109]

In 1958 Lawson enrolled at Vanderbilt Divinity School just as John Lewis enrolled at American Baptist Theological Seminary. Lewis and his friend Bernard Lafayette tried to bring classmate James Bevel to the Tuesday workshop, but Bevel was too brash and self-involved to be interested, and he ridiculed the idea of a social gospel. Lawson was intense, earnest, and low-key, never raising his voice. Always he talked about the social gospel, Gandhi, redemptive suffering, radical equality, and the power of love. He told his disciples that if they modeled the way of redemptive suffering, others would follow. If ten got arrested, fifty would follow; if fifty got arrested, two hundred would follow. Lewis later recalled of him, "He was God-sent. There was something of a mystic about him, something holy, so gathered, about his manner. . . . The man was a born teacher, in the truest sense of the word." For the cadre of what became SNCC, Lawson was the Gandhi figure. Lewis said it plainly: "In his own right, he was a great moral force. We regarded him as our real teacher in nonviolence." Lawson taught that nonviolence was the way of disarming oppressors by loving them enough to not strike back and not even want to strike back. He told trainees not to curl in a fetal position when they took a beating because passivity heightened the anger of violent segregationists, resulting in broken ribs and a failure to break the cycle of violence. The right method was to maintain eye contact with aggressors.[110]

Lewis had grown up in rural Pike County, Alabama, forty miles west of Montgomery. He was extremely country, having preached to chickens in his youth and conducted chicken baptisms and chicken weddings. His kindly parents allowed him to skip cotton picking on occasion because he was so keen to excel in school. Lewis was fourteen years old in the summer of 1955 when he heard King give a radio sermon on the apostle Paul admonishing American Christians for being lousy Christians. Lewis later recalled, "It was sort of the social gospel, making religion something real and using the emotionalism within religion to make it do something else for people." That was Lewis's first glimmer of the social gospel. The boycott commenced and Lewis dreamed of following King to Morehouse, but he could not afford the tuition. He ended up at the Baptist seminary in Nashville because it charged no tuition. Kelly Miller Smith taught homiletics at the seminary and became a role model to Lewis, who kept working on Bevel. Bevel was from Itta Bena, Mississippi, and a family of seventeen children. He had served in the navy, worked as a bricklayer, and read one book that really spoke to him, Tolstoy's *The Kingdom of God Is Within You*. Bevel found his way to seminary because he felt desperately his need of personal salvation. Social religion was superfluous, so Bevel wrote off Reinhold Niebuhr. Lewis dragged Bevel to a workshop at the Highlander Folk School in Monteagle, Tennessee, where Myles Horton became one of the few people ever to break through Bevel's self-containment. Horton had founded Highlander in 1932 as a labor education center, working with fledgling CIO unions. Later he emphasized civil rights work. Rosa Parks was a Highlander alumna, Septima Clark ran a citizen education center at Highlander, and Bevel met people who had given their lives to the social gospel, which made him reconsider it. Bevel joined the Lawson group and brought his powerful person-ality to it.[111]

The following fall Diane Nash transferred to Fisk from Howard University and quickly emerged as the group's student leader. Brilliant, brave, demanding, and a former beauty contestant, Nash had grown up in Chicago and was appalled by Nashville. She challenged the Lawson group to live by its ideals; it helped that most of the men were in love with her. She seemed wondrously fearless to them, although she later said that the early sit-ins terrified her. Lawson's workshop, by September 1959, had twenty core members. They were disciplined and passionate, and they struck hard in downtown Nashville, conducting sit-ins at segregated stores. The youth eruption had begun, albeit modestly, with much preparation. Then it exploded in Greensboro, North Carolina, with virtually no planning. On February 1, 1960, four freshman students at North Carolina A&T, David Richmond, Franklin McCain, Ezell Blair Jr., and Joseph McNeil, asked to be served at Woolworth's lunch counter in Greensboro and quietly held their seats as employees floundered with embar-rassment. The next day twenty students joined Richmond, McCain, Blair Jr., and McNeil. On the third day there were eighty protesters, and the next day there were over three hundred. Protests spread to five North Carolina towns: Winston-Salem, Durham, Raleigh, Charlotte, and High Point. Shuttlesworth happened to be guest preaching in High Point. He called Baker with an urgent message: "This is the thing. You must tell Martin that we must get with this."[112]

That week King moved to Ebenezer, as he needed a break from running Dexter and the floundering SCLC needed his attention. Daddy King finally got the ministerial partner he wanted, at a dramatic moment. The sit-ins escalated in Nashville and spread to Rock Hill, South Carolina, and Richmond, Virginia. For three years King had puzzled over the quandaries of nonviolent confronta-tion. He read books about Gandhi, went to India, organized seminars, and gave countless sermons about direct action—without doing any. The quandaries daunted him. What was nonviolent about coercive boycotts and sit-ins, espe-cially if they sparked a violent backlash? If CORE's demonstrations catalyzed nothing, what good were they? The student eruption cut through the quanda-ries with simple acts of bodily rebellion, compelling King to make a difficult decision. He lauded the students generously, declaring at Durham that the moment had come to fill up the jails of the South. But King balked at going to jail personally.

He had barely moved to Atlanta when the state of Alabama prosecuted him for felony tax evasion. King had reluctantly paid the state's assessment on his complicated taxes for 1956 and 1958, but the state charged him with perjury anyway. This naked display of vengeance shook King deeply. The prospect of being degraded and imprisoned frightened and sickened him. Nothing ever rattled him as deeply, not even his subsequent persecution by the FBI. Meanwhile he got an icy greeting from Daddy King's peers, who wanted no sit-ins in Atlanta. All six presidents of the Atlanta University colleges, including Mays, admonished King to confine his troublemaking to other cities. According to them, Atlanta worked better than other southern cities because of them. They had a proud record of channeling racial dissent toward constructive ends, and if sit-in turmoil came to Atlanta they would blame King. King's philosophy professor at Morehouse, Samuel Williams, joined in this plea, using his leverage as a charter member of SCLC.

King tried to have it both ways, cheering sit-in wildfire while making exceptions for Atlanta and himself. Atlanta students settled for a one-day march and rally at which students, the college presidents, King, and Borders said nice things about each other and dispersed. Vanderbilt Divinity School expelled Lawson for causing sit-in turmoil, and most of the Divinity School faculty resigned in protest. This did not go as Vanderbilt chancellor Harvie Branscomb expected. Lawson was flooded with scholarship offers from elite seminaries; Vanderbilt's medical and law faculties supported the Divinity faculty; Lawson chose Boston University; and the Divinity professors got their jobs back. Meanwhile King revved up SCLC by putting Walker in charge and supporting the founding of a youth organization. King needed a forceful type who would whip SCLC into shape and command respect from the ministers. That would never be Baker, so King replaced Baker with Walker, although he had to tell Walker that getting along with Rustin, Levison, and Baker was not optional. Baker and King had tense moments together at the founding of SNCC on April 15, 1960, but contrary to the dramatic myth of origin told by James Forman and other SNCC leaders, King did not oppose SNCC's independence or clash with Baker over this issue. King was willing to support a separate organization if SNCC wanted one, and his fondest wish was to hire Lawson and North Carolina firebrand Douglas Moore, King's former Boston University classmate, as field organizers.[113]

Lawson's disciples stood out at SNCC's founding conference. To the activists gathered at Shaw University, the Nashville protesters were already famous, they obviously trusted each other, and they exuded an attractive self-confidence. Hank Thomas, a Howard University student, envied the Nashville group and latched onto it. Lawson gave an electrifying keynote on his stock themes: Love is the central motif of nonviolence. Love matches the capacity of evil to inflict suffering with a greater capacity to absorb evil and remain loving. The movement needed to foster radical equality. Lawson believed ardently in radical equality and rotating leadership; at Shaw he put it negatively, blistering the stodgy, hierarchical, "too conservative" NAACP. *Crisis* was "the magazine of the black bourgeoisie," he chided. It was not enough to oppose segregation, especially only through the courts. The movement needed to stand for "nonviolent revolution," wholeheartedly opposing social evil: "It's against Uncle Tom Negroes, against the NAACP's over-reliance on the courts, and against the futile middle-class technique of sending letters to the centers of power." SNCC founders roared with approval, thrilled that Lawson said it so bluntly. Afterward Lawson and Moore told King they were willing to work for SCLC. King emoted jubilantly that this was the greatest news he had ever heard. But Lawson's speech infuriated Wilkins, who issued an ultimatum. If King hired Lawson or Moore, he would never get another favor or supportive anything from the NAACP. King was so crestfallen that he asked Muste to convey the news to Lawson. Lawson and Moore took it hard, as Lawson retreated to independent activism as a Methodist pastor, and Moore opted for missionary work in the Belgian Congo.[114]

King was vulnerable at the time plus dependent on the NAACP since three of his five lawyers were NAACP bigwigs, and all five told him he was headed to prison for tax fraud. The lawyers ran up staggering bills while assembling a messy defense. Rustin ran a fund-raising ad that yielded a libel suit from the state of Alabama, and King despaired over his dire situation. Levison endeared himself to King by scorching the lawyers for underperforming and overcharging. King was lucky to get late help from a sixth attorney, Chicago tax specialist Chauncey Eskridge, who pored through King's detailed diaries and ignored unhelpful advice. Eskridge discovered that King had fully paid his taxes and was guilty of nothing. The lawyers were astonished by this news, especially Daddy King's prickly friend and benefactor Jesse Blayton. Just before King went to trial, presidential candidate Jack Kennedy asked Harry Belafonte what he should do to improve his image among black Americans. Belafonte told him to forget about Belafonte and Jackie Robinson; the person to cultivate was King. JFK was incredulous: the Montgomery boycott preacher now headed to prison? Belafonte told Kennedy to believe it; he knew black Americans and Kennedy did not. In late May the King case went to court, and King expected to be convicted and marched off to prison. How could a white Alabama jury possibly acquit him? After they did, King choked out a single-sentence reaction, too overcome to speak. The crowd marched to Dexter Church to celebrate, where King asked Highlander alums to sing Highlander's new anthem, "We Shall Overcome," which Highlander troubadour Guy Carawan had adapted from a black church hymn—"I'll be all right, I'll be all right some day." For the rest of his life King said he had no idea what happened with that jury.

The sit-ins split the upper South and parts of Texas and Florida from the rest of the Deep South, eliminating segregated lunch counters in Nashville, San Antonio, and approximately ninety other towns and cities. Protesters exposed the moral bankruptcy of "separate but equal" ideology, reducing segregationists to a naked appeal to property rights and a naked resort to violence. Segregationists regained the upper hand in most of the South, expelling thousands of students from state-supported colleges and successfully repressing sit-ins in Louisiana, Mississippi, Alabama, Georgia, and South Carolina. Where gains were made, Wilkins wrote them off as low-hanging fruit. Elsewhere, to Wilkins, turmoil rebellion was counterproductive. King managed to say, "Fill the jails," which to Wilkins was an absurd objective, but King had only modest influence in the sit-in movement, and he navigated a tricky political situation. Daddy King and his peers wanted King to endorse Richard Nixon; Harris Wofford and Louis Martin lobbied King to endorse Kennedy; and SNCC implored King to get arrested at Rich's department store cafeteria in Atlanta. King begged off, and the protest was put off until October, when SNCC shamed King into joining its sit-in at Rich's.

To SNCC, the Atlanta sit-in marked a breakthrough—the first time King willingly got arrested. To King, the episode quickly turned nightmarish, as Judge Oscar Mitchell of DeKalb County Court declared that King's arrest violated his probation on a prior conviction of driving without a Georgia license and ordered his transfer to state prison. Being hauled to Reidsville and imprisoned shook King deeply; he wrote to Coretta, "This is the cross we must bear for the freedom of our people. . . . I am asking God hourly to give me the power of endurance. I have the faith to believe that this excessive suffering that is now coming to our family will in some little way serve to make Atlanta a better city, Georgia a better state, and America a better country. Just how I do not yet know, but I have faith to believe it will. If I am correct then our suffering is not in vain."[115]

This was the circumstance under which Coretta King called Wofford, JFK called Coretta King, and Robert Kennedy called Mitchell, swinging the 1960 election. It set a precedent, often repeated. Young protesters challenged King to relinquish his privileges, join them in the struggle, and practice what he preached. They always got to him, and sometimes they turned him. But King chafed at being admonished to endanger himself, and he remembered how he felt on the way to Reidsville. He vowed to make his own decisions about when he would sacrifice himself. Lawson's disciples were wholly committed to

Gandhian disruption, but King puzzled over what SCLC should do. SCLC had no strategy for abolishing segregation, and in 1961 the incoming president prized his white southern support more than he cared about civil rights. King proposed to concentrate on voter registration. Shuttlesworth preferred a barnstorming speaking tour to mobilize black clergy. Everyone grasped at straws until CORE struck hard in May 1961, replicating the beautiful simplicity of Greensboro with the Freedom Rides.

CORE executive secretary Jimmy Robinson held together a scrappy vanguard organization through the 1950s led by staffers James Peck, Jim McCain, and Gordon Carey. Peck, a clothing heir, had been a CORE stalwart since the 1940s. McCain was CORE's only black national staffer in the late 1950s, taking over as field secretary in 1957. Carey was an FOR veteran who became CORE's second field secretary in 1958. Peck, McCain, and Carey grasped that CORE had fallen behind the activist curve because it was too white and passive at the top. They pushed out Robinson and offered the leadership to King, who tried to imagine a fusion of CORE and SCLC. That was impossible, so CORE turned to its cofounder, Farmer, who had languished as a minor official at NAACP since 1959. Wilkins bade Farmer a surprisingly vulnerable farewell, telling him two things. First, clean house; Wilkins had made a terrible mistake by keeping Walter White's people, and now he was stuck with them. Second, appreciate his opportunity: "You're going to be riding a mustang pony, while I'm riding a dinosaur."[116]

Farmer's first day on the job was the first anniversary of the Greensboro sit-in. Carey and CORE veteran Tom Gaither had already hatched a plan to challenge interstate bus segregation—a reprise of the Journey of Reconciliation of 1947. The Freedom Rides were self-consciously a throwback to a storied moment in CORE/FOR history. This time there were thirteen riders divided between a Trailways bus and a Greyhound bus. Seven riders were black, six were white, and most were affiliated with CORE. Farmer and Carey started with Farmer and Peck, a veteran of the Journey of Reconciliation. They added two CORE staffers, Genevieve Hughes and Joe Perkins; a pacifist former navy captain, Albert Bigelow; and two SNCC veterans of the sit-ins, John Lewis and Hank Thomas. By then Lewis had five arrests on his activist record. The youngest Freedom Rider was eighteen-year-old Morehouse student Charles Person; the oldest was sixty-one-year-old retired Michigan school administrator Walter Bergman, a Norman Thomas Socialist who came with his wife, Frances, a retired elementary teacher. Both Bergmans were CORE stalwarts. The only minister was North Carolina Congregational pastor Benjamin E. Cox, one of the few southerners onboard. All but two of the original Freedom Riders were male, and both females were white, as Farmer was squeamish about sending women to be battered, and sending black women to be battered was out of the question.

On May 4 they set out for New Orleans from Washington, DC, planning to travel fifteen hundred miles in thirteen days. Along the way they asked for service at bus facilities. The Freedom Riders got icy stares in Fredericksburg, Richmond, and Petersburg, Virginia, but nothing worse, finishing their first day at Walker's former church in Petersburg. They got through North Carolina without incident, and the talkative Thomas kept saying this wasn't so bad, while Farmer said that things were sure to get worse. On the fifth day Lewis and Bigelow took a beating at a bus terminal in Rock Hill, South Carolina, and Lewis reluctantly dropped out to compete for an American Friends Service Committee scholarship for study in India—the same scholarship that Lawson won in 1954. In Atlanta the Freedom Riders had a festive dinner with King, who lauded their courage and privately trembled for them. King warned *Jet* reporter Simeon Booker that the group had no chance of making it through Alabama. Booker tried to laugh it off, telling King he would stick close to the portly Farmer, whom he would surely outrun. That night Farmer's father lapsed into a coma and died, and Farmer was called home; secretly he hated himself for feeling relieved.[117]

With Farmer and Lewis gone, Peck took charge of the Trailways bus, and Perkins became group captain on the Greyhound bus. Gaither warned that the first serious trouble would probably occur in Anniston, Alabama, after the Tallapoosa and Heflin stops. He was right; Anniston was a Klan stronghold. Approaching Anniston on Highway 78, the Greyhound was slowed by a mob that slashed the tires and pursued the wobbly fleeing bus. The tires went flat, and the driver fled into the countryside. The mob seized the bus, shook it, smashed windows with bricks and an ax, threw a firebomb inside, and sealed riders inside the burning bus. All might have been killed, except that Alabama state police chief Floyd Mann had planted a state investigator, E. L. Cowling, on the bus. Cowling got the riders out, brandishing a revolver, and some were beaten until state troopers arrived. Thomas was pummeled with a baseball bat. The battered Greyhound riders were taken to Anniston Hospital, where a mob gathered and the riders were refused treatment; Shuttlesworth rescued them by intervening with a caravan of his deacons. The next morning a spectacular photograph of the burning bus made front pages around the world. Meanwhile the Trailways group made it to Birmingham, where Peck and Walter Bergman were severely beaten and others were kicked and slugged. This mob, like others, doled out special vengeance to those it dubbed "nigger-lovers." It left Peck lying unconscious in a pool of his blood, presuming him dead. Turned away at

Carraway Methodist Hospital, Peck underwent surgery that night at Hillman Hospital. He told reporters he would be on the next day's bus to Montgomery.

Eighteen Freedom Riders showed up for the three o'clock bus to Montgomery, replenished with reinforcements. But Trailways had no driver, and the group had second thoughts. What was the point of taking more beatings? They had no protection, they had already garnered sensational publicity, and the atmosphere of hate got to them. The group decided to fly to New Orleans and proclaim victory, which alarmed the Lawson disciples in Nashville. It wasn't a victory if violence aborted the bus mission. Nash had already crossed her Deep South Rubicon, in Rock Hill, South Carolina, where she endured a thirty-day jail sentence in February 1961. Now she was as fearless as she seemed. Nash told Shuttlesworth that her group was coming to Birmingham to complete the Freedom Ride. Shuttlesworth was incredulous. Didn't Nash realize what happened to the Freedom Riders? She replied, "That's exactly why the ride must not be stopped. If they stop us with violence, the movement is dead. We're coming. We just want to know if you can meet us." Nash descended on King's home in Atlanta and begged him to join them. She offended King by pressing the point after he emphatically said no.[118]

Bevel selected ten Freedom Riders led by Lewis, who had returned, and not including Nash; the Nashville group needed Nash to run operations. The ten included six black males, two black females, and one white rider of each gender. Nash and Bevel asked the Nashville Christian Leadership Conference for support, and the ministers were horrified, calling the mission suicidal. Lawson, Kelly Miller Smith, and National Baptist Convention officer C. T. Vivian worked on the ministers, persuading them to provide support money. Lawson had moved to Scott Chapel Methodist Church in Shelbyville, sixty miles from Nashville. Smith habitually called Lawson's disciples "the children"; thus he was deeply conflicted. They were Smith's own children, whom he yearned to protect. Vivian, a fiery counterpoint to Smith, had long battled against the NBC's opposition to King. Lewis was struck by the pathos of the moment. Nearly all the young Freedom Riders had to overcome the terrified opposition of their parents. Now Smith had become another parental figure to look past because the crucial breakthroughs came with great risk. The Nashville group rushed to Birmingham, and Bull Connor hauled them to jail just before the bus to Montgomery boarded. Then he hauled them out of the state in a police caravan, dumping them at the border town of Ardmore, Tennessee; Connor told the Justice Department he couldn't stand their singing.

The Lawson disciples returned immediately to Birmingham to force the issue, and Attorney General Robert Kennedy, though angrily annoyed, pledged to help them continue the trip. On May 20 they rode to Montgomery in the company of sixteen highway patrol cars, which peeled off at the city limits. There were plenty of local police at the bus station, who fled just as the Freedom bus rolled in. Local authorities had given the Klan fifteen minutes. A crazed mob wielding pipes, clubs, and baseball bats destroyed *Life* and NBC cameras before heading toward the two Freedom Riders in the lead position, Lewis and a white exchange student at Fisk from Beloit College in Wisconsin, Jim Zwerg. The mob viciously beat Lewis and Zwerg, nearly killing them. Up to a dozen Freedom Riders would have been killed had Floyd Mann not intervened, firing his gun in the air. Justice Department official John Seigenthaler was smashed in the head by a lead pipe. A late-arriving police officer offered to call someone for Seigenthaler as he lay wounded. Seigenthaler asked him to call Mr. Kennedy. Who was that? Seigenthaler tried again: Either President Kennedy or Attorney General Kennedy, it didn't matter which one. Then he passed out. Robert Kennedy, always a fierce guardian of his brother's political interests, took civil rights more personally after his closest aide was nearly killed in Montgomery. He sent U.S. marshals to Montgomery and began to view civil rights in moral terms.

The next day Abernathy convened a mass rally at First Baptist Church to honor the Freedom Riders. King flew in from Chicago, and Walker from Atlanta. The Freedom Riders scattered through the congregation as a safety measure, while a thousand angry whites surrounded the packed church. Farmer arrived from Washington, DC, and Shuttlesworth hustled him through the mob; Farmer surmised that Shuttlesworth was either insane or the bravest soul he had ever met. The mob swelled and surged, breaking through the door, but the marshals pushed it back. The mob got angrier and bigger. Walker thought they were going to die that night in a blaze of fire. Abernathy said it would be better to give themselves to the mob. King had tense words with Robert Kennedy over the phone, protesting the lack of protection. The congregation was trapped and terrified. RFK got an implacably segregationist governor, John Patterson, to call out the National Guard, which allowed the congregants to leave at 4:30 a.m. King, Walker, Farmer, and Nash retreated to the home of a Montgomery pharmacist, across the street from the Dexter parsonage where King had lived for five years. Nash pressed King to join the Freedom Ride, and he refused. She called Baker repeatedly, who said that King only cared about "his little group," and the same thing was true of Farmer. It galled Nash that King took over as soon as he swept into town, pushing aside those who carried out his plea to dramatize the evil. In particular, he pushed her aside, after Nash had made every key decision that created this drama. Then he refused to join them.[119]

Seigenthaler awoke in a hospital, where Mann greeted him tearfully, feeling responsible. Seigenthaler ruminated that Mann was the only decent white official in Alabama and thus the only one to feel responsible. Farmer offended SNCC by telling reporters that "my show" would head immediately to Jackson. CORE had no riders in Montgomery except Farmer, who was not planning to ride. He later explained that he was frightened of being beaten to death. Mississippi was far more terrifying than Alabama. Alabama was a Klan state, long on semi-literate low achievers wearing hoods, but Mississippi was a White Citizens' Council state, flush at the top with well-off thugs. C. T. Vivian had to conceal from his wife, Octavia, that he planned to take the bus to Jackson. To Octavia, Alabama was bad enough, but Mississippi was out of the question. Even King never drew much of a crowd in Jackson, where people were too terrified to show up. Lewis and Lawson rounded up riders for the trip to Jackson, spurning Farmer as a pompous showboat, although a few CORE recruits from New Orleans got to Montgomery in time to ride. King was in another category; the Lawson disciples desperately wanted him to ride. Nash kept entreating King to change his mind. The cause of nonviolence would skyrocket if he got on the bus, she said. King agreed with that but explained that he was on probation; a Freedom Ride might land him in prison for six months.

This explanation offended the young protesters, who had jail records and an immediate future of prison or worse. King wilted perceptibly but stuck to his refusal, declaring, "I think I should choose the time and place of my Golgotha." According to Farmer, King's tortured declaration "evoked loud laughter and derisive comments." King identified with Jesus, not with mere mortals like them? He used that as a reason not to practice what he preached? Farmer recalled, "They were furious with him, and accused him of being yellow." Walker cut off the accusations, telling Nash and others to back off; King owed them no explanation for anything. At boarding time for Jackson, Farmer caught a look of terror and pleading from New Orleans teenager Doris Castle and surprised himself by climbing on the bus. Bevel rejoiced that Farmer redeemed himself by joining them. Meanwhile the Freedom Riders struggled with their feelings about King. Nash lost much of her admiration. Bevel said that King's decision was justified because of his leadership role. Paul Brooks said it would be easier to accept had King confessed his fear. Lewis cited Lawson's teaching that in nonviolence one does not badger people beyond their degree of commitment. Lewis still revered King, but he had to patronize him to rationalize what happened, while SNCC hung a derisive nickname on King, "De Lawd."[120]

On the way to Jackson they learned the game had changed. State officials, newly determined to avoid violence and cooperate with Robert Kennedy, sent out heavily armed escorts for Freedom buses. City officials smartened up, opting for low-key blanket arrests with no violence as soon as Freedom Rides arrived at central destinations. Jackson police captain J. L. Ray arrested the first riders so swiftly that Vivian almost failed to get arrested, having made a bathroom stop. The Freedom Riders did hard time in Mississippi's notorious Parchman prison, where they lost even their mattresses after they refused to stop singing. King, Walker, Nash, and Carey formed the Freedom Rides Coordinating Committee (FRCC), routing riders through Atlanta, Birmingham, Montgomery, and Jackson through the summer of 1961. Freedom Riders poured into the South, with patchy results leading to a legal victory. At summer's end, 328 Freedom Riders had been arrested in Jackson alone. In June Walker rode a Freedom Bus from Atlanta to Jackson, telling the Interstate Commerce Commission he was beaten in Hinds County Jail. In October the commission issued a ban on racial discrimination in interstate travel, which became effective on December 1, 1961.

The credit for this victory went primarily to CORE and SNCC. King and Walker earned some bandwagon credit for their work on FRCC, but tensions between SCLC and SNCC escalated during Freedom Summer, while SNCC had a bruising internal argument over direct action versus voter registration. Charles Jones, Ella Baker, Robert Moses, and Timothy Jenkins called for a switch to political action, anticipating the two-year Voter Education Project soon to be funded by the Field and Taconic foundations. The Nashville movement staunchly opposed any emphasis on voter registration, sticking to its concept of SNCC as a Gandhian nonviolent army. Nash said that voter registration was deradicalizing, a slick move by the Kennedy administration to co-opt a burgeoning protest movement. The voter registration faction was less religious and more political than the Lawson group; later it became more so. The two sides had it out at a summer conference at Highlander, where King urged that voter registration and direct action were both essential. Baker proposed that SNCC operate with two wings, a compromise that both sides reluctantly accepted, with Jones heading voter registration and Nash heading direct action. Both sides took offense that Walker habitually described SNCC as an adjunct of SCLC. SNCC got more snarky on this point after James Forman became the group's executive director. Forman had moved from Chicago to write about the movement; then he joined it. His flair for publicity and drama filled a void. However, SNCC *did* depend on the generosity of SCLC, which it rarely acknowledged. More important, the arguments over direct action versus higher righteousness faded as Moses, Charles Sherrod, and others encountered brutal violence doing the supposedly conventional work of voter registration.[121]

Moses epitomized the heroic SNCC freedom fighter, working in Deep South obscurity to instill democracy, in his case with high intelligence and a quiet manner. His quiet manner was essential to his charisma, a contrast to preacher volatility. Moses was born in Harlem in 1935 and graduated from Hamilton College in 1956. He first made contact with SCLC at its New York office, which hummed with efficiency, setting him up for disillusionment when he moved to Atlanta and witnessed the ramshackle languor of its Atlanta operation. Moses founded SNCC's Mississippi Project in 1961 and registered voters in Pike County and Amite County, facing unrelenting violence and intimidation in both cases. Meanwhile SNCC workers Charles Sherrod and Cordell Reagon moved to Terrell County in the southwest Georgia Black Belt to register voters, but Terrell was impossibly violent, so Sherrod and Reagon answered Carey's call to Albany, Georgia. Albany was not as repressive as Birmingham or Montgomery. Blacks could register and vote, the Klan was weak, and civic leaders took pride in the city's comparative calm. Rigid segregation and racial paternalism fit together in Albany, a 40 percent African American city lacking a single African American official. Moreover, Albany had a wily sheriff, Laurie Pritchett, who had gone to school on the mistakes of Birmingham, Anniston, and Montgomery.

Sherrod and Reagon entered Albany on November 1 on orders from Carey, who dispatched seven hundred activists to seven states as a follow-up to the Freedom Rides. Their assignment in Albany was to test the Trailways facilities, but they bonded with the town's black patriarch, C. W. King, a wealthy champion of liberal causes. Albany blacks were inflamed by a recent case of violence against a black field hand by county sheriff L. Warren Johnson. The local NAACP had done almost nothing for ten years, and NAACP Georgia field secretary Vernon Jordan was alarmed when SNCC showed up in Albany. Sherrod and Reagon organized prayer meetings at Shiloh Baptist Church, which led to a protest meeting on November 17, 1961, and the Albany movement was born. It called for fair employment practices and the abolition of segregation in municipal facilities, the bus station, and the train station. Five days later Pritchett arrested five Freedom Riders at the Trailways terminal. Two weeks after that, nearly five hundred people got arrested protesting on behalf of the Freedom Riders. Albany movement president William G. Anderson, a friend of Abernathy's from their school days at Albany State, asked King, Abernathy, and Walker to come to Albany.[122]

King had just made a bravura speech at the AFL-CIO convention in Miami, Florida, and was feeling exultant, exhaustion notwithstanding. The huge convention of steelworkers, carpenters, pipefitters, and assembly line operators gave

King a tepid welcome, but King impressed them with Levison's rendering of labor history and won them over with an appeal to solidarity. King chided that Randolph and black workers had long deserved better treatment from unionists. He stressed that black Americans were "almost entirely a working people" and their needs were "identical with labor's needs." He declared that the two most dynamic liberal forces in the nation were "the labor movement and the Negro freedom movement." Together, these two movements had the means to create a real democracy in America. He ended with a run on "we shall overcome," invoking the arc of the moral universe bending toward justice, no lie living forever, and truth crushed to earth rising again, all rushing toward the close he reprised at the March on Washington two years later, "Free at last, free at last." Three weeks earlier Randolph had accused this federation of laborers of "moral paralysis, pessimism, defeatism and cynicism." Now they gave King a thundering ovation, and he headed to Albany.[123]

In Albany he drew rapturous overflow crowds at Shiloh and Mt. Zion churches, declaring that the hour was late and they were not moving too fast: "The price that America must pay for the continued oppression of the Negro is a price of its own destruction." He preached on redemptive suffering, urging listeners to develop a willingness to die. They needed to go to jail without hating white jailors: "Say to the white man, 'We will win you with the power of our capacity to endure.' " He got a soaring refrain going on the "How long? Not long!" litany and seemed to be headed toward a closing crescendo when his voice trailed off. King stepped away from the pulpit, overwhelmed by the emotions he stirred in the crowd. Anderson, similarly transported, invited King to march with them, and King agreed to stay for an extra day. The following day a small crowd of 270 marched with King to city hall, as the most dedicated activists were already in jail, and King and Anderson were arrested for marching without a permit.[124]

Things had begun to go wrong just as King arrived. The city's negotiating committee teetered on a settlement with the Albany movement that city commissioners probably would have approved. Anderson, an osteopath, believed that King's sensational appearance would pressure city officials to settle. Bypassing the negotiating committee, Anderson issued an ultimatum to the commission, warning that new demands would be made if the commissioners did not settle. That backfired badly, as city officials would not be pressured into a settlement just because Martin Luther King came to Albany. They broke off negotiations, King felt trapped by Anderson's public invitation to stay for the march, King and Anderson were hauled to jail along with Abernathy, and Baker rushed to Albany to undercut King. Baker and Charles Jones resented that King had hijacked their campaign. They called a press conference at which a local organizer, Marion Page, read a statement composed by Baker that censured Walker and SCLC for trying to usurp the Albany movement. Reporters ran the story, and suddenly King and Walker looked like jerks. The new story was that King and Walker exploited the suffering of innocent locals and steamrollered SNCC organizers. King told reporters he would not accept bond or pay a fine; at the same time, he urged Walker to get Anderson, Abernathy, and him out of jail, partly because Anderson had deliriously flipped out in the harsh jail conditions. Walker needed a quick settlement; otherwise it would come out that King did not intend to stay in jail. City officials were eager to cut a deal that got King and other protesters out of jail without conceding anything concerning segregation. They cut that deal with Albany movement lawyer C. B. King and SNCC lawyer Donald Hollowell, and King was released after forty-eight hours in jail with a postponed trial date of sixty days.[125]

King told a cheering crowd they had won a huge victory that "thoroughly integrated" the bus and rail terminals and established a biracial commission to address segregation elsewhere. This boast was swiftly refuted, and the ridicule was ferocious. The *New York Herald Tribune* called the Albany truce a devastating and stunning defeat for King. The NAACP provided inside dope for reporters along this line, playing up the ambulance-chasing motif. Wilkins said that SCLC was competent only at causing turmoil and had birthed an out-of-control youth organization that was even worse. SNCC leaders told reporters anonymously that they were the responsible activists, whereas King flew around the country to heighten his fame while shirking his jail time. These scathing critiques brought unprecedented attention to SNCC, which became habituated to its insulting two-sided nickname for King, "De Lawd": King was pompous, and the church people who idolized him were submissive types. Few reporters pursued the irony that SNCC endorsed a weak settlement in Albany because it made King look bad. King, as usual, took his lumps and issued no recriminations. He told Belafonte that Walker and the students were not as alienated from each other as it looked. Walker told a different story, then and later. In his telling, SNCC routinely denigrated SCLC while taking advantage of King's charitable nature: "We should have won Albany and we could have won Albany but for the anxiety and the ambition of a Charlie Jones and the bitterness of an Ella Baker." SNCC manipulated city officials, Walker said, to win a "tribal" victory over SCLC.[126]

Albany dragged on for months of repetition and frustration. In July 1962 King tried to rally the protest movement, but federal judge Robert Elliott granted the city an injunction banning further marches, and King infuriated SNCC by canceling the planned marches. King argued that the movement should not defy court orders it disliked since the federal judiciary was the branch of government most supportive of civil rights. SNCC replied that King was an autocrat who no longer even made sense. Elliott's injunction was subsequently reversed, King went to jail briefly, and SNCC kept picketing; at one point SNCC had twenty field secretaries in jail. But the protests ran out of steam, and segregationists won the battle of nerves. Pritchett crowed that Albany set back the cause of integration by ten years. Movement historians Vincent Harding and Staughton Lynd said that King was too averse to being jailed and too above-it-all as a media star. King vowed to stop being a firefighter. SCLC needed to be a different kind of organization, he said—which it was becoming.[127]

In the Kennedy years SCLC no longer lived off King's fame alone. The state of Tennessee maliciously shut down the Highlander School, which put Septima Clark's citizenship training school out of business, but newcomer Andrew Young saved the citizenship school and created a job for himself by brokering a three-way deal among the Field Foundation, the United Church of Christ, and SCLC. The citizenship school moved to the SCLC office in Atlanta, where it soon possessed Voter Education Project grants. Meanwhile Levison and Jack O'Dell built a direct mail operation at the New York office. O'Dell, an autodidactic intellectual raised by his working-class black grandparents in Detroit, was a former organizer for the National Maritime Union, the first sea-workers' union to break the color line. He was a Communist in the 1940s and was purged from the union in 1950. He found a job in the insurance business, using his aptitude for numbers, and worked for Rustin on the 1959 Youth March for integrated schools. Through Rustin, O'Dell befriended Levison, who asked him to help promote the Sinatra–Davis benefit for SCLC at Carnegie Hall.

That got O'Dell into SCLC's New York office, where he and Levison built the fund-raising operation. It was so successful that King decided he needed O'Dell in both offices, raising money in New York and running voter registration in Atlanta. O'Dell commuted between the two cities and became indispensable to King, supervising more SCLC workers than Walker. On the side, he gave riveting lectures on African American history at citizenship school sessions sponsored by Clark and Young. O'Dell told King he was not a Communist; he was a Marxian Socialist with Communist friends, and he made no apology for his Communist past. O'Dell wanted King to say it forthrightly. Instead King dissembled in October 1962, claiming that O'Dell was "purely a technician" in the New York office and no longer worked in the Atlanta office; he barely knew the guy. These misrepresentations strengthened J. Edgar Hoover's hand in obtaining special leeway from the Justice Department. Hoover tracked Levison with four wiretaps and admonished RFK that King lied about O'Dell. To Hoover, King was nothing like the leader of America's greatest freedom movement. He was an enemy who plotted against the United States with two Soviet agents.[128]

TO BIRMINGHAM

King came out of Albany vowing that his next campaign would build from the ground up. Birmingham was the obvious choice. SNCC had no projects in Birmingham, the outlawed NAACP was not a factor in Alabama, Shuttlesworth had ministered in Birmingham from 1953 to 1961, and SCLC had its strongest affiliate in Birmingham, the Alabama Christian Movement for Human Rights (ACMHR). Shuttlesworth founded ACMHR in 1956, the same year that Bull Connor regained his position as commissioner of public safety. King believed, wrongly, that Shuttlesworth had a following among Birmingham ministers. Shuttlesworth was too autocratic and out-there for that, but the ministers admired his fearless eight-year track record in one of America's meanest cities. *New York Times* journalist Harrison Salisbury, in a vivid passage that yielded a lawsuit, described Birmingham as a racist tyranny: "Every channel of communication, every medium of mutual interest, every reasoned approach, every inch of middle ground has been fragmented by the emotional dynamite of racism, enforced by the whip, the razor, the gun, the bomb, the torch, the club, the knife, the mob, the police and many branches of the state's apparatus."[129]

Birmingham had to be done quietly, in tightfisted fashion, so King excluded the chatty, argumentative SCLC board. He started with Shuttlesworth, Walker, and Lowery plus three top SCLC officers from Atlanta: Abernathy, Andrew Young, and education director Dorothy Cotton. He added only a few others after Walker developed a plan of action: Bevel, O'Dell, Levison, Fred Bennett, and two ACMHR leaders, Edward Gardner and Abraham Woods. The opposition would be ruthless and King had to ward off infiltrators. He wanted to strike at Birmingham's Christmas trade, building on a boycott recently organized by students at nearby Miles College, but white business leaders came running to Shuttlesworth, agreeing to desegregate the water fountains and bathrooms in five downtown stores. To Shuttlesworth, a year after he took exile in Cincinnati, this victory was sweet and unprecedented. It was also short-lived, as Connor threatened to prosecute the stores, and segregation was reasserted. King's group worked quietly with ACMHR to strike at the Easter shopping season, reluctantly delaying the boycott after Birmingham's first mayoral election required a runoff. Walker, chastened by the overreach in Albany, vowed to focus the campaign on lunch counters and a boycott of downtown stores. If they could crack Birmingham, they could win anywhere. But failure in Birmingham would be a catastrophe.

The protest began on April 3 with twenty well-dressed sit-inners, one day after conventional segregationist Albert Boutwell defeated Connor in a mayoral runoff. Most Birmingham blacks were surprised and puzzled by King's timing, and many were appalled. Striking immediately after Connor's defeat seemed churlish, especially because Birmingham was making the transition to a mayoral system. The national media resoundingly shared that view, in contrast to the positive coverage that Montgomery received, which threw King on the defensive. Birmingham's black weekly dismissed King as a celebrity who did not live in Birmingham and Shuttlesworth as an irresponsible crank who no longer lived in Birmingham. Black ministers who had not been consulted in the first place were averse to letting King get them in trouble, and many had tired of Shuttlesworth years before. Everywhere King spoke he had to address the "outside agitator" issue and explain why he had not waited a bit longer. ACMHR was not an outside group, he said, and he had postponed Birmingham twice. These arguments cut little ice in Birmingham, which evoked King's edgy sarcasm when he wrote "A Letter from Birmingham City Jail."

King thought he had 250 volunteers ready to get arrested, but only 70 showed up. He tried to fill the jails with sit-ins at lunch counters, but only 35 protesters got arrested in the first three days. The protest in tiny Albany had put almost 300 protesters in jail on the first day; in Birmingham it took a week to get 140. King tried to light a fire at the mass meetings, putting off getting arrested. The boycott went better, and people turned out to watch the marches and attend the mass meetings. But the marches averaged 14 marchers, and King had to beg every night for new protesters. Sometimes he failed to persuade a dozen to get arrested. Always he implored audiences to see that the waiting argument was ludicrous. Black Americans had waited hundreds of years to be treated decently. Nothing would change in Birmingham if blacks waited for a new mayor to make one or two adjustments. In the early going Connor followed the Pritchett playbook, swiftly dispatching protesters to jail. King exhorted black audiences with the same arguments that he famously pressed a week later to white moderates and church leaders, later recalling, "Somehow God gave me the power to transform the resentments, the suspicions, the fears and the misunderstanding I found that week into faith and enthusiasm."[130]

On April 10 he caught a break when Connor obtained a state circuit court injunction banning further demonstrations. King's group had already talked it through and agreed to defy the injunction. The ridicule from the Albany fiasco was a factor; plus, Alabama courts were notorious for sitting on abusive injunctions for two or three years. The courts destroyed the protest movement in Talladega and got the NAACP barred from the entire state. King decided it was time to make some history in a state that routinely abused the judicial process. The prospect of defying an injunction both exhilarated and frightened him. Then he learned the bail fund had run out.

He held a grim meeting in which everyone said he had to raise a bundle of money, not go to jail. King went off by himself to decide—"I was standing at the center of all that my life had brought me to be." He felt compelled to risk everything by going to jail. He got arrested with Abernathy and spent the first day in solitary confinement, where he agonized at not knowing if his arrest would be catalyzing or a disaster. A phone call from President Kennedy got him out of solitary confinement, and Kennedy also called Coretta King. The latter call was deeply gratifying to King. Belafonte replenished the bail fund, while Clarence Jones made lawyerly visits. King had time on his hands and a swirl of arguments in his head. His recent sermons had wielded a sharp edge, criticizing ministers for caring about the wrong things. He gave black church and white church versions of the same accusatory lament. In Birmingham city jail King read a typically nauseating "Call to Unity" from eight local white clergy. The seven ministers and one rabbi bemoaned that King had been hasty and imprudent, he was an outsider anyway, it was best to fight segregation in the courts and electoral process, it was wrong to fight segregation in the streets, and now Birmingham was filled with unnecessary and harmful tension.[131]

King began to scrawl a response in the margins of the newspaper. *New York Times Magazine* editor Harvey Shapiro had urged King to write a prison letter during the Albany campaign, but King got out of jail, and Albany went badly. Then he had months to think about it, while critics piled on about Albany. King seized the chance to write a prison letter. The ministers provided a perfect foil for him, both personally and ideologically. King had been expounding on these themes for weeks, and the frustration of seeing the same lame arguments paraded as wisdom got to him. He rarely replied to criticism, as he rarely had time or inclination. Now he had both, and he sort-of respected the so-called unity callers, who numbered five bishops among them. King explained that he was in Birmingham because SCLC had an affiliate in Birmingham, injustice existed there, the Hebrew prophets ranged far beyond their hometowns to call for justice, and Paul carried the gospel of Jesus "to the far corners of the Greco-Roman world." Moreover, the very idea of an "outside agitator" was provincial and outdated; caring about injustice in Birmingham was not optional for him. King's first poster slogan in "Letter from Birmingham City Jail" was about the "network of mutuality" binding all people and things to each other: "Injustice anywhere is a threat to justice everywhere."[132]

King swatted away the ministers' dichotomy between negotiation and direct action, observing that direct action was about creating genuine negotiations. He cited the historical record and Reinhold Niebuhr: Gains in civil rights occurred only through pressure, and groups were more immoral than individuals: "We know through painful experience that freedom is never voluntarily given by the oppressor; it must be demanded by the oppressed." Somehow every campaign for racial justice was said to be hasty and impudent; thus justice delayed became justice denied. King grasped why white Americans did not perceive the urgency of abolishing racism. He went on a spectacular rhetorical run, fashioning a single sentence that got rolling on "when you have seen" and carried on for a page and a half: "When you have seen vicious mobs lynch your mothers and fathers at will and drown your sisters and brothers at whim; when you have seen hate-filled policemen curse, kick and even kill your black brothers and sisters; when you see the vast majority of your twenty million Negro brothers smothering in an airtight cage of poverty in the midst of an affluent society. . . ." He continued with images of children recognizing racism for the first time, being assaulted and wounded by it, acquiring the N-word as one's first name, never hearing one's mother or wife called "Mrs.," never knowing what to expect, and "forever fighting a degenerating sense of 'nobodiness.' "[133]

The ministers grieved that King-style protest broke laws and thus fostered disrespect for law. King replied that the civil rights movement deeply respected and supported just laws, as defined by Thomas Aquinas: laws rooted in eternal law and natural law. Any law that uplifted human personality was just, King argued. He probably considered a gloss on Brightman's moral laws of altruism and personality but cut straight to a shining example of just law, the *Brown* decision. Then he turned it over: Any law that degraded human dignity was unjust and thus undeserving of respect or support. Every segregation ordinance was an example of unjust law: "Segregation distorts the soul and damages the personality. It gives the segregator a false sense of superiority and the segregated a false sense of inferiority." King said that nonviolent resisters, by willingly accepting the legal penalties for breaking unjust laws, demonstrated "the highest respect for law." It pained him to have to spell this out to white moderates, who prized order higher than justice and who thus chastised King for causing trouble. King did not want to believe that white moderates were the chief enemy of the civil rights movement. So many had assured him privately of their sympathy for his goals. But he told Birmingham's white religious leaders that they epitomized the problem. It was painfully superficial of them to harp on King instigating violence because King merely brought the submerged violence of Jim Crow to the surface. These white clergy were the very people who should have explained the difference to white audiences. They accused King of extremism, and he replied that they needed to learn about black nationalism.[134]

There were two dominant opposing forces in black American life, King explained. One was the party of complacency, consisting mostly of the beaten-down and defeated plus a smattering of middle-class blacks who benefited from segregation. Black nationalists constituted the other force, which he called "one of bitterness and hatred," with a predisposition to violence. The very idea of the civil rights movement was to forge a church-based alternative to complacent despair and hateful despair. Put differently, King said, it was to provide a constructive, peaceable, Christian alternative to the "frightening racial nightmare" of black nationalism. If white moderates thought that King was extreme, they needed to get a clue. Black Americans had many grievances of long standing which had to find an outlet: "So let him march; let him make prayer pilgrimages to the city hall; let him go on freedom rides—and try to understand why he must do so." Black Americans were overdue to be allowed to vent their frustrations without setting off white anger.[135]

King mocked the phony moderation of his white critics, yet he posed as a moderate alternative to nationalist rage. Always he sought to be militant in a moderate way, whatever that meant in different contexts. In the mass meetings King was scathing about the brutality and barbarity of white oppression. In the prison letter he put it more puckishly, confessing that he got more comfortable with the extremist tag the more he thought about it because all his heroes were extremists. Jesus was an extremist for love; Amos was an extremist for justice; Paul was an extremist for the Christian gospel; even Thomas Jefferson and Abraham Lincoln were extremists in their contexts. King was an extremist like that—for love, justice, the gospel, and freedom. How could white southerners not see it? A few did, he allowed. There were noble white southern writers such as Lillian Smith, Ralph McGill, and Ann Braden, and some white southerners had been jailed with blacks "in filthy, roach-infested jails, suffering the abuse and brutality of policemen who viewed them as 'dirty nigger-lovers.' " But most white churches and political moderates were far from righteous. King longed to hear white ministers tell their congregations to abolish segregation "because integration is morally right and the Negro is your brother." Instead, most ministers said the church had no business preaching about social issues. King struggled to fathom how they could say it. How could they treat black people despicably and then prattle about Jesus? He shook his head in wonder when he saw a big white church: "What kind of people worship here? Who is their God?"[136]

King wrote the letter for the *New York Times Magazine,* but Shapiro's bosses didn't want it after the *New York Post Sunday Magazine* ran bootlegged excerpts without permission in May. The following month *Liberation* and the *Christian Century* published authorized versions, and in July the *Atlantic Monthly* launched the letter into its career as a famous King classic. Walker thrilled that King unleashed his scorn in the letter, which Walker transcribed during the wee hours while King was in jail. But the early reaction was weak and nonplussed. Clarence Jones worried that King had zoomed into irrelevant theology-land, and journalists viewed the letter as a rambling sermon lacking anything newsworthy.[137]

King was released on bail on April 20 after eight days in jail and convicted on April 26 of criminal contempt (unlawfully parading), which carried a penalty of five days and allowed twenty days to file an appeal. A conviction for civil contempt would have carried an indefinite sentence, but the court wanted to keep King out of jail. The protest was sputtering anyway and the journalists were leaving. One problem was that only 25 of the area's 225 black ministers supported the protest, but King had already tried to rally the ministers. Upon leaving jail he vowed to energize the movement by enlisting teenagers and young adults to it.

Bevel was the key to the coming of the children. Theatrical, hyperkinetic, and voluble, Bevel was the wild man of SNCC and then of SCLC, which he joined in 1962. He wore a yarmulke in homage to the Hebrew prophets and shaved his head so it wouldn't fall off. He combined Gandhi with radical Christian Socialism and Hebrew prophecy, prizing the five hand-knitted yarmulkes that his friend Candie Carawan gave him. In the summer of 1961 Bevel had gone straight from Parchman prison to the streets of Jackson, teaming with Lafayette to get a movement going. He was a magnet for youngsters, and he noticed that the youngest youth were the least fearful. In the fall of 1961 Bevel married Nash, confounding many activists who believed they better deserved her. Each was attracted to the intense brilliance of the other, though Bevel believed in free love, especially for himself, which doomed the marriage. In Birmingham Bevel conducted after-school workshops in churches. Young, Bernard Lee, and Dorothy Cotton fanned out to local schools, inviting students to the workshops. King worried about Bevel's appeal to youngsters, noting that Bevel had at least eighty counts pending against him in Jackson for exploiting minors. Bevel said that was exactly the problem; he hadn't reached enough young people. Had he recruited eighty thousand, nobody would have dragged him to court. Then as later King resisted Bevel's penchant for declaiming in absolutes, but Bevel got to him.

Bevel enthralled huge gatherings, telling students that segregation was a "water tower" standing on four legs: political disenfranchisement, economic deprivation, alienation from God, and lack of educational opportunity. Soon the workshops were bigger than the mass meetings. Youngsters poured into the mass meetings, too, but King balked at sending them into the streets. National press coverage was beginning to swing in favor of the protest. King knew he would be excoriated if he put children in danger, and he recoiled at doing so. But he also vowed to do something dramatic to rekindle press attention. He said it so bluntly that a local minister, John Thomas Porter, took offense, fearing that a spiritual movement had veered into something crassly political. At the end of April King left Bevel in charge in Birmingham while King, Abernathy, Shuttlesworth, and Walker attended an SCLC board meeting in Memphis. King was still waffling on filling the jails with children, but he authorized Bevel to convene a mass gathering of schoolchildren at noon on Thursday, May 2. That gave Bevel just enough time and leverage to organize a game-changer on his own, a spectacular children's march.[138]

Bevel called it "D Day," a gusher of marching children. The SCLC headliners returned on May 1 to learn that D Day was ready to roll. Walker was enraged at Bevel's insubordination, but King commended Bevel for acting boldly, and Walker came around, conceding that Bevel made a shrewd move. Walker later recalled, "We had run out of troops. We had scraped the bottom of the barrel of adults who could go." At the mass meeting on May 1 King said nothing about the explosion to come, but one of Bevel's young warriors, William "Meatball" Dothard, announced dramatically, "Tomorrow students are gonna show you old folks what you should have done forty years ago. They're gonna make you ashamed to see that they have to go through what you should have gone through earlier for them, to make their life better." Bevel and Walker worked together to pull it off. The following day, May 2, approximately one thousand students walked out of school, converged at Sixteenth Street Baptist Church, and marched toward city hall in waves of fifty students walking two abreast. They sang and laughed and clapped in high spirits, singing "Ain't Gonna Let Nobody Turn Me Around." They sang the usually dirge-like "We Shall Overcome" with buoyant, up-tempo bravado. They made a stunning sight, bewildering Connor on the first day. Over six hundred got arrested, and some were eight or nine years old. King emoted that he had never seen anything like it. He especially loved that the children sang the freedom songs with gusto and conviction. Finally he had filled the jails, after two years of trying. Jails built for eight people were stuffed with up to eighty youngsters. King did not say that he agonized over the decision to send the children; he said that any child old enough to accept Jesus was old enough to get arrested.[139]

The coming of the children electrified the Birmingham protest. Day two of the children's march brought out Connor's police dogs and fire hoses, just as King and Walker had hoped. There was no place to put new arrestees, so Connor tried to prevent demonstrators from entering the downtown business section without making arrests. He pummeled demonstrators with monitor-gunned water blasts and deployed eight police units armed with German shep-herds. The dogs lunged at the milling crowds, hospitalizing three teenagers with bites. The photos were dramatic, especially an Associated Press photo of a young bystander, Walter Gadsden, being grabbed by a police officer and dog-bitten in the abdomen. Walker had prayed that Connor would attack the chil-dren. He and Bevel provoked the police into lashing out, sometimes telling King about their tactics and sometimes not. Later Walker recalled, "Birmingham would have been lost if Bull had let us go down to the City Hall and pray; if he had let us do that and stepped aside, what else would be new? There would be no movement, no publicity. But all he could see was stopping us before we got there. We had calculated for the stupidity of a Bull Connor." Insiders debated whether Connor lost his head or shrewdly played to his segregationist base; Walker took the latter view: "He was a perfect adversary. Connor wanted publicity, he wanted his name in the paper. He believed that he would be the state's most popular politician if he treated the black violently, bloodily, and sternly. We knew that the psyche of the white redneck was such that he would inevitably do something to help our cause."[140]

The preachers poured it on at the mass meetings, which suddenly packed four churches. King ridiculed Connor for believing he could subdue black Baptists with water hoses. As for dogs, "Well, I'll tell you. When I was growing up, I was dog bitten"—dramatic pause—"for NOTHING! So I don't mind being bitten by a dog for standing up for freedom!" King waved off critics who censured him for exposing children to danger. Where was this tender solicitude when the children were brutalized by racism? A few dog bites didn't compare to millions of battered psyches and blighted lives. King's mood turned angry and scathing when he reflected on the depraved brutality of the police: "Let's let them get their dogs and let them get their hoses, and we'll leave them covered with their own barbarity. We will leave them standing before their God and the world splattered with the blood and reeking with the stench of our Negro brothers." That was an echo of "Who is their God?" King moved from the unfathomable barbarity of the white establishment to the movement's prosaic four demands: desegregation of stores and facilities, employment reform, dismissal of charges, and a biracial committee to negotiate total desegregation. He announced that the jail marches would go on, bigger than ever, which got a thunderous ovation. He dared to wait until the end to address the parents of the children in jail, declaring simply, "Don't worry about them. They are suffering for what they believe, and they are suffering to make this nation a better nation."[141]

President Kennedy was among the millions who were repulsed by the Gadsden photograph. JFK sent Assistant Attorney General Burke Marshall to Birmingham, and activists poured in from across the nation. Money poured in, too, as black churches took up special collections for Birmingham. Connor filled the state fairgrounds with arrestees, and Kelly Ingram Park became a site of guerrilla skirmishes between Walker/Bevel and Connor, which led to clashes between Walker and Bevel about who had greater authority to make decisions. To Walker, Bevel was a usurping newcomer. King implored his fiery aides to calm down and work together. In Albany he had aimed the marches at politicians, who did not need black votes. In Birmingham he aimed the marches at merchants, who needed black customers. King was eager to cut a deal with business leaders, from a position of strength, which the children gave him. By Monday, May 6, the schools were nearly empty. That day another one thousand demonstrators got arrested, and more than half were adults, some accompanied by their children. For four days Birmingham blacks had watched their children take the lead. Then they turned out for the largest single day of nonviolent arrests in American history, in a grimly determined mood.[142]

Abernathy lightened the mood that night at the mass meetings, comically jeering Connor and telling listeners not to worry about dying in Connor's jail or jail yard. More people died in bed than anywhere else, yet people crawled into one every night. King gave one of his talks about *eros*, *philia*, and *agape*, and Abernathy couldn't resist taking another turn, now spoofing King's high-minded seminary talk about "love that *moves ya*." The audience roared with delight at Abernathy's sexual innuendo; meanwhile King could feel the breakthrough coming. He recruited in the juke joints and pool halls, declaring that he *believed* in nonviolence as a creed, but they needed to know that nonviolence *worked* like nothing else. Sometimes he noted pointedly that most Birmingham whites had not rallied to Connor's side. A year earlier, Connor would not have had to do the dirty work. Now the white majority was acting neutral, and to King's astonishment, nobody shopped downtown. The business district resembled a ghost town. King and Walker had not dreamed that whites would boycott the stores, but it was happening, which pressured Birmingham's "Big Mules"—the very conservative business leaders who comprised the semisecret Senior Citizens Committee—to bargain with Marshall. King told a news conference at the Gaston Motel that Birmingham marked the nonviolent movement's coming of age.[143]

A complete victory for nonviolence seemed to be within reach, but King was losing control of the movement as he spoke, and the white backlash had not yet struck. Hundreds of newcomers and others untrained in nonviolence ran wild in Birmingham, daring police to chase them down. Walker accused Bevel of stoking chaos, and Shuttlesworth told King that an aggressive push into the business district might break the city's will. Walker cleared a path for a downtown march by setting off false fire alarms in distant corners of the city, without telling King. He also blew on high-pitched dog whistles. Shuttlesworth tried to lead a group of children downtown, but firefighters slammed him against Sixteenth Street Baptist Church with a monitor gun, blasting him until he collapsed from the pounding. An ambulance took Shuttlesworth to the hospital; Connor loudly regretted it was not a hearse. Glenn Evans, commander of Birmingham's uniform patrol division, witnessed the attack on Shuttlesworth and later recalled having thought, "What does this accomplish? What do we *hope* to do here by doing these kinds of things? How stupid can you be?"[144]

Evans viewed himself as a moderating figure, as did Birmingham police chief Jamie Moore, an officer in the Pritchett mold. For that matter, Connor viewed himself as a restrained alternative to Governor George Wallace's state troopers. Wallace had a thuggish highway patrol leader, Al Lingo, who had a roster of notoriously violent troopers. Though Connor was a strong ally of Lingo's, he knew that much of his department despised Lingo. Thus keeping the state troopers out of Birmingham was essential to Connor. Evans shook his head at the bottom-feeding illiterates Lingo hired: "Sorriest individuals that's ever been employed by the State of Alabama, he brought in. Wasn't fit to be highway patrolmen." But even Lingo said he was the real peacekeeper, as his troops were Alabama's last line of defense against the Klan and civil rights protesters. Every player in this picture, except the Klan leaders, boasted of limiting the death toll in Birmingham.[145]

As it was, King called on JFK to help, and Marshall pressed local bigwigs on both sides to settle. The key negotiators on the black side were motel owner A. G. Gaston, Miles College president L. H. Pitts, and lawyer Arthur Shores. On the Mule side, only businessman Sidney Smyer publicly acknowledged his role. On May 8 the negotiators struck a deal. The following day they sold it to reluctant politicians: a truce based on immediately desegregated dressing rooms, desegregated lunch counters within sixty days, and vagueness on everything else. The Big Mules despised King and refused to deal with him, but there was no deal without his approval, so they asked and he gave it. Shuttlesworth, already angry that King didn't visit him in the hospital, erupted at learning of the truce. It was pointless to scald a hog on one side, he railed; Connor had to be scalded on both sides to get clean. Shuttlesworth bolted from the hospital to the home of John Drew, where King was staying, and blistered King furiously in front of Abernathy, Marshall, Walker, Young, and others.

Everything about the truce offended Shuttlesworth: the deal itself, trusting white merchants, being ignored, King's presumption in making promises, and the fact that King and Kennedy had press conferences scheduled. Shuttlesworth said he had indulged King's prima donna lifestyle and chasing after the media spotlight, but look where that led! "You're in a hell of a fix, young man." An aide reminded King of the press conference, and Shuttlesworth erupted again. He would not obey King's truce, attend King's press conference, or shut up: "You're Mister Big but you're soon to be Mister Nothing." King reeled at the onslaught, pleading with Shuttlesworth not to walk out. To Marshall, King declared plaintively that they had to have unity. The appeal to unity just made Shuttlesworth madder, since it made him the problem. He lashed at King: "I'll be damned if you'll have it like this! You're Mr. Big, but you're going to be Mister S-H-I-T!" According to Abernathy, Shuttlesworth called King "a coward and a double-crosser." King made no attempt to defend himself, at least in front of others. He realized that the press conference especially offended Shuttlesworth. Nearly two hundred reporters were on hand, and most knew little or nothing about Shuttlesworth. King took Shuttlesworth to a back room, talked him down privately, and emerged with a smiling Shuttlesworth, although Young said it was a phone call from Robert Kennedy that "soothed his wounded ego, and saved me from punching him out." Young's patience was exhausted, "and I had none left for Fred." At the press conference Shuttlesworth announced that Birmingham had "reached an accord with its conscience." Then he collapsed from his wounds and exhaustion, while JFK gave the first press conference of his presidency dominated by the subject of race.[146]

The deal that King took was weak and trusting, winning only "the promise of concessions," as the *New York Times* put it, although King called it a great victory. Meanwhile it was backlash time in Alabama. Wallace announced that he was bound by no ostensible agreement to compromise segregation. A huge Klan rally in nearby Bessemer, featuring Imperial Wizard Bobby Shelton, condemned the "atheist so-called ministers of the nigger race" and pledged to protect segregation in Alabama. Alabama newspapers accused King of inciting riots in the name of phony justice. Connor jacked up the bonds for convicted marchers to $2,500 per person, which hauled King back to jail just after his rosy press conference, but King had second thoughts about returning to jail and paid the bail for himself and Abernathy. King's brother A.D., now a pastor in nearby Ensley, condemned the bond extortion and called for new demonstrations. All of this was on May 11. That night the Klan destroyed A.D.'s parsonage with two bombs while he was at home with his wife and five children. An anxious crowd came running to the parsonage, finding that no one had been injured. A.D. pleaded with his neighbors to keep calm. He was still pleading when another powerful explosion several miles away rocked the area. The crowd in Ensley, climbing to over two thousand people, rightly guessed the second target: King's room at the Gaston Motel. A.D. persuaded the crowd to go home quietly, at 1:30 a.m., and he headed for the Gaston Motel.[147]

For most of the evening Lingo and his troops had blanketed the area near the motel. They vanished just before a bomb ripped through the suite previously occupied by King and Abernathy. Abernathy had given the key to Lowery, but Lowery took the night train to Nashville. An angry crowd surged to the motel. Walker and other staffers worked hard at calming the crowd, assuring that King had returned to Atlanta and no one was hurt. Fighting broke out between the crowds and police, cars were set afire, and Lingo stormed in with 250 state troopers and irregular volunteers. Moore urged Lingo to leave, but Lingo's troops charged through the motel and down the street, busting the heads of any blacks they came across. A full-scale riot of brick throwing, torched buildings, and billy club smashing ensued. Several houses and six businesses were burned to the ground, and dozens of cars were destroyed. Walker found his wife, Ann, crumpled on the motel floor, bashed by a trooper's rifle butt. Later that night Walker was beaten after he visited Ann in the hospital. A.D. intervened in Kelly Ingram Park, telling crowds that if he could remain peaceful, they could. Lingo's rampage marked a new low in thuggish wilding. The next morning Robert Kennedy informed his brother that Wallace had taken over the state and everything was at stake in Birmingham. The president needed to show black Americans that "the federal government is their friend." JFK agreed, vowing to save the Birmingham accord. That night he gave a nationwide television address announcing that he would not allow the Birmingham settlement to be sabotaged by violence. He federalized the Alabama National Guard to block Wallace from using it and moved U.S. Army troops near Birmingham.[148]

JFK feared a bloodbath above all, and so did King. The federal government had never previously used military force to quell civil unrest lacking a specific legal injunction to enforce. Kennedy's threat to intervene held the state troopers in check, and the federal courts threw out Birmingham's expulsions of the student protesters. Birmingham became the template for direct action campaigns, despite all that went wrong. King overestimated Shuttlesworth's influence, Miles College did not come through, most black ministers never came around, and insiders complained that King still wavered far too much. King struck movement lawyer William Kunstler as "the most indecisive man I've ever seen. He really had trouble being decisive." Young put it more sympathetically, explaining that King made decisions "in an extremely circuitous way." That being the case, all they could do was wait for him to come around. But King surrounded himself with fiery commanders because he shrewdly grasped their value to him. Three of them made history in Birmingham: Bevel, Shuttlesworth, and Walker. Birmingham was Walker's zenith, where he discovered that filling the jails was not the ideal that he and King had thought. Merely drawing out crowds of bystanders could be equally effective. Reporters judged the success of a demonstration by the size of the crowd, and a thuggish adversary could be enticed to attack the crowd. Reaching City Hall was not the point or even desirable. It was better to win news coverage by being blocked. Walker put it boastfully: "There never was any more skillful manipulation of the news media than there was in Birmingham."[149]

Birmingham smashed the Jim Crow myth that black Americans would not fight for their freedom. It sparked over one thousand demonstrations with more than twenty thousand arrests in the summer of 1963 alone. And it led directly to the civil rights bill that Kennedy proposed a month after Birmingham, using moral arguments that didn't sound like Kennedy, which he cribbed from King. Journalist Diane McWhorter, in her sparkling memoir of the passing of "Our Way of Life" in her Birmingham hometown, remarked that the spectacle of Birmingham "seemed to belong in the Old Testament rather than the American mid-century." Birmingham nationalized the movement, swinging public opinion in its favor. Historian Glenn Askew similarly judged that Birmingham "ended the stalemate in national race relations." Communication theorist Gary S. Selby stressed that King pulled it off by employing the march as the principal mode of protest. At Birmingham the movement seized on a public ritual that bodily performed the Exodus myth of the Bible while singing the freedom songs of African American experience.[150]

King's creative reenactment of Exodus freedom marching yielded a triply ironic victory for nonviolence. He and Walker baited white violence with Gandhian moral cunning. Second, the riot of May 11 that King and Walker struggled so strenuously to avert played a role in winning the overt backing of the federal government. Third, this backing consisted of a threat of massive violence. Birmingham's historic victory for nonviolence rested on layers of covert, waged, and threatened violence, exactly as King understood after years of grappling with Niebuhr. Young later recalled that he and King routinely asked each other what Niebuhr would say when they plotted tactics and strategy. Always they remembered what Niebuhr said in *Moral Man and Immoral Society*: "The differences between violent and non-violent methods of coercion and resistance are not so absolute that it would be possible to regard violence as a morally impossible instrument of social change." Nonviolent resistance is a type of coercion, albeit one offering "the largest opportunities for harmonious relationship with the moral and rational factors in social life."[151]

King believed, with Niebuhr, in wringing as much as possible out of nonviolent coercion in fighting oppressors. But Niebuhr's dialectical spinning mattered less than King's persistent spiritual sincerity in preaching "Love your enemies." King was fully versed in the Niebuhrian ironies of nonviolence *and* fully convinced that violence is never redemptive. Otherwise he would not have identified with Gandhi so insistently. Otherwise he would not have been able to pull off a historic victory for nonviolence in arguably the nation's most violent city, where every black family was well armed, every white family was well armed, and the white majority deeply resented the coming of the SCLC. The sheer relentless preaching of "love your enemies," night after night in the mass meetings, won Birmingham's victory for nonviolence. King insisted tirelessly that redemptive *agape* was the guiding ideal of the movement. Bevel admonished that the protest would be ruined if a single police officer were maimed or killed. Demonstrators were required to surrender their weapons before entering the streets. King's aim was to provoke drama, not bloodshed. He was sincere about not inflicting violence despite being accused of it constantly.

Something novel erupted in northern cities after Birmingham: white mass rallies for civil rights. King encountered his first one on May 14, 1963, at St. Paul's Episcopal Church in Cleveland, after receiving a massive motorcade reception and posing with the Episcopal bishop of Ohio. He had five more overflow events in Cleveland before rushing off to similar treatment in Los Angeles, St. Louis, Chicago, New York, and Detroit. In Los Angeles he lit up a crowd of fifty thousand before heading to a glittering fund-raiser packed by Hollywood celebrities. In Chicago he headlined a gala extravaganza at McCormick Place featuring gospel queen Mahalia Jackson, blues queen Dinah Washington, and newcomer Aretha Franklin, not yet a crossover star. Where King lived, the only crossover celebrities were entertainers and sports stars. Now he became one, although not so much where he lived.

In Jackson, Mississippi, NAACP leader Medgar Evers got dragged into protests that his organization did not want but which he joined after six hundred

Jackson students got arrested and hauled to the state fairgrounds. The spirit of Birmingham was so powerful that even Wilkins got swept into a solidarity arrest in Jackson. On June 1 King shucked off indecisiveness, stunning Levison and Clarence Jones by telling them that he wanted a mass protest in Washington, DC. King pressured JFK every day on the stump, demanding an executive order against segregation. He knew that JFK and RFK were determined to get black protesters off the streets and were leaning toward a civil rights bill. He told aides that the president would probably propose a bill, which would probably fail, which would take JFK off the hook. What good was that? SCLC had to push for a civil rights bill whether or not Kennedy proposed one or at least for an executive order. On June 10, 1963, King announced that he was considering a march on Washington if the president did not come through on civil rights. The following morning Wallace barred the door at the University of Alabama, and that evening Kennedy proposed what became the Civil Rights Act of 1964.[152]

King was thrilled with JFK's speech, which settled the question of whether the March on Washington should be aimed at Kennedy or Congress. That night Evers was murdered outside his front door, and Jackson became the symbol of the struggle for racial democracy that Kennedy had just embraced. The Evers killing was interpreted as a political assassination, not a lynching. King learned of it while attending the Gandhi Society's first anniversary fundraiser. He and Mordecai Johnson announced that the Gandhi Society would establish a Medgar Evers Memorial Bail Fund to honor Evers. To Wilkins, this announcement was unspeakably obscene. As far as Wilkins was concerned, King had gotten Evers killed by whipping up protest fever in Birmingham; then King had the gall to raise bail funds for his organization off the memory of an NAACP martyr. Wilkins raged so vehemently against King that King nearly declined to attend the Evers funeral. He kept silent, trying not to exacerbate longtime tensions that had now erupted into an ugly public feud. Meanwhile Justice Department official John Doar dramatically held off a spontaneous funeral march that threatened to turn riotous, as King headed for the Jackson airport. King realized that no word from him would repair the rift between the NAACP and SCLC, but his aides believed he was long overdue to fight Wilkins.[153]

PURGING AND DREAMING

Robert Kennedy broke it to his brother that Wilkins really hated King. That complicated White House efforts to engage the civil rights movement. JFK settled on a three-step meeting on June 22 in which he met first with Wilkins, then with King, and then with a group of civil rights leaders. King came to the White House geared to make his pitch for a full-bore push for civil rights. Instead Marshall pulled him aside, telling King ominously that he had to get rid of Levison and O'Dell. The president was putting his political life on the line for civil rights, and he could not risk getting burned by King's Communist aides. King was incredulous, explaining that his friends had some Marxist beliefs, but Marshall cut him off. This was deadly serious business, and they knew the difference between Marxist intellectualism and being a paid agent of the Soviets. King disbelieved that his friends were Communist agents, so he was sent to Robert Kennedy, who made the same pitch. King asked for evidence, and Kennedy gave him the answer that worked for Hoover: The proof came from so high up in the machinery of American espionage that he could not discuss it. The attorney general saw that King was not convinced, so he had the president try.

JFK took King for a stroll in the Rose Garden and cautioned that King was "under very close surveillance." Merely to be told, by the president, was mind-boggling. What did it mean? Why was this conversation occurring in the Rose Garden? Was the president himself being bugged? King reeled at the thought, while Kennedy noted that conservatives in Congress were denouncing the March on Washington idea as a Communist ploy. Kennedy told King to cut loose from Levison and O'Dell because O'Dell was the "number five Communist in the United States," Levison's standing was too classified for details, and Levison had planted O'Dell in SCLC. King still didn't believe it, and Kennedy told him to consider the Profumo scandal in Britain. Prime Minister Harold Macmillan was loyal to his secretary of state, John Profumo, who had an affair with a prostitute who simultaneously romanced a Soviet diplomat. Now Macmillan was on the verge of losing his government because he stood by his aide. Kennedy told King they were in this together, and truth was only part of the equation. If King got shot down for having Communist aides, Kennedy would go down with him.[154]

In fact, except for Levison's past fund-raising for the Communist Party, Hoover had nothing on Levison and O'Dell, which he played to his advantage. The lack of evidence proved to Hoover that Levison and O'Dell were very high up in the Communist hierarchy. They were so high up that Hoover's spies had never met them! The Kennedys believed Hoover, and, more important, they feared him. JFK had to drop one of his mistresses, Judith Campbell, after Hoover warned that she also romanced mobster boss Sam Giancana. JFK also had to drop his favorite paramour, Ellen Rometsch, because Hoover suspected she was an East German spy. Hoover was annoying—JFK called him "that bastard. . . . He's the biggest bore"—but Hoover was not someone to offend. Kennedy lived in fear that Hoover would destroy him over the Rometsch affair. Meanwhile King had to weigh the sacrifice of his top aides against the extraordinary urging of the president of the United States that his administration teetered on King's decision. It wasn't fair, but bigger things were at stake. Absorbing the heavy pressure from Marshall, RFK, and JFK, King made his way from the Rose Garden to the Cabinet Room, where the civil rights leaders gathered to discuss with JFK and Lyndon Johnson whether there should be a march on Washington. For two hours King let others do the talking, while Randolph and Farmer assured the president there would be a march. The only question was whether it would be nonviolent and well organized. Kennedy said good luck with that; they had their problems, and he had his.[155]

Aside from the Bonus March of May–July 1932, when jobless World War I veterans descended on the nation's capital and were routed in their tent encampments by the army, there had never been a mass march on Washington. Had Wilkins gotten his way there would have been no March on Washington in 1963. As it was, King and Randolph needed Wilkins after Randolph assured JFK there would be a very big march. A major planning meeting on July 2 in New York had fifteen organizers. Wilkins joined the group dramatically, walked around the room, and tapped nine people on the shoulder, telling them to leave. Among those tapped were Rustin, Shuttlesworth, Forman, and CORE program director Norman Hill. The cast-offs exited promptly, leaving Wilkins, Randolph, King, Farmer, Lewis, and Whitney Young, thereafter called the Big Six. Wilkins said he had time only for chiefs. More important, he was determined to put his stamp on the biggest demonstration ever. Randolph wanted Rustin to lead the march, and Wilkins flatly refused, as did Young. King and Farmer lauded Rustin's superior ability but agreed with Wilkins that Rustin was a political liability; King had not worked with Rustin since the Powell fiasco in 1960. Wilkins wanted Randolph to lead the march, who agreed to do it only if Rustin were his deputy. So Rustin made his movement comeback by running the demonstration of the century. Using donated offices in Harlem, Rustin appointed Tom Kahn as his chief lieutenant, put Rachelle Horowitz in charge of transportation coordination, appointed Norman Hill as director of field staff, and shook down the Big Six organizations plus FOR and Students for a Democratic Society (SDS) for staff support.[156]

Wilkins surprised everyone by campaigning agreeably with King, though he chided that King's method had not integrated a single classroom in Albany or Birmingham. King replied good-naturedly that at least he had desegregated a few hearts. Meanwhile King tried to finesse his situation with the White House and got burned by Hoover and Robert Kennedy. King grieved at axing O'Dell. He realized that this was how purges worked—Hoover was dismembering the movement by striking at King's most vulnerable aides, a mere beginning for Hoover. Since King was tied to the Kennedys, he reluctantly sacrificed O'Dell, who was on the payroll with two major jobs. Levison was not on the payroll, so King pretended to cut his ties with Levison without actually doing so. He communicated with Levison through intermediaries, especially Clarence Jones, who tried to glean from Marshall which phones were being tapped. Marshall told RFK that King was trying to have it both ways concerning Levison, and RFK erupted, ordering wiretaps on King and Jones. When the authorizations came for his signature RFK had second thoughts about tapping King, as he was defending King in public. So he added wiretaps on Jones to the taps on Levison, telling a crestfallen Hoover that that should be enough.

Until now the FBI had heard King's conversations only with Levison, which were strictly business and filled with moral seriousness. Between King and Levison there was no gossip, profanity, or sex talk. As Taylor Branch puts it, "They spoke as blood brothers in the rush of a great cause, too busy for foolishness." The new wiretaps revealed a gossipy, profane King bantering with Jones about King's sexual partners and what he really thought of various players. It turned out that King talked with his road buddies—Jones, Abernathy, Walker, Andrew Young, and Bernard Lee—very differently from the way he talked with Levison. With them he let loose, enjoying raunchy banter and declaring that he needed sexual relief from the tensions he lived under. But he also felt bad about his secret, which showed in his Pauline sermons about the temptations of the flesh. King's road buddies qualified for insider status by going easy on his chronic adultery, telling him not to feel so guilty about it. Usually they shielded the inside story from their own wives; Jones, for example, was married to book publisher heiress Ann Norton, who idolized King. She took it very hard when she learned about King's personal life.[57]

To Hoover, the new wiretaps yielded a godsend trove of ammunition. He had always despised King, but now he had proof that King was a hypocrite and "tom cat," as he wrote in a racy summary that rocketed through the FBI and Justice Department to the president. One tidbit zoomed straight to the Senate floor, via Hoover and Strom Thurmond. A friend knowingly fretted to King, "I hope Bayard don't take a drink before the march." King replied, "Yes, and grab one little brother. 'Cause he will grab one when he has a drink." Hoover overplayed his hand by feeding this exchange to Thurmond, an icon of Jim Crow. Thurmond denounced Rustin on the Senate floor as a sexual pervert, but Randolph defended Rustin in high-minded fashion, and the press did not pursue the story. Ironically, Thurmond aided Rustin's movement comeback. That unleashed Hoover to try harder and less obviously, while feeling relieved of any duty to prove his accusation that King was a Communist.[158]

The March on Washington of August 28, 1963, was a stunning feat of orchestration. Many warned of terrible violence, but Rustin avoided confrontations by recruiting his own police force of out-of-uniform black officers. The National Council of Churches (NCC) joined the demonstration, as did the United Auto Workers (UAW), Steelworkers, and Ladies' Garment Workers, although AFL-CIO chief George Meany refused to endorse it. More than a hundred buses per hour poured south through the Baltimore tunnel, transporting church groups and activists singing freedom songs. The short shrift given to Rosa Parks, Diane Nash Bevel, and Ella Baker flowed directly from the chiefs, who decided who was important. Rustin told every speaker to focus on Congress and to submit his text in advance. Every speaker did so except Lewis and King. Lewis wrote a call for social revolution with Sherman-like marching through Dixie, and King had no text until the morning of the march, as he lacked any time to think about what he wanted to say.

Lewis's text set off an uproar among the march organizers and speakers. Every speaker represented an organization, but SNCC was not like the UAW, the NCC, the Urban League, the NAACP, or the SCLC. Many protested that Lewis's speech was inflammatory, radical, divisive, and not like the others. It spoke of burning Jim Crow to the ground and tearing the South into a thousand pieces, albeit nonviolently. Patrick O'Boyle, Catholic archbishop of Washington, DC, announced that he would not deliver the invocation or sit on the platform if Lewis gave this speech. Lewis refused to change anything. Wilkins hotly accused Lewis of double-crossing the march organizers. Lewis replied that Wilkins had no idea what it was like to organize in the Delta and Black Belt, so he had no business talking down to SNCC. Former NCC president Eugene Carson Blake objected that "revolution" and "the masses" were Communist words. Randolph replied that these were good words, and Lewis had every right to use them. Blake countered that the section about marching like Sherman violated the spirit of the march, and King added that it didn't sound like Lewis. But it did sound like SNCC, as King knew. King mostly held back as others pressed the argument.[159]

The Lincoln Memorial and reflecting pool were jammed with over two hundred thousand people when Randolph got through to Lewis in a room beneath Lincoln's seat: This was a special day; Randolph had waited twenty-two years for it; please don't ruin it; they had to stick together. Lewis folded and rewrote, eliminating the Sherman and Dixie references, a caustic judgment about "cheap" politicians, and SNCC's opinion that the Kennedy bill was "too little and too late." The speech he gave still had radical fire that distinguished him from the others. Lewis spoke of living "in constant fear of a police state." He asked where the federal government had been while black Americans were oppressed and abused. He announced that SNCC supported the proposed civil rights bill only "with great reservations" because it was so limited. He noted that JFK's party had southern segregationists and New York Senator Jacob Javits's party had Barry Goldwater reactionaries, which raised a question: "Where is our party? Where is the political party that will make it unnecessary to have Marches on Washington?" He declared that the civil rights movement would march through Jackson, Danville, Birmingham, and the entire South "with the spirit of love and with the spirit of dignity that we have shown here today." Lewis was the only speaker to shun the word "Negro" and the only one to speak of "black citizens" and "the black masses."[160]

The three-hour program was running a half-hour ahead of schedule when it reached its emotional peak, Mahalia Jackson's riveting singing of "I Been 'Buked and I Been Scorned." One speaker later it was time for King, who wobbled slightly until he ad libbed a set piece ending. The previous week he had spoken to the National Insurance Association (NIA) in Chicago and given the black insurers some tough love before going visionary. The NIA had been good to SCLC, King allowed, but more was required. The insurers needed to share with black Americans more of the wealth that they acquired from black Americans, and they needed to get ready for integration, which would abolish their protected market. King exhorted the insurers not to sleep through the civil rights revolution. He had a dream that down in Birmingham, "white men and Negro men, white women and Negro women, will be able to walk together as brothers and sisters." He had preached this dream in various speeches since 1960 and given a version of it in Detroit in June 1963. In Chicago he gave a robust version of it and the crowd responded thunderously. A week later, assembling the biggest speech of his life a few hours before he gave it, King wanted to make his customary pitch for a Second Emancipation Proclamation. But that would have undermined the ostensible purpose of this gathering, so he started with the blander metaphor from his "Bad Check" speech, the idea of a "promissory note" contained in the Constitution and the Declaration of Independence. This note, King began, was the promise of the rights to life, liberty, and the pursuit of happiness. America, however, handed black Americans a bad check, which came back marked "insufficient funds."[161]

That was a middling start, just after ABC and NBC cut away from afternoon soap operas to show King's speech; only CBS offered continuous live coverage of the march program. King had six minutes left, with the nation watching. He made a turn with a favorite phrase, "the fierce urgency of now." Everything was at stake, and the movement had to unite on a narrow path of righteous militancy that would change America. This was no time for cooling off or for taking the "tranquilizing drug of gradualism." Neither was it a time for "bitterness and hatred" because the "marvelous new militancy" of the civil rights movement would be wasted if it led merely to Negroes hating whites. A clueless question, "When will you be satisfied?" got King going on a run. Black Americans would never be satisfied as long as they were victimized by "the unspeakable horrors of police brutality," refused lodging in highway motels, confined to ghettoes, and prohibited from voting. He paid tribute to the "veterans of creative suffering," urging protesters to stay strong in the faith that "unearned suffering is redemptive." He implored them to return to the sites of American oppression. The speech was good enough, but it did not sing or soar, and by then King had wandered hopelessly off his text, trying to soar with something. Several platform performers urged him onward, and Mahalia Jackson called out, "Tell them about the dream, Martin." That may have been the trigger, although King said only that he had forgotten the speech and seized on the first run of oratory that came to him.[162]

It was all dream from there onward, more than one-third of the signature speech of the civil rights movement. King's dream was "deeply rooted in the American dream that one day this nation will rise up and live out the true meaning of its creed—we hold these truths to be self-evident, that all men are created equal." He dreamed of the sons of former slaves and slave owners eating together "at the table of brotherhood" on the red hills of Georgia. He dreamed that Mississippi, "sweltering with the heat of oppression," would be "transformed into an oasis of freedom and justice." He dreamed that his four children "will one day live in a nation where they will not be judged by the color of their skin but by the content of their character." He dreamed that down in Alabama, "with its vicious racists," black boys and girls would be able to join hands with white boys and girls "as sisters and brothers." He tied this dream to the biblical vision of the glory of the Lord being revealed "and all flesh shall see it together." King had faith and hope that the dream would come true: "This is the faith that I go back to the South with. With this faith we will be able to hew out of the mountain of despair a stone of hope. With this faith we will be able to transform the jangling discords of our nation into a beautiful symphony of brotherhood." His long ending rang nine rounds of chimes on "Let Freedom Ring," the closing phrase of "My Country 'Tis of Thee." King called for freedom to ring from the hilltops of New Hampshire, the Alleghenies of Pennsylvania, and the Rockies of Colorado, and from Stone Mountain of Georgia and the hills of Mississippi: "When we allow freedom to ring, when we let it ring from every village and hamlet, from every state and city, we will be able to speed up that day when all of God's children—black men and white men, Jews and Gentiles, Catholics and Protestants—will be able to join hands and to sing in the words of the old Negro spiritual, 'Free at last, free at last, thank God Almighty, we are free at last.' "[163]

Coretta Scott King later recalled, "At that moment it seemed as if the Kingdom of God appeared. But it only lasted for a moment." Certainly it was a peak moment, a national marker ranking with Lincoln's Gettysburg Address. In movement terms it was the apotheosis of civil rights liberalism. Most of the speech was new to most of the nationwide audience that heard it. Most of the television audience had never heard King give a full speech, including President Kennedy. A tidal wave of praise and adulation fell on King. Thousands of movement veterans and millions of newcomers appreciated that he ended the biggest demonstration ever with a spellbinding appeal to the promise of America. Black newspapers lauded the speech resoundingly and with rare unanimity. White papers stressed that the march was enormous, peaceful, and climaxed with King, although the *Washington Post* missed the story, failing to mention King. The *New York Times* ran five march articles on page one and stated emphatically that "I Have a Dream" was the story. The speakers trooped to the White House, and King was showered with effusive gratitude along the way. King's powerful unscripted ending impressed JFK, who told an aide, "He's damn good." King, growing embarrassed, asked the president if he heard Walter Reuther's forceful speech; JFK replied that he had heard Reuther "plenty of times." Wilkins, Randolph, and Reuther seized the moment with the president, pressing him to fight for a strong civil rights bill. JFK said the vote looked close in the House and bad in the Senate; they needed a bipartisan consensus on civil rights, not a Democratic crusade. King asked if someone might enlist Eisenhower to help with that, although he didn't mean himself; he was in the wrong denomination for the job. That evoked hilarity in the Cabinet Room until Blake agreed to work on Eisenhower.[164]

King had modeled the narrow path of moral and inclusive militancy that he prescribed for the movement, and he was inundated with praise for getting it right. The March on Washington was about winning the nation's attention and mobilizing support for the civil rights bill. On these counts it was a smashing success. The demands were emphatically moderate, only prescribed picket signs were allowed, and longtime liberals experienced the day as one of triumph, vindication, and mobilization. Now came the messy, grinding, and very political work of pushing the bill through, work that veteran politicos presumed to own. The March on Washington marked the end of the phase in which white and black civil rights liberals set the agenda for how things should go. It started Rustin on the path from Old Left pacifist protester to the liberal Democratic Party mainstream. The program insulted every female leader in the movement, although Rosa Parks and Diane Nash Bevel were allowed to take a bow. Ella Baker said quotable things about why this kept happening, and Malcolm X, James Baldwin, and Adam Clayton Powell Jr. delivered quotable zingers about the limitations of King's coalition. Malcolm derided the performers for letting Randolph tell them what song to sing and what speech to make.

Most telling of all, the march alienated many of the most dedicated exemplars of the "marvelous new militancy" lauded by King. Bevel had wanted a children's march to the nation's capital modeled on Gandhi's salt tax march of 1930. He refused to attend the march that occurred, protesting, "You all turned my march into a picnic." Young told Bevel that the march succeeded by attracting so many middle-class blacks and liberal whites. To Bevel, it felt more like a hijack; this was establishment liberalism celebrating itself. He had ample company in that reaction. The first players to say that King's speech and the march were dreamy and shallow and boring were SNCC stalwarts. Some were harsher than others; some showed up for the march and some did not; and some cut Lewis some slack after he and Forman toned down SNCC's speech. But many SNCC activists found the sentiments and conformism of the day to be unbearable. They nurtured a bitter legend about civil rights liberals ruining Lewis's speech in a demand for fake unity. To SNCC, the presumption of the liberals was nauseating. SNCC leaders Charles Sherrod, Robert Moses, Charles McLaurin, Courtland Cox, Charles McDew, and Avon Rollins had just spent three years being persecuted for community organizing in the Deep South. The experience had hardened them, yielding a contradictory agenda.[165]

Many of them no longer spoke the Lawson/King language of redemptive suffering and Christian love; some never had. Lewis evinced the moralistic radicalism of early SNCC, including its Christian inspiration and emphasis on nonviolent protest. He was the SNCC leader most like King. He did not sneer at King's talk about following Jesus and redeeming the soul of America because he had the same theology as King. SNCC increasingly conceived itself as a cadre of grassroots organizers dedicated to mobilizing blacks to coerce the federal government to enact gains for civil rights. This self-conception intensified and subsequently fractured in the summer of 1964, as SNCC bombarded Mississippi with thousands of white northern students in the Mississippi Summer Project, which fueled a searing internal debate over racial consciousness. SNCC

had two defining objectives: provoke the federal government to smash segregationist resistance in the Deep South and build strong black organizations. But
these two things did not go well together, and SNCC became a magnet for activists who spurned the binding power of King's theology.

Lewis, no less than Ella Baker and Stokely Carmichael, stood against making
a fetish of the proposed civil rights bill because there was so much more to
achieve. But Lewis did not share his organization's deepening alienation from
King and SCLC, even on August 28, 1963. Lewis believed there was a place for
hope-and-love optimism and a place for angry protest. It was wrong to make this
an either-or issue. It was dead wrong to say that King embarrassed the real
movement for racial justice at the March on Washington or to say that the
march was a laughable mistake. King was right to combine love and anger. He
did so at the march, contrary to later recollections of a purely dreamy speech.
He expressed, with perfect pitch, the hope of a moment. He wrung as much as
he could out of social gospel liberalism. He shifted gears when the moment
passed.

And then he grew truly radical.

6

NIGHTMARE FURY AND PUBLIC SACRIFICE

King was more angry and radical in 1960 than in 1955, more angry and radical in 1965 than in 1960, and more angry and radical at the end than ever. In his last years he was more of both than anyone around him, while cultivating a public image of being neither. The March on Washington sealed him in memory as the symbol of the civil rights movement and, later, the icon of a national holiday. But the Dream moment passed quickly, on Sunday morning, September 15, 1963, when fourteen-year-old Addie Mae Collins, eleven-year-old Denise McNair, fourteen-year-old Carole Robertson, and fourteen-year-old Cynthia Wesley were killed in a dynamite blast at Sixteenth Street Baptist Church in Birmingham. They were dressed in white from head to toe and had left a Sunday school discussion of a sermon titled "The Love That Forgives." Andrew Young, the father of three young girls, could not bring himself to attend the funeral in Birmingham. There King contrasted the innocent beauty of the murdered girls with the vicious savagery of the killers, praying that the crime would impel America to take "the high road of peace and brotherhood." But his customary call for "the white South to come to terms with its conscience" rang hollow even to him.[1]

A month later Robert Kennedy authorized the FBI to tap King's home phone, which yielded little because King was on the road 90 percent of the time, so the FBI bugged King's hotels and the SCLC headquarters. In November King was enjoying a respite at home when President Kennedy was assassinated. King sat, quiet and stunned, with Coretta King and Bernard Lee. "This is what is going to happen to me," he said. "I don't think I'm going to live to reach forty." As usual, Coretta asked him not to talk like that, but King persisted: "I keep telling you, this is a sick nation. And I don't think I can survive either." The Kennedy family wounded King by not inviting him to the funeral Mass,

355

and he returned the snub the following Sunday, barely mentioning Kennedy or the great national grieving in his sermon. King preached instead about breaking loose "from the Egypt of slavery." Elsewhere he declared that all Americans were implicated in Kennedy's killing: "We tolerated hate; we tolerated the sick stimulation of violence in all walks of life; and we tolerated the differential application of law." The United States was not merely wounded and grieving, King said; it was deeply sick. King urged that passing Kennedy's embattled civil rights bill was the best way to honor the fallen president. But he had already changed how he talked about it.[2]

He began to speak frankly about America's sickness simultaneously with accepting that the movement had taken over his life. From the Montgomery boycott to the March on Washington King complained about the demands placed upon him and dreamed of returning to a normal existence. Often he implored Walker and others to spare him the next engagement. Near the end of 1963, just before *Time* named him "Man of the Year," King finally accepted that no other life was in store for him. It was partly resignation, as King's exhaustion threw him into depression. Each day became a struggle to stir himself to battle, consumed by a movement that *was* his life. King gave himself to the movement under the ever-present fear that the time remaining to him would be short. He averted his final reckoning in St. Augustine, Florida, and outside Selma, Alabama, by avoiding known dangers, but he knew he was always in danger, and he preached about it as though heading toward Golgotha.

FREEDOM SUMMER

SCLC burned too hotly at the top to be sustainable. Walker and Bevel clashed over tactics and Walker's authority, Walker alienated other SCLC staffers by bossing and scolding them, too, and Walker resented that King refused to reprimand anyone, always imploring his aides to work together. To Walker, SCLC obviously needed a military commander at the top, which happened to be him. No staffer agreed with that view or Walker's insistence that he had to approve every meeting with King. Walker was drained after Birmingham, and he felt unappreciated. SCLC had soared on his watch, yet he got little acclaim or even credit. Staff meetings were fractious and angry. Walker fought with Bevel constantly, resenting that Bevel operated completely on his own. Walker tried to fire Bevel for insubordination, but King said no, and the staff revolted against Walker. In September 1963 Walker asked the SCLC convention for a pay raise and greater authority. He got no raise plus a demotion. Walker put out job feelers and drifted away, feeling disrespected and burned out. Young took over much of Walker's job, although King persuaded Walker to stay on officially until the summer of 1964. To King, it was important to make an amicable transition to whoever would succeed Walker. Walker later recalled that after three years of intense protest activism in the trenches, constant fighting with opponents and allies, and the drama of Birmingham, "I began to feel like I'd had it. I really felt a creeping bitterness coming over me."[3]

King wanted Bayard Rustin to take over, but a chorus of staffers and board members said no. Rustin was a movement player again after the success of the March on Washington. *Life* put him on its cover alongside Randolph. *Newsweek* put him at the center of its story about the march, commenting knowingly that Rustin had come "out of the shadows"—a common trope of gay life—into prominence. Though Rustin did not discuss his sexuality, *Newsweek* knew which form of prejudice had hurt him most, suggesting he had overcome it. Rustin was eager to see how much had changed for him. He wanted to keep the march going as an ongoing organization, but Wilkins refused, and Farmer agreed with Wilkins. Then Rustin campaigned for the SCLC job, telling friends that he welcomed the prospect of a steady income after thirty years of vagabond activism. The executive staffers pushed back, telling King that Rustin was still a nonstarter for being gay, a New York leftist, a former Communist, and nothing like a Baptist minister. Moreover, Rustin offended them by campaigning for the job, and some added that Rustin was no longer an independent leftist, having joined the labor wing of the Democratic Party via its most exotic sect, the Shachtmanites.[4]

Max Shachtman grew up in New York and dropped out of City College in 1921. That year he cofounded the legal arm of American Communism, the Workers Party of America, but was expelled from it seven years later. He became a close associate of Leon Trotsky in the 1930s, was expelled from the (Trotskyist) Socialist Workers Party in 1940, and founded the Workers Party that year, still lacking originality in nomenclature. In 1949 he renamed it the Independent Socialist League (ISL). Ideologically, Shachtman moved in the 1940s to a Marxist version of democratic Socialism, though his group never quite threw off its Leninist prejudice that Social Democracy watered down the real thing. The Shachtmanites thrived on Marxology, ideological critique, and sectarian intrigue. True Marxism, to them, was a feeling *and* a hybrid macro-theory that explained everything. They were ferociously anti-Stalinist but disdained the Socialist Party's undertheorized, broad-brush anti-Communism. They won staff positions in the United Auto Workers, supporting the purge of Communist-linked unions from the CIO, and in 1958 Shachtman folded his group into the Socialist Party, hoping to take it over. Michael Harrington, sociologist Bogdan

Denitch, literary critic Irving Howe, historian Hal Draper, and social theorist Julius Jacobson were leading Shachtmanites, as were numerous labor officials including United Federation of Teachers president Albert Shanker and many of the Cold War Social Democrats who later founded the neoconservative movement. Harrington, Shanker, Tom Kahn, and Rachelle Horowitz were Rustin's early links to the Shachtmanites. Although Rustin was still a pacifist—he came out against the Vietnam War in 1964—and a legend in the pacifist left, he had tired of pacifist left marginality. The Shachtmanites were ensconced in the AFL-CIO hierarchy; trade unions funded the Randolph Institute, which employed Rustin as director; Rustin wanted to work with Democrats to enact social programs; and he found a home among the Shachtmanites.[5]

Levison shuddered at seeing Rustin fall in with them. Levison and Rustin had parted ways in 1960 after King dropped Rustin, although Levison defended Rustin on the charges against his character. Still, Levison said, there was a problem with the new Rustin. It was no small matter that Rustin had fallen under the sway of sectarian ideologues, especially Kahn, whom Levison regarded as a Lenin-type schemer who manipulated Rustin. Corporate lawyer Harry Wachtel was the last SCLC insider aside from King to hold out for Rustin. Wachtel took over much of Levison's work for SCLC, without Levison's gentle manner. He was aggressive and connected, and he judged that King's knowledge base was sorely lacking. With Clarence Jones, Wachtel created a study group that met with King every two or three weeks in New York to beef up his knowledge of politics, policy, and world affairs. Wachtel greatly admired Rustin and consulted with him weekly, which led Wachtel to wonder if Levison had gone back to helping the American Communist Party. That would explain Levison's animus against some exotic breed of anti-Communist Socialists that Wachtel knew little about, aside from Levison's personal feelings of revulsion toward Kahn, which reeked of homophobia. But Wachtel relented, concluding that Rustin could not run SCLC in the face of so much internal opposition, so he joined Levison and Jones in advising King not to appoint Rustin. King grieved at the irony: This was exactly what Hoover did to them. They had already lost Levison and O'Dell to a witch hunt. Now they were doing it to themselves.[6]

Andrew Young, Walker's opposite temperamentally, held on to the job he was already doing. King wanted firebrands with huge egos on his team because SCLC existed to raise hell in hostile cities. But King reasoned that he needed a diplomatic, responsible type to hold the group together. Young was affable, suave, and an able manager plus comfortable with white people. He clashed with King's lieutenants less than anyone except King, partly because his autonomy allowed him to skirt the group's rivalries. Young also got along with SNCC, and he shared King's liberal seminary vocabulary and worldview. He had come from the black middle class and the white liberal church movement, both of which he knew better than any SCLC staffer. Young's forte was helping SCLC engage these two audiences, plus young people across racial lines, plus white southerners. He became SCLC's expert on dealing with the white media, teaching King to provide images and soundbites for television news. Young's father had taught him to approach white racists with condescending moral concern as people afflicted with a terrible illness. During the Albany campaign Young found himself in a confessor role with Laurie Pritchett, who pleaded that he was just following local laws and eager to become a federal marshal so he could get out of Albany. During the Birmingham campaign King relied on Young to make whatever breakthroughs were possible with local white officials and business owners. Every SCLC staff meeting was a clash of egos, so King relied on Young to prevent dysfunction—playing the house conservative in charge of the team while others declaimed in prophetic mode.[7]

Andy Young came to the black social gospel directly from the New England abolitionist story that helped to nurture it. Both of his parents were graduates of Straight College in New Orleans, a Congregational school founded in 1868 by the American Missionary Association (AMA). Young's father, Andrew Young Sr., went on to Howard University Dental School after college, graduating in 1921. Returning to New Orleans to establish a dental practice, he surveyed the Straight campus in search of a wife and found one in Daisy Fuller, a light-colored schoolteacher studying for her teaching certificate. Both of Young's parents were steeped in Afro-Saxon Congregationalism, believing deeply in its Puritan ethic of hard work and education. Much of his mother's New Orleans Creole family passed for white, an option that Young learned not to judge. Young's father had to live down the disappointment of his wife's family that he diminished her social standing and opportunities by marrying her. He taught his two sons to feel the same kind of compassion toward racist whites that they held for polio victims. Young grew up knowing about Booker T. Washington and W. E. B. Du Bois, although he later judged that he was taught the worst parts of both. His parents and teachers were models of Booker accommodation, and Du Bois was invoked as the great exhorter of the Talented Tenth.[8]

Earnestly raised for Talented Tenth success, specifically as a dentist, Young was rushed to college before he was ready, at age fifteen at Dillard University (a merger of Straight College and New Orleans University). He transferred to Howard University as a sophomore but never caught up. It gnawed at him that his parents expected him to be exactly like them: successful, churchgoing, and morally exemplary yet confined to segregated middle-class marginality. Howard was more of the same, except worse. Young recoiled at the haughty pretensions of Howard students who were comfortable with their privileges and career plans. Howard felt very northern, bourgeois, arrogant, and cold to him: "The girls were society-conscious to an extreme—some even wore high heels, cocktail dresses, and fur coats to class, as if their sole purpose was to snare a future physician or attorney." Young was a senior before he felt comfortable at Howard, by which time he had nearly flunked out. One more D would have got him expelled. He barely graduated but felt like a Howard student by the time he graduated in 1951, which made his career possible: "Had I failed to come to terms with my identity as a middle-class black person, I would never have accomplished very much in the civil rights movement or won elective office." He and King had to persuade the black establishment to embrace social change before they used the same arguments on the white establishment: "I understood the anxieties of the black middle class, but I also knew their most treasured hopes. I spoke the language of middle-class aspirations: it was my parents' language and it had become mine, as well."[9]

First, he broke the hearts of his parents, by opting for a low-status career as a minister. Young's Congregational background provided the hook, specifically the summer gatherings of black southern Congregationalists at Kings Mountain, North Carolina. Shortly after graduating from Howard, Young attended a United Christian Youth Movement conference in Lake Brownwood, Texas, where he was briefly the only black student before a few others arrived. He nearly left, feeling alone; then he met white students who were friendly toward him, a new experience for Young. He made new friends in United Christian Youth Action, a youth activist project of the National Council of Churches (NCC), which sent him to a youth conference sponsored by the Church of the Brethren at Camp Mack in Indiana, where he read Gandhi for the first time. Young had majored in biology at Howard and missed the Gandhian internationalist tradition that Mordecai Johnson and William Stuart Nelson kept alive there. He had also missed the social gospel, as religion was entirely personal and individual to him.

The two-week conference at Camp Mack changed Young's life. He converted to Gandhian nonviolence and the social gospel simultaneously, imagining himself as a Gandhian Christian activist. United Christian Youth Action sent him to Rhode Island and Connecticut to work as a youth organizer, where he took classes on the side at Hartford Theological Seminary in Hartford, Connecticut. Young enthused that seminary was like Camp Mack, only better. Hartford's architecture smacked of New England crustiness, but the seminary was a bastion of liberal theology, the social gospel, and internationalism. Its historic emphasis on missions had begun to morph into a pioneering emphasis on cultural internationalism. The seminary published a leading academic journal, the *Muslim World*; its curriculum engaged non-Western cultures; and Hartford had numerous students from Africa, Southeast Asia, and the Middle East. Many other Hartford students were worldly, hard-drinking World War II veterans.

Young soaked up all of it. His grades at Howard would have disqualified him for admission to Hartford, but he had enrolled as an unofficial student, which gave him a second chance. Young's heartbroken parents had no concept of the cosmopolitan world he had entered. They had not paid Howard's tuition for him to become a mere preacher, and they would not help him attend seminary, let alone a white liberal seminary. Young won admission to Hartford anyway, enrolling on a scholarship. He served a summer internship at a church in Marion, Alabama, in 1954; married a woman, Jean Childs, he met there; and graduated from Hartford in 1955. Young's wife, like his mother, was light-colored, very southern, middle class, and very Congregationalist. They moved to Thomasville, Georgia, where he served two congregations. Young took pride that his small congregation in Beachton had a history of civil rights militancy and had thus moved en masse, on two occasions, to find safety.[10]

In May 1957 Young and King met for the first time, while both addressed the Alpha Phi Alpha chapter at Talladega College in Talladega, Alabama. Young was eager to talk about theologians. He was reading Paul Tillich at the time, and he missed academic conversation. Young had read that King wrote his dissertation on Tillich. He wanted to talk about their theological interests and training, asking King how he made use of his academic training as a minister. King waved him off from academic conversation; all he wanted to talk about was his baby girl, Yoki. The only thing he said about Tillich was, "All that's behind me now." Young was crestfallen, taking King too literally. He had no idea, at the time, what deep exhaustion felt like. Subsequently Young learned that King still cared about academic theology and that exhaustion was too debilitating to permit King or him to pursue their intellectual interests. Young attended the Prayer Pilgrimage in 1957 and cheered King's "Give Us the Ballot" speech; then the NCC called, inviting Young to work for its Youth Department in New York. It was the heyday of the NCC, which wanted very much to play a bigger role in the civil rights movement. Young worried that he might become a token in the NCC's vast bureaucracy, but he figured, rightly, that he was suited to help the NCC become a movement player.[11]

Christian ministry had to change if the churches were to become relevant to American youths and society. Young said it at ecumenical youth conferences across the country, integrating many conferences simply by showing up. Often he met students who had never shared a cabin with a black American and who whispered that their parents would harshly disapprove if they knew. Young's work for the NCC linked him to the World Council of Churches and its Programme to Combat Racism, through which he met African youths who later became revolutionary leaders, notably Joshua Nkomo, Robert Mugabe, and N'dabinge Sithole of Rhodesia (Zimbabwe). His work for the NCC also facilitated friendships with James Lawson and C. T. Vivian before the youth eruption of 1960. Young was savoring a glass of wine in his living room in Queens when he saw a television report about Lawson's disciples striking in downtown Nashville. The program overjoyed and prodded Young, just as Lawson was beginning to grasp the power of a new force in American society: television news. Young told his close friend Robert Spike that he was maxed out on church work and eager to do the work of the church. Spike appreciated the difference; he was a white minister who had recently left Judson Church in Greenwich Village to run the United Church Board for Homeland Ministries and subsequently directed the NCC's Commission on Religion and Race. Young vowed to drag his wife and three daughters into the civil rights movement, and Jean complied, as she was eager to leave New York.[12]

King offered Young a job, and he declined it. He wasn't ready for the big time and he didn't want to work for high-strung Baptist preachers. Myles Horton offered him a job, and Young asked theologian-lawyer William Stringfellow to check out rumors that the Highlander School was Communist. Stringfellow wrote to the FBI, the Internal Security Committee of the House of Representatives, and the Senate Un-American Activities Committee. Did they have anything on Highlander? The government agencies said no, and Young quit his job to move to Highlander, just before the state of Tennessee spitefully shut it down. Now Young had no job, just as the sit-in movement exploded. He and Spike brokered a deal between the Field Foundation and the American Missionary Association Division of the United Church Board for Homeland Ministries. The Field Foundation had funded Septima Clark's Leadership Training Program at Highlander; now the Field grant went to the United Church Board, which was thrilled to expand its role in the civil rights movement. The citizenship school moved to the SCLC office in Atlanta, where Young officially worked for Wesley Hotchkiss of the United Church Board, but in King's shop.[13]

Nearly every move that Young made had taken him from one AMA-founded institution to another. He loved to tell the story of the AMA's founding in 1846 as an abolitionist mission society and its backstory in the *Amistad* slave ship revolt of 1839. Now he was working for the United Church of Christ (UCC), which united two denominations in 1957. His parents reeled at each blow—distressed that he quit his respectable job at the NCC, frightened that he associated with Highlander, and alarmed that he associated with King. Young's parents were Urban Leaguers, and his father was a down-the-line NAACP race man. Eleanor Roosevelt's support of Highlander was somewhat reassuring to them, but nothing redeemed King, just as their friends said. King caused mayhem wherever he went and he got people into trouble. Young reminded his parents that he worked for their denomination. How far-out could that be? The movement, he thought, had to win over people like his parents plus the white liberals and moderates and especially the children of the 1960s.

He moved to Atlanta and joined SCLC a year after Walker took over the organization. Walker held down one corner of the SCLC headquarters, with his secretary Edwina Smith. King and his buoyant secretary Dora McDonald—a gift from Mays—were in another corner. Abernathy had a corner with his secretary Lily Hunter, and Young shared a corner with Clark, Dorothy Cotton (who came with Walker from Petersburg), and Bernice Johnson. Walker and Abernathy resented that Young had his own power base, which Young safeguarded. Young worked closely with Cotton and Clark to expand the citizenship program, training grassroots leaders at the United Church Board's Dorchester Center in Dorchester, Georgia, near Savannah. He winced at the chauvinism of the Baptist ministers, believing that his Congregationalism helped him treat women more respectfully, although Young was no feminist. The program focused on the Deep South counties holding black majorities and almost no black voters. There were 188 of them, and the program trained everyone who showed up. One of its early graduates was Fannie Lou Hamer, a sharecropper from Ruleville, Mississippi, who became an electrifying speaker and voting rights activist. Young and Cotton traveled across the Deep South to recruit trainees. From 1961 to 1966 the program trained over six thousand people, and in 1964 Cotton took it over after Young succeeded Walker. Meanwhile Young worked with Burke Marshall and John Doar, after Birmingham, to pass the civil rights bill.[14]

King restocked SCLC in the early 1960s, as Bevel and Cotton held on, Young moved up, Walker fell away, and Abernathy pulled back from organizational work. Abernathy's loyalty was to King, not the organization. The key newcomers were C. T. Vivian and Hosea Williams. Vivian was born in Missouri and grew up in rural west-central Illinois (Macomb), graduating from high school in 1942 and from Western Illinois University in 1946. He preached in Peoria, Illinois, for eight years after graduating from college, moving to Nashville in 1954 to study at American Baptist Theological Seminary. There he became a Lawson disciple and SNCC cofounder. Vivian rode Freedom Ride buses in Mississippi and joined SCLC in 1961 as director of affiliates, coordinating the work of SCLC branches nationwide. He was as fiery and sharp-tongued as Bevel and Williams but also reflectively theological in King's mold, all of which drew King to him. Williams had a very different background. Born in Attapulgus, Georgia, in 1926, Williams was raised by his maternal grandparents, left home at the age of fourteen, and served in the U.S. Army during World War II under General George S. Patton Jr. On one occasion he was the only member of his unit to survive a bombing attack. On returning to the United States, still in uniform, he was beaten at a bus station for drinking from a segregated water fountain. Williams was a tempestuous brawler who called himself "Reverend" despite not being a minister. He earned a master's degree in chemistry at Atlanta University, worked in the early 1950s for the Department of Agriculture, and was boisterously procapitalist. SCLC's raucous staff meetings became dramatically more so after Williams joined the staff. He berated Bevel and Vivian for their Socialism, and they gave it right back, sowing a bitter rivalry between Williams and Bevel.

Williams lived to confront, which delighted King, who explained, "We need people who are confrontational." If Young got his way, King said, no confrontations would ever occur, and the worst violence would stay under the surface. Rational types like Young had a role to play, but SCLC was not going to reason America out of segregation. King put it bluntly: "You need some folks like Hosea and Bevel who are crazy enough to take on anything and anybody and not count the cost." King could be scathing about the foibles of his lieutenants; his favorite ploy was to tell them how he would preach their funerals. Always it was a humorously scalding roast of Williams's volatility, Bevel's extremism, Young's Uncle Tom persona, or the like. Were Young to be killed on a march, King planned to eulogize him by telling white America it made a terrible mistake because nobody ever loved white people more than Andy Young. That convulsed the staff with laughter every time.[15]

In Young's telling, every executive staffer was "high-strung, aggressive, and egotistical," including Cotton, and Bevel and Williams were more so, each regarding the other as "a menace to the movement." Young and Fred Bennett, a Baptist minister and SCLC insider, had a recurring joke in which Bennett warned that the "snakes are crawling" and Young replied not to worry, for he was a "sly mongoose." Bennett and King were the only SCLC insiders Young trusted, but Young held the group together, more or less willingly. He got the Presbyterian Church USA to pay Williams, who thus made a higher salary than everyone at SCLC. On one occasion Young took a break from reining in the others, pouting that if they were such geniuses he would let them have their way. King admonished him forcefully, declaring that he depended on Young to be the voice of common sense: "Now, if you decide you are going to start playing games, I don't see why I need you. I need you to take as conservative a position as possible, then I can have plenty of room to come down in the middle wherever I want to."[16]

That approach yielded a fizzled noncampaign in Atlanta and a beating in St. Augustine, Florida, the last two protest campaigns that Walker devised. Walker agreed with SNCC that not striking in Atlanta was indefensible. SCLC had shown too much deference to Daddy King's friends, and its credibility was on the line. If SCLC did not strike in Atlanta, critics would say that it only disrupted other peoples' towns, and they would be right. Walker designed a full-scale, Birmingham-style campaign of creative disruption for Atlanta, replete with frank instructions about provoking police violence. Daddy King and his friends opposed the campaign and vehemently denounced Walker's statements about provoking the police. Walker reluctantly scaled back to a minimal version of his plan, as King Junior had no stomach for provoking mayhem in his hometown. Walker and John Lewis got arrested at the Heart of Atlanta Motel restaurant, along with King's new aide Harry Boyte and Young's assistant, John Gibson. Meanwhile King stayed at home writing *Why We Can't Wait,* and Young frankly acknowledged that he did not want trouble in the city where his wife and children lived. It was enough, in Atlanta, for SCLC to promote voter registration and a jobs program, Operation Breadbasket. The Atlanta campaign petered out, Bevel said it was a waste of time, and Walker concurred, with disgust. Later he said it was the only time that getting arrested felt pointless to him.[17]

Bevel wanted to focus on one state, Alabama, and Williams pushed for one town, St. Augustine. The latter seemed more doable; plus St. Augustine was the nation's oldest city and Florida's most violently racist city. A tourist town on Florida's northern Atlantic coast, St. Augustine was a Klan stronghold policed by unabashedly racist thugs. Blacks who tried to enroll their children in public schools got their homes bombed in St. Augustine, and in 1963 the town won $350,000 from the federal government to celebrate its four hundredth anniversary in 1964. The NAACP protested that the government should send federal marshals to St. Augustine, not support its racist tourism industry. Local NAACP leader Robert B. Hayling founded a youth council that took a further step, a sit-in at Woolworth's that was harshly repressed, yielding an appeal to SCLC. King sent Cotton to work with Hayling, until Williams replaced her and implored King to go all-in. Young countered that SCLC was exhausted from Birmingham and it needed to focus on the civil rights bill; Williams was not exhausted because he had not worked on the Birmingham campaign.

Walker devised another Birmingham-style campaign, his last project for SCLC. King addressed a mass meeting on May 26, appointed Young as spokesperson, told him to keep a temperate tone, and left town. Williams and Hayling led dramatic night marches to the old slave market in the town's public square. Most of the marchers were women and children, whose men proved hard to shame into marching. On the third night Williams ambushed Young at a mass meeting, publicly goading him to lead that night's march. Young wanted to call off the march, as over 500 Klansmen had gathered in the slave market. Young led 350 protesters to the square, where he tried to initiate friendly conversation with the Klan mob and was savagely beaten. That changed Young's mind about pressing hard in St. Augustine, although he still wanted King to stay away, and Bevel refused to go.[18]

St. Augustine was too dangerous to risk losing King there, who made only brief appearances, once in tow with Walker. Police jabbed demonstrators with cattle prods, and many white locals belonged to the reactionary John Birch Society. There were tensions between Williams and Young over who was in charge, though Williams spent much of the campaign in jail. A local judge banned the night marches, and King rushed to Jacksonville to appeal the injunction in U.S. District Court. Judge Bryan Simpson asked for time to study the case, so King tried some outreach to local whites, calling Harold DeWolf to St. Augustine. DeWolf presented SCLC's demands and was harshly rebuffed, getting nowhere with a hostile crowd. On June 9 Simpson overturned the injunction. He excoriated St. Augustine's concrete sweatboxes, miniature cells, and chicken coops customized for civil rights prisoners: "Here is exposed, in its raw ugliness, studied and cynical brutality, deliberately contrived to break men physically and mentally." Simpson stood out among the noble federal judges who paved the way to the Civil Rights Act. The next day Senate Minority Leader Everett Dirksen of Illinois broke the Senate's filibuster against the civil rights bill, ensuring its passage.[19]

But St. Augustine was not for turning. Florida governor Farris Bryant ignored Simpson's injunction, and the thugs operated with impunity. Beatings were commonplace, including a second beating for Young, and the marches dwindled. SCLC staff meetings grew more fractious than ever. Bevel said that Williams got people killed so he could get his picture in the paper, and Williams said that Bevel had jealousy issues and was crazy. Williams wanted to fight on in St. Augustine, but King took the first face-saving offer to come, a proposal from Bryant to establish biracial negotiations. Walker took a job with the Negro Heritage Library and Young officially took over SCLC, in a strange moment. The NCC pushed hard for the civil rights bill, making a massive lobbying effort orchestrated by commissioner Bob Spike. Spike, Fannie Lou Hamer, and SCLC staffer Annelle Ponder worked the halls of Congress, swaying many votes. Young worked closely with them, gratified that the ecumenical churches came through. On July 2, fresh from battered defeat in St. Augustine, King stood behind President Lyndon Johnson in the East Ballroom of the White House as he signed the Civil Rights Act of 1964. St. Augustine felt like a humiliating defeat to SCLC because it was. But without the protests in St. Augustine there might not have been a Civil Rights Act.[20]

At the signing Johnson gave the strongest speech for civil rights equality ever delivered by a U.S. president. Then he told civil rights leaders in the Cabinet Room there was no need for any more direct action protests. The Civil Rights Act eliminated the last vestiges of racial injustice in the United States, and further demonstrations would only harm America's quest for racial harmony. Reporters asked King about that: Was there any reason to continue the movement? Wasn't LBJ right that further protests would only inflame racial resentments? King struggled to take the questions seriously. For months he heard them every day, replying as patiently as humanly possible: The Civil Rights Act had gaping holes on voting rights and fair housing, and nothing about poverty. It provided no protections for civil rights workers, and it did not mitigate the civil war that had just burned SCLC in St. Augustine. If the Greensboro students had been served at Woolworth's, King said, they probably could not have paid for their meal.

He wanted a Bill of Rights for the Disadvantaged, modeled on the GI Bill of Rights. It would make reparations for America's oppression of black Americans *and* cut across racial lines. No amount of money would ever compensate for 246 years of slavery and a century of segregation, but a program of massive federal aid to the poor would make a significant difference, much like the GI Bill: "It is a simple matter of justice that America, in dealing creatively with the task of raising the Negro from backwardness, should also be rescuing a large stratum of the forgotten white poor. A Bill of Rights for the Disadvantaged could mark the rise of a new era, in which the full resources of the society would be used to attack the tenacious poverty which so paradoxically exists in the midst of plenty."[21]

For a while this appeal folded into Johnson's War on Poverty, while King and Johnson officials cited Michael Harrington's *The Other America* as the book that launched the so-called war on poverty. Johnson had a gut-level passion about poverty that was fueled by his memory of growing up in it. He also had a prescient sense of the wild swing in national politics that would be his legacy. On the way to his Texas ranch after signing the civil rights bill Johnson told press secretary Bill Moyers and other White House staffers, "I think we just gave the South to the Republicans." In other renderings he told Moyers on the day after he signed the act, "We are turning the South over to the Republican Party for my lifetime and yours."[22]

Johnson officials debated this prediction in strict confidence. Was the politics of race really this powerful? Were they about to witness a realignment stampede? How could that be? Millions of white southern Democrats did not know any Republicans, and many black Americans routinely voted Republican. Republicans did not bother to run for office in the Deep South. In 1964 Republicans held zero House seats among the forty-one districts in the core Deep South of Georgia, Alabama, Mississippi, Louisiana, and South Carolina. The idea that Democrats owned the civil rights issue was very new and not true. Republicans voted in favor of the Civil Rights Act by 80 percent or more in the House and Senate. In the House, Republicans voted 136 yes and 35 no, while Democrats voted 153 yes and 91 no. In the Senate, Republicans voted 27 yes and 6 no, while Democrats voted 46 yes and 21 no. How could the fallout from these votes be so extreme? It was hard to fathom that LBJ might be right, even as one of the 6 no votes in the Senate, Barry Goldwater, rode a reactionary tide to the Republican nomination for president.[23]

Johnson campaigned in the summer of 1964 as though he believed it, treating the Goldwater surge as a threat to the Republic, not just his presidency. Two weeks after Johnson signed the Civil Rights Act, Republicans convened at the Cow Palace in San Francisco. Condemnations of big government and the Civil Rights Act coursed angrily through the convention, mortifying black Republican and Rockefeller-wing delegates. Jackie Robinson compared his experience on the convention floor to what Jews must have felt like in Nazi Germany. The *Chicago Defender* agreed that Nazi Germany was the best analogy, declaring that the tradition of black Republicanism was finished. From the Republican Convention in mid-July to the November election King denounced the Goldwater ticket nearly every day. Since King was the symbol of the civil rights movement, which belonged to no party, he carefully avoided saying he was for LBJ. Politically he walked a tightrope during Freedom Summer. Wilkins implored civil rights leaders to refrain from direct action protesting until the November election, King agreed to keep SCLC off the streets, and SNCC pressured King by building up the Mississippi Freedom Democratic Party (MFDP). King tried to support the Freedom Party *and*

Johnson, but he could not have it both ways when it mattered, fatefully, in Atlantic City, New Jersey.[24]

The MFDP was the brainchild of Robert Moses and former Stanford dean Allard Lowenstein. Formally, it was a new political party, founded in 1963 to create opportunities for black political agency in Mississippi. Operationally, it was designed to unseat Mississippi's official delegation to the Democratic Party presidential convention in Atlantic City. Lowenstein, a graduate of Horace Mann School in New York City, the University of North Carolina, and Yale Law School, was a hyperkinetic activist and former foreign policy assistant to Senator Hubert Humphrey. After Medgar Evers was murdered, Lowenstein moved to Greenwood, Mississippi, and teamed with Moses to create the MFDP. Moses served as director of voter registration for the Council of Federated Organizations (COFU), a state coalition of civil rights organizations to which SNCC belonged. SNCC had only 120 field-workers in the entire South, all working on their own to help people learn how to lead themselves. It was too small to topple the Mississippi Democratic Party, and the decision to try disrupted SNCC's regular work. Moreover, SNCC was a magnet for idealistic white activists; by 1963 20 percent of its field-workers and one-third of its conference participants were white. Moses and Lewis said this was mostly a good thing, as blacks and whites needed to change America together. Others countered that SNCC already had too many whites bearing white opinions and presumptions. The MFDP project exacerbated this in-house debate by recruiting a flood of white student volunteers.

In November 1963 the MFDP conducted a mock election alongside Mississippi's official election, running its own candidates—MFDP chair Aaron Henry and white Tougaloo chaplain Ed King—against the Democratic and Republican candidates for governor and lieutenant governor. Lowenstein recruited eighty white students, mostly from Stanford and Yale, to help organize the election. It was very successful, drawing eighty thousand voters. Freedom Summer was the follow-up, as Lowenstein recruited eight hundred white student volunteers to Mississippi to staff SNCC's freedom schools and register voters. Women taught in the schools and men conducted door-to-door canvassing, as canvassing was more dangerous. Liberal stalwart Joseph Rauh worked closely with Moses, serving as MFDP's legal counsel. Students poured into Mississippi, and on the first day of Freedom Summer three young CORE workers were lynched. Mickey Schwerner, a white field secretary; Andrew Goodman, a white sophomore at Queens College; and James Chaney, a black field secretary, were dumped in an earthen cattle pond dam. The FBI searched for their bodies while extensive media coverage spotlighted the spectacle of white victims. The bodies of blacks previously killed and dumped, with no media notice, were found before the CORE workers were found. Meanwhile Johnson signed the Civil Rights Act, and SNCC mobilized Mississippi blacks to participate in the Democratic Party's precinct, county, and state conventions. SNCC leaders appreciated the Civil Rights Act but did not celebrate its passage, as they were in the middle of a war, registering seventeen thousand brave souls. The new registrants showed up at Democratic gatherings and were excluded, so MFDP offered its own slate of sixty-eight delegates to the Democratic Convention.[25]

Rauh believed the Freedom Democrats would win if the issue got to the convention floor in Atlantic City. The acid test was getting through the 110-member Credentials Committee, on which he served. On August 21, the day before the convention opened, the Freedom Democrats made their case to the Credentials Committee. Television reporters flocked to the hearing as the only interesting thing happening that day. Rauh called on Aaron Henry and Ed King, who gave strong testimonies. Rauh called on Fannie Lou Hamer, seated next to Schwerner's mother. Hamer told the committee that when she tried to register, the state highway police dragged her to a cell and forced two black prisoners to beat her with a blackjack: "I laid on my face and the first Negro began to beat. And I was beat by the first Negro until he was exhausted. . . . I began to scream and one white man got up and began to beat me in my head and tell me to hush. . . . All of this on account we want to register, to become first-class citizens. And if the Freedom Democratic party is not seated now, I question America. Is this America, the land of the free and the home of the brave, where we have to sleep with our telephones off of the hooks because our lives be threatened daily, because we want to live as decent human beings, in America?"[26]

Johnson erupted in fury at the broadcast, fretting that Hamer's riveting testimony might blow up his convention. Texas governor John Connally put it brutally, warning LBJ, "If you seat those black buggers, the whole South will walk out." LBJ wheedled and threatened in customary Johnson fashion, devising a compromise that delayed the issue. Humphrey wanted to be vice president, so Johnson made him earn it by championing LBJ's compromise: two seats for the MFDP, with LBJ choosing the delegates (Aaron Henry and Ed King). The president was determined to exclude Hamer, who had hurt his campaign. Humphrey defended LBJ's exclusion of "that illiterate woman," and Moses denounced Humphrey as a racist. Since Rauh made his living as the general counsel of the United Auto Workers, LBJ reached out to Walter Reuther, who put the squeeze on Rauh, telling him to accept the compromise or find another job. Johnson floated the word that Humphrey's place on the ticket rested on MFDP's decision. The Freedom Democrats dramatically infiltrated the convention floor, producing the convention's signature images, to Johnson's distress. King and Rauh were tortured over what to do, especially Rauh. On the fifth day of the convention King and Rauh accepted the compromise. Rustin and King spoke to the Freedom Democrats, quite differently. For Rustin it was a coming-out moment, epitomizing his move "from protest to politics," as he put it. Rustin implored the Freedom Democrats not to betray their friends in the labor movement. They had won a breakthrough victory in a long, grinding, and very political struggle for justice. The time had come to move beyond moral protest, claiming their historic victory and building upon it. The Freedom Democrats listened to Rustin politely but disagreed; he did not speak their language, and they did not know him. King went next, more gingerly. As a national movement leader, he said, he hoped they would accept the compromise and move on: "But if I were a Mississippi Negro, I would vote against it."[27]

That was exactly what happened, as the Freedom Democrats voted unanimously for self-respect and defying Johnson. They had risked their lives to vote at this convention, not to win a symbolic victory. A compromise that did not acknowledge their right to represent Mississippi and to choose their own representatives failed the test of decency, no matter that Rustin, Young, Wilkins, King, and a chorus of white liberals implored them to accept a symbolic victory. Johnson's insistence on naming the delegates cut deeper than the two token seats he offered, but both were offensive. Moreover, his proposal would have opened party meetings to blacks with no guarantee that they would be allowed to register to vote. The MFDP declared that it would have accepted "any honorable compromise." As it was, "this kind of dictation is what Negroes in Mississippi face and have always faced, and it is precisely this that they are learning to stand up against." On the issue of rejecting the compromise, SNCC leaders did not pressure the MFDP to agree with them; they stepped back as MFDP leaders Hamer, Victoria Gray, Unita Blackwell, and others made the case for saying no. The two organizations shared the same bitter disappointment at the outcome but responded to it differently, as the MFDP kept battling within the Democratic Party—campaigning for the Johnson–Humphrey ticket in a state that cast 87 percent of its votes for Goldwater. The corner-turning farewells and conversions came from SNCC.[28]

Atlantic City convinced Moses that his brave registration work was pointless. He never again spoke to Rauh, and he swore off working with whites or in the system. He fell into silence at meetings, resisting the deference that others gave him, which heightened his mystique until he walked out in February 1965, telling SNCC leaders they should vanish too. On his way out, Moses dropped his last name, going by Bob Parris. He went underground in Montreal for two years, fleeing the military draft, and settled in Tanzania. Charles Sherrod took a similarly dramatic turn, but within SNCC. Sherrod was a trusted friend and ally of Lewis, he had sparred with SNCC workers over his employment of white field secretaries and his commitment to Christianity, and he resisted the coup against Lewis when it came. But Sherrod joined the swing toward racial militancy that redefined SNCC. He argued that the crucial question for black Americans was whether they wanted to share power in reconciliation with whites or seize power "in rioting and blood." Winning a few positions changed nothing, he said. The MFDP was defeated at Atlantic City because blacks had no real power at the convention. Black Americans needed to build their own base of political power, not make alliances with white liberals that forced blacks to be satisfied with token gains. Blacks needed to become powerful as a people and for their own people instead of helping white liberals become more powerful. Sherrod spoke for an emerging majority that reconceptualized SNCC as a new-style black nationalist organization devoted to building up racial power: "We are a country of racists with a racist heritage, a racist economy, a racist language, a racist religion, a racist philosophy of living, and we need a naked confrontation with ourselves."[29]

Atlantic City went down in SNCC lore as the epitome of liberal betrayal and the proof that civil rights liberalism was bankrupt. Johnson, Humphrey, Rustin, and Reuther were marked as chief offenders, and Reuther's bully role showed why power was what mattered. New Left critic Staughton Lynd charged that Rustin had become "a labor lieutenant of capitalism" who pathetically prized his friendships with regular Democrats. The quintessential symbol of liberal betrayal, however, was Rauh. Being the best of the establishment liberals set up Rauh for singular ridicule; he was pilloried after Atlantic City. If the establishment liberal closest to SNCC could not be trusted to stand with oppressed blacks in Mississippi, to hell with the establishment white liberals. Rauh got squeezed in more ways than King because Rauh was a Humphrey liberal who didn't want to blow his friend's chance to be vice president, and much of Rauh's influence depended on the UAW. Yet Rauh stuck with the Freedom Democrats through the summer, when King confessed to being ambivalent about the MFDP challenge. Rauh wrote seamless, detailed legal briefs for the Freedom Democrats, saving SNCC from having to rely on National Lawyers Guild activists William Kunstler, Arthur Kinoy, and Ben Smith. Rauh forced the Democratic Party to hear the MFDP challenge, and, as Lewis reflected, he was "a serious, skillful, brilliant attorney, very polite and very passionate about basic human rights." Lewis recoiled as SNCC workers heaped condemnation on Rauh: "Joe Rauh would be seen as a villain, a traitor, a back stabber. And that was a shame. He was a good man who worked incredibly hard to bring this moment about. It's ironic that the situation he had worked so hard to create wound up skewering his reputation, at least among the black community."[30]

Atlantic City did not disabuse all white liberals of their innocence about integration and their roles in the civil rights movement. But it ended the innocence phase for all white liberals who were not willfully oblivious. To sing "We Shall Overcome" now evoked awkward feelings of self-consciousness in white liberals, whose typical concept of racism as personal bias did not help them comprehend their situation. Lewis realized that white Americans were overdue to interrogate their cultural privilege, as even the idealistic whites who poured into SNCC and Freedom Summer routinely exacerbated racial tensions in SNCC. Many were patronizing, and some were pushy. Even those who were neither caused problems simply by being themselves. It happened in SNCC before Freedom Summer; then the gusher of Freedom Summer students magnified the issue. Lewis recalled, "A skilled, college-educated white volunteer would arrive from someplace like Smith College, a well-meaning coed just brimming with earnestness, and she would get right down to business, typing like the wind, cranking out newsletters, speaking at meetings, just shining, giving us everything we could want in terms of office and organizational and public relations skills." Meanwhile her fellow worker felt humiliated: "It might be all she could do to tap out maybe thirty words a minute, and here comes this white college woman doing seventy-five with one hand tied behind her back. That was bound to cause resentment, and it did." Some white activists pushed into leadership roles, with variable degrees of self-promotion: "This was always a sensitive area, and even the most self-aware whites sometimes had trouble knowing where the boundaries were."[31]

Having begun as a small, southern, black, Christian, Gandhian movement organization that operated by consensus, SNCC took fierce pride in its antiauthoritarianism and its respect for the individual freedom of every SNCC worker. Moses said as little as possible at meetings, holding back from exercising his personal authority, and he let workers set their own schedules. By Freedom Summer, however, SNCC had two hundred staff workers and a flood of white volunteers. Forman ran its daily operations with little regard for SNCC's Gandhian origins, which he had never shared. Northern intellectuals gained the upper hand, operating by consensus no longer worked, and Lewis became a throwback. In that case, why should he still be chair? If SNCC was truly radical, perhaps it should have no leaders at all.[32]

The surge for a new ideology came from northern intellectuals with very different backgrounds from the SNCC founders. Carmichael, Courtney Cox, and Charles Cobb were more political, intellectual, and aggressive than the southern blacks they joined, having lived in white northern contexts where they had white friends. Then they joined SNCC in its Deep South work and disowned their cultural backgrounds, reinventing themselves as racial radicals. For them it was a liberating experience of empowerment to affirm their blackness. Lewis and civil rights lawyer Roger Wilkins put it psychologically, stressing that the Carmichael faction purged itself of the self-hatred that came from being validated by white teachers and role models. Lewis recalled, "They disowned their own experiences with whites in the North, as they came south and were swept up by ugliness and anger. I saw it happen so many times." Lewis and his closest SNCC allies—Bob Mants and Don Harris—felt the irony as SNCC debated its racial identity and ideology. They had lived their entire lives in a black world and had never been conflicted or confused about their racial identity. Mants put it bluntly at a SNCC meeting: "A Southern Negro doesn't need to wear a sign saying he's black. We don't need to wear Afros to show that we are black. We *know* we are black."[33]

Freedom Summer exhausted Lewis, blunting his awareness of how fast the organization was changing. At Atlantic City Lewis told reporters and delegates that the Freedom Democrats had shed too much blood to be treated as honorary guests. In less than two months the Mississippi Summer Project yielded sixty beatings, eight unsolved killings, seventeen church burnings, thirteen bombings, and twenty-three shootings. Lewis grieved that King sided with the liberals at Atlantic City, but he was grateful that King found the least offensive way of selling out. Then Lewis offended SNCC comrades by refusing to join them in bashing King. Lewis never wavered in admiring and emulating King. As a board member of SCLC, Lewis straddled the two organizations. Like Bevel and Vivian, who had come out of SNCC, Lewis prized King for approximating a Gandhian ideal. Observers sometimes scoffed that King was the only SCLC leader who really believed in redemptive suffering and Gandhian pacifism; his preacher lieutenants only went along with it out of deference to King and strategic necessity. But that did not describe Lewis, Bevel, Lawson, Lafayette, or Young, for whom King exemplified the way of the cross.

SNCC was long on youthful activists who lived for the movement, deferred their graduate education, and had no personal lives not enmeshed with the movement. After Atlantic City Harry Belafonte recognized that his SNCC friends were in trouble emotionally, so he helped them get to newly independent Guinea, to recharge. Belafonte's friend Ahmed Sékou Touré was president of Guinea and eager to meet civil rights leaders. Lewis made the trip along with Moses, Forman, Hamer, Don Harris, Julian Bond, and five others, and Lewis spent two extra weeks touring Liberia, Ghana, Ethiopia, and Kenya with Harris. Everywhere that Lewis and Harris went, Africans asked about Malcolm X. King's rhetoric seemed boring and staid to them. Malcolm was the electrifying figure who spoke to them. On their way to Zambia Lewis and Harris got waylaid in Nairobi, Kenya, where they passed an afternoon at a hotel courtyard café and were astonished to encounter Malcolm. The three Americans compared their travel experiences, and Malcolm spoke expansively about his changing worldview. Egypt's light-colored Muslims had made a deep impression on him, Malcolm said; he no longer believed that racial color was so important. Black Americans were obsessed with the United States, but he wanted to be part of a movement that focused on the world's poor of all races in their struggles against hegemonic governments.[34]

Malcolm was in transition during Freedom Summer. He broke with the Nation of Islam in March 1964 and expressed a desire to work with civil rights leaders, explaining that Nation leader Elijah Muhammad had forbidden him to do so. The following month Malcolm made a pilgrimage to Mecca as a Sunni Muslim, and he traveled twice to Africa in the spring and summer, meeting numerous heads of state, including Kwame Nkrumah of Ghana, Gamal Abdel Nasser of Egypt, and Ahmed Ben Bella of Algeria. To SNCC leaders Malcolm had long been an iconic figure but walled off from them. Now Malcolm was starting over, like them. They, too, were recalibrating the importance of Pan-African unity and thinking globally. Lewis looked forward to talking about it when he returned to the United States. But when he got home in late November his friends chastised him for staying too long. Derision of Lewis had gone public and nasty, and SNCC took a battering in the press, accused of harboring Communist agents and relying on Communists from the National Lawyers Guild. Lowenstein provided knowing quotes on the Communist issue, charging that SNCC did nothing to ward off Communist infiltrators. Lewis waged a counteroffensive, insisting that he was still chair of SNCC, Moses was still director of the Mississippi project, and Communists had not overtaken SNCC. But Lewis's days at SNCC were numbered.[35]

SNCC needed an organizational overhaul with structures of accountability or, failing that, a galvanizing leader who held things together. It needed money to pay its mushroomed staff, and it needed a sage or therapist to help with burnout. None of these things happened. Lewis was marginalized, the insurgent faction disdained organizational restructuring and accountability, Moses refused to be the unifying leader, the bad publicity after Atlantic City killed

SNCC's sporadic fund-raising, burnout spread like a contagion, and SNCC disagreed about its fundamental objectives.

Meanwhile King won the Nobel Peace Prize, which incurred Hoover's wrath, and Johnson crushed Goldwater, which convinced King to strike as soon as possible for voting rights. King reaped wave after wave of acclaim—feted by West Berlin mayor Willy Brandt, greeted warmly by Pope Paul VI, and speaking to throngs in London. He barely endured all of it, as he was deeply depressed from exhaustion and anxiety. Many days King had to struggle to crawl out of bed. He took a desperate vacation in Bimini, accepting Powell's offer of an island escape, but it was cut short by Hoover's sensational declaration to a group of female journalists that King was America's "most notorious liar" and, off the record, "one of the lowest characters in the country." En route to London, King poured out his dread and fear to Wachtel, worrying that Hoover would expose his sexual affairs. Then he risked everything on a big, dangerous, nervy campaign in Selma.[36]

SELMA

The Nobel Prize, despite King's depression, touched him deeply. He took other awards in stride, barely feeling anything besides speech-obligation. The Nobel Prize registered differently, thrilling and gratifying him. Many wanted to share the moment, so King brought twenty-six friends, relatives, and SCLC officers, the largest entourage in Nobel history. Abernathy, Rustin, Walker, Young, Cotton, Wachtel, and Reddick were among them. Daddy King stole the opening night by declaring emotionally why it mattered so much: He had always wanted to make a contribution, and God heard his prayer by giving him Martin Luther King Jr. Now the King family would go down in world history, not only American history. Abernathy behaved badly in Oslo, pouting that half of everything awarded to King should go to him. Many were offended, but King indulged his road and prison partner, as always. King was visibly moved when Gunnar John, chair of the Norwegian Parliament's Nobel Committee, introduced him as the first Westerner to show that a great struggle for justice could be waged without violence.[37]

He accepted the prize on behalf of a still-struggling civil rights movement and the millions of black Americans still living in "debilitating and grinding poverty." King eschewed Niebuhrian dialectics about violence in nonviolence and justice, declaring flatly, "Civilization and violence are antithetical concepts." This was an occasion for nonviolent religious idealism: "Man must evolve for all human conflict a method which rejects vengeance, aggression and retaliation.

The foundation of such a method is love." The road from Montgomery to Oslo had been torturous, King said, beginning a run of metaphors, but it opened "for all Americans a new era of progress and hope." This road had already led to a new civil rights bill, and it was leading to "a superhighway of justice" for all Americans: "I accept this award today with an abiding faith in America and an audacious faith in the future of mankind." King refused to believe that human beings were morally incapable of "reaching up for the eternal 'oughtness'" that all morally conscious human beings felt. He refused to believe that humankind was so "tragically bound to the starless midnight of racism and war that the bright daybreak of peace and brotherhood can never become a reality." He refused to believe that the nations "must spiral down a militaristic stairway into the hell of thermonuclear destruction."[38]

To have faith was precisely to refuse to believe these supposed truisms. King still believed in Gandhian social gospel nonviolence, and thus he still believed in the triumph of peace and redemptive goodwill. His deepening anger at white presumption and bigotry, however, blunted his earlier tendency to charm white audiences with his affability. King's daily drill wore on him. Wherever he went he got the same stupid questions about why there still needed to be a civil rights movement and why he seemed angry. In the summer of 1964 journalist Alex Haley started asking King for a high-profile interview in *Playboy*. It took two months to win an appointment, which King broke with apologies, pressed by his usual schedule and emergencies. Haley tracked King for a week, estimating that King worked twenty hours per day and never had enough time for anything.

Finally King cleared time for the longest interview he ever gave, conversing with an interviewer who knew what to ask. Haley, identified only as "Playboy," found King to be grimly serious, aside from an occasional flash of irony. What were King's worst mistakes? King cited three: He should not have bailed out of jail in Montgomery, which cost the movement publicity; he should have struck for something specific in Albany instead of campaigning too generally against segregation; and he overestimated the spiritual integrity of white southern ministers. King's deepest regret, by far, was the ministers. The essence of Pauline Christianity, he said, was to rejoice at being deemed worthy to suffer for the divine good: "The projection of a social gospel, in my opinion, is the true witness of a Christian life." The white ministers who sat out the civil rights movement flunked that test.[39]

Haley asked if black churches did better at projecting a social gospel and King gave his only evasive answer, hedging on no. Trying to mobilize black ministers was "almost always a problem," he said. Ministers were averse to movements they did not organize, and most had no experience with movement

activism. Many just wanted to preach about heaven. King stressed the difference, however, between the situations of the white and black churches. White
churches were not oppressed in America, while black churches were subjected
to the worst brutality ever inflicted on Christian churches anywhere: "Not since
the days of the Christians in the catacombs has God's house, as a symbol,
weathered such attack as the Negro churches." King recalled that when the
Birmingham girls were slaughtered he had a despairing moment: "I can
remember thinking that if men were this bestial, was it all worth it?"[40]

Haley asked how it felt to be called De Lawd and Booker T. King. King
said it went with being a public leader. He identified with Lincoln's remark
that if he responded to his critics he would lack time for anything else. Haley
asked how one could be militant and nonviolent at the same time; King said
this was like realism and idealism. A seeker of justice *had* to be realistic *and*
idealistic, holding to both in tension. Nonviolence was a healing sword, "a
weapon fabricated of love." Haley observed that many whites believed the civil
rights movement had gone far enough and should not incur resentment by
pressing on. King had waited for this moment. His blistering response made the
interview:

> Why do white people seem to find it so difficult to understand that the Negro
> is sick and tired of having reluctantly parceled out to him those rights and
> privileges which all others receive upon birth or entry in America? I never
> cease to wonder at the amazing presumption of much of white society,
> assuming that they have the right to bargain with the Negro for his freedom.
> This continued arrogant ladling out of pieces of the rights of citizenship has
> begun to generate a *fury* in the Negro.[41]

The fury in King was a harbinger of the rage that retired the word "Negro"
the following summer. King told Haley that black Americans wanted "absolute
and unqualified freedom and equality" and nothing else and nothing less.
There was nothing new about this demand, he noted. *Every* black American
leader since 1900 said it in some way. The only new thing was that black
Americans as a whole were finished with being abused. American society was
in a crisis because blacks were fed up and whites were tired of hearing
about blacks. King observed that "abysmal ignorance" prevailed among white
Americans on racial justice. Three groups were especially significant. One
was the whole class of "bigots and backlashers" that attacked the civil rights
movement. Another group, woefully ignorant public officials, discharged their
responsibilities without recognizing the harm they caused, grossly ignorant of
why blacks were angry. The third group was the hardest to take—"enlightened"

types who gave nauseating counsel about proceeding gradually: "I wonder at men who dare to feel that they have some paternalistic right to set the time-table for another man's liberation. . . . America today is an extremely sick nation."[42]

Haley had questions about civil rights leaders, Communists, and Malcolm. Who were the "most responsible" civil rights leaders? King started with Wilkins, who was "very articulate," and Whitney Young, who kept the Urban League going. He praised Farmer for being courageous and thoughtful, and Lewis for being courageous and creative. The greatest civil rights leader, however, was Randolph because of his integrity and statesmanship. Concerning Communism King blasted typical nonsense, saying he was "sick and tired" of hearing about Communist infiltration because the civil rights movement had no more Communists than Florida had Eskimos. Haley noted that Malcolm had "recently renounced his racist past," not mentioning that he and Malcolm were collaborating on what became *The Autobiography of Malcolm X*. What did King think of Malcolm? King regretted that his sole encounter with Malcolm lasted less than a minute—a photo-op at the Capitol during the debate over the Civil Rights Act. He was wary of seeming judgmental, and he acknowledged that he did not know to what extent Malcolm's views had changed. But he totally disagreed with Malcolm's philosophy, and he deeply regretted that Malcolm specialized in "fiery, demagogic oratory in the black ghettos," urging blacks to arm themselves and prepare to wage violence. Malcolm expressed "the despair of the Negro," but he offered no "positive, creative alternative," which was a tragedy; Malcolm's approach "can reap nothing but grief." Haley asked if King meant grief for blacks or whites. King said it was bad for everyone, but especially for the blacks that Malcolm influenced.[43]

Malcolm had begun to say that King owed him because he scared whites into accepting King. Malcolm said it in February 1965 upon visiting the Selma campaign, three weeks before he was assassinated. But the *Playboy* interview was scathing compared to King's usual speeches to white audiences. The "fury in the Negro" burned in him. Bigots and backlashers aside, he seethed at the casual racism of ordinary Americans. White Americans got a glimpse of King's anger in an unlikely magazine just after Hoover obscenely tried to blackmail King and SCLC struck in Selma. King sent Vivian to explore the situation in Selma, wanting the worst place they could find. Vivian reported that Selma was perfectly terrible and the ideal place to protest, with one caveat: SNCC was already there. Selma had notoriously hostile police and courts, a fearful and depressed black population, a powerful circuit judge, James Hare, and a vitriolic county sheriff, James G. Clark Jr. When the historic Freedom Bus from

Montgomery to Jackson bypassed Selma, nobody on the bus wanted to stop in Selma. Dallas County, though 60 percent black, had 335 black voters and more than 10,000 white voters. It had a registration test on the Constitution, government, reading, and dictation, replete with one hundred permutations that kept the electorate very white. The Dallas County Voters League, in a bravely desperate move, asked SCLC to come.[44]

White Selma was so mean that early SNCC field-workers got nowhere and SNCC briefly gave up on it. In August 1962 Bernard Lafayette asked Forman for a new assignment. Lafayette's quiet geniality got him less attention than other Lawson disciples, but he was deeply committed to Gandhian Christian protest, and he wanted something on his own. Thus he turned down Forman's proposal that he team up with Moses. Forman reconsidered, telling Lafayette that SNCC had nobody in Selma, so Lafayette moved there with his wife, Colia, in January 1963. He gave nine months to Selma before moving on to Fisk and the SCLC staff, long enough to start something. Lafayette held a few meetings and won a few allies, notably home economics teacher Amelia Boynton. On the same night that Medgar Evers was killed Lafayette was viciously beaten and left for dead. He broke through in Selma by staying on after he was beaten. Local blacks were shamed into attending Lafayette's meetings, and the wall of fear eroded slightly, creating an opening. Throughout the Deep South three groups worked on voter registration: SCLC, SNCC, and the civil rights division of the Justice Department. All three began to regard Selma as a showdown site, but Forman and other SNCC leaders recoiled at SCLC's new interest in Selma. SNCC leaders were fond of saying, not without warrant, that they put their lives on the line and SCLC reaped the credit.

That did not dissuade King from launching the Selma protest on January 2, 1965. Back in Atlanta Coretta King, still opening mail that piled up during the Nobel trip, opened a package containing a letter and audio recording. The letter was relentlessly vile:

> King, look into your heart. You know you are a complete fraud and a great liability to all of us Negroes. . . . You are a colossal fraud and an evil, vicious one at that. You could not believe in God. . . . Clearly you don't believe in any personal moral principles. King, like all frauds your end is approaching. . . . Satan could not do more. What incredible evilness. . . . The American public, the church organizations that have been helping—Protestant, Catholic and Jews will know you for what you are—an evil, abnormal beast. So will others who have backed you. You are done. King, there is only one thing left for you to do. You know what this is. . . . You better take it before your filthy, abnormal fraudulent self is bared to the nation.

The recording was a pastiche of bawdy remarks and the sounds of people having sex, featuring King's voice and others who partied with him, notably at the Willard Hotel in Washington, DC.[45]

King and Coretta listened to the recording along with Abernathy, Young, Joseph Lowery, and Chauncey Eskridge. The culprits were obvious: Hoover and his FBI sidekick William C. Sullivan. Everyone in King's group knew that King had a mistress and several lovers plus trysts with tall, beautiful, light-colored, model-like women who flocked to him. No one said anything about that, out of deference to King. Coretta King later said she never discussed this issue with her husband during their entire marriage, as her relationship with him was on a "very high level" transcending such things. What mattered immediately, as King despaired to a friend, was that Hoover was trying to break him. Hoover hated King for criticizing the FBI and for supposedly being a Communist. Then Hoover's bugs—sixteen by 1965—yielded salacious material that Hoover seized upon. King objected that his private life should have been off-limits to the FBI. As it was, the FBI message rattled him deeply, worsening his depression. Young protested to Hoover aide Deke DeLoach that the FBI harassment and leaks were out of bounds. DeLoach brazenly denied that the FBI took any interest in King's private life, which offended and frightened Young: If the FBI was going to lie about it there was no basis for a negotiation. But lying about it tied Hoover's hands, limiting what he could do to King without exposing the lie.[46]

Selma started slowly, with daily mass meetings and planning sessions, all of it more localized and grassroots than Birmingham had been. Local leaders Frederick Reese, Amelia Boynton, and Marie Foster played key roles in the planning. King counted on Clark's inability to hold his volatility in check, although for a while Clark denied SCLC a media spectacle. The real power in Selma, James Hare, was a self-styled intellectual who told reporters and Justice Department officials that all blacks were hopelessly inferior and that Selma sadly inherited West Africa's most inferior tribes. This was known in the Justice Department as the "bad boatload" theory of segregation. On January 15 Johnson promised King by telephone that he would send voting rights legislation to Congress as soon as he could muster votes for it, which would take a while—probably a year. Voting rights, LBJ declared, was the highest priority for civil rights. He advised King to spotlight registration abuses, such as requiring black Americans to recite Longfellow or the first ten amendments. King and LBJ agreed about that, but King was not for waiting.[47]

Three days later King and Lewis launched the campaign's direct action phase, leading 400 prospective voters to the Dallas County Courthouse, where they scrupulously obeyed the city's parade ordinance, waiting all day to register.

None were allowed into the courthouse. Like most days of most campaigns, nothing happened except the long waiting outside a closed door. That night a National States Rights Party activist slugged King at the Hotel Albert and was quickly pulled away by police chief Wilson Baker. The following day Clark forced the demonstrators into an alley and roughed up Boynton, which sparked protests and 67 arrests. The next day another 150 people got arrested, angering Baker, a former hardliner turned Pritchett-schooler who tried to avoid arrests and drama. Vivian and Bevel goaded Clark into lashing out, and King escalated the protest on February 1 by violating the parade ordinance and getting arrested. There were 265 parade protesters, followed by 500 schoolchildren; Baker reluctantly arrested all of them. From jail King told Young to seize the moment: Hold a protest every day, push hard, recruit more teachers, rally the politicians, and call the celebrities to Selma—"We must have a sense of drama." Selma made a breakthrough with teachers, usually a conservative group that guarded its privileged status. Selma was about voting, not lunch counters, and teachers took special offense at not being allowed to vote. In jail King told white SCLC staffer Charles Fager, "If we are going to achieve real equality, the United States will have to adopt a modified form of socialism." He told Young that he would stay in jail until the politicians and famous people arrived because they responded best when he was in jail.[48]

On February 4 Malcolm showed up in Selma—his first visit to a southern movement campaign—and King bridled at his appearance. Young, Bevel, and Coretta King had an amicable meeting with Malcolm, which surprised Coretta, though not Young, who had met Malcolm several times at the SCLC office. Young and Bevel cautioned Malcolm not to incite violence; he replied, as always, that nobody put words in his mouth. Malcolm said he was there to help the campaign, and he tried to visit King in jail but was turned away. At Brown Chapel Malcolm gave a bland—for him—talk about the divide between house Negroes and field Negroes, but he gave it with his customary strident, rapid-fire, northern style, which put off most of the audience. They were used to warm southern preachers with singsong cadences. Malcolm won cheers from the SNCC activists and a politely tepid response from the rest of the crowd. Then he told a press conference that white America needed to hurry up and support King "before some other factions come along and try to do it another way."[49]

Fifteen members of Congress arrived in Selma the next day and King bonded out to greet them. He pressed for a meeting with Johnson in the White House, who did not want to be lobbied but took the meeting anyway. King lauded LBJ's support of voting rights legislation and implored him to force the issue. Protests spread to Marion, Alabama, where police officers violently attacked protesters marching to the Perry County jail. Officers chased young Jimmie Lee Jackson into a café, beat him, and shot him; eight days later, on February 26, Jackson died. Meanwhile Malcolm was slain in a hail of bullets on February 21 in Harlem. Young and Lewis attended Malcolm's grim, stoic, intensely quiet funeral. King let the horror of it wash over him, banishing the usual distractions.

The previous November King had resolved to reach out to Malcolm, but Malcolm made an anti-Semitic outburst that changed King's mind; the new Malcolm was too much like the old one. King took seriously, however, that Young, Lewis, and Bevel respected Malcolm and that SNCC radicals revered him. Then even Coretta warmed to him. Malcolm's death pushed King to think about his own death. He announced that he wanted Abernathy to succeed him, disregarding that SCLC insiders had minimal respect for Abernathy. King preached Jimmie Lee Jackson's funeral in a deeply morbid mood, half expecting to be assassinated during the service. He made his first public reference to Vietnam, protesting that America poured blood and treasure into Vietnam without protecting its own citizens in Alabama. Then he held another meeting with LBJ, who had good news: Everett Dirksen promised to support a voting rights act. Johnson advised King to discuss the details of the bill with Attorney General Nicholas Katzenbach, who had confronted Wallace at the University of Alabama in 1963. King hustled back to Atlanta to decide what role he should play in Bevel's climactic drama in Selma: a march from Selma to Montgomery.[50]

The idea of marching fifty miles from Selma to Montgomery had occurred to Bevel during the Jackson funeral procession. In February Clark's deputies beat Bevel nearly to death after Bevel provoked Clark, which temporarily deterred Nash from telling Bevel their marriage was over. Bevel had left her to raise their two children by herself while continuing to romance his female admirers. Then Bevel crawled out of Clark's jail cell and had one of his visions, the perfect ending to Selma. Wallace banned the march, vowing to stop it. Katzenbach pleaded with King not to march because the risk of assassination was too great. King, Rustin, Wachtel, and Young hatched a compromise: King would join the march but with limited participation, catching up to it on the second day. SNCC leaders ridiculed King's decision as cowardly and typical, never mind that SNCC opposed the march anyway, deriding it as typical SCLC showboating. Lewis was the only SNCC leader who supported the march, making him feel lonelier than ever.

On Sunday, March 7, Lewis and Williams led six hundred backpacking marchers two-by-two across the Edmund Pettus Bridge. They had no plan or arrangements, and they would not have gotten far, as many marchers came straight from church in their Sunday best. The mood was somber, tense, and quiet, like a funeral procession. Lewis later recalled, "There was something holy about it, as if we were walking down a sacred path." At the end of the bridge two hundred state troopers led by Clark brutally carried out Wallace's vow to stop the march. The troopers charged headlong into the marchers, some on horseback, attacking with billy clubs and tear gas. Lewis took a beating that cracked his skull and gave him a brain concussion. Seventeen demonstrators had to be hospitalized, including Lewis. Young prevented the carnage from escalating by scurrying frantically in every direction, pleading against retaliation. Network television captured all of it vividly, nationalizing the Selma campaign in one evening. The images were graphic and revolting. "Bloody Sunday" aroused the nation like nothing before it—more than the Freedom Rides, Birmingham, the March on Washington, or Freedom Summer. That evening the battered marchers regrouped at Brown Chapel and resolved to march again in two days. The call went out to come to Selma. Approximately five hundred white clergy did so, surging to Selma from across the country.[51]

King hurried back to Selma, and the SCLC lawyers petitioned Federal District Judge Frank M. Johnson Jr. for an order barring any obstruction of Tuesday's march. Judge Johnson said a full hearing had to be convened first, which stymied King as the ministers poured into Selma. Forman, suddenly a proponent of the march, urged King not to wait for the hearing, and Hosea Williams also implored King to push ahead with the Tuesday march. John Doar urged King to wait for Judge Johnson's support, which would come if King respected the court process. King agonized over the decision until Doar and Community Relations Service Director LeRoy Collins talked him into a compromise: a symbolic march that crossed the Pettus Bridge and returned to Selma. King led an unknowing parade of marchers across the bridge. He halted, prayed, led a chorus of "We Shall Overcome," winced as the troopers stepped aside, and looped back across the bridge to Brown Chapel, where Forman and others berated him for betraying the movement.

It was a deeply embarrassing moment, threatening to end Selma badly. King never settled on which bad explanation to adopt. If he said he had cut a deal with the government, he looked like a sellout. If he said there was no deal, he risked a contempt of court citation and a no from Judge Johnson. At first King dissembled, claiming that the troopers would not have allowed the march to proceed; two days later he admitted in Johnson's court that there was a tacit agreement; in other contexts he continued to dissemble. Meanwhile a Boston Unitarian minister, James Reeb, was murdered by a Selma mob, which yielded a huge national outpouring of grief and protest, and LBJ embraced the Selma campaign at a press conference in the Rose Garden. The following Monday evening, on

March 15, Johnson gave a powerful speech to Congress inviting all Americans to support "the dignity of man and the destiny of Democracy." LBJ linked Selma to Lexington, Concord, and Appomattox as places where history and fate met "to shape a turning point in man's unending search for freedom." He said the issue of racial justice laid bare "the secret heart of America itself." He condemned racist restrictions on voting and the "crippling legacy of bigotry and injustice," vowing dramatically, "And we shall overcome." He used the phrase a second time in vowing to overcome "poverty, disease, and ignorance," adding, "The real hero of this struggle is the American Negro. His actions and protests, his courage to risk safety, and even to risk his life, have awakened the conscience of this nation." King watched the speech on television, surrounded by friends. In nine years of campaigning King had never publicly shed tears, until the president said, "We Shall Overcome."[52]

Forman protested that that ruined a good song; at a Selma rally he added, "If we can't sit at the table of democracy, we'll knock the fucking legs *off*." The crowd was stunned by Forman's vulgarity, as Lewis, the ministers, and the churchgoing locals gasped with embarrassment. King followed Forman to the pulpit, announcing that Judge Johnson had approved a march to Montgomery beginning on Sunday, March 21. This time there were five days of elaborate preparations. LBJ lined the highway with eighteen hundred Alabama National Guardsmen and two thousand U.S. Army troops. There were three thousand marchers for most of the way, with the largest infusion ever of white church leaders. Rabbi Abraham Joshua Heschel made his protest debut. King marched and departed and returned, frustrated that he had to hustle to other appointments, and Belafonte organized a star-studded concert outside Montgomery. Some marchers expressed disappointment that King seemed so ordinary, not a galvanizing leader. Kentucky politician Georgia Davis Powers, not yet romantically involved with King, reacted very differently, appreciating King's genial humility during the march: "Many times he went to the side of the road to shake hands with an old person in tatters, say a kind word to a drunk, and rub the head of a child. He talked to them personally, and he listened."[53]

At the concluding rally in Montgomery Lewis noticed that the Alabama and Confederate flags flew high above the rotunda dome, with no U.S. flag. Coretta King enthused that the rally offered the church's greatest witness "since the days of the early Christians." Nine speakers preceded Lewis, who preceded King, who expounded memorably on God and the movement marching on: "We are on the move now. The burning of our churches will not deter us. We are on the move now. The bombing of our homes will not dissuade us. We are on the move now. The beating and killing of our clergymen and young people will not divert us. . . . I must admit to you there are still jail cells waiting for us, dark and difficult moments. We will go on with the faith that nonviolence and its power transformed dark yesterdays into bright tomorrows." He asked rhetorically how much longer the struggle would take: "How long? Not long, because the arm of the moral universe is long but it bends toward justice."[54]

Selma marked four turning points. It led to the Voting Rights Act of August 6, 1965. It turned King into the political leader of millions of white Americans, outnumbering his black following. It marked the end of King's influence over black militants in SNCC and the Black Power movement. And it marked the end of King's willingness to confine SCLC campaigns to the South. The Selma march was not supposed to end SCLC's Alabama campaign. Viola Gregg Liuzzo, a white homemaker from Detroit who took part in the march, was murdered by a carload of Klan nightriders shortly after the Montgomery rally. King could not let the Klan provide the ending of the Alabama campaign, and he vowed to keep fighting against Wallace's "reign of terror." With no advanced planning King announced an economic boycott against the entire state. He wanted the federal government to cut off all federal program funds into Alabama, the U.S. Treasury to withdraw all federal funds from Alabama banks, and unions to transport no Alabama goods. The liberal establishments, white and black, howled in objection. Whitney Young, Jacob Javits, and the Johnson administration said a boycott would harm blacks and poor whites, and Rustin said the idea was flat-out stupid. The worst problems confronting the civil rights movement were class-based, not race-based, Rustin argued. He wanted SCLC to push for national health insurance, a public works jobs program, and a two-dollar minimum wage.[55]

King was for all these things but not for settling for liberal politics. His best opportunity to retire from movement politics came after Selma, when King was asked every day if the civil rights movement was over. The question galled him, fueling his resolve to double down in the North. Discrimination was still the worst problem faced by black Americans everywhere in America. In the North racism was structural and threefold in every city. Segregated housing led to segregated schools, and segregated housing and schools handicapped black Americans in the job market. King vowed to keep the heat on Alabama and to push harder than ever somewhere else—a northern city to be determined.

CHICAGO AND BLACK POWER

King and Young narrowed the list to Chicago, Cleveland, New York, Philadelphia, and Washington, DC. Chicago was a showcase of urban misery, and it had a coalition of activist groups, the Coordinating Council of Community Organizations (CCCO), led by black schoolteacher Al Raby. The CCCO had a militant flank led by Chicago CORE and the Chicago Area Friends of SNCC and a moderate flank led by the Chicago Urban League and the Chicago Catholic Interracial Council. King made a whirlwind tour of Chicago in late July, leading fifteen thousand marchers down State Street on July 26, which he enjoyed despite teetering on exhaustion. He made a less interesting tour of Cleveland and would have gone next to New York, but Powell told him to stay out of New York. He visited Philadelphia only briefly; by then King had nearly settled on Chicago.

His visit to the nation's capital coincided with Johnson's signing of the Voting Rights Act, where King told the president he wanted new housing and job-training programs, a cutoff of federal aid to segregated school systems, and a crackdown on slumlords. LBJ was supportive, asking King to submit a detailed proposal. From there King headed to SCLC's annual convention in Birmingham, where he called for the United States to negotiate with the Viet Cong and halt the bombing of North Vietnam. King asked the board to support him; many board members were appalled. This was how King proposed to treat their friend in the White House? The board commended King for having a conscience about such things but rebuffed his request, declaring that SCLC existed to secure full citizenship rights for black Americans, and it lacked the resources to add the peace issue to its agenda. King responded graciously, explaining that he did not believe SCLC should lift the peace issue to the same level as civil rights. Still, he would not be silent about the war because he had a Christian conscience about war and he was more than a civil rights leader.[56]

LBJ, upon signing the Voting Rights Act, implored King to carry through on the voting issue by registering every possible black voter. King had already put voter registration in the hands of Williams, who founded SCLC's Summer Community Organization and Political Education Project (SCOPE) in the summer of 1965. But Williams mismanaged the program, alarming Young, King, and Voter Education Project program director Randolph Blackwell. Blackwell told King to shut down SCOPE before its waste and scandal brought down SCLC. That was painfully debated at SCLC's convention, where Rustin, Bevel, and Young offered competing visions of its future. Rustin made a twofold pitch for focusing on national economic issues and continuing direct action protests in the South. Bevel countered that civil rights organizations were no longer needed: "There is no more civil rights movement. President Johnson signed it out of existence when he signed the voting rights bill."[57]

Bevel was a font of brilliant ideas and bizarre ones. He had always been eccentric, hearing only his own voice. Sometimes he argued loudly with himself while walking alone. After Selma Bevel zoomed further out there; at the convention staffers rolled their eyes that Bevel was off again. But Bevel had earned his right to be heard even on his worst days. He burned with righteous idealism; he was fiercely devoted to King even as he took no counsel from King or anyone else; and he was dead serious. Bevel could not bear to watch SCLC drift into irrelevance. He feared that Rustin's proposal would turn it into a mere lobbying operation, and he still held Lawson's original vision of a nonviolent army that intervened wherever violence and oppression existed. Bevel wanted to take a peace army to Vietnam. Lawson himself and Ella Baker chided Bevel for taking leave of the real world, as Vietnam was far away. Young countered with a King-like blend of religious idealism and political realism, telling the convention, "We are not an especially brilliant people. We are not, God forgive us, even a particularly industrious people. And we are hardly what moralists would call a good people. But somehow, God has chosen us as his people." Christian-Gandhian nonviolence was still the basis of SCLC and its work, Young urged: "If we are true to Gandhi, and seek to attack issues rather than people, we can hope to inspire even our opposition to new moral heights, and thereby overcome."[58]

King was desperate for a break, so he headed to San Juan, Puerto Rico. But the Watts section of Los Angeles erupted in a riot and King stopped in Miami. LBJ, stunned and mortified by the riot, could not bring himself to look at the cables from Los Angeles. He did nothing, stewing in grief; Watts was a terrible omen for Johnson. Rustin, meanwhile, implored King not to go to Watts. If he helped to quell the violence, he would be tagged as an Uncle Tom. If he failed to quell the violence, that would be worse. King held out for two days before telling Rustin to meet him in Los Angeles—an awkward destination for Rustin, as it was the site of his two great humiliations. His arrest for gay "perversion" had occurred in Los Angeles, seven years before the Powell fiasco. The first episode cost Rustin his sonlike relationship with Muste; the second banished him from King's inner circle. Rustin reluctantly came to Watts and walked the streets with King and Young.

King, mounting a platform, was jeered when he tried to speak. He called for nonviolence and working together, noting that whites had been jailed and killed along with blacks in the civil rights struggle. He met with Mayor Sam Yorty and Police Chief William Parker, who told him that blacks in Los Angeles had no legitimate grievances. King told a press conference the riot was "a class revolt of underprivileged against privileged." Poor blacks were angry at white liberals and the black middle class, he said. Robert Kennedy wounded King by telling reporters that the civil rights movement overemphasized middle-class issues. King told Young that the rioting was a judgment on SCLC for precisely that reason. Young hated it when King talked like that. How were they supposed to save America with one hundred staff members and a $600,000 budget? King insisted that RFK was right, however much it hurt. A young Watts protester boasted to Rustin that "our manifesto" had finally brought the likes of him to Watts. Rustin asked to see a copy: "He pulled out a matchbox; he pulled out a single match; he lit it. He said, 'Daddy, that was our manifesto,' and the slogan was 'Burn, baby, burn.' "[59]

The riot raged for six days, killing thirty-four people. Rustin later recalled, "Martin was absolutely shaken by it. He was absolutely undone." Rustin said it was pointless to make speeches about law and order because order did not come from enforcing or piling up laws. Dwelling on police brutality missed the point, too, because Watts would have exploded even with model police officers. Watts exploded because life in Watts was hellish and desperate. Watts had thrived on the defense industry during World War II, but afterward the jobs dried up and Watts decayed badly. Blacks watched their unemployment soar to 50 percent while the civil rights movement did almost nothing for them. Rustin acknowledged that the Fair Employment Practices Committee provisions in the Civil Rights Act were an exception; otherwise, the movement seemed to care only about the civil rights of southern blacks. The War on Poverty, he said, at least targeted the right issue. But settling for Sargent Shriver's literacy programs and summer camps would be a disaster, making the beneficiaries more frustrated after they returned to their miserable neighborhoods. Rustin called for a "massive public works program" coupled with training for modern jobs: "I'll tell you what those boys are: they are sticks of dynamite with a time fuse, planted in the ghetto with their frustrated expectations." In 1863, Rustin recalled, the Irish were denigrated as lazy, dirty, and ugly; they rioted in New York, killing over three hundred people and lynching thirty-one blacks; and their murderous rampaging was much worse than what happened in Watts, notwithstanding that Watts was repeatedly said to be the worst riot in American history. Rustin had nothing against the Irish: "No, I only say that poor frustrated people will riot."[60]

Only a month earlier King had fantasized about taking a year off to regain his health. Now he had to reinvent SCLC, while fencing nervously with LBJ about Vietnam. Johnson dramatically escalated the war in February 1965 by bombing North Vietnam in Operation Flaming Dart and pouring ground troops directly into South Vietnam's fight against the Viet Cong. He and King had awkward conversations in which Johnson defended his escalation and claimed not to be a warmonger, while King defended his waffling criticisms of the war and claimed to believe Johnson. That spring a three-pronged antiwar movement surged. It had a pacifist left flank led by FOR, the War Resisters League, and the Catholic Worker, which had protested the war since 1963. It had a liberal left flank led by the Committee for a SANE Nuclear Policy and a trickle of war critics from Americans for Democratic Action. Above all, it had a burgeoning radical left led by Students for a Democratic Society (SDS), a New Left youth organization founded in 1960. SDS was stocked with veterans of the Freedom Rides and Freedom Summer. It organized the first big demonstration against the war, on April 17, 1965, in Washington D.C., drawing a crowd of twenty-five thousand. There, Bob Moses asked plaintively if Americans had the right to kill Vietnamese in the name of defending American society. In October a handful of religious leaders organized an ecumenical forum that morphed three months later into an important antiwar organization, the National Emergency Committee of Clergy Concerned About Vietnam. Founded in the apartment of Union Theological Seminary president John C. Bennett, Clergy Concerned About Vietnam was led by Bennett, Heschel, Yale chaplain William Sloane Coffin Jr., Lutheran pastor Richard John Neuhaus, Jesuit priest Daniel Berrigan, Stanford theologian Robert McAfee Brown, NCC deputy secretary David Hunter, and King. Its national board had twenty-eight Protestants, seven Jews, and five Catholics. Coffin provided quotable zingers to the press, and the group won ample publicity, much of it alarmed that a coalition of distinguished antiwar clerics existed. King realized that Vietnam changed everything politically, and he could not avoid offending Johnson—although he tried to avoid it.[61]

Meanwhile King faced a decision about mounting a big, risky, expensive campaign in Chicago. He called the entire SCLC brain trust and senior staff to Atlanta to debate it. Bevel was the leading pro-Chicago advocate, urging that SCLC needed to show that nonviolent activism worked in the North. Black Chicago was not significantly different from the black South, Bevel argued; in fact, black Chicago *was* the black South moved to the North. Bevel cautioned, however, that the Chicago campaign had to focus on something bigger than ousting School Superintendent Benjamin Willis. Thus far CCCO had aimed too low. Rustin led the opposition, urging that Chicago was very different from the Deep South; SCLC needed to stick to its sphere of competence. He got personal in pressing the point, telling Bevel and King, "You don't know what you are talking about. You don't know what Chicago is like. You're going to be wiped out." Young sided with Rustin, though awkwardly. In theory Young wanted to strike somewhere in the North; on the other hand, Chicago was very problematic. Chicago was huge, complex, foreign to SCLC, and forbidding.

Moreover, CCCO had no history of exacting economic pressure; all it did was protest. King announced that he would pray about it. That angered Rustin, knowing what it meant. The discussion was over, and King had decided: They had to strike somewhere in the North, and it might as well be Chicago.[62]

It helped that Diane Nash lived in Chicago, though her marriage to Bevel was ending, and Lafayette worked there with the American Friends Service Committee. Above all, the Chicago campaign brought Jesse Jackson onto the SCLC staff as Bevel's protégé and SCLC's liaison with CCCO. Born in 1941 in Greenville, South Carolina, to a high school student and her married neighbor, Jackson was taunted as a youth for his out-of-wedlock birth, which scarred him. He grew up in Greenville, enrolled at the University of Illinois on a football scholarship, and transferred to North Carolina A&T in Greensboro, where he joined the student movement and graduated in 1964. That fall he enrolled at Chicago Theological Seminary, studying under CCCO leader Alan Pitcher. The following year Jackson brought a group of seminarians to Selma, where he caught King's attention.

King liked Jackson's energetic self-confidence and his lack of SNCC-like romanticism about the proletariat. Jackson was eager to be a leader in the Baptist social gospel preacher mold. Young surmised early on that Jackson looked to King as a father figure, which was not going to work. Young later explained, "While neither Martin nor I had any trouble being a brother to Jesse, we were struggling ourselves with our own identity development and in no position to play a fatherly role." That was slightly misleading as applied to Jackson, who had relationships with his biological father and stepfather, and ironic in Young's case since King routinely roasted Young for being too well adjusted. King enjoyed and relied upon the quirks and bullishness of Bevel, Williams, Abernathy, Vivian, Shuttlesworth, Walker, and, now, Jackson. He teased SCLC's staff member in Washington, DC, Walter Fauntroy, that Fauntroy was too smooth and temperate, like Young. To push into Chicago King needed an aggressive personality who knew Chicago and sought leadership roles. That described Jackson, so he dropped out of seminary to became a full-time activist.[63]

The Chicago campaign began in January 1966 and focused on Chicago's lack of adequate housing for blacks. Bevel called it a "war on slums." King called it a struggle against a structure of economic oppression "crystallized in the SLUM," which he described as "a system of internal colonialism not unlike the exploitation of the Congo by Belgium." Virtually every long-standing institution in Chicago played a role in perpetuating its slums, including the trade unions, welfare boards, and city government. King said he had previously believed that northern blacks would "benefit derivatively from the Southern struggle," but by 1965 he had changed his mind, having surveyed "the Negro's repellent slum life" in the North. He dramatized the housing issue by renting a dilapidated fourth-floor walk-up apartment on South Hamlin Avenue near Sixteenth Street, in the Lawndale section, which at first did not impress the neighbors. To them it was a publicity stunt by an unwelcome celebrity. King rarely stayed there, but the apartment became a symbol plus the unofficial headquarters of a campaign focused on open housing.[64]

Young stayed there often, always fearfully. Getting lynched in Alabama would have been one thing, Young said. Getting knifed by a Chicago junkie was very different, and nothing he could accept. For the first time in his life Young lived in fear of being killed. Every night he climbed the stairs with his heart racing, picturing himself dying far from his wife and children. He kept telling himself that this situation showed why they needed to take the struggle north, without believing it. If a junkie murdered him it would be "the ultimate absurdity," lacking any redeeming value. Jackson, Jimmy Collier, and other field-workers organized block meetings to mobilize tenants, and Bevel organized a protest campaign. But SCLC faced stiff opposition from black ministers who were unwilling to support something they did not control. Jackson had greater success with Operation Breadbasket. Founded in Philadelphia by Baptist minister Leon Sullivan, Operation Breadbasket enlisted businesses in black communities to provide jobs for blacks. Fred Bennett administered SCLC's first Breadbasket program, in Atlanta. The Chicago version was modestly successful, with a rotating chair, when Jackson got there. Formally, he kept the rotating chair, but in effect, Jackson took over the organization and built it into a powerful employment vehicle that long outlasted SCLC's Chicago campaign.[65]

The work in Chicago was grinding and slow, and it lacked a unifying focus. LBJ pushed a new civil rights act in Congress that would have barred racial discrimination in the sale and rental of all housing. It passed the House in August 1966 but stalled in the Senate as Democrats failed to muster a cloture vote against a threatened filibuster. The Civil Rights Act of 1966 died in the Senate in September after a second failed cloture attempt. In the months leading up to the Senate failure SCLC got a bitter taste of the shifting politics and the sheer difficulty of mobilizing around the housing issue. Bevel, Lafayette, Young, and other SCLC workers got hostile treatment on a daily basis from the housing industry, city government, homeowners, and putative allies. Bevel and Lafayette concentrated on East Garfield, organizing tenants that were hard to pull together and harder to mobilize for specific goals. At King's request Lawson made periodic visits from Memphis to provide pastoral counseling to the organizers, as King worried that his staffers were burning out. Young felt conflicted much of the time. King relied on Young as his chief operative and alter ego, but Young paid for it by taking constant barbs from staffers, including King. In Chicago Young missed the spirituality and warmth of southerners, who readily talked about God bringing them thus far. He missed the clarity of the struggle for dignity and citizenship in the South, where class factors seemed less important. Young sympathized that Chicago ministers probably had good reasons to resist the SCLC newcomers in their midst. It took months to nurture even tenuous relationships, though at least the churches were repositories of black spiritual culture in Chicago.

Young was just beginning to get traction in Chicago when James Meredith got shot on June 6, 1966, and the civil rights movement rushed to Memphis to complete Meredith's march. Young had minimal regard for Meredith, a prickly individualist who could not be bothered with organizations or other people. Marches were supposed to dramatize concrete community demands, not somebody's need for attention. Young disliked that "an ego trip by one man" hijacked the entire movement. He clashed with Williams over that reaction, as Williams accused Young of being scared of Mississippi, and Young said he was sick of being bullied by Williams. As always, there was a turf issue at play: Williams resented that the Chicago campaign swung the media's attention away from his work in the Deep South. But Young rushed to Memphis to join Williams and King, who were in a staff meeting in Atlanta when word came that Meredith had been shot. King hastened to Meredith's hospital bed and rejoiced that Meredith was not seriously wounded. Lawson brokered an agreement between CORE's new executive director, Floyd McKissick, and SNCC's new leader, Stokely Carmichael, to join King in carrying out the march. They also agreed to invite other civil rights leaders to join them. Carmichael, however, had to overcome SNCC's opposition to joining the march, and he had no intention of marching with Wilkins and Whitney Young.[66]

SNCC had had a dramatic half-year. SNCC identified with the New Left as much as it identified with civil rights, yet it was a bit slow to oppose the Vietnam War. In January 1966, just before LBJ gave his epic "guns and butter" State of the Union speech, SNCC came out against the war. To Lewis it felt belated, as he and most SNCC workers had opposed the war from the beginning. To Wilkins and Whitney Young, SNCC's announcement was a shocking disgrace. They condemned SNCC indignantly, telling Humphrey that SNCC did not deserve to be treated as a respectable organization. Humphrey agreed that SNCC's opposition to LBJ and the war was outrageous. That got a media bonfire going, which King handled cautiously. At Ebenezer he warned that America was "perpetuating white colonialism" in Vietnam, taking up where

France left off. But to the press King declined to support or oppose SNCC's position; all he said was that SNCC had a right to dissent. SNCC communications director Julian Bond was due that month to be seated in the Georgia state legislature. The son of Lincoln University's first black president, Bond was eloquent, urbane, and a close friend to Lewis. He had dropped out of Morehouse College in 1961 to work for SNCC, confining his SNCC work to press conferences on account of his chronic hives. Then the U.S. Supreme Court created a black Atlanta district in the state legislature, and in November 1965 Bond won the seat. On January 10 a reporter asked Bond if he supported SNCC's opposition to the war. He said yes, and the bonfire engulfed him. The state legislature said that Bond had committed a treasonous act and thus disqualified himself from being seated. A special election was held in February, Bond was reelected, and the legislature still refused to seat him. It took until December for the U.S. Supreme Court to put Bond in his seat, by which time he was nationally renowned and no longer a member of SNCC. For SNCC, in May, veered away from Bond and Lewis.[67]

Carmichael and Cox demanded that Lewis resign from the SCLC board, which he refused to do. There were murmurs that Lewis should resign as chair of SNCC, which he resisted. On May 8 Lewis sought to be reelected at SNCC's retreat at Kingston Springs, near Nashville. Separatist feeling was gaining in SNCC but not dominant. SNCC had a separatist flank named the Atlanta Project, led by Bill Ware and John Churchville. It was deeply influenced by Malcolm X and by Frantz Fanon's books on revolutionary anticolonialism, and it wanted a complete purge of SNCC's forty white staffers, including stalwarts Casey Hayden, Mary King, Bill Hansen, Bob Zellner, Danny Lyon, Sam Shirah, and Betty Garman. Heading into the May meeting, Lewis and Carmichael were proponents of limited white participation in SNCC. Both contended that SNCC should be a predominately black organization and that whites should play a subordinate role in it.

The separatist faction was lightly represented at the May meeting, but others spoke up for racial militancy. Veteran organizer Ivanhoe Donaldson said that SNCC's devotion to interracial democracy was outdated now that most of the country gave lip service to it; he wanted SNCC to support nationalist projects such as the germinating Black Panther Party. Forman wanted SNCC to think in global terms from the perspective of revolutionary anticolonial blackness. Others said that SNCC had nothing to learn from white theorists like Karl Marx. Some noted that CORE was going through a similar transformation, having replaced Farmer with McKissick. Lewis said that SNCC workers were prone to assume they had a "monopoly on truth" and were the best organizers.

Ella Baker called for seminars on revolutionary ethics taught by Third World revolutionaries. On the staff issue of the moment, SNCC decided to keep only white workers who were willing to work only in white communities. Lewis grieved that this compromise went too far, and it would not hold. Some of his closest friends in SNCC were being purged. Then it was time to elect a chairperson. Many people criticized Lewis for coddling King and for attending planning sessions for a White House conference on civil rights, which compared poorly with Carmichael's founding of an independent political party in Lowndes County symbolized by a Black Panther. There was a lot of macho talk about grabbing LBJ and King by the balls and making them kiss SNCC's ass. The vote began to look worrisome to Lewis, but near midnight he won by 60 to 22, with many abstentions by staffers who had slipped off to bed.[68]

Lewis hung around for afterglow conversation, while most of his friends headed for bed. Worth Long, a former SNCC staffer, and Julius Lester, a SNCC staffer from Fisk, arrived late from Mississippi, and Long asked what happened. He erupted at the answer: "John Lewis? How'd y'all do *that?* You can't do that." Long admired Lewis's courage, but SNCC had changed. Long challenged the election, charging that Forman should not have conducted the vote with so many absentees. Suddenly the election was back in play. More speeches commenced, with high emotion, and all were against Lewis's idealistic, Christian, King-supporting leadership. Jack Minnis, a white staffer who headed SNCC's research department, stressed that Lewis's Christian orientation represented the SNCC of the past. It went on for five hours, while Lewis said nothing. Lewis was deeply wounded that no one spoke up for him, but this was a select group. At 5:30 a.m. they elected Carmichael as the new chair. Lewis was heartbroken, blaming his longtime critic, Forman, not his friend, Carmichael. In this bitter telling Forman used Carmichael to get rid of Lewis. To Lewis it felt like a coup, not an election, and a personal repudiation. In public, he took it graciously. In private, Lewis confided to *Time* reporter Arlie Schardt that the coup hurt him badly. Later he recalled, "When I was alone, it hurt. It hurt more than anything I'd ever been through." The fact that Lewis was so deeply wounded convinced many SNCC workers that he wanted it too much; Forman said so pointedly. Some said Lewis was too much like King. Lewis told himself he had to somehow keep going. Later he wrote, "What happened that night was devastating for me, yes, but even more so for SNCC. Breaks were created; wounds were opened that would never heal. I didn't consider it so much a repudiation of me as a repudiation of ourselves, of what we *were*, of what we stood for. We denied and denounced ourselves that night. It was a very sad thing, very tragic."[69]

SNCC was fresh from that drama when Meredith was shot, and King resolved to finish Meredith's march. Most SNCC workers dismissed the march as another celebrity spectacle not worth supporting. Carmichael had to convene an emergency session of SNCC's central committee on June 10 to get SNCC into the march. On June 7 officials in Greenwood, Mississippi, illegally excluded black voters in a local election, and John Doar promptly filed a U.S. lawsuit. Greenwood, a SNCC foothold since Moses moved to the Mississippi Delta in 1962, was straight in the path of the Meredith March. Moreover, Carmichael and SNCC veteran Willie Ricks were field testing a new slogan for SNCC in the towns along Highway 7 leading to Greenwood. Ricks told Carmichael that every time he used the phrase "Black Power" in a speech the crowd lit up: "They're going wild for it." Carmichael wasn't sure what to make of that experience, but he was intrigued. This was his first shot at national media coverage, and he wanted to test the electricity of "Black Power" for himself. Though SNCC usually complained about King's media power, Carmichael was eager to exploit it.[70]

Carmichael had star ambitions that conflicted with what SNCC still claimed to be. Born in Port of Spain, Trinidad and Tobago, in 1941, Carmichael joined his parents in Harlem at the age of eleven, won admittance to the elite Bronx High School of Science, and graduated from Howard University in 1964. At Howard he was active in the campus chapter of SNCC along with classmate Tom Kahn, who was already Rustin's romantic partner and a key player in the Shachtmanite Old Left. Kahn introduced Carmichael to Rustin and other left activists, and Carmichael was arrested over thirty times as a Freedom Rider. He became a field organizer for SNCC in 1964, working on the Greenwood voting project with Moses, and helped organize the MFDP, burning with outrage at the Atlantic City convention. In November 1964, after Casey Hayden and Mary E. King presented a paper on women in the movement, Carmichael famously opined, "The position of women in the movement is prone." Mary King took the remark as a friend's jest, but it was frequently cited as an example of SNCC's prevalent sexism. In 1965 Carmichael organized the Lowndes County Freedom Organization as an independent political party. The Atlantic City convention ended his interest in the Democratic Party. Carmichael quotably explained, "Negroes vote as a bloc in the Democratic Party but it lied. It said it was good, it said it was nice, it said it was liberal, it said it was for peace, it said it was for Negroes. And it lied."[71]

His charismatic radicalism might have lifted him to fame anyway, but Carmichael took a shortcut by latching onto King. Wilkins and Whitney Young, arriving from New York, wanted the Meredith March to promote the Civil

Rights Act of 1966, which was moving toward passage in the House. Carmichael was contemptuous of their agenda and determined to shoo them away. To Carmichael, the march only worked if he deprived King of a right flank. Carmichael excoriated Wilkins and Young, saying "very terrible things" with full-throttle derision—they were has-been Uncle Toms who didn't belong in the Meredith March. He was not aiming for a place at the civil rights table or the next White House conference. King said nothing as Carmichael chased Wilkins and Young back to New York. This march was to be different. King felt it immediately, walking down Highway 7. Some marchers shouted that they were against "that nonviolence stuff." Some said they were hoping for a violent confrontation. Some said the white marchers should leave. King asked a group why they refused to sing "We Shall Overcome." They said they were done with that song; they wanted to sing "We Shall Overrun." Though most of the four hundred marchers supported King, the march felt hostile and alien to him: "As I listened to all these comments, the words fell on my ears like strange music from a foreign land."[72]

As usual, he had to cut away. King was away, on June 16, when Carmichael first tried the Black Power slogan, in Greenwood. Carmichael said he was done with getting arrested, blacks had no business fighting in Vietnam, and they needed to fight for Black Power in places like Greenwood. "We want Black Power!" he exclaimed, five times, jabbing his finger in the air. "That's right. That's what we want, Black Power. We don't have to be ashamed of it. We have stayed here. We have begged the president. We've begged the federal government— that's all we've been doing, begging and begging. It's time we stand up and take over. Every courthouse in Mississippi ought to be burned down tomorrow to get rid of the dirt and the mess. From now on, when they ask what you want, you know what to tell 'em. 'What do you want?' " The response was as thunderous as Ricks had predicted.[73]

King felt it when he returned the next day. According to Carmichael, the struggle was now about achieving political, economic, and cultural self-determination. King was for all these things, but not in Carmichael's style, as the march dramatized. The atmosphere was tense as the marchers proceeded to Leflore County courthouse in Greenwood. Ricks gave a fiery speech about Black Power, stressing his commitment to separatism. Ricks and Williams led dueling chants, as the Ricks group chanted "Black Power!" and the Williams group chanted "Freedom Now!" A reporter asked Carmichael about the new slogan, and he said that blacks had to become powerful enough to institute justice and not be shot down like dogs. King replied that of course he agreed with that; the problem was that "Black Power" reverberated with additional connotative meanings. He asked Carmichael to stop using the phrase, who refused. King cut away to Detroit, where he raised money for the Meredith March at a UAW rally, and to Philadelphia, Mississippi, where he spoke at a memorial for Andrew Goodman, James Chaney, and Mickey Schwerner. In Philadelphia, where some of the Meredith Marchers took a detour, King remarked knowingly that the murderers of the three young civil rights workers were probably in the audience, which evoked a sickening murmur of chuckles, grunts, "Right behind you" and "You're damn right." The sinister atmosphere repulsed him. King told reporters that Philadelphia "is a terrible town, the worst city I have ever seen. There is a complete reign of terror here."[74]

He was depressed and exhausted, the Carmichael challenge shook him, and the depravity of Philadelphia battered him. Then King encountered a frontal challenge upon rejoining the march in Yazoo City. Ernest Thomas, a leader of the gun-toting Louisiana Deacons for Defense and Justice, ridiculed King's request for federal protection, winning many cheers from the marchers. King stirred himself to a passionate sermon on nonviolence that won back the crowd: "I would be misleading you if I made you feel that we can win a violent campaign. It's impractical even to think about it. The minute we started, we will end up getting many people killed unnecessarily. Now I'm ready to die myself. Many other committed people are ready to die. If you believe in something firmly, if you believe in it truly, if you believe it in your heart, you are willing to die for it, but I'm not going to advocate a method that brings about unnecessary death. . . . We have another method, and I've seen it, and they can't stop it."[75]

In that mood he pleaded with Carmichael, Ricks, and McKissick for five hours to turn off the inflammatory rhetoric. The denotative meaning of "Black Power" was sound, he said, but its connotations of burning, killing, separatism, and nationalism were disastrous for the movement. Carmichael countered that the issue of violence versus nonviolence was irrelevant. What mattered was whether blacks consolidated their resources to achieve power. Every other ethnic group was self-respecting and strategic in this way, Carmichael said, citing Jewish, Irish, and Italian Americans. Why should blacks not do the same thing? King replied that this question proved his point, not Carmichael's. Jews and Italians did not chant about Jewish or Italian power; they acquired real power through constructive achievements and solidarity. Chanting about Black Power merely publicized that Black Power enthusiasts had no power and did not know how to acquire it. The violence issue was far from irrelevant, and chanting about Black Power was self-defeating.

King urged that power is the ability to achieve a purpose. The inflammatory appeal to Black Power literally thwarted blacks from gaining real power, something they needed desperately. Carmichael objected that the movement needed a new slogan as a rallying cry, one with the word "black" in it. King was not against that. If the slogan had to be black something, why not "black consciousness" or "black equality"? These terms were more accurate, King said; they conveyed what the movement actually meant. Carmichael replied that neither slogan had the emotive power of Black Power. His only concession was to suspend the chanting of rival slogans for the rest of the Meredith March. The two sides agreed to that truce, and Carmichael, feeling his victory, made a confession: "Martin, I deliberately decided to raise this issue on the march in order to give it a national forum and force you to take a stand for Black Power." King was gracious and accommodating, as always, when confronted by infighting, replying that he had been used before and "one more time won't hurt."[76]

King told himself and Andrew Young that Carmichael was a minor distraction and not a serious challenge to him. SNCC wanted a more militant image, and Carmichael wanted to be famous. Lawson told King not to kid himself about that. Lawson argued strenuously with Carmichael on the Meredith March, he believed that Carmichael had never embraced or seriously studied nonviolence, and he worried that the gifted Carmichael was perfectly suited to derail the movement. Young, having opposed this month-long detour "into the psychological zone," was anxious for the Meredith March to end, especially since it cast a spotlight on Carmichael. Later he reflected, "The real work of the struggle is not sensational, it does not garner headlines. Black Power was a dead end. It provided emotional release and the illusion of manhood, without the content."[77]

The Meredith March wounded King, and it ended dismally despite swelling to fifteen thousand marchers for the final eight miles from Tougaloo to Jackson. SNCC and CORE allowed Whitney Young, but not Wilkins, to join the final lap. Walter Reuther and Harold DeWolf came too, amid taunts of "We don't need whitey" from marchers, and DeWolf collapsed of heatstroke. James Peck, bitter at being expelled from CORE after thirty years of activism in it, assured King that he was still in the movement "despite the dirty deal I have received from CORE." Meredith was cranky with pretty much everyone and did not like what became of his march: "The whole damn thing smells to me." King made little attempt to hide his despondency, a first for him. Reporters were stunned that he seemed so shaken and down. King admitted to friends that the March pulled him to a new low. He doubted that he could work with SNCC anymore; he and Young steamed that SCLC got stuck with the bills, an echo of the NAACP's longtime complaint; and King was asked about Black Power wherever he went. Repeatedly he said that he was dedicated to transforming black powerlessness into constructive and creative power. He did not conceive power as an end in itself; power was a means to the achievement of a good society, the beloved community. Wilkins protested that the march did nothing for the civil rights bill except perhaps hurt it; King ruefully agreed: "Because Stokely Carmichael chose the March as an arena for a debate over black power, we didn't get to emphasize the evils of Mississippi and the need for the 1966 Civil Rights Act. Internal dissension along the March helped Mississippi get off the hook somewhat."[78]

He returned to Chicago in that mood. On July 10 the Chicago campaign held a rally at Soldier Field that aimed for a crowd of one hundred thousand and mustered only thirty-five thousand, compounding King's discouragement. He gave a strong speech demanding color-blind real estate listings and banking policies, a civilian review board for the police department, expanded low-cost public housing, school desegregation, tenant protection, and a federal guaranteed income, declaring, "We shall begin to act as though Chicago were an open city." King stressed that black Americans needed to be proud without stigmatizing all whites as the enemy. He touted nonviolence as the best strategy, leading a march to City Hall, where he taped the movement's demands to the outside door. Mayor Richard J. Daley refused to comment on the demands, even when King asked him to endorse LBJ's pending civil rights bill. Two days later the nation's first riot of the summer broke out in Chicago. King tried valiantly to converse with angry youth; one night he kept two assistant attorneys general of the United States waiting until 4:00 a.m. as he implored rioters not to burn their city. Later, King got his first taste of repudiation at a protest gathering. A group of youths protesting police brutality jeered King as he tried to address them; King fled the gathering, hiding in the office of West Side Organization director Chester Robinson. Burning and looting went on for two days, until Governor Otto Kerner called out the Illinois National Guard.[79]

There had to be a synthetic ideal, King said—a position sufficiently militant to satisfy militants but sufficiently disciplined not to scare off moderate blacks and supportive whites. He seemed to believe that saying it would help him find the ideal and attract others to it. King urged Chicago's major gangs—the Cobras, Vice Lords, and Roman Saints—to join the campaign for nonviolent revolution. He called on white Chicago to abolish segregation and got violently hostile responses in Gage Park and Marquette Park, places where Irish, Italians, and Poles had moved to get away from blacks. White mobs pelted protesters with rocks and bottles. There were Confederate flags and chants about go-back-to-Africa. An enraged mob of ten thousand in Gage Park cursed and screamed at King, hitting him with a rock. Gage Park, Young said, felt like a war zone. King shook off the attacks, saying he was used to it, but added that Chicago had the most vicious mobs he had ever seen. Three days before a summit negotiation King and the CCCO struck back as Bevel led four hundred demonstrators through Jefferson Park, Jackson led three hundred through Bogan, and Raby led five hundred through Gage Park and Chicago Lawn. An interfaith organization, the Conference on Religion and Race, convened a summit on August 17 at the Episcopal diocesan headquarters. Daley was desperate to end the marches, so he floored nearly everyone in the room by accepting the movement's demands. Quickly the discussion swung to the Board of Realtors, whom Daley squeezed to go along. The realtors pleaded that they did not create housing market racism; they merely reflected it. They were not civic leaders; they were in business. King admonished the realtors to take responsibility for their role in keeping white neighborhoods white.[80]

The first summit ended with a deal on the table that each party had to clear with somebody. Then Daley thwarted new protests by obtaining a court injunction, claiming that Chicago police were depleted. King was infuriated, ripping Daley for bad faith, double-dealing, and bad governance. The movement for racial justice had no political power, King said. All it had were the bodies of protesters and their right to protest. They were not trying to overthrow the system; they were trying to get into it. Nothing, he warned, could be worse for America than to engulf black ghettos with walled-off white suburbs. King got around the injunction by leading marches in suburban Chicago Heights, Evergreen Park, and South Deering. He threatened to march in Cicero, a stronghold of white nationalists where eleven thousand blacks worked by day and not a single black lived at night. The specter of protest martyrs in Cicero frightened Daley. At a second summit on August 26 at the Palmer House Daley pressed for the deal on the table. Civic and religious leaders—notably Catholic archbishop John Cody—said they wanted an open city, and real estate board president Ross Beatty nearly blew up the deal by stumbling awkwardly with his make-believe script. Beatty was supposed to say that realtors would rent and sell to black people. He knew that was untrue, so he groped through an embarrassing assurance that assured nobody. Daley saved the deal by pretending to believe in it, and King saved it by going along with Daley, ending the campaign. Daley got what he wanted, an end to the marches, as King felt obliged to take yes for an answer. The alternative was a bloody war against Daley and the Chicago Democratic machine, starting in Cicero.[81]

The reviews from near and far, both allied and enemy, were brutal. It was open season on King as soon as he settled with Daley. Critics howled that King got real people assaulted for a fake agreement. The *Christian Century*, trying to be optimistic, called it "the beginning of the beginning," but the *Chicago Daily News* called it "a paper victory," and the *New Republic* scolded that King declared victory prematurely. He got a scathing reaction upon reading the terms of settlement at Chicago's Liberty Baptist Church. King was booed during the introduction and heckled after he starting speaking. It got so bad that he asked if the (SNCC-organized) hecklers had a spokesperson who wanted the pulpit. SNCC activist Monroe Sharp came forward to blast King for doing a bad job of something he should not have tried. Black Americans, Sharp said, needed to solve their own problems, not beg Daley and white suburbanites for favors; moreover, it was wrong to back down from Cicero. A rump coalition vowed to march in Cicero, and King recouped some local respect by wishing it good luck. Two hundred blacks and fifty whites marched across the Belt Line Railroad into Cicero and were pelted with a savage barrage of rocks and hostility. Chicago, it turned out, was very much like Selma, only worse. For a while the postmortems on Chicago cut King so deeply that he seriously considered moving the SCLC's headquarters to Chicago to prove his seriousness about holding Daley to his promises.[82]

Meanwhile Carmichael skyrocketed to national fame. He crammed his schedule with media appearances, spreading the message of Black Power with spectacular success. He spoke at CORE's national convention in July, applauding CORE's embrace of Black Power and declaring that the movement did not need white liberals. He wrote a book with Charles Hamilton that became an instant classic, *Black Power: The Politics of Liberation.* Carmichael said that blacks in America were colonized subjects and integration was a middle-class goal championed by a professional elite of middle-class blacks. More important, integration was "a subterfuge for the maintenance of white supremacy," a "despicable" scheme that sprinkled a few blacks into the white middle class on token terms to hold down all others. Carmichael was done with that and with redemptive suffering. In his telling, the Deep South blacks he had tried to organize were "steaming mad" at being oppressed: "We had nothing to offer that they could see, except to go out and be beaten again. We helped to build their frustration. We had only the old language of love and suffering. And in most places—that is, from the liberals and middle-class—we got back the old language of patience and progress." Carmichael urged that blacks in America needed to hook up with revolutionary struggles in the Third World, overthrowing racism itself. If that sounded like "black racism" to fearful whites, he could not help them: "The final truth is that the white society is not entitled to reassurances, even if it were possible to offer them."[83]

He got an early boost from King's church-world, as a new group called the National Committee of Negro Churchmen (NCNC), headquartered in New York City, issued a manifesto endorsing Black Power. Spearheaded by Presbyterian official Gayraud Wilmore and NCC official Benjamin F. Payton, the group consisted of forty-eight clergy from the AME, AMEZ, Baptist, Christian Methodist, Congregational, Episcopal, Methodist, and Presbyterian churches, including six bishops. This group still assumed that integration was the ideal, but it cheered the rise of liberationist rhetoric. Black Power, it declared, was controversial only because white men were all-powerful and black men had no power: "Powerlessness breeds a race of beggars. We are faced now with a situation where conscienceless power meets powerless conscience, threatening the very foundations of our nation."[84]

As long as blacks had no power and could not safely say they wanted it, whites would disrespect blacks and blacks would disrespect themselves. The ministers declared, "We fail to understand the emotional quality of the outcry of some clergy against the use of the term today." Integration was saving only if blacks had the power to make it work for them and society: "Without this capacity to *participate with power*—i.e., to have some organized political and economic strength to really influence people with whom one interacts— integration is not meaningful." It was nonsense to say that Black Power rhetoric endangered the gains of the civil rights movement because there were hardly any to lose. The NSNC stressed that every major city was more segregated than before the *Brown* decision, black unemployment increased during the same period, and income inequality worsened. The only gains were "limited mainly to middle-class Negroes," a small minority of the black community. The NSNC ministers were still in King's mode and camp, but they wanted him to accentuate what was good about Black Power ideology.[85]

Lewis had the same conflicted feelings as King about Black Power. "I had so many thoughts about this concept," he later wrote. Lewis was for black power as self-determination and self-reliance and against it as separatism and black supremacy. He regretted that the latter version electrified the media and that his friend Carmichael had become a divider: "He delighted in scaring white people, and this did the trick." Interviewed by Associated Press reporter Don McKee, Lewis said he was for programs and working together, not slogans and divisiveness. McKee wrote the story, and Lewis learned at a rally in Canton, Mississippi, that he was finished in SNCC. It was July 22, the toughest day of the Meredith March. State troopers tear-gassed the marchers and beat several of them, throwing Carmichael into a panic attack. Lewis mounted a speaker's box to restore calm, declaring that the "whole man must say no nonviolently, his entire Christian spirit must say no to this evil and vicious system." There were no jeers or catcalls; the marchers simply fell away, ignoring Lewis. *New York Times Magazine* reporter Paul Good captured the moment: "The speaker's credentials were in order, but his time was out of joint. He spoke the old words of militant love, but the spiritual heart of the movement that for years had sent crusaders up and down American roads, trusting in love, was broken and Lewis had become that most expendable commodity, a former leader. It was not so much that he was losing his audience; the audience was already lost."[86]

Lewis told Good that he felt like an uninvited guest in Canton. A month later he cleaned out his desk at SNCC, telling friends that SNCC had changed and he had not: "The organization was riddled with bitterness and talk of retaliation and violence, actions that might deliver some quick comfort but that in the long run were debasing." He was twenty-six years old and starting over, lacking any resume except six years of movement activism and arrests. After three years of chairing SNCC, Lewis was too proud to be one of King's lieutenants. He took a job with the Marshall Field Foundation and shook his head in December 1966 as SNCC fired its last five white workers. Carmichael wavered over the final purge, voting against it; Forman, fuming that posturing latecomers had hijacked SNCC, urged the organization to completely disband; Carmichael lasted only a year as chair, giving way to H. Rap Brown.[87]

Chicago yielded mostly frustration and bad publicity, and Rustin provoked insider heartburn by disparaging King and the "disaster" in Chicago, declaring, "I knew he had to fall on his face. Daley cut Martin Luther King's ass off." Many exaggerated things were said about the superiority of the Birmingham and Selma campaigns, overlooking that both accomplished almost nothing locally. Birmingham and Selma were saved by national victories that bathed the campaigns in reflected glory. The Chicago campaign had nothing like that going for it, even though it made a bigger dent in local arrangements. Friends noticed that King no longer shucked off criticism like a politico. It ate at him and wore him down.[88]

Blackwell quietly slipped away from SCLC, concluding that King would never rein in Williams. King grieved at losing Blackwell, apologizing that his impossible schedule left him no time to deal with organizational problems. The civil rights bill died in the Senate, Williams got in trouble for mismanaging federal funds, and archracist Lester Maddox won the Democratic nomination for governor in Georgia. King reeled from each blow, blaming Dirksen for bailing on civil rights, admonishing Williams, and assailing the sickening coming of Maddox. Two signs of a gathering political backlash were especially ominous. Paul Douglas, one of SCLC's strongest allies in the U.S. Senate, fell behind in his Illinois race, and newcomer Ronald Reagan mounted a commanding lead over Governor Pat Brown in California. Reagan came from the far right, a strident opponent of the civil rights movement and the welfare state. He had seemed unelectable until the civil rights bills passed; then he mastered the coded language of racial backlash. King was appalled that Maddox and Reagan soared so high on racial resentment. He told friends that he wanted to shock decent white Americans into waking up but didn't know how. He considered resigning from SCLC, but Levison said that wouldn't work. King considered attacking the Black Power upsurge, which yielded a crisis gathering of King and Young with the advisors Levison, Rustin, Jones, and Wachtel.

The immediate question was whether King should sign a declaration censuring the Black Power rhetoric of separation and anti-nonviolence. Rustin was scathing on this subject, repelled by the style and content of the new racial militancy. He hated the masculine bravado of Black Power and its repudiation of coalitional economic justice politics. "Anybody who talks about a black agenda is a reactionary," Rustin said. "As soon as you move into the economic struggle you're in a totally new universal ball game with universal objectives." In that vein he wrote a declaration titled "Crisis and Commitment" that Randolph, Wilkins, and Whitney Young promptly endorsed. It reaffirmed the movement's commitment to integration, nonviolence, and democracy, without referring explicitly to Black Power. King balked at signing the statement, and Rustin stressed that it reiterated King's core beliefs. King, Young, Levison, Jones, and Wachtel worried that the subtext was obvious and damaging: Black Power caused much of the white backlash. King did not want to be associated with that accusation, so he turned down Rustin. He was still the apostle of bringing people together, as he emphasized to reporters. But after the statement was published King told reporters that of course he agreed with its substance; he refused to sign only because he stood for unity. That was a serious mistake. King realized it after his endorsement became the story, and Levison told him he had to take it back; he was in danger of sabotaging his unifying capacity. King, deeply embarrassed, agreed to eat some crow. He told Levison that he made mistakes of this kind only when he dealt with Rustin.[89]

That week tragedy struck in a manner that foreshadowed justice movements still to come. Robert Spike was found bludgeoned to death in a guest room of the Christian Center at Ohio State University. The tributes were profuse and heartfelt, notably from Humphrey, Moses, Carmichael, and Urban League official Edwin Berry. King was eloquent: "He was one of those rare individuals who sought at every point to make religion relevant to the social issues of our times. He lifted religion from the stagnant arena of pious irrelevancies and

sanctimonious trivialities. His brilliant and dedicated work will be an inspiration to generals yet unborn. We will always remember his unswerving devotion
to the legitimate aspirations of oppressed people for freedom and human
dignity." White ecumenists vowed to remember the best of their tribe and to
find his killer. NCC officials prepared to hire detectives and then backed off.
Spike's lawyer, Jack Pratt, cautioned that Spike was gay and would not have
wanted his wife and son to know about his furtive trysts or be shamed by public
exposure. Paul Spike, a student at Columbia University, confirmed that his
mother would be shattered if the story came out, whether or not it was true,
which the family also resisted believing. The church liberals hushed out of
embarrassment unspeakable, and the case was never solved. News stories about
it strained to say nothing about why silence had descended. For years to come,
on the rare occasions that the Spike case was publicly remembered it usually
got rolled into a conspiracy narrative about the FBI or somebody else killing off
the heroes of the left. Andrew Young, grieved that his friend was forgotten, never
gave up believing that Spike was killed because he opposed the war in Vietnam.[90]

The election approached and King oscillated between saying what he really
believed and trying not to hurt liberals running for office. He had not said previously that white Americans never intended to integrate their schools or neighborhoods or to support economic equality. Then he got pelted with rocks in
Chicago, and King began to say it. He said it bitterly to the Alabama Christian
Movement at its tenth anniversary dinner in Birmingham. He turned it around
in *Ebony*, mocking blacks who told him they would not march because they
didn't believe in nonretaliation. Every facet of their lives reeked of oppression,
King said, yet they were willing to fight only if someone spat on them at a
demonstration! The election came and the backlash was fierce, though King
spurned backlash talk. Democrats lost 47 House seats, 3 Senate seats, 8 gover-
norships, and 677 seats in state legislatures. Reagan cruised to a landslide
victory, Douglas lost, Wallace stayed in power via his wife, and pundits crowned
Reagan as the new leader of the American Right, annoying Wallace. LBJ told
aides that black Americans caused this disaster, not him, and the backlash he
had feared was terribly real. In public he said he had no idea what to say about
it. Officially, almost every major player denied there was a backlash or denied
having courted it; even Wallace claimed to avoid the race issue. Richard Nixon,
plotting a comeback, said that Republicans had no racial agenda and that LBJ
was the first American president to fail to unite his party behind a war. Pat
Brown, relieved of office and careful speaking, declared that race was obviously
the major issue in 1966: "Whether we like it or not, the people want separation
of the races."[91]

King denied that a backlash was occurring because that story always blamed him for something, and it obscured what mattered: The civil rights movement merely surfaced the animosity that had always existed. Calling it a backlash suggested that racism was increasing and he should do something differently. Backlash talk was a species of denial. After the election King convened a retreat for the financially bleeding SCLC, now down to seventy-five staffers, at Frogmore, near Savannah. He was bleak and grim, admitting that he didn't know what to do next. King gave a long, personal, vulnerable summary of the movement's shortcomings and a lowball assessment of its accomplishments from 1954 to 1965. He appreciated that some legislative and judicial victories had been won, but they "did very little to improve the lot of millions of Negroes in the teeming ghettos of the North." The movement did not touch "the lower depths of Negro deprivation." It was hard to say this, but "we must admit it: the changes that came about during this period were at best surface changes, they were not really substantive changes." American racism, King noted, was distinctly vicious: "The white man literally sought to annihilate the Indian. If you look through the history of the world this very seldom happened." That was what black Americans were up against—a genocidal impulse fueled by the pervasive white American belief in white superiority. "The ultimate logic of racism is genocide," King cautioned. By that optic the current talk about a backlash was superficial.[92]

King sympathized with Black Power because it instilled something (racial pride) and sought something (real power) that were both desperately needed. But the Black Power ideology currently in vogue, he said, had three fatal problems: It was nihilistic and separatist, and these things combined to justify violence. SCLC had to stand for power as "the right use of strength," the capacity to achieve a positive and creative purpose. They could not wave off the problem of how things were heard. King believed deeply that Swedish social democracy was better than American capitalism, but he couldn't say that without hurting the movement, so he laid off Socialism. He believed that getting rid of the class system was essential, though King teased that Williams didn't believe it. SCLC needed to become a flat-out, passionately antipoverty organization, pressing for a minimum guaranteed income. King observed that it took Gandhi forty years to liberate India, so SCLC needed to think in a longer time frame than previously: "I believe that with this kind of moral power, with this kind of determination, with this willingness to suffer, we'll get across the goal-line."[93]

King had a mind-boggling sideline ambition in mind: a peace treaty between Israel and the Palestinians. At Frogmore he chastised Young for losing control of the Chicago campaign, just before telling Young to pack his bags for Israel.

Young's next job was to organize a pilgrimage of five thousand people to the Holy Land. Young staggered at this assignment, collapsed from exhaustion, and found himself on a bathroom floor. Then he crawled off to Tel Aviv, after his physician told him that organizing in Israel might be restful compared to his usual drill. For twelve days Young laid the groundwork for an extravaganza that was not to be, as the Six Day War of June 1967 terminated King's fantasy of mediating the Israeli–Palestinian conflict.[94]

Back in Chicago, Young and the SCLC fought losing battles with the Daley machine on voter registration, job training, slumlords, and open occupancy. Daley kept voting rolls low and he wanted all patronage in Chicago to come through his organization. He fought off downstate Republican voters by tightening his urban machine—a shortsighted strategy as the suburbs grew in size and anti-urban hostility. Young and King urged Daley to work with them to change Chicago, but that was never a serious option for Daley, who used his leverage with the federal government to get his way. Then Douglas was punished for championing open occupancy, and Daley announced that he had never really supported it; the Open Housing Summit Agreement was merely aspirational. King was crestfallen, realizing that his deal with Daley was worthless. The Chicago campaign yielded a reform organization—the Metropolitan Chicago Leadership Council for Open Housing—that did commendable work over the long haul, and Jackson won job commitments from soft drink firms and grocery store chains, building up Operation Breadbasket. Otherwise SCLC got very little for its grinding, painful, much-criticized work in Chicago. Many pundits crowed that they had warned King that Daley would play him. King, as usual, responded by doubling down on the course he had already taken—moving from insider prophecy to radical outsider prophecy.[95]

ECONOMIC JUSTICE AND VIETNAM

Most of the Hebrew prophets operated within the power structure while reminding the kings and people of Israel of their covenant with God. They said hard things, speaking for God, but played the political game. The radical prophets, epitomized by Amos, were outsiders who criticized the monarchy, championed the poor and oppressed, and opposed war. King was mindful of the difference as he moved from insider prophecy to outsider prophecy. He did not make a fetish of his increasingly outsider status, and drifting to the outside did not make him any less political. He strove to get practical things done, and he hoped for a role in a better administration to come. His new galvanizing idea was a wonky legislative proposal: a guaranteed income of $4,000. Achieving it would have required a powerful inside game fusing the civil rights movement, labor, and political liberalism. But even this magic-bullet approach to antipoverty politics pushed King, from 1965 on, to the outside.

Levison pushed the idea of a new book featuring the income idea. McGeorge Bundy, fresh from disaster in Vietnam as national security advisor for Kennedy and Johnson, took over the Ford Foundation with hopes of repairing his reputation. Though Bundy had no history of caring about civil rights, he reached out to King after taking over at Ford. In December 1966 Senator Abraham Ribicoff invited King to address the Government Operations Committee. Levison and two Ford aides wrote a forty-four-page statement, and King delivered a summary on December 15, protesting that the war on poverty had been sidelined by the war in Vietnam. The war on poverty never reached the battle stage, he said. It was wrongly divided into separate programs targeting education, employment, and housing. Money that should have helped the poor paid for four hundred thousand troops in Vietnam, and there was a simpler solution to poverty: a guaranteed income. Ribicoff asked if the civil rights movement had entered a new stage. King said yes, because the movement needed to stand for the human right to an adequate living. America could afford to abolish poverty. Americans needed only to decide that doing so was more important than fighting in Vietnam or waging an arms race: "It was easier to integrate public facilities, it was easier to gain the right to vote, because it didn't cost the Nation anything, and the fact is that we are dealing with issues now that will call for something of a restructuring of the architecture of American society. It is going to cost the Nation something. We can't talk about the economic problem that the Negro confronts without talking about billions of dollars."[96]

The Frogmore speech and the Senate testimony provided the foundation for King's last book, which he was eager to write. By January 1967 spending for the Office of Economic Opportunity plateaued at $1.5 billion while the lowballed estimate for Vietnam zoomed to $10 billion. King and Levison tried to focus on the book, but Levison's updates got in the way. Levison told King that Norman Thomas, Allard Lowenstein, and William Sloane Coffin Jr. wanted King to campaign against Vietnam. King greatly admired Thomas, calling him "the bravest man I ever met" and an unsurpassed champion of peace and "a society free of injustice and exploitation." King aspired to Thomas's standard of social justice bravery, but he told Levison he was not ready to burn his bridge to LBJ. Then the House unseated Powell, King said nothing, and Levison prodded for a statement. King said he didn't care how it looked because he didn't care what happened to Powell. If Wilkins wanted to defend Powell, so be it, but King would not pretend. Levison pressed for something, and King relented slightly, saying he felt bad for Powell; later that week Powell uncorked his first reference to "Martin Loser King."[97]

Finally in mid-January King got away, to Jamaica, along with Bernard Lee, to a secluded house in Ocho Rios lacking a telephone. It was the only extended getaway he ever made. In Ocho Rios King labored on the book, writing in his sloping longhand. Lee and Dora McDonald typed pages, sending each chapter to Levison, who smoothened and rewrote; eventually Coretta and Young came for one of the four weeks that King spent in Jamaica. There were a few bumpy moments in a compressed writing period, while King tried to relax. He recycled a section of *Why We Can't Wait,* and his editor, Hermine Popper, reminded King that he had already written that book. Popper also worried, having worked with King and Levison on *Why We Can't Wait,* that the new book sounded more like Levison than King. Levison and King replied that Levison was a mere enabler who knew King's mind. King had barely arrived in Jamaica when he had a turning point. Leafing through the January *Ramparts,* he came across a twenty-four-page photo essay depicting the burned and mutilated bodies of Vietnamese war victims. The pictures filled King with revulsion. He told Lee that he had to face up to being an antiwar leader.[98]

Clergy and Laity Concerned About Vietnam (CALCAV, the group's next-to-last name) had pined for that decision for months. CALCAV staged vigils against the war and assembled a petition signed by over two thousand theologians and religious leaders. Heschel, Coffin, and Robert McAfee Brown beseeched King to speak out. Levison was wary of doing so, fretting that King would diminish his standing by speaking for two movements that did not work together. Becoming an antiwar leader would mean losing LBJ, probably the Ford Foundation, and much of the Democratic Party and civil rights movement. If King lost influence in civil rights to become one peace leader among others, what good was that? King wrestled with that question, criticized the war, agreed with Levison, agonized, and felt he should do more. Then he crossed a line upon seeing the *Ramparts* pictures, unbeknownst to Bevel, who could not wait for King to emerge from Jamaica.[99]

Young turned away all who demanded to know King's whereabouts, except Bevel, who would not be denied. Bevel told Young he had a message from Jesus. Young gave up the secret and Bevel showed up in Ocho Rios with a wild look on his face and a passionate plea. He told King that Jesus had appeared to him, sitting on a dryer, while Bevel did laundry, telling him to help the suffering children of Vietnam. Bevel wanted King to take a peace boat across the Pacific into the rivers of the Vietnamese countryside, preaching against war. He reasoned that if King and other prominent Americans risked their lives as shields, the U.S. military would stop bombing in the Mekong Delta. Bevel scared King but also got to him. King admonished Young that Bevel was clearly "off his rocker" and needed psychiatric help. How had Young failed to see it before sending Bevel to interrupt King's getaway? The shield idea, however, was brilliantly ahead of its time—American peace activists employed it in El Salvador in the 1980s—and Bevel's worrisome, somewhat unhinged visit helped King decide for risky, out-there righteousness.[100]

King granted Bevel a brief leave to join Muste's staff at FOR, where Bevel organized a huge antiwar demonstration scheduled for April 15 at the United Nations Plaza. Shortly after Bevel returned to New York and before King left Jamaica Muste died of a heart attack. Muste had trained the people who trained King in Gandhian nonviolence. His last antiwar coalition was dominated by SDS and other left groups holding little interest in Gandhian nonviolence. Rustin, Bevel, and Thomas spoke at Muste's memorial service, emphasizing his religious wellspring; meanwhile King's advisors and the SCLC board implored King to reject Bevel's invitation to speak at the United Nations protest. Levison and Wachtel often disagreed but not about this. They dreaded that King seemed bent on squandering his civil rights leadership for a role in the white, left-wing, increasingly shrill antiwar movement. Young attended a meeting of the April 15 organizers and was appalled. Wild talk about smashing the fascist American government prevailed. Young told King the only sane organizer was the Communist representative. Moreover, King's advisors were wary of Bevel, and King wearied of the hostility between Bevel and Williams, which was worse than ever. King took seriously Young's warning about SDS and the pleas of his advisors not to let Bevel drag him down. Young worried that King would not have time, at a rally speech, to develop a thoughtful argument and that media coverage would not distinguish King from ranting SDS speakers. Besides, Bevel's erratic outbursts frightened the CALCAV activists, who wanted King to stand with them.

King turned the issue over and over in his mind. At least he was refreshed, zinging Young and others with his mimicry and bawdy humor. Insiders measured King's exhaustion by how much they saw his comic side; it came back briefly after Ocho Rios. April 15 approached, King accepted a speaking role, and Young scrambled to cushion the impact. King had to speak first and leave, to avoid being associated with Carmichael and other extremists. In addition, King needed to make a thoughtful speech to his wing of the movement—religious progressives—before the April 15 rally defined him. Young made arrangements with Bennett and Heschel for King to speak at Union. But the buffer event grew too large for Union's chapel, necessitating a move across the street to Riverside Church and its seating capacity of thirty-nine hundred.[101]

The Riverside Speech required special preparation. None of King's advisors wanted to write it, so Young farmed it out to two professors, Vincent Harding of Spelman College and John Maguire of Wesleyan University. Meanwhile King spoke against the war during the run-up to Riverside. He gave an antiwar speech in Beverly Hills, California, marched with best-selling pediatrician Benjamin Spock in a peace parade in Chicago, and reprised the Beverly Hills speech at Chicago's Coliseum. King wanted Rustin to write the Beverly Hills speech, still underestimating Rustin's loyalty to Johnson–Humphrey Democrats and the AFL-CIO. LBJ demanded to know why King canceled two meetings with him, and the speeches provided the answer.

King said he protested the war out of love for America. To Levison, that was weak and naïve because the antiwar movement boiled with anti-American feeling. If King ended up in an angry, white, alienated antiwar movement, it would be disastrous for racial justice. SCLC board members, including Daddy King, refused to endorse King's position, although at least the board refrained from taking the opposite position. King brushed off the rebuff and the fears behind it, believing that most black Americans were bitter about the war. Every black community saw its sons pushed to the front to defend a country that denigrated them. King judged that civil rights leaders were overdue to speak for an embittered majority. Harding and Maguire drafted the speech, Young polished it, and the buffer event, by April 4, 1967, was a very big deal. Levison could not bring himself to attend; temperamentally, King's house Communist was cautious about politics.

"I come to this magnificent house of worship tonight because my conscience leaves me no other choice," King declared. He saluted CALCAV and a recent statement by its executive committee, written by Brown: "A time comes when silence is betrayal." King felt morally obligated "to break the betrayal of my own silences and to speak from the burnings of my own heart." For a while he had been hopeful about the fight against poverty, but "then came the build-up in Vietnam, and I watched the program broken and eviscerated as if it were some idle political plaything of a society gone mad on war, and I knew that America would never invest the necessary funds or energies in rehabilitation of its poor so long as Vietnam continued to draw men and skills and money like some demonic, destructive suction tube."[102]

French-American critic Bernard Fall's book, *The Two Viet-Nams*, was an essential text for war resisters in the 1960s. King read it in Jamaica to bolster his contention that Vietnam was a recycled colonial war. At Riverside he recounted that France and Japan colonized Vietnam, which declared its independence in 1954, yielding nine years of French colonial aggression backed by the United

States, followed by America taking over the recolonizer role. King ridiculed America's liberator self-image: "We have destroyed their two most cherished institutions: the family and the village. We have destroyed their land and their crops. We have cooperated in the crushing of the nation's only non-Communist revolutionary political force—the unified Buddhist church. We have supported the enemies of the peasants of Saigon. We have corrupted their women and children and killed their men. What liberators!"[103]

Sadly he declared that the United States was on the wrong side of anticolonialist movements throughout the world. King still believed in the dream of America realizing the revolutionary promise of its Declaration of Independence. But America was rich, privileged, short on compassion, and morbidly afraid of communism, he said. Thus the first modern country had become the world's foremost counterrevolutionary power. "I am convinced that if we are to get on the right side of the world revolution, we as a nation must undergo a radical revolution of values." Americans, King charged, prized profit, property, and machines above human beings. This profoundly warped value system defeated all attempts to overcome "the giant triplets of racism, materialism, and militarism." The revolution that was needed—"a true revolution of values"—would not tolerate extreme inequality in the United States or the pillage of Third World countries by American capitalism. Neither would it stand for imperial American wars: "This business of burning human beings with napalm, of filling our nation's homes with orphans and widows, of injecting poisonous drugs of hate into veins of peoples normally humane, of sending men home from dark and bloody battlefields physically handicapped and psychologically deranged, cannot be reconciled with wisdom, justice and love. A nation that continues year after year to spend more money on military defense than on programs of social uplift is approaching spiritual death."[104]

America needed a spiritual reawakening to its own revolutionary democratic ideals: "Our only hope today lies in our ability to recapture the revolutionary spirit and go out into a sometimes hostile world declaring eternal hostility to poverty, racism and militarism." Personally, King could not go on speaking for nonviolence or against the violence of the oppressed in America's cities "without having first spoken clearly to the greatest purveyor of violence in the world today—my own government." The war poisoned America's soul, he pleaded: "It can never be saved so long as it destroys the deepest hopes of men the world over." At the end he reached for his biggest what-is-needed statement, a creed about love divine that he called "this Hindu-Moslem-Christian-Jewish-Buddhist belief about ultimate reality," citing 1 John 4: "Let us love one another; for love is God and everyone that loves is born of God and knows God. He that loves not knows not God; for God is love. If we love one another God dwells in us, and his love is perfected in us."[105]

At Riverside there were two standing ovations, bursts of applause when King endorsed draft resistance and called the United States to negotiate with China, and no real surprises. The crowd hushed when King described America as the world's leading purveyor of violence, and it cheered his announcement that seventy Morehouse students and alums were conscientious objectors to the draft. Bennett declared that King spoke to America's conscience more powerfully than anyone. Daddy King astonished himself by changing his mind about the war and his son's opposition to it. The Riverside crowd knew that King had said most of this before and much of it numerous times. Many knew his favorite riffs and set pieces by heart, joining in when King closed with sixteen lines of James Russell Lowell's "Once to Every Man and Nation."

Elsewhere shock and condemnation prevailed. King assumed that this episode would be like Birmingham: White editorialists would disapprove, middle-class black journalists would say that King was egotistical and harmful to blacks, the usual defenders would push back, and the story would turn in his favor. That *is* what happened eventually, but each part went worse than he expected.

The chief organs of liberal Protestantism, *Christian Century* and *Christianity & Crisis*, and the left-liberal *Nation* were exceptions to an onslaught of condemnation. The *Century* praised the speech as "a magnificent blend of eloquence and raw fact, of searing denunciation and tender wooing, of political sagacity and Christian insight, of tough realism and infinite compassion." *Life* countered that King exceeded his "personal right to dissent" by connecting civil rights to his espousal of "abject surrender in Vietnam." Former U.S. Information Agency chief Carl Rowan skewered King in *Reader's Digest*. The real civil rights leaders grieved over King's egotism, Rowan claimed. They also chafed at his habit of fleeing jail to accept honors, his rude treatment of White House allies, and his reliance on Communist advisors. Wilkins, Whitney Young, the *New York Times*, and the *Washington Post* denounced the speech as politically disastrous. The *Post* put it frostily, charging that King's "sheer inventions of unsupported fantasy" inflicted "grave injury" on his allies and worse injury on himself: "Many who have listened to him with respect will never again accord him the same confidence. He has diminished his usefulness to his cause, to his country and to his people. And that is a great tragedy." The *Pittsburgh Courier* said the same thing, ripping King for "tragically misleading" black Americans about issues that were "too complex for simple debate." Levison defended King publicly but told him privately that the speech was politically inept and poorly structured, rambling too long about distant matters. Rustin and Randolph, glaringly, refused to comment publicly. Rustin, after decades of lonely antiwar activism, did not join the major antiwar movement of his time. King reeled at the outpouring of condemnation, the worst he ever received.[106]

The battering went on, stunning King and shaming him. Friends saw him shed tears more than once. It was hard to maintain that he was competent to speak about Vietnam when so many critics insisted he was not. For a while it seemed that Levison and Rustin were right, but the controversy helped to lift the April 15 mobilization into a spectacle: the takeoff of a skyrocketing antiwar movement. King felt it happening as huge crowds surged into Central Park. He marched with Young from Central Park down Fifth Avenue to Forty-second Street and the U.N. Plaza. Viet Cong flags were unfurled, and the first mass burning of draft cards occurred. King compared the mobilization to the March on Washington, and Young claimed the sea of marchers exceeded one million, although the *New York Times* guessed one hundred thousand. Security concerns kept King off the platform, which was fine with him; his camp did not want him on stage with Carmichael. King repeated much of the Riverside Speech, to tumultuous acclaim, adding, "I am disappointed with our failure to deal positively and forthrightly with the triple evils of racism, extreme materialism, and militarism. We are presently moving down a dead-end road that can only lead to national disaster."[107]

King teased Harding that the Riverside Speech ruined an entire month of his life. Jackson replaced Bevel as director of Chicago SCLC, and Rap Brown replaced Carmichael at SNCC. To King, it was a bitter irony that SNCC activists considered themselves more radical than he was since he stuck with Gandhian nonviolence while they discarded it like a pair of training wheels. They weren't students anymore, either, and they no longer operated as an egalitarian coordinating committee. Every word of their name was obsolete. SNCC committed no actual violence, but the repudiation from SNCC cut King deeply, much more than the flak he took from Wilkins. The civil rights establishment charged that King damaged its relationship with LBJ and King replied that he was still a civil rights leader who appreciated LBJ's support; on the other hand, he had taken too long to oppose the war. It galled King that the same white liberals and moderates who cheered his nonviolence in the civil rights struggle reacted with shock and scorn when he applied it to Vietnam. Summer polling in 1967 showed that 70 percent of Americans supported the war, including 50 percent of African Americans. King knew what he risked in the Riverside Speech and that he could not live with himself if he did not give it.[108]

By the summer of 1965 the United States had tried every conceivable military strategy in Vietnam except using atomic weapons. Counterinsurgency failed, and bombing North Vietnam merely strengthened the determination of the insurgents. By the spring of 1967 two years of saturation bombing had done nothing to turn the war and U.S. Commander William Westmoreland called for 200,000 additional troops, upping the total to 670,000. Westmoreland told a joint session of Congress in April 1967 that winning in Vietnam was solely a question of resolve; Congress boisterously agreed with nineteen rounds of applause. Meanwhile Defense Secretary Robert McNamara, famous for escalating the war and issuing cocksure pronouncements about it, moved ahead of the Congress and public on the meaning of the war. McNamara, at least, was willing to let facts change his opinion. What good was it to win every battle when the enemy persevered? McNamara warned Johnson that America looked bad in Vietnam—a superpower killing tens of thousands of noncombatants in a desperately poor and tiny nation for debatable reasons with no end in sight. McNamara stewed in this fashion for seven months until November 1967, when he resigned or was fired, shortly after advising LBJ to freeze troop levels, stop bombing in the north, and turn the ground war over to South Vietnam.[109]

Viewed politically, King's timing was perfect for embracing and influencing the antiwar movement. But King judged himself in politics by the standard of righteousness and thus did not congratulate himself for shrewd timing. It gnawed at him that he dithered through 1965 and 1966 to find his courage. At Frogmore he told SCLC, "My name then wouldn't have been written in any book called *Profiles in Courage*. But now I have decided. I will not be intimidated." King's pacifist friends agreed that he should not have taken so long. They were against all wars, and Vietnam was not remotely a close call.[110]

But the religious antiwar allies that mattered most to King were not pacifists. CALCAV was a stronghold of Niebuhrian realism. Its Niebuhrian leaders, especially Bennett, Coffin, Brown, and a fading Niebuhr, though staunchly anti-Communist, were appalled that a militaristic and ideological concept of anti-Communism had led to disaster in Vietnam. They were also liberal Christian pro-Zionists. Reinhold Niebuhr regarded the state of Israel as an invaluable outpost of Western civilization in the Middle East and a fitting compensation for the Holocaust. Before Israel was founded, Niebuhr acknowledged that a Jewish homeland in Palestine would infringe the rights of Arabs living there, and he advocated transferring Arab Palestinians to Iraq. His case for Zionism rested on moral, cultural, and political arguments; Niebuhr was too liberal theologically to press theological arguments in this area. Describing the emergence of Israel as "a kind of penance of the world for the awful atrocities committed against the Jews," Niebuhr clashed with two successive presidents of Union Seminary—Henry Sloane Coffin and Henry Pitney Van Dusen—over Zionism. For Niebuhr and Heschel, who were close friends, it was a breakthrough for Jewish–Christian friendship when Bennett became president of Union in 1963. Bennett was mostly a caretaker president, sticking to the legacies of his two predecessors, but he made Union more ecumenical by adding Roman Catholics to the faculty and by asserting his pro-Zionism. During the buildup to the Six Day War Bennett rallied support for Israel, wrote a solidarity statement, and enlisted Zionists in Union's orbit to sign it. On May 29, 1967, it was published in the *New York Times.* Niebuhr and Orthodox theologian Alexander Schmemann were among the signatories; less predictably, King was there too.[111]

King tried to play it down, complaining that the *New York Times* treated his signature as a blanket endorsement of Israel, which it was not. Had he gotten his way King would have spent the summer of 1967 making peace between Israelis and Palestinians in a two-state solution. Still, faced with a threat to Israel's existence, King set aside his pacifism to side with Niebuhr, Bennett, Heschel, and Israel. To many religious progressives that settled the question whether King's adherence to Gandhian nonviolence was absolute or situational. In this telling, he was closer to the pragmatic, generally antiwar, Zionist religious progressivism of CALCAV than to FOR pacifism. That was a credible reading, but Brown, Coffin, and Heschel did not lead the greatest nonviolent resistance movement in U.S. American history. The burden of holding fast to nonviolence weighed heavily on King. Thus he declared repeatedly that he believed in nonviolence more than ever, it was a faith and way of life for him, and he would never retreat from it.

Where Do We Go from Here: Chaos or Community? said it emphatically. King began with a blistering riposte to the white American view that America was "a middle-class Utopia" committed to fair play and racial harmony. This ridiculous self-perception was "a fantasy of self-deception and comfortable vanity," he declared. American society was less racist and repressive than before Montgomery but only by a small degree, which most white Americans refused to acknowledge: "It is an aspect of their sense of superiority that the white people of America believe they have so little to learn." King allowed that most white Americans were uneasy and defensive about the race issue, but they were unwilling to do anything to abolish racism that cost them anything. Moreover, white goodwill and even white guilt were diminishing in supply; thus he gave up saying there was no backlash: "There is a strong mood to bring the civil rights movement to a halt or reduce it to a crawl. Negro demands that yesterday evoked admiration and support, today—to many—have become tiresome, unwarranted and a disturbance to the enjoyment of life."[112]

Where Do We Go retold the story of the Meredith March and repeated King's much-quoted belief that Carmichael-style activism was a misguided approach to a crucially necessary thing, creating black power. This time he recycled his Frogmore theme that it was nihilistic and self-defeating: "Beneath all the satisfaction of a gratifying slogan, Black Power is a nihilistic philosophy born out of the conviction that the Negro can't win. It is, at bottom, the view that American society is so hopelessly corrupt and enmeshed in evil that there is no possibility of salvation from within." Black Power carried "the seeds of its own doom" by capitulating to hate. Until Gandhi came along, King said, all revolutions were based on love and hate: hope in the expectation of freedom and justice and hate for oppressors. Gandhian nonviolence was more revolutionary than all previous revolutions because it rested on hope and love, breaking the cycle of revenge. From Montgomery to Selma the civil rights movement ran on hope that gave power to the way of nonviolence. More recently, many black Americans lost hope that they would ever live in a just society: "They were now booing because they felt that we were unable to deliver on our promises." King sympathized and even agreed but countered that despair never sustained any revolution for long. This was "the ultimate contradiction of the Black Power movement." It snuffed out the flame of hope in the name of revolution, ignoring that a revolution stripped of hope inevitably "degenerates into an indiscriminating catchall for evanescent and futile gestures."[113]

King denied that Black Power was a species of racism since its proponents did not go on about the innate inferiority or worthlessness of white people. Racism was very much a white specialty. Still, Carmichael and others called for retaliatory violence, which King called "the most destructive feature of Black Power," and they repudiated racial integration. King rejected the new separatism, avowing that liberation and integration go together. No oppressed group can be liberated without integrating, or integrate without being liberated, because power has to be shared in a just society. The sharing of power is the very definition of a just society: "I cannot see how the Negro will be totally liberated from the crushing weight of poor education, squalid housing and economic strangulation until he is integrated, with power, into every level of American life." King tired of being asked if he still believed in nonviolence and integration, especially nonviolence. He reached for a way of saying it that settled the question. He believed that most blacks agreed with him about nonviolence, but even if it turned out that they did not he would still believe in it. He was committed to molding a consensus about nonviolence and took no interest whatsoever in being a consensus leader. The latter type merely searched and represented, conforming to whatever happened to be. King was nothing like that; to him, it was convictional leadership or bust, and his conviction remained a burning fire in him: "Occasionally in life one develops a conviction so precious and meaningful that he will stand on it till the end. That is what I have found in nonviolence."[114]

He circled back to the white backlash, acknowledging that this ubiquitously employed phrase named something terribly significant, albeit misleadingly. The backlash ripping through U.S. American politics and society would have happened had there been no riots in American cities and no Black Power movement, King argued. It was caused, as usual, by America's centuries-old racial pathology. Every breakthrough for racial justice in American history swiftly yielded a setback, now called a backlash: "White America has been backlashing on the fundamental God-given and human rights of Negro Americans for more than three hundred years." The only thing new was that blacks now spoke for themselves with confidence and pride, which hurt the feelings of white liberals, who wanted to speak for blacks. King told the wounded whites to get over their hurt feelings. The civil rights movement still needed white marchers, and they needed to accept a certain amount of black anger. When told to get lost, they needed to respect why they were hearing it, without actually leaving. There was a place in the movement for white supporters who accepted black leadership, King said. He believed that white liberals who backed the movement for the right reasons would find the right posture and usually be welcomed. The whites who made a fuss about being excluded or silenced lacked the right motivation: "If he supported the movement for the wrong reasons, he will find every available excuse to withdraw from it now, and he will discover that he was inoculated with so mild a form of commitment that he was immune to the genuine moral article."[115]

King stressed that black Americans had precious few on-ramps to "the economic highway to power." Higher education afforded access to some black Americans, but not many. Union organizing was no longer segregated, but blacks tended to shun unions; King regretted that Randolph was the only prominent labor leader ever produced by black America. Black leaders were nearly always middle-class professionals lacking street credibility to working-class blacks. The civil rights movement had more success with the consumer lever, especially consumer boycotts. King touted that Operation Breadbasket had spread to twelve cities and that Chicago's chapter directed funds to black-owned banks. The growing power of the black vote was another hopeful trend, although King judged that black Americans still disdained black politicians too much.

Powell was the nation's only respected black political leader, and he commanded nowhere near the respect that whites conferred on JFK and Adlai Stevenson. King lauded the community-organizing groups and training centers "now proliferating in some slum areas," which created a new generation of community leaders and built democracy from the bottom up. Community organizing was tremendously important, and it rightly agitated for a full-employment economy. But community organizing was very limited by comparison to the transforming potential of a single, simple, sweeping reform measure: abolishing poverty by instituting a minimum guaranteed income. Economist John Kenneth Galbraith figured that a $20 billion federal program would do the job; King said that lifting the poor from poverty would be good for the economy and America's moral health. There was no reason for any American citizen to be poor: "The time has come for us to civilize ourselves by the total, direct, and immediate abolition of poverty."[116]

Where Do We Go was King's best book: eloquent, practical, timely, judicious, and visionary. It had King's trademark blend of reformist common sense and liberationist militancy. It spoke to the moment with passion while keeping its balance. On his book tour he prepared audiences for its militancy, occasionally declaring that he had watched his dream turn into a nightmare. The book evoked little response at first and very little that was not tepid, until the response turned scathing. A few reviewers said it was pretty good or at least not too bad. Milton Konvitz, in *Saturday Review,* called the book "moderate, judicious, constructive, [and] pragmatic." Eliot Fremont-Smith in the *New York Times* said that King made a credible plea not to despair of nonviolence before he did. Then came a downpour of dismissal and ridicule. David Steinberg in *Commonweal* censured King for misrepresenting Black Power and his own relation to it. Many reviewers said that King seemed confused or weary. Some said that he groped unsuccessfully to be relevant in a time that had passed him by; others said he never figured out what the book was about.[117]

One scalding, much-quoted review set the standard for fashionable left-wing King bashing. White journalist Andrew Kopkind pronounced in *New York Review of Books* that King was no longer someone serious people had to take seriously. King was boringly middle-class, still bragging about black inventors, and hopelessly outdated: "He has been outstripped by his times, overtaken by the events which he may have obliquely helped to produce." According to Kopkind, King did not understand his own statements about structural change, he had no strategy for pursuing it, and he did not understand that morality is like politics in beginning at the barrel of a gun. Up until Chicago King still mattered; after Chicago and this book he no longer mattered: "He is not likely to regain command. Both his philosophy and his techniques of leadership were products of a different world, of relationships which no longer obtain and expectations which are no longer valid." King was irrelevant, Kopkind said, because liberalism was dead. Vietnam and Black Power killed liberalism, as all informed people knew, although King was not among them. In short, King "had simply, and disastrously, arrived at the wrong conclusions about the world."[118]

The bad reviews had just begun when rioting broke out, in July, in Newark and Detroit. In Detroit fires and gunfire raged through entire neighborhoods. More than fourteen hundred fires, many set off by Molotov cocktails, ravaged a 140-block area. There were pitched battles between snipers and police and house-to-house combat. The National Guard moved in with armored personnel carriers, and forty-three people were killed before army paratroopers restored order. King told a conference call of advisors that he had hit bottom; Detroit marked a new low in modern U.S. American history. Powell declared from Bimini that more riots were surely coming, "a necessary phase of the black revolution." Rap Brown said it with enthusiasm: "Violence is necessary. It is as American as cherry pie." King, speaking at the National Conference for New Politics, was jeered with "Kill whitey, kill whitey" before he said anything. The conference was a coalition of nearly four hundred groups meeting at the Coliseum and Palmer House in Chicago. More-radical-than-you was very much in fashion, with much chanting about burning down fascist Amerika. Black nationalists heckled King and he struggled to be heard. It was awful, he told Levison: "The black nationalists gave me trouble. They kept interrupting me, kept yelling things at me." White wannabe radicals came out against liberalism and all things American. One day of this was enough for King, who made an early exit with four days of conferencing still to go. The atmosphere of chaotic hostility repelled him. If the antiwar coalition that he wanted had already veered into crazed ultra-leftism, he could not speak for it.[119]

Meanwhile SCLC boiled over with problems deferred and worsening. Bevel rejoined the executive staff, refueling Bevel versus Williams issues, and King missed Blackwell, needing a manager desperately. Williams was angry that his southern field-worker team had been cut from 180 to 12, while some believed that Williams retained more sway at SCLC than he deserved. There were bruising arguments over the organization's highest priority. Antipoverty? The war? Open housing? Voter registration? Bevel likened antipoverty campaigning to scrounging for bus fare. Wachtel said that Operation Breadbasket merely shook down corporations for token jobs and write-offs. Marian Wright, a lawyer working for the NAACP Legal Defense Fund in Mississippi, had an idea that King liked: marching poor people from Mississippi to Washington, DC, to stage sit-ins. Levison added the idea of a tent city, recalling the Bonus March of 1932. King had come to regret that he cut short the antislum campaign in Chicago. Had he marched into Cicero it would have been bloody, but he would have earned street credibility before Newark and Detroit erupted. King's lieutenants objected that poverty was an abstraction and that squatting in the nation's capital would go badly. King took their brusque rebuttals personally. Their fractiousness no longer seemed creative to him. One night, as King wailed about it, Young had to pry a whiskey bottle from his hand and send him to bed. King decided, against Rustin and most of the staff, for a "Poor People's Campaign for Jobs or Income." Bevel and Jackson told him vehemently that he was wrong.

All such debates were academic if King did not hire a manager to whip SCLC into shape. Mail piled up unopened, bills went unpaid, and private agendas abounded. King reached out to a corporate high-flyer, William Rutherford, who had to leave his home in Zurich, Switzerland, to take the job. Rutherford was a black public relations executive and founder of management companies. He got a frosty greeting from SCLC staffers and a sharp you-don't-belong-here from Williams, both of which he took in stride. Rutherford was shocked, however, by the sexual banter of the ministers (he had no idea) and the extreme disorder of the office (so much worse than King had said). He cleaned up years of backlogged mail, checks, bills, and policies, to King's delight, and advised King on personnel changes. King promoted Young to executive vice president and appointed Lafayette to run the Washington campaign, banking on Lafayette's quiet competence and his background in Quaker antislum activism. Then he asked Rutherford to make a major decision. Most of the staff disliked Jackson, and King had misgivings about him. Did Jackson's value to the organization outweigh his egotism and opportunism? Was he loyal enough to keep? Or should he go? Rutherford was still thinking about it, leaning toward "go," when time ran out on King's earthly life. In addition, King asked Rutherford to learn how Williams and SCLC comptroller James Harrison managed to afford a shared apartment at the University Plaza on their meager salaries. Rutherford found no evidence of pilfering by Williams or Harrison, which relieved King greatly, and the matter was closed. King never learned that his comptroller was a Hoover spy.[120]

In November and December 1967 King gave the seventh annual Massey Lectures, broadcast by the Canadian Broadcasting Corporation. He moved straight to a two-sided argument about the decade from 1955 to 1965: "Everyone underestimated the amount of violence and rage Negroes were suppressing and the amount of bigotry the white majority was disguising." Both illusions were dispelled, King said, because for three summers in a row Americans watched their cities burn. Victor Hugo, describing France in the eighteenth century, remarked, "If the soul is left in darkness, sins will be committed. The guilty one is not he who commits the sin, but he who causes the darkness." That was King's verdict exactly: "The policy-makers of the white society have caused the darkness: they created discrimination; they created slums; they perpetuate unemployment, ignorance, and poverty." The crimes committed by black looters were small and derivative: "They are born of the greater crimes of the white society." In a crucial sense, King allowed, it was true to say that the civil rights movement had ended. In the South SCLC's protest demonstrations had felt like social earthquakes, but in the North the same tactics barely impacted "the normal turbulence of city life." King felt the difference acutely. More important, something had happened to young people. During the heyday of SCLC young people flocked to the protests and felt represented by them. But that had "fallen apart under the impact of failures, discouragement, and consequent extremism and polarization."[121]

They had to march on the nation's capital to spark a new generation of protest against denigration and oppression. King put it dramatically in his last Massey Lecture, a Christmas sermon. It was his usual message in a context of worse-than-ever despair: "Somehow we must be able to stand up before our most bitter opponents and say, 'We shall match your capacity to inflict suffering by our capacity to endure suffering. We will meet your physical force with soul force. Do us what you will and we will still love you.' " Now, however, he said it by counterposing the dream and the nightmare, invoking four nightmares. He had a dream but saw it turn into a nightmare when four young girls were murdered. He saw the nightmare again in the vicious poverty gripping urban black American neighborhoods. He saw it again as black Americans set fire to their own neighborhoods. He saw a fourth nightmare rage out of control as America ravaged Vietnam. King lived on the edge of despair but dared not give up hope: "Yes, I am personally the victim of deferred dreams, of blasted hopes, but in spite of that I close today by saying I still have a dream, because, you know, you can't give up in life."[122]

Erecting a city of the poor in Washington would show dramatically that he had not given up. There was much grumbling that King committed SCLC to a bad campaign, and he stiffed his top aides in choosing Lafayette for it. Bevel and Jackson angered King by continuing to deride the campaign after King committed to it. Rustin said that herding poor people to Washington would not accomplish anything. King replied that they had to find a way to dramatize what poor people were up against. He wished he could do it without protesting and going to jail because he was tired of protesting and going to jail. He wanted to talk about democratic Socialism, but that was out of play. All he could do was stand with the poor and dramatize their situation. This was the best way to expand the civil rights movement into a human rights movement that show-cased the struggles of oppressed peoples across racial lines. King reached out to Harrington for help, who agreed with Rustin that King needed a political victory, not a sprawling shantytown spectacle in the nation's capital. Harrington was stunned by King's battered condition. The King he had known was ebullient, warm, funny, and self-confident. Now King seemed grimly sad to Harrington and barely recognizable—a tortured figure who looked seriously ill. But Harrington could not say no to King, so he set aside his personal opinion to work on the Washington campaign, scheduled to begin on April 22, 1968.[123]

On February 4 King adapted a sermon by evangelist Wallace Hamilton, "The Drum Major Instinct," to his own situation and moment. The sermon was based on Mark 10: 35–45. Two disciples asked Jesus for seats next to him in heaven, the other ten disciples were angry when they heard about it, and Jesus declared that whoever wished to be great must be the servant of others. King liked that Jesus did not rebuke James and John for their ambition, which King called "the drum major instinct." Harnessing this instinct was "the great issue in life," he declared. For the most part the drum major instinct was a baleful thing; King spent most of the sermon dwelling on it: "I must be first. I must be supreme. Our nation must rule the world. And I am sad to say that the nation in which we live is the supreme culprit. And I'm going to continue to say it in America, because I love this country too much to see the drift that it has taken." Americans were criminals in an unjust war: "We have committed more war crimes almost than any nation in the world, and I'm going to continue to say it." King circled back to Jesus, saying that to be great, one has to serve others. Everybody can serve others, King reasoned, so, according to Jesus, everybody can be great. One doesn't have to be a genius or highly educated: "You only need a heart full of grace. A soul generated by love."[124]

King pushed to the close, stressing that Jesus stirred up controversy, agitated for justice, practiced civil disobedience, broke injunctions, and was tortured and cursed on his way to the cross. The ministry of Jesus led to his martyrdom, which led King to muse on his own death: "Every now and then I think about my own death, and I think about my own funeral." He didn't want the preachers to run long or enumerate his hundreds of awards. He wanted them to say that King "tried to give his life serving others" and he tried to love others: "I want you to say that day, that I tried to be right on the war question. I want you to be able to say that day, that I did try to feed the hungry." He finished the gloss on Matthew 25 and returned to the drum major motif: "If you want to say that I was a drum major, say that I was a drum major for justice; say that I was a drum major for peace; I was a drum major for righteousness. And all the other shallow things will not matter. I won't have any money to leave behind. I won't have the fine and luxurious things of life to leave behind. But I just want to leave a committed life behind."[125]

He had two months left, and nothing came easily anymore. At the end King was tense, drained, overweight, and constantly teetering on collapse. He could not sleep, and he startled friends by snapping at them. Longtimers who had never seen him yell at anyone were stunned to see him yell at Young, Rutherford, Jackson, and others. On the day after his drum major sermon King attended a meeting of the National Welfare Rights Organization (NWRO) in Chicago, where he expected to be among friends. George Wiley, a chemist and former CORE official, had founded the NWRO the previous summer with foundation grants. Wiley primed thirty welfare mothers to give King a bruising welcome. King endorsed the organization's demands for a federal legal aid program, a welfare bill, and grassroots antipoverty activism, but the NWRO board grilled him anyway with aggressive questions, exposing his weak grasp of amendments to H.R. 1280 and other policy specifics. Young and Lafayette bristled at the hostile treatment, but King submitted to it good-naturedly, empathizing with the women and Wiley's power move. Having deferred to his mother while brushing off his blustery father, he knew when to defer.[126]

On February 23 King headlined a tribute to Du Bois at Carnegie Hall in New York. Organized and sponsored by James O'Dell's *Freedomways* magazine, the event featured speeches by King, James Baldwin, and Ossie Davis. Thinking about Du Bois lifted King to special eloquence, brushing off how it might play in the *New York Times*. Nearly fifty years later this speech is still too radical to be included in the corporate-funded archive of King's works. Du Bois, King said, was an "intellectual giant" and teacher who surpassed all others in demolishing the pernicious idea of racial inferiority. Du Bois shredded "the army of white propagandists—the myth-makers of Negro history." He was "first and always a black man," in later life he became a Communist, and he was persecuted by the U.S. government. King was defiantly admiring: "He confronted the establishment as a model of militant manhood and integrity. He defied them and though they heaped venom and scorn on him his powerful voice was never stilled." More than ever King appreciated what it must have been like for Du Bois—"a radical all his life"—to battle on. It was time to stop "muting the fact" that Du Bois was a genius *and* a Communist, for "irrational, obsessive anti-Communism has led us into too many quagmires." The crowd erupted in passionate applause. King concluded that Du Bois had many virtues but his greatest "was his committed empathy with all the oppressed and his divine dissatisfaction with all forms of injustice."[127]

The Poor People's Campaign called for a $30 billion federal antipoverty program, a full-employment bill, a guaranteed annual income, and at least $500,000 for low-cost housing per year. King and Young designed a plan for SCLC's most ambitious protest ever, and King vowed to be militant. It would begin with a lobbying campaign; caravans of the poor would descend on Washington; and the marching around Capitol Hill would start on May 5. At Carnegie Hall King said they had to march on Washington because the government "declared an armistice in the war on poverty while squandering billions to expand a senseless, cruel, unjust war in Vietnam." Afterward he acknowledged that there would be traffic jams and disruption plus a spectacle encampment. Rustin pleaded with King in the press to call off the whole thing. Electing Democrats and stumping for a new civil rights bill with an open-housing title were crucial. Making a mess in Washington was crazy.[128]

But King had grown accustomed to being more radical than everyone around him. In his last weeks he doubled down on the path of public sacrifice, dragging others along. He had never taken care of himself, and he was not about to change his ways merely because he was ill and exhausted. As a child he had sung that he wanted to be more and more like Jesus. In his last years he bore his cross so intently and with such disregard for his health that friends suspected a death wish. The Poor People's Campaign, which King launched at the lowest point of his life, topped his previous forays into risky, controversial, chaotic protest. He would not be moved by strategic arguments about political reforms. He would not be shamed into reverting to middle-class politics. Now he outflanked even Bevel, his usual barometer of too-far extremism. King had to stand with the poorest of the poor and afflicted; otherwise he was not really a follower of Jesus. In March he told a New York City union consisting mostly of blacks and Puerto Ricans that the next march on Washington would have black Americans "because black people are poor" and Puerto Ricans because they were poor too and Mexican Americans and Native Americans "because they are mistreated" and poor Appalachian whites who repudiated racism. King knew what he needed to do and with whom he needed to be. He only did not know where this was heading politically.[129]

Young believed that King's emotional and spiritual despair was far more disabling than his physical exhaustion. As long as King knew where he wanted to go he could bull through everything that the road threw at him. After King fell into trouble emotionally he brushed off Young and others who tried to talk to him about it. Occasionally King acknowledged that he might be too exhausted to go on and he needed to take a year off. He fantasized about teaching at Union or living in Switzerland. But mostly he bulled forward, bearing his cross, enduring one sleepless night after another, and rousing himself with sermonic riffs about the view from the mountaintop. He told the SCLC staff, "When I took up the Cross, I recognized it's meaning. The Cross is something that you bear, and ultimately that you die on."[130]

King tried to hire Lawson because Lawson was more like him than any SCLC staffer, and King wanted Lawson to help him rebuild the SCLC staff. But Lawson doubted that King would make the necessary changes, which would leave Lawson to deal with the egos and volatility of lieutenants who would not get fired. It didn't help that SCLC ministers chortled about Lawson's marriage-only sex life. So Lawson stayed at Centenary Methodist Church in Memphis, where he had served since 1962. From an activist standpoint Memphis was much harder than Nashville had been. Memphis was more conservative politically and socially; very few black ministers in Memphis had any theological training; most of the preaching on both sides of the color line was pure fundamentalism; and Lawson slowly built up his credibility there, having arrived with "radical Northern agitator" pinned to his chest.

Sanitation workers in Memphis were mostly black, poorly paid, and unpaid in bad weather, and had no benefits. They had a fledgling union, AFSCME Local 1733, which the city did not recognize. Thus when the union struck in February 1968 Mayor Henry Loeb treated it as illegitimate—a wildcat strike. AFSCME national president Jerry Wurf got nowhere with Loeb, and the strike moved quickly from a local labor dispute to a national racial flashpoint. Lawson organized a strike support group named COME (Community on the Move for Equality) and asked for King's help. King was struggling, and failing, to get the Poor People's Campaign off the ground. He recruited few volunteers and spent more money than he raised. His staffers had tense encounters with Latino activists not inclined to take orders. Young told King they could not afford to spend any time in Memphis, even as Young presumed that Lawson had trained the Memphis protesters in rigorous Nashville movement fashion. That presumption turned out to be false, but King showed up for a speech at Mason Temple and returned on March 28 for a march that turned disastrous.

To Lawson, Memphis had never been like Nashville, and 1968 was far removed from 1960. Lawson worked hard at mobilizing solidarity for the thirteen hundred striking workers, but some of the protesters in Memphis were unruly marchers belonging to no group, and some were young militants belonging to a group called the Invaders. Both spurned nonviolence and Lawson. King did not know about the tensions between Lawson and the Invaders. King's plane arrived late, ratcheting up tensions as the marchers waited for him. He sensed trouble when he arrived, as the mood and the placards were angry. Finally the march began, with King at the head. The ministers bunched up to the front to be near King, neglecting their duties as marshals, which left the young marchers unsupervised. The rear ranks had barely begun to march when they began smashing store windows. Looting and turmoil commenced, Lawson swung to the back to survey the situation, and he aborted the march, which covered only seven blocks and lasted only twenty-five minutes. King caught a ride from a passing motorist and fled the scene as soon as Lawson ended the march. It was King's last march.

Lawson tried unsuccessfully to reverse the march. The looting got worse, the police dispensed tear gas and beatings indiscriminately, and television reporters chastised King for cutting out. Deeply distraught, King ended up at a Holiday Inn in nearby Rivermont. He told Abernathy, "Maybe we'll have to let violence run its course. Maybe the people will listen to the voice of violence. They certainly won't listen to us." Abernathy demurred, but King said it repeatedly; America was sick, the day of violence had come, and nonviolence was finished. A group of Invaders came to the hotel to apologize to King, which helped briefly. King pulled himself together, gave a winsome performance at a press conference, and implored reporters to distinguish between most of the marchers, who were dignified and disciplined, and a handful of rioting interlopers. He got hostile questions in reply, which wounded him. Afterward he asked Abernathy to get him out of Memphis. By telephone King told Levison that the movement was in terrible trouble because violence was winning. Levison pushed back, and King assured him that he was only fearful and distressed, not defeated. But the press coverage was every bit as harsh and reproachful as King feared, pronouncing that he had embarrassed himself, nonviolence was losing, and King needed to call off the Poor People's Campaign.[131]

A second march in Memphis was organized to redeem the first one. King preached at Washington Cathedral on March 31, Palm Sunday, and promised that the upcoming Poor People's Campaign would be huge, well organized, and historic. That night LBJ told a stunned nation that he would not seek reelection. King was too exhausted and pressed for time to think about Johnson's demise. On Wednesday he returned to the Lorraine Motel in Memphis, too drained to face a rally crowd at the Mason Temple, so he sent Abernathy to speak for him. Mason was the headquarters church of the Church of God in Christ (COGIC), whose bishop and COGIC cofounder James Patterson strongly supported the strike. A storm lessened the crowd, but two thousand people showed up along with all three national television networks. Lawson warmed up the crowd, but nobody applauded when Abernathy, Jackson, and Young appeared. Abernathy realized that the crowd yearned for King. Earlier that week King had rebuked Jackson, who was still smarting from it; Jackson wanted badly to speak, urging Abernathy not to call King. King had told Jackson he might have to take an extended sabbatical because of his terrible exhaustion. The prospect that King might leave the movement was very real to Jackson that night. Abernathy made the call, stressing the network cameras and the rows of sanitation workers, and King, surprisingly, agreed to come. According to Young, King was more depressed that night than ever. But Abernathy knew how to motivate King, and Mason Temple was a special venue—huge in seating capacity, yet intimate. Abernathy repeated what Lawson told him: the movement rarely gathered this many people in the South, let alone during a storm. So King crawled out of bed. Abernathy, to his own puzzlement, felt compelled to speak first, giving a prolonged introduction to King. He went on for almost an hour, regaling the crowd with a cheeky imitation of the drum major sermon and a lavish tribute to King's life and greatness. The crowd roared with approval when Abernathy finished, and King declared that Abernathy was his best friend in the world.[132]

The long introduction inspired King to reach down. He did not know this crowd, and he was mindful that he had not meant to come to Mason Temple. But King was impressed that these strangers braved a storm to hear him. It said something about what was happening in Memphis and the world, not merely something about King's fame. He began with the former something, taking the crowd from Egypt and the Hebrew exodus to Mount Olympus and Plato and Aristotle, to the heydays of the Roman Empire and the Renaissance, to Abraham Lincoln and the Emancipation Proclamation, to the present day in Johannesburg, Nairobi, Accra, New York City, Atlanta, Jackson, and Memphis, where people cried for their freedom. He was happy to be alive in 1968 and in Memphis, even in the midst of such trouble. In the past, King said, people debated violence versus nonviolence, but in 1968 there was no choice to debate; now the issue was nonviolence or nonexistence: "That is where we are today." The issue in the human rights revolution was very similar to the threat of a global nuclear holocaust: "If something isn't done, and in a hurry, to bring the colored peoples of the world out of their long years of poverty, their long years of hurt and neglect, the whole world is doomed."[133]

They were going to march again in Memphis because violence had broken out during the first march and the press saw nothing else to write about. King noted that every article was about gunfire and broken windows, not about why thirteen hundred sanitation workers were on strike. The movement would not be stopped by a little violence, just as Bull Connor's dogs had not stopped it.

Memphis was very much like Birmingham, King said. There was an injunction in place against demonstrating, and the usual court battle was ongoing. But they were going to march whether or not the injunction was lifted. King gave thanks that Memphis had ministers like Lawson, Ralph Jackson, and Billy Kyles. It was fine to preach about heaven, but Jesus cared about more than heaven. Many preachers still worried mostly about themselves, but Memphis had some relevant ministers: "And I'm always happy to see a relevant ministry."[134]

Every good campaign, King observed, had direct action protests backed by the threat of economic withdrawal. Black Americans were poor compared to white Americans, but not poor compared to most of the world's peoples. Black Americans had significant power at their disposal, which had nothing to do with "acting bad with our words" or throwing Molotov cocktails. Memphis blacks, to assert their power, needed to boycott Coca-Cola, Sealtest, Wonder Bread, and other enterprises that refused to hire blacks. They also needed to support black banks and insurance companies and to develop "a kind of dangerous unselfishness."[135]

King had a set piece on the Good Samaritan parable that he cribbed partly from eminent preacher George Buttrick. The Good Samaritan was terribly relevant to the Memphis strike, King said. In the story told by Jesus, a man was robbed by thieves, a Levite and a priest passed by the stricken man without helping him, and a Samaritan—"a man of another race," King noted—took compassion on the man and came to his aid. King raced through three standard interpretations. The Levite and priest were rushing to a religious engagement, or they were blocked by legalistic religious scruples, or they were system reformers who spurned individual efforts. King favored a fourth reading: these respectable religious figures were afraid of getting into trouble, so they looked the other way. What if the thieves lurked nearby, waiting for more prey? What if the victim was faking, ready to pounce? King asked the crowd to be like the Good Samaritan, who opted for dangerous unselfishness. Instead of asking the wrong questions, they needed to follow the Samaritan in asking the right question: "If I do not stop to help the sanitation workers, what will happen to them?"[136]

Now he needed to close. The long introduction and King's surprise at being there militated against a poem or hymn. He was too fully present—too much *there* in spirit and body—not to go personal at the end. King recalled the time he was nearly stabbed to death at Blumstein's in Harlem. Had he sneezed, the tip of the blade would have punctured his aorta and killed him. In the hospital he got many letters, including one from a white girl who told him she was happy he had not sneezed. King told the crowd at Mason Temple that he was happy, too, for not having sneezed. Had he sneezed, he would not have witnessed the sit-ins at lunch counters, the Freedom Rides, the Albany campaign, the Birmingham campaign, the Civil Rights Act, the March on Washington, and the Selma campaign. It was generous of King to suggest that these things would have happened anyway had he died. He personalized only one event, describing the March on Washington as his attempt "to tell America about a dream I had had." His voice climbed as he reviewed the history of the civil rights movement and implied that God spared him to play the role he played.[137]

"If I had sneezed" was a staple of King's oratory, but it usually came early in a speech, as the first run. Always it got a big reaction, as it did in Mason Temple, but King had never closed with it, and he had never paired it with the mountaintop, another staple. Whenever King used the mountaintop piece, Young knew he was almost unbearably depressed and exhausted. For a moment King stumbled at moving from one to the other. Awkwardly he remarked, "And they were telling me, now it doesn't matter now." Nobody knew what that meant; King clarified it by owning it: "It really doesn't matter what happens now." He meant, what happened to him; King cared greatly what happened to the sanitation strikers. Still a bit awkwardly, he told the crowd about his day. That morning his Eastern Airlines flight was delayed by a bomb threat. The pilot said everyone had to de-plane to wait for a bomb search because Martin Luther King was aboard. After the flight landed in Memphis, King heard about new threats to kill him. He hung an eerie, pensive question in the air, changing tenses: "What would happen to me from some of our sick white brothers?"[138]

King said he did not know what would happen next; there were difficult days ahead: "But it doesn't matter with me now." He paused briefly, flushed with emotion, before belting out the line that took him home: "Because I've been to the mountaintop!" Cheers and clapping broke out. "Like anybody, I would like to live a long life. Longevity has its place. But I'm not concerned about that now. I just want to do God's will." Many called out, "Yes!" at doing God's will. "And he's allowed me to go up to the mountain. And I've looked over. And I've s-e-e-e-e-n the promised land." He paused, with a slight smile, holding the moment. "I may not get there with you. But I want you to know tonight, that we, as a people, will get to the promised land!" The cheering got louder, and the ministers behind King moved toward him. King exclaimed over the cheering, not waiting for a lull, "So I'm happy tonight! I'm not worried about *any*thing I'm not fearing *any* man. Mine eyes have seen the *glo-o-ry* of the coming of the Lord!"[139]

He broke off the quotation, drained and finished, falling into Abernathy's arms. The crowd roared with tumultuous, gut-level, raucous emotion, while the ministers helped King to a chair. The roaring went on as the ministers surrounding King compared him to Moses atop Mount Nebo, glimpsing Canaan across the Jordan River. King revived at hearing the ministers gush; preacher talk was therapeutic and energizing for him. He did not hear what the ministers told each other—that the dying Moses bit was too much, no matter that it enthralled the crowd. Some were embarrassed that King indulged his morbid martyr streak; Young said the ending seemed almost macabre. Though the ministers winced at the ending, they marveled that King pulled off one of his most powerful sermons despite being miserably exhausted. Abernathy thought that King soared higher than ever at Mason Temple. But King had spoken brilliantly on countless occasions despite being miserably exhausted; he relied on his inspirations. Then he partied all night in Memphis, too wired for sleeping. Young later acknowledged, "He may have seen, as we could not, that his time was passing, that he had done all he could on earth."[140]

On his last day King dispatched Young and Eskridge to federal court, hoping to not have to defy a federal injunction. The Invaders urged King to respect their belief in tactical violence, which he rebuffed, chastising Williams for indulging the Invaders. A. D. King had come to Memphis, so the brothers called their mother together, a rare family moment. Young and Lawson were grilled in court, where they denied that SCLC nonviolence instigated violence, imploring that a second march was the best way to prevent more violence. King spent much of the afternoon in bed, "just staring at the ceiling," according to Georgia Davis Powers. "He was withdrawn and meditative, almost prayerful." When Young returned to the Lorraine Motel, King admonished him for failing to provide telephone updates, which led to a playful pillow fight. The mood brightened further when they heard that Judge Bailey Brown had approved a second march featuring a prescribed route, no weapons, and narrow ranks. King's entourage gathered in the parking lot, awaiting a trip to Kyles's home for dinner. King teased Kyles that his wife was too good-looking to be a good cook. Jackson asked King if he remembered Ben Branch, a Memphis musician. King assured him that he did, asking Branch to play "Precious Lord, Take My Hand" at the meeting that night: "Play it real pretty." Those were his last words. A call went out to grab some coats, but before they were delivered King stepped onto the balcony and was assassinated.[141]

THE DREAMER SLAIN

All the foreboding made it no less shocking. Blood poured from King's exploded cheek and neck, Young and others pointed in the direction of the shooter, and Abernathy pleaded with King to open his eyes or say something. Abernathy claimed that King moved his lips, and Young felt a very weak pulse. An ambulance took King to St. Joseph's Hospital, accompanied by Abernathy and Lee. Young telephoned Coretta King, who took it with remarkable calm, and Young followed close behind the ambulance. The physicians tried to save King before stepping aside to let Abernathy have a last moment with him. Young was outside the emergency room when Lee came out to say quietly, "He's gone."[142]

Except for Dorothy Cotton, the entire SCLC senior staff was in Memphis. Coretta went to the Atlanta airport but turned back after King was pronounced dead. Young made calls to Belafonte, Levison, and Cotton, while Lawson rushed to black radio stations, pleading for calm, to no avail. Rioting broke out in Memphis, spread to 110 cities, and was worst in Chicago and Washington, DC. Abernathy fell into a catatonic trance. A reporter asked Abernathy about King's last moments, the crime scene, and the rioting. Nothing got a reaction, until a throwaway question about the early days of the movement evoked an Abernathy gusher about Vernon Johns. Jackson offended Williams and others by telling reporters that King said his last words while Jackson cradled him in his arms. Young, Abernathy, Lee, Williams, Bevel, Jackson, and Lawson returned to the hotel but could not bear to watch television reports of the assassination and rioting. Abernathy told the group they had to go on; it would be a betrayal of King not to do so. Bevel declared that he had loved King even more than he loved Jesus, but now King was gone and they had to follow Abernathy's leadership. No one disputed that King wanted it that way, though Bevel soon changed his mind about trying to follow Abernathy.[143]

Jackson told Abernathy he was returning to Chicago to urge Chicagoans on to the funeral in Atlanta. The others tried to sleep, which was impossible, so they regathered to hold each other up, surprised that Jackson had already left. Jackson appeared on television with King's blood on his jacket, further offending the lieutenants. Young burned with anger and denial at King's death. He did not want to carry on without King but saying so was unthinkable. Young felt trapped and condemned; otherwise he felt nothing, being the type to shut down: "Martin couldn't leave us with all this mess. It seemed unfair that he was 'free' from innumerable problems, while we, the living, were left to try to cope without him. We had been just getting by with him, how could we get along without him?"[144]

James Earl Ray, a fugitive criminal and segregationist, shot King from a rooming house across the street and made it to Canada, England, and the Continent before a worldwide manhunt tracked him down. SCLC veterans found it bitterly unbelievable that the low-functioning Ray pulled off King's murder all by himself, then got to Canada and somehow came up with a forged passport. They did not trust the FBI to explain what happened since the FBI had persecuted King. King was denied a state funeral because Georgia governor Lester Maddox considered him an enemy of the United States. Ebenezer was too small to handle the funeral, so there was a private funeral at Ebenezer followed by a public funeral three miles away at the Morehouse College quadrangle, linked by a mule-drawn wagon procession through the streets of Atlanta.

At Ebenezer Abernathy conducted the service, and DeWolf gave the eulogy. Rows of white dignitaries displaced longtime members and friends, and the service ran long, in sweltering heat. The eulogy section of the drum major sermon was played, every speaker except DeWolf ignored King's request to be brief, and Abernathy poignantly invoked the Joseph story in Genesis: "Let us slay the dreamer, and see what shall become of his dream." DeWolf said that his friendship with King was the "highest privilege" of his life and that King exemplified the eternal virtues of faith, hope, and love "in the greatest intensity." King's faith enabled him to endure the hate and violence of oppression. His hope enabled him to dream of global human fellowship. His love enabled him to love hate-filled enemies and pour himself out for strangers and friends. DeWolf praised the "little band of nonviolent crusaders" that lit a fire in Montgomery and kept the struggle going: "They are too few, they who have already made such a costly sacrifice." He ended with a call to complete King's mission: "It is now for us, all the millions of the living who care, to take up his torch of love. It is for us to finish his work, to end the awful destruction in Vietnam, to root out every trace of race prejudice from our lives, to bring the massive powers of this nation to aid the oppressed and heal the hate-scarred world."[145]

The procession to Morehouse and the scorching heat wilted many marchers and observers. Fifty thousand jammed into the Morehouse quad, where Abernathy invited a few dignitaries to speak and compensated by canceling several scheduled speakers, including Joseph Lowery. Daddy King pressed Abernathy to bring on Mays because people were passing out. The mood was somber and flat; no speaker or performer stirred the crowd, not even Mahalia Jackson. Finally it was time for Mays, who said he had wanted King to eulogize him. As it was, he thanked God for calling King to "speak to America about war and peace; about social injustice and racial discrimination; about its obligation to the poor; and about nonviolence as a way of perfecting social change in a world of brutality and war." King had faith in America, Mays said. He believed that America was capable of curing its racial pathology, and he dreamed of a nation that achieved social justice, "where our nation will be militarily strong but perpetually at peace; economically secure but just; learned but wise; where the poorest—the garbage collectors—will have bread enough and to spare; where no one will be poorly housed; each educated up to his capacity; and where the richest will understand the meaning of empathy." Mays stressed that King's commitment to nonviolence combined love, courage, and intelligence. He viewed all people as equal, and he identified with oppressed people in their struggles for justice, dignity, and freedom: "He was supra-race, supra-nation, supra-denomination, supra-class and supra-culture. He belonged to the world and to mankind."[146]

Millions of people hated King for these very things, Mays noted. King was in the prophetic line of Amos, Micah, and Hosea. He was not ahead of his time because nobody is. He had one life to live, he belonged to his time, and he could not wait. Thus he was like Abraham, Moses, Jesus, Paul, Galileo, Copernicus, Martin Luther, Lincoln, Woodrow Wilson championing the League of Nations, Gandhi, and Nehru: He did what was right, believing that the time is always ripe to do right. Mays said it should not have been necessary for King to sacrifice his life. He spent most of his career struggling to restore the Thirteenth, Fourteenth, and Fifteenth Amendments—achievements of the Reconstruction era. At the end he was struggling to help garbage workers attain minimally decent treatment in a strike that should not have dragged on. "We, too, are guilty of murder," Mays declared. "It is time for the American people to repent and make democracy equally applicable to all Americans." Mays challenged the crowd to ensure that King's redemptive suffering was redemptive. If they loved King, they could not condone violence or rioting, and they had to fight against the social conditions that caused rioting. If they did so, "Martin Luther King, Jr. will have died a redemptive death from which all mankind will benefit."[147]

SCLC cadre knew what that meant for them: The Poor People's Campaign had to resume. It did not matter that they were battered and exhausted. It did not matter that King's successor had always been loyal to King personally, not to SCLC. It did not matter that King himself had barely managed to hold together his fractious band of movement leaders. Nor did it matter that the crowd at King's funeral could not bring itself to actually sing "We Shall Overcome" after Mays finished speaking. The seething mood of the time compelled King's disciples to the nation's capital, carrying out an antipoverty campaign they had opposed, all in the name of nonviolence, which was more derided than ever. McKissick tartly declared that King-style activism was finished. Four days before King's funeral McKissick told the *New York Times* that nonviolence was a "dead philosophy" and that King was its last "prince." A week after the funeral McKissick put it quotably: "The way things are today, not even Christ himself could come back and preach nonviolence."[148]

Abernathy felt the ending of the King era very personally. He had never worried about being killed; now he worried about it constantly. He needed the "comfort and counsel" of a loyal friend, such as he had given to King, but that was different too: "He had Ralph Abernathy. I had no one." At the Rivermont Holiday Inn he had tried to buck up King by telling him they had to stand up for nonviolence in Washington. Later Abernathy recalled, "It broke Martin's heart to be attacked by his own people, and it was also extremely difficult for me to bear." Abernathy dreaded the new militants: "They were filled with hatred and anger and they wanted to stir up the same emotions in their followers. We saw them on the rise, and tried to persuade the best of them to join us, but they were beyond listening to reasons." He was wary of his putative comrades, too, knowing they had little respect for him. For years they rolled their eyes as Abernathy snoozed through strategy meetings. Now that mattered, while they resumed the Poor People's Campaign that King's assassin had presumably tried to cancel.[149]

King had aimed for fifteen hundred marchers and fallen short. Now there were almost five thousand marchers, who began arriving on May 11. Fauntroy secured a Department of Interior permit to assemble in West Potomac Park between the Lincoln and Washington monuments. Coretta King and Robert Kennedy addressed an opening rally on May 12, and a plywood and canvas city—Resurrection City—sprang up overnight. By early June there were nearly seven thousand dwellers. Many had no training in nonviolence, some belonged to street gangs, and petty crime plagued the encampment from the beginning. Abernathy announced that Resurrection City would be integrated, which did not happen, as each group kept to itself. Abernathy remarked, "It rapidly became a camp full of ghettos, with no one having a great deal to do with anyone else." Mexican Americans from the Southwest, Native Americans from the Dakotas, and Puerto Ricans from New York City complained of bad treatment from SCLC leaders. Mexican American leader Reies Tijerina put it bluntly: "They do not consult us." Torrential rains turned the encampment into a quagmire, which became the main story, topping Bevel's pitched battle with Abernathy over who should be mayor. Bevel told Abernathy he lacked the requisite ability to lead SCLC and should step aside in favor of Jackson. No other SCLC staffer was willing to defer to Jackson, so Abernathy muddled on. At one point Abernathy hired, and later fired, Jackson as city manager. Young recalled, "I was in a daze, functioning on autopilot. I remember thinking that there was no way I was going to jail with this crew." Young had been willing to spend a year in prison with King, assuming that federal courts would disapprove of Resurrection City. But he was unwilling to be jailed with undisciplined allies: "I had never felt so despondent."[150]

Two things kept Young going: his own call to be faithful to King and the presidential campaign. Robert Kennedy had converted to peace and antipoverty activism, and he backed the Poor People's Campaign. Young supported Kennedy, while Lewis campaigned with RFK in Indiana, Oregon, and California, bonding with him personally. On June 5, after RFK won the California primary, he teased Lewis that he had gotten more votes from Mexican Americans than from black Americans; what had happened? Kennedy went downstairs at the Ambassador Hotel for his victory speech, looking, Lewis recalled, "as if he could have floated out of the room. He was in such wonderful spirits." Lewis exulted too, cheering as RFK called his followers to the Democratic Convention in Chicago. Then Kennedy was assassinated. "I dropped to my knees, to the carpet," Lewis wrote. "I was crying, sobbing, heaving as if something had been busted open inside." Young and Coretta watched the assassination coverage at the Willard Hotel. To Young, Lewis, and many others, the King era ended that day. Young recalled, "After he died I sank into a depression so deep it was impossible for me to go on. We had thought we might be able to rebuild a forceful national consensus around Kennedy, salvaging at least something in the wake of Martin's death. Now even that hope was gone." It was no longer possible to repress what had happened in April. Kennedy's assassination ended the denials: "We were all trying to pretend that Martin's death had not devastated us, but it had. And with the compounding shock and grief of Robert Kennedy's murder, I couldn't even pretend anymore."[151]

Lewis and Abernathy served as honor guards at RFK's funeral, after which Abernathy put off the Memorial Day ending of the Poor People's Campaign, deferring for a better ending. Abernathy tried to get the media to focus on poverty, the right to a job, and the case for a guaranteed annual income. But the story was always the muddy disorder of Resurrection City and the squabbling among SCLC leaders. Abernathy hired Rustin to organize a rally on June 19, "Juneteenth," the day that slaves in the Deep South heard of the Emancipation Proclamation. Hiring Rustin was immediately problematic since he had opposed the campaign. Rustin compounded the problem by dropping most of SCLC's demands, not mentioning Vietnam, and making no reference to the demands of Latinos and Native Americans. Young was fine with that—he just wanted to go home—and Abernathy hesitated; others objected that Rustin did not speak for them, so Rustin resigned. Urban League official Sterling Tucker replaced Rustin, organizing a Solidarity Day rally that attracted fifty thousand protesters. The crowd inspired Abernathy to go militant, vowing in his speech to keep the campaign going in spite of the mud and an expired permit.[152]

That yielded a dismal ending. Police cleared the site five days later, and Abernathy led ragged marches for two more weeks. He was left wondering if King would have done better. The unwieldy coalition of the poor gathered in the nation's capital was the first of its kind in U.S. history. It was the beginning of something revolutionary—a broad-based antipoverty movement still in the making nearly fifty years later. Every organizing effort like it invokes its memory, recalling that this is where King left off.[153]

The Democratic Convention nominated Humphrey—the winner of zero primaries—amid riotous dissension and fury, which helped to deliver the White House to Nixon. To Democratic Party bosses, the party belonged to them; democracy had nothing to do with it. To Young and Lewis, Humphrey was a longtime friend of the movement and a hapless casualty of Johnson's blunder in Vietnam. To Rustin, Humphrey was a good liberal meriting full-throttle support. Rustin worked hard for Humphrey, riding with him in motorcades and speaking alongside him at rallies. But many white liberals spurned Humphrey, resenting his record on Vietnam and his dependence on party bosses. Many others were like Young and Lewis in being too traumatized to resume the struggle. Black voters supported Humphrey but in lukewarm fashion. The march of civil rights leaders into electoral politics was still to come; meanwhile, black communities were convulsed by trauma and rage. Rustin believed that white antiwar liberals were the key to the election. He begged them not to stay home out of pique at the war; too much was at stake for civil rights and social justice.

Instead, Rustin's nightmare scenario came to be. Nixon won the presidency with a racially coded appeal to a newly Republican South, and the King era ended. SCLC had a last hurrah of direct action in Charleston, South Carolina, in 1969, regrouping sufficiently to win a union campaign at the South Carolina Medical College Hospital. But the Charleston strike lasted only a few days, and it was the last time that SCLC and the AFL-CIO pulled together to win a campaign. SCLC splintered into competing agendas and projects, Abernathy was unsuited to run the organization, Coretta was blocked from playing a leadership role in SCLC, and Bevel was fired in 1970 for going rogue. King's death had seared Bevel, a loner who needed King. Holding forth at Spelman College to starstruck coeds, Bevel wrote on the walls with a Magic Marker, effused expansively about free love, peed into a cup, and told the students to drink it; otherwise they were not really his followers. Bevel protégé James Orange called Young to say that this time Bevel had flipped out. Young and the

SCLC board committed Bevel to a hospital psychiatric ward for two days, which enraged Bevel. SCLC convened an emergency meeting at which Young made the case for not expelling Bevel: Martin had prized Bevel precisely for his eccentricity, and they were all in Bevel's debt for his brilliant contributions to the movement. Young and Lewis voted for therapy, not expulsion, and everyone else voted for expulsion. They were done with Bevel. Later that year Young ran for Atlanta's Fifth District seat in Congress. To Young, entering electoral politics was another marker that the King era was over. King did not want his lieutenants to be ensnared in the system, but Young chafed at being stuck in the remnants of a disintegrating SCLC.[154]

Young lost his congressional election in 1970 and won it in 1972, becoming the first black member of Congress from Georgia since Reconstruction. He entered the House of Representatives along with Barbara Jordan of Houston, assuring himself that King would have approved. Many others subsequently took that path, winning state and federal offices, while others who had been in the second rank of civil rights leaders during the King era became leaders of the civil rights organizations, notably Lowery, Benjamin Hooks, and Vernon Jordan. Jackson split with SCLC in 1971 after clashing for the last time with Abernathy, taking the Chicago chapter of Operation Breadbasket with him, which he renamed Operation Push. There he built a national reputation as a civil rights leader and presidential candidate. In 1984 and especially 1988 Jackson's brilliant campaigns for the Democratic presidential nomination symbolized for many campaign workers, including me, and millions of others the hope of a liberationist politics fired by veterans of the civil rights movement and a new generation of "Rainbow Coalition" activists. Jackson distinctly championed Martin's Dream of a better society and created movement vehicles through which youthful, middle-aged, and elderly activists seized the opportunity to espouse it. Meanwhile Abernathy hung on at SCLC until 1976, when the board pushed him out in favor of Lowery.

The black social gospel had a bountiful legacy in the careers of civil rights leaders who became politicians, especially Young, Jackson, Lewis, Jordan, Fauntroy, and Marian Wright Edelman. A cadre of black scholars enhanced King's influence in theological education, notably J. Deotis Roberts, Major Jones, Preston Williams, C. Eric Lincoln, Pauli Murray, Vincent Harding, Samuel Roberts, Peter Paris, and James Washington, just before black women entered the academy and ordained ministry. Some black scholars followed Johnson and Mays into schoolmaster service, notably Bernard Lafayette at American Baptist Theological Seminary. The black social gospel reverberated in countless black churches in which it became a kind of new orthodoxy. There were full-fledged disciples of King in black pulpits across the country who preached the social gospel and supported the surge into electoral politics. Samuel DeWitt Proctor restored Abyssinian Church to its glory days of every-week scintillating preaching and national public leadership. Gardner Taylor held forth at Brooklyn's mammoth Concord Baptist Church for forty-two years, until 1990. Kelly Miller Smith, revered in Nashville, could not resist the lure of a big-steeple church in Cleveland, soon regretted the move, and returned to a distinguished career in Nashville. Lawson finished his ministerial career with a successful run in Los Angeles and graciously conversed with scholars and reporters who asked him about Nashville, King, and what happened in Memphis. Jerry Wurf observed that Lawson was too selfless to realize how much he had been reviled in white Memphis: "They feared him because he was a totally moral man, and totally moral men you can't manipulate and you can't buy and you can't hustle."[155]

Lawson was like Lewis in possessing a record of movement heroism and a rock-of-ages moral integrity that partly inoculated both men from criticism after the tide turned against racial integration. Lawson continued to oppose Black Power ideology along the lines that he and King expounded on the Meredith March. But the rhetoric of "fulfilling King's dream" and keeping faith with King's legacy became problematic for many as soon as King was gone. The more that white liberals embraced King as a hero, the more ambiguous he became for blacks still denigrated by white society. It became hard to remember that King was radical, militant, and angry. He seemed to be wholly outstripped by Carmichael and Rap Brown, failing to break through his image as the civil rights leader best suited to prop up white liberalism. Even King's sympathetic biographer, David Levering Lewis, writing two years after King's death, contended that King specialized in making his audiences feel good. King, Lewis wrote, evoked "deeply pleasurable emotions" in the middle-class blacks and whites who flocked to hear him, never threatening anyone: "Almost until the end, the meliorism of the Social Gospel—and more viscerally, that of the black bourgeoisie—stayed with Martin, despite the instructive lessons in Marx and Niebuhr."[156]

That was true—and misleading. King did not become the most hated man in America on a misunderstanding. His supposedly unthreatening meliorism obliterated more structural evil than all his critics combined. He struck with audacity and forcefulness in the most hateful southern cities he could find. He raised hell in Chicago in the same fashion, forcing the northern white liberals who had cheered him to confront their own racism. But Lewis's judgment that King was too peaceable, generous, and eager to be liked was spot-on for the mood that succeeded King. Social gospel nonviolence reeked unavoidably of "compromise and gradualism," as Lewis said, no matter that King preached it with passionate militancy.[157]

Every sermon that King ever gave was a gloss on the beloved community—the kingdom hope of a regenerated society. He was an exemplar of his theme that freedom has no reality apart from power. Power is integral to hope and liberation. Integration requires equal access to political and economic power. Freedom is participation in power. To King, the goal of the civil rights movement was precisely to transform the lack of power of black Americans into creative, vital, interpersonal, organized power. All could be free, but only if all were empowered to participate. Freedom and integration went together to build the beloved community, a universal goal embracing all peoples and nations. King epitomized the black social gospel at its best and most radical, which made him the true founder of black liberation theology.

But that was not how it seemed at the time. Liberation theology arose within the Black Power movement, where King was problematic. He exemplified the ethic of self-sacrificial love and nonviolent resistance to oppression not merely as a method but as a way of life. He insisted that integration was an essential goal of the civil rights movement, notwithstanding the movement's lack of any workable or comprehensive concept of integration. SCLC veterans like Abernathy who retained a simple concept of integration were disabused of it in the Poor People's Campaign, when they tried to impose it and failed. The pendulum swung toward liberation by any means necessary, away from King's emphasis on integration and nonviolence. Violence versus nonviolence was not the issue, because giving primacy to it preempted what might be necessary for liberation and self-respecting community. In the aftermath of King's assassination, young theologian James Cone took for granted that King was a major source and inspiration of the liberating theology that was needed. But the King valorized by white liberals and black church leaders struck Cone as the exemplar of a white liberal ideal, not a symbol of black liberation. Cone's respect for King jostled with feelings of ambivalence, and he hated what white liberals made of King. In that conflicted brew of feelings and reactions black liberation theology was born.

7

Theologies of Liberation

The idea of a black social Christianity that carried on King's legacy was commonplace and inadequate. Civil rights leaders and organizations pledged to continue his legacy. Hundreds of ministers preached King's blend of evangelical religion, racial dignity, social justice politics, and nonviolent philosophy. For fifteen years King Day celebrations invoked the Dream, sang "We Shall Overcome," and called for a King holiday. Every King Day celebration had speeches on King as the martyr of civil rights, the one who died to redeem America. King's reputation in white America climbed ever higher, putting a national holiday in reach. People who had spurned or reviled King while he lived now claimed to admire him; many "forgot" having reviled him. King became the icon of racial integration just as many black Americans decided they were done with singing about that.

The campaign for a King holiday, pushed by Coretta King and the AFL-CIO, lost a House of Representatives vote in 1979 and won a veto-proof majority in Congress in 1983, compelling President Ronald Reagan to sign it. The campaign fixed on "I Have a Dream" imagery and race-blind ideals. King's views about capitalism and militarism were still out of play, smacking of way-out-there leftism, better not mentioned. It was considered bad form to dwell on such things or on what he actually said about Black Power; only reactionary warhorses like North Carolina senators Jesse Helms and John Porter East did that. To win the iconic status that King deserved, he had to be domesticated, and was.[1]

King became safe and ethereal, registering as a noble moralist. His later emphasis on economic justice was routinely ignored, which in turn obscured that he had cared about it from the beginning, which obscured why the social gospel mattered. The black social gospel was hardly ever mentioned. Before the King era the black social gospel had not been recognized as a credible or important tradition of social Christianity. After he was gone it still got little credit for being a tradition, much less for shaping King's idea of prophetic Christianity. But without the black social gospel, King would not have known what to say when history called on December 3, 1955.

The domestication of King began by stripping him of his black church formation and identity—which came easily to writers lacking any acquaintance with the black church. King contributed to it by offering a seminary-oriented account of his development that emphasized personalist philosophy. There were two problems here, which folded together. His account played down the radical aspects of the social gospel, including the things he took from black social gospel mentors. Boston University was not merely a bastion of integrationist liberalism and personalism. King's dean at Boston University, Walter Muelder, epitomized the wing of the social gospel that was Socialist, pacifist, antiracist, anticolonial, and feminist. More important, King entered the ministry fully persuaded that Mays, Barbour, Johnson, and Thurman were viable models of a radical social gospel ministry—models for him personally, especially on economic justice. He said it to Coretta in 1952 after she knowingly gave him a copy of Edward Bellamy's utopian Socialist classic, *Looking Backward*. Capitalism, King said, played a constructive role in the eighteenth century by disrupting the trade monopolies of the nobles: "But like most human systems it fell victim to the very thing it was revolting against. So today capitalism has outlived its usefulness. It has brought about a system that takes necessities from the masses to give luxuries to the classes." King told Coretta that he was an idealist who believed in evolutionary Socialism, not a Marxist materialist or revolutionary. Moreover, Bellamy was unrealistic about how long it would take: "I don't think he gave capitalism long enough time to die." But "radical change" was coming, King said, and it was desperately needed.[2]

King did not consider himself daring or exceptional for having a Socialist worldview because he was schooled in the social ethics of the social gospel, and the best social gospelers were Socialists. The figures who influenced King in this area were steeped in the writings of Rauschenbusch and the Christian Socialist tradition. Even Reinhold Niebuhr remained a Socialist long after he repudiated social gospel idealism. This was hard to talk about in ordinary congregations, and King realized that even the tamest talk about Social Democracy was perilous in middle-class black congregations. He played a careful hand, though no differently from other ministers who admired Rauschenbusch or Du Bois. Throughout King's career in SCLC he quietly confirmed to surprised newcomers that he was a democratic Socialist. Yet even after King was killed this worldview remained something of an insider secret. King's defenders had enough trouble without getting into that. Even those who shared his politics usually held back on what they knew about him. The campaign to put King in the rank of George Washington and Abraham Lincoln stressed his civil rights liberalism, sometimes crediting his opposition to the Vietnam War. King became identified in the dominant national imagination with a race-blind idea of racial justice during the very period that many black Americans stopped believing in it. They loved him, but he belonged to a bygone age, the King era.

BLACK THEOLOGIES OF LIBERATION

Theologian J. Deotis Roberts felt the passing of the age immediately—on the evening of King's assassination. Roberts was a black pioneer in American theology before black theology existed. Born in 1927 in Spindale, North Carolina, to working-class parents, he graduated from Johnson C. Smith University in 1947, earned bachelor of divinity degrees from Shaw University (1950) and Hartford Seminary Foundation (1951), studied Platonism at the University of Cambridge in 1956, and completed his doctorate in philosophical theology at the University of Edinburgh in 1957. Like King, Roberts was drawn to the battle of philosophical ideas. Like King, Roberts found just enough white liberal mentors to become an academic theologian. Roberts's crucial mentors were Edinburgh theologian C. S. Duthie and Cambridge theologian Charles E. Raven, plus theologians John Baillie, Herbert H. Farmer, and J. S. McEwen.

In his early career Roberts taught and wrote European and American philosophy of religion, in the manner of his teachers. He specialized in the seventeenth-century Cambridge Platonism of Benjamin Whichcote, Ralph Cudworth, Henry More, and John Smith, whom Roberts described as forerunners of modern ecumenical Christianity. The Cambridge Platonists blended the Puritan and Platonist passions for truth, uniting faith and reason, and they had a social conscience, paving the way to the progressive Platonist Anglicanism of Raven and William Temple. This intellectual tradition, however, was foreign to the schools and churches in which Roberts spent his early career. He preached at Baptist churches in Tarboro, North Carolina, and Hartford, Connecticut, and taught at Georgia Baptist College and Shaw University. He wanted to teach at a prominent university or seminary, but none were interested in him. He looked for a role model—a black professor at a major divinity school—and could not find one. In 1958 he joined the faculty of Howard University as a field education supervisor, seized the chance to teach theology and philosophy of religion, and settled into an academic home.[3]

Roberts published his first book, *Faith and Reason,* in 1962, comparing the religious philosophies of Blaise Pascal, Henri Bergson, and William James. He argued that Pascal's critique of rational knowledge, though more subjective than similar arguments by Bergson and James, was also more reasonable and Christian. Roberts was slow to imagine himself as a theologian of the black experience. He admired King but viewed himself as having taken the academic path that King eschewed. To Roberts, the turning point occurred when King was assassinated. German theologian Jürgen Moltmann spoke that evening at Duke University, and Roberts tried to listen; Moltmann's "theology of hope" had attracted great attention. The following day Roberts asked Moltmann what his theology had to say to black Americans such as himself whose hope had been smashed. Moltmann replied that his theology had been forged in the context of Germany's reconstruction after World War II and that Americans had to rethink the meaning of Christianity for themselves. Roberts later recalled, "It was then that the seed of 'black theology' began to germinate in my own mind. It was Moltmann's conception of theology as 'political' rather than the particular content of it that aroused my interest."[4]

Six months later he had a working idea of what was needed, which he called "a theological alternative to Black Power" that appropriated the best aspects of the new black consciousness. The Black Power movement spurned theology, while current theological fads about the "death of God" and the "secular city" meant nothing to the black community. Roberts called for a black theology that expressed the religious meaning of the new black consciousness. He believed that Stokely Carmichael's call for Black Power launched a new era in black American history, making it "almost impossible for any Negro to think the same and be satisfied with anything less than a revolution in the churches in reference to race relations." Culturally and personally the King era already seemed long past. Carmichael's moment had come; Roberts observed that a season of "Black Rage" had descended upon the United States. Though Roberts cautioned that he did not "personally envisage a 'Theology of Violence,' " America was overdue for theologies that focused on black experience and bolstered the new black pride: "Nothing like a systematic formulation of the Christian faith by a Negro writer has ever appeared. There has been no system of theology informed by a profound grasp of theology and Christian history projected by a Negro." Citing religious historian Joseph Washington for support, Roberts reached for the strongest way of saying it: "Three hundred years of American history have not witnessed one major Black theologian."[5]

Now he knew what his life and career needed to be about. "Black Theology must be radical and militant," Roberts declared. "It must move men to act upon the ethical imperatives of their faith. To the assertion that 'Black is beautiful,' it must answer *Amen*, but to the call for violence it must say *No*. Black Theology must be informed by biblical exegesis and historical theology." The new black theology, he contended, had to hold together faith and ethics, and it had to reject separatism. Black Americans like him, by virtue of their long acquaintance with subjection and 'suffering-victory' experiences," were able to relate to all people: "The easy identification of the Negro theologian with all races and classes will lead him to a universal theological position." Latin American liberation theology, just emerging at the time, won sympathetic attention in divinity schools and the ecumenical movement. Roberts found it amazing that many white North American progressives showed deeper concern for Latin Americans than for North American blacks. It was time for black and white North Americans to cultivate their own garden: "The theology to make human life human for the American Negro has not been written. This will be the task of a Black Theology."[6]

The following year James Cone published a searing attack on the established white and black churches, calling for a theology of Black Power. If not for the summer riots of 1967 Cone might not have been a theologian by the time that King was cut down. Cone was in the library during the climactic years of the civil rights movement, earning a doctorate in theology. Then he taught theology during the rise of the Black Power movement. By 1967 the ironies were galling to him. He savored the writings of James Baldwin, Richard Wright, and LeRoi Jones (later, Amiri Baraka), which pulsated with existential meaning, but he was stuck with Karl Barth, Paul Tillich, and Reinhold Niebuhr, who epitomized the culture of whiteness without noticing it. Cone decided that he was in the wrong field. He would have to get another doctorate, this time in a field that spoke to him, black literature: "How could I continue to allow my intellectual life to be consumed by the theological problems defined by people who had enslaved my grandparents?" To have something worthwhile to contribute to the new black consciousness and to keep himself from falling into despair he had to get out of theology. Then Detroit erupted, and Cone decided he lacked time for another doctorate. He would have to make do with the education he had already, to say something on behalf of the struggle of oppressed American blacks for freedom.[7]

Cone was born in Fordyce, Arkansas, in 1938 and raised in nearby Bearden, a rural community of four hundred blacks and eight hundred whites. Bearden and his parents, Charles and Lucy Cone, deeply influenced him. Lucy Cone was a faithful churchgoer and believer in God's righteousness, and Charles Cone was a guardian of the family's dignity who said that blacks could not survive white oppression without constant struggle and that "no black should ever expect justice from whites." After Cone became a renowned theologian he remarked that all his writing and speaking amounted to mere "dim reflections of what my parents taught and lived." If his father, lacking any social protection, could fearlessly oppose the evils of white society, how could he, protected by doctorate and tenure, dare to do less?[8]

Cone was a transfer student at Philander Smith College in Little Rock when he first heard of King, in 1956. In Little Rock he witnessed the gut-wrenching integration of a large urban high school. "Those were very rough and tense days," he later recalled. Every black person Cone knew opposed "the satanic force of white supremacy" and took for granted "that God was on our side," while every white person, as far as he could tell, was too blinded by hate and privilege even to comprehend that justice was God's will.[9]

At Philander Smith, a United Methodist college, Cone discovered the world of scholarship, taking special interest in black history. Frederick Douglass, Booker T. Washington, and W. E. B. Du Bois were exciting to him; on the other hand, in disciplinary terms they belonged to history, while Cone wanted to change the world through religion. The past interested him only as a clue to how things got the way they were; he did not want to live there. At the age of sixteen he had started preaching at his brother's AME congregation in Spring Hill, Arkansas; during his college years he ministered to two AME congregations, taking for granted that ministry would be his vocation. On that assumption Cone and his brother Cecil enrolled at Garrett Biblical Institute (later, Garrett-Evangelical Theological Seminary) in Evanston, Illinois, in 1958. Both were immediately disillusioned. Northern relatives had told them for years that things were better for blacks in the North; it took Cone a single day to conclude differently: "I was rudely awakened to the fact that white America is the same everywhere."[10]

Excelling in his studies, Cone found a mentor in theologian William Hordern, completed his divinity degree in 1961, and applied for Garrett's joint doctoral program with Northwestern University. Garrett's graduate advisor told Cone not to bother applying for the doctoral program; Hordern told him he would resign if Cone was not admitted. To Cone, that was a realized impossibility, "the first time that any white person ever put himself on the line for me."[11]

Thus he found himself in the library studying European theology, while many black classmates, including Cecil Cone, threw themselves into civil rights activism. Cone felt the contradiction deeply, telling himself he had to seize the opportunity to become a theologian. From the beginning he was surprised at what theologians took to be important. The reward structure of North American theology was geared to learning German, studying in Germany, and mastering German debates; meanwhile American Christian racism had no standing as a theological topic. "The failure to discuss it as a central problem in theology appeared strange and racist to me," he later recalled. "Most North American theologians identified their task as keeping up with the problems defined by European theologians." Reading King and Malcolm X on the side, Cone found it tormenting to sit through lectures on European topics. On one occasion he erupted in protest, calling his teacher a racist, which terminated class for that day. The professor, a close acquaintance of Cone's, was devastated to be called a racist; Cone later explained that he "had no capacity for understanding black rage." After that, Cone made the best of a dismal situation at Garrett, which he later described as a little better than average for liberal white seminaries: "I hardly knew who I was as a theologian; I was a graduate student who mimicked white male Europeans and Americans." Keeping his feelings mostly to himself, he got his degree in 1965 with a dissertation on Barth's theological anthropology.[12]

He taught at Philander Smith College, where he stewed over the irrelevance of his training. Cone wrote articles that meant nothing to him and were rejected anyway. Alienating the school's trustees, he left after two years and moved to Adrian College in Adrian, Michigan, in 1966, where his feeling of isolation proved to be something of a spur to find his own subject and voice. After a lonely year in Adrian, Cone told himself it was not too late to change fields, but he changed his mind after Detroit exploded. Whatever he had to say, he would have to say as a theologian. He later recalled that upon hearing white theologians and pastors admonish blacks to follow Jesus instead of resorting to violence, he found his voice: "I was so furious that I could hardly contain my rage. The very sight of white people made me want to vomit. 'Who are they,' I said, 'to tell us blacks about Christian ethics?'" How did whites muster the gall to lecture oppressed blacks about love and nonviolence? "My rage was intensified because most whites seemed not to recognize the contradictions that were so obvious to black people."[13]

That was the wellspring of emotion and conviction that produced his electrifying first book, *Black Theology and Black Power* (1969). Alone in Adrian aside from his wife, Rose, and a trusted white friend, Lester Scherer, Cone identified with the Black Power movement, meeting Carmichael in early 1968. He also met black religious historian C. Eric Lincoln and took his first pass at writing a theological manifesto for Black Power radicalism. Lincoln's support and influence were crucial to Cone, opening doors to lecture invitations, job offers, and publishers; eventually he smoothed the way for Cone to become his colleague at Union Theological Seminary.[14]

King's murder supplied extra motivation for Cone to write a theology of Black Power, which he described as "equating Black Power with the Christian gospel." Putting it that way steeled him for the charge that he reduced the gospel to an ideology. Theologically, Cone was a Barthian, so part of him agreed that equating the gospel with an ideology was problematic. Barth said that liberal theology contaminated the gospel by accommodating it to modern cultural agendas. On the other hand, Barthian theology had done nothing to abolish racism, so Cone looked past his Barthian misgivings: "By the summer of that year, I had so much anger pent up in me I had to let it out or be destroyed by it." King's murder was merely the last straw: "My anger stretched back to the slave ships, the auction block, and the lynchings. But even more important were my personal encounters with racism in Bearden, Little Rock, Evanston, and Adrian."[15]

If theology was to be his work, he would not do it in a way that compromised his integrity. More precisely, Cone vowed to himself, he would never compromise with the evils of white racists: "Racism is a deadly disease that must be resisted by any means necessary. Never again would I ever expect white racists to do right in relation to the black community." Flushed with emotion, Cone wrote *Black Theology and Black Power* in four weeks; he described it as a conversion experience: "It was like experiencing the death of white theology and being born again into the theology of the black experience."[16]

Malcolm's phrase "by any means necessary" was fundamental to Cone's definition of his object, Black Power: "Complete emancipation of black people from white oppression by whatever means black people deem necessary." Black Power, he explained, used boycotts when necessary, demonstrations when necessary, and violence when necessary. Cone's first book contained the liberationist principle of responding to a world that defined the oppressed as nonpersons; however, neither personhood nor the word "liberation" was a key concept for him as yet. He focused on why Black Power rejected white liberalism and black reformism. White liberals, Cone observed, took pride in their liberality toward blacks and howled with wounded defensiveness when he and Carmichael placed them "in the same category with the George Wallaces." Cone told them to deal with it. Invoking Malcolm's analogy of the rapist asking his victim to like him, Cone said it was pathetic for white liberals to ask blacks to like them. Some whites protested that it was unfair to lump them with racists; others told Cone that things were better in their town because they supported the civil rights movement. Cone replied that all whites were responsible for white oppression, and American whites had always had "an easy conscience."[17]

Black Power was an announcement that all whites were responsible for white oppression. Cone reflected that King seemed less threatening to whites, so many whites claimed to admire him, never mind that King was hated in his time for threatening white supremacy, until greater threats emerged: "What whites really want is for the black man to respond with that method which best preserves white racism." Cone preferred Malcolm on the basic problem of American society, who was "not far wrong when he called the white man 'the devil.' " American society was gripped by demonic forces, which so controlled the lives of white racists that they seemed incapable of distinguishing themselves from the alien power.[18]

Was that racism in reverse? Was there such a thing as "black racism," which triggered the white backlash feared by liberals? Cone replied, "While it is true that blacks do hate whites, black hatred is not racism." He explained that racism rested on two pillars: (1) Biological race is a determinant of psychocultural traits and capacities. (2) One race is thus superior over others, possessing the right to dominance over them. By contrast, Cone argued, Black Power made no assertion of racial superiority or right to dominance. It was simply an assertion of the right to liberation from white oppression. Black Muslim theology, admittedly, offered a partial exception, describing blacks as a superior race and whites as devils. But Black Muslims claimed no right to enslave whites, and the Nation of Islam was hardly a serious threat to white American hegemony. The Black Muslim movement, a "justifiable reaction to white racism," did not represent the Black Power movement, which focused on black empowerment and self-identity: "Black Power seeks not understanding but conflict; addresses blacks and not whites; seeks to develop black support, but not white good will."[19]

Black Power was against integration, especially its humiliating assumption that white institutions were superior. The last thing that black people needed, Cone contended, was to be assimilated into white culture. White liberals, to the extent that they acknowledged white racism, sought to cure their culture of it by integrating blacks into it. They claimed to believe that race should not matter; white liberal Christians added that Jesus was above race. Cone replied that race mattered everywhere in real-world America, assimilation was deadly for blacks, and in the American context of black oppression Christ was a black liberator.

White people in general had amazingly short memories, Cone noted. They persecuted blacks viciously for centuries but puzzled over the black anger that sparked urban riots. White liberals, in particular, wanted to be morally innocent of racism while enjoying the privileges of whiteness. Cone remarked that the white liberal was a "strange creature" who often said "the right things" and was even capable of defending Carmichael or allowing his daughter to marry a black man: "But he is still white to the very core of his being. What he fails to realize is that there is no place for him in this war of survival." The humiliating

phase of linking arms with white liberals was over. The black struggle for liberation would get nowhere if blacks got tied up with the anxieties and superiority
complexes of white liberals, Cone argued. There was a place in the justice
struggle for white radicals—the John Browns who burned with hatred of white
racism. They didn't get in the way of black liberation or presume to tell blacks
what to do, and they risked their lives for freedom. Cone later placed some
of the Freedom Riders in that category. But a theology of Black Power had to
repudiate the white liberal quest of innocence, its bogus "solidarity" with black
freedom, and its myth of a "raceless Christ."[20]

"White liberal preference for a raceless Christ serves only to make official
and orthodox the centuries-old portrayal of Christ as white," Cone wrote. If
Christ was the redeemer and liberator of the scriptural witness, in the American
context he had to be black, "working through the activity of Black Power."
Cone's next book developed this thesis, conceptualizing blackness as a racial
marker and as a symbol of liberation from various forms of oppression. In the
meantime he enunciated the basic principles of liberation theology, condemned
white churches for perpetuating white oppression, and took an ambivalent view
of black churches, stressing the negative. The historic black churches offered a
social haven to blacks but also facilitated white oppression. King and the civil
rights movement offered the beginning of a corrective, but only a beginning.
The next step was for the black church to become relevant "by joining Christ in
the black revolution."[21]

Cone admonished black pastors to stop being " 'nice' to white society."
The riots threw many pastors on the defensive, activating their moralizing
impulse. Cone urged that a relevant black church had to *fight* racism, taking a
rebellious attitude: "It cannot condemn the rioters. It must make an unqualified identification with the 'looters' and 'rioters,' recognizing that this stance
leads to condemnation by the state as law-breakers. There is no place for 'nice
Negroes' who are so distorted by white values that they regard laws as more
sacred than human life. There is no place for those who deplore black violence
and overlook the daily violence of whites. There is no place for blacks who want
to be 'safe,' for Christ did not promise security but suffering." Instead of draining
the black community of its rebellious spirit, black churches needed to embrace
the new era of Black Power: "It is an age of rebellion and revolution. Blacks are
no longer prepared to turn the other cheek; instead, they are turning the gun."
The black revolution was already happening; the only question was whether
black churches would join it.[22]

Black Theology and Black Power was a sensational debut that won a large
readership and changed Cone's life. A prime example of late-sixties revolutionary

oracle, it was published in March 1969, a month before James Forman presented a galvanizing "Black Manifesto" to the National Black Economic Development Conference in Detroit. Forman demanded a $500 million program of reparations for slavery and racial discrimination, called for the seizure and "total disruption" of church agencies, and called black Americans to "fight our enemies relentlessly." On May 4 he interrupted the Sunday service at Riverside Church in New York, dramatically repeating his demands. Forman won extensive media coverage that stressed his attack on white churches and often mentioned his similarity to Cone. Besides sweeping Cone's book into the media spotlight, the manifesto impacted Cone's career institutionally. At Union Theological Seminary a group of approximately seventy students pressed Union president John Bennett to respond to Forman's demands. Several days of demonstrations and hurried board meetings produced a twofold response: Union contributed $100,000 to black enterprise development in Harlem, promising to raise an additional $1 million, and created a new faculty position for Cone, who had several offers to consider. Cone chose Union, joined the National Conference of Black Churchmen (NCBC), forged relationships with several black nationalist groups, and accepted Amiri Baraka's invitation to play a leading role in the Congress of African People (CAP), a major nationalist group.[23]

But Cone had chastening experiences at nationalist conferences. Speakers at the 1970 CAP conference in Atlanta ridiculed religion and black churches unsparingly, with hostile name calling, teaching Cone a bitter lesson: "The mere agreement that white people are devils is not enough to attain our freedom." He had similar experiences with the Black Panthers and other revolutionary groups. Panther leader David Hilliard, addressing an NCBC conference in Oakland, insulted black ministers with vulgar and threatening invective, telling them to choose between shooting white police officers and being shot by the Panthers. That reordered Cone's strategic priorities. Threatening to harm black people was beyond the pale; he shuddered at the "twisted" minds of Hilliard and other revolutionary leaders, which showed the destructive force of white oppression. Neither did Cone want any revolution that excluded his Christian mother. He was willing to support nationalist organizations on a secondary basis but resolved that his primary loyalty was to the liberationist wing of black Christianity.[24]

Organizationally that meant the NCBC, not a denominational home, as Cone left the AME Church to join the predominantly white United Methodist Church. To many observers that was a puzzling move, if not self-contradictory. To Cone, it was analogous to teaching at Union Seminary. AME bishops and ministers rebuffed Cone for criticizing the "moral corruption" of AME Church politics, its lack of Episcopal accountability, and its stodgy conformity. Since AME leaders did not recognize Cone as a theologian, he joined the United Methodist Church, notwithstanding that he called it the anti-Christ, because it offered a workable base for him to develop liberation theology. In that respect the Methodist Church was much like Union Seminary. Cone wanted the AME Church to support black liberation and him, but when it did neither he reasoned that he was better off in a place that provided a "meaningful context" for doing liberation theology. Being half-accepted in the Methodist Church was less intolerable than being half-accepted in the AME Church because the Methodist Church was not founded on the idea of black self-determination and had no prospect of moving in that direction. Yet in that denomination he was recognized as a leading theologian.[25]

Shortly after Cone joined the faculty at Union he explained the logic to Bennett, who inquired about Cone's description of the white church as the anti-Christ. "Jim, you don't mean that literally, do you?" Bennett asked. Cone replied that he was dead serious; he was not spinning metaphors. From a black liberationist perspective the white church was the enemy of Jesus Christ. Bennett asked, "But why did you choose to teach at Union if you mean it literally?" Cone explained that his father cut billets and logs for a living, and he taught at Union. Neither situation was very agreeable, but as long as he had to make a living he might as well do it at Union: "Living in a racist society, every black person has to assume that his job may not meet all the requirements for which he or she may have been called." Subsequently Cone found his way back to the AME Church while remaining at Union.[26]

His epochal work *A Black Theology of Liberation* (1970) launched the North American tradition of liberation theology by expounding what it meant to interpret Christianity from a black liberationist perspective. At the time, Cone was unaware of similar stirrings in Latin America and South Africa, but he defined "blackness" as a symbol of oppression extending beyond the North American context. The object of black theology, he declared, was "liberation from whiteness." Black theology was "theology of and for the black community, seeking to interpret the religious dimensions of the forces of liberation in that community." Cone stressed that whites were "in no position whatever" to make judgments about the truth claims or legitimacy of black theology. The very point of black theology was to "analyze the satanic nature of whiteness" and offer a liberating alternative to it. No white theologian had ever taken white America's oppression of blacks as the point of departure for theology: "Apparently white theologians see no connection between whiteness and evil and blackness and God." Even white theologians who wrote about racial injustice failed to attack white racism in its totality. Thus white theology was not Christian theology at all, but its enemy. Every Christian theology worthy of the name was a liberation theology, and, in a North American context, Christ was black.[27]

Cone contended that black theology was of and for the black community, declaring that it was "accountable only to the black community." Black theology did not claim a universal starting point or aim. It was intrinsically communal, refusing to be separated from the black community of faith; it identified liberating activity with divine action; and it rejected all abstract principles of right and wrong. It lived by a single principle, liberation, which was always partial and contextual: "There is only one principle which guides the thinking and action of black theology: an unqualified commitment to the black community as that community seeks to define its existence in the light of God's liberating work in the world." The test of truth in black theology was whether a statement or action served the end of black liberation.[28]

Identifying six sources of black theology—black experience, black history, black culture, revelation, Scripture, and tradition—Cone ontologized blackness in the sense of identifying blackness with qualities of being, without saying that blacks and whites were different *kinds* of human beings. "The black experience is possible only for black persons," he declared. White musicians tried to play like Johnny Lee Hooker or B. B. King but could never replicate black soul: "Black soul is not learned; it comes from the totality of black experience, the experience of carving out an existence in a society that says you do not belong." The black experience was about struggling for survival under racist oppression, loving "the spirit of blackness," and hearing soaring sermons on God's love in black congregations. It was also, Cone wrote, the rush of feeling that one got from bombing a white-owned building "and watching it go up in flames. We know, of course, that getting rid of evil takes something more than burning down buildings, but one must start somewhere."[29]

Barth claimed to start with revelation; Cone replied that the sources of theology were interdependent even if one claimed to start with revelation. What mattered about revelation was its content, not its methodological priority: "As a black theologian, I want to know what God's revelation means right now as the black community participates in the struggle for liberation. *Revelation is a black event*—it is what blacks are doing about their liberation." Affirming that black theology took seriously the shaping authority of the scriptural witness, Cone lifted up the scriptural themes of exodus from slavery and liberation from oppression. In Scripture and revelation, God is a partisan, liberating power. The God of the Bible called blacks to liberation, not redemptive suffering: "Blacks are not elected to be Yahweh's suffering people. Rather we are elected because we are oppressed against our will and God's, and God has decided to make our liberation God's own undertaking." Cone sympathized with militants who rejected Christianity because they loathed the "Uncle Tom approach of black churches," especially its "deadly prattle about loving your enemies and turning the other cheek." But there was another Christianity that fought the enslavement of African Americans in the name of God's blackness and liberating will: "The blackness of God means that God has made the oppressed condition God's own condition. This is the essence of the biblical revelation."[30]

Because liberation was the very essence of the divine nature, God was black. Cone drew the sharpest contrast between his theology and that of his teachers at this point: "White religionists are not capable of perceiving the blackness of God, because their satanic whiteness is a denial of the very essence of divinity. That is why whites are finding and will continue to find the black experience a disturbing reality." To blacks, evil was anything that arrested or negated liberation; salvation was liberation. To whites, evil was normal life, benefiting from the privileges of whiteness; salvation was the abolition of whiteness. White theologians, preferring their privileges, pleaded that color should not matter. Cone replied, "This only reveals how deeply racism is embedded in the thought forms of their culture." Black liberation was not a relative option in theology: "Those who want to know who God is and what God is doing must know who black persons are and what they are doing." That did not mean joining the "war on poverty" or making other "sin offerings" promoted by white liberals to assure themselves of their goodness: "Knowing God means being on the side of the oppressed, becoming one with them, and participating in the goal of liberation. *We must become black with God!*"[31]

How could whites do that? Cone did not claim to take the question seriously: "This question always amuses me because they do not really want to lose their precious white identity, as if it is worth saving." But salvation was not moral anyway, he cautioned. The solution was spiritual, not moral. In Cone's rendering black theology had to break not only from the reformist moralism of liberal theology but also from its academic agenda. Liberal theology was preoccupied with justifying religious belief in the face of scientific, historical, and philosophical criticism, "but most blacks never heard of Aristotle, Anselm, Descartes, or Kant, and they do not care about the interrelationship of theology and philosophy. Unless God's revelation is related to black liberation, blacks must reject it." The test of black theology was whether it reflected the religious experience of oppressed blacks and contributed to their liberation. This claim was original to Cone, although it soon gained wide currency as the defining principle of Latin American, feminist, and other liberationist theologies.[32]

Wherever he spoke Cone got troubled questions about race and violence. In 1975 he declared, "With Marcus Garvey, we say: 'Any sane man, race or nation that desires freedom must first of all think in terms of blood.' " That seemed to cross the line of treating race as biologically significant, which Cone did not intend. To Cone, race was ontological as a marker of black suffering and a blues-inflected cultural authenticity, not as a claim that biologically different kinds of human beings exist, though he was often interpreted otherwise. White people, he charged, cared only about the violence that harmed them: "Why did we not hear from the 'non-violent Christians' when black people were *violently* enslaved, *violently* lynched, and *violently* ghettoized in the name of freedom and democracy?" To whites, violence was a threat to personal safety in what was supposed to be a white world; to blacks, violence was systemic and pervasive. At lectures whites asked Cone if he really supported violence. He replied, "Whose violence? What the hell are you talking about?" Sometimes violence was an instrument of liberation and reconciliation, just as the Bible said. Cone remarked, "According to the Bible, reconciliation is what God does for enslaved people who are unable to break the chains of slavery." Reconciliation was the divine gift of being set free from bondage, participating in God's liberating activity. Thus for black theology, reconciliation with white people had to mean one thing before it could mean anything else: "Destroying their oppressive power."[33]

Many white reviewers complained that Cone's books were emotional, intellectually thin, obsessed with race, infatuated with violence, and dependent on the accusative mode. Sometimes they accused in return, calling him a racist; Catholic sociologist Andrew Greeley won the prize for invective, describing Cone as a racist with a "Nazi mentality." Cone alternated between brushing off white critics and raging in reply. In his brushing-off mode he recalled Malcolm's observation that whites were skilled at making "the victim look like the criminal and the criminal look like the victim." In both cases Cone seethed inside: "I could barely contain my rage whenever I read their books or found myself in their presence. They were so condescending and arrogant in the way they talked about black theology, always communicating the impression that it was not genuine theology, because it was too emotional and anti-intellectual."[34]

But liberation theology was too profound in its critique and constructive import even for defensive white critics to dismiss it. Why did racial justice disappear from the agenda of white American theology after slavery was abolished? How was one to account for the stupendous silence of white American theologians through decades of segregation and racist lynching? How should the Enlightenment be viewed if one took seriously that Europe was deeply involved in the slave trade throughout the eighteenth century? What would it mean if theology interpreted history from the standpoints of oppressed and excluded peoples?

Cone was the apostle of the revolutionary turn in American theology that privileged liberationist questions. He had gotten that way by reading Du Bois, Baldwin, Malcolm, Fanon, and King, not his theological teachers, and he pressed hard on the point that white theology had bad priorities. In Cone's early career several white theologians recognized the historic and normative significance of his critique, notably Paul Lehmann, Frederick Herzog, William Hordern, Helmut Gollwitzer, and John Bennett. Lehmann and Herzog were, to Cone, especially significant interlocutors. Lehmann, a Union Seminary ethicist, debated Cone at length, mostly privately, on the perils of conflating Christian faith with an ideology. Hordern, Bennett, and Gollwitzer echoed the same concern, while Bennett added that Cone's work smacked of self-righteousness and wrongly claimed immunity from public criticism. All of them acknowledged, however, the importance of Cone's indictment of the white liberal failure to focus on racial oppression. Herzog, a Duke Divinity School theologian, did something about it, offering the first theological work by a white American to take up Cone's challenge.[35]

Lehmann agreed with Cone that black theology was the crucial point of departure for exploring the truth of Christian theology; on the other hand, he said that Cone identified too unqualifiedly the truth of Christian theology with the concrete reality of blackness. Black theology was certainly Christian theology, but Christian theology was not black theology without remainder, for the ultimate object of Christian theology was the transcendent divine mystery that could not be grasped. Lehmann allowed that such a statement had to be suspended as soon as it was set down or put in scare quotes; otherwise it became an excuse to ignore Cone's criticism. But Cone wrongly erased the distinction between God's story and the black story of liberation.[36]

Herzog praised Cone for offering the first American theology devoted to the liberation of oppressed people. The social gospel was a liberal reform project lacking a real theology, Herzog judged, and neo-orthodoxy was devoted to alleviating middle-class anxiety. Cone was the first American theologian to base his theology on God's question: "Your neighbor is oppressed. What is your responsibility?" Instead of attending to modern intellectuals, Cone attended to the needs of blacks and other oppressed peoples. That was the way to a better theology, Herzog contended, although he urged Cone to develop an economic critique. As for white American supporters of liberation theology, what mattered was to change white America. Herzog backed off on integration and the beloved community. The task for white radicals was to change the values of white society, not to work in or with black communities.[37]

There was no feminist movement in theology when Cone began writing, and for many years after one existed he dismissed it as a farcical attempt to change the subject. Two early feminist judgments on his project, however, outlasted in memory those of his white male colleagues. Mary Daly, in 1973, panned Cone's theology as a fiercely patriarchal and vindictive "cry for vengeance." It had biblical support but was bad for women. It transcended religion as a crutch but settled for "religion as a gun." Daly argued that Cone's simplistic either/ors and "will to vindication" never got beyond the dualistic, sexist models internalized by Western selves and societies. Thus he had a one-dimensional solution that never got to the root of racism.[38]

Rosemary Radford Ruether, in 1972, criticized Cone on two points, the first of which she applied subsequently to Daly. It was terribly important for a liberation theology not to denigrate or deny the humanity of any group, she argued. For a theology to be liberating, it had to condemn the demonic powers that possessed oppressive groups but always in the name of an emancipating community reality that lay beneath the alienating power. Liberation lost its moral basis when it dehumanized the oppressor. Ruether acknowledged that Cone occasionally suggested the possibility of a universal salvation. But his constant rhetoric of destroy-the-oppressor gave "the overwhelming impression that theological categories have been wedded to racial identities in such a way that denies the humanity, as well as the false power, of white people." Identifying whiteness with the demonic, Cone failed to distinguish between whiteness as the nature of white people and whiteness as the destructive power possessing white society.[39]

The second problem with Cone was closely related to the first, Ruether said: His theology was not very black in a cultural sense. The idioms, theology, and preaching of the black church were rooted deeply in African American experience, but Cone was alienated from the black church. Black church preaching was hopeful, unselfconscious, involved in ordinary politics, and universalistic, but Cone was none of these things. He represented a "black intelligentsia in theology" that lacked a living relation to black culture, which left him with no communal basis for doing black theology. Ruether argued that although Cone condemned white theology, he lived in it and through it, promoting an abstract theory of blackness that had more to do with German theology than the black experience: "The result of this reversal in the thought of a man like Cone is that his 'blackness' and 'whiteness' are peculiarly flat and 'formal' in character. There is little living black culture reflected in Cone's sense of blackness." Just as black people were more than the oppressed, white people were more than oppressors.[40]

Similar critiques of Cone were commonplace among black clergy, which Ruether heard while teaching at Howard University, where she and Roberts were colleagues. Roberts protested repeatedly that Cone's preeminence was undeserved because he represented only himself and gave the movement a bad image. According to Roberts, Cone was wrong to denigrate racial reconciliation, his language was too violently antiwhite, his theology was too Barthian, his thinking as a whole was narrow and exclusive, and he was disastrously cut off from black culture, the black church, and African sources of black religion. In a signature work, *Liberation and Reconciliation* (1971), Roberts declared, "The narrowness that Cone has sought to impose upon Black Theology must be rejected. This must be done for the sake of Black Theology itself."[41]

Black nationalist theologian Albert Cleage contended that Jesus was literally black; Roberts sharply replied, "I do not need to find black Jews." Against the religious exclusivism of Cleage and Cone, he added, "I would like to hold on to a universal Christ who reveals himself existentially." Roberts conceived the black Messiah as a liberating religious symbol of a universal reality, Jesus Christ. Black theology had to speak to all people of an all-embracing Christ whom blacks experienced as the black Messiah, "a symbol or a myth with profound meaning for black people."[42]

Identifying Christ's atonement with the incarnation, Roberts emphasized the close relation between the Jesus of history and the Christ of faith. Christianity was founded on the redemptive and transforming impression that the divine indwelling in Jesus made upon the disciples. Jesus was the savior of all oppressed people as the black Messiah and the reconciling savior of all people as the universal Word. The same Jesus who revealed God to the apostles became existentially real to black Christians as the black Messiah. Roberts wrote, "In and through the black Messiah, the good news of salvation is presented to us in our own dialect in terms and ideas that are familiar to us as black persons. The black Messiah meets us against the background of our history and our culture." Many Christians had only a "secondhand experience" of the cross, but black Christians inherited a cross at birth and were never unburdened of it. With special feeling they sang "Must Jesus Bear the Cross Alone?" expressing their experience: "When the hymn says, 'no, there is a cross for everyone, and there is a cross for me,' it goes right to the heart of the black religious experience."[43]

Roberts insisted that liberation and reconciliation went together and were equally indispensable. Greater polarization was not an acceptable outcome; he grieved at "the drifting apart of the races." White racism pervaded American society, its quiet forms were no less toxic than outright bigotry, and black Americans were giving up on integration. Roberts told them not to settle for separatism: "I am aware that some blacks have elected themselves judges and executioners of whites for their evil deeds. For these prophets of hate, revenge and revolt have become their only creed. My understanding of the Christian faith leads me to reject this path." Black theology, he urged, had the "awesome task" of speaking for black emancipation from white oppression at the same time that it admonished blacks against believing they had no sins to confess: "It must speak of reconciliation that brings blacks together and of reconciliation that brings blacks and whites together, both in a multiracial fellowship of the body of Christ and within the world where a multiracial society must be built." Black liberation was a precondition for racial reconciliation, but blacks had to be willing to advance the cause of black–white fellowship and cooperation.[44]

Cone replied that this position was self-contradictory nonsense: "If liberation is the precondition of reconciliation, why then should enslaved blacks assure white oppressors that we are ready to be reconciled when the latter have no intention of loosing the chains of oppression?" He advised Roberts to decide whether he wanted to be a liberation theologian. Liberation was very different from the liberal reformism of the social gospel. If Roberts did not conceive liberation as the uncompromised normative principle of black theology, he was still a liberal. Cone argued that interracial cooperation was the acid test. To work with whites on religious and political causes was to sabotage the cause of liberation by forfeiting the right of blacks to define for themselves the meaning of liberation and reconciliation. "Reconciliation and liberation on white terms have always meant death for black people," Cone warned. There was no such thing as cooperation or fellowship with whites that did not lead to further oppression. Virtually all whites were oppressors, and even progressive whites wanted to tell blacks what racial justice meant. For that reason, Cone argued, the Black Power radicals had been right to expel white liberals from SNCC and CORE. Black liberation was the defining objective of black theology and was definable only by black liberationists.[45]

Roberts agreed that liberation had to be the primary goal of black theology, but he rejected Cone's separatist concept of it. The black theology movement could have unity without subscribing to a uniform ideology, he urged: "There are going to be several Black theologies. My program combines liberation and reconciliation. Many feel that I am neither fish nor fowl. Some have observed that it is too soon to talk of reconciliation. Others rule reconciliation out altogether." Roberts had a three-layered response to this situation: It was never too soon to advocate racial reconciliation, the immediate problem of human estrangement was larger and more complex than that of white oppression versus black liberation, and he was in solidarity with black liberationists who disagreed with him on these points: "Reconciliation is a theological way of seeing the essential nature of this interracial society. We must not only co-exist; we must in-exist in a pluralistic society."[46]

His exemplar was King. Roberts judged that the early King overemphasized sacrificial love as an ethical norm, taking too literally the Lundensian school theory of agape as the moral ideal. His early preaching shortchanged the robust idea of love in biblical prophecy, which included eros and philia. But King had Amos's prophetic fire for social justice, which showed especially in King's later career. Roberts stressed that King moved "to the very edge of violence" in his later career: "His brinkmanship was so pronounced that even though he did not advocate violence, he created a climate in which violence sprang to the surface." King contributed to racial fears that produced greater violence by contending that his strategy was the only alternative to violence. His dream of a promised land of integration was shattered by the entrenched rage of the white majority and the rage of Black Power. Roberts observed that the riots of the 1960s broke the "magnolia myth" of the contented black, leading whites to wonder what had happened to the nice blacks "who had for so long accommodated themselves to inhuman treatment."[47]

Thus it was true, as white racists charged, that King's campaigns for civil rights incited violence; Roberts agreed that King practiced creative destruction. After King's death Roberts sympathized with ministers who told him that nonviolent resistance was self-disrespecting and ineffectual. At the same time, he urged that King's brinkmanship was still the best option: "What we need is a constructive, deeply motivated, long-range, massive reorientation in black–white relations." Niebuhr, Roberts said, was right about the stubbornly collective character of racism. Thus America needed more nonviolent crusaders of King's type who healed and destroyed at the same time, pressing hard for social change but just short of violent rebellion: "Even blacks themselves are not safe in the hands of those who hate sufficiently to destroy whites. Hate is blind whether it comes from blacks or whites." Roberts felt reasonably certain that violence failed the test of pragmatism, and certain it was un-Christian: "Those who argue for counterviolence, even self-defense, encourage the hatemongers, black and white." At best, violent revolutions were the lesser of two evils, and most of the time they led to wholesale slaughter and a new set of unworthy bosses. As bad as the situation was in the United States, it did not compare to "slavery, death camps, or even South Africa." There was still enough goodwill between American whites and blacks to justify the dream of a decent society. The Christian understanding of God and the divine good compelled black and white Christians to find "the very best means to overcome racial strife."[48]

Roberts ranged widely, writing about African and Asian religions, African American folklore, and interreligious dialogue. He embraced William Temple's principle that either all occurrences are revelatory or revelation does not exist; there is nothing that is not revelation. On that ground he rejected Cone's Christocentrism, judging that Cone stuck too rigidly to a dogmatic lens: "He often seems indifferent to sound historical criticism and careful exegesis. Even a black theology should be oriented toward the unity of the Bible and the whole gospel." Cone's major work, *God of the Oppressed* (1975), deepened his reliance on African American sources, but Roberts protested that he still spoke from the standpoint of a dogmatic position, not an inductive search for truth and wholeness: "What we have is a monologue. What we need is a black ecumenical theology and an operational unity."[49]

That was the model that Roberts set for himself and the next generation of black theologians. "I am pleading for a theology of the black experience that grows out of the soil of our heritage and life," he wrote. Black theology needed to refuse the dichotomy between the sacred and secular, in the manner of African religion. To say "Jesus means freedom" was to affirm that Jesus is the Lord of all life and that his salvation applies to all cultures and civilizations. Black theology, Roberts argued, needed to be Christian without being provincially American or European: "We have been lured away by our white teachers to seek religious insights from the Euro-American tradition, which has never given birth to a great religion. Our black fathers had a rich religious heritage in Africa when the Norsemen were living in caves."[50]

Roberts believed in this agenda before he believed in his capacity to pull it off. In his early career he judged that African religions were too diffuse in their tribal customs, languages, and religious systems to be manageable. Then he read African religious scholars John Mbiti and E. Bolaji Idowu, who convinced him that his first impression was wrong. "I discovered that African religion, at the core, is similar across Black Africa," Roberts wrote. "The beliefs in a supreme god, lesser spirits, and reverence for ancestors are held in common. These are the *esse*, the vital core beliefs of African traditional religion." Drawing on the ethnotheological analyses of Mbiti and Aylward Shorter, Roberts contended that African religion was ultimately monotheistic, contained myths of redemption, and, long before Judaism and Christianity existed, conceived God as a provident creator. These aspects of the traditional African religious worldview reinforced his Christian faith; Roberts urged students and colleagues not to fear that studying African religion would weaken their devotion to Jesus. Like Shorter, Roberts commended the sense of wholeness and relationality in African religion, its emphasis on symbolism, its belief in a spiritual connection between the living and the dead, and its celebration of the fecundity and sharing of life.[51]

Like Mbiti, Roberts lamented that African religion lacks any sense of the future or eschatology. In African thinking, time consists of events, which occur only in the past and present; thus only these dimensions are real. The future is nothing because it is not experienced. Roberts believed that African religion had much to gain from biblical religion in this area and that the Christian doctrine of the communion of saints improved upon the African notion that every death takes place by the will of ancestors. Surprisingly, Roberts did not focus on North African ancient Christianity, which included Clement, Origen, Cyprian, Athanasius, and Augustine or the subsequent history of Christianity in Africa, which produced the very integration of traditions that he theorized. He stuck to a harder project, showing that traditional African religion and biblical religion hold similar conceptions of the nondualistic sense of the wholeness of things. To interpret Christianity from an African perspective, Roberts argued, is to cut through the Greek dualism and German dialectics that turned Christianity away from its holistic biblical roots.

In 1973 Roberts took a leave from Howard University to serve for a year as dean of the School of Theology at Virginia Union School of Theology. Completing a major work, *A Black Political Theology* (1974), he bluntly expressed his sense of the time, charging that white America had lost its conscience about racial injustice and was in danger of losing its soul. Black Americans had better politics than most white Americans, but the state of black America's soul was increasingly dubious, at least among the young: "It is disturbing to see the young repudiate the faith that sustained their black forefathers and made life possible for him. The youths have only experienced the minor blows resulting from racism, whereas their black forefathers marched by faith through the very flames of hell and into the present, undaunted and unafraid." Roberts implored young black Americans not to spurn the faith that sustained generations of black survivors: "Yet almost daily we see black youth snap their fingers in derision against one of the richest spiritual traditions known to man." Human beings needed religious meaning, "especially if they are an oppressed people seeking liberation." His hope for black theology was restorative, revisionist, and postcolonial, not revolutionary. It was that black theology would help to instill and renew a genuine appreciation for "the deep religious roots of black culture."[52]

LIBERATIONISM AS CULTURAL POLITICS: C. T. VIVIAN

These were the arguments that launched black theology, which yielded new black theologies in which women entered the field of academic theology and changed the discourse of liberation theology. Cone changed his position about feminist criticism after he acquired black female students at Union, and he made a painstaking shift to a more deeply cultural perspective after Charles H. Long, Cecil Cone, and others criticized his abstract theologizing. All of this preceded Cone's rethinking of how he should talk about the legacies of King and Malcolm, which produced his book *Martin & Malcolm & America* (1991). In that book Cone interpreted King as the first liberation theologian and Malcolm as the indispensable corrective to King's liberal integrationist tropes. All of Cone's later work operated with this dialectic, until late in his career, when his teaching and scholarship lifted James Baldwin to the stature of King and Malcolm.[53]

In the beginning black theology was a liberationist Christian response to the Black Power movement. It long outlasted the Black Power movement because black liberation theology fixed on the gospel demand to take the side of the poor and oppressed, viewing the world from the perspectives of oppressed people. Soon there were many liberation theologies, a development inherent in the liberationist idea. In the beginning, however, the centrality of the integration-and-reconciliation issue threw into question whether King could be claimed for liberation theology. Even if one believed, as Cone and Roberts agreed, that King qualified on other counts, his legacy on the bellwether issue yielded different kinds of liberation theology. It was not a simple question of keeping faith with King or not, for some of King's most ardent disciples became libera-tionists in Cone's mold, and others pulled Cone aside at conferences to quietly cheer him on.

C. T. Vivian became a prominent example of the former—a close associate of King's who moved to liberationist anti-integrationism. His civil rights activism had begun in 1947 in Peoria, Illinois, in a lunch-counter protest. He had been a Lawson disciple in Nashville, a cofounder of SNCC, and a King lieutenant in SCLC, coordinating SCLC branches. In Nashville his fiery temperament and edgy style contrasted effectively with the pastoral geniality of his close colleague, Kelly Miller Smith. Vivian was a veteran of the campaigns in Birmingham, St. Augustine, and Selma, taking a jailhouse beating in Selma. He resembled Walker so closely in appearance and preaching style that insiders called them "the Civil Rights twins." In 1966 Vivian took a job in Chicago as director of the Urban Training Center for Christian Mission; he was just getting started as a founder of black organizations. In 1968 he cofounded the Coalition for United Community Action, a coalition of sixty-one black organizations opposed to racial discrimination in the building trade unions. The following year he founded the Black Action Strategies and Information Center, the nation's first African American think tank. Working with Jesse Jackson, Vivian urged black youths to stay in school, and in 1969 Vivian and Jackson helped to forge a civil rights agreement with the Chicago construction industry. For a while in 1971 Vivian tried to revive the Chicago chapter of SCLC, acceding to Abernathy's plea. But Abernathy failed to come through with promised support, and Vivian resigned in 1972. Reestablishing Chicago SCLC was quixotic, and not only because Vivian tried to do it in his basement. He had already moved on, having published, in 1970, a vivid manifesto that tapped the zeitgeist, *Black Power and the American Myth.*[54]

Vivian said that the myth of a free and open America did not apply to black Americans because white Americans always had to look down on somebody. He admired King immensely, claiming that King was the first black leader to lift the freedom struggle above economic survival to the higher realm of moral and spiritual concern. But Vivian believed that the civil rights movement ended with King, in failure. It failed because it wrongly believed that integration was the solution to racism and that legislation would lead to justice. Vivian explained, "The Movement sprang from Christian morality, and its strategy and tactics evolved from that morality." He did not regret King's deep commitment to Christian nonviolence or the movement's Pauline sermons on the coming of a new age. The movement wrung as much as it could from these sources; at the time, nothing would have worked better. But Vivian judged that King and the movement took too seriously the self-descriptions of white liberals. Thus the civil rights movement failed: "We assumed that integration was the model for our success. We assumed that the barriers of segregation would be broken when enough good men saw the justice of our cause. We assumed that we were dealing with an open, democratic, and Christian nation, a nation which *had*, and would, implement the solutions to our condition. And we assumed that a single ideology of movement would be sufficient to our success."[55]

Every one of these assumptions derived from white America's conceits about itself, Vivian said. Having come from the Nashville movement, Vivian was schooled in early SNCC skepticism about King and leaders, which he some-times conveyed to King. He had reality-checked King's optimistic liberalism, and he took part in SCLC's brawling disputes about campaigns and strategy. But Vivian and King bonded over their theological, political, and tempera-mental affinities, and Vivian believed fervently in King; surely they were on the right track. It was not until Watts, Vivian said, that he and King realized "the extent of our failure." King felt burned in Watts, and refuted. He belatedly questioned his governing assumptions and strategy, and thus he got more radical, breaking from the liberal mainstream. Vivian wrote, "As long as we believed what the nation said about itself we chose strategies which in no way corresponded to the reality we faced, strategies which were bound to fail." The goals were not the problem. The civil rights movement had the right goals from the beginning, and it made substantial progress toward them. But there was no justice when justice did not exist for all. King was dead serious about that, and the movement for it was stuck and floundering when King was slain. Two years later the utter failure of the movement seemed undeniable to Vivian, who winced "with pained nostalgia" at the memory of "those grand days" in Selma.[56]

One thing was certain, Vivian argued: White liberalism was not a basis for making any further progress toward the goals of the civil rights movement. White American racism was so toxic and pervasive that it drove whites into two groups. A small tradition of white radicals shared John Brown's hatred of racism; the rest were psychologically unable to acknowledge the "unspeakable and intolerable crime" of American racial tyranny. The only true white allies were the ones who hated racism enough to purge themselves of it. They recognized their complicity in white supremacy and worked to abolish it. Vivian said there were more of them than black nationalists sometimes suggested; he had trusted white allies, and even John Brown had sixteen white comrades at Harpers Ferry. But this was a small group, and the genuine white allies did not ask blacks for validation or a place at the table.[57]

The "new separatism," as Vivian called it, was finished with helping white liberals with their problems. The movement that mattered was a black freedom movement that sang its own songs. King and Vivian had pledged allegiance to integration because this concept fit their understanding of how people should relate to each other. A good society had integrationist values. But this idea did not fit American society, Vivian said, "and the measure by which we misjudged that reality is precisely the measure of the yawning gulf between Blacks and whites." Holding out for integration in racist America was demeaning and self-defeating for African Americans. It masked the oppressive relation of whites to blacks, making white liberals the brokers of racial integration. Vivian declared, "Almost everything we learned in the Movement makes integration impossible as a goal for the Black community today." Integration was dead as a value and goal because most whites only pretended to believe in it, "and Blacks, in response, have realized that they must develop their own distinctive culture."[58]

Vivian lauded the "exciting new mood" of the new separatism and its social policy agenda. Welfare policy was a major example. Welfare was an assault on human dignity, Vivian argued, exactly as conservatives said. Welfare programs provided cushy jobs for government administrators, ensnaring recipients in a ruinous system of dependency that stripped them of self-respect and personal responsibility. Vivian sought to avoid Moynihan Report controversy by not saying "women," but the debate over welfare policy at the time fixed on poor, unmarried mothers. Sociologist Daniel Patrick Moynihan, in a paper for the Johnson administration in 1965, updated E. Franklin Frazier's critique of matriarchal family structure in black American life. Frazier's classic text of 1939, *The Negro Family in the United States* (updated in 1948) lamented that many black youths grew up without appropriate parental care or guidance because their homes lacked fathers. Moynihan showed that single parenthood had increased significantly in African American households since Frazier had drawn attention to it. Religious communities, Moynihan argued, had a major role to play in establishing moral norms, but "the Negro churches have all but lost contact with men in the Northern cities." Moynihan allowed that urban life usually eroded the moral authority of religious congregations in this area. Still, he had a patronizing image for it in this case: "The tangle of pathology is tightening." Citing Frazier on this theme, Moynihan admonished against looking away and could not resist another pass at his pathology image: "Three centuries of injustice have brought about deep-seated structural distortions in the life of the Negro American. At this point, the present tangle of pathology is capable of perpetuating itself without assistance from the white world. The cycle can be broken only if these distortions are set right."[59]

Moynihan called for policies designed to strengthen two-parent black families, which ignited a firestorm over social engineering, cultural chauvinism, out-of-wedlock childbirth, and the racial prejudices of white liberals like Moynihan. Black nationalism had a long history of pressing the Frazier argument, powerfully in the case of Alexander Crummell. Civil rights ministers typically walked a tightrope in this area, advocating two-parent families, Christian morality, welfare rights, and goodwill. King exemplified the approach of civil rights ministers who supported the expansion of the welfare state; he even commended the Moynihan Report before pulling back from it. Aid to Dependent Children (ADC), a New Deal component of the Social Security Act of 1935, provided meager assistance to poor, white, unwed mothers. The civil rights movement won for poor black mothers the right to receive welfare benefits (renamed, in 1962, Aid to Families with Dependent Children). This mere gain by black Americans of a right to receive benefits from the existing welfare system racialized welfare politics, fueling a long-running political backlash. Political candidates rode to office with racially coded attacks on poor, unwed mothers, notwithstanding that most welfare recipients were still white, most black female recipients continued to work, and there was no evidence that welfare programs caused marriages to break up.[60]

King was in the mainstream of the civil rights movement on these issues, speaking for two-parent families *and* welfare rights. This part of his legacy long outlasted him. But defending welfare rights was deeply political, grinding, and bureaucratic work, and it allied civil rights ministers with welfare state liberals like Moynihan and Hubert Humphrey, implicating the movement in draining debates over AFDC regulations and "man in the house" regulations. Vivian's excitement about the new racial militancy had much to do with cutting that cord. He called for the abolition of the welfare system, a position that put him in line with black nationalists and white reactionaries. He stressed the point, observing that white reactionaries would be surprised to learn who agreed with them. According to Vivian, "Black organizations that have organized around welfare have almost universally called for the abolishment of that system." The only organizations meriting the title of "Black organizations" were nationalist groups that repudiated integration and liberal politics. Moynihan noted that Black Muslims were the only black religious group to buck the tide of religious erosion in northern cities, "a movement based on total rejection of white society, even though it emulates white mores." To Vivian, this exception was salutary and another reason to get as far as possible from the likes of Moynihan.[61]

Welfare was a big government idea resting on liberal integrationist politics, and so was integrated public education. The new black consciousness, Vivian said, had no use for integrated public schools and refused to be co-opted by liberal demands for them. It demanded black community control of black schools, not mere decentralization. The new black consciousness absorbed the true history of ethnic struggle in the United States, not the whitewashed history taught in schools. Vivian had been taught, all the way through Western Illinois University and Colgate Rochester, that Irish and German Americans won success in America by working hard and being thrifty. He had not been told that the Irish rioted in New York and Boston or that Germans in Chicago marched on city hall with guns: "They did not work in isolation, they worked together. They organized political clubs and used the power of bloc voting. They took over labor unions and kept the membership exclusive. They created their own banks for their own use. They built up businesses and brought their own people into them. They took care of their own." That was exactly what African Americans needed to do, despite having long preceded the Irish and Germans in America. Vivian still believed in King's dream, but King's strategy for achieving it was obsolete: "Separatism has taken the place of integration as the strategy and tactic of the Movement. It is tactically necessary in order to achieve the kind of unity needed to accomplish the aims of the Black community. It will also function as a strategy until those ends are met."[62]

Vivian had perfect pitch for the moment, distilling for many what had just happened. He spoke with authority as a movement veteran, and his judgments were clear and emphatic. Nearly every reviewer noted that the book came from King's inner circle, which reviewers variously rendered as instructive, chastening, confusing, or enraging. Evangelical theologian James Daane hoped that Vivian was "too cynical about the moral decency of the American conscience." This was merely a hope, however, as Daane acknowledged that Vivian had reasons to give up on integration, beginning with his movement experience. Writing in the conservative *Reformed Journal*, Daane wanted to believe that King would have done better had he been theologically orthodox and committed to biblical realism. But orthodoxy and realism had not saved conservative white churches from a bad record on racial justice, and Daane deferred to Vivian's hard-won authority. If white America was truly incapable of treating black Americans as human beings, "then this book is a profound warning about America's future." Legal scholar Arthur Selwyn Miller had a similar take from a nontheological standpoint. Commenting on Vivian's verdict that white Americans needed to look down on somebody, Miller said that Black Power and separatism were "only too understandable" under this circumstance: "Our constitutional law proclaims equality, a sentiment deeply carved in the façade of the Supreme Court building in Washington, but that law is by and large a farce. The hour is late, possibly too late; let no one be sanguine about this struggle, this stain upon the American Conscience."[63]

The favorable reviews outnumbered the defensive and angry ones, and Vivian went on to a distinguished career in black freedom activism. In 1979 he and white southern civil rights activist Ann Braden founded the National Anti-Klan Network, which later morphed into the Center for Democratic Renewal, a community-based, multiracial human rights organization combating hate groups. Vivian exemplified the history of left-leaning civil rights and black freedom organizing. He stayed in the mainstream of the freedom movement by responding creatively to its generational twists and turns, later tacking away from his nationalism of the 1970s. He battled and endured, having been claimed early on by the gospel demand to stand at the cross with victims, long before he heard of King. The same thing was true of a forerunner of womanist theology, Pauli Murray, but with very different politics from Vivian's post-King, 1970s nationalism. Murray combined civil rights militancy, social gospel religion, and a cosmopolitan concept of racial identity long before King was famous. She was marginalized in every post she ever took because of her gender or race or class or sexuality, often without knowing which factor weighed most against her. And she kept acquiring "firsts" after King was gone.

PAULI MURRAY AND THE BLACK SOCIAL GOSPEL

Pauli Murray worked at the edges of the entire story told in this book. She was disqualified by gender from being a minister until late in her life, and from playing a leadership role in civil rights organizations, although she tried. She was prolific, energetic, accomplished, and extroverted, though often alone. She had a queer identity but no language for it or places of affirmation. She was alone of all her sex at Howard Law School's graduation in 1944 and later became the first black woman to be ordained an Episcopal priest. She had a lonely, barely surviving career as a lawyer before she clawed her way to a tenured chair at Brandeis University, which she quit to study for the priesthood. She struggled with her racial identity and her sexual identity, the former in public and the latter in private, although she renamed herself to mark her feeling of being a man who was attracted to women. She hated the sexism of King and the SCLC, which marginalized her along with every other woman who worked in the civil rights movement. She made historic contributions to feminist legal theory and to the creation of a feminist movement. She urged the feminist movement, unsuccessfully, not to marginalize black women. And she spurned the sexism and nationalism of early black theology, which made her a pioneer yet again.

She was named Anna Pauline Murray on her birth in Baltimore in November 1910, the same year that Du Bois launched *The Crisis*, a fixture in her childhood homes. Murray was a seventh-generation Episcopalian descending from families of teachers on both sides. Her mother, Agnes, was a nurse from Durham, North Carolina; her father, Will, was a graduate of Howard University and a school principal. Murray, the fourth of six children, lost both of her parents as a toddler. Will Murray caught typhoid fever when Anna Pauline was an infant, he nearly died, and he only partly recovered, suffering terrible mood swings and depression for the rest of his life. The memory of his struggle with mental illness scarred his gifted fourth child throughout her life. Agnes Murray coped with six children and a disabled husband until March 1914, when she suffered a massive cerebral hemorrhage and died; she was thirty-five years old and in the fourth month of another pregnancy. Murray's siblings were sent to live with her father's family in Baltimore, but she was sent to Durham to live with her Fitzgerald relatives—principally her mother's sister Pauline Dame plus her maternal grandparents and her Aunt Sally Fitzgerald, who later married an Episcopal priest. Will Murray ended up in a state psychiatric hospital, where he spent the last ten years of his life until he was murdered by a guard. Murray's first experience of being an orphan was thus literal, although she grew up in the loving embrace of her mother's elderly family.[64]

Her grandfather Robert Fitzgerald was a biracial veteran of the Union army who moved to Orange County, North Carolina, after the Civil War to found a school for former slaves. His tenacity eventually caused the local Klan to back off, and his siblings followed him to Durham to found a bank and a brick-making business. The Fitzgeralds were cultured and industrious lovers of literature and the Episcopal Church. Both of Murray's aunts were schoolteachers. They might have passed for white but took pride in their light-colored black American multiplicity, urging Murray to take pride in her complex family heritage. Murray, telling their story years later, titled her book *Proud Shoes*. Robert Fitzgerald had gone blind by the time that Murray joined the family, and her aunts made very modest salaries; thus her family of readers teetered financially on the bottom rung of the middle class. Murray avoided streetcars and other sites of encounter with white people, "a confusing world to me because I was both related to white people and alienated from them." The contrasts between her dilapidated, rickety, tobacco-road school and the shiny school for whites cut her deeply: "We got the greasy, torn, dog-eared books; they got the new ones. They had field day in the city park; we had it on a furrowed stubbly hillside. They got wide mention in the newspaper; we got a paragraph at the bottom. . . . We were bottled up and labeled and set aside." Everything that she learned about race, outside her nurturing home and church, was oppressively threatening: "Race was the atmosphere one breathed from day to day, the pervasive irritant, the chronic allergy, the vague apprehension which made one uncomfortable and jumpy. We knew the race problem was like a deadly snake coiled and ready to strike, and that one avoided its dangers only by never-ending watchfulness."[65]

Henry B. Delany, one of the first two black Americans to serve as an Episcopal bishop, was a close friend of Murray's family. He was highly respected, magnanimous, and had ten children, all of whom achieved professional success. The Delany children were "beacon lights to younger people like me," Murray said. On Delany's deathbed in 1927 he told her, "You are a child of destiny." Murray and Aunt Pauline took this blessing to heart for the rest of their days, often citing it; Anthony Pinn aptly says that Murray had "a soft sense of destiny," a belief that her life had a purpose and direction. In 1926 Murray graduated from high school and moved to New York City, spurning the South's segregated colleges.

She lived with an aunt in Queens who had been quietly passing for white until Murray's arrival exposed her; Murray shuddered at the mediocrity and sheltered humiliation of the passing strategy. She heard about Hunter College, only to learn that her spotty education disqualified her for admission. Murray studied for a year to pass the entrance exams, enrolling at Hunter in 1928, and changed her name to Pauli, feeling that its gender ambivalence fit her better. Hunter took pride in its racial inclusivity and free tuition, though Murray felt isolated as one of two black female students in her class at the Brooklyn Annex. Moreover, the college had no campus. One summer Murray rented a room at the Harlem YWCA, where she caught a glimpse of civic role models Anna Arnold Hedgeman and Dorothy Height and occasionally attended nearby Abyssinian Church. Excelling in her academic work, Murray had only one bad racial experience at Hunter: an American history course in which the professor never mentioned black Americans, except as a drag on American society. Murray traced her passionate interest in black American history to this course.[66]

Restless, adventurous, and curious about the world and herself, Murray graduated from Hunter in 1933, "the worst possible time to come out of school and try to begin one's career." The Depression made a mockery of the career ambitions of most graduates. By the time she graduated Murray was a veteran hitcher of freight trains. She hitched rides up and down the Northeast and then across the country, determined to see as much of it as possible. She performed odd jobs for townspeople to buy food, spent many nights in public accommodations and county jails, and posed as a male, ostensibly for safety. Murray never wrote for publication about her sexuality, but she began puzzling about it in her diary as an adolescent and later read assiduously about sexual identity. Her letters and journals conveyed that she was romantically attracted to women and that she conceived herself as a "boy-girl" who was more boy than girl. In college she married a shy young man, but they parted after a few months. Murray was slow to find friends whom she trusted, but she also had a gift for friendship. Her buoyancy and volatility attracted friends and detractors throughout her life, and her closest friends kept her secrets. Between 1937 and 1947 Murray had three emotional breakdowns that put her in hospitals. Each time she pressed the medical staff to investigate whether she had a set of testes. Finally in 1954 she had surgery that yielded a definitive answer—no. Sarah Azaransky, in her excellent book *The Dream Is Freedom*, observes that Murray resorted to "pseudo-hermaphrodite" as a self-description, making her way before the language of transgender sexuality existed. In 1943 Murray wrote to Aunt Pauline, "This little 'boy-girl' personality as you jokingly call it sometimes gets me into trouble . . . but where you and a few people understand, the world does not accept my pattern of life. And to try to live by society's standards always causes me such inner conflict that at times it's almost unbearable."[67]

In college she spurned an obvious career track—teaching—because she wanted to be a writer and poet. Afterward Murray wrote prolifically for publication. She published only one account of her gender-bending hitchhiking—a short story—until she wrote her autobiography five decades later, in which Murray said that traveling as a man saved her from danger. Privately, however, she compiled photographic albums of herself dressed in male attire, sometimes playfully experimenting with her gender persona. Her poems during the same period probed her multiracial identity. One poem, "Mulatto's Dilemma," cursed the summer sun "that burned me thus to fateful recognition," yearning for "the pride of blackness." Murray had not seemed tortured about her racial identity while growing up under the care of strong and loving elderly relatives. The racial problem was simply that whites treated all "colored" despicably. Then Murray threw herself into New York City and wherever the trains took her, and found herself a puzzle to others and herself. Strangers stared at her to determine her race and gender. She was not as white-looking as her aunts, but she was close enough that blacks in northern climes often made her feel not really black. "Mulatto's Dilemma" was a variation on a literary trope, the "tragic mulatta" who confused whites and blacks alike and was thus rejected by both. Murray said it for the rest of her life—her mixed heritage threw her into "a no man's land between the whites and the blacks, belonging wholly to neither, yet irrevocably tied to both."[68]

She cast her first vote in a presidential election for Norman Thomas. Supporting a Democrat was unthinkable to Murray, and Republican contempt for blacks put Republicans beyond the pale too. Murray landed her first career job as a field representative for *Opportunity* magazine, the house organ of the National Urban League. She promoted the magazine at social work conferences and also wrote for it, until her low pay and failing health compelled her to resign. She took a job with the Federal Relief Administration, running a recreational camp for women, but Murray was cocky and outspoken, two things that her patronizing white boss did not tolerate in black employees, so that fizzled. In 1935 the New Deal's Works Progress Administration (WPA) created the Workers Education Project (WEP). Murray took a WEP job near Greenwich Village, teaching night classes in remedial English and community organizing. Her supervisor was Ella Baker. To Murray, WEP teaching was a lifesaver and a political education. Communists, Lovestonite former Communists, and Socialists battled for control of the trade unions. Murray, navigating the New York left, spurned the Communist slogan "Self Determination for the Black Belt," which smacked of Jim Crow. For a while she was a Lovestonite, taking a course from Jay Lovestone himself—the expelled former leader of the Communist Party USA—but in 1937 the Lovestonites supported the Communist Party, and Murray went back to Norman Thomas Socialism, without joining the Socialist Party.[69]

She had never thought of white people as victims of oppression until she heard white students in her WEP classes tell their stories of being beaten, starved, and jailed for trying to organize unions. Murray surprised herself by concluding that blacks were not alone in struggling for human dignity. She did not like the ideological warfare that consumed Communists and Socialists, but she embraced their conviction that politics was unavoidable in the struggle for justice and human dignity. African and Asian colonial peoples were rebelling against British and French imperialism, Nazi fascism menaced Europe, and New York leftists like Thomas were returning from Soviet Russia with grim tales of oppression. Murray reasoned, like Thomas, that democracy was the most radical and liberating possibility. Democracy, if paired with Christianity, "could be made to work for all its people, including Negroes." She wrote in her notebook, "It seems to me that the testing ground of democracy and Christianity in the United States is in the South; that it is the duty of Negroes to press for political, economic and educational equality for themselves and for disinherited whites; that it is the responsibility of socially-minded Negro and white Southerners to work out this problem; and that the job of interpretation and leadership falls to those of both races with a knowledge of the problems and an understanding of the tremendous task to be accomplished."[70]

Murray struggled with her conscience, eager to build a career while knowing that her aunts needed her. Aunt Pauline scraped by at age sixty-eight, with no pension coming, and Aunt Sally had returned to Pauline's home with two children in tow after her husband died. Feeling guilty about stranding them, Murray applied for graduate study in sociology at the University of North Carolina (UNC). Meanwhile President Franklin Roosevelt gave a speech at UNC commending his own liberalism and that of UNC, which grated on Murray. What was so liberal about a university that had never enrolled a black student or employed a black faculty member? How did FDR qualify as a liberal when he said little or nothing about the rights of black Americans? Murray wrote a blistering letter to the president that pressed these questions, telling him that southern blacks like her were political refugees exactly like the Jews struggling to get out of Germany. She resented being ignored while the president congratulated himself, UNC, and UNC president Frank Graham on their liberalism. Graham was a noted liberal who said Murray-like things about democracy and Christianity fusing together to change the world. Applying these beliefs to his university, however, was out of play. Murray sent her letter to FDR and a copy to Eleanor Roosevelt, who replied that the South was changing slowly but surely, "don't push too fast." That was a breakthrough, even as Murray cringed from the advice.[71]

UNC denied admission to Murray because she was black, and she promptly informed the NAACP. There was an offended family affinity involved, as one of Murray's Fitzgerald ancestors had attended UNC and another served on the board of trustees. Murray got her first taste of press notoriety, which pleased her at first, until a terrified Aunt Pauline told her by telephone that angry white locals were threatening to burn down her house. Murray grieved that having loved ones and risking public bravery did not go together. The WPA was phased out, and Murray scratched for a living. The urge to write kept her going, as did the encouragement of her literary hero, Stephen Vincent Benét, author of *John Brown's Body*, who befriended Murray after she wrote to him. Speaking for "we, the disinherited," Murray published a letter in the *New York Herald Tribune* lamenting the plight of "these miserable, frustrated, unused people." Eleanor Roosevelt cited the letter in her syndicated column, "My Day," and a friendship was born; Murray had her first tea with Roosevelt in January 1940. Each prized the integrity of the other, and for many years to come Roosevelt would caution Murray against rashness and Murray would reply that Roosevelt still did not fathom what it felt like to be black.[72]

She was a pioneer Freedom Rider long before the name or movement existed. In 1940 Murray took a bus from New York to Durham with her West Indian housemate and likely romantic partner, Adelene McBean. Murray had recently read Krishnalal Shridharani's *War Without Violence*, so she knew a little about Gandhi's method, and she had qualms about traveling in the South with McBean because her peppery activist friend opined that black Americans were timid toward Jim Crow. Nothing eventful happened until the pair reached Richmond, Virginia. A relief bus running from Richmond to Durham was uncomfortable and half empty; McBean took a decent seat near the front for greater comfort, and the pair were arrested in Petersburg. McBean was defiant, until she passed out, and Murray ended up in jail with her. In Murray's telling, the local jailed riffraff treated her rudely, with vulgar sexual banter, until she won them over with a compelling display of her nobility; she was there so they could ride the bus with dignity. Word of the arrest reached local NAACP attorneys Raymond Valentine and Robert H. Cooley Jr., who represented Murray and McBean at their trial for disorderly conduct, where they were convicted.[73]

The lawyers filed an appeal that brought Thurgood Marshall, William H. Hastie, and Leon A. Ransom into it, hoping for a test case. But the locals shrewdly kept the segregation statutes out of it, and the appeal was denied. Murray was appalled and fascinated. Was this how the system worked? The South retained segregation by keeping it out of the courtroom? The episode put her on a new path, having discovered something about the power of nonviolent resistance and the reach of legal reasoning.

Odell Waller, a black sharecropper, was sentenced to death in 1940 for murdering his white landlord in Pittsylvania, Virginia. The jury convicting him was compiled from voter lists in a county with a poll tax, and Murray joined a national campaign protesting that his Fourteenth Amendment rights had been violated. Murray spoke for Waller across the country, employed by the Workers Defense League, and lectured on sharecropping at Young People's Socialist League meetings. She aimed for larger audiences through her writing but failed; William Hastie and Leon Ransom urged her to apply to Howard Law School. Waller was executed, and Murray enrolled at Howard, aided by Ransom's recommendation.[74]

Her life turned a corner. Murray found the racial oppression of the nation's capital hard to bear after living in New York, but her training at Howard Law School was enthralling. She soaked up case law and loved the drama of dress rehearsals, especially when the entire school assembled to hear a professor's rehearsal arguments for a Supreme Court case. Murray's teachers included Ransom, Hastie, George E. C. Hayes, George M. Johnson, James N. Nabrit, and Spottswood W. Robinson III. She marveled at Ransom's combination of kindly geniality in personal relations and ruthless interrogation in the classroom and courtroom. Trials were war, she learned, and courtroom battle was legal combat. Murray would have welcomed equal treatment on these terms, but she had to fight to be respected by her teachers and friends. She told them there was such a thing as sexual bias in the practice of law, and they had a bad case of it. She coined a term for it, "Jane Crow." Murray bridled against being drowned out in classroom discussions. Excluded from Sigma Delta Tau, a well-connected legal fraternity, she protested that excluding her was not funny or fair. She fought this battle alone, as she was the only woman in her class. The law school acquired only two additional female students while Murray was there, and the professional staff had only one woman, the registrar.[75]

She joined FOR and supported CORE's early attempts to light a fire. She read the Gandhian literature of the time, adopting Howard's theology of Christian pacifist redemptive suffering, although Murray did not reference Johnson, Mays, or Thurman in her writings, and she referenced James Farmer only in connection with CORE and FOR. In an article titled "An Alternative Weapon" Murray and fellow FOR activist Henry Babcock said that black American pacifists had a prophetic role to play in creating a genuine American democracy. There was something odd, they acknowledged, even troubling, in the notion that out of "the Negro's struggle and suffering may come the answer to the very problem which troubles so many Americans today." One probably had to be Christian or at least religious to appreciate that suffering could be redemptive; Murray and Babcock affirmed that pacifism itself was essentially religious, a type of faith: "Through his suffering, through his bitter conflicts and frustrations of his personal situation, the Negro is led to a thorough-going pacifism at home and abroad which may prove itself the means of giving the movement its greatest impetus." The suffering of black Americans showed that the struggle between fascism and democracy ravaging the world was internal within each nation, not merely a fight between nations. American racism, they implored, undermined the claim that America fought to rid the world of fascist racism. Democracy was indeed the better way, but America was far from a genuine democracy. Religious pacifism had to be personal before it was social, but to be truly redemptive it had to be personal and social.[76]

The military draft seized upon Howard students notwithstanding that they could not eat in local restaurants. Murray organized a caucus within Howard's NAACP chapter that applied what she called "the stool-sitting technique"—the direct action method used by CORE. In April 1943 and April 1944 Howard students picketed two downtown restaurants. Johnson wanted to support the pickets but bowed to his political reality: Howard depended on the federal government. Johnson told the students to shut down and the students refused, believing they had the support of at least Hastie, Ransom, and Thurman. On the second go-round Johnson spelled out the problem: 60 percent of Howard's income came from the federal government. For that reason, it turned out, even Hastie, Ransom, and Thurman supported Johnson's demand. Murray sought out Thurman in the midst of the controversy, who told her that evil is persistent: "When we beat it down in one place, it pops up in another." Murray rued the irony that Howard University opposed the very things that Johnson promoted every week on the lecture circuit. Her group "had been aborted by our own black administrators, held hostage themselves to the forces of bigotry in government."[77]

Meanwhile Murray risked her friendship with Eleanor Roosevelt by ripping FDR's continued silence about Jim Crow, and Eleanor Roosevelt replied that the Fair Employment Practice legislation was FDR's answer; the president was a political leader constrained by politics. Murray retorted that white American racism was very much like Nazi racism and thus a powerful refutation of the American claim to being in the right. Black Americans were angry and alienated because they were treated abominably, much as Jews were treated in

Germany. Murray thought that might terminate their friendship. Instead the First Lady greeted her warmly at their next meeting, and a deeper trust formed between them. Upon realizing that Eleanor Roosevelt was reviled in the South for advocating racial justice, Murray swore off returning to the Deep South, except for family funerals. On the other hand, after Detroit erupted in June 1943, Murray published a bitter poem in *Crisis* titled "Mr. Roosevelt Regrets," begging the president to say something about racism that wasn't bland and innocuous. Eleanor Roosevelt replied, "I am sorry but I understand."[78]

Murray's deep friendship with another distinguished white woman, historian Caroline Ware, germinated during this period. Lina Ware belonged to a Boston Brahmin Unitarian family long associated with Harvard. A pioneering cultural historian who taught during her early career at Vassar, she was married to a renowned New Deal economist, Gardiner C. Means, who worked for the Department of Agriculture, applying his theory of administered prices. Ware worked for the Department of Agriculture until 1942, when she took a job at Howard teaching constitutional history. Murray heard that the history department had an accomplished feminist scholar who had a friendship with Eleanor Roosevelt, and Murray promptly audited Ware's undergraduate class, introducing herself. A deep friendship developed, as Murray pulled Ware into the local protest movement and Ware brought Murray into her social circle. In July 1943 Murray told Ware that she had recently joined the Socialist Party because "FDR is unhappily wedded to white supremacy, I am afraid." For forty years afterward Murray and Ware helped each other see how racism and sexism fed on each other. In person they were said to banter as equals, although in their letters Ware stuck persistently to the teacher role.[79]

The same summer that she joined the Socialist Party Murray tried to find a doctor in New York or Baltimore who would give her hormone injections. She told Pauline that she needed to get herself "straightened out sort of once and for all." There were rumors on campus that Murray had a female lover, perhaps a college student; Murray was terrified that her career would be destroyed before it began. In that state of anxiety she completed a twelve-part epic poem, "Dark Testament," on which she had labored for years. "America was the dream of freedom," Murray wrote, but this dream turned into a nightmare through the slave trade, the genocide of Native Americans, and especially America's lust for wealth. This was a story of "blood streaking the Atlantic," nothing suited for children or optimism. Murray excoriated the white America that stripped a black man of his manhood and gave him "a white God." Yet Christianity also spoke a language of freedom that sustained her hope. If God cared about justice, there had to be hope for America.[80]

Howard law professors did not teach that *Plessy v. Ferguson* was sure to be overthrown, much less within ten years. They taught their students to look for the inequalities between schools, voting requirements, and the like, nibbling away at *Plessy* without challenging it fundamentally. In 1944 Murray argued in class that this strategy was woefully inadequate. Instead of treating *Plessy* and the Supreme Court's disastrous 1883 edict against civil rights as settled law, NAACP lawyers should challenge the legitimacy of existing law, dispensing with the usual emphasis on the equality side of the *Plessy* equation. Her class-mates thought that was the most ridiculous thing they had ever heard; Murray later recalled that she might as well have proposed to tear down the Statue of Liberty. Attacking *Plessy* would surely be disastrous for the civil rights move-ment, erasing decades of torturously achieved legal progress. Murray's legendary teacher Spottswood Robinson was less heated but equally dismissive: Howard Law School was about making a positive difference in the real world, not finding ways to make it worse. Robinson bet Murray ten dollars that *Plessy* would still be standing in twenty-five years.[81]

Murray had entered law school as a civil rights activist and came out describing herself as equally committed to racial and sexual justice. She wanted to study labor law at Harvard after graduating from Howard in 1944, but Harvard informed her that it did not accept students of her gender. Murray's resentment burned hotter when classmates found her situation amusing. She was still steaming at her graduation, when Johnson got her attention with a stirring address about changing America. Johnson challenged the graduates to flood the Deep South with their idealism and commitment to social justice. It didn't happen until Freedom Summer; the *Baltimore Afro-American* tersely summa-rized Johnson's pitch as "Go South — Commit Suicide." But the idea stuck in Murray's head for years, setting the gold standard for her idealism, and she smiled with appreciation when a succeeding generation did it.[82]

For four years Murray clerked at law offices, and for fifteen years she strug-gled to make a living. She applied to New York firms but failed to find one that would hire a black female attorney. She befriended a municipal court judge, Dorothy Kenyan, who confirmed that women were barely tolerated in the legal profession and rarely hired. In 1949 the Women's Division of the Christian Service Board of Missions of the Methodist Church hired Murray for a research project. Thelma Stevens, a Women's Division official from Mississippi and anti-segregation activist, asked the NAACP and the American Civil Liberties Union (ACLU) for a compilation of the laws of states concerning racial segregation. Stevens sought out Murray after learning that no such compilation existed, and Murray holed up at the New York County Law Library. Laboriously, Murray spent entire days and evenings transcribing state statutes in longhand, as she had no budget for Photostats. Stevens hired her to write a pamphlet; Murray, with typical diligence, produced a 746-page tome titled *States' Laws on Race and Color*. The book exhaustively documented laws discriminating against black Americans, Native Americans, and Americans of Chinese and Japanese ancestry. It was an invaluable resource for the ACLU, which distributed one thousand copies to its staff attorneys and allied groups, and for the NAACP; Thurgood Marshall called it "the bible" of segregation laws. The book had a brief career, contributing to its own obsolescence by helping the NAACP win the *Brown* decision, and Murray stressed that she experienced zero excitement or intellectual stimulation in producing it.[83]

Her work almost won her a research position at Cornell University in 1952. Cornell's School of Industrial and Labor Relations had a State Department contract to codify the laws of Liberia, one of President Harry Truman's Point Four programs. Murray wanted the job desperately. Her research skills were a perfect match for it, and she got strong letters of support from Hastie, Marshall, Randolph, New York attorney Lloyd K. Garrison, and Eleanor Roosevelt. Cornell dean M. P. Catherwood balked at the letters, noting that all were from lefty-liberals, and none played up she-is-not-a-Communist. Didn't Murray know any conservatives who might recommend her? The question floored Murray. Her references epitomized respectability, to her, and no, she had no conservative mentors to call upon. Catherwood reviewed Murray's political history, shuddered at the Workers Defense League, the National Negro Congress, the Socialist Party, and the like, and concluded that Murray was not worth the risk of a HUAC spectacle. He told Murray that her "past associations" put her out of play and told project director Milton Konvitz to get Murray to withdraw her application, to avoid a formal rejection.[84]

Murray was crushed. She appealed the decision, to no avail. She grieved and fumed, telling Ware, "I have no alternative but to fight. Every tack with every job I have tried has failed. Either I must lie down and let the passerby kick me into the dirt or I must fight back. It's as basic as the law of survival." She wondered if Catherwood was a closet racist or just amazingly spineless or both. Did somebody claim to know that she was a lesbian? Since gays and civil rights activists were routinely lumped with Communists anyway, how could she know? Murray told Ware, "Would prefer not to fight—but the issues are so entertwined—race, sex, liberal academic tradition—each of us must hold his ground wherever he is." She tried to move past this "shattering blow to my self-esteem," accepting Pauline's counsel that it was a test of her character. But this time she couldn't move on: "I was undergoing a crisis of my own faith, screaming against the unfairness of life and asking myself whether my years of struggle to prepare myself had been worth it if I was to be chopped down at the very moment I reached for my greatest opportunity. I was standing at a cross-roads in my career, not knowing which way to turn." Her family tradition called her to abide in faith and hope, but Cornell had "ruthlessly stripped me of individuality and discarded me like unwanted refuse."[85]

In that intensely grieving state she had a moment of illumination, triggered by the phrase "past associations." Cornell had shamed her by identifying her with left-wing organizations of questionable loyalty. But the Workers Defense League was not the story of Murray's life. She was deeply American and proud of it, by family tradition. Her grandfather Fitzgerald was of African, French, and Irish descent, born a free person in Delaware. He fought for the Union, American democracy, and freedom, and he fathered a quintessentially American family. Murray's past associations that really mattered were the Fitzgeralds: "They had instilled in me a pride in my American heritage and a rebellion against injustice." Her "best answer" to Cornell, she reflected, was to tell her family story.[86]

Proud Shoes, which Murray published in 1956, centered on Robert Fitzgerald and his wife, Cornelia Fitzgerald, a woman of African and Native American descent who had a slave-owning white father. Robert came off better because Cornelia esteemed prominent white people and her own white heritage too highly, notwithstanding that her mother was repeatedly raped. Robert Fitzgerald was a teenager when the *Dred Scott* decision denied his humanity. Murray stressed that *Dred Scott* left her grandfather and all other free persons of color "stranded at a halfway station between slaves and citizens." Robert Fitzgerald, in her telling, devoted his life to showing that he was worthy of citizenship. Thus he helped to expand the idea of American citizenship to include black Americans. Whites and blacks in America, Murray said, were more deeply and widely related than they usually acknowledged. America became great by producing strong, civic-minded, multiracial families like the Fitzgeralds, and America would become greater when it embraced its relatedness. Murray compared America's racial tangle to the biblical story of Abraham, Sarah, and Hagar. Abraham banished his slave Hagar and their son Ishmael to the desert after his wife Sarah belatedly gave birth to Isaac. To Murray, Cornelia Fitzgerald's mother epitomized the Hagar figure, and America itself was an Ishmaelite tangle, still in denial about tangible relatedness steeped in slavery and rape.[87]

Relatedness was not an optimistic trope for Murray; it was realistic, blood-soaked, complex, and geared toward reconciliation. Murray ended *Proud Shoes* with a poignant image. Robert Fitzgerald died in 1919 and was buried on a

cemetery hillside just outside a white cemetery, between Durham and Chapel
Hill. At the age of ten Murray adopted a Memorial Day tradition of planting a
U.S. flag on her grandfather's grave. This solitary American flag waved amid a
sea of Confederate flags, representing, to Murray, "an act of hunger and defiance." Murray lingered at the grave, wanting white people to see her. The flag
"bore mute testimony to the irrefutable fact that I was an American," she wrote.
It refuted the symbols of inferiority that white southerners paraded: "Whatever
else they denied me, they could not take from me this right and the undimin-
ished stature it gave me. For there at least at Grandfather's grave with the
American flag in my hands, I could stand very tall and in proud shoes."[88]

Proud Shoes won mostly favorable reviews and few readers. Murray took
particular delight in the *New York Herald Tribune* review, which accurately
described the book as a fusion of personal memoir, history, biography, and
dramatic fiction, "written in anger, but without hatred." She began writing
the book just before Adlai Stevenson launched his first presidential campaign,
and she finished it just before Stevenson launched his second campaign.
Murray liked Stevenson very much, having worked with Lloyd Garrison in 1952
to win black votes for Stevenson in New York. Four years later the national politics of race had changed dramatically. The *Brown* decision had come down,
Montgomery erupted, and Stevenson tried to placate angry southern Democrats
with his fateful statement about proceeding gradually, which divided his
defenders. Then he proposed a moratorium on the integration issue for all presidential candidates. Eleanor Roosevelt rallied embarrassed liberal Democrats,
urging that this was political and Stevenson was still as liberal as they were.
Murray furiously disagreed, writing to Roosevelt, "Civil rights cannot be dealt
with with moderate feelings. It involves a passion for justice and for human
decency, and if Mr. Stevenson has not felt this passion, then he does not belong
in the White House." Back and forth they debated whether Stevenson should
prize party unity or defend the *Brown* decision. Stevenson stuck to the Roosevelt
strategy of courting southern support, and Murray went through the motions
with Garrison in New York, wanly asking black New Yorkers to vote for Stevenson
again. The campaign was frustrating and demoralizing for her plus futile.
Shortly after the campaign ended, however, Murray's life turned another corner,
as Garrison persuaded his prestigious firm, Paul, Weiss, Rifkind, Wharton, and
Garrison, to hire her as an associate attorney. Murray's years of scratching for a
bare living were over.[89]

It helped that Garrison strongly identified with his fabled family tradition of
civil rights militancy, and he had represented the poet Langston Hughes when
he was hauled before HUAC. Murray struggled at first, negotiating Garrison's

world of corporate clients and gleam, and she never felt comfortable in it. But she gave three years to corporate law and marked it as a valuable experience, especially for the personal bond she developed with Garrison's office manager, Irene (Renee) Barlow. In 1959 Murray defended the Monroe, North Carolina, NAACP president Robert F. Williams after Wilkins fired him for making aggressive statements to the press about retaliatory violence. Murray told the NAACP national board that Williams had merely defended—verbally and heatedly—the right to self-defense that every board member took for granted. Williams operated in a context of flagrant white violence against blacks, which had to be taken into account. The board listened respectfully to Murray and upheld Williams's firing. Williams had embarrassed the NAACP; more important, he represented a shifting, angry mood among black Americans that made the NAACP board nervous.[90]

That year Murray's friend Maida Springer went to a conference in Ghana and returned with news that the newly established law school in Accra had faculty openings. Murray applied immediately. She was restless and not disposed to spend the rest of her career in a corporate assembly line. She had never traveled outside the United States and had no inkling of the coming sit-in explosion. Murray arrived in Accra in February 1960 to a just-completed law school wedged between the Parliament House and Supreme Court building. The National Assembly convened, debating a proposed constitution and plebiscite. Three months later the plebiscite voted to make Ghana a republic and elected Kwame Nkrumah as president. Murray found much of it exciting but opposed Nkrumah's authoritarian impulse, and she grieved at missing the sit-ins back home: "The moment of action had come when I was thousands of miles from home."[91]

She gave sixteen months to Ghana, teaching the new republic's first course on constitutional and administrative law at a law school. She suffered through malaria, bridled at the slow pace of life, marveled at the dignified bearing and courtesy of even the poorest locals, and protested that she had never employed a servant and did not want one. On most things, Murray coped and adjusted. On Nkrumah, her days were numbered from early on, as Murray held out for Western civil liberties and supported Nkrumah's rival, J. B. Danquah, a distinguished lawyer and former independence leader. Murray found herself feeling more and more American. In December 1960 she wrote an essay, "What Is Africa to Me?—A Question of Identity." She answered that she was very much an American. No longer would she say, "I am American, too," which implied in the "too" that black Americans were additions to America, not integral to it. She was American, period. She denied that embracing her multiple origins made her ashamed of her race. Her family came from too many unknown places for her to have sentimental feelings about any putative ancestral site. In Ghana she flushed with revulsion upon hearing a chief banter casually about his family's longtime involvement in the slave trade. Every day people commented on her light color and her American speech, gait, and thinking. Murray reflected, "I am beginning to understand that I am the product of a new history which began on African shores but which has not been shared by Africans, a history accompanied by such radical changes in a new environment that over time it produced a new identity. For me, the net gain of coming to Africa has been to reexperience imaginatively this break in continuity as well as to gain an appreciation for the peoples and cultures who remained on the African side of the historical divide."[92]

She caught a break when Yale legal scholar Fowler Harper visited Ghana and befriended her. Harper shared Murray's apprehension that Nkrumah did not respect the rule of law and would not tolerate, for long, her approach to constitutional law. Harper stunned her with a proposal: Why not come to Yale to earn a doctorate? It was not too late for her to do it, and he would secure a fellowship for her. Murray had never considered such a thing, but Harper was persistent; the following fall she was a graduate student, with classmates fresh from the sit-ins, notably Eleanor Holmes (Norton) and Marian Wright (Edelman). Eleanor Roosevelt died in November 1962; Murray grieved at the passing of her beloved friend: "She had filled the landscape of my entire adult life." Murray marched twice in the March on Washington, first with the Washington, DC, chapter of the ACLU, then with members of her congregation at St. Mark's Church-in-the-Bowery of New York City. She enjoyed the day but bristled at the token attention given to women. She respected King's achievements but considered him a typical preacher chauvinist. Murray was offended when King hauled a huge delegation to Oslo without taking Rosa Parks. Then she protested that King and the ministers consigned women to support work.[93]

In 1964 Murray had a role in the lobbying campaign to keep the word "sex" in Title VII of the Civil Rights Act after it passed the House of Representatives. Murray knew from a lifetime of struggle that it was often impossible to determine whether race or gender was the primary cause of discrimination against a black woman. She pressed the point forcefully after Title VII was adopted with the word "sex" included, imploring legal scholars and movement activists not to compel a false choice. Murray's work in this area put her at the forefront of a fledgling women's movement and subsequently contributed to feminist versions of critical race theory emphasizing intersectional or synthetic identity.

Essentially she extended her theory of complex identity to the American legal system, writing her dissertation on this subject, although American courts subsequently compelled the false choice, requiring claims about discrete acts of discrimination. Murray's dissertation surveyed the role of black inferiority myths in nineteenth-century American history and law, contending that deliverance from America's racial pathology was a complex matter because multiple factors produced it.[94]

In 1965 Murray became the first black American to earn a doctor of juridical science degree at Yale University. Her friend and advisor, Harper, died before she graduated, requiring an emergency advisor switch. Murray knew what she owed to the white liberals who opened doors for her. She relied on her capacity to make friends and was good at giving and receiving. Her next influential friend, Betty Friedan—the mother of American second-wave feminism—came along shortly after Harper died and Murray graduated from Yale. Murray blasted the Equal Employment Opportunity Commission (EEOC) for failing to enforce the Title VII prohibition, and Friedan reached out to Murray. A friendship bloomed. The following June Friedan and Murray launched the National Organization for Women (NOW) at an EEOC conference, beginning with twenty women in Friedan's hotel room. Murray and Friedan are officially credited with writing the organization's statement of purpose, although Murray said in her memoir that Friedan wrote it: "To take action to bring women into full participation in the mainstream of American society now, exercising all privileges and responsibilities thereof in truly equal partnership with men." Murray wanted to believe that this civil rights movement would not marginalize her like the other one, but that is what happened. She resigned from the NOW board in 1967, privately but angrily, and subsequently fell away from the organization. NOW fixated on white middle-class issues, it did not want to hear that things were different for black women, and Murray clashed with the founders.[95]

Though Murray made friends wherever she went, she also had a record of repelling people, especially prospective employers and colleagues, for which she reproached herself. She applied for numerous faculty positions that seemed promising but never panned out. She pinned her hopes on the EEOC, applying for a commissioner position, but did not get it. In 1967 Murray took an administrative position at Benedict College in Columbia, South Carolina, running a school retention program with minimal satisfaction. That December she made a list of her faults in her journal. It was unsparing: "Undue sensitivity; fierce outbursts of resentful anger; acquisitive in an egotistic way; lack of cooperation with associates; intuitive rather than professional; redoubtable opponent; administrative talents not outstanding; selfishness; deceit; vanity; much self-approbation;

vindictive; bullying; unscrupulous disposition; cunning methods in gaining goals; slow to admit error; fault-finding; ill-nature; tendency toward copying and plagiarism." Blaming herself seemed to help, at least a little. Murray wanted to believe that some of this situation was in her control. If she got hold of her volatility and ego, she might still get what she wanted.[96]

On April 4, 1968, Murray happened to be reading *The Autobiography of Malcolm X*. Malcolm said that nobody knew whether he or King would be killed first, and that the same thing was true of the fate of his approach and of King's. That evening Murray made a pledge: "The foremost advocate of nonviolence as a way of life—my own cause—was stilled and those who had embraced Dr. King's religious commitment to nonviolence were called upon to keep his tradition alive and to advance the work for which he gave his life."[97]

BLACK POWER AND THE WAY OF KING

Her life accelerated dramatically. Murray resigned from Benedict and returned to New York just before Robert Kennedy was assassinated. Eugene Carson Blake's office cabled from Geneva, asking Murray to participate in the upcoming World Council of Churches Assembly in Uppsala, Sweden. Blake had taken over as general secretary of the WCC in 1966, which proposed at Uppsala to combat the racism of European civilization and its long-reaching ravages. Murray regarded herself as a secular type who belonged to an Episcopal congregation. She had no experience in the ecumenical movement, partly owing to her lay status in a clerical denomination. She was too worldly to have considered ordination, which was not open to her anyway. And she held stereotypes about other denominations, which she happily discarded at Uppsala, "one of those peak experiences seldom duplicated in a lifetime."[98]

The Uppsala assembly gathered 704 delegates from 235 member churches. It issued strong statements against racism, economic injustice, and war, and the shadow of King hung over the assembly, as King had been slated to give the opening address. Murray worked as a WCC staffer and made new friends, especially WCC staffer Rena Karefa-Smart, who later taught at Howard University. The pageantry and devotional atmosphere of the assembly enthralled Murray. She heard James Baldwin address the assembly, she participated in a Women's Caucus that demanded female speakers and officials, and she was disappointed when Eleanor Roosevelt went unmentioned on Human Rights Night. Altogether it was a transforming experience for Murray, changing her sense of herself and her story. Religion had not been the wellspring or context of her work, but the ecumenical movement was undeniably committed to antiracist activism, and now she had friends who conceived the church as an important site of the battle against sexism. Murray returned to New York inspired "to proclaim through my own life and work the universal sisterhood and brotherhood I experienced during those eighteen days."[99]

In that mood and moment she joined the faculty of Brandeis University, a triumph that quickly turned traumatizing, followed by ambiguous success. Brandeis president Morris Abram tracked down Murray just before she headed to Uppsala. A one-year teaching offer arrived just after Murray returned, asking her to teach in the American Civilization program and to help develop a program in Afro-American studies. Murray was excited, viewing the offer as a career breakthrough. She reasoned that she was uniquely qualified to combine prelaw courses with establishing Afro-American studies as a field. She felt like a "teenage college freshman" while pulling into the Brandeis campus in Waltham, Massachusetts, not anticipating how she would be received. To Murray, racial integration was fundamentally an experience of individual mind and spirit, a coming to awareness of the interconnectedness and common humanity of all humankind. She conceived Afro-American studies as an integral part of the study of American civilization; thus the two halves of her teaching position folded together. Immediately her classroom at Brandeis felt like a battleground to her. Brandeis had recently doubled its black student enrollment from 58 to 120, in a student body of 1,200. It launched a "pre-freshman" program for students lacking a high school diploma or a college preparatory background, and Murray drew a difficult mix of white seniors and black "pre-freshmen" in the first class she taught. More important, as she later put it, Brandeis was like many other predominantly white colleges in 1968, rocked by "the convulsions of Negro student rebellion [that] spread like a contagious madness."[100]

Murray defended her use of the term "Negro," to her a term of pride and dignity, unlike "black," a term pressed into confusing double duty as a describing word (color) and a naming word (race). Most of her black students were less individualistic than she was and far more strengthened by a collective identity claim. Murray grasped the difference intellectually, but that did not help her communicate with her students. She was uncomfortable in any group that was not racially and sexually diverse. Murray's sense of herself as individuated, intersectional, and complex militated against any single category of self-identification: "To thrive, I needed a society that was hospitable to all comers." Some students lectured her about Black Power, which offended her: "From the moment I arrived on campus, I was thrown into fundamental philosophical and moral conflict with the advocates of a black ideology as alien to my nature and as difficult for me to accept as white ethnocentrism. This emerging racial rhetoric smacked of an ethnic 'party line' and made absolutely no sense to me; in turn, some of my most deeply held values about universal human dignity were considered obsolete by young black radicals."[101]

Murray tried not to bait the militant students, always a minority in her classes, but her resentment showed through. If they were really against white society and integration, why were they at Brandeis? Her students at Benedict, she recalled, had faced much worse repression with more grace: "Thus at Brandeis I was wholly unprepared for the bellicose postures of their northern counterparts in the peaceful, friendly surroundings of a New England suburban campus." Murray was heartbroken to be scorned as a Big House servant after years of waiting for this professional opportunity: "Far from providing leadership in a new and constructive phase of civil rights, I found myself in a head-on collision with those whom I most wanted to serve." Classroom discussions were strained, punctuated by tense exchanges between Murray and black students. There was a lot of looking down and looking away, especially by white students, while Murray pined for honest give-and-take. By her lights she stood her ground, judging that the new cultural nationalism was "misplaced." When Murray thought about cultural nationalism, she remembered the derision she received in West Africa. She shuddered at witnessing demands for separate residence halls and dining areas: "For a time, I was living in a world turned upside down."[102]

A group of white female students complained to Murray that she pitched her course too low, aiming at the back row of students. Murray was mortified; she wanted a tenure-track appointment and could not afford to disappoint high-achieving students. Promptly she switched to engaging the front row. In January 1969 a group of black students at Brandeis went on strike, at first in solidarity with a strike at San Francisco State College. Both strikes were part of the Black Campus Movement sweeping the country, demanding autonomous Afro-American studies departments. At Brandeis the students occupied the building containing Murray's office, which infuriated her: "I could barely suppress my rage over the violation of my privacy, which I considered just short of a physical violation of my person." Murray sorted out her feelings, aware that she was not reacting to just one thing. The new cultural nationalism offended her morally and ideologically, and she loathed its sexist ethos. Above all, the new militancy seemed crude and self-defeating to her, a "withdrawal into a self-imposed segregation" that masked a fear of failing in an open and competitive society. Murray protested that the academy was supposed to operate on the basis of reason and dialogue, not coercion, blackmail, and extortion. She wrote in her journal, "Why can't I be proud of these kids for what they have done? Because I think they have used the lowest, crudest form of protest and they are getting away with it and this will lead them to believe that this is the only way to win victories."[103]

She could not see the Black Campus Movement as an extension of the civil rights movement to the academy, even after it transformed the academy, creating over three hundred departments, centers, and institutes in black studies, and even though Murray benefited from it. The movement made her suddenly very employable, with leverage. Murray's position was converted to tenure track; later she was named to an endowed chair, as Louis Stulberg Professor of Law and Politics; and she watched Brandeis struggle to meet the demand for additional black faculty: "We were competing with other major colleges and universities seeking the same scholars." In her telling, however, the "suddenly burgeoning demand for 'black studies taught by black faculty' " diminished her achievements and the integrity of the academy, creating walled-off departments reserved for blacks. She said it angrily, which shaped her legacy at Brandeis. Brandeis built an Afro-American studies program in which Murray played almost no role. She became a popular teacher, offering courses on the Constitution, civil rights, and women and society, all in American studies. In this work she made seminal contributions to legal studies and women's studies, deepening her own feminist identity and helping Brandeis make the transition from a mushy American Civilization program to a credentialed American Studies Department. Nearly all of Murray's students were white; as she put it, "Only a handful of black students ventured into my classes." Murray insisted that black students shunned her courses because she taught rigorous courses. To her, she said, the ideological issue was secondary; the main thing was academic integrity. She did not indulge the "intellectual laziness" of students seeking an easy pass because that would not help them become intellectually competent. In her later years at Brandeis Murray attracted a few more black students, but never more than a few.[104]

This was not the career she had sought. Murray did not like Forman's Black Manifesto, finding it narrow and sexist. She implored her home parish, St. Mark's Church-in-the-Bowery, and her Massachusetts bishop, John Burgess, to stop taking it seriously. During her Brandeis years Murray renewed close relationships with two friends from her experience in Ghana, Harold Isaacs and Viola Isaacs. Harold was a political scientist at the Massachusetts Institute of Technology, Viola was a social worker, and both had worked with the Crossroads Africa project. Harold Isaacs reasoned that Murray was like Viola and him in being a rootless type who found her way to an identity through migration and cross-cultural mingling. His book *Idols of the Tribe* was a touchstone for Murray, as was Murray's friendship with a young, white feminist she met through Ware, Mary Norris. Norris made a suggestion that proved enlightening for Murray: Whenever she was tempted to erupt over black militancy at Brandeis, try substituting the words "women" or "women's liberation" for "black." The women's movement, too, had plenty of angry separatist voices, but Murray sympathized with them, mostly cheered them on, and did not feel diminished by them. Murray later reflected, "Mary helped to soften my harsh estimate of what was happening at Brandeis. I began to see that much of my barely disguised hostility toward the Black Revolution was in reality my feminist resentment of the crude sexism I perceived in many of the male leaders of that movement."[105]

Had Murray not cut herself off from black freedom activists in Boston, she might have met women who shared her feelings. As it was, she relied on white friends for feminist insight. In 1970, contributing to a landmark feminist reader, Mary Lou Thompson's *Voices of the New Feminism*, Murray put it bluntly: "Reading through much of the current literature on the Black Revolution, one is left with the impression that for all the rhetoric about self-determination, the main thrust of black militancy is a bid of black males to share power with white males in a continuing patriarchal society in which both black and white females are relegated to a secondary status." Murray countered that black women suffered under interlocking triads of racial, sexual, and class oppression. Oppression was weblike; thus every one-factor concept of liberation was inadequate. Though she opposed the triumph of "black" over "Negro," Murray bowed to its usage in Thompson's book: "In the face of their multiple disadvantages, it seems clear that black women can neither postpone nor subordinate the fight against sex discrimination to the Black Revolution." It was a matter of "sheer survival" for black women to do so on behalf of themselves and their children, she urged. Otherwise "the outlook for their children will be bleak indeed." Black women had an "equal stake in women's liberation and black liberation" and thus stood distinctly at the juncture of both movements: "By asserting a leadership role in the growing feminist movement, the black woman can help to keep it allied to the objectives of black liberation while simultaneously advancing the interests of all women."[106]

Murray had two lodestars as she made her way in the 1970s: Eleanor Roosevelt and Martin Luther King Jr. To her, these were the two great exemplars of her time because they showed the power of ethical, democratic, Christian love in the struggle for universal human dignity. Murray did not anticipate, in the early 1970s, where she was heading. Winning the Stulberg chair was a great honor for her, she enjoyed teaching constitutional law, and she was a leading figure in the feminist movement, albeit embattled behind the scenes. She had begun to write her memoir, fitfully but with determination. Ware told Murray that her first draft was not in a league with *Proud Shoes*, a book that knew what it was about from the title page onward. The new book, still lacking a title, also lacked an organizing idea. Ware advised Murray to decide whether the book was primarily psychological or sociopolitical. Murray agreed completely. She told Ware that she had known what she was doing in *Proud Shoes:* telling a family story that refuted Cornell University, back when she was a hungry artist "with tremendous nervous energy." Now she was a big-name professor and not so hungry.[107]

But that was a superficial explanation. Murray was on a spiritual journey without realizing it. The first draft of her memoir was scattered and laborious, with flashes of brilliance, because her own deepest story was missing from it. She wrote *Song in a Weary Throat* before realizing how important her Christian faith was to her. Then she spent the rest of her life periodically touching it up and writing the last chapter. When Murray thought about Roosevelt and King, she thought about their ethical religion—how it drove and sustained them. She was supposedly less religious than her exemplars, and it still mattered that she had a clerical Episcopalian idea of holiness in her head, although the ecumenical movement shook some of that out of her.

Her involvement in feminist church activism carried her to the brink of a religious awakening. Murray gave her name to various feminist church groups, willing to be the first or only person of color in some of them. Thelma Stevens hooked Murray for Church Women United, and Murray had a role in numerous ad hoc groups advocating the ordination of women and support of gays and lesbians in the Episcopal Church. For a while, in 1970, Murray stopped going to church out of anger that the church did not ordain women. Feminist activism in the church came readily to her, whether or not she attended services. Being present to her own spiritual being was something else. It did not happen to her until her beloved partner Renee Barlow fell ill with a brain tumor in January 1973. Barlow and Murray had taken vacations together in Montego Bay, Jamaica, and Barlow took care of her frail, aged mother in New York City. Murray had no experience of end-of-life care giving or decision making until Barlow fell gravely ill. While Barlow lay dying, it occurred to Murray that she had never thought about her own death. Belatedly thinking about it drove Murray to seek holy orders, knowing that the movement for women's ordination was gaining ground in the Episcopal Church.

This explanation of her call to ministry would not have satisfied many bishops and Commissions on Ministry. Murray wavered between saying that her whole life had led to this moment and saying that Barlow's death threw her into a dazed and overwhelmed conviction of being called, an unexpected intrusion that she struggled against. Pinn rightly says that Murray was not certain of what she believed about the call to ministry, notably her own. But many ordination candidates go through a similar process of questioning, doubting, and being challenged. Murray's vivid sense of being called won the support of Burgess, and Murray told her department chair at Brandeis, Lawrence Fuchs, that her academic obligations had become draining to her "without replenishing one's spiritual reservoir." She resigned her chair and headed for General Theological Seminary in New York at the age of sixty-three, telling her friends and family, "As most of you know, I am in the tradition of the late Dr. Martin Luther King and more and more have been led to believe that the core of our troubles—alienation because of race and sex, political corruption, economic dislocation, senseless violence—is in the moral and spiritual realm. I have felt increasingly inadequate as both a lawyer and a teacher in addressing myself to these social issues as well as to human interrelationships. The missing element in my training was theological."[108]

To become fully herself, she had to become a theologian. She needed to know what King absorbed before his ministry began. And she wanted to minister to aging people, as she had done for Barlow, and serve them as a priest at the end, unlike what she was able to do for Barlow. Seminary was hard for Murray, "the most rigorous discipline I had ever encountered, surpassing by far the rigors of my law school training." She struggled with theological scholarship and the scrutiny of teachers and students. General Seminary seethed and stewed over the ordination controversy. It had female candidates for ordination in a denomination that did not ordain women; it had students, professors, and administrators who chafed at the controversy; and Murray acquired a reputation as an aggressive, snarky student. She was the only black female student and the oldest student. Her legal training accustomed her to thrust-and-parry wrangling, which failed seminary standards of pastoral sensitivity. Students complained that she interrupted them in midsentence and dominated class discussions. Murray had not given up a prestigious chair at Brandeis to be silenced at seminary. She could be wounded by criticism but did not let it stifle her voice. The coursework, to her, was challenging; otherwise the school was sadly mediocre. Murray told a classmate that she held "a dim view of the institution," especially the students: "There are times when I look at my fellow Seminarians and say, 'God, help the Church!' THIS DOES NOT HAVE TO BE." General Seminary, she judged, was long on individual talent and woefully short on leadership and fellowship.[109]

The General Convention of 1973 approached, and Murray declined to go: "Given my volatile temperament, it was providential that I did not go to the General Convention of 1973." The pioneers of women's ordination got rough treatment at the convention. Murray later recalled ruefully that one of them, Carter Heyward, admonished her for playing it safe. There were fractious debates at General Seminary about using direct action tactics at religious observances, and in 1974 three bishops ordained Heyward and ten other women without permission of the convention, setting off an uproar in the national church. Two years later the General Convention approved women's ordination. Murray completed her studies amid this drama, learning that seminaries brawled much like other institutions over things political. She threw herself as fully as possible into the life, rhythms, idioms, and practices of General Seminary, adjusting to its Anglo-Catholic conservatism, although Murray had spent most of her life in progressive modernist congregations. She pushed the seminary to expand its provincial canon of topics, and she pushed back when criticized, telling a classmate, "Try to imagine for 24 hours what it must be like to be a Negro in a predominantly white seminary, a woman in an institution dominated by men and for the convenience of men, some of whom radiate hostility even though they do not say a word, who are patronizing and kindly as long as I do not get out of my place, but who feel threatened by my intellect, my achievements, and my refusal to be suppressed." Murray accepted that Christians were called to be Suffering Servants, "but nobody said a Suffering Servant couldn't scream when it hurts."[110]

She took her third year of seminary at Virginia Theological Seminary in Alexandria, Virginia. To Murray, the rural and commuter ethos of Virginia Seminary was a welcome respite from the urban, residential, and boiling atmosphere of General. It was also welcome for a sentimental reason. Murray undertook her field training at Saint Philip's Chapel in Maryland, where her uncle John E. G. Small had long served during her youth and she had visited him. Her papers at Virginia built upon two years of theological training, although Murray concluded that seminaries should add one year to their basic degree programs, as three years were not enough to absorb a seminary curriculum. At General and Virginia she tracked the debate between Cone and Roberts over the future of black theology and similar arguments between Mary Daly and Rosemary Ruether over feminist theology. Murray wrote several papers on these topics, culminating in a master's thesis that called for intersectional fusions of black theology and feminist theology.

The early Cone epitomized what Murray did not like in the new black radicalism, and Murray rejected more abruptly the separatist arguments of Daly, since Daly was on her way out of Christianity. Murray judged that Cone was narrow and dogmatic, his "racial exclusiveness" smacked of arrogance, and all of this went hand in hand with the sexism of Black Power militancy. On every major point Roberts came out better in Murray's rendering. Roberts was not narrow or dogmatic, he was interested in other religions, he put reconciliation at the center of Christian theology, and he did not employ invective against whites in general. Murray judged that Roberts was much closer than Cone to King's ethic of reconciliation and nonviolence. Moreover, Roberts was right not to disavow King's dream of the beloved community. All three figures were sexists, Murray noted. She tried to imagine Roberts expounding on a female Christ and could not do it. Even Roberts fixated on one kind of oppression, despite his generous spirit. But otherwise she liked Roberts, telling friends she wanted to engage him personally, which happened in 1975.[111]

In Murray's rendering of Cone versus Roberts, they had profoundly different projects. She missed the crucial point of commonality between Cone and Roberts because it was the root of everything else that she rejected in Cone— his emphasis on blackness. Murray rejected the claim to blackness that defined black theology, notwithstanding that Roberts shared it. Murray censured Cone for fixating on a false polarity of black against white, overlooking that Cone conceived blackness as a racial term *and* as a symbol of the struggle against complex forms of oppression implicated in various relations of power. Cone could imagine white people becoming black to be saved, even if it rarely happened. His double use of "black" exploited the ambiguity that Murray had resisted when "Negro" gave way to "black" in American usage. To Cone and Roberts, the point of black theology was to privilege black experience, and blackness was a symbol of liberation. Murray believed deeply, and rightly, that a flat concept of blackness was an obstacle to grasping the intersectional complexity of identities. She long anticipated the influential critique of onto-logical blackness that Vanderbilt ethicist Victor Anderson put forth in 1995. But the concept of blackness that fired early black theology countered white supremacy like nothing else. It remained a powerful source of identity claims and antiracist politics long after it was challenged by poststructuralist criticism, and there would have been no early black theology without it—a point that Murray misconstrued in obscuring Roberts's debt to it.[112]

Murray's seminary career culminated with a thesis in which she contended that black theologians and feminist theologians needed to learn from each other. Cone and Daly, Murray wrote, had too much in common as "ultraradi-cals," despite being opposites. Her exposition of Cone centered on two quota-tions. The first was about God: "Black theology refuses to accept a God who is not identified totally with the goals of the black community. If God is not for us and against white people, then he is a murderer, and we had better kill him." The second was about reconciliation: "All talk about reconciliation with white oppressors, with mutual dialogue about its meaning, has no place in black power or Black Theology." Murray said that Cone's statement about God was "foreign to Christian doctrine," but she did not explain what he meant by it, dismissing it on shock value and doctrinal "foreignness." Thus she missed her chance to explicate the liberationist logic of Cone's version of black theology. The second quotation raised an ethical question that she probed a bit more deeply, explaining that Cone was averse to letting white people say what reconciliation should mean. Here, at least, was a familiar issue straight from the founding of the Black Power movement. Cone conceived the black struggle for liberation as "a closed circle," Murray explained. He did not prize mutual dialogue, and his understanding of the Christian gospel did not compel him to do so. Murray engaged this claim more seriously because it exactly contradicted—or seemed to in the mid-1970s—what she believed about black theology and feminist theology needing each other.[113]

Murray rejoiced that finally there were prominent theologians who privileged the experiences of women in construing the meaning of Christianity and everything else. Daly and Ruether were most prominent; Murray also mentioned Yale theologian Letty Russell. Murray aligned herself with Ruether's inclusive, multidimensional perspective and confirmed Ruether's warning that an "undeclared war" was brewing between the black and feminist theological movements. This conflict was a throwback to the schism in the abolitionist movement over the Reconstruction amendments, Murray said. It was avoidable, but not if black theologians continued to spurn what Ruether called "reciprocal solidarity with the women's movement." Murray quoted Ruether again: "Far from being open to the question of female oppression, the model of black liberation has appeared to be modeled after the super-male chauvinist traditions." Murray endorsed Ruether's diagnosis, and her prescription that racism and sexism should be conceived as "interstructural elements within the overarching system of white male domination." Black theology, Ruether said, had to become feminist, and feminist theology had to "integrate the experience of black and poor women." Otherwise each was an obstacle to liberation.[114]

Murray did not mention that Ruether herself had not yet done it. It was enough that she had the right project. Murray knew very well what might go wrong in feminist theology; she had already seen it in the upper reaches of NOW. The liberation theology that was needed, she urged, would interrogate the intersections of sex, race, and class oppression. It would not identify "the suffering of a particular group with righteousness and redemption," a tendency that was "particularly strong in Cone's writings." Closed circles were notorious for producing self-righteousness, a mistake that no feminist theology should make, although Murray noted that closed-off feminist theologies already existed. She could imagine a better liberation theology on the way, but to be truly better it had to resist the hierarchy-of-oppression models that fixed on one source of evil at the expense of universal liberation. Murray had a definite idea of where it would come from. "There is a dearth of black women theologians," she observed. That had to change. It remained to be seen who would come forward to interrogate theologically the intersections of racism and sexism within black culture and experience. Murray did not quite live to see the emergence of womanist theology and ethics in the late 1980s. Most of the founders came out of Union Theological Seminary, where nearly all studied under Cone and were supported by him, notably Katie Cannon, Jacquelyn Grant, and Delores S. Williams.[115]

Murray's ministry was surprisingly quiet, even traditional, serving as an associate pastor for two years at Church of the Atonement in Washington, DC, and briefly as a supply priest at a mission church in Baltimore. Her sermons were grounded in the social gospel and theologically liberal, with an existentialist bent. She lauded King as the exemplar of social justice religion and cited him far more than anyone else. On matters theological she usually cited Tillich or Anglican theologian John Macquarrie, favoring existential tropes in both cases. In 1975 she declared, "I do not need to make special pleading for my sex—male or female, or in-between—to bolster self-esteem. When I truly believe that God is my Father and Mother, in short, my Creator, I am bound also to believe that all men, women, and children of whatever race, color, creed, or ethnic origin, are my sisters-and-brothers-in-Christ, whether they are Anglicans, Roman Catholics, Methodists, Black Muslims, members of the Judaic faith, Russian Orthodox, Buddhists, or atheists." Repeatedly she expounded on that theme, often citing "our own great prophet of the twentieth century, the late Dr. Martin Luther King Jr."[116]

Sometimes she started with her own story and moved outward: "My entire life's quest has been for spiritual integration, and this quest has led me ultimately to Christ, in whom there is no East or West, no North or South, no Black or White, no Red or Yellow, no Jew or Gentile, no Islam or Buddhist, no Baptist, Methodist, Episcopalian, or Roman Catholic, no Male or Female. There is no Black Christ, no White Christ, no Red Christ—although these images may have transitory cultural value. There is only Christ, the Spirit of Love and reconciliation, the healer of deep psychic wounds, drawing us all closer to that goal of perfection that links us to God our Creator and to eternity." Sometimes she enlisted a text such as the Mary and Martha story in Luke 10 to support her social gospel universalism: "I believe that the heart of the gospel message in the two Great Commandments means that Christians are called by God to transform the world, to work for a more just and humane history to the end that God's will *is* done on earth."[117]

Repeatedly she spoke about suffering and the Suffering Servant in Anglican fashion, which emphasized the Incarnation, not Calvary. Murray's sermonizing on redemptive suffering was always a page from King, usually citing King's personal example. Christians, she said, are able to identify with the humanity of Jesus through their suffering. This subject was especially difficult and perilous for black American Christians, Murray acknowledged: "On the one hand, we strive for self-respect and pride in ourselves and our achievements against those who would deny our humanity and our personhood. On the other hand, we are told that self-pride is a stumbling block to salvation." Murray did not claim that she had a solution to this problem; thus she was compelled to wrestle with it constantly. Always she got her bearings and held her position by thinking about King. King's critics accused him of exaggerating the power of nonviolence and sacrificial love divine, but King stood on the word of Jesus, and he glimpsed the true problem when he added a word to Jesus: "The struggle is not between black and white, but between good and evil."[118]

Murray had studied Macquarrie's *Principles of Christian Theology* in seminary, which became her theological base-text for sermons. She expounded Macquarrie's concept of the ministry of reconciliation as human cooperation in the divine work of letting-be. She cited Macquarrie on the gradual coming together of divinity and humanity in Jesus and all human beings, which Murray called "Christhood." She cited the fourteenth-century English mystic Julian of Norwich on the motherhood of God, commending Dame Julian's belief that "Divine Love holds the clue to all problems of existence, particularly the problem of evil." On Palm Sunday 1974, Murray asked her congregants to recall how they felt at Easter season six years previously, when "our own Dr. Martin Luther King made a triumphal march in Memphis." On the day of his death, she recalled, "he had planned to eat a meal of special delight with his disciple, colleague, and successor, the Reverend Abernathy." Moreover, "with his death by an assassin's bullet, the dream of justice with reconciliation seemed to die and throughout our nation cities went up in flames."[119]

Many ministers influenced by the social gospel and the civil rights movement preached in a similar fashion. Murray was a trailblazer of what progressive Christianity sounded like after liberal feminists entered the ministry in large numbers in the 1970s. She preached an all-are-welcome version of the social gospel with a feminist sensibility and a passionate commitment to renewing the civil rights movement. She preached redemptive suffering without saying that suffering itself is redemptive; suffering could be made redemptive when people accepted it in the spirit and way of Christ. She favored Macquarrie and Tillich on matters theological because their transhistorical existentialism fit her universalizing aim; plus Macquarrie was a convert to Anglicanism. Azaransky, commenting on Murray's sermons, was surprised that she preached King-style social gospel religion with a light feminist touch. Where were the debates about the historical Jesus, liberationist interpretations of Scripture, and feminist reconstructions of doctrine that Murray wrote about in her seminary papers? Murray, however, had a strong sense of what preached and what was appropriate in the pulpit. She had it long before she went to seminary, and she was reflective about what kept her in the faith. Theology was important to her, but she realized, unlike many newly minted clergy, that her seminary papers would not make good sermons. She became a priest in order to participate in the priesthood of Christ. A sermon, in her Episcopalian context, was never more than fifteen minutes and never the central thing. She was there to ask herself and help others discern what it meant to follow Christ in the modern world.[120]

That was King's question, as Murray emphasized. It linked her more profoundly to King after he was gone than it had during his lifetime because King's sexism repelled Murray and she had come late to her defining Christian commitment. For most of her life Murray was religious in the compartmentalized fashion of many churchgoers, which had room for ample skepticism and years of off-and-on actual churchgoing. Her family's Episcopal faith was an important feature of her story and identity, but she was more worldly, she thought, than the truly religious people she knew. Murray's churchy clericalism hindered her from claiming the spiritual sensibility she already had, and her early commitment to nonviolence was strategic and political. Even after her powerfully moving experience at Uppsala she had no clue about where she was heading because she was secular and priests were male. Though Murray embraced nonviolence as a strategy just before enrolling in law school, and she vowed on various occasions afterward to become more like King by making nonviolence her way of life, it never quite happened until she dropped Brandeis for seminary. In 1973, newly imbued with conviction, she explained, "I can no longer accept a purely fellowship role in the Church. It is not undue vanity to say that a comparatively long life of struggle, of prayer, of trying to follow Christ and the Cross should have produced some fruit which the Church could use to advance the kingdom of Heaven."[121]

Thus she got a late start on thinking theologically about racial justice. Murray did not read theology until she went to seminary. Then she immersed herself in it and reconsidered King's legacy. Her many subsequent references to King in her sermons were crafted to fit her sermon points: King exemplified the way of spirit of Christ. Though imperfect like all human beings, King was a Jesus figure who died for us. The King movement was a renewal of the Jesus movement, which had to be refashioned to address the challenges of a new age. Murray's appeals to King were usually idealized in way-of-Jesus fashion and short on sociohistorical or political complexity. She was comfortable with paradox and historical messiness on other subjects, most notably her trademark emphasis on intersectional identity, but when she appealed to King or the gospel, idealism prevailed and history got short shrift.

Murray did not place King in his black church and freedom movement contexts. King, in her telling, exemplified a gospel ideal that hurtled through the ages from Jesus to the present day. On occasion Murray told a story about Mary McLeod Bethune or National Woman's Party founder Alice Paul, but her rendering of the civil rights movement was habitually King-centered, ahistorical, and fixated on ideals, much like the King legend then taking shape. Johnson, Mays, and Thurman had no role in her account of the King movement, even though Murray knew all of them. Like the black social gospel forerunners she did not cite and the one she cited constantly, Murray conceived the love ethic of Jesus as a desperately needed and relevant social ideal. Had she historicized her references to King and the civil rights movement, Murray surely would have felt compelled to expound on its exploitation and marginalization of women; she was Example A of marginalization. But the church audiences to which she preached had not come to hear about that.

THE SOCIAL GOSPEL IN BLACK THEOLOGY

When Murray forecast beyond 1975, she started with a Tillichian premise that human existence is ambiguous and contradictory and so is the church, both individually and collectively. All victories over the problems of human life are transitory and fragmentary, and even breakthrough victories can be overturned by a succeeding generation. It was no easy thing to carry on King's legacy after he was gone, but Murray believed in taking moral responsibility for one's time. She predicted that a quaint nineteenth-century term, "people of color," was sure to make a comeback because no other term was sufficiently inclusive. "I categorically reject the term 'black,' " she declared. "Black" did not describe the multiple origins of many black Americans such as herself. It was a polarizing term marking racial separation, just like its opposite, "white"—another misguided category. Replacing "Negro" with "black" negated the dignity associated with uppercase identifications. "Black" did not register that Americans were more deeply related by social and cultural bonds than they were separated from each other. Murray urged her church audience not to assume that "black" had prevailed for all time. It would surely pass, hopefully soon, just as her generation had replaced "Colored" with "Negro." She comprehended, she said, why "black" suddenly became normative in the mid-1960s. She knew all about struggling for self-respect in a society that denigrated one's humanity on racial grounds. But in 1974 they were still living in the afterglow of the King era, and Murray said that the church needed to press ahead, standing for liberation *and* reconciliation.[122]

Murray did not say that the progressive religion she preached belonged to a tradition of black social Christianity. The social gospel had always been black *and* white, and Murray saw no reason to lift up forgotten social gospel leaders of any particular color, unless they were women. She knew very little about black social gospel founders such as Reverdy Ransom and Alexander Walters. The social gospel that mattered to her was the ecumenical one that crossed the color line—although Murray was an outsider to it for most of her career. Mordecai Johnson, to Murray, was the person who quashed her direct action organizing at Howard. Moreover, she knew many Howard faculty and students who tagged Johnson as a bully. So Johnson got minimal credit from Murray for his national civil rights activism. Murray and Mays never quite overlapped anywhere, and Mays was an insider in religious and activist organizations that marginalized Murray, so she never mentioned him in a memoir running 435 pages. Murray and Thurman had much in common, including FOR affiliations, universalism, mystical religion, and loner tendencies. Murray sought out Thurman for counseling at a low point at Howard, and later she supported Fellowship Church as a national associate. But neither wrote about the other. Had Murray come sooner to spiritual theology she could have found tropes in Thurman's work that she took from mystical scholar Evelyn Underhill and other authors assigned at General Seminary. But her theological education came late, and Thurman was not in it.

When history turned in 1968 it was said that black American Christianity had never produced a significant theologian and never privileged black experience as a point of departure for religious thinking. Roberts said it unequivocally, usually citing Joseph Washington for historical ballast. This oft-repeated judgment was spectacularly false as applied to King. It wrongly dismissed Mays and Thurman as religious thinkers. It unjustly erased the black social gospel tradition as though it had never existed. The existing black social gospel sustained the dream of a new abolition during the notorious "nadir" era. It provided allies for Du Bois in black churches and produced public intellectuals who crossed the color line. It provided the theology of social justice that fueled the King-era civil rights movement, and it struggled in a myriad of ways with the nationalist tradition that Black Power renewed. The black social gospel was not only a significant intellectual tradition; it was more accomplished and influential than its famous white counterpart. Usually the black social gospel was not granted the status of being a tradition, period. The usual alternative was to tag it as intellectually derivative and middle class, the dream of a tiny black bourgeoisie to integrate with white society.

The former dismissal was flat-out wrong, and the latter dismissal, though at least based on something real, had two problems. The first problem was that black social Christianity was more diverse ideologically than a simplistic idea of assimilation. All four traditions of black social Christianity engendered versions of nationalist feeling, and three of them produced versions of civil rights militancy. Even the exception on civil rights militancy—the school of Booker Washington—covertly supported resistance initiatives that it refrained from endorsing publicly. The language of black pride and social justice reverberated through the work of Ransom, Walters, William Simmons, Ida B. Wells, Adam Clayton Powell Sr., Nannie Burroughs, Richard R. Wright Jr., and J. Pius Barbour, laying social gospel groundwork for the figures featured in this book. All of the major founders took black experience as their point of departure, not imagining that they had any choice in the matter anyway. Moreover, the Socialist stream of black social Christianity later embraced by Johnson, Barbour, Mays, arguably Thurman, and King had wellsprings in black social gospel founders Ransom, George W. Woodbey, Robert W. Bagnall, and George Frazier Miller and in two lodestar allies, W. E. B. Du Bois and A. Philip Randolph.

Second, the idea that the black social gospel was discredited by its middle-class ethos is powerful as a species of corrective criticism, not as a basis for an alternative politics. Virtually every social justice movement acquires middle-class leaders and theorists who have to interrogate their complicity in the system. All reform movements rely on middle-class leaders and funding, and so do virtually all proletarian and liberationist movements, whatever they may say about from-the-bottom-only activism. The black social gospel was like the white social gospel in coming out of largely middle-class congregations where the ministers were seminary-educated and schooled in modern criticism. It preached about staying in school and building a better society for everyone. It would not have been more relevant or effective had its Socialist proponents like Ransom,

Johnson, Barbour, or King ridiculed middle-class values. Even democratic Socialism is a middle-class ideology, an attempt to lift the poor out of poverty and to curtail the excessive rewards of success under capitalism. King, more than anyone in his line, eventually rebelled against the limitations of a civil rights movement that benefited a select group and did not reach the teeming urban poor. But King would not have done better by saying that ministers like Johnson, Barbour, Thurman, and Mays spent their careers talking about the wrong things.

These figures provided King's model of what ministry should be. King knew that the social gospel reached further than Daddy King thought because King's middle-class models and graduate education had proved it. Soon King found himself at the head of a social movement that stormed into cities and raised hell, something his high-minded mentors never modeled. He got more and more radical along the way because the gospel pulled him far beyond his comfort zone, calling him to stand with the poorest of the poor, seeing the world from their purview. The fact that King was more radical than anyone around him proved hard to absorb after he was gone. There was too much to appropriate in the volatile aftermath of his death, and a powerful stereotyped image of him stood in the way of trying. Then the demands of domestication took over, making King unreal. The turn in this story did not occur until the 1980s, when Garrow's pioneering scholarship and the launch of the King Papers Project restored King's social gospel radicalism and Socialism, unleashing King's associates to confirm what they knew.

Cone, seemingly an unlikely candidate for revisionism about King, made a major contribution to it by contending that King and Malcolm complemented and corrected each other. Cone conferred with Garrow and other King scholars through the 1980s while working on his seminal text, *Martin & Malcolm & America*. All of that lay far ahead and was hard to imagine at the mid-1970s endpoint of the present book. The theological field that my generation entered in the 1970s, besides having no books about the black social gospel, had no books acknowledging that such a thing ever existed. Simmons, Ransom, Walters, Woodbey, Burroughs, and Wright were totally forgotten. Powell Senior was remembered chiefly for fathering a famous politician. Wells-Barnett was just beginning to be remembered after forty years of oblivion. Incredibly, Mays, Thurman, and Johnson were forgotten, too, despite having only recently passed on. The idea that Mays or Thurman might be a resource for black theology or cultural criticism had no currency at the graduate institutions that produced black social gospel leaders. Mays had a marginal role in early King biographies, and Thurman had less than that. All were consigned to the self-negating "Negro church" lampooned by Frazier. Early black theology soared by stepping into a putative void.[123]

C. Eric Lincoln put it aggressively in 1974, declaring that the "Negro church" was dead and gone:

> It died an agonized death in the harsh turmoil which tried the faith so rigorously in the decade of the "Savage Sixties," for there it had to confront under the most trying circumstances the possibility that "Negro" and "Christian" were irreconcilable categories. The call to full manhood, to *personhood*, and the call to Christian responsibility left no room for the implication of being a "Negro" in contemporary America. With sadness and reluctance, trepidation and confidence, the Negro Church accepted death in order to be reborn. Out of the ashes of its funeral pyre there sprang the bold, strident, self-conscious phoenix that is the contemporary Black Church.

The new Black Church was not the Negro Church radicalized, Lincoln said: "Rather it is a conscious departure from the critical norms which made the Negro Church what it was." To be sure, he allowed, the Negro Church produced a few freedom-fighting leaders, notably Nat Turner, Henry McNeil Turner, Adam Clayton Powell Jr., Martin Luther King Jr., and Malcolm X. Lincoln was trying to be generous, giving the church credit for Malcolm. But all were products of something that no longer existed. The Negro Church had never believed that it held the power to effect historic social change. King was the Moses figure who showed otherwise, and thus, Lincoln urged, what mattered about King was that he killed the Negro Church, not that he exemplified some ideal of it.[124]

Lincoln first presented this argument at Duke University in 1970 and published it in 1974. He made a powerful case for radical rupture, a story about agonizing death and triumphant rebirth. Lincoln's story suggested that King was the first liberation theologian—the verdict that Cone took up in the 1980s, a bit surprised to be saying it. Cornel West, in the 1980s, similarly reconsidered how he thought about King and talked about him. But 1974 was at the far edge of the period in which scholars inspired by liberation theology described the black church as bold, strident, and phoenix-like. The Black Power movement had already faded. Civil rights activism became deeply institutionalized, King's disciples ran for political office, and prosaic everydayness prevailed in the churches. The idea that some dramatic breakthrough had occurred in the 1960s did not ring true, to put it mildly. That was the trend-line that yielded a womanist movement emphasizing survival issues and, later, efforts to recover the black social gospel sources of King's theology and activism.

Theologies of Liberation

The black social gospel had an ample career after King was gone, usually
under other names. It fired the preaching and witness of progressive black
congregations throughout the nation. It gave ballast to the careers of numerous
politicians, most notably Young, Jackson, and Lewis. There were traces of it in
the rise of womanist theology in the late 1980s and early 1990s. Slowly it began
to be recovered on its own terms, as scholars reconsidered the sources of King's
theology and activism. If there was such a thing as a black social gospel tradition
that challenged white supremacy and paved the way to King, the back story to
liberation theology had to be reconceived and renarrated. But if King epitomized the black social gospel and was more radical than his image, there was a
deeper affinity between the two movements than it had seemed in 1970. The
case for considering black social Christianity as a tremendously significant
tradition, far outstripping its famous white social gospel counterpart, was always
there in the writings and activism of William Simmons, Reverdy Ransom, Ida
B. Wells-Barnett, Alexander Walters, Nannie Burroughs, George W. Woodbey,
Adam Clayton Powell Sr., Adam Clayton Powell Jr., Mordecai Johnson, Vernon
Johns, Benjamin E. Mays, Howard Thurman, Martin Luther King Jr., Wyatt
Walker, James Bevel, James Lawson, Pauli Murray, Andrew Young, Jesse
Jackson, Gardner Taylor, Samuel Proctor, and John Lewis, to name only the
headliners. It played a key role in creating America's greatest liberation move-
ment and played a large role in carrying it out. And it remains the basis on
which many hold fast to the dream of the Beloved Community.

---◆---

NOTES

CHAPTER 1. ACHIEVING THE BLACK SOCIAL GOSPEL

1. Gary Dorrien, *The New Abolition: W. E. B. Du Bois and the Black Social Gospel* (New Haven: Yale University Press, 2015).

2. Joseph R. Washington Jr., *Black Religion: The Negro and Christianity in the United States* (Boston: Beacon Press, 1964); Washington, *The Politics of God* (Boston: Beacon Press, 1967), quotes, 161.

3. Gayraud S. Wilmore, *Black Religion and Black Radicalism: An Interpretation of the Religious History of African Americans* (New York: Doubleday, 1973; 3rd rev. ed., Maryknoll, NY: Orbis Books, 1983).

4. Ibid., 163, 190.

5. See Calvin S. Morris, *Reverdy C. Ransom: Black Advocate of the Social Gospel* (Lanham, MD: University Press of America, 1990); Walter E. Fluker, *They Looked for a City: A Comparative Analysis of the Ideal of Community in the Thought of Howard Thurman and Martin Luther King Jr.* (Lanham, MD: University Press of America, 1989); Wallace D. Best, *Passionately Human, No Less Divine: Religion and Culture in Black Chicago, 1915–1952* (Princeton: Princeton University Press, 2005); Barbara Dianne Savage, *Your Spirits Walk Beside Us: The Politics of Black Religion* (Cambridge: Harvard University Press, 2008); Lawrence Edward Carter Sr., ed., *Walking Integrity: Benjamin Elijah Mays, Mentor to Martin Luther King Jr.* (Macon, GA: Mercer University Press, 1998); Anthony Pinn, *The African American Religious Experience in America* (Westport, CT: Greenwood, 2005); Quinton H. Dixie and Peter Eisenstadt, *Visions of a Better World: Howard Thurman's Pilgrimage to India and the Origins of African American Nonviolence* (Boston: Beacon Press, 2011); Juan M. Floyd-Thomas, *The Origins of Black Humanism in America: Reverend Ethelred Brown and the Unitarian Church* (New York: Palgrave Macmillan, 2008).

6. See Mohandas K. Gandhi, *Autobiography: The Story of My Experiments with Truth* (Washington, DC: Public Affairs, 1948), 1–86; Gandhi, "From Slave to College President," *Indian Opinion* (October 9, 1903); Louis Fischer, *The Life of Mahatma*

505

Gandhi (New York: Harper & Row, 1950), 3–40; Yogesh Chadha, *Gandhi: A Life* (New York: John Wiley, 1997), 1–43; Eknath Easwaran, *Gandhi the Man: The Story of His Transformation* (Tomales, CA: Nilgiri Press, 1972), 11–26.

7. Editorial [W. E. B. Du Bois], "The Woes of India," *Crisis* 22 (May 1921): 27; Editorial, "India's Saint," *Crisis* 22 (July 1921): 124–125; Reverdy C. Ransom, "Gandhi, Indian Messiah and Saint," *AME Church Review* 38 (October 1921): 87–88; W. E. B. Du Bois, "As the Crow Flies," *Crisis* 39 (November 1932), "there is," 342; see Du Bois, "Gandhi Strikes a Snag," *Pittsburgh Courier*, September 22, 1934, 10; Sudarshan Kapur, *Raising Up a Prophet: The African-American Encounter with Gandhi* (Boston: Beacon Press, 1992), 26; Nico Slate, *Colored Cosmopolitanism: The Shared Struggle for Freedom in the United States and India* (Cambridge: Harvard University Press, 2012), 123.

8. Editorial, "If We Had a Ghandi [*sic*]," *Pittsburgh Courier*, February 28, 1931, 10; Editorial, "Will a Gandhi Arise?" *Chicago Defender*, November 5, 1932.

9. W. E. B. Du Bois, "Postscript," *Crisis* 38 (January 1931): "magnificent," 29; Du Bois, "The Wide, Wide World," *New York Amsterdam News*, October 28, 1931, 8; Du Bois, "As the Crow Flies," *New York Amsterdam News*, March 13, 1943, "still."

10. See Edward W. Said, *Orientalism* (New York: Vintage, 1979); Said, *Culture and Imperialism* (New York: Vintage, 1994); Gayatri Chakravorty Spivak, *A Critique of Postcolonial Reason* (Cambridge: Harvard University Press, 1999); Albert Rabateau, *Canaan Land: A Religious History of African Americans* (Oxford: Oxford University Press, 2001); Peter J. Paris, *The Spirituality of African Peoples: The Search for a Common Moral Discourse* (Minneapolis: Fortress Press, 1995).

11. See Jervis Anderson, *A. Philip Randolph: A Biographical Portrait* (New York: Harcourt Brace Jovanovich, 1973), 85–109; Lillie Patterson, *A. Philip Randolph: Messenger for the Masses* (New York: Facts on File, 1996), 19–45; William H. Harris, *Keeping the Faith: A. Philip Randolph, Milton P. Webster, and the Brotherhood of Sleeping Car Porters, 1925–1937* (Urbana: University of Illinois Press, 1977).

12. James Farmer, *Lay Bare the Heart: An Autobiography of the Civil Rights Movement* (New York: Arbor House, 1985; reprint, Fort Worth: Texas Christian University Press, 1998), quote, 153.

13. Aldon D. Morris, *The Origins of the Civil Rights Movement: Black Communities Organizing for Change* (New York: Free Press, 1984), 17–25; Elliott Rudwick, *Along the Color Line* (Urbana: University of Illinois Press, 1976), 365–366.

14. Morris, *Origins of the Civil Rights Movement*, 30–35, 17–25; Rudwick, *Along the Color Line*, 366–367; Patricia Sullivan, *Lift Every Voice: The NAACP and the Making of the Civil Rights Movement* (New York: New Press, 2009), 384–428.

15. See David J. Garrow, "King's Plagiarism: Imitation, Insecurity, and Transformation," *Journal of American History* 78 (June 1991): 89–90; Keith D. Miller, "Martin Luther King, Jr., and the Black Folk Pulpit," *Journal of American History* 78 (June 1991): 120–121; David Levering Lewis, "Failing to Know Martin Luther King Jr.," *Journal of American History* 78 (June 1991): 84–85.

16. Richard Lischer, *The Preacher King: Martin Luther King, Jr. and the Word That Moved America* (New York: Oxford University Press, 1995), 53–57; William Newton Clarke, *An Outline of Christian Theology* (New York: Charles Scribner's Sons, 1898; 15th ed.,

1906), 227–259; William Adams Brown, *Christian Theology in Outline* (New York: Scribner's, 1906), 235–300; Walter Rauschenbusch, A *Theology for the Social Gospel* (New York: Macmillan, 1917), 31–94.

17. Lischer, *The Preacher King*, quote, 60.

18. Cornel West, "The Religious Foundations of the Thought of Martin Luther King Jr.," in *We Shall Overcome: Martin Luther King, Jr., and the Black Freedom Struggle*, ed. Peter J. Albert and Ronald Hoffman (New York: Pantheon, 1990), 113–129, quote, 129.

CHAPTER 2. PROPHETIC SUFFERING AND BLACK INTERNATIONALISM

1. Mordecai Wyatt Johnson, "Autobiography of Mordecai W. Johnson, President Emeritus of Howard University," unpublished typescript in Moorland-Spingarn Research Center, Mordecai Wyatt Johnson Papers, Howard University, Biographies Box; Johnson, Obituary for Wyatt J. Johnson, Johnson Papers.

2. Johnson, "Autobiography of Mordecai W. Johnson," n.p.; Mary White Ovington, "Mordecai W. Johnson," in Ovington, *Portraits in Color* (Freeport, NY: Books for Libraries Press, 1927), 46; Walter Dyson, *Howard University: Capstone of Negro Education, A History* (Washington, DC: Graduate School of Howard University, 1941), 398–399; Richard I. McKinney, *Mordecai: The Man and His Message* (Washington, DC: Howard University Press, 1997), 5–7, quote, 7; Edwin R. Embree, *Thirteen Against the Odds* (New York: Viking, 1944), 176–178; Howard University, *Education for Freedom: A Documentary Tribute to Celebrate the Fiftieth Anniversary of the Election of Mordecai W. Johnson as President of Howard University* (Washington, DC: Moorland-Spingarn Research Center, 1976).

3. Ovington, *Portraits in Color*, 47; Mordecai W. Johnson, "On Giving and Receiving," Sermon at First Baptist Church, Charleston, West Virginia, July 20, 1924, Mordecai Wyatt Johnson Papers; reprinted in McKinney, *Mordecai*, 176–177.

4. Ridgely Torrence, *The Story of John Hope* (New York: Macmillan, 1948), 10–12; Inventory of the Samuel Howard Archer Collection, Auburn Avenue Research Library on African American Culture and History, Atlanta-Fulton Public Library System, Atlanta, GA; Marc Moreland, "Samuel Howard Archer: Portrait of a Teacher," *Phylon* (1949).

5. Johnson, "Autobiography of Mordecai W. Johnson"; McKinney, *Mordecai*, 11–12; Embree, *Thirteen Against the Odds*, 182.

6. See Leroy Davis, *A Clashing of the Soul: John Hope and the Dilemma of African American Leadership and Black Higher Education in the Early Twentieth Century* (Athens: University of Georgia Press, 1998); Jacqueline Anne Rouse, *Lugenia Burns Hope: Black Southern Reformer* (Athens: University of Georgia Press, 1989); John Hope to W. E. B. Du Bois, January 17, 1910, *The Correspondence of W. E. B. Du Bois, Volume 1, Selections, 1877–1934*, ed. Herbert Aptheker (Amherst: University of Massachusetts Press, 1973), 165–167; Du Bois to Hope, January 22, 1910, ibid., 167.

7. Johnson, "Autobiography of Mordecai W. Johnson"; McKinney, *Mordecai: The Man and His Message*, 17–18; Torrence, *The Story of John Hope*, 30–34.

8. Mordecai Johnson, "The Social Responsibility of the Administrator," in *Academic Freedom in the United States: Papers Contributed in the Fifteenth Annual Spring Conference of the Division of the Social Sciences*, ed. Gustave Auzeene (Washington, DC: Howard University Press, 1953), "it will," 128; Edward A. Jones, *A Candle in the Dark: A History of Morehouse College* (Valley Forge, PA: Judson Press, 1967), 149–151.

9. Johnson, "Autobiography of Mordecai W. Johnson"; Fawn Brody, *Thomas Jefferson: An Intimate Biography* (New York: Norton, 1974); McKinney, *Mordecai*, 15.

10. McKinney, *Mordecai*, 23–24.

11. Ovington, *Portraits in Color*, 48.

12. Ibid., 48–49.

13. Embree, *Thirteen Against the Odds*, quotes, 185.

14. Newton Theological Institution ended its policy of racial discrimination after Everett Carlton Herrick became president in 1925. The following year Newton affiliated with Andover Theological Seminary, a Congregational seminary founded in 1808 in the wake of the Unitarian takeover of Harvard. For two decades in the early twentieth century Andover had a formal affiliation with Harvard University; it relocated to Cambridge, built Andover Hall on the Harvard campus, and sought to merge with Harvard Divinity School. But the merger effort collapsed and Andover moved, in 1931, to the Newton campus in Newton Centre. In 1965, after three decades of coexistence on the same campus, the two schools officially merged, becoming Andover Newton Theological School. See Gary Dorrien, *The Making of American Liberal Theology: Imagining Progressive Religion, 1805–1900* (Louisville: Westminster John Knox Press, 2001), 4–5, 290–293; Andover Newton Theological School, "About Andover Newton: A Short History of the School," www.ants.edu/history.

15. Walter Rauschenbusch, *Christianity and the Social Crisis* (New York: Macmillan, 1907); see Gary Dorrien, *Social Ethics in the Making: Interpreting an American Tradition* (Oxford: Wiley-Blackwell, 2009), 83–109.

16. Walter Rauschenbusch, *Christianizing the Social Order* (New York: Macmillan, 1912), quotes, vii; *The Social Creed of the Churches*, ed. Harry F. Ward (New York: Eaton and Mains, 1912).

17. Rauschenbusch, *Christianizing the Social Order*, 124–125, 130–138.

18. See Rauschenbusch, *Christianity and the Social Crisis*, quotes, 276–279; Rauschenbusch, "Some Moral Aspects of the 'Woman Movement,'" *Biblical World* 42 (October 1913): 195–198; Rauschenbusch, "What About the Woman?" Box 20, Rauschenbusch Family Papers; Peter Gabriel Filene, *Him Her Self: Sex Roles in Modern America* (New York: Harcourt Brace Jovanovich, 1974), 23–29; Janet Fishburn, *The Fatherhood of God and the Victorian Family* (Philadelphia: Fortress, 1981), 120–127; Susan Curtis, *A Consuming Faith: The Social Gospel and Modern American Culture* (Baltimore: Johns Hopkins University Press, 1991), 107–108, 112.

19. Rauschenbusch, *Christianizing the Social Order*, 317; see Daniel Bell, *The Cultural Contradictions of Capitalism* (New York: Basic Books, 1976).

20. Rauschenbusch, *Christianizing the Social Order*, 341–354, quote, 353.

21. Walter Rauschenbusch, "The Belated Races and the Social Problems," *Methodist Review* 40 (April 1914): 258.

22. Rauschenbusch, *Christianizing the Social Order*, 60; Walter Rauschenbusch, *A Theology for the Social Gospel* (New York: Macmillan, 1917), 79.

23. Mordecai Johnson to John Hope, March 29, 1914, Johnson Papers.

24. McKinney, *Mordecai*, 37–38; Walter Rauschenbusch, "Be Fair to Germany: A Plea for Open-mindedness," *The Congregationalist*, October 15, 1914; Rauschenbusch, "The Contribution of Germany to the National Life of America," Rauschenbusch Family Collection, Colgate Rochester Crozer Seminary, Rochester, New York; "Methodists Do Not Want to Hear Pro-German Divine," *Regina Morning Leader*, November 5, 1914.

25. McKinney, *Mordecai*, 42; Patricia Sullivan, *Lift Every Voice: The NAACP and the Making of the Civil Rights Movement* (New York: New Press, 2009).

26. Embree, *Thirteen Against the Odds*, "there must," 188.

27. Mordecai W. Johnson, "The Blindness of Obsession," Sermon at First Baptist, Charleston, July 13, 1924, in McKinney, *Mordecai*, quotes, 161, 163, 167.

28. Ibid., 171.

29. Ibid., 172–173.

30. Johnson, "On Giving and Receiving," 175, 176.

31. Ibid., 179, 181, 182.

32. Ibid., 185.

33. Mordecai W. Johnson, "The Social Consequences of Sin," July 12, 1924, ibid., quotes, 190, 191.

34. Ibid., quotes, 199, 192.

35. Ibid., 195.

36. Ibid., 197, 198.

37. Mordecai W. Johnson, "Work, Business, and Religion," August 10, 1924, ibid., 202–213, quote, 209.

38. Mordecai W. Johnson, "The Radical Commitment," August 17, 1924, ibid., quotes, 215, 216, 217, 218, 219.

39. Ibid., quotes, 219, 224.

40. See Conrad Wright, "The Election of Henry Ware: Two Contemporary Accounts Edited with Commentary," *Harvard Library Bulletin* 17 (1969): 245–278; Daniel Walker Howe, *The Unitarian Conscience: Harvard Moral Philosophy, 1805–1861* (Cambridge: Harvard University Press, 1970), 4–5; Dorrien, *Social Ethics in the Making*, 10–36.

41. George Foot Moore, *History of Religions: China, Japan, Egypt, Babylonia, Assyria, India, Persia, Greece, and Rome* (New York: Scribner's, 1922); Moore, *The Literature of the Old Testament* (New York: Henry Holt, 1913); Moore, *The Birth and Growth of Religion* (New York: Scribner's, 1923); George La Piana, *Within Our Gates* (Boston: Welfare Society of Boston, 1923); La Piana, *The Italians in Milwaukee, Wisconsin* (Milwaukee: privately published, 1915).

42. Mordecai W. Johnson, Eulogy for Wyatt Johnson, April 1922, Johnson Papers, Box 178.

43. Mordecai W. Johnson, "The Faith of the American Negro," Commencement Address, Harvard University, June 22, 1922, in McKinney, *Mordecai*, quotes, 247, 249.

44. Ibid., quotes, 249, 250.

45. Ibid., quotes, 250, 251.

46. Johnson Papers, Box 178.

47. Mordecai W. Johnson to Jesse Moorland, June 10, 1922, in McKinney, *Mordecai*, 51.

48. Walter Dyson, *Howard University, the Capstone of Negro Education—A History, 1867–1940* (Washington, DC: Graduate School, Howard University, 1941), 44–69, quote, 387; Rayford W. Logan, *Howard University: The First Hundred Years, 1867–1967* (New York: New York University Press, 1969), 140–148.

49. Dyson, *Howard University*, quote, 391; Sterling N. Brown, "What About Howard University?" *Washington Sentinel*, August 7, 1926.

50. Michael R. Winston, *The Howard University Department of History, 1913–1973* (Washington, DC: Howard University Press, 1973; reprinted, Washington, DC: Association for the Study of African American Life and History, 1998), 1–2; Dyson, *Howard University*, 368–375; Logan, *Howard University*, 188–192; Zachery R. Williams, *In Search of the Talented Tenth: Howard University Public Intellectuals and the Dilemmas of Race, 1926–1970* (Columbia, MO: University of Missouri Press, 2009), 18–20.

51. Dyson, *Howard University*, 375, 391–396; Logan, *Howard University*, 188–192; James M. McPherson, "White Liberals and Black Power in Negro Education, 1865–1915," *American Historical Review* 75 (1970): 1364–1365.

52. George Marsden, *The Soul of the American University: From Protestant Establishment to Established Nonbelief* (New York: Oxford University Press, 1994), 150–164; L. L. Bernard and Jesse Bernard, *Origins of American Sociology: The Social Science Movement in the United States* (New York: Crowell, 1943); Dorrien, *Social Ethics in the Making*, 10–20.

53. Dyson, *Howard University*, 156–168; Logan, *Howard University*, 69–107; Winston, *The Howard University Department of History*, 2–3.

54. See Kelly Miller, "The Ultimate Race Problem," *Atlantic Monthly* (April 1909): 2–8; Miller, *Race Adjustment: Essays on the Negro in America* (New York: Neale, 1909); Carter G. Woodson, "Kelly Miller," *Journal of Negro History* (January 1940): 137–138; August Meier, "The Racial and Educational Philosophy of Kelly Miller, 1895–1915," *Journal of Negro Education* (July 1960): 121–127.

55. *The New Negro*, ed. Alaine Locke (New York: Albert & Charles Boni, 1925; reprint, New York: Simon & Schuster, 1992); Locke, "Art or Propaganda?" *Harlem* 1 (1928): 12–13; Locke, "The Concept of Race as Applied to Social Culture" (1924), reprinted in Locke, *The Philosophy of Alain Locke: Harlem Renaissance and Beyond*, ed. L. Harris (Philadelphia: Temple University Press, 1989), 188–199; Locke, "Values and Imperatives," 1935, in *The Philosophy of Alain Locke*, 34–50; C. Eze, *The Dilemma of Ethnic Identity: Alain Locke's Vision of Transcultural Societies* (New York: Mellen Press, 2005); Leonard Harris, "The Great Debate: W. E. B. Du Bois vs. Alain Locke on the Aesthetic," *Philosophia Africana* 7 (2004): 15–39; Leonard Harris and Charles Molesworth, *Alain Locke: Biography of a Philosopher* (Chicago: University of Chicago Press, 2008).

56. Carter G. Woodson, *The Education of the Negro Before 1861* (New York: Putnam, 1915); Woodson, *The Negro in Our History* (Washington, DC: Associated Publishers,

1922); Williams, *In Search of the Talented Tenth*, quote, 21; Charles H. Wesley, "Carter G. Woodson as a Scholar," *Journal of Negro History* 36 (January 1951): 12–24; Claire Corbould, *Becoming African Americans: The Public Life of Harlem, 1919–1939* (Cambridge: Harvard University Press, 2009), 87–88; Raymond Wolters, *The New Negro on Campus: Black College Rebellion of the 1920s* (Princeton: Princeton University Press, 1975), 86–91; George B. Hutchinson, "Jean Toomer and the 'New Negroes' of Washington," *American Literature* 63 (December 1991): 683–687.

57. J. Stanley Durkee, President's Address, Opening Convocation at Howard University, October 4, 1922, *Howard University Record* 27 (November 1922): "the ignorant," 10; Chancellor James Williams, "Teacher: As Seen by a Former Student," in *A Tribute to the Memory of Professor William Leo Hansberry* (Washington, DC: Howard University Department of History, 1972), 17–18; Winston, *The Howard University Department of History*, 7–8; Logan, *Howard University*, 192–214; Dyson, *Howard University*, 397.

58. Albert Rhys Williams, *The Bolsheviks and the Soviets: Seventy-Six Questions and Answers on the Workingman's Government of Russia* (Brooklyn: Socialist Press, 1918); *Congressional Record*, 66th Congress, 2nd Session (January 8, 1920), 1213; President J. Stanley Durkee to Senator Reed Smoot, January 10, 1920, in Dyson, *Howard University*, 430–432; "Funds for Howard Slashed by House," *Evening Star*, January 30, 1924.

59. *Howard University Record* (February 1919), quote, in Logan, *Howard University*, 220; Wolters, *The New Negro on Campus*, 111–120; Dyson, *Howard University*, 363–375; Seymour Martin Lipset, *Rebellion in the University* (Boston: Little, Brown, 1971), 158–178.

60. Alumnus [G. David Houston], "Alumni Plan to Picket Howard Univ. Unless President Durkee Resigns," *Baltimore Afro-American*, July 18, 1925.

61. Alumnus, "Durkeeism," *Baltimore Afro-American*, November 1, 1925; Alumnus, "Alumni Plan to Picket Howard"; Logan, *Howard University*, 234–238, quotes, 236; Wolters, *New Negro on Campus*, 101–107; Williams, *In Search of the Talented Tenth*, 23–26. According to the stenographic report, forty-five professors testified, but Logan, at the time a student at Howard, counted forty-seven.

62. McKinney, *Mordecai*, "I think," 57; J. Stanley Durkee to B. F. Seldon, June 20, 1927, "I did," in Dyson, *Howard University*, 397.

63. W. E. B. Du Bois, "Howard and Lincoln," *Crisis* 32 (1926): 7–8; Wolters, *New Negro on Campus*, 28, 130; Williams, *In Search of the Talented Tenth*, 28–29.

64. Richard R. Wright Jr., *The Bishops of the African Methodist Episcopal Church* (Nashville: AME Sunday School Union, 1963), 199–200; *New York Age*, June 12, 1926; Wolters, *New Negro on Campus*, 133.

65. Logan, *Howard University*, 242–243; Dyson, *Howard University*, 370–375; McKinney, *Mordecai*, 58–59.

66. Editorial, "Negro at Last Heads Howard University," *Washington Post*, August 1, 1926; Neval H. Thomas to *Washington Tribune*, August 6, 1926, in Dyson, *Howard University*, quote, 400; Editorial, *Messenger* 8 (1926): 167–168; Wolters, *New Negro on Campus*, 133; Williams, *In Search of the Talented Tenth*, 35–36.

67. Sherwood Eddy, *Eighty Adventurous Years: An Autobiography* (New York: Harper & Brothers, 1955), 127–128; *Kirby Page: Social Evangelist: The Autobiography of a Twentieth-Century Prophet for Peace*, ed. Harold E. Fey (Nyack, NY: Fellowship Press,

1975), 99–100; Eddy, *What Shall We Do About War?* (New York: Eddy and Page, 1935); Robert Moats Miller, *American Protestantism and Social Issues* (Chapel Hill: University of North Carolina Press, 1958), 46, 251; McKinney, *Mordecai,* 60.

68. Mordecai W. Johnson, "Autobiographical Statements," Johnson Papers, Box 178-14, "dangerously" and "I would be," 1–2; Johnson, "The Social Responsibility of the Administrator," Address to the Fifteenth Annual Spring Conference, Division of Social Sciences, Howard University, March 11, 1953, in McKinney, *Mordecai,* "this was," 288.

69. Mordecai W. Johnson, "Inaugural Presidential Address of Mordecai Wyatt Johnson at Howard University," June 10, 1927, in McKinney, *Mordecai,* 252–267, quotes, 255, 257, 257–258; see Jon Michael Spencer, "The Black Church and the Harlem Renaissance," *African American Review* 30 (1996): 454–455.

70. Dyson, *Howard University,* 201–218; Miles Mark Fisher IV, "The Howard Years," in *Walking Integrity: Benjamin Elijah Mays, Mentor to Martin Luther King Jr.,* 131–151; Jelks, *Benjamin Elijah Mays: Schoolmaster of the Movement,* 114–115; Jonathan Holloway, *Confronting the Veil: Abram Harris, Jr., E. Franklin Frazier, and Ralph Bunche, 1919–1941* (Chapel Hill: University of North Carolina Press, 2002), 46–49.

71. Johnson, "Inaugural Presidential Address," quotes, 258; Dyson, *Howard University, the Capstone of Negro Education—A History, 1867–1940,* 173–174; Fisher, "The Howard Years," 132–135; Logan, *Howard University,* 157; D. Butler Pratt to Howard Thurman, August 30, 1932, in Thurman, *The Papers of Howard Washington Thurman,* ed. Walter Earl Fluker (Columbia: University of South Carolina Press, 2009), 1: 167–169.

72. Johnson, "Inaugural Presidential Address," 263, 265–266.

73. Ibid., 254, 266.

74. Johnson, "Autobiography of Mordecai W. Johnson"; Logan, *Howard University,* 251–265, 590.

75. Brian Urquhart, *Ralph Bunche: An American Life* (New York: W. W. Norton, 1993); Anthony Platt, *E. Franklin Frazier Reconsidered* (New Brunswick, NJ: Rutgers University Press, 1991); Joanne V. Gabbin, *Sterling A. Brown: Building the Black Aesthetic Tradition* (Westport, CT: Greenwood Press, 1985); Kenneth Robert Janken, *Rayford W. Logan and the Dilemma of the African American Intellectual* (Amherst: University of Massachusetts Press, 1993); Logan, *Howard University,* quote, 284.

76. Dyson, *Howard University,* 400–404; Logan, *Howard University,* 249.

77. Genna Rae McNeil, *Groundwork: Charles Hamilton Houston and the Struggle for Civil Rights* (Philadelphia: University of Pennsylvania Press, 1983), 69–75, 84–88; Michael D. Davis and Hunter H. Clark, *Thurgood Marshall: Warrior at the Bar, Rebel on the Bench* (New York: Carol Publishing, 1992), 55; McKinney, *Mordecai,* 71–73; Logan, *Howard University,* 266–268, 313.

78. Logan, *Howard University,* "in those," 268; McKinney, *Mordecai,* "my," 74; Gilbert Ware, *William Hastie: Grace Under Pressure* (New York: Oxford University Press, 1984), 16–19.

79. Charles H. Thompson, "The Prospect of Negro Higher Education," *Journal of Educational Sociology* 32 (1959): 309–316; Thompson, "The Present Status of the Negro Private and Church-Related College," *Journal of Negro Education* 29 (1960): 227–244; *The Negro Caravan,* ed. Sterling Brown, Arthur Paul Davis, and Ulysses Lee

(New York: Dryden, 1941); Ralph J. Bunche, "A Critique of New Deal Social Planning as It Affects Negroes," *Journal of Negro Education* 5 (January 1936); Bunche, *A World View of Race* (Washington, DC: Associates in Negro Folk Education, 1936); E. Franklin Frazier, *Black Bourgeoisie* (New York: Free Press, 1957); Arthur P. Davis, "E. Franklin Frazier (1894–1962): A Profile," *Journal of Negro Education* 31 (1962): 429–435; Abram Harris, "A White and Black World in American Labor and Politics," *Social Forces* 4 (December 1925); Harris, *The Negro as Capitalist* (Philadelphia: American Academy of Political and Social Sciences, 1936); John Hope Franklin, *From Slavery to Freedom* (New York: Knopf, 5th ed., 1980).

80. Kenneth R. Manning, *Black Apollo of Science: The Life of Ernest Everett Just* (New York: Oxford University Press, 1983); Darlene R. Stille, *Percy Levon Julian: Pioneering Chemist* (Washington, DC: Capstone, 2009); NOVA, "Forgotten Genius: Percy Julian," www.pbs.org.wgbh; Logan, *Howard University*, 286–292.

81. Logan, *Howard University*, 288.

82. Ibid., 340–341, "supplicant," 341; McKinney, *Mordecai*, 85–86; Clifford L. Muse Jr., "Howard University and the Federal Government During the Presidential Administrations of Herbert Hoover and Franklin D. Roosevelt, 1928–1945," *Journal of Negro History* 76 (1991): 3–12.

83. "Special Reporter," *Baltimore Afro-American*, December 1, 1934, in McKinney, *Mordecai*, 88; "much more," ibid., 88; Muse, "Howard University and the Federal Government," 9–12; Embree, *Thirteen Against the Odds*, 175.

84. Dyson, *Howard University*, 437; Logan, *Howard University*, 293; McKinney, *Mordecai*, 87.

85. "Capital, Nation Join in Fight for H.U. Prexy," *Baltimore Afro-American*, April 18, 1931, in Dyson, *Howard University*, 434–436, quotes, 435.

86. "Johnson Wins Student Cheer," *Baltimore Afro-American*, April 18, 1931, "a vision," in Dyson, *Howard University*, 436; Logan, *Howard University*, "arrogant" and "this man," 294.

87. Mordecai W. Johnson, Baccalaureate Sermon, June 4, 1933, quoted in *Chicago Defender*, June 13, 1933, cited in Logan, *Howard University*, 295.

88. *Baltimore Afro-American*, June 24, 1933, in Dyson, *Howard University*, 437.

89. Alvin B. Tillery Jr., *Between Homeland and Motherland: Africa, U.S. Foreign Policy, and Black Leadership in America* (Ithaca, NY: Cornell University Press, 2011), 89–90.

90. Kelly Miller to the *Baltimore Afro-American*, June 1, 1935.

91. McKinney, *Mordecai*, quotes, 83; Harold Ickes, "The Need for Academic Freedom," Speech on March 27, 1935, reprinted in *Bulletin of the American Association of University Professors* 21 (November 1935): 562–565.

92. Logan, *Howard University*, quote, 348; Muse, "Howard University and the Federal Government," 10–12; Williams, *In Search of the Talented Tenth*, 53–54; McKinney, *Mordecai*, 89–90.

93. "The Case Against Mordecai Johnson," *Howard University Alumni Journal*, Johnson Papers; Logan, *Howard University*, quotes, 336; Muse, "Howard University and the Federal Government," 11–12; Williams, *In Search of the Talented Tenth*, 54; Margaret Wade-Lewis, *Lorenzo Dow Turner: Father of Gullah Studies* (Columbia, SC: University of South Carolina Press, 2007).

94. Benjamin E. Mays, "The Relevance of Mordecai Wyatt Johnson," Inaugural Address, Mordecai Wyatt Johnson Lecture Series, Howard University, January 27, 1978, Johnson Papers; Mordecai Johnson to John Q. Taylor King Jr., quoted in interview with Richard I. McKinney, November 11, 1987, in McKinney, *Mordecai*, "people have," 94; "The Trials of a President," *Time*, March 20, 1938, "almost equivalent."

95. Seventeenth Day Charter Day Dinner Program, Howard University, March 1941, Johnson Papers; Williams, *In Search of the Talented Tenth*, "the major," 53.

96. Harold Ickes, Speech at Interior Department dinner, March 1935, in *Atlanta World*, March 22, 1935, in McKinney, *Mordecai*, 91; Logan, *Howard University*, 338; Seventeenth Annual Charter Day Dinner Program.

97. Howard Thurman, *With Head and Heart: The Autobiography of Howard Thurman* (New York: Harcourt Brace Jovanovich, 1979), quotes, 87; D. Butler Pratt to Howard Thurman, August 30, 1932, in Howard Thurman, *The Papers of Howard Washington Thurman*, ed. Walter Earl Fluker (Columbia, SC: University of South Carolina Press, 2009), 1: 167–169.

98. Logan, *Howard University*, "an extraordinary," 257; Benjamin E. Mays, *Born to Rebel* (Athens: University of Georgia Press, 1971; reprint, 2003), 139–140.

99. Mays, *Born to Rebel*, 140–141.

100. Ibid., 141.

101. Ibid., 142.

102. Ibid., quote, 143; Benjamin E. Mays, "My View: Thirty-Four Years of Distinguished Leadership," *New Pittsburgh Courier*, July 16, 1960; Holloway, *Confronting the Veil*, 46–49; Fisher, "The Howard Years," 131–151.

103. George Schuyler, "Views and Reviews," *Pittsburgh Courier*, March 29, 1930, Johnson quotes, 10. Schuyler, a popular syndicated columnist, blasted Johnson's "unadulterated nonsense," contending that Gandhi was likely to fail against British might and that Christianity was the leading hindrance to the advancement of African Americans. See Nico Slate, *Colored Cosmopolitanism: The Shared Struggle for Freedom in the United States and India* (Cambridge: Harvard University Press, 2012), 108–109.

104. Seventeenth Annual Charter Day Dinner Program.

105. Abram Harris to Alain Locke, May 10, 1947, Alain C. Locke Papers, Moorland-Spingarn Research Center, Howard University, "my disgust"; William A. Darity Jr., "Abram Harris: An Odyssey from Howard to Chicago," *Review of Black Political Economy* 15 (1987): 4–40; Williams, *In Search of the Talented Tenth*, 115.

106. Logan, *Howard University*, 366; see John Hope Franklin, *Mirror to America: The Autobiography of John Hope Franklin* (New York: Farrar, Straus and Giroux, 2005).

107. Logan, *Howard University*, 375–378.

108. Embree, *Thirteen Against the Odds*, 175.

109. Mordecai W. Johnson, Address at the Inauguration of Charles S. Johnson, Fisk University, November 27, 1947, in *Washington Afro-American*, November 27, 1947, and McKinney, *Mordecai*, quotes, 269, 270.

110. McKinney, *Mordecai*, quotes, 271, 273.

111. Ibid., quotes, 274, 275.

112. Ibid., 276.

113. Douglas Hall, *Baltimore Afro-American*, November 27, 1947; McKinney, *Mordecai*, 113.

114. Mordecai W. Johnson, Address to the Woman's Auxiliary, National Council of the Episcopal Church, Denver, Colorado, n.d., in McKinney, *Mordecai*, quotes, 279; see John Egerton, *Speak Now Against the Day: The Generation Before the Civil Rights Movement in the South* (Chapel Hill: University of North Carolina Press, 1994), 15–47.

115. Johnson, Address to the Woman's Auxiliary, quotes, 282, 285.

116. Mordecai W. Johnson, "Presidential Address Given at the Formal Opening of School Exercises," Howard University, September 22, 1953, Johnson Papers, quotes, 4–5, 13, 24; Johnson, "Gandhi's Purity of Heart," Johnson Papers; Sudarshan Kapur, *Raising Up a Prophet: The African-American Encounter with Gandhi* (Boston: Beacon Press, 1992), 148–149.

117. See David Caute, *The Great Fear: The Anti-Communist Purge Under Truman and Eisenhower* (New York: Simon & Schuster, 1978); Richard Fried, *Nightmare in Red: The McCarthy Era in Perspective* (New York: Oxford University Press, 1990); David M. Oshinsky, *A Conspiracy So Immense: The World of Joe McCarthy* (New York: Free Press, 2005); Richard M. Freeland, *The Truman Doctrine and the Origins of McCarthyism: Foreign Policy, Domestic Politics, and Internal Security, 1946–1948* (New York: New York University Press, 1985).

118. Johnson, "The Social Responsibility of the Administrator," quote, 288.

119. Ibid., quote, 298.

120. Ibid., quotes, 301–302, 303.

121. Ibid., quote, 307.

122. Ibid., quotes, 307, 308.

123. Ibid., 310.

124. Ibid., 310–311; see Mordecai W. Johnson, "The Heart of the Matter," *Progressive* (March 1952).

125. Mordecai W. Johnson, "Emancipation Day Address," January 10, 1954, Baltimore, Maryland, in *Rhetoric, Religion and the Civil Rights Movement, 1954–1965*, ed. Davis W. Houck and David E. Dixon (Waco, TX: Baylor University Press, 2006), quotes, 20, 21, 22; Johnson, "Platform for Freedom," *Baltimore Afro-American*, January 15, 1954.

126. Johnson, "Emancipation Day Address," quotes, 25, 27.

127. Ibid., 30.

128. McKinney, *Mordecai*, "some teachers," 93; Logan, *Howard University*, 449, "he increasingly," 410.

129. *Brown et al. v. Board of Education of Topeka et al.*, 347 U.S. 483 (1954); James M. Nabrit Jr., "Resort to the Courts as a Means of Eliminating Legalized Segregation," *Journal of Negro Education* 20 (Summer 1951): 460–474; William H. Hastie, "Toward an Equilibrium Legal Order, 1930–1950," *Annals of the American Academy of Political and Social Science* 407 (May 1973): 18–31; Kenneth B. Clark, *Argument: The Oral Argument Before the Supreme Court in Brown v. Board of Education of Topeka*, ed. Leon Friedman (New York: Chelsea House, 1969), xxxi; Winston, *The Howard University Department of History*, 8.

130. Dennis C. Dickerson, "William Stuart Nelson in India: The Making of a Religious Intellectual," American Academy in Berlin, www.americanacademy; Logan, *Howard University*, "remained," 378.

131. William Stuart Nelson, "Gandhiji" (January 30, 1950), William Stuart Nelson Papers, Howard University; Dickerson, "William Stuart Nelson in India"; Martin Luther King Jr., *Stride Toward Freedom: The Montgomery Story* (1958; reprint, Boston: Beacon Press, 2010), xv–xvii, 83–86.

132. Mordecai W. Johnson to the *Washington Times Herald*, December 16, 1957, "ruthlessly."

133. Mordecai W. Johnson, "The Need for a Program of International Economic Aid," Speech to the First Atlantic Congress, North Atlantic Treaty Organization, London, England, June 6, 1959, in McKinney, *Mordecai*, quote, 327.

134. Ibid., 330.

135. Ibid., 334–335.

136. "President Johnson's Citations: Martin Luther King Jr.," *Howard University Bulletin*, July 15, 1957, in *The Papers of Martin Luther King Jr.*, ed. Clayborne Carson (Berkeley: University of California Press, 2000), 4: 225.

137. Martin Luther King Jr. to Mordecai W. Johnson, July 5, 1957, *The Papers of Martin Luther King Jr.*, 4: "please know," 234; Johnson to King Jr., August 3, 1957, ibid., "there are," 233–234.

138. Logan, *Howard University*, "his magnificent," 447; Mays, "My View: Thirty-Four Years of Distinguished Leadership."

139. McKinney, *Mordecai*, "I want to," 105.

140. Johnson, "Autobiography of Mordecai W. Johnson"; Rayford Logan, "Howard University," undated [probably 1962], Rayford Logan Papers, Moorland-Spingarn Research Center, Howard University; Williams, *In Search of the Talented Tenth*, 118–119.

141. Mordecai W. Johnson to Richard McKinney, May 1966; McKinney, *Mordecai*, 105–106; Embree, *Thirteen Against the Odds*, 194; Logan, *Howard University*, 446.

142. McKinney, *Mordecai*, 124.

143. Ibid., 129.

144. Obituary for Mordecai W. Johnson, *Washington Evening Star*, September 15, 1976.

145. Obituary for Mordecai W. Johnson, *Hilltop*, September 17, 1976; Obituary for Johnson, *Washington Post*, September 17, 1976.

146. Logan, "Howard University," "awful"; Williams, *In Search of the Talented Tenth*, 119–121; Janken, *Rayford W. Logan*, 225–227.

147. Embree, *Thirteen Against the Odds*, "is our," 175.

CHAPTER 3. MORAL POLITICS AND THE SOUL OF THE WORLD

1. Benjamin E. Mays, "A Negro Educator Gives His Views," *Christian Science Monitor*, January 19, 1957, "I am," 22; Lerone Bennett Jr., "The Last of the Great Schoolmasters," in *Walking Integrity: Benjamin Elijah Mays, Mentor to Martin Luther King Jr.*, ed. Lawrence Edward Carter Sr. (Macon, GA: Mercer University Press, 1998), 333–339.

2. Benjamin E. Mays, *Born to Rebel: An Autobiography* (New York: Scribner, 1971; paperback ed., Athens: University of Georgia Press, 2003), quote, 33–34; see Stephen Kantrowitz, *Ben Tillman and the Reconstruction of White Supremacy* (Chapel Hill: University of North Carolina Press, 2000). According to local legend, the town of Ninety Six got its name from an event in the Revolutionary War: the town was ninety-six miles from the Old Star Fort in North Carolina, which was then occupied by the British. My discussion of Mays adapts material from Gary Dorrien, *The Making of American Liberal Theology: Idealism, Realism, and Modernity, 1900–1950* (Louisville: Westminster John Knox Press, 2003), 415–430.

3. Benjamin E. Mays, "In My Life and Time," in *Benjamin E. Mays: His Life, Contribution, and Legacy*, ed. Samuel DuBois Cook (Franklin, TN: Providence House, 2009), "never," 7; Mays, *Born to Rebel*, "all too," 9, 10; see Benjamin E. Mays, *Lord, the People Have Driven Me On* (New York: Vantage Press, 1981), 1–2.

4. Mays, *Born to Rebel*, 23.

5. Ibid., "trying," 45; Mays, "In My Life and Time," "I have lived" and "the wings," 12, 7.

6. Benjamin E. Mays, "Why I Believe There Is a God," *Ebony* (December 1961), reprinted in *Why I Believe There Is a God: Sixteen Essays by Negro Clergymen*, introduction by Howard Thurman (Chicago: Johnson Publishing, 1965), "very" and "so I," 3; Mays, "In My Life and Time," "genuine" and "this story," 9, 10.

7. Mays, *Born to Rebel*, 14, 15; Randal Maurice Jelks, *Benjamin Elijah Mays: Schoolmaster of the Movement* (Chapel Hill: University of North Carolina Press, 2012), "first," 15.

8. Ibid., "they gave me," 17; Benjamin E. Mays, "I Have Been a Baptist All My Life," in *A Way Home: The Baptists Tell Their Story*, ed. James S. Childers (Atlanta: Tupper and Love, 1964), "I felt," 166; Jelks, *Benjamin Elijah Mays: Schoolmaster of the Movement*, "my fifth," 17; Mays, "In My Life and Time," 8.

9. Mays, "In My Life and Time," quotes, 8, 7; Carrie M. Dumas, *Benjamin Elijah Mays: A Pictorial Life and Times* (Macon, GA: Mercer University Press, 2006), 102.

10. Mays, *Born to Rebel*, quote, 41.

11. Ibid, quote, 40.

12. Benjamin E. Mays, "Why I Went to Bates," *Bates College Bulletin*, January 1966, "where I could," n.p.; Mays, *Born to Rebel*, "worthy," 52; Mays, "In My Life and Time," 9.

13. Laurence Veysey, *The Emergence of the American University* (Chicago: University of Chicago Press, 1965), 203–212; William Anthony, *Bates College and Its Background: A Review of Origins and Causes* (Philadelphia: Judson Press, 1936); Jelks, *Benjamin Elijah Mays*, 38–39; Mays, *Born to Rebel*, quotes, 54, 55; Mays, "In My Life and Time," 10.

14. Mays, *Born to Rebel*, quotes, 60; Mays, "Why I Went to Bates," n.p.

15. Mays, *Born to Rebel*, quotes, 50, 58, 60.

16. Eugene Debs, "Statement to the Court," September 14, 1918, in *Writings and Speeches of Eugene V. Debs* (New York: Hermitage Press, 1948), quote, 437; Benjamin E. Mays, "Address of Dr. Benjamin Elijah Mays at the Ceremony Dedicating the Historic Marker at Mays Crossroads near the Birthplace of Dr. Mays at Epworth, SC, November 7, 1981," "Eugene Debs" quote, cited in Orville Vernon Burton, foreword to Mays, *Born to Rebel*, x; Herbert Purinton, "Some Recent Books on Religion," *Bates Alumnus*

(May 1928): 11; Randal M. Jelks, "Mays's Academic Formation, 1917–1936," in *Walking Integrity: Benjamin Elijah Mays, Mentor to Martin Luther King Jr.*, 114–118.

17. Mays, *Born to Rebel*, quote, 65; Dorrien, *The Making of American Liberal Theology: Idealism, Realism, and Modernity, 1900–1950*, 151–285.

18. Mays, *Born to Rebel*, quote, 65; Allan H. Spear, *Black Chicago: The Making of a Negro Ghetto, 1890–1920* (Chicago: University of Chicago Press, 1967), 22–23, 129–150; Lawrence Edward Carter Sr., "The Life of Benjamin Elijah Mays," in *Walking Integrity: Benjamin Elijah Mays, Mentor to Martin Luther King Jr.*, 2–3.

19. Leroy Davis, *A Clashing of the Soul: John Hope and the Dilemma of African American Leadership and Black Higher Education in the Early Twentieth Century* (Athens: University of Georgia Press, 1988), 259; Jelks, *Benjamin Elijah Mays*, 53; Mays, *Born to Rebel*, "temptations" and "detours," 134.

20. Mays, *Born to Rebel*, quotes, 67, 80. Carter began his long career as dean of the chapel at Morehouse in 1979; see Lewis V. Baldwin, "Models of the Scholar-Activist Type: Lawrence E. Carter, Sr. in the Shadows of Benjamin Elijah Mays and Martin Luther King Jr.," in *In the Beginning: The Martin Luther King, Jr., International Chapel at Morehouse College*, ed. Echol Nix Jr. (Macon, GA: Mercer University Press, 2015), 1–18; Edward A. Jones, *A Candle in the Dark: A History of Morehouse College* (Valley Forge, PA: Judson Press, 1967), 17–78.

21. Mays, *Born to Rebel*, quotes, 90, 93.

22. Benjamin E. Mays, unpublished eulogy for Mordecai Johnson, 1976, cited in Carter, "The Life of Benjamin Elijah Mays," quote, 3; McKinney, *Mordecai: The Man and His Message*, 37–76.

23. Benjamin E. Mays, "Pagan Survivals in Christianity" (Master's thesis, University of Chicago Divinity School, 1925), quotes, 1; Shirley Jackson Case, *The Evolution of Christianity: A Genetic Study of First-Century Christianity in Relation to Its Religious Environment* (Chicago: University of Chicago Press, 1914); Case, *The Social Origins of Christianity* (Chicago: University of Chicago Press, 1923); Mays, *Born to Rebel*, 99–100; Spear, *Black Chicago: The Making of a Negro Ghetto, 1890–1920*, 125–137.

24. Mays, "Pagan Survivals in Christianity," 19–41, quote, 89.

25. Benjamin E. Mays, *Quotable Quotes of Benjamin E. Mays* (New York: Vantage Press, 1983), "it is," 18–19; Samuel DuBois Cook, "Benjamin E. Mays: Rebel, Dreamer, Emancipator, Prophet, and Impossible Possibility and Reality," in *Benjamin E. Mays: His Life, Contributions, and Legacy*, "he was," 21.

26. Mays, *Born to Rebel*, 106–124.

27. Benjamin E. Mays, "The Kings Mountain Student Conference," *Intercollegian* 1 (March–April 1929): 1–2; Aldon Morris, *The Origins of the Civil Rights Movement: Black Communities Organizing for Change* (New York: Free Press, 1984), 138–139; Mays, *Born to Rebel*, "the sky" and "surely," 125, 127; Jelks, *Benjamin Elijah Mays*, 76–77; Nina Mjagkij, *Light in the Darkness: African Americans and the YMCA, 1852–1946* (Lexington: University Press of Kentucky, 1994), "sanctuaries," 129.

28. William A. Daniel, *The Education of Negro Ministers* (New York: George H. Doran, 1925); C. Luther Fry, *The U.S. Looks at Its Churches* (New York: Institute of Social and Religious Research, 1930); Pero Daghovie, *The Early Black History Movement, Carter*

G. *Woodson, and Lorenzo Johnston Greene* (Urbana: University of Illinois Press, 2007), 141–142; Jacqueline Goggins, *Carter G. Woodson: A Life in Black History* (Baton Rouge: Louisiana State University Press, 1993), 69–70; Barbara Dianne Savage, *Your Spirits Walk Beside Us: The Politics of Black Religion* (Cambridge: Harvard University Press, 2008), 50–51; Jelks, *Benjamin Elijah Mays*, 80–81.

29. A. Philip Randolph, "The Negro Church and Economic Relations," and Benjamin E. Mays, "The Negro Church and Economic Relations," Yale Divinity School seminar, "Whither the Negro Church?" cited in Jelks, *Benjamin Elijah Mays*, 82–83.

30. Benjamin E. Mays and Joseph W. Nicholson, *The Negro's Church* (New York: Institute of Social and Religious Research, 1933), quotes, 3, 278; see Benjamin E. Mays, "Christianity in a Changing World," *National Educational Outlook among Negroes* 1 (December 1937): 18–21.

31. Mays and Nicholson, *The Negro's Church*, 16–19, 38–93, quotes, 17, 85, 91; see Benjamin E. Mays, "The Negro Church in American Life," *Christendom* 5 (Summer 1940): 387–389.

32. Mays and Nicholson, *The Negro's Church*, 278–292, quotes, 281; Benjamin E. Mays, "The American Negro and the Christian Church," *Journal of Negro Education* 8 (July 1939): 530–538.

33. Mays and Nicholson, *The Negro's Church*, 288–289.

34. Walter White, review of *The Negro's Church*, by Benjamin E. Mays and Joseph W. Nicholson, *New York Herald Tribune Book Review* (1933); Howard Thurman, review of *The Negro's Church*, by Benjamin E. Mays and Joseph W. Nicholson, *Intercollegian* 50 (June 1933): 258, in *The Papers of Howard Washington Thurman*, ed. Walter Earl Fluker et al., 4 vols. (Columbia: University of South Carolina Press, 2009), 1: 173.

35. See Robert E. Park and Ernest W. Burgess, *Introduction to the Science of Sociology* (Chicago: University of Chicago Press, 1924), 870–952; Booker T. Washington and Robert E. Park, *The Man Farthest Down: A Record of Observation in Europe* (1912; reprint, New Brunswick, NJ: Transaction, 1984); Dorothy Ross, *The Origins of American Social Science* (Cambridge: Cambridge University Press, 1991), 357–361, 438–440; Jelks, "Mays's Academic Formation," 123–124. For critiques of Park and his influence, see Morris, *Origins of the Civil Rights Movement: Black Communities Organizing for Change*; and Morris, *The Scholar Denied: W. E. B. Du Bois and the Birth of Modern Sociology* (Oakland: University of California Press, 2015), 100–118.

36. See Shailer Mathews, *The Faith of Modernism* (New York: Macmillan, 1924); Mathews, *The Atonement and the Social Process* (New York: Macmillan, 1930); Mathews, *The Growth of the Idea of God* (New York: Macmillan, 1931); Dorrien, *The Making of American Liberal Theology: Idealism, Realism, and Modernity, 1900–1950*, 203–215.

37. See Henry Nelson Wieman, *Religious Experience and Scientific Method* (New York: Macmillan, 1926); Wieman, *The Wrestle of Religion with Truth* (New York: Macmillan, 1928).

38. Alfred North Whitehead, *Process and Reality: An Essay in Cosmology* (New York: Macmillan, 1929); Henry Nelson Wieman, "A Philosophy of Religion," review of *Process and Reality*, by Alfred North Whitehead, *Journal of Religion* 10 (January 1930): 137–139; Wieman, "Theocentric Religion," in *Contemporary American Theology:*

Theological Autobiographies, ed. Vergilius Ferm (New York: Round Table Press, 1932), 1: 345–346; Bernard E. Meland, "A Long Look at the Divinity School and Its Present Crisis," *Criterion* 1 (Summer 1962): 24–25.

39. See *A Gospel for the Social Awakening: Selections from the Writings of Walter Rauschenbusch*, ed. Benjamin E. Mays (New York: Association Press, 1950), reprint, *A Rauschenbusch Reader: The Kingdom of God and the Social Gospel* (New York: Harper Brothers, 1957).

40. Carter G. Woodson, *The Mis-Education of the Negro* (Washington, DC: Associated Publishers, 1933), quotes, 43, 45; see Albert Raboteau et al., "Retelling Carter Woodson's Story: Archival Sources for Afro-American Church History," *Journal of American History* 77 (June 1990): 183–199; Jelks, *Benjamin Elijah Mays: Schoolmaster of the Movement*, 93.

41. Benjamin E. Mays, *The Negro's God as Reflected in His Literature* (1938; reprint, New York: Atheneum, 1968), preface, n.p.

42. Ibid., preface, 14, 15.

43. Ibid., 25, 26.

44. Ibid., 19–53, 97–127.

45. Ibid., 78–79, cited from Mays and Nicholson, *The Negro's Church*, 64–65.

46. Mays, *The Negro's God*, 80.

47. Ibid., 218–244, quote, 244. See Countee Cullen, *Color* (New York: Harper & Brothers, 1925), 3, 20–21, 39–40; Cullen, *The Black Christ* (New York: Harper & Brothers, 1929), 77–85; James Weldon Johnson, *Along This Way* (New York: Viking Press, 1933), 414, 431.

48. Mays, *The Negro's God*, 253.

49. Carter G. Woodson, review of *The Negro's God* by Benjamin E. Mays, *Journal of Negro History* 24 (1939): 119; see Woodson, *The Mis-Education of the Negro*, 1–10, 34–48.

50. Mays, *The Negro's God*, 254, 255.

51. Ibid., 255.

52. Jelks, *Benjamin Elijah Mays*, "he missed," 101; Mays, *The Negro's God*, "the Negro's life," 255.

53. Benjamin E. Mays, "The Education of the Negro Ministers," *Journal of Negro Education* 2 (1933): 350–351.

54. Miles Mark Fisher IV, "The Howard Years," in *Walking Integrity: Benjamin Elijah Mays, Mentor to Martin Luther King Jr.*, 131–151; Jonathan Holloway, *Confronting the Veil: Abram Harris, Jr., E. Franklin Frazier, and Ralph Bunche, 1919–1941* (Chapel Hill: University of North Carolina Press, 2002), 46–49; Mays, *Born to Rebel*, quotes, 144.

55. James Farmer Jr., *Lay Bare the Heart: An Autobiography of the Civil Rights Movement* (New York: Arbor House, 1985), quotes, 136.

56. Ibid., 136.

57. Thurman, *With Head and Heart: The Autobiography of Howard Thurman* (New York: Harcourt Brace Jovanovich, 1979), 4–6; Howard Thurman, *Footprints of a Dream: The Story of the Church for the Fellowship of All Peoples* (New York: Harper, 1959), 15–16. This discussion adapts material from Dorrien, *The Making of American Liberal Theology: Idealism, Realism, and Modernity, 1900–1950*, 559–566.

58. Thurman, *Footprints of a Dream*, quote, 17; Howard Thurman, *Jesus and the Disinherited* (New York: Abingdon-Cokesbury Press, 1949; reprint, Boston: Beacon Press, 1996), 30–31.

59. Thurman, *With Head and Heart*, quote, 10; see Audrey Thomas McCluskey and Elaine M. Smith, eds., *Mary McLeod Bethune: Building a Better World: Essays and Selected Documents* (Bloomington: Indiana University Press, 1999).

60. Thurman, *Jesus and the Disinherited*, quote, 39–40.

61. Howard Thurman, introduction to *A Track to the Water's Edge: The Olive Schreiner Reader*, ed. Howard Thurman (New York: Harper & Row, 1973), "face" and "vast," xxvii–xxviii; Thurman, *With Head and Heart*, "a sense," "the boundaries," and "a certain," 8; see William Ellery Channing, "Christian Worship: Discourse at the Dedication of the Unitarian Congregational Church, Newport, Rhode Island, July 27, 1836," in *The Works of William E. Channing, D.D.*, 6 vols. (Boston: James Munroe, 1841–1843), 4: 341–348; Dorrien, *The Making of American Liberal Theology: Imagining Progressive Religion, 1805–1900*, 9–10.

62. Thurman, *With Head and Heart*, 24–26; Walter Earl Fluker, "Biographical Essay," in *The Papers of Howard Washington Thurman*, 1: xlvi–xlvii.

63. Howard W. Thurman to Mordecai Wyatt Johnson, June 18, 1918, in *The Papers of Howard Washington Thurman*, quotes, 1: 1, 2, 3.

64. Mordecai Wyatt Johnson to Howard W. Thurman, July 8, 1918, ibid., quotes, 1: 4–5; Thurman, *With Head and Heart*, 27–28.

65. Thurman, *With Head and Heart*, 40–41; Fluker, "Biographical Essay," lvii; E. A. Burtt, *The Metaphysical Foundations of Modern Physical Science* (New York: Harcourt, Brace, 1924). Burtt used two textbooks in the course: John Dewey, *How We Think* (Boston: Heath, 1910), and Laurence Buermeyer et al., *An Introduction to Reflective Thinking* (New York: Houghton Mifflin, 1923).

66. Thurman, *With Head and Heart*, "I found," 265.

67. "Howard Washington Thurman," *The Torch*, Morehouse College Yearbook, 1923, in *The Papers of Howard Washington Thurman*, "he is," 1: 25; Benjamin E. Mays to Mary Jenness, February 12, 1936, in Thurman, *The Papers of Howard Washington Thurman*, "the average," 1: 324–325; Quinton H. Dixie and Peter Eisenstadt, *Visions of a Better World: Howard Thurman's Pilgrimage to India and the Origins of African American Nonviolence* (Boston: Beacon Press, 2011), 20–21.

68. Thurman, *With Head and Heart*, quotes, 46, 48.

69. Ibid., 51; Howard Thurman, "Let Ministers Be Christians!" *Student Challenge* (January 1925): 1, 14; Thurman, "The Perils of Immature Piety," *Student Volunteer Movement Bulletin* (May 1925): 110–113; Thurman, "Negro Youth and the Washington Conference," *The Intercollegian and Far Horizons* (December 1925): 77–78, in *The Papers of Howard Washington Thurman*, 1: 43–46, 47–51, 67–69.

70. Howard Thurman, "Can It Be Truly Said That the Existence of a Supreme Spirit Is a Scientific Hypothesis?" Fall 1925 Term Paper, in *The Papers of Howard Washington Thurman*, 1: 56–63, see editors' discussion, 55; Thurman, *With Head and Heart*, 60.

71. Thurman, *With Head and Heart*, quotes, 60–61.

72. Olive Schreiner, *The Story of an African Farm* (1885; reprint, Boston: Little, Brown, 1924); Schreiner, *Trooper Peter Halket of Mashonaland* (Boston: Roberts Brothers, 1897); Schreiner, *Women and Labor* (New York: Frederick A. Stokes, 1911); Shreiner, *Dreams* (Boston: Little, Brown, 1900); Schreiner, *Stories, Dreams and Allegories* (New York: Frederick A. Stokes, 1923); Ruth First and Ann Scott, *Olive Schreiner: A Biography* (New Brunswick, NJ: Rutgers University Press, 1990); Dixie and Eisenstadt, *Visions of a Better World*, 35; Karenna Aitcheson Gore, "A Vastly Creative Spiritual Insight: Howard Thurman and the Redemption of Religion," M.A. thesis, Union Theological Seminary, April 10, 2013, 38.

73. Thurman, introduction to *A Track to the Water's Edge*, quote, xxvi.

74. Dixie and Eisenstadt, *Visions of a Better World*, quote, 37; Howard Thurman, "The Basis of Sex Morality: An Inquiry into the Attitude Toward Premarital Sexual Morality Among Various Peoples and an Analysis of Its True Basis," BD thesis, Rochester Theological Seminary, April 1926, in Thurman, *The Papers of Howard Washington Thurman*, 72–106.

75. Thurman, "The Basis of Sex Morality," quotes, 86, 88. Thurman's historical account relied on E. Westermarck, *The Origin and Development of the Moral Ideas*, 2 vols. (New York: Macmillan, 1906); W. E. Lecky, *History of European Morals*, 2 vols. (London: Longmans, Green, 1869); and H. C. Lea, *History of Sacerdotal Celibacy* (New York: Macmillan, 1907).

76. Thurman, "The Basis of Sex Morality," quotes, 102; George A. Coe, *What Ails Our Youth?* (New York: Charles Scribner's Sons, 1924).

77. Thurman, "The Basis of Sex Morality," quote, 104; see Havelock Ellis, *Little Essays of Love and Virtue* (New York: Doran, 1922); Ellis, *Studies in the Psychology of Sex* (Philadelphia: F. A. Davis, 1924); Ellis, *Men and Women* (New York: Scribner's, 1914).

78. Dixie and Eisenstadt, *Visions of a Better World*, 41.

79. Howard Thurman, "Finding God," *Religion on the Campus: Report of the National Student Conference, Milwaukee, December 28, 1926 to January 1, 1927*, ed. Francis P. Miller (New York: Association Press, 1927), 48–52, in Thurman, *The Papers of Howard Washington Thurman*, 1: 110–113, "I go" and "I am," 112; Thurman, *With Head and Heart*, "as I," 73.

80. Thurman, *With Head and Heart*, 73–74.

81. Ibid., 74; Rufus M. Jones, *Finding the Trail of Life* (New York: Macmillan, 1931). This discussion adapts material from Dorrien, *The Making of American Liberal Theology: Idealism, Realism, and Modernity, 1900–1950*, 364–371.

82. Rufus M. Jones, "Why I Enroll with the Mystics," in *Contemporary Theology: Theological Autobiographies*, 2 vols., ed. Vergilius Ferm (New York: Round Table Press, 1932), 1: 191–215; Jones, *The Story of George Fox* (New York: Macmillan, 1919); Jones, *George Fox, Seeker and Friend* (New York: Harper & Brothers, 1930); Jones, *Practical Christianity* (Philadelphia: John C. Winston, 1899); Jones, *Quakerism: A Religion of Life* (London: Headley Brothers, 1908); Elizabeth Gray Vining, *Friend of Life: The Biography of Rufus M. Jones* (Philadelphia: J. B. Lippincott, 1958); Dorrien, *The Making of American Liberal Theology: Idealism, Realism, and Modernity*, 364–371.

83. Jones, *Practical Christianity*, "the moment," "a revelation," and "it is," 188–189, 196.

84. Rufus M. Jones, *Social Law in the Spiritual World: Studies in Human and Divine Inter-Relationship* (Philadelphia: J. C. Winston, 1904), "facts" and "we must," 43–44.

85. Jones, *Social Law in the Spiritual World*, quotes, 70–71, 30–31.

86. Thurman, *With Head and Heart*, quotes, 76; Howard Thurman to Mordecai Wyatt Johnson, May 23, 1928, and Katie Thurman to Florence M. Read, July 18, 1928, in Thurman, *The Papers of Howard Washington Thurman*, 1: 125–126.

87. Thurman, *With Head and Heart*, 77.

88. Ibid., quote, 79.

89. Howard Thurman, "General Introduction," *Deep River and the Negro Spiritual Speaks of Life and Death* (Richmond, IN: Friends United Press, 1975,) quote, iii–iv;

90. Howard Thurman, "The Message of the Spirituals," *Spelman Messenger* 45 (Fall 1928): 4–12, in Thurman, *The Papers of Howard Washington Thurman*, 1: 127–137; Thurman, "Religious Ideas in Negro Spirituals," *Christendom* 4 (Autumn 1939): 515–528; Thurman, *Deep River: An Interpretation of Negro Spirituals* (Mills College, CA: Eucalyptus, 1945); Dixie and Eisenstadt, *Visions of a Better World*, 57–58; E. Franklin Frazier, *The Negro Church in America* (New York: Schocken Books, 1963), 9–25; Melville J. Herskovits, *The Myth of the Negro Past* (1924; reprint, New York: Harper & Brothers, 1941).

91. Howard Thurman, "Peace Tactics and a Racial Minority," *World Tomorrow* (December 1928); expanded edition published as " 'Relaxation' and Race Conflict," in *Pacifism in the Modern World*, ed. Devere Allen (Garden City, NY: Doubleday, 1929), 67–78, and in Thurman, *The Papers of Howard Washington Thurman*, 1: 145–151, quote, 147; George A. Coe, *The Psychology of Religion* (Chicago: University of Chicago Press, 1916), 138–140.

92. Thurman, " 'Relaxation' and Race Conflict," quotes, 147, 149, 151.

93. Devere Allen, "Introduction: Pacifism Old and New," *Pacifism in the Modern World*, quotes, xviii, 3–12; Allen, "The New White Man," ibid., 49–64; Rufus Jones, "Overcoming Evil," ibid., 39–48; Rabindranath Tagore, "Nationalism and the New Age," ibid., 203–218; Paul Jones, "The Meaning of Pacifism," ibid., 3–12; Reinhold Niebuhr, "The Use of Force," ibid., 13–26; A. J. Muste, "Pacifism and Class War," ibid., 91–102; Lucius L. Jones, "Ministers' Confab at Shaw Closed by Thurman," *Atlanta Daily World*, August 20, 1932; Jones, "Society Slants," *Atlanta Daily World*, October 7, 1932; Fluker, "Biographical Essay," lxxiii.

94. Myra Scovel, *I Must Speak: The Biography of Augustine Ralla Ram* (Allahabad: North India Christian Literature Society, 1961), 8–15; "A Great Christian from India," *Spelman Messenger* 48 (October 1931): 24–25; Dixie and Eisenstadt, *Visions of a Better World*, 69–70.

95. Daniel Johnson Fleming, *Whither Bound in Missions?* (New York: Association Press, 1925); William R. Hutchinson, *Errand to the World: American Protestant Thought and Foreign Missions* (Chicago: University of Chicago Press, 1987), 150–155; Dixie and Eisenstadt, *Visions of a Better World*, 71–72; Fluker et al., "Pilgrimage of Friendship," editorial comments in Thurman, *The Papers of Howard Washington Thurman*, 1: 184.

96. Winnifred Wygal to Howard Thurman, May 16, 1934; A. Ralla Ram to Frank T. Wilson, June 28, 1934; Muriel Lester to Howard Thurman, January 21, 1935; Howard Thurman to Elizabeth Harrington, July 11, 1935; Howard Thurman to the Members of the India Committee, December 20, 1935, in Thurman, *The Papers of Howard Washington Thurman*, 1: 192, 193–194, 231–233, 273–274, 312–317; "Thurmans, Carrolls, Embark for India," *Baltimore Afro-American*, October 5, 1935.

97. Howard Thurman, Colombo Journal, October 1935–December 1935, in Thurman, *The Papers of Howard Washington Thurman*, 1: 300–304; Detailed Schedule of the Negro Delegation in South Asia, October 21, 1935 to April 1, 1936, ibid., 283–297; see E. Stanley Jones, *The Christ of the Indian Road* (New York: Abingdon Press, 1925).

98. Thurman, Colombo Journal, quotes, 1: 303.

99. Ibid.

100. Ibid., 1: 303–304; Thurman, *With Head and Heart*, quotes, 115.

101. Thurman, *With Head and Heart*, quotes, 130, 129; see Rabindranath Tagore, *The Religion of Man* (London: George Allen and Unwin, 1931); Kshiti Mohan Sen, *Hinduism* (New York: Penguin, 2005).

102. Mahadev Desai, "With Our Negro Guests," *Harijan* (March 14, 1936), Thurman, *The Papers of Howard Washington Thurman*, 1: 333–337; Thurman, *With Head and Heart*, 132–135; Mohandas Gandhi, "From Slave to College President," *Indian Opinion*, October 9, 1903; Gandhi, "An Example to Copy," July 29, 1933; Nico Slate, *Colored Cosmopolitanism: The Shared Struggle for Freedom in the United States and India* (Cambridge: Harvard University Press, 2012), 21–22.

103. Desai, "With Our Negro Guests," 1: 335; see Leo Tolstoy, *The Kingdom of God Is Within You: Christianity Not as a Mystic Religion but as a Theory of Life* (London: Heinemann, 1894).

104. Desai, "With Our Negro Guests," 1: 335–336.

105. Ibid., 1: 336.

106. Ibid., 1: 336–337.

107. Ibid., quotes, 1: 337; Thurman, *With Head and Heart*, "he was striking," 134.

108. Thurman, *With Head and Heart*, "Christianity as it," 135; "Thurman Finds Indian, Negro Problem Same, Tells Howard Faculty of His Talk with Mahatma Ghandi," *Norfolk Journal and Guide*, May 9, 1936; Farmer, *Lay Bare the Heart*, quote, 135; Sudarshan Kapur, *Raising Up a Prophet: The African-American Encounter with Gandhi* (Boston: Beacon Press, 1992), 90–91; Dyson, *Howard University*, 68; Walter Fluker, "Biographical Essay," Thurman, *The Papers of Howard Washington Thurman*, 2: xxxv; G. James Fleming, "Preacher-At-Large," *Crisis* 46 (August 1939): 251–253.

109. Benjamin E. Mays, "Introduction," *God and Human Freedom: A Festschrift in Honor of Howard Thurman*, ed. Henry James Young (Richmond, IN: Friends United Press, 1983), xiii–xiv, "people knew," xiii; Farmer, *Lay Bare the Heart*, 135; Holloway, *Confronting the Veil: Abram Harris, Jr., E. Franklin Frazier, and Ralph Bunche, 1919–1941*; E. Franklin Frazier, *Black Bourgeoisie* (New York: Free Press, 1957); Howard Thurman to Ralph Bunche, November 9, 1934, in Thurman, *The Papers of Howard Washington Thurman*, 1: 216.

110. Howard Thurman, "India Report," February 10, 1938, in Thurman, *The Papers of Howard Washington Thurman*, 2: 122–139, quotes, 137.

111. Howard Thurman, "A 'Native Son' Speaks," *The Advocate*, May 17, 1940, in Thurman, *The Papers of Howard Washington Thurman*, 2: 247–251, quotes, 248, 249; E. Franklin Frazier, *The Negro Family in Chicago* (Chicago: University of Chicago Press, 1932).

112. Thurman, "A 'Native Son' Speaks," 250–251.

113. Howard Thurman to Ralph Harlow, November 6, 1936, in Thurman, *The Papers of Howard Washington Thurman*, 2: 190–234.

114. Howard Thurman, "Mysticism and Social Change," February 13–16, 1939, in Thurman, *The Papers of Howard Washington Thurman*, 2: 190–234; see Rufus M. Jones, *New Studies in Mystical Religion* (New York: Macmillan, 1927); Jones, *Some Exponents of Mystical Religion* (New York: Abingdon Press, 1930); Jones, *The Faith and Practice of the Quakers* (London: Methuen, 1927).

115. Logan, *Howard University*, quote, 379; McKinney, *Mordecai: The Man and the Message*, 77–97; Mays, *Born to Rebel*, 142; Walter Fluker, "Biographical Essay," Thurman, *The Papers of Howard Washington Thurman*, 2: xxxix; Howard Thurman to Mordecai Wyatt Johnson, August 13, 1938, in Thurman, *The Papers of Howard Washington Thurman*, 2: 187; Benjamin E. Mays to Howard Thurman, September 11, 1938, ibid., 2: 188; Samuel H. Archer to Howard Thurman, July 19, 1938, ibid., 173–174.

116. Mays, *Born to Rebel*, 156; Benjamin E. Mays, "Gandhi and Non-Violence," *Norfolk Journal and Guide*, May 22, 1937, 8.

117. Mays, *Born to Rebel*, 157, quotes, 159.

118. C. F. Andrews, *Mahatma Gandhi's Ideas: Including Selections from His Writings* (New York: Macmillan, 1930), 8, 37, 128; Andrews, "Christianity and Race Prejudice," *Crisis* 36 (August 1929): 271, 284; [Mahatma Gandhi], "Gandhi Hits Racial Bar," *Baltimore Afro-American*, June 16, 1934, quotes, 1; Kapur, *Raising Up a Prophet*, 78–79; Slate, *Colored Cosmopolitanism*, 123.

119. Mays, *Born to Rebel*, 157–158; "Mays Back from YMCA Conference," *Baltimore Afro-American*, March 6, 1937, 9.

120. Benjamin E. Mays, "The Color Line Around the World," *Journal of Negro Education* (March 1937): quote, 143.

121. Benjamin E. Mays, "Gandhi and Non-Violence," *Norfolk Journal and Guide*, May 22, 1937, "the first," 8; Mays, "Gandhi Rekindled Spirit of Race Pride in India, Dr. Mays Finds," *Norfolk Journal and Guide*, May 29, 1937, "has gone" and "a leader," 19.

122. Benjamin E. Mays, "What Are the Differences Between Gandhi and Nehru? Dr. Mays Asks, Gives Answer," *Norfolk Journal and Guide*, June 5, 1937, 19.

123. Mays, "The Color Line Around the World," 141.

124. Ibid.

125. Editorial, "Until Then," *Norfolk Journal and Guide*, June 12, 1937, 8; see Kapur, *Raising Up a Prophet*, 95–97; Muriel Lester, *It Occurred to Me* (New York: Harper & Brothers, 1940), 139–140.

126. See Gary Dorrien, *The Barthian Revolt in Modern Theology* (Louisville: Westminster John Knox, 2000), 47–130.

127. Edwin E. Aubrey, "The Oxford Conference, 1937," *Journal of Religion* 17 (October 1937): 379–396, quotes, 385; Reinhold Niebuhr, "The Christian Church in a Secular Age," reprinted in Niebuhr, *The Essential Reinhold Niebuhr*, ed. Robert McAfee Brown (New Haven: Yale University Press, 1986), "Christianity is," 85; J. H. Oldham, *The Oxford Conference: World Conference on Church, Community, and State (Official Report)* (New York: Willett, Clark, 1937), 25–27.
128. Aubrey, "The Oxford Conference, 1937," 386.
129. Ibid., 392; see Graeme Smith, *Oxford 1937: The Universal Christian Council for Life and Work Conference* (New York: Peter Lang, 2004).
130. Benjamin E. Mays, "The Church Surveys World Problems," *Crisis* 44 (October 1937): 316–317.
131. Samuel H. Archer to Howard Thurman, July 19, 1938, Thurman, *The Papers of Howard Washington Thurman*, 2: 173–174; Howard Thurman to Samuel H. Archer, July 26, 1938, ibid., 176–177; "Dr. Mays Elected President of Morehouse," *Atlanta Daily World*, May 11, 1940, 1; "Morehouse Has a New President," *Georgia Baptist*, May 15, 1940, quotes, 2; Mays, *Born to Rebel*, 170–177; Jones, *A Candle in the Dark*, 123–132.
132. Jelks, *Benjamin Elijah Mays*, 149; Dereck Rovaris, "Developer of an Institution: Dr. Benjamin E. Mays, Morehouse College President, 1940–1967" (Ph.D. dissertation, University of Illinois, Urbana-Champaign, 1990), 151; Mays, *Born to Rebel*, 177.
133. Benjamin E. Mays, "Interracial Leadership in This Time of Crisis," *Georgia Observer* 3 (1942): 3–4.
134. Benjamin E. Mays, "Have You Forgotten God?" *Our World*, November 1952, 40–41, "forsaking," 40; Mays, *Quotable Quotes of Benjamin E. Mays* (New York: Vantage Press, 1983), "a spiritual," 18–19.
135. Jonathan Reider, *The Word of the Lord Is Upon Me: The Righteous Performance of Martin Luther King Jr.* (Cambridge: Harvard University Press, 2008), quotes, 100–101; Jelks, *Benjamin Elijah Mays*, 153.
136. "Protestants at Pittsburgh," *Time*, December 11, 1944; Mays, *Born to Rebel*, 252; Jelks, *Benjamin Elijah Mays*, 166; Martin Luther King Sr. with Clayton Riley, *Daddy King: An Autobiography* (New York: William Morrow, 1980), 303–304; Derek Joseph Rovaris, "Mays's Leadership at Morehouse College," in *Walking Integrity: Benjamin Elijah Mays, Mentor to Martin Luther King Jr.*, 353–376; Robert Moats Miller, *Bishop G. Bromley Oxnam: Paladin of Liberal Protestantism* (Nashville: Abingdon Press, 1970), 254. Between 1945 and 1970 Mays received twenty-eight honorary doctorates.
137. Benjamin E. Mays, "The Christian in Race Relations," Henry B. Wright Lecture, Yale University Divinity School, April 16, 1952, in *Rhetoric of Racial Revolt*, ed. Roy L. Hill (Denver: Golden Bell Press, 1964), quotes, 127–128, 135.
138. Benjamin E. Mays, "Christianity and Race," *Pulpit* 25 (May 1954): 11–12.
139. Benjamin E. Mays, "The Church and Racial Tensions," *Christian Century* 71 (September 8, 1954): 1068.
140. Mays, *Born to Rebel*, quote, 253; Barbara Dianne Savage, "Benjamin Mays, Global Ecumenism, and Local Religious Segregation," *American Quarterly* 59 (September 2007): 790–791; Jelks, *Benjamin Elijah Mays*, 166; David W. Wills, "An Enduring

Distance: Black Americans and the Establishment," in *Between the Times: The Travail of the Protestant Establishment in America, 1900–1960*, ed. William R. Hutchison (New York: Cambridge University Press, 1989), 184–186.

141. Mays, "The Christian in Race Relations," quotes, 124–125; Mays, "Christianity and Race," 13; Benjamin E. Mays, "The South's Racial Policy," *Presbyterian Outlook* 132 (November 6, 1950): 2–6; Mays, "The Church Will Be Challenged at Evanston," *Christianity & Crisis* 14 (August 9, 1954): 106; David M. Reimers, *White Protestantism and the Negro* (New York: Oxford University Press, 1965).

142. Benjamin E. Mays, "Democratizing and Christianizing America in This Generation," *Journal of Negro Education* 14 (Fall 1945): 527–534, quotes, 528; Reinhold Niebuhr, "A Theologian's Comments on the Negro in America," *Reporter*, November 29, 1956, "slow erosion," 24; *A Gospel for the Social Awakening*, ed. Mays.

143. Benjamin E. Mays, "Mays: Whether Robeson Should or Should Not Speak Is Irrelevant, U.S. Should Wake Up," *Pittsburgh Courier*, October 15, 1949, 15; Mays, "If Man Is Neither Good Enough Nor Wise Enough to Avoid War, Perhaps He Should Die," *Pittsburgh Courier*, July 22, 1950, 19; Mays, "Mays: We Must Spell Out D-e-m-o-c-r-a-c-y at Home as Well as Abroad for Victory Over Reds," *Pittsburgh Courier*, February 3, 1951, 19.

144. Benjamin E. Mays, "Non-violence," *Pittsburgh Courier*, February 28, 1948, quote, 6; Mays, "Peace and Bombs," *Pittsburgh Courier*, August 9, 1947, 7; Mays, "World Aspects of Race and Culture," *Missions: American Baptist International Magazine* 147 (1949): 85; Associated Press, "300 Ask President to Talk With Reds," *Washington Post*, April 11, 1949, 2; Jelks, *Benjamin Elijah Mays*, 176–177; James L. Roark, "American Black Leaders: The Response to Colonialism and the Cold War, 1943–1953," *African Historical Studies* 4 (1971): 253–270; Reinhold Niebuhr, "A Theologian's Comments on the Negro in America," *Reporter*, November 29, 1956, 24; Niebuhr, *Christian Realism and Political Problems* (New York: Scribner's, 1953).

145. Benjamin E. Mays, "We Are Unnecessarily Excited," *New South* 9 (February 1954): quote, 2–3; Mays, "Dr. Mays: Negroes Will Win Even if High Court Oks Separate but Equal," *Pittsburgh Courier*, March 13, 1954, 8; Richard Kluger, *Simple Justice: The History of Brown v. Board of Education and Black America's Struggle for Equality* (New York: Knopf, 1975).

146. Benjamin E. Mays, "My View: Negroes Should Protest More," *Pittsburgh Courier*, March 19, 1955, quotes, 15; Mays, "My View: The Dark and Bright Side," *Pittsburgh Courier*, October 22, 1955, 24.

147. Mays, *Born to Rebel*, "strengthened," 265; author's conversation with Lawrence E. Carter Sr., November 19, 2015.

148. Farmer, *Lay Bare the Heart*, 101–108; August Meier and Elliott Rudwick, *CORE, A Study in the Civil Rights Movement, 1942–1968* (New York: Oxford University Press, 1973).

149. Peter Dana, "Dr. Thurman Speaks on Indian Question," *Pittsburgh Courier*, August 29, 1942; Dixie and Eisenstadt, *Visions of a Better World*, 117–118.

150. Lerone Bennett Jr., "Howard Thurman: 20th Century Holy Man," *Ebony* 33 (February 1978): "I'm glad," 76, "I have never," 84; Benita Eisler, "Keeping the Faith," *Nation*

(January 5, 1980), 24; Thurman, "don't ask," www.goodreads.com/author/quotes/56230. HowardThurman.

151. A. J. Muste to Howard Thurman, September 9, 1940; Howard Thurman to A. J. Muste, September 20, 1940, *The Papers of Howard Washington Thurman*, 2: 264, 265.

152. See *Ambassador of Reconciliation: A Muriel Lester Reader*, ed. Richard Deats (Santa Cruz, CA: New Society, 1991).

153. Thurman, *With Head and Heart*, 139–162; Thurman, *Footprints of a Dream*, 22–30; Dixie and Eisenstadt, *Visions of a Better World*, 166–177.

154. Thurman, *Jesus and the Disinherited*, quotes, 7, 30.

155. Ibid., 29.

156. Ibid., 16.

157. Ibid., 78.

158. Thurman, *With Head and Heart*, 155–156.

159. Thurman, *Jesus and the Disinherited*, 78–79.

160. Ibid., 100.

161. Reinhold Niebuhr, *Moral Man and Immoral Society: A Study in Ethics and Politics* (New York: Charles Scribner's Sons, 1932); Niebuhr, *An Interpretation of Christian Ethics* (New York: Harper & Brothers, 1935); Howard Thurman to Reinhold Niebuhr, December 28, 1934, *The Papers of Howard Washington Thurman*, 1: 229; Niebuhr to Thurman, December 31, 1934, ibid., 1: 230.

162. Howard Thurman, *Deep Is the Hunger: Meditations for Apostles of Sensitiveness* (New York: Harper & Brothers, 1951), quotes, 44–45; see Kenneth E. Kirk, *The Vision of God: The Christian Doctrine of the Summum Bonum* (New York: Longmans, Green, 1931), 451.

163. Thurman, *Deep Is the Hunger*, "with all" and "with renewed," 176, 177; Howard Thurman, *The Inward Journey* (New York: Harper & Brothers, 1961), "to focus," 7; Rufus M. Jones, "How Shall We Think of Christ?" in *Religious Foundations*, ed. Rufus Jones (New York: Macmillan, 1923), 15–29.

164. Howard Thurman, *Meditations of the Heart* (New York: Harper & Row, 1953), quotes, 120–121.

165. Benjamin E. Mays, *Seeking to Be Christian in Race Relations* (New York: Friendship Press, 1957; rev. ed., 1964), 79.

166. Ibid., 79; see Barbara Dianne Savage, *Your Spirits Walk Beside Us: The Politics of Black Religion* (Cambridge: Harvard University Press, 2008), 217.

167. Thurman, *Footprints of a Dream*, 157; see Dixie and Eisenstadt, *Visions of a Better World*, 178–179; Albert S. Broussard, *Black San Francisco: The Struggle for Racial Equality in the West, 1900–1954* (Lawrence: University of Kansas Press, 1993), 185–190.

168. Mays, *Born to Rebel*, quote, 265.

169. Howard Thurman, *A Strange Freedom: The Best of Howard Thurman on Religious Experience and Public Life*, ed. Walter Earl Fluker and Catherine Tumber (Boston: Beacon Press, 1998), "the overflowing" and "it is," 95; Thurman, *Mysticism and the Experience of Love* (Wallingford, PA: Pendle Hill Publications, 1961), "he gave," 3.

170. Thurman, *Mysticism and the Experience of Love*, quote, 19; Thurman, *Footprints of a Dream*, 144.

171. Niebuhr, *Moral Man and Immoral Society*, quotes, 254.

172. Mays, "Why I Believe There Is a God," 7; Thurman, *Jesus and the Disinherited*, "the disinherited," 108–109; see Howard Thurman, *The Search for Common Ground: An Inquiry into the Basis of Man's Experience of Community* (Richmond, IN: Friends United Press, 1986).

173. See Martin Luther King Jr., "A Religion of Doing" (July 4, 1954), *The Papers of Martin Luther King Jr.*, 6: 170–174; King Jr., "Overcoming an Inferiority Complex" (July 14, 1957), ibid., 6: 303–316; King Jr., "Living Under the Tensions of Modern Life," (September 1956), ibid., 6: 262–270.

CHAPTER 4. PROTEST POLITICS AND POWER POLITICS

1. Adam Clayton Powell Jr., *Marching Blacks* (New York: Dial Press, 1945; reprint, with postscript, 1972), "first love," 93; Adam Clayton Powell Jr., *Adam by Adam: The Autobiography of Adam Clayton Powell Jr.* (1971; reprint, New York: Kensington, 2002), "the sheer," 11.

2. Adam Clayton Powell Sr., *Against the Tide: An Autobiography* (New York: Richard R. Smith, 1938), 6–7; Lenworth A. Gunther III, "Flamin' Tongue: The Rise of Adam Clayton Powell Jr., 1908–1941" (Ph.D. dissertation, Columbia University, 1985), 5–7; Samuel D. Proctor, "Adam Clayton Powell, Sr.," *Dictionary of American Negro Biography*, 501–502; Edward L. Queen II, "Adam Clayton Powell, Sr.," in *The Encyclopedia of American Religious History*, ed. Edward L. Queen II, Stephen R. Prothero, and Gardiner H. Shattuck Jr., 2 vols. (New York: Facts on File, 1996), 517–518; Ben Richardson, *Great American Negroes* (New York: Thomas Y. Crowell, 1956), 201–203; "Dr. A. C. Powell, Sr., Minister, 88, Dead," *New York Times* (June 13, 1953), 15; "Thousands Mourn Rev. Powell's Death," *New York Amsterdam News*, June 20, 1953, 1.

3. Powell, *Marching Blacks*, "that P.," 15; Powell, *Adam by Adam*, "who forgave," 11, "I am," 12.

4. Powell, *Adam by Adam*, 14.

5. Powell, *Marching Blacks*, quotes, 92; Adam Clayton Powell Sr., *Upon This Rock* (New York: Abyssinian Baptist Church, 1949), 15–16; Powell, *Against the Tide*, 68–71; Gilbert Osofsky, *Harlem: The Making of a Ghetto* (New York: Harper & Row, 1966), 112–117; Roi Ottley and William Weatherby, eds., *The Negro in New York: An Informal Social History, 1626–1940* (New York: Praeger, 1967), 182–187; John William Kinney, "Adam Clayton Powell, Sr. and Adam Clayton Powell, Jr.: A Historical Exposition and Theological Analysis" (Ph.D. dissertation, Columbia University, 1979), 79–80; William Welty, "Black Shepherds: A Study of the Leading Negro Churchmen in New York City, 1900–1940" (Ph.D. dissertation, New York University, 1969), 142–144; Claude McKay, *Harlem: Negro Metropolis* (New York: E. P. Dutton, 1940), 143–180; Neil Hickey and Ed Edwin, *Adam Clayton Powell and the Politics of Race* (New York: Fleet, 1965), 22–24.

6. Powell, *Adam by Adam*, quote, 15; Powell, *Against the Tide*, 70–71; Lawrence Rushing, "The Racial Identity of Adam Clayton Powell Jr.: A Case Study in Racial Ambivalence and Redefinition," *Afro-Americans in New York Life and History* 34 (January 2010), www.questia.com/library.

7. Dan Wakefield, interview with Adam Clayton Powell Jr. in Wakefield, "Adam Clayton Powell Jr.: The Angry Voice of Harlem," *Esquire* (November 1959); Powell, *Adam by Adam*, 23–24; Hickey and Edwin, *Adam Clayton Powell and the Politics of Race*, 33.

8. Powell, *Adam by Adam*, quote, 24.

9. Claude Lewis, *Adam Clayton Powell* (Greenwich, CT: Fawcett, 1963), quotes, 38.

10. Powell, *Adam by Adam*, quotes, 27, 30.

11. Ibid., 31; Lewis, *Adam Clayton Powell*, 37.

12. David Balch, interview with Ray Vaughn, "God, Caesar and Powell—Adam Clayton Saves 'em All," *New York World Telegram*, April 3, 1963, 49, 62; Wil Haygood, *King of the Cats: The Life and Times of Adam Clayton Powell Jr.* (Boston: Houghton Mifflin, 1993; reprint, New York: HarperCollins, 2006), 10–15; Charles V. Hamilton, *Adam Clayton Powell Jr.: The Political Biography of an American Dilemma* (New York: Scribner, 1991), 49–50; Hickey and Edwin, *Adam Clayton Powell and the Politics of Race*, 34–35; Powell, *Adam by Adam*, 31.

13. Powell, *Adam by Adam*, 32; Haygood, *King of the Cats*, 14–15.

14. Powell, *Adam by Adam*, 34–35.

15. Ibid., 35.

16. Balch, interview with Ray Vaughn, 62; Powell, *Adam by Adam*, 34.

17. Powell, *Adam by Adam*, quotes, 37; John Dewey, *Schools of Tomorrow* (New York: E. P. Dutton, 1915); Dewey, *Democracy and Education* (New York: Macmillan, 1916); Dewey, "Education for a Changing Social Order," *NEA Addresses and Proceedings* 72 (1934): 754–770; George Counts, *Dare the School Build a New Social Order?* (Carbondale: Southern Illinois University Press, 1932).

18. Powell, *Adam by Adam*, quote, 55; Oliver E. Allen, *The Tiger: The Rise and Fall of Tammany Hall* (New York: Addison-Wesley, 1993); Alfred Connable and Edward Silberfarb, *Tigers of Tammany: Nine Men Who Ran New York* (New York: Holt, Rinehart and Winston, 1967).

19. Powell, *Marching Blacks*, quote, 85; Haygood, *King of the Cats*, 37–41; Hamilton, *Adam Clayton Powell Jr.*, 51–52; Hickey and Edwin, *Adam Clayton Powell and the Politics of Race*, 37–39; Powell, *Adam by Adam*, 58–59.

20. Isabel Powell, interview with Charles V. Hamilton, November 16, 1988, quoted in Hamilton, *Adam Clayton Powell Jr.*, 85; Haygood, *King of the Cats*, 28–29; Hickey and Edwin, *Adam Clayton Powell and the Politics of Race*, 36–37; Powell, *Adam by Adam*, 59–60.

21. Powell, *Against the Tide*, "preach with," 290; Haygood, *King of the Cats*, "not," 73; Robert Jakoubek, *Adam Clayton Powell Jr.: Political Leader* (New York: Chelsea House, 1988), 41.

22. Powell, *Marching Blacks*, 92.

23. Powell, *Adam by Adam*, 39.

24. Ibid., 41–42; Adam Clayton Powell Jr., "Do You Really Believe in God?" January 23, 1955, in Powell, *Keep the Faith, Baby!* (New York: Trident Press, 1967), 285–287; Powell, "Thy Will Be Done," ibid., 255–257.

25. Powell, *Adam by Adam*, 43.

26. Ibid., 43–44; Adam Clayton Powell Jr., "You Cannot Limit Christ," in *Keep the Faith, Baby!*, 200–201; Powell, *Marching Blacks*, 92–93.

27. U.S. Supreme Court, *New Negro Alliance v. Sanitary Grocery Company*, 303 U.S. 552 (1938), decided March 28, 1938, http://supreme.justia.com/cases; "New Negro Alliance," in *Organizing Black America: An Encyclopedia of African American Associations* (New York: Garland, 2001).

28. Powell, *Marching Blacks*, "I was," 94; Roi Ottley, *New World A-Coming* (Boston: Houghton Mifflin, 1943), 229; Hamilton, *Adam Clayton Powell Jr.*, "backbiting," 97; McKay, *Harlem: Negro Metropolis*, 193–195; Hickey and Edwin, *Adam Clayton Powell and the Politics of Race*, 52–57.

29. Powell, *Marching Blacks*, quotes, 95, 96; Ottley, *New World A-Coming*, 228–229.

30. Powell, *Marching Blacks*, quotes, 98; see Mark Naison, *Communists in Harlem During the Depression* (New York: Grove Press, 1983).

31. Powell, *Marching Blacks*, quotes, 89, 99.

32. Adam Clayton Powell Jr., Commencement Address at Shaw University, 1938, in Haygood, *King of the Cats*, 78.

33. Ottley, *New World A-Coming*, 232–233; Hamilton, *Adam Clayton Powell Jr.*, 102–104; Haygood, *King of the Cats*, 82–83.

34. Powell, *Marching Blacks*, quote, 48.

35. Powell, *Adam by Adam*, quote, 69; Haygood, *King of the Cats*, 80–81.

36. Powell, *Adam by Adam*, 69; Ottley, *New World A-Coming*, 233; see Gilbert Osofsky, *Harlem: The Making of a Ghetto* (New York: Harper & Row, 1966).

37. "Look Out for Surrender," *Amsterdam News*, reprinted in *People's Voice*, February 14, 1942, "ambitious"; Editorial, *People's Voice*, February 14, 1942, "working" and "a just"; Adam Clayton Powell Jr., "Soap Box," *People's Voice*, March 28, 1942, "it is"; Hamilton, *Adam Clayton Powell Jr.*, 119–120; Haygood, *King of the Cats*, 88–89; Ottley, *New World A-Coming*, "we are," 234.

38. Karen Chilton, *Hazel Scott: The Pioneering Journey of a Jazz Pianist from Café Society to Hollywood to HUAC* (Ann Arbor: University of Michigan Press, 2008), 5–21; Kristin McGee, "Swinging the Classics: Hazel Scott and Hollywood's Musical–Racial Matrix," in *Some Liked It Hot: Jazz Women in Film and Television, 1928–1959* (Middletown, CT: Wesleyan University Press, 2009), 113–133; E. Taubman, "Café Music Heard at Carnegie Hall," *New York Times*, April 24, 1941.

39. Isabel Washington Powell, interview with Charles V. Hamilton, November 16, 1988, in Hamilton, *Adam Clayton Powell Jr.*, 115; Powell, *Adam by Adam*, "one day," 224; Adam Clayton Powell Jr., "Mickey Mouse vs. Mayor La Guardia—The Winner, Mickey!" *People's Voice*, May 23, 1942, "one of the," 20; Powell, *Marching Blacks*, 153–154; Dominic J. Capeci, "From Different Liberal Perspectives: Fiorello H. La Guardia,

Adam Clayton Powell Jr., and Civil Rights in New York City, 1941–1943," *Journal of Negro History* 62 (April 1977): 168; see Arthur Simon, *Stuyvesant Town, USA: Pattern for Two Americas* (New York: New York University Press, 1970), 34.

40. Adam Clayton Powell Jr., "Soap Box," *People's Voice*, April 18, 1942, "a direct," 5; Hamilton, *Adam Clayton Powell Jr.*, "countenance," 140.

41. Adam Clayton Powell Jr., Speech at Madison Square Garden, June 16, 1942, in Powell, *People's Voice*, June 19, 1942; Haygood, *King of the Cats*, 93.

42. Powell, *Adam on Adam*, "time," 224; Lewis, *Adam Clayton Powell*, "tossed," 109; Haygood, *King of the Cats*, 103–104.

43. Powell, *Marching Blacks*, 5, 6.

44. Ibid., "secretly copied," "except," "ingratiate," "today," 13–14; "the men," 79; Haygood, *King of the Cats*, "a fantastic," 89.

45. Powell, *Marching Blacks*, quotes, 25, 28, 49.

46. Ibid., quotes, 67.

47. Ibid., quote, 140; Gunnar Myrdal, *An American Dilemma: The Negro Problem and Modern Democracy* (New York: Harper & Row, 1944).

48. Powell, *Marching Blacks*, 178, 180–181, 183–184.

49. Ibid., 186, 187–188.

50. Ibid., 194–195, 198.

51. Edwin Embree, "Democracy and Race Relations," Address to the National Conference of Social Work, Cleveland, Ohio, May 26, 1944, cited ibid., 205–206.

52. Ben Richardson, review of *Marching Blacks* by Adam Clayton Powell Jr., *People's Voice*, February 2, 1946, "I say"; Adam Clayton Powell Jr., "Soap Box—Washington, DC," *People's Voice*, March 30, 1946, "white"; Haygood, *King of the Cats*, 133.

53. Powell, *Adam by Adam*, 70–72, quote, 70; Hamilton, *Adam Clayton Powell Jr.*, 137.

54. Haygood, *King of the Cats*, quotes, 126; Lewis, *Adam Clayton Powell*, 111.

55. "Tea for Fifty Ladies," *Newsweek*, October 22, 1945; Haygood, *King of the Cats*, 128–129; Robert J. Donovan, *Conflict and Crisis: The Presidency of Harry S. Truman, 1945–1948* (New York: Norton, 1977), 147–148; Powell, *Adam by Adam*, 79.

56. Donovan, *Conflict and Crisis*, quote, 148; Editorial, "Doesn't the DAR Know That the Civil War Is Over?" *Philadelphia Record*, October 13, 1945; Powell, *Adam by Adam*, 79; Haygood, *King of the Cats*, 130; Hamilton, *Adam Clayton Powell Jr.*, 165.

57. Powell, *Adam by Adam*, 74.

58. See William W. Freehling, *The Road to Disunion: Secessionists at Bay, 1776–1854* (New York: Oxford University Press, 1990), 144–150; William Lee Miller, *Arguing About Slavery: John Quincy Adams and the Great Battle in the United States Congress* (New York: Random House, 1995), 48–49; Gordon W. Gunderson, "National School Lunch Program," United States Department of Agriculture, www.fns.usda.gov/nsip/history.

59. Haygood, *King of the Cats*, 135–146; Earl Brown, "Timely Topics," *Amsterdam News*, June 22, 1946, 10; Hamilton, *Adam Clayton Powell Jr.*, 182–185.

60. Robert A. Divine, "The Cold War and the Election of 1948," *Journal of American History* 59 (1972): 90–110; Thomas W. Devine, *Henry Wallace's 1948 Presidential Campaign and the Future of Postwar Liberalism* (Chapel Hill: University of North

Carolina Press, 2013); Zachary Karabell, *The Last Campaign: How Harry Truman Won the 1948 Election* (New York: Knopf, 2001); Michael Bowen, *The Roots of Modern Conservatism: Dewey, Taft, and the Battle for the Soul of the Republican Party* (Chapel Hill: University of North Carolina Press, 2011).

61. Hamilton, *Adam Clayton Powell Jr.*, 189–190; Roy Wilkins, *New Leader*, January 1950, quote; see Yvonne Ryan, *Roy Wilkins: The Quiet Revolutionary and the NAACP* (Lexington: University Press of Kentucky, 2014), 44–46.

62. Roy Wilkins, *Standing Fast: The Autobiography of Roy Wilkins* (New York: Da Capo Press, 1994), quote, 189; Matthew J. Countryman, *Up South: Civil Rights and Black Power in Philadelphia* (Philadelphia: University of Pennsylvania Press, 2006), 32–40; Hamilton, *Adam Clayton Powell Jr.*, 191–192.

63. Benjamin J. Davis, "Rep. Powell's New Line," *Daily Worker*, March 15, 1951, quote; "Testimony of Hazel Scott," Hearing before the Committee on Un-American Activities, 81st Congress, Second Session (September 22, 1950), 3611–3615, "we should," 3615; Hamilton, *Adam Clayton Powell Jr.*, 195–196; Haygood, *King of the Cats*, 162.

64. Hamilton, *Adam Clayton Powell Jr.*, 197–198; Haygood, *King of the Cats*, 167–173; see Porter McKeever, *Adlai Stevenson: His Life and Legacy* (New York: Morrow, 1989); Jeff Broadwater, *Adlai Stevenson and American Politics: The Odyssey of a Cold War Liberal* (Ann Arbor: Twayne, 1994).

65. Robert Frederick Burk, *The Eisenhower Administration and Black Civil Rights* (Knoxville: University of Tennessee Press, 1984), 15–28; Arthur Larson, *Eisenhower, the President Nobody Knew* (New York: Scribner's, 1968), 127–128; Robert J. Donovan, *Confidential Secretary: Ann Whitman's 20 Years with Eisenhower and Rockefeller* (New York: E. P. Dutton, 1988), 112–115; Hamilton, *Adam Clayton Powell Jr.*, 200–201.

66. Haygood, *King of the Cats*, 183.

67. "Hobby Note Flouts Segregation Order, Powell Charges," *Washington Evening Star*, June 4, 1953; *Congressional Record* (1953), Appendix A3555; Haygood, *King of the Cats*, 187; Hamilton, *Adam Clayton Powell Jr.*, 201–202.

68. *Congressional Record* (1953), Appendix A3555, "we have," "a Magna Carta"; Hamilton, *Adam Clayton Powell Jr.*, 203; Haygood, *King of the Cats*, "I guess," 189, "he was," 191.

69. Adam Clayton Powell Jr., "The President and the Negro: A New Era!" *Reader's Digest*, October 1954, quotes; Richard Kluger, *Simple Justice: The History of Brown v. Board of Education and Black America's Struggle for Equality* (New York: Knopf, 1975), 656–657.

70. Adam Clayton Powell Jr., "Walking Under a Cloud," Sermon Preached at Abyssinian Church (December 13, 1953), in Powell, *Keep the Faith, Baby!*, "the abolition," 151; Powell, *Adam by Adam*, "but something," 121.

71. Homer Bigart, "Powell Tells Asia About U.S. Negro; Red Newsmen Find Him Off the 'Line,' " *New York Herald Tribune*, April 18, 1955; "Adam Powell at Bandung," *New York Mirror*, April 20, 1955; "Madden Praises Powell, Representative Says Colleague Upset Red's Bandung Plans," *New York Times*, April 27, 1955; "Powell's Asia Reports Are Criticized," *Amsterdam News*, May 21, 1955; Editorial, "The New Cong. Powell," *Pittsburgh Courier*, June 4, 1955; Hamilton, *Adam Clayton Powell Jr.*, 237–258; Haygood, *King of the Cats*, 199–204.

72. Powell, *Adam by Adam*, 124; Joseph E. Treaster, "James E. Folsom, Colorful Politician and Twice Governor of Alabama, Is Dead at 79," *New York Times*, November 22, 1987; Associated Press, "J. E. (Big Jim) Folsom Dies; Ex-Governor of Alabama," November 22, 1987.

73. Haygood, *King of the Cats*, 204–206; Powell, *Adam by Adam*, 124–125.

74. Haygood, *King of the Cats*, 206; see Dan T. Carter, *The Politics of Rage: George Wallace, the Origins of the New Conservatism, and the Transformation of American Politics* (New York: Simon & Schuster, 1995).

75. Hamilton, *Adam Clayton Powell Jr.*, 249–251; Haygood, *King of the Cats*, 196–198.

76. Hamilton, *Adam Clayton Powell Jr.*, 257–258.

77. Ibid., 261–263; E. Frederick Morrow, *Black Man in the White House* (New York: Coward-McCann, 1963), 46–48.

78. Editorial, "Mr. Stevenson and Gradualism," *New York Age*, February 18, 1956, "we must proceed"; Editorial, "Adlai Speaks Out," *Baltimore Afro-American*, March 6, 1956; Haygood, *King of the Cats*, 214–215; John Bartlow Martin, *Adlai Stevenson and the World* (Garden City, NY: Doubleday, 1977), "evidently," 256; Wilkins, *Standing Fast*, "we must," 232–233; C. Vann Woodward, *The Strange Career of Jim Crow* (New York: Oxford University Press, 1955; 3rd ed., 1974; reprint, 2002), 164; Joseph B. Gorman, *Kefauver: A Political Biography* (New York: Oxford University Press, 1971).

79. Hamilton, *Adam Clayton Powell Jr.*, 270; interview with Adam Clayton Powell Jr., *New York Mirror*, October 16, 1956; "Rep. Powell Admits: He Misquoted Eisenhower on Jailing Segregationists," *New York Herald Tribune*, October 24, 1956; Powell, *Adam by Adam*, 130.

80. Hamilton, *Adam Clayton Powell Jr.*, 266–269; Haygood, *King of the Cats*, 219; Lewis, *Adam Clayton Powell*, 113; Powell, *Adam by Adam*, 130–131.

81. Powell, *Adam by Adam*, quote, 131.

82. Ibid., quotes, 132; William F. Buckley Jr., "Death of an Investigation: The Wheels of Justice Stop for Adam Clayton Powell, Jr.," *National Review*, December 14, 1957, 537–541; Don Hogan, "Powell Tells Flock He Is Persecuted," *New York Herald Tribune*, April 28, 1958; Editorial, "Chastise Powell," *Amsterdam News*, November 17, 1956; Hamilton, *Adam Clayton Powell Jr.*, 276–277; Haygood, *King of the Cats*, 122–123.

83. Adam Clayton Powell Jr., "Why I Am a Christian," Sermon at Abyssinian Church, October 2, 1955, in *Keep the Faith, Baby!*, quotes, 109, 113, 114.

84. Ibid., quotes, 111, 112.

85. Ibid., quotes, 114, 115.

86. Adam Clayton Powell Jr., "The New Church," ibid., "we are not," 122; Powell, "Democracy and Religion," ibid., "lay more stress," 158.

87. Adam Clayton Powell Jr., "The Temptation of Modernity," ibid., 208.

88. Powell, *Adam by Adam*, 136; L. D. Reddick, *Crusader Without Violence: A Biography of Martin Luther King Jr.* (New York: Harper & Brothers, 1959), 194–197; James L. Hicks, Editorial, *Amsterdam News*, June 1, 1957; Taylor Branch, *Parting the Waters: America in the King Years, 1954–63* (New York: Simon & Schuster, 1988), 220–221; Hamilton, *Adam Clayton Powell Jr.*, 281–290; Haygood, *King of the Cats*, 237–238; David Garrow, *Bearing the Cross: Martin Luther King Jr. and the Southern Christian Leadership Conference* (New York: William Morrow, 1986), 90.

89. Powell, *Adam by Adam*, "and so," 138; Branch, *Parting the Waters*, 234–236; "Powell Dares Democrats to Drop Him," *New York Post*, February 10, 1958, 18; David Hapgood, *The Purge That Failed: Tammany v. Powell* (New York: McGraw-Hill, 1960), 11–19.

90. "Powell Dares Democrats to Drop Him," *New York Post*, February 10, 1958, 18; Lewis, *Adam Clayton Powell*, "hat," 68; Hapgood, *The Purge That Failed: Tammany v. Powell*, 11–19.

91. Hamilton, *Adam Clayton Powell Jr.*, 295.

92. Adam Clayton Powell Jr., "Let's Give Up Our Own Prejudices," Sermon on July 3, 1960, in Powell, *Keep the Faith, Baby!*, quotes, 79, 80.

93. Garrow, *Bearing the Cross*, 138; Branch, *Parting the Waters*, 314–315, quote, 291; John D'Emilio, *Lost Prophet: The Life and Times of Bayard Rustin* (Chicago: University of Chicago Press, 2003), 296–297.

94. Branch, *Parting the Waters*, 315; D'Emilio, *Lost Prophet*, 298; Garrow, *Bearing the Cross*, 138.

95. D'Emilio, *Lost Prophet*, quotes, 298–299; Branch, *Parting the Waters*, 329; Clayborne Carson, *In Struggle: SNCC and the Black Awakening of the 1960s* (Cambridge: Harvard University Press, 1995), 26–27.

96. Adam Clayton Powell Jr., "A New Frontier of Faith," in Powell, *Keep the Faith, Baby!*, 83–86; Haygood, *King of the Cats*, 270–272; Harris Wofford, *Of Kennedys and Kings: Making Sense of the Sixties* (New York: Farrar, Straus, Giroux, 1980), 64–65; Branch, *Parting the Waters*, 343–344.

97. Editorial, "Why Nixon Lost the Negro Vote," *Crisis* (January 1961): 12; Wofford, *Of Kennedys and Kings*, 23–26; Morrow, *Black Man in the White House*, 212–213; Branch, *Parting the Waters*, 374–376; Theodore C. Sorensen, *Kennedy* (New York: Harper & Row, 1965), 216; Theodore White, *The Making of the President, 1960* (New York: Atheneum, 1961), 321–354. Kennedy mythologists refused to acknowledge what JFK and some of them owed to Wofford and Martin. Sorensen said that Kennedy would have won a landslide in the black vote even without the King calls because Kennedy's economic policies were (somehow) obviously better for blacks than Nixon's. White famously turned the story on its head, claiming that Kennedy's kitchen cabinet employed its astonishing brilliance to brilliantly court black voters.

98. Frederick W. Roevekamp, "Storms Weathered, Harlem's Powell Garners Tributes," *Christian Science Monitor*, January 31, 1961; Branch, *Parting the Waters*, 385; Haygood, *King of the Cats*, 275–276; Hamilton, *Adam Clayton Powell Jr.*, 339–340.

99. Hamilton, *Adam Clayton Powell Jr.*, 340–342; Sorensen, *Kennedy*, 474–477; Wilkins, *Standing Fast*, 278–288; Murray Kempton, "The Payoff," *New York Post*, June 20, 1960.

100. Wilkins, *Standing Fast*, quote, 279.

101. Powell, *Adam by Adam*, "miserable," 201; Kempton, "The Payoff," "terrible"; Hamilton, *Adam Clayton Powell Jr.*, 344–357; Sorensen, *Kennedy*, 350–353.

102. Branch, *Parting the Waters*, "I'm not," 807–808; Hamilton, *Adam Clayton Powell Jr.*, "the white man" and "I don't agree," 360.

103. NAACP, *Adam . . . Where Art Thou?* (New York: NAACP, April 1963); Hamilton, *Adam Clayton Powell Jr.*, 364.

104. Lewis, *Adam Clayton Powell*, 33. Powell and Malcolm spoke together in Harlem at a rally for the Mississippi Relief Committee on March 23, 1963, and Malcolm preached at Abyssinian that summer, on June 23, 1963.

105. John F. Kennedy, "The Civil Rights Address," June 11, 1963, www.americanrhetoric.com/speeches.

106. Robert Dallek, *An Unfinished Life: John F. Kennedy, 1917–1963* (New York: Little, Brown, 2003), "sweeping," 606; Hamilton, *Adam Clayton Powell Jr.*, 366; Adam Clayton Powell Jr., Speech at NAACP Labor Banquet, Sheraton Hotel, Philadelphia, July 14, 1963, NAACP Papers, Library of Congress.

107. See William P. Jones, *The March on Washington: Jobs, Freedom, and the Forgotten History of Civil Rights* (New York: Norton, 2013); Charles Euchner, *Nobody Turn Me Around: A People's History of the March on Washington* (Boston: Beacon Press, 2010); Lucy G. Barber, *Marching on Washington: The Forging of an American Political Tradition* (Berkeley: University of California Press, 2002); Leonard Freed, *This Is the Day: The March on Washington* (Los Angeles: Getty, 2013).

108. Haygood, *King of the Cats*, quotes, 294, 295; Jakoubek, *Adam Clayton Powell Jr.*, 87.

109. Powell, *Adam by Adam*, quote, 216.

110. Hamilton, *Adam Clayton Powell Jr.*, quote, 374; see John C. Donovan, *The Politics of Poverty* (New York: Pegasus, 1967).

111. Lyndon B. Johnson, Remarks Upon Signing the Civil Rights Act of 1964 (July 2, 1964), *Public Papers of the Presidents of the United States: Lyndon B. Johnson, 1963–64*, vol. 2, entry 446 (Washington, DC: Government Printing Office, 1965), quote, 843–844; Charles Whalen and Barbara Whalen, *The Longest Debate: A Legislative History of the 1964 Civil Rights Act* (New York: New American Library, 1985).

112. David J. Garrow, *Protest at Selma: Martin Luther King Jr. and the Voting Rights Act of 1965* (New Haven: Yale University Press, 1978), 21–22; Adam Fairclough, *To Redeem the Soul of America: The Southern Christian Leadership Conference and Martin Luther King Jr.* (Athens: University of Georgia Press, 1987), 208–209; James Farmer, *Lay Bare the Heart: An Autobiography of the Civil Rights Movement* (Fort Worth: Texas Christian University Press, 1985), 298–299; Charles Fager, *Selma, 1965: The March that Changed the South* (Boston: Beacon Press, 1985); Garrow, *We Shall Overcome: The Civil Rights Movement in the United States in the 1950s and 1960s* (Brooklyn, NY: Carlson, 1989); Chandler Davidson, *Quiet Revolution in the South: The Impact of the Voting Rights Act, 1965–1990* (Princeton: Princeton University Press, 1994).

113. Lyndon B. Johnson, *The Vantage Point: Perspectives of the Presidency, 1963–1969* (New York: Holt, Rinehart, 1971), 210–211.

114. "Powell Convenes Ad Hoc Sub-Committee on De Facto School Segregation; Announces Investigation," March 7, 1966, press release, in Hamilton, *Adam Clayton Powell Jr.*, 391.

115. Carson, *In Struggle*, "this is," 209–210, and John Lewis, *Walking with the Wind: A Memoir of the Movement* (New York: Harcourt, Brace, 1998), 388–389; Adam Clayton Powell Jr., "Black Power: A Form of Godly Power," in Powell, *Keep the Faith, Baby!*, 9–19, "to demand," 9–10; see Richard Wright, *Black Power: A Record of Reactions in a Land of Pathos* (New York: Harper, 1954).

116. Haygood, *King of the Cats*, 324–325, 398–399, "this new," 324; Taylor Branch, *At Canaan's Edge: America in the King Years 1965–68* (New York: Simon & Schuster, 2006), "Adam is," 377; "Powell, Denying Rift, Welcomes King to Harlem," *New York Times*, November 15, 1965; Stokely Carmichael and Charles Hamilton, *Black Power: The Politics of Liberation in America* (New York: Random House, 1967), 34–56; Wyatt Tee Walker, *Road to Damascus: A Journey of Faith* (New York: Martin Luther King Fellows Press, 1985); "Wyatt Tee Walker," Martin Luther King Jr. Research and Education Institute, http://mlk-kpp01.stanford.edu.

117. Powell, "Black Power," quotes, 10; Haygood, *King of the Cats*, 325; Peniel E. Joseph, *Stokely: A Life* (New York: Basic Books, 2014), 129–130.

118. Powell, "Black Power," quotes, 11.

119. Ibid., 14, 15.

120. Ibid., "the economic," 16; Haygood, *King of the Cats*, "you're dealing," 324, quoted in *New York Post* (July 28, 1965).

121. Powell, "Black Power," quotes, 17, 18; see Powell, *Marching Blacks*, 208.

122. Bruce Perry, *Malcolm: The Life of a Man Who Changed Black America* (Barrytown, NY: Station Hill, 1991), "it's hard," 304; Powell, *Adam by Adam*, "a dear," "I also," 243, 244; Taylor Branch, *Pillar of Fire: America in the King Years, 1963–65* (New York: Touchstone, 1998), 96; Manning Marable, *Malcolm X: A Life of Reinvention* (New York: Viking, 2011); Malcolm X, *Malcolm X Speaks*, ed. George Breitman (New York: Grove, 1965).

123. Farmer, *Lay Bare the Heart*, 303–304.

124. Ibid., quotes, 304, 305; Editorial, "Mr. Powell Defaults," *New York Times*, December 10, 1966, 36; Drew Pearson, "Who Is Mrs. James?" *New York Post*, February 14, 1967, 34.

125. Hamilton, *Adam Clayton Powell Jr.*, 407–417, quote, 410; Lewis, *Adam Clayton Powell*, 114–118.

126. Lewis, *Adam Clayton Powell*, 74–75, quote, 118; James L. Hicks, "I Traveled in Europe with Congressman Powell," *Amsterdam News*, September 22, 1962.

127. Drew Pearson, "The Washington Merry-Go-Round: Negroes Found Ashamed of Powell," *Washington Post*, September 22, 1966; Haygood, *King of the Cats*, 329.

128. "Must Adam Leave Eden?" *Newsweek*, January 16, 1967; Haygood, *King of the Cats*, 346–352.

129. Editorial, "Rebuke for Powell," *New York Times*, January 10, 1967, 42; Editorial, "Disciplining of Powell," *New York Times*, January 13, 1967, 12; Jakoubek, *Adam Clayton Powell Jr.*, quote, 94; Andy Jacobs, *The Powell Affair: Freedom Minus One* (New York: Bobbs-Merrill, 1973), 3–11.

130. "Investigations: Adam & Yvette," *Time*, February 24, 1967; Editorial, "Disciplining of Powell," 12; Haygood, *King of the Cats*, 355–359, quote, 359; Jakoubek, *Adam Clayton Powell Jr.*, 99; Jacobs, *The Powell Affair*, 3–11.

131. "Wilkins Accuses Powell of Apathy," *New York Times*, January 14, 1967; Martin Luther King Jr., A. Philip Randolph, Bayard Rustin, Roy Wilkins, and Whitney M. Young, "Statement on Adam Clayton Powell," press release, NAACP, January 23, 1967, NAACP Papers; Editorial, "In Defense of Powell," *Pittsburgh Courier*, January 21, 1967; "Rebuke for Powell," *New York Times*, 42; Joseph, *Stokely*, 174; Jacobs, *The Powell Affair*, 8–9.

132. Joseph, *Stokely*, 174.

133. Haygood, *King of the Cats*, 368–375.

134. *Powell v. McCormack*, 395 U.S. 486, Opinion of the Court, by Chief Justice Earl Warren, Decided June 16, 1969, http://en.wikisource.org.; Kent M. Weeks, *Adam Clayton Powell and the Supreme Court* (New York: Dunellen, 1971).

135. Haygood, *King of the Cats*, 396–398, 402.

136. See Samuel DeWitt Proctor, *My Moral Odyssey* (Valley Forge, PA: Judson Press, 1989); Proctor, *The Substance of Things Hoped For: A Memoir of African-American Faith* (Valley Forge: Judson Press, 1995).

137. Haygood, *King of the Cats*, 52–53.

138. Ottley, *New World A-Coming*, 220–221.

139. Haygood, *King of the Cats*, 406.

140. Powell, *Adam by Adam*, quote, 234.

141. Wayne Morse to Adam Clayton Powell Jr., October 5, 1964, *Congressional Record*, Appendix 5512.

CHAPTER 5. REDEEMING THE SOUL OF AMERICA

1. Martin Luther King Jr., *Stride Toward Freedom: The Montgomery Story* (New York: Harper & Brothers, 1958), 20; Marshall Frady, *Martin Luther King Jr.: A Life* (New York: Penguin, 2002), 11–13; Lewis V. Baldwin, *There Is a Balm in Gilead: The Cultural Roots of Martin Luther King Jr.* (Minneapolis: Fortress, 1991), 16–17; Taylor Branch, *Parting the Waters: America in the King Years, 1954–63* (New York: Simon & Schuster, 1988), 40–41.

2. L. D. Reddick, *Crusader Without Violence* (New York: Harper & Row, 1959), 43–51; Martin Luther King Sr. with Clayton Riley, *Daddy King: An Autobiography* (New York: William Morrow, 1980), 26, 88; Branch, *Parting the Waters*, 46–47. Reddick was close to the King family and is an invaluable source on the tangled name story; Daddy King's memoir sought to straighten out long-standing confusions about it.

3. King Jr., *Stride Toward Freedom*, 90; David Levering Lewis, *King: A Biography* (1970; 3rd ed., Urbana: University of Illinois Press, 2003), 5–6; Frady, *Martin Luther King Jr.*, 12–14; Branch, *Parting the Waters*, 48, 62; David J. Garrow, *Bearing the Cross: Martin Luther King, Jr., and the Southern Christian Leadership Conference* (New York: William Morrow, 1986), 34–35; Baldwin, *There Is a Balm in Gilead*, 31; Clayborne Carson, "Martin Luther King Jr., and the African-American Social Gospel," in *African American Religion: Interpretive Essays in History and Culture*, ed. Timothy E. Fulop and Albert J. Raboteau (New York: Routledge, 1997), 346.

4. Martin Luther King Jr., "An Autobiography of Religious Development," *The Papers of Martin Luther King Jr.*, Volume 1, *Called to Serve, January 1929–June 1951*, ed. Clayborne Carson, Ralph E. Luker, and Penny A. Russell (Berkeley: University of California Press, 1992), 1: 359–363, quotes, 359, 360; Reddick, *Crusader Without Violence*, 50–61; King Sr., *Daddy King*, 109; Stephen B. Oates, *Let the Trumpet Sound: A Life of Martin Luther King Jr.* (New York: Harper & Row, 1982), 13; Lewis, *King*, 13–14.

5. King Jr., *Stride Toward Freedom*, "the oppressive," 19, "all of these," 90; King Jr., "An Autobiography of Religious Development," 1: 359–363, "would always," "how could I," 362; Martin Luther King Jr. interview with John Freeman, "Face to Face," British Broadcasting Corporation, October 29, 1961, Martin Luther King Jr. Center Papers, Center for Nonviolent Social Change, Atlanta, GA, 3; Lewis, *King*, 13; Garrow, *Bearing the Cross*, 655; Andrew Young, *An Easy Burden: The Civil Rights Movement and the Transformation of America* (Waco, TX: Baylor University Press, 2008), 139, 400; Coretta Scott King, *My Life with Martin Luther King Jr.* (New York: Holt, Rinehart and Winston, 1969), 80.

6. King Jr., "An Autobiography of Religious Development," 362; interview with Martin Luther King Jr., "Man of the Year," *Time*, January 3, 1964, "I don't think I have ever been so deeply angry in my life," 14; King Jr., *Stride Toward Freedom*, 90–91; Lewis, *King*, 17.

7. Martin Luther King Jr., transcript of courses at Morehouse College, *The Papers of Martin Luther King Jr.*, 1: 39–40; Richard Lischer, *The Preacher King: Martin Luther King Jr. and the Word That Moved America* (New York: Oxford University Press, 1995), 45; Christine King-Farris, "The Young Martin: From Childhood through College," *Ebony* 41 (January 1986): 58.

8. Ibid., 1: 39–40; King Jr., "An Autobiography of Religious Development," 361; Oates, *Let the Trumpet Sound*, 17–21; see William D. Watley, *Roots of Resistance: The Nonviolent Ethic of Martin Luther King Jr.* (Valley Forge, PA: Judson Press, 1985), 18; King-Farris, "The Young Martin," 58; Walter R. Chivers, "Current Trends and Events of National Importance in Negro Education," *Journal of Negro Education* 12 (Winter 1943): 104–111.

9. King Jr., "An Autobiography of Religious Development," quotes, 362, 363; Renee D. Turner, "Remembering the Young King Jr.," *Ebony* 43 (January 1988): 42–46; see George D. Kelsey, *Racism and the Christian Understanding of Man* (New York: Charles Scribner's Sons, 1965); Kelsey, "Protestantism and Democratic Intergroup Living," *Phylon* 7 (1947): 77–82; Kelsey, "Negro Churches in the United States," in *Twentieth Century Encyclopedia of Religious Knowledge*, ed. Lefferts A. Loetscher (Grand Rapids, MI: Baker Book House, 1953), 2: 789–791; Kelsey ran an annual Institute for the Training and Improvement of Baptist Ministers that enhanced his standing among ministers.

10. Benjamin Elijah Mays to Charles E. Batten, February 28, 1948, *The Papers of Martin Luther King Jr.*, 1: 152–153; George D. Kelsey to Charles E. Batten, March 12, 1948, ibid., 1: 155.

11. Branch, *Parting the Waters*, 69–73; Kenneth L. Smith and Ira G. Zepp Jr., *Search for the Beloved Community: The Thinking of Martin Luther King Jr.* (Valley Forge, PA: Judson Press, 1998), 6–10; see James B. Pritchard and Sidney Smith, eds., *Enuma elish (Creation)/Ancient Near Eastern Texts Relating to the Old Testament* (2nd ed., Princeton: Princeton University Press, 1955); Morton Scott Enslin, *Christian Beginnings* (New York: Harper & Brothers, 1938). Enslin used his book in his introductory course; Pritchard used Robert H. Pfeiffer's *An Introduction to the Old Testament* (New York: Harper & Brothers, 1944). This section adapts material from Gary Dorrien,

The Making of American Liberal Theology: Crisis, Irony, and Postmodernity, 1905–2005 (Louisville: Westminster John Knox Press, 2006), 144–154.

12. Martin Luther King Jr. to Alberta Williams King Jr., October 1948, *The Papers of Martin Luther King Jr.*, "I never," 1:161; Horace Bushnell, *The Vicarious Sacrifice, Grounded in Principles Interpreted by Human Analogies*, 2 vols. (New York: Charles Scribner, 1877); William Newton Clarke, *An Outline of Christian Theology* (New York: Charles Scribner's Sons, 1898); William Adams Brown, *How to Think of Christ* (New York: Charles Scribner's Sons, 1948); Walter Rauschenbusch, *Christianity and the Social Crisis* (New York: Macmillan, 1907); Edgar S. Brightman, *A Philosophy of Religion* (New York: Prentice-Hall, 1940); Martin Luther King Jr., "The Christian Pertinence of Eschatological Hope," 29 November 1949–15 February 1950, *The Papers of Martin Luther King Jr.*, 1: 268–273, "will be a society," 272–273; King Jr., "The Humanity and Divinity of Jesus," 29 November 1949–15 February 1950, ibid., 1: 257–262, "the true significance," 262; King Jr., "Six Talks in Outline," 13 September–23 November 1949, ibid., 1: 242–251; King Jr., "A View of the Cross Possessing Biblical and Spiritual Justification," 29 November 1949–15 February 1950, ibid., 1: 263–267; King Jr., "Preaching Ministry," September 14–November 24, 1948, *The Papers of Martin Luther King Jr.*, Volume 6, *Advocate of the Social Gospel*, ed. Clayborne Carson et al. (Berkeley: University of California Press, 2007), 69–72, "I am a," 72.

13. King Jr., *Stride Toward Freedom*, "a book," "during," 91, 95; Martin Luther King Jr., "Pilgrimage to Nonviolence," *Christian Century* 77 (April 13, 1960): 439–441, "turn," 440; Coretta Scott King, *My Life with Martin Luther King Jr.*, 71; Garrow, *Bearing the Cross*, 41; see Charles E. Cobb Jr., *This Nonviolent Stuff'll Get You Killed* (New York: Basic Books, 2014).

14. King Jr., *Stride Toward Freedom*, quote, 96; see Smith and Zepp Jr., *Search for the Beloved Community*, 43–44; Richard B. Gregg, *The Power of Nonviolence* (2nd rev. ed., New York: Schocken Books, 1959); Charles F. Andrews, *Mahatma Gandhi's Ideas* (New York: Macmillan, 1930); King Jr., "Pilgrimage to Nonviolence," *The Christian Century*, 440; Harris Wofford, "Non-violence and the Law: The Law Needs Help," *Journal of Religious Thought* 15 (Autumn–Winter 1957–1958): 25–36; William Stuart Nelson, "Satyagraha: Gandhian Principles of Non-violent Non-cooperation," *Journal of Religious Thought* 15 (Autumn–Winter 1957–1958), 15–24.

15. Lewis V. Baldwin, "Martin Luther King Jr., the Black Church, and the Black Messianic Vision," *Journal of the Interdenominational Theological Center* 12 (Fall 1984–Spring 1985), 93–108; Baldwin, "Family and Church: The Roots of Martin Luther King Jr.," *National Baptist Union-Review* 91 (January 1987): 1, 3; Baldwin, "Understanding Martin Luther King Jr., Within the Context of Southern Black Religious History," *Journal of Religious Studies* 13 (1987): 1–26; Baldwin, *There Is a Balm in Gilead*, "many books," 3; Baldwin, *To Make the Wounded Whole: The Cultural Legacy of Martin Luther King, Jr.* (Minneapolis: Fortress Press, 1992); David J. Garrow, "The Intellectual Development of Martin Luther King Jr.: Influences and Commentaries," *Union Seminary Quarterly Review* 40 (January 1986): "the least," 5; Garrow, *Bearing the Cross*, 111–112; James H. Cone, "The Theology of Martin Luther King Jr.," *Union Seminary Quarterly Review* 40 (January 1986): 21–39; Cone, *Malcolm & Martin & America: A*

Dream or a Nightmare (Maryknoll, NY: Orbis Books, 1991), 26–30; Watley, *Roots of Resistance*, 17–18.

16. Keith D. Miller, "Martin Luther King, Jr. Borrows a Revolution: Argument, Audience and Implications of a Secondhand Universe," *College English* 48 (March 1986): 249–265; Miller, "Composing Martin Luther King Jr.," *PMLA* 105 (January 1990): 70–82. See Keith D. Miller, *Voice of Deliverance: The Language of Martin Luther King Jr., and Its Sources* (New York: Free Press, 1992; reprint, Athens: University of Georgia Press, 1998), 53–66. Miller's early articles expanded on discoveries reported by Ira G. Zepp Jr. in his 1971 dissertation on King that King appropriated passages from Richard Gregg, Harris Wofford, and Paul Ramsey in his book *Stride Toward Freedom.* See Ira G. Zepp Jr., "The Intellectual Sources of the Ethical Thought of Martin Luther King Jr." (Dissertation, St. Mary's University, 1971). Zepp's and King's teacher at Crozer, Kenneth L. Smith, coauthored one of the standard intellectual biographies of King Jr., *Search for the Beloved Community.* This book essentially fills out the sketch of King's development that King offered in three versions of his memoir, "Pilgrimage to Nonviolence," and briefly mentions King's use of Gregg and Ramsey.

17. Martin Luther King Jr. Papers Project, "The Student Papers of Martin Luther King, Jr.: A Summary Statement on Research," *Journal of American History* 78 (June 1991): 23–31; David Thelen, "Becoming Martin Luther King, Jr.: An Introduction," ibid., 11–22; David J. Garrow, "King's Plagiarism: Imitation, Insecurity, and Transformation," *Journal of American History* 78 (June 1991): 86–92; Keith D. Miller, "Martin Luther King Jr., and the Black Folk Pulpit," ibid., 120–123, "his professors," 121; David Levering Lewis, "Failing to Know Martin Luther King Jr.," ibid., 81–85, "who" and "a picture," 84, 85; Clayborne Carson, with Peter Holloran, Ralph E. Luker, and Penny Russell, "Martin Luther King, Jr., as Scholar: A Reexamination of His Theological Writings," ibid., 93–105; John Higham, "Habits of the Cloth and Standards of the Academy," ibid., 106–110; Bernice Johnson Reagan, " 'Nobody Knows the Trouble I See': or, 'By and By I'm Gonna Lay Down My Heavy Load,' " ibid., 111–119; Miller, "Composing Martin Luther King Jr.," 70–82; Theodore Pappas, "A Doctor in Spite of Himself: The Strange Career of Martin Luther King Jr.'s Dissertation," *Chronicles* 15 (January 1991): 25–29; Pappas, *Plagiarism and the Culture War: The Writings of Martin Luther King, Jr., and Other Prominent Americans* (Tampa, FL: Hallberg, 1998), 85–103.

18. Miller, "Composing Martin Luther King Jr.," 70–82; see Miller, *Voice of Deliverance: The Language of Martin Luther King, Jr., and Its Sources*, 45–92; Miller, "Martin Luther King, Jr. Borrows a Revolution," 249–265; Garrow, "The Intellectual Development of Martin Luther King Jr.," reprinted in *Martin Luther King, Jr.: Civil Rights Leader, Theologian, Orator*, 3 vols., ed. David J. Garrow (New York: Carlson, 1989), 2: 443.

19. John D'Emilio, *Lost Prophet: The Life and Times of Bayard Rustin* (Chicago: University of Chicago Press, 2003), "a hoax," 231; Branch, *Parting the Waters*, 87; Smith and Zepp, *Search for the Beloved Community*, 43.

20. Martin Luther King Jr., *Strength to Love* (1963; reprint, Philadelphia: Fortress Press, 1981), 146–154, quotes, 147. This chapter, also titled "Pilgrimage to Nonviolence," is a third version of King's chapter 6, "Pilgrimage to Nonviolence," in *Stride Toward*

Freedom and his *Christian Century* essay, "Pilgrimage to Nonviolence." See Miller, "Composing Martin Luther King Jr.," 76–77.

21. King Jr., *Strength to Love*, 147.
22. King Jr., *Stride Toward Freedom*, "false optimism," 99; King Jr., *Strength to Love*, "if liberalism," 147.
23. King Jr., *Stride Toward Freedom*, 98–99.
24. King Jr., *Strength to Love*, "one of the most," 150; King Jr., *Stride Toward Freedom*, "in other words," 99; Garrow, "The Intellectual Development of Martin Luther King Jr.," 443; Garrow, *Bearing the Cross*, 67–68; Harris Wofford, "Nonviolence and the Law," *Gandhi Marg* 3 (January 1959): 27–35.
25. Martin Luther King Jr., "How Modern Christians Should Think About Man," *The Papers of Martin Luther King Jr.*, 29 November 1949–15 February 1950, 1: 273–279, quotes, 272.
26. Clayborne Carson, *Martin's Dream: My Journey and the Legacy of Martin Luther King Jr.* (New York: Palgrave Macmillan, 2013), "the girls," 201; Baldwin, *There Is a Balm*, "he would go," 37–38.
27. J. Pius Barbour to Martin Luther King Jr., July 21, 1955, *The Papers of Martin Luther King Jr.*, 2: 564–566; Lischer, *The Preacher King Jr.*, quotes, 68–69; Lewis, *King*, 33; Garrow, *Bearing the Cross*, 41.
28. Lischer, *The Preacher King Jr.*, 38–53; Branch, *Parting the Waters*, 76–77; Garrow, *Bearing the Cross*, 42; Michael Eric Dyson, *I May Not Get There With You: The True Martin Luther King Jr.* (New York: Simon & Schuster, 2000), 137–154.
29. Martin Luther King Jr., "A Conception and Impression of Religion Drawn from Dr. Brightman's Book Entitled *A Philosophy of Religion*," *The Papers of Martin Luther King Jr.*, 1: 407–416, quotes, 410, 415–416.
30. King Sr., *Daddy King*, 147, also cited in *The Papers of Martin Luther King Jr.*, Volume 2, *Rediscovering Precious Values, July 1951–November 1955*, ed. Clayborne Carson, Ralph E. Luker, Penny A. Russell, and Peter Holloran (Berkeley: University of California Press, 1994), 1; Walter G. Muelder, "Philosophical and Theological Influences in the Thought and Action of Martin Luther King Jr.," *Debate and Understanding* 1 (1977): quote, 183; see "Conversation between Cornish Rogers and David Thelen," *Journal of American History* 78 (June 1991): 41–62; Martin Luther King Jr., "Fragment of Application to Boston University," September–December 1950, *The Papers of Martin Luther King Jr.*, 1: 390; Raymond J. Bean, "Confidential Evaluation of Martin Luther King Jr.," 4 February 1951, *The Papers of Martin Luther King Jr.*, 1: 392; Muelder, "Recruitment of Negroes for Theological Studies," *Review of Religious Research* 5 (Spring 1964): 152–156.
31. "Conversation between Cornish Rogers and David Thelen," Rogers quote, 45; Baldwin, *There Is a Balm*, Lenud quote, 40.
32. Borden Parker Bowne, *Theory of Thought and Knowledge* (New York: Harper & Brothers, 1897); Bowne, *Metaphysics* (New York: Harper & Brothers, 1898); Bowne, *Personalism* (Boston: Houghton Mifflin, 1908); Gary Dorrien, *The Making of American Liberal Theology: Imagining Progressive Religion, 1805–1900* (Louisville: Westminster John Knox Press, 2001), 370–392.

33. See Gary Dorrien, *The Making of American Liberal Theology: Idealism, Realism, and Modernity*, 1900–1950 (Louisville: Westminster John Knox Press, 2003), 286–355; Dorrien, *The Making of American Liberal Theology: Crisis, Irony and Postmodernity*, 9–39.

34. Martin Luther King Jr., "Final Examination Answers, Personalism," January 1952, *The Papers of Martin Luther King Jr.*, 2: 110–112; Dorrien, *The Making of American Liberal Theology: Crisis, Irony and Postmodernity*, 17–28.

35. King Jr., "An Exposition of the First Triad of Categories of the Hegelian Logic— Being, Non-Being, Becoming," 4 February–22 May 1953, *The Papers of Martin Luther King Jr.*, 2: 196–201; King Jr., *Stride Toward Freedom*, 100–101; "favorite philosopher" statement, Martin Luther King Jr., interview with Tom Johnson, *Montgomery Adviser*, January 19, 1956; cited in John J. Ansbro, *Martin Luther King, Jr.: Nonviolent Strategies and Tactics for Social Change* (Lanham, MD: Madison Books, 2000), 122; Miller, "Composing Martin Luther King Jr.," 76–77.

36. Martin Luther King Jr., "Reinhold Niebuhr's Ethical Dualism," 9 May 1952, *The Papers of Martin Luther King Jr.*, 2: 142–151, quotes, 150; see Muelder, "Reinhold Niebuhr's Conception of Man," *The Personalist* 26 (July 1945): 284–292; King Jr., *Stride Toward Freedom*, 100; King Jr., "The Theology of Reinhold Niebuhr," April 1953–June 1954, *The Papers of Martin Luther King Jr.*, 2: 269–279. Taylor Branch mistakenly claims that King took courses with Muelder; Branch, *Parting the Waters*, 94.

37. Martin Luther King Jr., "A Comparison and Evaluation of the Theology of Luther with That of Calvin," 15 May 1953, *The Papers of Martin Luther King Jr.*, 2: 174–191, quotes, 189; Albert C. Knudson, *Basic Issues in Christian Thought* (New York: Abingdon-Cokesbury, 1950), "simply," 137, 144; see Anders Nygren, *Agape and Eros*, trans. Philip Watson (Philadelphia: Westminster Press, 1953).

38. King Jr., "A Comparison and Evaluation of the Theology of Luther with That of Calvin," 189–190; Albert C. Knudson, *The Doctrine of Redemption* (New York: Abingdon-Cokesbury, 1933), 222–333; Borden Parker Bowne, *Studies in Christianity* (Boston: Houghton Mifflin, 1909), 85–193.

39. Martin Luther King Jr., "Qualifying Examination Answers, Systematic Theology," *The Papers of Martin Luther King Jr.*, 17 December 1953, 2: 228–233, quotes, 228, 232.

40. Martin Luther King Jr., "Contemporary Continental Theology," 13 September 1951–15 January 1952, *The Papers of Martin Luther King Jr.*, 2: 113–138. In addition to its extensive copying of Horton's book, King's paper for DeWolf's seminar also lifted numerous passages from an article by George Davis, "Crisis Theology," *Crozer Quarterly* (July 1950): 208–213. King's paper for Bertocci, "An Exposition of the First Triad of Categories of the Hegelian Logic—Being, Non-Being, Becoming," lifted numerous passages from W. T. Stace, *The Philosophy of Hegel* (London: Macmillan, 1924), 42, 60–61, 69, 82–83, 87, 90–92.

41. See Walter Marshall Horton, "Tillich's Role in Contemporary Theology," in *The Theology of Paul Tillich*, ed. Charles W. Kegley and Robert W. Bretall (New York: Macmillan, 1952), 36–37; Jack Stewart Boozer, "The Place of Reason in Paul Tillich's Concept of God" (Ph.D. dissertation, Boston University, 1952); Raphael Demos, Review of *Systematic Theology*, Volume 1, by Paul Tillich, *Journal of Philosophy* 49 (October 23, 1952): 692–708; George F. Thomas, "The Method and Structure of

Tillich's Theology," *The Theology of Paul Tillich*, 86–105; David E. Roberts, "Tillich's Doctrine of Man," ibid., 109–130; *The Papers of Martin Luther King Jr.*, 2: 339–340; L. Harold DeWolf, "First Reader's Report," 26 February 1955, *The Papers of Martin Luther King Jr.*, 2: 333–334; S. Paul Schilling, "Second Reader's Report," 26 February 1955, ibid., 2: 334–335. The committee's members were DeWolf, Schilling, Bertocci, John H. Lavely, Richard M. Millard, Jannette E. Newhall, and, at least formally, Muelder.

42. Reddick, *Crusader Without Violence*, 90–107, "I am like," 105; Lewis, *King*, 41; Martin Luther King Jr. to George W. Davis, December 1, 1953, *The Papers of Martin Luther King Jr.*, "to the," "saturated," 2:223–224; see Branch, *Parting the Waters*, 94–96; Garrow, *Bearing the Cross*, 45; George W. Davis, "Reasonable Christianity," *Journal of Bible and Religion* 21 (October 1953): 268–269; Martin Luther King Jr. to Dexter Avenue Baptist Church, April 14, 1954; and R. D. Nesbitt to Martin Luther King Jr., April 19, 1954, *The Papers of Martin Luther King Jr.*, 2: 260, 262–263. Having used William Newton Clarke's *Outline of Christian Theology* and William Adams Brown's *Christian Theology in Outline* as his theology textbooks for many years, Davis switched to DeWolf's *Theology of the Living Church* after it was published in 1953; see Smith and Zepp Jr., *Search for the Beloved Community*, 16.

43. Martin Luther King Jr., "A Comparison of the Conceptions of God in the Thinking of Paul Tillich and Henry Nelson Wieman," *The Papers of Martin Luther King Jr.*, 2: 339–544; Paul Tillich, *Systematic Theology*, 3 vols., Volume 1 (Chicago: University of Chicago Press, 1951); Henry Nelson Wieman, *Religious Experience and Scientific Method* (New York: Macmillan, 1927), quote, 9; Cone, *Martin & Malcolm & America*, "as if," 31.

44. Henry Nelson Wieman, Douglas Clyde Macintosh, Max Carl Otto, *Is There a God? A Conversation* (Chicago: Willett, Clark, 1952), Macintosh quote, 22–23; King Jr., "A Comparison of the Conceptions," 404–421, 493–497, 503–508, "by drastically," "personality," 506, 511; see Bowne, *Personalism*, 266; Macintosh, *The Reasonableness of Christianity* (New York: Scribner's, 1925), 74–83; Macintosh, "Experimental Realism in Religion," in *Religious Realism*, ed. D. C. Macintosh (New York: Macmillan, 1931).

45. King Jr., "A Comparison of the Conceptions," 512–513; Knudson, *The Doctrine of God*, 307.

46. King Jr., "A Comparison of the Conceptions," 533.

47. Miller, *Voice of Deliverance*, "today almost," 62; David L. Chappell, *A Stone of Hope: Prophetic Religion and the Death of Jim Crow* (Chapel Hill: University of North Carolina Press, 2004), "from thousands," 53.

48. King Jr., *Stride Toward Freedom*, quote, 100; Chappell, *A Stone of Hope*, 53–54; David Garrow, *Protest at Selma: Martin Luther King, Jr. and the Voting Rights Act of 1965* (New Haven: Yale University Press, 1978), 221; see Garrow, "The Intellectual Development of Martin Luther King Jr.," 2: 451; Miller, *Voice of Deliverance*, 7, 17, 61; Gary Dorrien, *Kantian Reason and Hegelian Spirit: The Idealistic Logic of Modern Theology* (Oxford: Wiley-Blackwell, 2012), 530–567. Chappell recognizes that Niebuhr was much closer to Rauschenbusch's version of the social gospel than Niebuhr's polemical rhetoric about it suggested, which helps Chappell get the main thing right:

"The prophetic core of the Social Gospel at its best may explain the attraction it held for Martin Luther King Jr." (quote, 310).

49. Reddick, *Crusader Without Violence*, "ambivert" and "a touch," 6, 7; King Jr., *Stride Toward Freedom*, 16–18; Lewis, *King*, "a guilt-ridden," 254; "Conversation between Cornish Rogers and David Thelen," 49–50; Branch, *Parting the Waters*, "that's," 104.

50. Branch, *Parting the Waters*, 1–26; Ralph Luker, "Johns the Baptist," www.ralphluker.com, 1–3; Vernon Johns, *Human Possibilities: A Vernon Johns Reader*, ed. Samuel Lucius Gandy (Washington, DC: Hoffman Press, 1977); Charles Emerson Boddie, *God's "Bad Boys"* (Valley Forge, PA: Judson, 1972).

51. Vernon Johns, "Transfigured Moments," in *Best Sermons*, ed. Joseph Fort Newton (New York: Harcourt, Brace, 1926), quotes, 334, 335, 345, 346, 347.

52. Branch, *Parting the Waters*, 15–16; Luker, "Johns the Baptist," 2–3; Lischer, *The Preacher King Jr.*, 74–75.

53. Johns, "Transfigured Moments," 348.

54. Ralph David Abernathy, *And the Walls Came Tumbling Down* (New York: Harper & Row, 1989), 125–126; Branch, *Parting the Waters*, 108–109, quote, 109.

55. Martin Luther King Jr., "The Three Dimensions of a Complete Life," in King Jr., *The Measure of a Man* (Philadelphia: Pilgrim Press, 1968; reprint, Minneapolis: Augsburg Fortress, 2001), 39–49, "you can," 48; Phillips Brooks, "The Symmetry of Life," in Brooks, *Selected Sermons*, ed. Will Scarlett (New York: Dutton, 1949), 195–206; Joshua Liebman, *Peace of Mind* (New York: Simon & Schuster, 1946); Lischer, *The Preacher King Jr.*, "the awesome," 98; Miller, *Voice of Deliverance*, 75.

56. King Jr., "The Three Dimensions," quotes, 40–41.

57. King Jr., *Stride Toward Freedom*, 16–17, "at least," 21; Barbour to King, July 21, 1955, 2:564–566; see Stephen B. Oates, "The Intellectual Odyssey of Martin Luther King Jr.," in *Martin Luther King, Jr.: Civil Rights Leader, Theologian, Orator*, 3: 713.

58. Barbour to King, July 21, 1955, 2: 565–566.

59. Abernathy, *And the Walls Came Tumbling Down*, 126.

60. Martin Luther King Jr., September 5, 1954, "Recommendations to the Dexter Avenue Baptist Church for the Fiscal Year 1954–1955," *The Papers of Martin Luther King Jr.* 2: 287–294, quote, 287.

61. Rosa L. Parks to Martin Luther King Jr., August 26, 1955, *The Papers of Martin Luther King, Jr.*, 2: 572; Howell Raines, *My Soul Is Rested: The Story of the Civil Rights Movement in the Deep South* (New York: G. P. Putnam's Sons, 1977; reprint, New York: Penguin Books, 1983), 44–45; Jo Ann Robinson, *The Montgomery Bus Boycott and the Women Who Started It: The Memoir of Jo Ann Gibson Robinson* (Knoxville: University of Tennessee Press, 1987).

62. King Jr., *Stride Toward Freedom*, 62; Branch, *Parting the Waters*, quotes, 136; Raines, *My Soul Is Rested*, 49.

63. Garrow, *Bearing the Cross*, quotes, 23; Raines, *My Soul Is Rested*, 49; Branch, *Parting the Waters*, 137–138.

64. Martin Luther King Jr., "MIA Mass Meeting at Holt Street Baptist Church," December 5, 1955, *The Papers of Martin Luther King Jr.*, 3: 71–74; King Jr., Holt Street Baptist

Church Address, December 5, 1955, audiotape, Martin Luther King Center, Atlanta, GA; King Jr., *Stride Toward Freedom*, 48–52.

65. King Jr., "MIA Mass Meeting at Holt Street Baptist Church," quotes, 72; King Jr., "Holt Street Baptist Church Address," audiotape.

66. King Jr., "MIA Mass Meeting at Holt Street Baptist Church," quotes, 72; King Jr., "Holt Street Baptist Church Address," audiotape.

67. King Jr., "MIA Mass Meeting at Holt Street Baptist Church," quotes, 73; King Jr., "Holt Street Baptist Church Address," audiotape.

68. King Jr., "MIA Mass Meeting at Holt Street Baptist Church," quotes, 73, 74; King Jr., "Holt Street Baptist Church Address," audiotape.

69. King Jr., "MIA Mass Meeting at Holt Street Baptist Church," quote, 74; King Jr., "Holt Street Baptist Church Address," audiotape; King Jr., *Stride Toward Freedom*, 48–52; Branch, *Parting the Waters*, 136–142; Lischer, *The Preacher King Jr.*, 86–88; Raines, *My Soul Is Rested*, 49.

70. King Jr., *Stride Toward Freedom*, quotes, 124; King Jr., *Strength to Love*, quotes, 113–114. King told this story with slightly varying details on various occasions, but the basic version is the one he recounted in *Stride Toward Freedom* and in his sermon "Our God Is Able" in *Strength to Love*.

71. King Jr., *Stride Toward Freedom*, "I have" and "stand up," 125; King Jr., *Strength to Love*, "he promised," 113–114.

72. Reddick, *Crusader Without Violence*, 134, 166–167, "a psychological," 166; Lewis, *King*, 70; Oates, *Let the Trumpet Sound*, 88–89; Branch, *Parting the Waters*, 162; Garrow, *Bearing the Cross*, 57; Baldwin, *There Is a Balm*, "liberal training," 189; Nathan I. Huggins, "Commentary," in *We Shall Overcome: Martin Luther King Jr. and the Black Freedom Struggle* (New York: Da Capo Press, 1993), 88; Frady, *Martin Luther King Jr.*, "kitchen," 46.

73. King Jr., *Stride Toward Freedom*, 128.

74. Reddick, *Crusader Without Violence*, quote, 145; King Jr., *Stride Toward Freedom*, 134–136; Steven Miller, "The Montgomery Bus Boycott: Case Study in the Emergence and Career of a Social Movement," in *The Walking City: The Montgomery Bus Boycott, 1955–1956*, ed. David J. Garrow (Brooklyn, NY: Carlson, 1989), 432–433.

75. Bayard Rustin, "Nonviolence vs. Jim Crow" (1942), Rustin, "The Negro and Nonviolence" (1942), and Rustin, "Twenty-Two Days on a Chain Gang," in Rustin, *Time on Two Crosses: The Collected Writings of Bayard Rustin*, ed. Devon W. Carbado and Donald Wise (San Francisco: Cleis Press, 2003), 1–5, 6–10, 31–57; Raines, *My Soul Is Rested*, 53–56; August Meier and Elliott Rudwick, *CORE: A Study in the Civil Rights Movement, 1942–1968* (New York: Oxford University Press, 1973), 9–38; D'Emilio, *Lost Prophet*, 7–38; Milton Viorst, *Fire in the Streets: America in the 1960s* (New York: Simon & Schuster, 1979), 200–211.

76. Bayard Rustin, Montgomery Diary, February 21, 25, and 26, 1956, in *Time on Two Crosses*, quotes, 59, 63; D'Emilo, *Lost Prophet*, 224–229.

77. Rustin, Montgomery Diary, quotes, 64, 65; Bayard Rustin, "New South, Old Politics," *Liberation* (October 1956): 23–26.

78. D'Emilio, *Lost Prophet*, quote, 234; Farmer, *Lay Bare the Heart*, 178, 186–187.

79. Glenn Smiley to John Swomley and Alfred Hassler, February 29, 1956, Fellowship of Reconciliation Papers, John Swomley Files, Swarthmore College, "he had"; Smiley to Swomley, n.d. [March 1, 1956], "we can"; D'Emilio, *Lost Prophet*, "Bayard was," 234; Garrow, *Bearing the Cross*, 70; Reddick, *Crusader Without Violence*, 123–124.

80. Martin Luther King Jr., "Our Struggle," *Liberation* (April 1956): 3–6; Michael Harrington, *Fragments of the Century* (New York: Saturday Review Press, 1973), 101–102.

81. King Jr., *Stride Toward Freedom*, "there is" and "whatever," 54, 55; Garrow, *Bearing the Cross*, "the oppressed" and "he wanders," 63, 76; Reddick, *Crusader Without Violence*, 129–130; L. D. Reddick, "The Bus Boycott in Montgomery," *Dissent* (Spring 1956): 111.

82. Martin Luther King Jr., "The Ethical Demands of Integration," in *Religion and Labor* (May 1963), quotes, 4; Nygren, *Agape and Eros*, 75–81; Paul Ramsey, *Basic Christian Ethics* (New York: Charles Scribner's Sons, 1950), 2–3, 13, 94–105; Smith and Zepp Jr., *Search for the Beloved Community*, 61–66.

83. Ella Baker, "Bigger Than a Hamburger," *Southern Patriot* 18 (June 1960): 4; Baker, "Tent City: Freedom's Front Line," *Southern Patriot* 19 (February 1961): 1; Barbara Ransby, *Ella Baker and the Black Freedom Movement: A Radical Democratic Vision* (Chapel Hill: University of North Carolina Press, 2003); Reddick, *Crusader Without Violence*, 157; Garrow, *The FBI and Martin Luther King Jr.*, 42–45; Adam Fairclough, *To Redeem the Soul of America: The Southern Christian Leadership Conference and Martin Luther King Jr.* (Athens: University of Georgia Press, 1987), 29–31.

84. A. Philip Randolph to Ella Baker, March 7, 1956, A. Philip Randolph Papers, Library of Congress; Fairclough, *To Redeem the Soul of America*, 32; Aldon D. Morris, *The Origins of the Civil Rights Movement: Black Communities Organizing for Change* (New York: Free Press, 1984), 82–83; Ella Baker, "The Black Woman in the Civil Rights Struggle," in *Ella Baker: Freedom Bound*, ed. Joanne Grant (New York: Wiley, 1998), 227–231.

85. Branch, *Parting the Waters*, 185–186; Garrow, *Bearing the Cross*, quotes, 81, 84; King Jr., *Stride Toward Freedom*, 163–165; Reddick, *Crusader Without Violence*, 154; Harris Wofford, *Of Kennedys and Kings: Making Sense of the Sixties* (New York: Farrar, Straus and Giroux, 1980; reprint, Pittsburgh: University of Pittsburgh Press, 1992), 115.

86. Morris, *Origins of the Civil Rights Movement*, quotes, 84, 85; Fairclough, *To Redeem the Soul of America*, 32; Reddick, *Crusader Without Violence*, 184–186; King Jr., *Stride Toward Freedom*, 167–168.

87. Morris, *Origins of the Civil Rights Movement*, 84–87; Fairclough, *To Redeem the Soul of America*, 33–34; Branch, *Parting the Waters*, 199; Kenneth B. Clark, "The Civil Rights Movement: Momentum and Organizations," *Daedalus* 95 (Winter 1996): 611–612.

88. Fairclough, *To Redeem the Soul of America*, 33–34; Morris, *Origins of the Civil Rights Movement*, quote, 88.

89. Reddick, *Crusader Without Victory*, quote, 179; J. Mills Thornton III, "Challenge and Response in the Montgomery Bus Boycott of 1955–1956," *Alabama Review* 33 (July 1980): 163–235.

90. Bayard Rustin, "New South . . . Old Politics" (1956), in Rustin, *Time on Two Crosses*, 95–101; Fairclough, *To Redeem the Soul of America*, 37–55; Adam Fairclough, *Martin Luther King Jr.* (Athens: University of Georgia Press, 1995), 34–47; Branch, *Parting the Waters*, 206–216.

91. Branch, *Parting the Waters*, quotes, 217; Reddick, *Crusader Without Victory*, 194–196.

92. Martin Luther King Jr., "Give Us the Ballot—We Will Transform the South," May 17, 1957, in King Jr., *Testament of Hope: The Essential Writings and Speeches of Martin Luther King Jr.*, ed. James M. Washington (New York: HarperCollins, 1991), quotes, 197, 198.

93. Ibid., 198, 199.

94. Ibid., 199, 200.

95. Ibid., 200.

96. Fairclough, *To Redeem the Soul of America*, 42–46; Morris, *Origins of the Civil Rights Movement*, 126–128; Farmer, *Lay Bare the Heart*, 190.

97. Ransby, *Ella Baker and the Black Freedom Movement*, 180–192; Oates, *Let the Trumpet Sound*, 514; Morris, *Origins of the Civil Rights Movement*, "I have," 113; Fairclough, *To Redeem the Soul of America*, "whatsoever," 50.

98. Raines, *My Soul Is Rested*, "I'm proud," 50; Morris, *Origins of the Civil Rights Movement*, "fit into," 115, "Dr. King Jr.," 93.

99. Reddick, *Crusader Without Violence*, quote, 205.

100. Martin Luther King Jr., "The Vision of a World Made New," *The Papers of Martin Luther King Jr.*, September 9, 1954, 6: 181–183, "we stand" and "the old," 183; Martin Luther King Jr. to Thomas Kilgore, July 7, 1958, ibid., 4: 447; Martin Luther King Sr. to Joseph H. Jackson, July 29, 1957, ibid., 4: 18; "Dr. King Is Accused in Baptist Dispute," *New York Times*, September 10, 1961.

101. Reddick, *Crusader Without Violence*, "neither by," 233; *Time*, February 18, 1957, 13.

102. Harrington, *Fragments of the Century*, 108–114, "I marveled," 114; Gary Dorrien, *Economy, Difference, Empire: Social Ethics for Social Justice* (New York: Columbia University Press, 2010), 111–132.

103. Harrington, *Fragments of the Century*, quotes, 114–115, 115.

104. Martin Luther King Jr., "The Power of Nonviolence," Speech at University of California, Berkeley, June 4, 1957, in King Jr., *A Testament of Hope*, 12–15, "nonaggressive," 12; King Jr., "The Social Organization of Nonviolence," 1959, ibid., 31–34; King Jr., *Stride Toward Freedom*, "sensitive," 71, "spirit," 72, "infinitely," 92.

105. King Jr., *Stride Toward Freedom*, "we will," 213; Reddick, *Crusader Without Violence*, "from his," 233.

106. Reddick, *Crusader Without Violence*, "the discipline," 233; Martin Luther King Jr., "Address at the Thirty-sixth Annual Dinner of the War Resisters League," *The Papers of Martin Luther King Jr.*, 5: 120–125, "the colored," 125; King Jr., "My Trip to the Land of Gandhi," *Ebony*, July 1959, in King Jr., *A Testament of Hope*, 23–30, "virtually every," 25, and King Jr., *The Papers of Martin Luther King Jr.*, 5: 231–238; "Account by Lawrence Dunbar Reddick of Press Conference in New Delhi on 10 February 1959," *The Papers of Martin Luther King Jr.*, 5: 125–129, "but to India," 126; Coretta Scott King, *My Life with Martin Luther King Jr.*, 176; see Nico Slate, *Colored*

Cosmopolitanism: The Shared Struggle for Freedom in the United States and India (Cambridge: Harvard University Press, 2012), 224–228.

107. "Account by Lawrence Dunbar Reddick of Press Conference," "I have come" and "not more," 5: 127, 128; King Jr., "My Trip to the Land of Gandhi," "the bourgeoisie," and "I left," 27, 25; Martin Luther King Jr., "Farewell Statement for All India Radio," March 9, 1959, *The Papers of Martin Luther King Jr.*, 5: 135–136, "have not shown," 135; King Jr., "The American Dream," Sermon at Ebenezer Church, July 4, 1965, in King Jr., *A Knock at Midnight: Inspiration from the Great Sermons of Martin Luther King Jr.*, ed. Clayborne Carson and Peter Holloran (New York: Warner Books, 1998), 79–100; King Jr., "The American Dream," Commencement Address at Lincoln University, June 6, 1961, in *A Testament of Hope*, 208–216.

108. Author's conversation with James Lawson, February 21, 2005; David Halberstam, *The Children* (New York: Random House, 1998), 34–35.

109. Author's conversation with James Lawson; Halberstam, *The Children*, 18–53.

110. John Lewis, with Michael D'Orso, *Walking with the Wind: A Memoir of the Movement* (San Diego: Harcourt Brace, 1998), 75–77, "there was," 76; Fairclough, *To Redeem the Soul of America*, "in his own," 60; Branch, *Parting the Waters*, 259–260; Viorst, *Fire in the Streets*, 117.

111. Raines, *My Soul Is Rested*, "it was," 73; Lewis, *Walking with the Wind*, 80–82; Halberstam, *The Children*, 94–100.

112. Morris, *The Origins of the Civil Rights Movement*, "this is," 201; Clayborne Carson, *In Struggle: SNCC and the Black Awakening of the 1960s* (Cambridge: Harvard University Press, 1995), 21–25; Halberstam, *The Children*, 3–5.

113. James M. Lawson, Gene L. Davenport, Langdon Gilkey, Lou H. Silberman, John Compton, Charles Roos, and Dale A. Johnson, "The Lawson Affair, 1960: A Conversation," in *Vanderbilt Divinity School: Education, Context, and Change*, ed. Dale A. Johnson (Nashville: Vanderbilt University Press, 2001), 131–177; Dorrien, *The Making of American Liberal Theology: Crisis, Irony, and Postmodernity*, 326–327; Branch, *Parting the Waters*, 284–300; Morris, *The Origins of the Civil Rights Movement*, 197–217; Oates, *Let the Trumpet Sound*, 217; Raines, *My Soul Is Rested*, 116; Halberstam, *The Children*, 204–205; James Forman, *The Making of Black Revolutionaries* (New York: Macmillan, 1972), 215–216.

114. James Lawson, "Non-violent Way," *Southern Patriot*, April 1960; Howard Zinn, *SNCC: The New Abolitionists* (Boston: Beacon Press, 1964), 17–34; Carson, *In Struggle*, 19–24; Halberstam, *The Children*, 216.

115. Martin Luther King Jr. to Coretta Scott King, October 26, 1960, *The Papers of Martin Luther King Jr.*, 5: 531.

116. Farmer, *Lay Bare the Heart*, quote, 195; Raymond Arsenault, *Freedom Riders: 1961 and the Struggle for Racial Justice* (New York: Oxford University Press, 2006), 56–58.

117. Arsenault, *Freedom Riders*, 93–139; Carson, *In Struggle*, 32–34; Halberstam, *The Children*, 255; Farmer, *Lay Bare the Heart*, 195–204.

118. Arsenault, *Freedom Riders*, 140–182; Branch, *Parting the Waters*, quote, 430; Halberstam, *The Children*, 272–273; Carson, *In Struggle*, 34–35; Farmer, *Lay Bare the Heart*, 201–202.

119. Fairclough, *To Redeem the Soul of America*, 78–79; Branch, *Parting the Waters*, quote, 466; Arsenault, *Freedom Riders*, 229–242; Halberstam, *The Children*, 308–311; Farmer, *Lay Bare the Heart*, 203–204.

120. Farmer, *Lay Bare the Heart*, quotes, 207; Branch, *Parting the Waters*, 466–468; Arsenault, *Freedom Riders*, 265–269.

121. Arsenault, *Freedom Riders*, 304–342; Fairclough, *To Redeem the Soul of America*, 81–83; Farmer, *Lay Bare the Heart*, 208–213; Branch, *Parting the Waters*, 486–489.

122. Arsenault, *Freedom Riders*, 452–458; Branch, *Parting the Waters*, 524–533.

123. Martin Luther King Jr., "Address Delivered to the Fourth Constitutional Convention of the AFL-CIO," December 11, 1961, *The Papers of Martin Luther King Jr.*, 7: 333–341, quotes, 336, 339, 341; Stanley Levy, "Negro Union Head Scores AFL-CIO," *New York Times*, November 12, 1961, Randolph quote.

124. Claude Sitton, "Negroes' Unrest Grows in Georgia," *New York Times*, December 16, 1961; Sitton, "Dr. King Among 265 Negroes Seized in March on Albany, Ga., City Hall," *New York Times*, December 17, 1961; Martin Luther King Jr., "Address Delivered at Albany Movement Mass Meeting at Mt. Zion Baptist Church," December 15, 1961, *The Papers of Martin Luther King Jr.*, 7: 342–344, "the price," 343; Branch, *Parting the Waters*, "we will," 546; Bruce Galphin, "Albany Shaping Racial Settlement," *Atlanta Constitution*, December 15, 1961.

125. Claude Sitton, "Dr. King Among 265 Negroes Seized in March on Albany, Ga., City Hall," *New York Times*, December 17, 1961; Sitton, "Negro Groups Split on Georgia Protest," *New York Times*, December 18, 1961; "Albany Balks at Truce Price; Rev. King Rallies Negroes," *Atlanta Constitution*, December 16, 1961.

126. "Confused Crusade," *Time*, January 12, 1962, 15; Forman, *The Making of Black Revolutionaries*, 254; Branch, *Parting the Waters*, 553–557, "thoroughly" and "devastating," 556, 557; Claude Sitton, "Rivalries Beset Integration Campaigns, *New York Times*, December 24, 1961; Fairclough, *To Redeem the Soul of America*, "we should," 90–91.

127. Vincent Harding and Staughton Lynd, "Albany, Georgia," *Crisis* 70 (February 1963): 69–78; Fairclough, *To Redeem the Soul of America*, 103–106; Carson, *In Struggle*, 56–65.

128. Branch, *Parting the Waters*, 574–575, "purely," 674; Young, *An Easy Burden*, 171–172.

129. Harrison Salisbury, "Fear and Hatred Grip Birmingham," *New York Times*, April 12, 1960; The *New York Times* Company, Appellant, v. Eugene Connor, Appellee, No. 22362, United States Court of Appeals, Fifth Circuit, August 4, 1966. Birmingham minister John Thomas Porter said that ACMHR "was a one-man show. It was Fred all the way. . . . He was just a dictator. That was his style." Garrow, *Bearing the Cross*, 238. Smiley described Shuttlesworth as a "courageous leader, but devoid of organizational knowledge, headstrong and wild for publicity, almost to the point of neurosis, undemocratic and willing to do almost anything to keep the spotlight on himself." Fairclough, *To Redeem the Soul of America*, 442–443.

130. Martin Luther King Jr., *Why We Can't Wait* (1963; reprint, New York: Signet Classics, 2000), quote, 74; William M. Kunstler, *Deep in My Heart* (New York: William Morrow, 1966), 172–184; Fairclough, *To Redeem the Soul of America*, 118–122; Garrow, *Bearing the Cross*, 231–250.

131. King Jr., *Why We Can't Wait*, "I was standing," 80; Branch, *Parting the Waters*, 695. The "Call to Unity" was authored by Episcopal bishops Charles C. J. Carpenter and George Murray, Methodist bishops Nolan Harmon and Paul Hardin, Roman Catholic bishop Joseph Durick, Southern Baptist minister Earl Stallings, Presbyterian minister Edward Ramage, and Rabbi Milton Grafman.

132. King Jr., *Why We Can't Wait*, quotes, 86, 87; Diane McWhorter, *Carry Me Home: Birmingham, Alabama: The Climactic Battle of the Civil Rights Movement* (New York: Simon & Schuster, 2001), 356.

133. King Jr., *Why We Can't Wait*, 92–93.

134. Ibid., 94–95; see Edgar S. Brightman, *Moral Laws* (New York: Abingdon Press, 1933); Walter Muelder, *Moral Law in Christian Social Ethics* (Richmond, VA: John Knox Press, 1966); Gary Dorrien, *Social Ethics in the Making: Interpreting an American Tradition* (Oxford: Wiley-Blackwell, 2009), 317–319.

135. King Jr., *Why We Can't Wait*, 100–101.

136. Ibid., quotes, 103, 105, 106; see Jonathan Rieder, *Gospel of Freedom: Martin Luther King Jr.'s Letter from Birmingham Jail and the Struggle that Changed a Nation* (New York: Bloomsbury Press, 2013).

137. Martin Luther King Jr., "Letter from Birmingham Jail," *Liberation*, June 1963, 10–16, 23; King Jr., "Letter from Birmingham Jail," *Christian Century* (June 12, 1963), 767–773; and King Jr., "The Negro Is Your Brother," *Atlantic Monthly* 212 (August 1963): 78–81; see McWhorter, *Carry Me Home*, 356–357; Jonathan S. Bass, *Blessed Are the Peacemakers: Martin Luther King Jr., Eight White Religious Leaders, and the "Letter from Birmingham Jail"* (Baton Rouge: Louisiana State University Press, 2001), 139–140.

138. McWhorter, *Carry Me Home*, 358–360; Bass, *Blessed Are the Peacemakers*, 143; Young, *An Easy Burden*, 236; Branch, *Parting the Waters*, 754; Fairclough, *To Redeem the Soul of America*, 124; Halberstam, *The Children*, 391–392; King Jr., *Why We Can't Wait*, 115; Garrow, *Bearing the Cross*, 247.

139. Wyatt T. Walker, interview with John Britton, October 11, 1967, "we had" in Garrow, *Bearing the Cross*, 247, and Fairclough, *To Redeem the Soul of America*, 124; Rieder, *Gospel of Freedom*, "Tomorrow," 114.

140. Garrow, *Bearing the Cross*, Walker quotes, 251; see Raines, *My Soul Is Rested*, 167–178; King Jr., *Why We Can't Wait*, 116; Kunstler, *Deep in My Heart*, 188–189.

141. Branch, *Parting the Waters*, "Well, I'll" and "Don't worry," 763; Rieder, *Gospel of Freedom*, "Let's let," 118.

142. Claude Sitton, "Birmingham Jails 1,000 More Negroes," *New York Times*, May 7, 1963; Foster Hailey, "U.S. Seeking Truce in Birmingham; Hoses Again Drive Off Demonstrators," *New York Times*, May 5, 1963; McWhorter, *Carry Me Home*, 386–390; Branch, *Parting the Waters*, 771.

143. Branch, *Parting the Waters*, "love," 774; King Jr., *Why We Can't Wait*, 119, 125.

144. Interview with Glenn V. Evans, in Raines, *My Soul Is Rested*, quotes, 174.

145. Ibid., quote, 176.

146. Garrow, *Bearing the Cross*, "you're in" and "you're Mister," 257; Branch, *Parting the Waters*, "I'll be," 783; Abernathy, *And the Walls Came Tumbling Down*, "a coward," 268; Young, *An Easy Burden*, "soothed" and "and I had," 247; Fairclough, *To Redeem*

the Soul of America, "reached," 129; Raines, *My Soul Is Rested*, 159; Michael Dorman, *We Shall Overcome* (New York: Delacorte Press, 1964), 181–185; McWhorter, *Carry Me Home*, 420–428.

147. Claude Sitton, "Birmingham—Impact of Racial Tensions on the Deep South," *New York Times*, May 12, 1963, "the promise"; Sitton, "Birmingham Pact Sets Timetable for Integration," *New York Times*, May 11, 1963; McWhorter, *Carry Me Home*, "the atheist," 425; Abernathy, *And the Walls Came Tumbling Down*, 270.

148. Garrow, *Bearing the Cross*, quote, 261; Claude Sitton, "50 Hurt in Negro Rioting After Birmingham Blasts," *New York Times*, May 12, 1963; McWhorter, *Carry Me Home*, 425–428; Irving Bernstein, *Promises Kept: John F. Kennedy's New Frontier* (New York: Oxford University Press, 1991), 90–93; Branch, *Parting the Waters*, 794–799.

149. Garrow, *Bearing the Cross*, "the most" and "there never," 671, 264; Young, *An Easy Burden*, "approached," 179.

150. McWhorter, *Carry Me Home*, "Our Way," 25, "seemed to," 15; Glenn T. Eskew, *But for Birmingham* (Chapel Hill: University of North Carolina, 1997), "ended," 17; Gary S. Selby, *Martin Luther King and the Rhetoric of Freedom* (Waco, TX: Baylor University Press, 2008), 38.

151. Reinhold Niebuhr, *Moral Man and Immoral Society: A Study in Ethics and Politics* (New York: Scribner's, 1932), quotes, 250–251.

152. "Dr. King Denounces President on Rights," *New York Times*, June 10, 1963; Branch, *Parting the Waters*, 816–817.

153. Roy Wilkins, *A Man's Life: An Autobiography* (Woodbridge, CT: Ox Bow Press, 1991), 122–123; "NAACP Leader Assails Other Civil Rights Groups," *New York Times*, June 23, 1963; Branch, *Parting the Waters*, 828–830; Garrow, *Bearing the Cross*, 269–270; Yvonne Ryan, *Roy Wilkins: The Quiet Revolutionary and the NAACP* (Lexington: University Press of Kentucky, 2014), 111–112; see Adam Nossiter, *Of Long Memory: Mississippi and the Murder of Medgar Evers* (Reading, MA: Addison Wesley, 1995).

154. Branch, *Parting the Waters*, quotes, 837, 838; Garrow, *Bearing the Cross*, 272–273.

155. Athan Theoharis, ed., *From the Secret Files of J. Edgar Hoover* (Chicago: I. R. Dee, 1991), 40–41; Anthony Summers, *Official and Confidential: The Secret Life of J. Edgar Hoover* (New York: G. P. Putnam's, 1993), 309–311; Branch, *Parting the Waters*, quote, 569; Garrow, *The FBI and Martin Luther King Jr.*, 26–57; McWhorter, *Carry Me Home*, 564–565; Wofford, *Of Kennedys & Kings*, 399–402.

156. See William P. Jones, *The March on Washington: Jobs, Freedom, and the Forgotten History of Civil Rights* (New York: Norton, 2013); Charles Euchner, *Nobody Turn Me Around: A People's History of the March on Washington* (Boston: Beacon Press, 2010); Lucy G. Barber, *Marching on Washington: The Forging of an American Political Tradition* (Berkeley: University of California Press, 2002); Leonard Freed, *This Is the Day: The March on Washington* (Los Angeles: Getty, 2013).

157. Branch, *Parting the Waters*, quote, 859; Garrow, *The FBI and Martin Luther King Jr.*, 67–68; Dyson, *I May Not Get There With You*, 155–222.

158. Branch, *Parting the Waters*, quotes, 861; Remarks by Sen. Strom Thurmond, *Congressional Record*, August 13, 1963, S14836; D'Emilio, *Lost Prophet*, 348–349.

159. Lewis, *Walking with the Wind*, 225–231, quotes, 225, 226; see Thomas Gentile, *March on Washington: August 28, 1963* (Washington, DC: New Day, 1983), 176–180.

160. John Lewis, Speech at the March on Washington, August 28, 1963, *Student Voice* (October 1963), quotes, 1, 2, 3, 4; Lewis, *Walking with the Wind*, 227–228.

161. Branch, *Parting the Waters*, "white men," 871; Martin Luther King Jr., "I Have a Dream," August 28, 1963, in King Jr., *A Testament of Hope*, "promissory," 217; see D. D. Hansen, *The Dream: Martin Luther King Jr. and the Speech That Inspired a Nation* (New York: HarperCollins, 2003).

162. King Jr., "I Have a Dream," quotes, 218, 219; Branch, *Parting the Waters*, "tell them," 882.

163. King Jr., "I Have a Dream," 219, 220.

164. King Jr., *A Testament of Hope*, "At that," 217; James Reston, "'I Have a Dream . . .' Peroration by Dr. King Sums Up a Day the Capital Will Remember," *New York Times*, August 29, 1963; Branch, *Parting the Waters*, "He's damn" and "plenty," 883; Garrow, *Bearing the Cross*, 281–283.

165. Young, *An Easy Burden*, quote, 270; Carson, *In Struggle*, 96–99; Charles Marsh, *The Beloved Community: How Faith Shapes Social Justice, from the Civil Rights Movement to Today* (New York: Basic Books, 2005), 87–100.

CHAPTER 6. NIGHTMARE FURY AND PUBLIC SACRIFICE

1. Martin Luther King Jr., "Eulogy for the Martyred Children," in King Jr., *A Testament of Hope: The Essential Writings and Speeches of Martin Luther King Jr.*, ed. James M. Washington (New York: HarperCollins, 1991), quotes, 221; Andrew Young, *An Easy Burden: The Civil Rights Movement and the Transformation of America* (Waco, TX: Baylor University Press, 2008), 276.

2. Stephen B. Oates, *Let the Trumpet Sound: A Life of Martin Luther King Jr.* (New York: HarperCollins, 1982), "This is," "I don't think," and "I keep," 270; Taylor Branch, *Pillar of Fire: America in the King Years, 1963–65* (New York: Touchstone, 1999), "from the," 183; Martin Luther King Jr., *Why We Can't Wait* (1963; reprint, New York: Signet Classics, 2000), "we tolerated," 180.

3. Adam Fairclough, *To Redeem the Soul of America: The Southern Christian Leadership Conference and Martin Luther King Jr.* (Athens: University of Georgia Press, 1987), "I began," 165.

4. "In Color: Spectacle of the March," *Life*, September 6, 1963, cover; "On the March," *Newsweek* 62 (September 2, 1963), quote, 18; see "Man of the Year: Martin Luther King Jr.," *Time*, January 3, 1964; Nat Hentoff, "Socrates of the Civil Rights Movement," *New York Herald Tribune Sunday Magazine*, June 28, 1964, 6–8.

5. See Gary Dorrien, *The Neoconservative Mind: Politics, Culture, and the War of Ideology* (Philadelphia: Temple University Press, 1993), 3–6, 30–34; Max Shachtman, *Bureaucratic Revolution: The Rise of the Stalinist State* (New York: Ronald Press, 1962); Julius Jacobson, "The Two Deaths of Max Shachtman," *New Politics* 10 (Winter 1973): 96–99; Tom Kahn, "Max Shachtman: His Ideals and His Movement," *New America* 10 (November 16, 1972): 5; Maurice Isserman, *If I Had a Hammer . . .: The Death of the Old Left and the Birth of the New Left* (New York: Basic Books, 1987), 35–75; Peter Drucker, *Max Shachtman and His Left* (Highland Park, NJ: Humanities Press, 1994), 90–112, 180–190.

6. Branch, *Pillar of Fire*, 292–293; John D'Emilio, *Lost Prophet: The Life and Times of Bayard Rustin* (Chicago: University of Chicago Press, 1963), 365, 372.

7. Young believed that Pritchett's recent conversion to Roman Catholicism played a role in giving him a bad conscience and in treating Young as a confessor; see Young, *An Easy Burden*, 178.

8. Ibid., 7–23, 30.

9. Ibid., quotes, 43, 45. Andrew Young, *A Way Out of No Way: The Spiritual Memoirs of Andrew Young* (Nashville: Thomas Nelson, 1994), 9–10.

10. Young, *A Way Out of No Way*, 15–33; Young, *An Easy Burden*, 48–77; Hartford Seminary, "Our History," http://www.hartsem.edu/about/our-history.

11. Young, *An Easy Burden*, "All that's," 97; Young, *A Way Out of No Way*, 36–44.

12. See Robert W. Spike, "Address to the National Council of Churches of Christ in the USA," Philadelphia, Pennsylvania, December 2, 1963, and Spike, "Sermon at Deering Community Church," Deering, New Hampshire, July 12, 1964, in Davis W. Houck and David E. Dixon, eds., *Rhetoric, Religion, and the Civil Rights Movement, 1954–1965* (Waco, TX: Baylor University Press, 2006), 670–676, 769–773.

13. James F. Findlay Jr., *Church People in the Struggle: The National Council of Churches and the Black Freedom Movement, 1950–1970* (New York: Oxford University Press, 1993), 113; Young, *An Easy Burden*, 129–133; Young, *A Way Out of No Way*, 51–52.

14. Grace Jordan McFadden, "Septima P. Clark and the Struggle for Human Rights," in *Women in the Civil Rights Movement: Trailblazers and Torchbearers, 1941–1965*, ed. Vicki L. Crawford, Jacqueline Anne Rouse, and Barbara Woods (Bloomington: Indiana University Press, 1993), 85–97; Katherine Mellen Charron, *Freedom's Teacher: The Life of Septima Clark* (Chapel Hill: University of North Carolina Press, 2009); Young, *An Easy Burden*, 153–154; Earnest N. Bracey, *Fannie Lou Hamer: The Life of a Civil Rights Icon* (Jefferson, NC: McFarland, 2011), 53–60.

15. Lydia Walker, *Challenge and Change: The Story of Civil Rights Activist C. T. Vivian* (Alpharetta, GA: Dreamkeeper Press, 1993); Daniel Lewis, "Hosea Williams, 74, Rights Crusader, Dies," *New York Times*, November 17, 2000; Henry Hampton and Steve Fayer, eds., *Voices of Freedom* (New York: Bantam, 1991), 66; Young, *An Easy Burden*, quotes, 281, 299.

16. Young, *An Easy Burden*, quotes, 285, 299, 288, 285.

17. David R. Colburn, *Racial Change and Community Crisis: St. Augustine, Florida, 1877–1980* (New York: Columbia University Press, 1985), 92–102; Fairclough, *To Redeem the Soul of America*, 176–177; Paul Good, *The Trouble I've Seen* (Washington, DC: Howard University Press, 1975), 25–45.

18. Good, *The Trouble I've Seen*, 80–88; William M. Kunstler, *Deep in My Heart* (New York: William Morrow, 1966), 273–282; Colburn, *Racial Change and Community Crisis*, 99–110; Young, *An Easy Burden*, 289–296; Young, *A Way Out of No Way*, 90–92; David J. Garrow, *Bearing the Cross: Martin Luther King Jr. and the Southern Christian Leadership Conference* (New York: Quill, 1986), 323–338.

19. Branch, *Pillar of Fire*, quote, 333; Oates, *Let the Trumpet Sound*, 293–301; Martin Luther King Jr., "The Hammer of Civil Rights," *Nation* (March 9, 1964), 230–234.

20. Findlay, *Church People in the Struggle*, 48–65; Michael B. Friedland, *Lift Up Your Voice Like a Trumpet: White Clergy and the Civil Rights and Antiwar Movements, 1954–1973* (Chapel Hill: University of North Carolina Press, 1998), 70–92.

21. Martin Luther King Jr., *Why We Can't Wait* (1963; reprint, New York: Signet Classics, 2000), quote, 171.

22. Nicholas Lemann, *The Promised Land: The Great Black Migration and How It Changed America* (New York: Knopf, 1991), "I think," 183; Joseph A. Califano Jr., *The Triumph and Tragedy of Lyndon Johnson: The White House Years* (New York: Simon & Schuster, 1991), "we are turning," 43; Michael Harrington, *The Other America: Poverty in the United States* (Baltimore: Penguin Books, 1963).

23. Branch, *Pillar of Fire*, 404–405; Robert Loevy, *The Civil Rights Act of 1964: The Passage of the Law that Ended Racial Discrimination* (Albany: State University of New York Press, 1997), 173–177; Loevy, "A Brief History of the Civil Rights Act of 1964," in David C. Kozak and Kenneth N. Ciboski, eds., *The American Presidency* (Chicago: Nelson Hall, 1985), 411–419; Branch, *Pillar of Fire*, 404–405.

24. Editorial, "The Grand Old Party," *Chicago Defender*, July 16, 1964; Branch, *Pillar of Fire*, 405; Fairclough, *To Redeem the Soul of America*, 200; Dan T. Carter, *The Politics of Rage: George Wallace, the Origins of the New Conservatism, and the Transformation of American Politics* (New York: Simon & Schuster, 1995), 218–222.

25. Howell Raines, *My Soul Is Rested: Movement Days in the Deep South Remembered* (New York: G. P. Putnam's, 1977; reprint, New York: Penguin, 1983), 233–285; Milton Viorst, *Fire in the Streets: America in the 1960's* (New York: Simon & Schuster, 1979), 247–265; John Lewis, with Michael D'Orso, *Walking with the Wind: A Memoir of the Movement* (New York: Harcourt Brace, 1998), 274; William H. Chafe, *Never Stop Running: Allard Lowenstein and the Struggle to Save American Liberalism* (Princeton: Princeton University Press, 1998).

26. Fannie Lou Hamer, "Testimony Before the Credentials Committee at the Democratic National Convention, Atlantic City, New Jersey, August 22, 1964," in Hamer, *The Speeches of Fannie Lou Hamer: To Tell It Like It Is*, ed. Maegan Parker Brooks and Davis W. Houck (Jackson: University Press of Mississippi, 2011), quotes, 45; Kay Mills, *This Little Light of Mine: The Life of Fannie Lou Hamer* (Lexington: University of Kentucky Press, 2007), 111–123; Raines, *My Soul Is Rested*, 249–255.

27. Lewis, *Walking with the Wind*, "if you seat," 288; Bayard Rustin, "From Protest to Politics: The Future of the Civil Rights Movement," *Commentary* (February 1965), reprinted in Rustin, *Time on Two Crosses: The Collected Writings of Bayard Rustin*, ed. Devon W. Carbado and Donald Weise (San Francisco: Cleis Press, 2003), 116–129; Fairclough, *To Redeem the Soul of America*, "that illiterate" and "but if," 203, 204; Viorst, *Fire in the Streets*, 265–267; Raines, *My Soul Is Rested*, 254

28. Clayborne Carson, *In Struggle: SNCC and the Black Awakening of the 1960s* (Cambridge: Harvard University Press, 1995), quotes, 127; Lewis, *Walking with the Wind*, 289.

29. Carson, *In Struggle*, quotes, 127, 128.

30. Staughton Lynd, "Coalition Politics or Nonviolent Revolution?" *Liberation* (June 1965), 18–21, "labor," 20; David McReynolds, "The March on Washington and Its Critics," *Liberation* (May 1965), 6–7; Lewis, *Walking with the Wind*, "a serious" and "Joe," 285, 289.

31. Lewis, *Walking with the Wind*, 249.

32. See Carson, *In Struggle*, 134–135; Charles Marsh, *The Beloved Community: How Faith Shapes Social Justice, from the Civil Rights Movement to Today* (New York: Basic Books, 2005), 100–109.

33. Lewis, *Walking with the Wind*, quotes, 306, 307; Peniel E. Joseph, *Stokely: A Life* (New York: Basic Books, 2014), 77–78; Carson, *In Struggle*, 129; Marsh, *The Beloved Community*, 117–118.

34. Lewis, *Walking with the Wind*, 295–296.

35. Malcolm X, with Alex Haley, *The Autobiography of Malcolm X* (New York: Grove Press, 1965), 385–394; Malcolm X, "A Declaration of Independence, March 12, 1964," and "The Ballot or the Bullet, April 3, 1964), in *Malcolm X Speaks*, ed. George Breitman (New York: Grove Press, 1965), 18–22, 23–44; Carson, *In Struggle*, 134–135; Lewis, *Walking with the Wind*, 308–311; Joseph, *Stokely*, 78.

36. Garrow, *Bearing the Cross*, quotes, 360.

37. David Levering Lewis, *King: A Biography* (3rd ed., Urbana: University of Illinois Press, 2013), quote, 261.

38. Martin Luther King Jr., "Nobel Prize Acceptance Speech," in King Jr., *A Testament of Hope*, quotes, 224, 225, 226.

39. Martin Luther King Jr., interview with Alex Haley, *Playboy* (January 1965), in King Jr., *Testimony of Hope*, 340–377, quote, 345.

40. Ibid., quotes, 346, 347.

41. Ibid., quotes, 348, 349, 353.

42. Ibid., quotes, 353, 354, 355.

43. Ibid., quotes, 361, 362, 364, 365.

44. Coretta Scott King, *My Life with Martin Luther King Jr.* (1969; rev. ed., New York: Henry Holt, 1993), 255–256; Fairclough, *To Redeem the Soul of America*, 209–210.

45. Garrow, *Bearing the Cross*, quotes, 373; Ralph David Abernathy, *And the Walls Came Tumbling Down* (New York: Harper & Row, 1989), 309–311; Jimmie Lewis Franklin, "Review Essay: Autobiography, the Burden of Friendship, and Truth," *Georgia Historical Quarterly* 74 (Spring 1990), 83–98; Georgia Davis Powers, *I Shared the Dream: The Pride, Passion, and Politics of the First Black Woman Senator From Kentucky* (Far Hills, NJ: New Horizon Press, 1995), 145–162; Michael Eric Dyson, *I May Not Get There With You: The True Martin Luther King Jr.* (New York: Touchstone, 2001), 155–174.

46. Garrow, *Bearing the Cross*, quote, 374.

47. Califano, *The Triumph and Tragedy of Lyndon Johnson*, 43–44; Nick Kotz, *Judgment Days: Lyndon Baines Johnson, Martin Luther King Jr., and the Laws That Changed America* (Boston: Houghton Mifflin, 2005), 272–279; David Halberstam, *The Children* (New York: Random House, 1998), 495; J. L. Chestnut Jr. and Julia Cass, *Black in Selma: The Uncommon Life of J. L. Chestnut, Jr.* (New York: Farrar, Straus and Giroux, 1990), 164–168.

48. Fairclough, *To Redeem the Soul of America*, 231–234, "we must," 234; Garrow, *Bearing the Cross*, 382–386, "if we are," 382.

49. Lewis, *Walking with the Wind*, "before some," 324; Malcolm X, *By Any Means Necessary*, 218–220; Malcolm X, *Malcolm X Speaks*, 225; Young, *An Easy Burden*, 350–351.

50. Roy Reed, "Wounded Negro Dies in Alabama," *New York Times* (February 27, 1965); Reed, "Memorial Service Honors Negro Slain in Alabama Rights March," *New York Times* (March 1, 1965); Coretta Scott King, *My Life with Martin Luther King Jr.*, 240; Branch, *Pillar of Fire*, 584; Nick Kotz, *Judgment Days: Lyndon Baines Johnson, Martin Luther King Jr., and the Laws that Changed America* (Boston: Houghton Mifflin), 272–279.

51. Lewis, *Walking with the Wind*, "there was," 338; Branch, *Pillar of Fire*, 599.

52. Lyndon B. Johnson, "We Shall Overcome," March 15, 1965, http://www.historyplace.com/speeches, quotes; Garrow, *Bearing the Cross*, 406–408; Lewis, *Walking with the Wind*, 347–349.

53. Lewis, *Walking with the Wind*, "if we can't," 354; Garrow, *Bearing the Cross*, 412; Powers, *I Shared the Dream*, "many times," 128.

54. Coretta Scott King, *My Life with Martin Luther King Jr.*, "since," 249; Martin Luther King Jr., "Our God is Marching On!" March 25, 1965, in *A Testament of Hope*, 227–230, "we are on," 229, "How long," 230.

55. Garrow, *Bearing the Cross*, "reign" and "stupid," 414, 415; Young, *An Easy Burden*, 367–370; Lewis, *Walking with the Wind*, 361–362; Bayard Rustin, "From Protest to Politics: The Future of the Civil Rights Movement," *Commentary* (February 1965), reprinted in Rustin, *Time on Two Crosses: The Collected Writings of Bayard Rustin*, 116–129; Alvin Pitcher, "An American Crisis," *Criterion* 4 (Spring 1965): 3–14.

56. Taylor Branch, *At Canaan's Edge: America in the King Years, 1965–68* (New York: Simon & Schuster, 2006), 249–274; Garrow, *Bearing the Cross*, 434–438; Fairclough, *To Redeem the Soul of America*, 254–255.

57. August Meier and Elliott Rudwick, *CORE: A Study in the Civil Rights Movement, 1942–1968* (New York: Oxford University Press, 1973), "there is no," 329.

58. Branch, *At Canaan's Edge*, "we are not" and "if we are," 284, 286; Young, *An Easy Burden*, 375–376; Garrow, *Bearing the Cross*, 441; Fairclough, *To Redeem the Soul of America*, 258–260.

59. Garrow, *Bearing the Cross*, "a class," 440; Bayard Rustin, "Some Lessons from Watts" (1965), in Rustin, *Time on Two Crosses*, "our manifesto" and "He pulled," 132; Young, *An Easy Burden*, 380; Doris Kearns, *Lyndon Johnson and the American Dream* (New York: St. Martin's, 1991), 304–305; Anthony Oberschall, "The Los Angeles Riot of August 1965," *Social Problems* 15 (1968): 322–341; Vincent Jeffries and H. Edward Ransford, "Interracial Social Contact and Middle-Class White Reaction to the Watts Riot," *Social Problems* 16 (1969): 312–324.

60. Rustin interview with Viorst, cited in D'Emilio, *Lost Prophet*, "Martin was," 420; Rustin, "Some Lessons from Watts," "massive" and "I'll tell," 136, "No, I," 138.

61. "Clergy Concerned About Vietnam," *Christian Century* 83 (January 26, 1966), 99–100; John C. Bennett, "From Supporter of War in 1941 to Critic in 1966," *Christianity & Crisis* 26 (February 21, 1966), 13; Mitchell Hall, "CALCAV and Religious Opposition to the Vietnam War," in *Give Peace a Chance: Exploring the Vietnam Antiwar Movement*, ed. Melvin Small and William D. Hoover (Syracuse: Syracuse University Press, 1992), 36–37; Hall, *Because of Their Faith: CALCAV and Religious Opposition to the Vietnam War* (New York: Columbia University Press, 1990), 1–12; Adam

Garfinkle, *Telltale Hearts: The Origins and Impact of the Vietnam Antiwar Movement* (New York: St. Martin's, 1995), 57–68; Kirkpatrick Sale, *SDS* (New York: Random House, 1974).

62. Young, *An Easy Burden*, 382–385; Garrrow, *Bearing the Cross*, "you don't," 455; Fairclough, *To Redeem the Soul of America*, 279–286; Branch, *At Canaan's Edge*, 320–321; Alan B. Anderson, "The Issue of the Color Line: Some Methodological Considerations" (Ph.D. dissertation, University of Chicago, 1975), 305–335.

63. Young, *An Easy Burden*, "while neither," 386; Joyce Purnick and Michael Oreskes, "Jesse Jackson Aims for the Mainstream," *New York Times*, November 29, 1987; Seth G. King Jr., "Jackson Quits Post at SCLC in Policy Split with Abernathy," *New York Times*, December 12, 1971.

64. Garrow, *Bearing the Cross*, "war," 456; Martin Luther King Jr., "Next Stop: The North," *Saturday Review* 48 (November 13, 1965), "benefit" and "the Negro," 33; Anderson, "The Issue of the Color Line," 332–335; George W. Pickering, "The Issue of the Color Line: Some Interpretive Considerations" (Ph.D. dissertation, University of Chicago, 1975); Anderson and Pickering, "The Issue of the Color Line: A View from Chicago" (Joint Appendix to Ph.D. dissertations, 1975), 329–335.

65. Young, *An Easy Burden*, "the ultimate," 388; "King Comes to Chicago," *Christian Century* 82 (August 11, 1965), 979–980; Leon Sullivan, *Moving Mountains: The Principles and Purposes of Leon Sullivan* (Valley Forge, PA: Judson Press, 1998); David T. Beito and Linda Royster Beito, *Black Maverick: T. R. M. Howard's Fight for Civil Rights and Economic Power* (Urbana: University of Illinois Press, 2009), 205–210.

66. Young, *An Easy Burden*, "an ego," 395; Branch, *At Canaan's Edge*, 476; Martin Luther King Jr., *Where Do We Go from Here: Chaos or Community?* (New York: Harper & Row, 1967; reprint, Boston: Beacon Press, 2010), 23–25.

67. Carson, *In Struggle*, "outrageous," 189; Branch, *At Canaan's Edge*, "perpetuating," 413; "King Defends Bond's Right to Views," *Atlanta Journal-Constitution*, January 9, 1966; Roy Wilkins, "SNCC Does Not Speak for Whole Movement," *Los Angeles Times*, January 17, 1966; James Forman, *The Making of Black Revolutionaries* (New York: Macmillan, 1972), 440–445; James Finn, *Protest, Pacifism and Politics: Some Passionate Views on War and Nonviolence* (New York: Vintage Books, 1967), 304–305; Julian Bond, *A Time to Speak, A Time to Act: The Movement in Politics* (New York: Simon & Schuster, 1972).

68. Carson, *In Struggle*, 191–203, "monopoly," 202; Lewis, *Walking with the Wind*, 382–383; Branch, *At Canaan's Edge*, 466.

69. Branch, *At Canaan's Edge*, "John Lewis," 466; Lewis, *Walking with the Wind*, "but when" and "what happened," 385, 386; Halberstam, *The Children*, 523–524; Forman, *The Making of Black Revolutionaries*, 449–455.

70. Branch, *At Canaan's Edge*, "they're going," 485; Peniel E. Joseph, *Stokely: A Life* (New York: Basic Books, 2014), 101; Carson, *In Struggle*, 207.

71. Kwame Ture, *Ready for Revolution: The Life and Struggles of Stokely Carmichael* (New York: Simon & Schuster, 2003), 15–35; Mary E. King Jr., *Freedom Song: A Personal Story of the 1960s Civil Rights Movement* (New York: William Morrow, 1988), "the position," 451; Joseph, *Stokely*, 13–73, "Negroes vote," 99; Bruce Watson, *Freedom*

Summer: The Savage Season that Made Mississippi Burn and Made America a Democracy (New York: Viking, 2010), 176–178.

72. King Jr., *Where Do We Go from Here*, "that nonviolence," "We shall," and "As I listened," 25, 26; Garrow, *Bearing the Cross*, "very terrible," 477.

73. Branch, *At Canaan's Edge*, "We want," 486; Joseph, *Stokely*, 107–115.

74. Branch, *At Canaan's Edge*, "Black Power" and "right behind," 487, 488; Garrow, *Bearing the Cross*, "a terrible," 483; Joseph, *Stokely*, 116.

75. Martin Luther King Jr., Rally Speech in Yazoo City, Mississippi, June 21, 1966, The King Center, www.thekingcenter.org/archive/document/transcript, 1–6, quotes, 3, 4.

76. King Jr., *Where Do We Go from Here*, quotes, 31, 32.

77. Young, *An Easy Burden*, quotes, 404; Halberstam, *The Children*, 525–532.

78. Branch, *At Canaan's Edge*, "we don't," "despite the," and "the whole," 492, 493; Garrow, *Bearing the Cross*, "because Stokely," 489; Young, *An Easy Burden*, 395–398.

79. Martin Luther King Jr., "Address to the Chicago Freedom Movement Rally," Soldier Field, Chicago, July 10, 1966, The King Center, www.thekingcenter.org/archive/document/transcript, "we shall"; Coretta Scott King, *My Life with Martin Luther King Jr.*, 283–288; Alvin Pitcher, "The Chicago Freedom Movement—What Is It?" November 1966, unpublished paper; Anderson, "The Issue of the Color Line: Some Methodological Considerations," 345–347; Barbara A. Reynolds, *Jesse Jackson: The Man, the Movement, the Myth* (New York: Nelson-Hall, 1975), 57–58.

80. "Dr. King—Housing March in Gage Park, Chicago, 1966," www.youtube.com; "Dr. King Is Felled by Rock, *Chicago Tribune*, August 6, 1966; Young, *An Easy Burden*, 413; Alan J. Matusow, *The Unraveling of America* (New York: Harper & Row, 1984), 205.

81. David Halvorsen, "Cancel Right Marches," *Chicago Tribune*, August 27, 1966; Paul Good, "Bossism, Racism, and Dr. King Jr.," *Nation* 203 (September 19, 1966), 237–242; Pitcher, "The Chicago Freedom Movement"; Garrow, *Bearing the Cross*, 508–525; Branch, *At Canaan's Edge*, 521–522.

82. "Still King Jr.," *Christian Century* (September 7, 1966), 1071–72; Editorial, *Chicago Daily News* (September 6, 1966); Editorial, *New Republic* (September 17, 1966), 9–10; Nicholas von Hoffman, "King Hails Accord but Problem Still Terrifies Chicago," *Washington Post* (August 29, 1966); Rowland Evans and Robert Novak, "King's Chicago Pillow," *Washington Post* (August 29, 1966); "Cicero March Called Off," *Chicago Defender* (August 27-September 2, 1966); Garrow, *Bearing the Cross*, 530; Branch, *At Canaan's Edge*, 524.

83. Stokely Carmichael and Charles Hamilton, *Black Power: The Politics of Liberation* (New York: Random House, 1967; reprint, Kwame Ture and Charles Hamilton, Vintage, 1992), quotes, 53, 54, 50, 49; see Bayard Rustin, " 'Black Power' and Coalition Politics," *Commentary* (September 1966), in Bayard Rustin, *Down the Line: The Collected Writings of Bayard Rustin* (Chicago: Quadrangle Books, 1971), 154–165.

84. National Committee of Negro Churchmen, "Black Power," *New York Times*, July 31, 1966, reprinted in *Black Theology: A Documentary History*, 2 vols., ed. James H. Cone and Gayraud S. Wilmore (Maryknoll, NY: Orbis Books, 1993), 19–26, "powerlessness," 19.

85. National Committee of Negro Churchmen, "Black Power," quotes, 21.

86. Lewis, *Walking with the Wind*, quotes, 389, 390.

87. Ture, *Ready for Revolution*, 566–571; Forman, *The Making of Black Revolutionaries*, 475–479; Carson, *In Struggle*, 236–238; Lewis, *Walking with the Wind*, quote, 390.

88. D'Emilio, *Lost Prophet*, "I knew," 455.

89. "Dr. King Weighing Plan to Repudiate 'Black Power' Bloc," *New York Times*, October 10, 1966; "Crisis and Commitment," *New York Times*, October 14, 1966; "7 Negro Leaders Issue a Statement of Principles Repudiating 'Black Power' Concepts," *New York Times*, October 14, 1966; "King Clarifies His Stand," *New York Times*, October 18, 1966; Bayard Rustin interview with Milton Viorst, cited in D'Emilio, *Lost Prophet*, "anybody," 449; Thomas Brooks, "A Strategist Without a Movement," *New York Times Magazine*, February 16, 1969, 24–27; Garrow, *Bearing the Cross*, 533–534; Branch, *At Canaan's Edge*, 538–539.

90. "Theologian, a Rights Advocate, Slain at Ohio State," *New York Times*, October 18, 1966; "Robert Spike: The Movement Loses a Voice," *Southern Courier*, October 29–30, 1966; Findlay, *Church People in the Struggle*, 176; King telegram in Houck and Dixon, *Rhetoric, Religion, and the Civil Rights Movement*, "he was," 668; Branch, *At Canaan's Edge*, 541; Paul Spike, *Photographs of My Father* (New York: Knopf, 1973), 201–225; Young, *An Easy Burden*, 472–473.

91. Lemann, *The Promised Land*, 195–196; Garrow, *Bearing the Cross*, 536; Martin Luther King Jr., "Nonviolence: The Only Road to Freedom," *Ebony* 21 (October 1966): 27–30; "Reagan Emerging in 1968 Spotlight," *New York Times*, November 10, 1966; Branch, *At Canaan's Edge*, 549–550; Matusow, *The Unraveling of America*, quote, 214; John L. Sullivan and Robert E. O'Connor, "Electoral Choice and Popular Control of Public Policy: The Case of the 1966 House Elections," *American Political Science Review* 66 (December 1972): 1256–1268.

92. Martin Luther King Jr., "Dr. King's Speech—Frogmore—November 14, 1966," The King Center, www.thekingcenter.org/archive, quotes, 6, 7.

93. Ibid., quotes, 13, 30.

94. Young, *An Easy Burden*, 414–415.

95. Adam Cohen and Elizabeth Taylor, *American Pharaoh: Mayor Richard J. Daley–His Battle for Chicago and the Nation* (Boston: Little, Brown, 2000), 426–427.

96. Martin Luther King Jr., Testimony to the Subcommittee on Executive Reorganization of the Committee on Government Operations, U.S. Senate, 89th Congress, 2nd Session, December 15, 1966, college.cengage.com/history, quote.

97. Martin Luther King Jr., "The Bravest Man I Ever Met," *Pageant*, June 1965, reprinted in Cornel West, ed., *The Radical King* (Boston: Beacon Press, 2015), 229–234, quotes, 225; "Dr. King Will Write Book During Leave," *New York Times*, December 14, 1966; Branch, *At Canaan's Edge*, 575–576.

98. William F. Pepper, "The Children of Vietnam," with a preface by Benjamin Spock, *Ramparts*, January 1967, 44–67; Garrow, *Bearing the Cross*, 544.

99. Friedland, *Lift Up Your Voice Like a Trumpet*, 177–178; William Sloane Coffin Jr., *Once to Every Man* (New York: Atheneum, 1977), 223–229; Branch, *At Canaan's Edge*, 577–578.

100. Young, *An Easy Burden*, 425; Branch, *At Canaan's Edge*, "off his," 577.

101. Young, *An Easy Burden*, 428; Garrow, *Bearing the Cross*, 549–550; Branch, *At Canaan's Edge*, 584–588.

102. Martin Luther King Jr., "A Time to Break Silence," Speech at Riverside Church, April 4, 1967, in King Jr., *A Testament of Hope*, quotes, 231, 232–233.

103. Ibid., quote, 236; see Bernard Fall, *The Two Viet-Nams: A Political and Military Analysis* (New York: Praeger, 1963).

104. King Jr., "A Time to Break Silence," quotes, 240, 241.

105. Ibid., "our only" and "this Hindu," 242; Martin Luther King Jr., "Declaration of Independence from the War in Vietnam," April 4, 1967, in *Two, Three ... Many Vietnams: A Radical Reader on the Wars in Southeast Asia and the Conflicts at Home*, ed. Banning Garrett and Katherine Barkley (San Francisco: Harper & Row, 1971), "without having" and "it can never," 207, 208.

106. Editorial, *Christian Century* (April 19, 1967), "a magnificent," 492–493; Editorial, *Christianity & Crisis* (May 1, 1967), 89–90; Editorial, *Nation* (April 24, 1967), 515–516; "Dr. King's Disservice to His Cause," *Life* (April 21, 1967), "his personal" and "abject," 4; Carl Rowan, "Martin Luther King's Tragic Decision," *Reader's Digest* (September 1967), 37–42; Rowan, *Breaking Barriers: A Memoir* (Boston: Little, Brown, 1991), 246–248; Editorial, "Dr. King's Error," *New York Times*, April 7, 1967; Editorial, "A Tragedy," *Washington Post*, April 6, 1967, "sheer inventions" and "many who"; "NAACP Decries Stand," *New York Times*, April 11, 1967; Editorial, *Pittsburgh Courier*, April 16, 1967, "tragically"; Max Lerner, "The Color of War," *New York Post*, April 7, 1967; Garrow, *Bearing the Cross*, 553–554; Branch, *At Canaan's Edge*, 595.

107. Martin Luther King Jr., "Dr. King's Speech in Front of U.N., April 15, 1967," "I am," www.thekingcenter.org/archive/document; Wofford, *Of Kennedys and Kings*, 223.

108. Carson, *In Struggle*, 244–264; Branch, *At Canaan's Edge*, 613.

109. Stanley Karnow, *Vietnam: A History* (New York: Penguin Books, 1991), 493–525; "General Westmoreland to CINCPAC, June 13, 1965," in *Vietnam and America: A Documented History*, ed. Martin E. Gettleman, Jane Franklin, Marilyn B. Young, and H. Bruce Franklin (New York: Grove Press, 1995), 280–281; Robert S. McNamara, *In Retrospect: The Tragedy and Lessons of Vietnam* (New York: Vintage, 1996), 259–269; Gabriel Kolko, *Anatomy of a War* (New York: Pantheon, 1985), 293–299.

110. Martin Luther King Jr., "To Charter Our Course for the Future," Speech to Southern Christian Leadership Conference, May 22, 1967, Penn Community Center, Frogmore, SC, "my name," King Papers.

111. Reinhold Niebuhr, "My Sense of Shame," *Hadassah Newsletter* 19 (December 1938), 59–60; Niebuhr, "The Partition of Palestine," *Christianity and Society* 13 (Winter 1948): 3–4; Niebuhr, "The Future of Israel," *Messenger* 13 (June 8, 1948), 12; Niebuhr, "Christians and the State of Israel," *Christianity and Society* 14 (Fall 1949): 3; Niebuhr, "Our Stake in the State of Israel," *New Republic* 136 (February 4, 1957), 9–12; Niebuhr, *Pious and Secular America* (New York: Scribner's, 1958), "a kind of," 109; Niebuhr, "David and Goliath," *Christianity & Crisis* 27 (June 26, 1967), 141.

112. King Jr., *Where Do We Go from Here*, quotes, 5, 10, 12.

113. Ibid., quotes, 45, 46, 47.

114. Ibid., quotes, 56, 64, 66.

115. Ibid., quotes, 87, 100.

116. Ibid., quotes, 147, 165, 175.

117. Garrow, *Bearing the Cross*, "my dream," 567; Martin Luther King Jr., "A Christmas Sermon on Peace," 1967, in King Jr., *The Trumpet of Conscience* (New York: Harper & Row, 1967), 67–78; Milton R. Konvitz, review of *Where Do We Go*, *Saturday Review* (July 1967), 28–29; Eliot Fremont-Smith, review of *Where Do We Go*, *New York Times*, July 12, 1967; David Steinberg, review of *Where Do We Go*, *Commonweal* (November 17, 1967), 215–216; review of *Where Do We Go*, *Washington Post Book Week* (July 9, 1967), 1; David J. Garrow, "Where Martin Luther King Jr. Was Going: *Where Do We Go from Here* and the Traumas of the Post-Selma Movement," *Georgia Historical Quarterly* 75 (Winter 1991): 719–721.

118. Andrew Kopkind, "Soul Power," *New York Review of Books* (August 24, 1967), 3–6.

119. Branch, *At Canaan's Edge*, "a necessary" and "violence is," 633, "kill" and "awful," 637, 638; John Hersey, *The Algiers Hotel Incident* (New York: Knopf, 1968), 90–91; Kerner Commission, *Report of the National Advisory Commission on Civil Disorders* (New York: Bantam, 1968), 20–32; Nancy Zaroulis and Gerald Sullivan, *Who Spoke Up? American Protest Against the War in Vietnam* (New York: Doubleday, 1984), 128–129; Renata Adler, "Letter from the Palmer House," *New Yorker* (September 23, 1967), 71.

120. Fairclough, *To Redeem the Soul of America*, 358–362; Garrow, *Bearing the Cross*, 584–586; Young, *An Easy Burden*, 443–445.

121. Martin Luther King Jr., *Conscience for Change* (Boston: Beacon Press, 1968; reprint, *The Trumpet of Conscience* [Boston: Beacon Press, 2010]), quotes, 7, 8, 15, 48.

122. Ibid., quotes, 76, 78, 79.

123. D'Emilio, *Lost Prophet*, 457–471; Fairclough, *To Redeem the Soul of America*, 364; Branch, *At Canaan's Edge*, 678–679; Michael Harrington, *Fragments of the Century* (New York: Saturday Review Press, 1973), 128–129.

124. Martin Luther King Jr., "The Drum Major Instinct," February 4, 1968, Ebenezer Baptist Church, in King Jr., *A Testament of Hope*, 259–267, quotes, 260, 264, 265, 266.

125. Ibid., quotes, 266–267.

126. Nick Kotz and Mary Lynn Kotz, *A Passion for Equality: George Wiley and the Movement* (New York: Norton, 1977), 248–252.

127. Martin Luther King Jr., "Honoring Dr. Du Bois," in John Henrik Clarke, Esther Jackson, Ernest Kaiser, and James H. O'Dell, *Black Titan: W. E. B. Du Bois* (Boston: Beacon Press, 1970), reprinted in Cornel West, ed., *The Radical King* (Boston: Beacon Press, 2015), 113–121, quotes, 114, 118, 119, 120.

128. King Jr., "Honoring Dr. Du Bois," quote, 120.

129. Martin Luther King Jr., "Salute to Freedom," Address to New York City Local 1199, March 10, 1968, in West, *The Radical King*, 235–244, quotes, 240.

130. Martin Luther King Jr., Address to the Southern Christian Leadership Conference, Penn Community Center, Frogmore, SC, May 22, 1967, in West, *The Radical King*, 126.

131. Ralph David Abernathy, *And the Walls Came Tumbling Down: An Autobiography* (New York: Harper & Row, 1989), "maybe," 420; Lerone Bennett Jr., *What Manner of Man: A Biography of Martin Luther King Jr.* (3rd ed., Chicago: Johnson Publishing, 1968), 237; Raines, *My Soul Is Rested*, 465; Garrow, *Bearing the Cross*, 614.

132. Abernathy, *And the Walls Came Tumbling Down*, 431–433; Jesse Jackson, panel presentation at American Academy of Religion, November 19, 2016, San Antonio, TX, and author's conversation with Jackson, November 19, 2016.

133. Martin Luther King Jr., "I See the Promised Land," address on April 3, 1968, at Mason Temple, Memphis, in King Jr., *A Testament of Hope*, quotes, 280; King Jr., "I've Been to the Mountaintop," video.

134. King Jr., "I See the Promised Land," quote, 282.

135. Ibid., quotes, 283, 284.

136. Ibid., quotes, 284, 285; see George Buttrick, *The Parables of Jesus* (New York: Harper, 1928); Keith D. Miller, *Martin Luther King's Biblical Epic: His Final, Great Speech* (Jackson: University Press of Mississippi, 2012), 56–61.

137. King Jr., "I've Been to the Mountaintop,"

138. Ibid.

139. Ibid.

140. Young, *An Easy Burden*, 461–463, quote, 463; Abernathy, *And the Walls Came Tumbling Down*, 433–437; Branch, *At Canaan's Edge*, 757–758; Lewis, *King*, 387.

141. Powers, *I Shared the Dream*, "just staring," 229; Abernathy, *And the Walls Came Tumbling Down*, 439–441; Branch, *At Canaan's Edge*, "play," 766.

142. Young, *An Easy Burden*, quote, 466; Abernathy, *And the Walls Came Tumbling Down*, 441.

143. Earl Caldwell, "Guard Called Out: Curfew Is Ordered in Memphis, but Fires and Looting Erupt," *New York Times*, April 5, 1968; Thomas A. Johnson, "Sporadic Violence Occurs in Harlem and Brooklyn," *New York Times*, April 5, 1968; Tom Wicker, "Thousands Leave Washington as Bands of Negroes Loot Stores," *New York Times*, April 6, 1968; Young, *An Easy Burden*, 466; Branch, *At Canaan's Edge*, 767; Abernathy, *And the Walls Came Tumbling Down*, 446.

144. Young, *An Easy Burden*, "Martin," 466; Abernathy, *And the Walls Came Tumbling Down*, 447–449.

145. L. Harold DeWolf, "Tribute," *New York Times*, April 10, 1968; L. Harold DeWolf, "Funeral Tribute to Martin Luther King Jr.," April 9, 1968, www.pbs.org/wnet/religionandethics/2006/01/13; Abernathy, *And the Walls Came Tumbling Down*, 461–462.

146. Benjamin E. Mays, "Eulogy at the Funeral Services of Martin Luther King Jr., at Morehouse College, Atlanta, Georgia, April 9, 1968," Appendix C in Mays, *Born to Rebel: An Autobiography* (Athens: University of Georgia Press, 1971), 357–360, quotes, 357, 358, 359.

147. Ibid., quotes, 359, 360.

148. "McKissick Says Nonviolence Has Become Dead Philosophy," *New York Times*, April 5, 1968; "April 1968: Benjamin Mays '20 Delivers Final Eulogy for the Rev. Martin Luther King Jr.," www.bates.edu/150-years/months/april/benjamin-mays-king-eulogy, "the way"; Philip Meyer, "Aftermath of Martyrdom: Negro Militancy and Martin Luther King Jr.," *Public Opinion Quarterly* 33 (Summer 1969): 160–173; Harry A. Reed, "Martin Luther King, Jr.: History and Memory, Reflections on Dreams and Silences," *Journal of Negro History* 84 (Spring 1999): 150–166.

149. Abernathy, *And the Walls Came Tumbling Down*, "comfort" and "he had," 460, "it broke" and "they were," 497.

150. Fairclough, *To Redeem the Soul of America*, "they do," 386; Abernathy, *And the Walls Came Tumbling Down*, "it rapidly," 516–517; Young, *An Easy Burden*, "I was," "I had," 485; Halberstam, *The Children*, 679.

151. Lewis, *Walking with the Wind*, "as if," "I dropped," 415; Young, *An Easy Burden*, "after he," "we were," 486.

152. Fairclough, *To Redeem the Soul of America*, 386–387; Tom Kahn, "Why the Poor People's Campaign Failed," *Commentary* (September 1968), 52–54.

153. Willie Baptist and Jan Rehmann, *Pedagogy of the Poor: Building the Movement to End Poverty* (New York: Teachers College Press, 2011).

154. Fairclough, *To Redeem the Soul of America*, 395–396; Lewis, *Walking with the Wind*, 428–429; Halberstam, *The Children*, 680–681; Abernathy, *And the Walls Came Tumbling Down*, 540–577.

155. Samuel DeWitt Proctor and William D. Watley, *Sermons from the Black Pulpit* (Valley Forge, PA: Judson Press, 1984); Proctor, *The Substance of Things Hoped For: A Memoir of African-American Faith* (Valley Forge, PA: Judson Press, 1995); Gardner C. Taylor, *The Words of Gardner Taylor*, 5 vols., ed. Edward L. Taylor (Valley Forge, PA: Judson Press, 1999–2002); Halberstam, *The Children*, quote, 555.

156. Lewis, *King*, 394–395.

157. Ibid., 394.

CHAPTER 7. THEOLOGIES OF LIBERATION

1. See Don Wolfensberger, "The Martin Luther King, Jr. Holiday: The Long Struggle in Congress; An Introductory Essay," Seminar on "The Martin Luther King, Jr. Holiday: How Did It Happen?" Woodrow Wilson International Center for Scholars, January 14, 2008, http://www.wilsoncenter.org/events/docs/King; Helen Dewar, "Helms Stalls King's Day in Senate," *Washington Post*, January 16, 2011.

2. Martin Luther King Jr. to Coretta Scott, July 18, 1952, in *The Papers of Martin Luther King Jr.*, Volume 6: *Advocate of the Social Gospel*, ed. Clayborne Carson (Berkeley: University of California Press, 2007), 6: 123–126, quotes, 125, 126. King's early letters to Coretta and his sermon notes remained in a box under her bed until 1997, five years after Carson published the first volume of the collected papers, where they otherwise would have been published. His letter of July 18, 1952, was especially revealing and may have contributed to Coretta King's slowness in delivering these materials to Carson. See Clayborne Carson, *Martin's Dream: My Journey and the Legacy of Martin Luther King Jr.* (New York: Palgrave Macmillan, 2013), 173–183. For works that emphasize King's commitment to democratic socialism, see Douglas Sturm, "Martin Luther King Jr. as Democratic Socialist," *Journal of Religious Ethics* 18 (Fall 1990): 79–105; Thomas F. Jackson, *From Civil Rights to Human Rights: Martin Luther King, Jr. and the Struggle for Economic Justice* (Philadelphia: University of Pennsylvania Press, 2007); Obery M. Hendricks Jr., "The Uncompromising Anti-Capitalism of Martin Luther King Jr.," *Huffington Post*, January 20, 2014, http://www.huffingtonpost.com/obery-m-hendricks-jr.

3. James Deotis Roberts, *From Puritanism to Platonism in Seventeenth-Century England* (The Hague: Martinus Nijhoff, 1968); Roberts, "Afterword," *Black Religion, Black Theology: The Collected Essays of J. Deotis Roberts*, ed. David Emmanuel Goatley (Harrisburg, NJ: Trinity Press International, 2003), 200. This section adapts material from Gary Dorrien, *The Making of American Liberal Theology: Crisis, Irony and Postmodernity* (Louisville: Westminster John Knox, 2006), 161–163.

4. James Deotis Roberts, *Faith and Reason: A Comparative Study of Pascal, Bergson and James* (Boston: Christopher, 1962); Roberts, "Black Theology and the Theological Revolution," *Journal of Religious Thought* 28 (Spring/Summer 1971): 5–20, reprinted in Roberts, *Black Religion, Black Theology*, 31–49, quote, 46; Roberts, "Christian Conscience and Legal Discrimination," *Journal of Religious Thought* 19 (1962–1963): 157–161; Roberts, "Black Theology in the Making," *Review and Expositor* 70 (Summer 1973): 321–330, reprinted in *Black Theology: A Documentary History*, Volume 1, 1966–1979, ed. James H. Cone and Gayraud S. Wilmore (Maryknoll, NY: Orbis Books, 1993), 114–124; see Roberts, "Kierkegaard on Truth and Subjectivity," *Journal of Religious Thought* 28 (1961): 41–56; Roberts, "Bergson as a Metaphysical, Epistemological and Religious Thinker," *Journal of Religious Thought* 20 (1963–1964): 105–114; Roberts, "Religious and Political Realism in Kautilya's Arthasastra," *Journal of Religious Thought* 22 (1965–1966): 153–166; Roberts, "Karma-Yoga in Tilak's Gita Rahhaysa," *Journal of Religious Thought* 24 (1967–1968): 83–98.

5. J. Deotis Roberts, "The Black Caucus and the Failure of Christian Theology," *Journal of Religious Thought* 26 (1969): 15–25, reprinted in James Deotis Roberts, *Black Theology Today: Liberation and Contextualization*, ed. Frank Flinn (New York: Edwin Mellen Press, 1983), 140–150, quotes, 140, 141, 144, 145; Joseph R. Washington Jr., *Black Religion* (Boston: Beacon Press, 1964).

6. Roberts, "The Black Caucus and the Failure of Christian Theology," quotes, 148, 149.

7. James H. Cone, *My Soul Looks Back* (Maryknoll, NY: Orbis Books, 1986), 42–43; this discussion adapts material from Gary Dorrien, *Social Ethics in the Making: Interpreting an American Tradition* (Oxford: Wiley-Blackwell, 2009), 396–406.

8. Cone, *My Soul Looks Back*, quotes, 20, 22.

9. Ibid., quotes, 21, 25.

10. Ibid., quote, 29.

11. Ibid., quote, 34.

12. Ibid., "the failure," 37; Cone, *Risks of Faith: The Emergence of a Black Theology of Liberation, 1968–1998*, "devastated," xv; James H. Cone, "*Martin & Malcolm & America*: A Response by James Cone," *Union Seminary Quarterly Review* 48 (1994): 52–57, "I hardly," 53.

13. Cone, *My Soul Looks Back*, 44.

14. Cone's first publication, an essay titled "Christianity and Black Power," was rejected by the *Christian Century* and *Motive* magazines before Lincoln published it in his book *Is Anybody Listening to Black America?* ed. C. Eric Lincoln (New York: Seabury Press, 1968), 3–9; see Cone, *My Soul Looks Back*, 140, n. 2.

15. Cone, *My Soul Looks Back*, quotes, 46, 47; see "Statement by the National Committee of Negro Churchmen," July 31, 1966, in *Black Theology: A Documentary History*,

2 vols., ed. James H. Cone and Gayraud S. Wilmore (2nd rev. ed., Maryknoll, NY: Orbis Books, 1993), 1: 19–26; Gayraud S. Wilmore, *Black Religion and Black Radicalism: An Interpretation of the Religious History of African Americans* (3rd rev. ed., Maryknoll, NY: Orbis Books, 1998), 226–230.

16. Cone, *My Soul Looks Back*, quotes, 47, 48.

17. James H. Cone, *Black Theology and Black Power* (New York: Harper & Row, 1969; 2nd ed., 1989; reprint, Maryknoll, NY: Orbis Books, 2005), quotes, 6, 22, 23.

18. Ibid., quotes, 56.

19. Ibid., quotes, 15–16.

20. Ibid., 27–28, 68.

21. Ibid., quotes, 68, 48, 111.

22. Ibid., 113–114.

23. James Forman, "The Black Manifesto," adopted by the National Black Economic Development Conference, Detroit, Michigan, April 26, 1969, reprinted in *Black Theology: A Documentary History*, 1: 27–36, quotes, 33, 35; Robert T. Handy, *A History of Union Theological Seminary in New York* (New York: Columbia University Press, 1987), 280–283. The Black Manifesto was originally called "Manifesto to the White Christian Churches and the Jewish Synagogues." Most of the additional $1 million was raised by 1974.

24. *African Congress: A Documentary of the First Modern Pan-African Congress*, ed. Amiri Baraka/LeRoi Jones (New York: Morrow, 1972); Cone, *My Soul Looks Back*, quotes, 55, 57; see James H. Cone, "Black Theology and the Black College Student," *Journal of Afro-American Issues* 4 (Summer/Fall 1976): 420–430.

25. Cone, *My Soul Looks Back*, 72.

26. Ibid., 73.

27. James H. Cone, *A Black Theology of Liberation* (Philadelphia: J. B. Lippincott, 1970; 20th anniversary ed., Maryknoll, NY: Orbis Books, 1990), quotes, 5, 7, 8, 9.

28. Ibid., 10.

29. Ibid., quotes, 25.

30. Ibid., quotes, 30, 56, 57, 63.

31. Ibid., 64, 65.

32. Ibid., 65, 66; James H. Cone, "Black Theology on Revolution, Violence, and Reconciliation," *Union Seminary Quarterly Review* 31 (Fall 1975): 5–14, "nothing to do," 13.

33. Cone, "Black Theology on Revolution, Violence, and Reconciliation," quotes, 5–6, 10, 13, 14.

34. Andrew M. Greeley, "Nazi Mentality in This Country," *Inter/Syndicate* (1971): 1971; *Malcolm X Speaks*, ed. George Breitman (New York: Grove Press, 1966), 165; James H. Cone, "Preface to the 1986 Ed.," *A Black Theology of Liberation*, xii–xiii, "I could," xiv.

35. See Paul Lehmann, *The Transfiguration of Politics* (New York: Harper & Row, 1975), 259–275; James H. Cone and William Hordern, "Dialogue on Black Theology," *Christian Century* 88 (September 15, 1971), 1079–1082; Frederick Herzog, *Liberation Theology* (New York: Seabury Press, 1972); Peter C. Hodgson, *Children of Freedom: Black Liberation in Christian Perspective* (Philadelphia: Fortress Press, 1974); Hodgson,

New Birth of Freedom: A Theology of Bondage and Liberation (Philadelphia: Fortress Press, 1976); Helmut Gollwitzer, "Why Black Theology?" *Union Seminary Quarterly Review* 31 (Fall 1975): 38–58; John C. Bennett, *The Radical Imperative: From Theology to Social Ethics* (Philadelphia: Westminster Press, 1975), 126–128.

36. Paul Lehmann, "Black Theology and 'Christian' Theology," *Union Seminary Quarterly Review* 31 (Fall 1975): 31–37.

37. Frederick Herzog, "Theology at the Crossroads," *Union Seminary Quarterly Review* 31 (Fall 1975): 59–70, quote, 61.

38. Mary Daly, *Beyond God the Father: Toward a Philosophy of Women's Liberation* (1973; reprint, Boston: Beacon Press, 1985), 25.

39. Rosemary Radford Ruether, *Liberation Theology: Human Hope Confronts Christian History and American Power* (New York: Paulist Press, 1972), 134–137, quote, 137.

40. Ibid., 137–139, quotes, 137, 138.

41. J. Deotis Roberts, *Liberation and Reconciliation: A Black Theology* (Philadelphia: Westminster Press, 1971; 2nd ed., Maryknoll, NY: Orbis Books, 1994), quotes, 5, 75–76.

42. Roberts, "Black Theology and the Theological Revolution," "I would," 45; Roberts, *Liberation and Reconciliation,* "a symbol," 68.

43. Roberts, *Liberation and Reconciliation,* quotes, 75, 76; see Roberts, "Black Theology in the Making," 121–122.

44. Roberts, *Liberation and Reconciliation,* quotes, 9, 21, 80.

45. James H. Cone, *God of the Oppressed* (San Francisco: HarperCollins, 1975), 239–240.

46. Roberts, "Black Theology in the Making," quotes, 118, 119.

47. Roberts, *Liberation and Reconciliation,* 98–99; J. Deotis Roberts, "Christian Liberation Ethics: The Black Experience," *Religion in Life* 48 (Summer 1979): 227–235, reprinted in Roberts, *Black Religion, Black Theology,* 50–60.

48. Roberts, *Liberation and Reconciliation,* 102–103; see Roberts, "Christian Liberation Ethics: The Black Experience," 55–57.

49. J. Deotis Roberts, "Folklore and Religions: The Black Experience," *Journal of Religious Thought* 27 (1970): 5–15; Roberts, "Afro-Arab Islam and the Black Revolution," *Journal of Religious Thought* 28 (1972): 95–111; Roberts, "Religio-Ethical Reflections Upon the Experiential Components of a Philosophy of Black Liberation," *Journal of the Interdenominational Theological Center* 1 (Fall 1973): 80–94; Roberts, "Theology of Religions: The Black Religious Heritage," *Journal of the Interdenominational Theological Center* 1 (Spring 1974): 54–68; Roberts, "Black Theologies and African Theologies," *Insight: A Journal of World Religions* 3 (1978–1979): 14–27; Roberts, *A Black Political Theology* (Philadelphia: Westminster Press, 1974), 20–21; Roberts, "The Methodological Crisis in Black Theology: Major Jones, William Jones and James Cone," in Roberts, *Black Theology Today,* quotes, 40, 43.

50. J. Deotis Roberts, "Black Liberation Theism," *Journal of Religious Thought* 33 (Spring/Summer 1976): 25–35, reprinted in Roberts, *Black Theology Today,* 48–57, "I am pleading," 54; Roberts, "A Black Ecclesiology of Involvement," *Journal of Religious Thought* 32 (Spring/Summer 1975): 36–46, reprinted in Roberts, *Black Religion, Black Theology,* 73–86, "we have been," 74.

51. J. Deotis Roberts, "Traditional African Religions and Christian Theology," *Studia Africana* 1 (Fall 1979): 206–218, reprinted in Roberts, *Black Religion, Black Theology*, 128–144, quote, 137; see Roberts, "Africanisms and Spiritual Strivings," *Journal of Religious Thought* 30 (Spring/Summer 1973): 16–27; John S. Mbiti, *New Testament Eschatology in an African Background* (New York: Oxford University Press, 1971); Mbiti, *African Religions and Philosophy* (Garden City, NY: Doubleday, 1970); E. Bolaji Idowu, *African Traditional Religion: A Definition* (Maryknoll, NY: Orbis Books, 1973); Aylward Shorter, *African Christian Theology* (Maryknoll, NY: Orbis Books, 1977).

52. Roberts, *A Black Political Theology*, 13–14, quotes, 59.

53. See James H. Cone, *Martin & Malcolm & America: A Dream or a Nightmare* (Maryknoll: Orbis Books, 1991); Cone, *For My People: Black Theology and the Black Church* (Maryknoll, NY: Orbis Books, 1984), 78–98; Charles H. Long, "Perspectives for a Study of Afro-American Religion in the United States," *History of Religion* 11 (August 1971): 54–66; Long, "Structural Similarities and Dissimilarities in Black and African Theologies," *Journal of Religious Thought* 32 (Fall/Winter 1975): 9–24; Cecil Cone, *Identity Crisis in Black Theology* (Nashville: African Methodist Episcopal Church, 1975); Cecil W. Cone; "The Black Religious Experience," *Journal of the Interdenominational Theological Center* 2 (Spring 1975): 137–139.

54. Lydia Walker, *Challenge and Change: The Story of Civil Rights Activist C. T. Vivian* (Alpharetta, GA: Dreamkeeper Press, 1993), 21–48, quote, 44; David Halberstam, *The Children* (New York: Fawcett, 1998), 56–57; Henry Hampton and Steve Fayer, eds., *Voices of Freedom* (New York: Bantam, 1991), 65–66.

55. C. T. Vivian, *Black Power and the American Myth* (Philadelphia: Fortress Press, 1970), quotes, 55–56.

56. Ibid., quotes, 56, 57.

57. Ibid., quote, 6.

58. Ibid., quotes, 60, 61.

59. Ibid., "exciting," 65; Daniel P. Moynihan, *The Negro Family: The Case for National Action* (Washington, DC: U.S. Government Printing Office, 1965), reprinted in *Black Matriarchy: Myth or Reality?* ed. John H. Bracey Jr., August Meier, and Elliott Rudwick (Belmont, CA: Wadsworth, 1971), "the Negro churches" and "a tangle," 157, "a large" and "three centuries," 158; E. Franklin Frazier, *The Negro Family in the United States* (Chicago: University of Chicago Press, 1939); Moynihan used the 1948 edition of Frazier's book.

60. Alexander Crummell, "The Black Woman of the South: Her Neglects and Her Needs," in Crummell, *Africa and America: Addresses and Discourses* (Springfield, MA: Wiley, 1891), 59–82; William Graebner, "The End of Liberalism: Narrating Welfare's Decline, from the Moynihan Report (1965) to the Personal Responsibility and Work Opportunity Act (1996)," *Journal of Policy History* 14 (2002): 170–190; Robert F. Schoeni and Rebecca M. Blank, "What Has Welfare Reform Accomplished? Impacts on Welfare Participation, Employment, Income, Poverty, and Family Structure," National Bureau of Economic Research Working Paper 7627 (Cambridge, MA: National Bureau of Economic Research, 2000); Gregory Acs, Kenneth Braswell, Elaine

Sorenson, and Marjorie Austin Turner, "The Moynihan Report Revisited," Urban Institute, June 13, 2013, http://www.urban.org/research/publication/moynihan-report-revisited.

61. Vivian, *Black Power and the American Myth*, "black organizations," 62; Moynihan, *The Negro Family*, "a movement," 157.

62. Vivian, *Black Power and the American Myth*, "they did not," 90, "separatism has," 66.

63. James Daane, "Civil Rights and Wrongs: Review of *Black Power and the American Myth*, by C. T. Vivian, and *My Life with Martin Luther King Jr.*, by Coretta Scott King, *Reformed Journal* (May–June 1971): 27–28, "too cynical" and "then this," 27; Arthur Selwyn Miller, review of *Black Power and the American Myth*, by C. T. Vivian, *Annals of the American Academy of Political and Social Science* 393 (January 1971): 150–151, "only too" and "our," 151.

64. Pauli Murray, *Song in a Weary Throat: An American Pilgrimage* (New York: Harper & Row, 1987), 1–13; Murray, *Proud Shoes: The Story of an American Family* (Boston: Beacon Press, 1999), 1–23.

65. Murray, *Song in a Weary Throat*, "a confusing," 31, "race was," 36; Murray, *Proud Shoes*, "we got," 269–270.

66. Murray, *Song in a Weary Throat*, 59–91, "beacon," 49, "you are," 70; Anthony B. Pinn, *Becoming "America's Problem Child": An Outline of Pauli Murray's Religious Life and Theology* (Eugene, OR: Pickwick, 2008), "a soft," 38.

67. Murray, *Song in a Weary Throat*, "the worst," 92; Pauli Murray, "Three Thousand Miles on a Dime in Ten Days," in *Negro Anthology: 1931–1934*, ed. Nancy Cunard (London: Wishart, 1934), 90–93; Pauli Murray to Pauline Dame, June 2, 1943, Pauli Murray Papers, Schlesinger Library, Radcliffe Institute for Advanced Study, Harvard University, Box 10, "this little"; Sarah Azaransky, *The Dream Is Freedom: Pauli Murray and American Democratic Faith* (New York: Oxford University Press, 2011), 23; Nancy Ordover, *American Eugenics: Race, Queer Anatomy, and the Science of Nationalism* (Minneapolis: University of Minnesota Press, 2003), 107; Leila J. Rupp and Verta Taylor, "Pauli Murray: The Unasked Question," *Journal of Women's History* 14 (2002): 83–87.

68. Pauli Murray, "Mulatto's Dilemma," in Murray, *Dark Testament and Other Poems* (Norwalk, CT: Silvermine, 1970), "that burned" and "the pride," 32–33; Murray, *Song in a Weary Throat*, "a no," 390; see Werner Sollors, *Neither Black nor White Yet Both: Thematic Explorations of Interracial Literature* (New York: Oxford University Press, 1997), 240–242.

69. Murray, *Song in a Weary Throat*, 92–104.

70. Ibid., quotes, 107, 107–108.

71. Pauli Murray to President Franklin Roosevelt, December 8, 1938, Pauli Murray Papers, Box 15; "Roosevelt's Address at Chapel Hill," *New York Times*, December 6, 1938; Eleanor Roosevelt to Pauli Murray, December 19, 1938, "don't push," Pauli Murray Papers, Box 15; Murray, *Song in a Weary Throat*, 112–113; Glenda E. Gilmore, "Admitting Pauli Murray," *Journal of Women's History* 14 (2002): 62–67; John Egerton, *Speak Now Against the Day: The Generation Before the Civil Rights Movement in the South* (New York: Knopf, 1994), 188; Azaransky, *The Dream Is Freedom*, 16–17.

72. Murray, *Song in a Weary Throat*, quotes, 134

73. Ibid., 138–148; Mark V. Tushnet, *Making Civil Rights Law: Thurgood Marshall and the Supreme Court, 1936–1961* (Oxford: Oxford University Press, 1994), 72–73; Azaransky, *The Song Is Freedom*, 148.

74. Richard B. Sherman, *The Case of Odell Waller and Virginia Justice, 1940–1942* (Knoxville: University of Tennessee Press, 1992), 32–33; Murray, *Song in a Weary Throat*, 164–176.

75. Murray, *Song in a Weary Throat*, 182–184.

76. Pauli Murray and Henry Babcock, "An Alternative Weapon," *South Today* (Winter 1942–1943): 53–57, quotes, 53, 56; see Anthony B. Pinn, ed., *Moral Evil and Redemptive Suffering: A History of Theodicy in African-American Religious Thought* (Gainesville: University Press of Florida, 2002), 218–219.

77. Pauli Murray, "A Blueprint for First Class Citizenship," *Crisis* 51 (1944): "the stool," 358; Howard University NAACP Chapter pledge, in August Meier, Elliot Rudwich, and Francis L. Broderick, ed., *Black Protest Thought in the Twentieth Century* (New York: Bobbs-Merrill, 1971), 246; Murray, *Song in a Weary Throat*, "When" and "had been," 228.

78. Eleanor Roosevelt to Pauli Murray, August 3, 1943, Pauli Murray Papers, Box 15; Pauli Murray, "Negroes Are Fed Up," *Common Sense* (August 1943), 274–275; Murray, "And the Riots Came . . . " *The Call* (August 13, 1943); Murray, "Harlem Riot, 1943," in Murray, *Dark Testament*, 35; Murray, "Mr. Roosevelt Regrets," *Crisis* (August 1943); Murray, *Song in a Weary Throat*, "I am," 212.

79. Pauli Murray to Caroline Ware, July 31, 1943, in *Pauli Murray and Caroline Ware: Forty Years of Letters in Black and White*, ed. Anne Firor Scott (Chapel Hill: University of North Carolina Press, 2006), "FDR is," 26; see Caroline F. Ware, *The Early New England Cotton Manufacture: A Study in Industrial Beginnings* (Boston: Houghton Mifflin, 1931); Ware, *Greenwich Village* (New York: Columbia University Press, 1935); Adolph Berle and Gardiner C. Means, *The Modern Corporation and Private Property* (New York: Columbia University Press, 1932).

80. Pauli Murray to Pauline Dame, June 2, 1943, "straightened," Murray Papers, Box 10; Murray, *Dark Testament*, "America," "blood," and "a white," 13, 17, 21; Azaransky, *The Dream Is Freedom*, 32.

81. Murray, *Song in a Weary Throat*, 221–222; Pauli Murray, "An American Credo," *Common Ground* 5 (1945): 24.

82. Murray, *Song in a Weary Throat*, 246–247; see Flora R. Bryant, "An Examination of the Social Activism of Pauli Murray" (Ph.D. dissertation, University of South Carolina, 1991).

83. Pauli Murray, *States' Laws on Race and Color* (Cincinnati: Women's Division of Christian Service, Board of Missions and Church Extension, Methodist Church, 1951); Murray, *Song in a Weary Throat*, 285–289, quote, 289.

84. Murray, *Song in a Weary Throat*, 294–305, "past," 297.

85. Pauli Murray to Caroline Ware, May 10, 1952, in *Pauli Murray and Caroline Ware*, "I have," 73; Murray to Ware, May 13, 1952, ibid., "Would prefer," 75; Murray, *Song in a Weary Throat*, "shattering," 294, "I was" and "ruthlessly," 298.

86. Murray, *Song in a Weary Throat*, quotes, 298.

87. Murray, *Proud Shoes*, "stranded," 110.

88. Ibid., "an act" and "bore," 275, "whatever," 276.

89. Ibid., "written," 311, "civil," 308.

90. Timothy Tyson, *Radio Free Dixie: Robert F. Williams and the Roots of Black Power* (Chapel Hill: University of North Carolina Press, 1999), 159–160; Azaransky, *The Dream Is Freedom*, 51; Pauli Murray, "Memorandum to Mrs. Daisy Bates, Re: Facts on Robert F. Williams," June 5, 1959, Murray Papers, Box 127.

91. Murray, *Song in a Weary Throat*, "the moment," 322.

92. Pauli Murray, "What Is Africa to Me?—A Question of Identity," December 1960, Murray Papers, Box 85, 1–13; excerpt reprinted in Murray, *Song in a Weary Throat*, quote, 332; see Azaransky, *The Dream Is Freedom*, 56; Kevin Gaines, *African Americans in Ghana: Black Expatriates and the Civil Rights Era* (Chapel Hill: University of North Carolina Press, 2006), 111–113.

93. Murray, *Song in a Weary Throat*, "she had," 351; Lynn Olson, *Freedom's Daughters: The Unsung Heroines of the Civil Rights Movement from 1830–1970* (New York: Scribner, 2001), 289.

94. Pauli Murray and Mary O. Eastwood, "Jane Crow and the Law: Sex Discrimination and Title VII," *George Washington Law Review* 34 (December 1965): 243; Jo Freeman, "How 'Sex' Got into Title VII: Persistent Opportunism as a Maker of Public Policy," *Law and Inequality* 9 (1991): 163–164; Pauli Murray, "Reexamination of the Roots of the Racial Crisis: Prologue to Policy," 3 vols. (JSD dissertation, Yale University, 1965); Kimberlé Crenshaw, "Demarginalizing the Intersections of Race and Sex: A Black Feminist Critique of Antidiscrimination Doctrine, Feminist Theory, and Antiracist Politics," *University of Chicago Legal Forum* (1989), 140.

95. National Organization for Women, "Statement of Purpose," October 29, 1966, http://coursesa.matrix.msu.edu/~hst306/documents/nowstate.html, "to take"; "Founding," http://now.org/about/history/founding; Murray, *Song in a Weary Throat*, 368; Betty Friedan, *The Feminine Mystique* (New York: Norton, 1963).

96. Pauli Murray, Journal entry of December 4, 1967, reprinted in *Pauli Murray and Caroline Ware*, "undue," 145.

97. Murray, *Song in a Weary Throat*, "the foremost," 377.

98. Ibid., "one," 381.

99. Ibid., "to proclaim," 385; World Council of Churches, "Uppsala 1968," http://oikoumene.net/hostudies/gerecht.book/one.book.

100. Murray, *Song in a Weary Throat*, "teenage" and "the convulsions," 389.

101. Ibid., "to thrive," 391, "from the," 392.

102. Ibid., "thus at" and "far from," 393, "for a," 396.

103. Ibid., "I could," 410, "withdrawal," 396; Murray, Journal entry of January 1, 1969, "why can't," Murray Papers, Box 2; Azaransky, *The Dream Is Freedom*, 84; Ibram Rogers, "The Marginalization of the Black Campus Movement," *Journal of Social History* 42 (Fall 2008): 176–177.

104. Murray, *Song in a Weary Throat*, quotes, 413, 414; Joyce Antler, "Pauli Murray: The Brandeis Years," *Journal of Women's History* 14 (2002): 78–82; Rogers, "The Marginalization of the Black Campus Movement," 176.

105. Murray, *Song in a Weary Throat*, "rootless," 414, "Mary helped," 415–416; Harold Isaacs, *Idols of the Tribe: Group Identity and Political Change* (Cambridge: Harvard University Press, 1975); John Burgess to Pauli Murray, October 24, 1969, Murray Papers, Box 62.

106. Pauli Murray, "The Liberation of Black Women," in *Voices of the New Feminism*, ed. Mary Lou Thompson (Boston: Beacon Press, 1970), 87–102, quotes, 92, 101, 102; see Susan M. Hartmann, "Pauli Murray and the 'Juncture of Women's Liberation and Black Liberation,'" *Journal of Women's History* 14 (2002): 74–77.

107. Caroline Ware to Pauli Murray, August 15, 1971, in *Pauli Murray and Caroline Ware*, 148–150; Murray to Ware, August 19, 1971, 150–152, "with tremendous," 151.

108. Pauli Murray to Lawrence Fuchs, April 18, 1973, "without," Murray Papers, Box 63; Murray to Family and Friends, December 20, 1973, "As most," Murray Papers, Box 99; Murray, *Song in a Weary Throat*, 426–427; Pinn, *Becoming "America's Problem Child,"* 41–42.

109. Murray, *Song in a Weary Throat*, "the most," 427; Pauli Murray to Bob Godley, April 11, 1973, "dim" and "There are," Murray Papers, Box 23; Pinn, *Becoming "America's Problem Child,"* 54.

110. Murray, *Song in a Weary Throat*, "given," 429; Carter Heyward, *A Priest Forever: One Woman's Controversial Ordination in the Episcopal Church* (Cleveland: Pilgrim Press, 1999); Suzanne Hiatt, "How We Brought the Good News from Graymoor to Minneapolis: An Episcopal Paradigm," *Journal of Ecumenical Studies* 20 (Fall 1983): 579–580.

111. Pauli Murray, "J. Deotis Roberts on Black Theology: A Comparative View," November 20, 1975, Term Paper at General Theological Seminary, "racial," 4, Murray Papers, Box 23; Murray, "Black Theology: Heresy, Syncretism, or Prophecy?" April 16, 1975, Murray Papers, Box 23; Pauli Murray to J. Deotis Roberts, May 20, 1975, Murray Papers, Box 99.

112. See J. Deotis Roberts, *Black Theology Today: Liberation and Contextualization* (New York: Edwin Mellen, 1983), 38–39; Victor Anderson, *Beyond Ontological Blackness: An Essay on African American Religious and Cultural Criticism* (New York: Continuum, 1995).

113. Pauli Murray, "Black Theology and Feminist Theology: A Comparative Study," MDiv thesis, General Theological Seminary, March 20, 1976, Murray Papers, Box 23; rev. ed., Murray, "Black Theology and Feminist Theology: A Comparative View," *Anglican Theological Review* 60 (January 1978): 3–24, reprinted in *Black Theology: A Documentary History*, 1: 304–322, "ultraradical" and "foreign," 309, "closed," 311; Cone, *A Black Theology of Liberation*, "black theology," 59–60; Cone, *God of the Oppressed*, "all talk," 241.

114. Murray, "Black Theology and Feminist Theology," 316–317; Rosemary Radford Ruether, *New Woman/New Earth: Sexist Ideologies and Human Liberation* (New York: Seabury, 1975), quotes, 115, 116.

115. Murray, "Black Theology and Feminist Theology," "the suffering" and "particularly," 318, "there is," 317; Katie Cannon, *Black Womanist Ethics* (Atlanta: Scholars Press, 1988); Jacquelyn Grant, *White Women's Christ and Black Women's Jesus: Feminist*

Christology and Womanist Response (Atlanta: Scholars Press, 1989); Delores S. Williams, *Sisters in the Wilderness: The Challenge of Womanist God-Talk* (Maryknoll, NY: Orbis Books, 1993).

116. Pauli Murray, "Father's Day Sermon," June 15, 1975, St. Philip's Church in New York, in Murray, *Pauli Murray: Selected Sermons and Writings*, ed. Anthony B. Pinn (Maryknoll, NY: Orbis Books, 2006), quotes, 15, 16.

117. Pauli Murray, "Healing and Reconciliation," February 13, 1977, Chapel of the Cross, Chapel Hill, North Carolina, in *Pauli Murray: Selected Sermons and Writings*, "my entire," 87; Murray, "Sermon on Luke 10: 42," July 14, 1977, Good Shepherd Episcopal Church, Silver Spring, Maryland, ibid., "I believe," 78.

118. Pauli Murray, "The Dilemma of the Minority Christian," June 9, 1974, St. John's Episcopal Church, Hempstead, New York, in *Pauli Murray: Selected Sermons and Writings*, quotes, 9, 10.

119. Pauli Murray, Untitled sermon at Wisconsin Avenue Nursing Home, Washington, DC, July 22, 1979, in *Pauli Murray: Selected Sermons and Writings*, 37; Murray, untitled sermon of December 23, 1979, ibid., "Christhood," 40; Murray, "Has the Lord Spoken to Moses Only?" May 8, 1977, Church of Our Savior, Washington, DC, ibid., "that Divine," 74; Murray, "Palm Sunday Sermon," April 4, 1974, "our own," Murray Papers, Box 64; John Macquarrie, *Principles of Christian Theology* (London: SCM, 1966; 2nd ed., 1977), 276–279.

120. Azaransky, *The Dream Is Freedom*, 107.

121. Pauli Murray to John Burgess, March 30, 1973, "I can," Murray Papers, Box 95; Pinn, *Becoming "America's Problem Child*," 57–58.

122. Pauli Murray, "What the Protestant Episcopal Church of the USA Could Be Doing the Next Century: 1975–2075," Paper for the Commission on Ordained and Licensed Ministries, 1974, Murray Papers, Box 67, in *Pauli Murray: Selected Sermons and Writings*, quotes, 190.

123. E. Franklin Frazier, *The Negro Church in America* (New York: Schocken Books, 1963).

124. C. Eric Lincoln, *The Black Church Since Frazier*, quotes 105–106, 106–107, in E. Franklin Frazier, *The Negro Church in America*, and Lincoln, *The Black Church Since Frazier* (New York: Schocken Books, 1974).

INDEX

Page numbers in *italics* indicate illustrations.

Louis, Joe, 204

Louisiana Deacons for Defense and
 Justice, 398

Lovestone, Jay, 473–74

Lowell, James Russell, 414

Lowenstein, Allard, 369, 375, 409

Lowery, Joseph, 302–3, 308, 331, 342, 381,
 434, 439

Lowndes County Freedom Organization,
 396

Lucy Laney Normal and Industrial
 Institute, 32

Lynd, Staughton, 330, 372

Lyon, Danny, 394

Macintosh, D. C., 278

Mack, Julian, 48, 57

Macmillan, Harold, 346

MacNutt, Paul, 84

Macquarrie, John, 496–98

Maddox, Lester, 404–5, 434

Maguire, John, 412

Mahatma Gandhi's Ideas (Gandhi), 149

Malcolm X, 2; African fascination with,
 375; assassination of, 383; black
 separatist movement and, 394; black
 theology and, 504; civil rights leaders
 and, 375–76; Cone's study of, 448–50,
 456–58, 464; King and, 379; March on
 Washington and, 237; Murray and, 486;
 Powell and, 231–34, 244; Selma march
 and, 382

Malone, Vivian, 234

Mann, Floyd, 322, 324–25

Mants, Bob, 374

Marcantonio, Vito, 181, 202, 205–7

March Against Fear, 241

Marching Blacks (Powell), 196–201, 233,
 243

March on Washington for Jobs and
 Freedom (1963), 15, 236–37, 242, 345–54;
 Murray's participation in, 484

March on Washington Movement (1941),
 13–14, 189

Marshall, Burke, 339–40, 346–48, 363

Marshall, James F., 99–100

Marshall, Thurgood, 65, 88, 222; King and,
 307; Murray and, 475, 480

Marshall Field Foundation, 404

Martin, Dean, 228

Martin, Louis, 226, 235, 320, 535n97

Martin & Malcolm & America (Cone),
 464, 502

Marxism, King's distance from, 310

Massey Lectures, 422–24

Mathews, Shailer: at Chicago Divinity
 School, 112–13, 116; Mays and, 104, 107,
 121; social gospel and, 32

Matthews, Red, 128

Mays, Benjamin E., *xiii*, 2, 7; on African
 American Christianity, 109–20; black
 church and, 98–100, 109–12; on black
 intellectuals, 118–20; on black
 seminaries and theology education,
 120–21; black social gospel and, 96–97,
 107–12, 158–59, 443, 501–4; at Chicago
 Divinity School, 103–5, 112–16;
 ecumenical theology and, 153–54,
 157–58; eulogy for King by, 434–35;
 Farmer and, 15, 122; Gandhi's influence
 on, 10, 12, 77, 148–51, 159; at Howard
 University, 64, 75–78, 88–89, 121–22, 145;
 in India, 148–51, 314; interracial
 solidarity advocacy of, 105, 156–58, 168;
 Johnson and, 73, 76–77, 92, 94–95,
 105–6; King and, 20, 97, 160–61, 260–61,
 269–71, 276, 281, 311, 318; life and career
 of, 10–12, 21, 31, 97–109; as Morehouse
 College president, 11, 18, 154–56, 160,
 259; Murray and, 500; racial justice
 advocacy of, 156–60, 168–71;
 Rauschenbusch and, 18; on school
 desegregation, 159–60; SCLC and, 302;
 on spirituals, 116–17; Thurman and, 127;
 trip to India by, 139; Whitehead and,
 114–15; Woodson and, 114–15; as YMCA
 World Conference delegate, 148

Mays, Ellen Harvin, 101, 103, 105–6

Progressive era: anti-corruption campaigns during, 181; black social gospel and, 2–4; Mays's analysis of, 120

Progressive National Baptist Convention, 310

progressive theology, social justice and, 6

prophetic religion, post–World War I rise of, 117–18

Prosser, Seward, 181

protest activism for racial justice, 3

Proud Shoes (Murray), 471, 481–82, 491

Psychology of Religion (Coe), 136

Pullman Company, 13, 101

Purinton, Herbert, 103

Quakerism. *See* Society of Friends

Rabb, Maxwell, 209–10, 212, 215–16, 221

Raby, Al, 387, 401

racial justice: Cone's liberation theology and, 448–58; Eisenhower and, 208–9; Gandhi's influence on, 149–51; Johnson's discussion of, 79–83, 87–88; King's advocacy for, 287; Mays's advocacy for, 156–60, 168–71; Murray's advocacy for, 476–86, 498–500; Myrdal on, 198–99; northern discrimination and, 386–408; Powell's activism on behalf of, 175–217; Rauschenbusch's discussion of, 34–35; Thurman's views on, 145–47, 165–71; Vivian's analysis of, 465–70

Radhakrishnan, Sarvapalli, 313

Railway Labor Act, 13

Ralla Ram, Augustine, 138

Ramji Ambedkar, Bhimrao, 149

Ramparts magazine, 410

Ramsey, Paul, 299

Randolph, A. Philip, 2; on black churches, 109–10; black social gospel and, 13–15, 501; civil rights movement and, 220, 224–25; economic justice and, 419–20; Eisenhower and, 305; employment discrimination and, 328; Johnson and,

245; King and, 308, 311–12, 379; March on Washington and, 236–37, 347, 349–50, 352; Montgomery bus boycott and, 295–96; Murray and, 480; politics and, 216, 226; Powell and, 189–90, 195, 204, 208, 215, 217, 228–29, 248; Rustin and, 295, 348–49, 357, 405; SCLC and, 300–301

Randolph Institute, 358

Rangel, Charles, 251

Rankin, Jeremiah E., 50

Rankin, John, 199, 203–4

Ransom, Leon A., 79, 475–77

Ransom, Reverdy C., ix–x, 3, 5, 7; black social gospel and, 23–24, 96, 282, 500–502, 504; on Gandhi, 9, 77

Rap Brown, H., 249, 404, 421, 440

Rauh, Joseph, 217, 239, 369–73

Rauschenbusch, Walter, 18, 20, 32–35; influence on Mays of, 114, 121–22, 158–59; King's study of, 262–66, 269, 311–12; Niebuhr and, 544n48; on substitutionary atonement, 42; World War I and, 37–38

Raven, Charles E., 444

Ray, James Earl, 433–35

Ray, J. L., 326

Rayburn, Sam, 201

Read, Florence, 135

Reader's Digest, 414

Reagan, Ronald, 405–6, 442

Reagon, Cordell, 327

Recovery Party, 183

Reddick, Lawrence D., 281, 293, 302–3, 309–11, 313–14, 376

Red Scare, 54, 83–84

Reeb, James, 384

Reed, Daniel A., 63

Reese, Frederick, 381

Reeves, Frank, 250

Reformation, Rauschenbusch's discussion of, 33–34

Reformed Journal, 469

Reid, Arthur, 187

Simmons, William, 23, 302, 501–2, 504

Simpson, Bryan, 366

Sinatra, Frank, 228

Sithole, N'dabinge, 362

sit-ins: in Birmingham, 332; Murray's participation in, 477, 483–84; in Southeast, 364–66; student participation in, 317–18, 320

Six-Day War (1967), 408, 417

skyrocket sermon structure, 270

slavery: African American Christianity and, 116–18; economic impact on whites of, 81–82; Johnson's discussion of, 42–43; Pauline theology and, 123; spirituals and, 136

Slowe, Lucy, 73

Small, Albion, 29

Small, John E. G., 493

Smiley, Glenn, 2–3; King and, 265–67; Montgomery bus boycott and, 295–98, 300; SCLC and, 312, 314, 550n129

Smith, Al, 181

Smith, Ben, 372

Smith, Celestine, 139

Smith, Edwina, 363

Smith, John, 444

Smith, Kelly Miller, 302, 315–16, 323, 440, 464

Smith, Kenneth, 266

Smith, Lillian, 335

Smoot, Reed, 54

Smyer, Sidney, 340

Social Creed of the Churches, 33

social gospel: Christian Socialism movement and, 49; ecumenical theology and, 153; King's study of, 262–63, 275; Mays's study of, 103, 158–59; ministry of, 37–49; post-Kantian idealism and, 272–73; at University of Chicago Divinity School, 112–16

Socialism: black political leadership and, 13; FCSO and, 59; Johnson's study of, 29, 90, 501; King and, 18–19, 313, 443–44; Mays and, 103; Murray and, 473–74,

478; Randolph and, 224–25; Rustin and, 295; Thurman and, 127, 147

Socialist Workers Party, 357

social justice: black social gospel and, 3–4, 172–73, 501–4; ecumenical theology and, 152–53; at Howard University, 77–78; King's advocacy for, 287; Powell on, 198–99; progressive theology and, 6; Rauschenbusch and, 35–36; Thurman and, 147

social science, black social gospel and, 7, 112–16

Society of Friends (Quakers), 132–34, 163; Rustin and, 295

Söderblom, Nathan, 151–52

Song in a Weary Throat (Murray), 491

Sorensen, Theodore, 226, 235–36, 535n97

South Africa, Gandhi's activism in, 8, 141–42

South Carolina State College, 100–101, 108

Southern Baptist Convention, 43

Southern Christian Leadership Conference (SCLC), 2; assassination of King and, 435–41; Birmingham protests and, 331–45; Carnegie Hall benefit for, 330; Chicago campaign and, 390–91, 399–402, 408; Civil Rights Act lobbying by, 367; civil rights movement and, 234, 255, 345; clerical-gender problem in, 22–23; FBI surveillance of, 355; financial crisis at, 407, 421–22; founding of, 299–303; Johnson and, 91; King and, 17–18, 220, 225, 228, 299–311, 317–21, 387–90; Lawson and, 318–19; leadership struggles within, 303–11, 357–59, 366–67, 387–88, 421–22; Lewis and, 374; Meredith March and, 399; middle-class black dominance of, 389; NAACP and, 224–25, 302–4, 309–11, 329–30, 345; Poor People's Campaign and, 426; Powell and, 243–44; Prayer Pilgrimage for Freedom and, 305–7; presidential politics and, 368–69; Resurrection City